# Pollution Prevention and Abatement Handbook 1998

*Toward Cleaner Production*

The World Bank Group
in collaboration with the
United Nations Environment
Programme and the United Nations
Industrial Development Organization

*The World Bank Group*
*Washington, D.C.*

**Library of Congress Cataloging-in-Publication Data**

Pollution prevention and abatement handbook, 1998 : toward cleaner
    production / in collaboration with the United Nations Environment
    Programme and the United Nations Industrial Development Organization.
        p.   cm.
    Includes bibliographical references.
    ISBN 0-8213-3638-X
    1. Factory and trade waste—Management.   2. Pollution prevention.
I. United Nations Industrial Development Organization.   II. United
Nations Environment Programme.   III. World Health Organization.
IV. World Bank Group.
TD897.5.P645     1998
    363.73'1—dc21                                             98-34574
                                                                 CIP

 The text and the cover are printed on recycled paper, with a flood aqueous coating on the cover.

# Contents

# Acknowledgments

The *Pollution Prevention and Abatement Handbook* was prepared by a team from the World Bank and the International Finance Corporation (IFC), led by Richard Ackermann (subsequently by David Hanrahan) and comprising Gordon Hughes (Part I), David Hanrahan (Part II), and Anil Somani, Sanjeev Aggarwal, and Arthur FitzGerald (Part III). Among the principal authors of individual guidelines were John Dixon, Arundhati Kunte, Magda Lovei, and Kseniya Lvovsky. Sari Soderstrom provided the information in Table 3 of the chapter on Indicators of Pollution Management. The *Handbook* is based on technical documents from the United Nations Environment Programme (UNEP) and the United Nations Industrial Development Organization (UNIDO) and on numerous commissioned reports by consultants. The documents have been extensively reviewed by several governments, nongovernmental organizations, industry associations, and individual companies, as well as by the World Bank's Industry and Mining Division (IENIM), the IFC, and a World Bank/IFC Steering Committee. Hans-Roland Lindgren and Yasuhide Koga reviewed the guidelines, with particular attention to consistency with national and European Union standards.

The production of the *Handbook* and the many related administrative tasks have depended critically on the tireless assistance of Sriyani Cumine (desktop publishing), Clare Fleming, Karen Danczyk, and Virginia Hitchcock (editing), Olivia McNeal, and Luz Rivera.

The *Handbook* was developed in collaboration with UNIDO (Ralph Luken), the Industry and Environment Office of the UNEP (Jacqueline Aloisi de Larderel and Fritz Balkau), and the World Health Organization (Dieter Schwela). The World Bank Group is thankful for the generous financial support provided by the governments of Canada, the Netherlands, and Norway and for the comments and guidance provided by the United States Environmental Protection Agency (USEPA), by Frank van den Akker (Netherlands Ministry of Housing, Physical Planning and Environment), and by the World Health Organization in providing technical comments and guidance.

Special thanks is owed to the German government for carrying out an exhaustive review of the entire *Handbook* and for hosting two lengthy meetings at which the technical issues were discussed in detail. The involvement of these organizations and of the many individuals who contributed to the development of the *Handbook* is gratefully acknowledged.

# Foreword

In 1988, the World Bank published *Environmental Guidelines* to provide technical advice and guidance to staff and consultants involved in pollution-related projects. In the years since then, there have been significant changes in technologies, in pollution management policies and practices, and in the activities and portfolio of the World Bank Group. This *Pollution Prevention and Abatement Handbook* has been prepared to update and replace the 1988 guidelines.

The *Handbook* is specifically designed to be used in the context of the World Bank Group's environmental policies, as set out in Operational Policy (OP) 4.01, "Environmental Assessment," and related documents.[1] World Bank Group policy stresses the primacy of the project-specific or site-specific environmental assessment process in setting the requirements for environmental performance. The guidelines contained in this *Handbook* are therefore subject to interpretation in light of the results of the environmental assessment.

The guidelines apply to all Bank Group–funded projects approved in principle on or after July 1, 1998, unless the project sponsor can demonstrate that a significant investment has already been made (or that a legally binding agreement has been entered into) on the basis of the 1988 guidelines.

The *Handbook* promotes the concepts of sustainable development by focusing attention on the benefits—both environmental and economic—of pollution prevention, including cleaner production and good management techniques.

The *Handbook* consists of three parts.

*Part I* contains a summary of key policy lessons in pollution management, derived from practical experience inside and outside the World Bank Group over the past decade. Although Part I is aimed primarily at government decision-makers, other readers will derive considerable benefit from a better understanding of the issues facing government agencies.

*Part II* presents good-practice notes on implementation of policy objectives, based on experience with World Bank Group projects and on lessons from the policies and practices of other agencies and organizations in this field.

*Part III* provides detailed guidelines to be applied in the preparation of World Bank Group projects. The guidelines, which cover almost 40 industrial sectors, represent state-of-the-art thinking on how to reduce pollution emissions from the production process. In many cases, the guidelines provide numerical targets for reducing pollution, as well as maximum emissions levels that are normally achievable through a combination of cleaner production and end-of-pipe treatment. The guidelines are designed to protect human health; reduce mass loadings to the environment; draw on commercially proven technologies; be cost-effective; follow current regulatory trends;

---

1. The World Bank consists of the International Bank for Reconstruction and Development (IBRD) and its concessional-lending affiliate, the International Development Association (IDA). The World Bank Group includes, in addition to the IBRD and IDA, the International Finance Corporation (IFC), which focuses on cooperation with the private sector in developing countries, and the Multilateral Investment Guarantee Agency (MIGA). The World Bank's Operational Policy 4.01 is a conversion of the existing Operational Directive 4.0 and contains the same basic principles as the directive. The IFC and MIGA have parallel policies.

and promote good industrial practices, which offer greater productivity and increased energy efficiency.

The application of the guidelines set out in Part III can minimize the use of resources and reduce the quantity of wastes requiring treatment and disposal. The guidelines represent good environmental management practices that can be implemented and maintained with the skills and resources typically available in countries in which the World Bank Group operates. The World Bank Group is committed to strengthening management and technical skills and to supporting the development of the necessary institutions in these countries. Where relevant national regulations do not exist, the guidelines may provide a basis for negotiating site-specific agreements between regulators and enterprises.

The *Handbook* was compiled by staff members of the Environment Departments of the World Bank and the International Finance Corporation (IFC). Contributions and advice came from many other technical and operational units within the World Bank Group and from outside consultants. A number of drafts were circulated and discussed, including a full Annual Meetings edition in September 1997. The guidelines related to thermal power plants were the subject of a two-day international expert panel workshop held at the World Health Organization (WHO) in Geneva in April 1997. Officials of key borrowing countries, other government and private sector representatives, and WHO and Bank experts attended the workshop.

The IFC and the World Bank's Industry and Mining Division carried out and coordinated detailed technical reviews of the relevant industry-specific guidelines. Technical background material, as well as advice and comments, were provided by the United Nations Environment Programme (UNEP), the United Nations Industrial Development Organization (UNIDO),

WHO, and several bilateral agencies, including those of Canada, Germany, the Netherlands, Norway, Sweden, and the United States.

In addition, extensive informal consultation and discussions with other international financing institutions, industry organizations, regulatory agencies, and nongovernmental organizations have taken place. Many comments have been received and have been incorporated into the *Handbook* to the extent possible. It is intended and hoped that the *Handbook* represents a broad consensus of what is achievable through current good practice in pollution management.

This *Handbook* is envisaged as a living document: its implementation will be monitored over the next year, further industry guidelines will be issued, and the need for revision will be weighed in the light of the accumulated experience. The full text of the *Handbook* is available on the environmental section on the World Bank Group's website (www.worldbank.org), where any revisions or additional guidelines will be posted.

Formal and informal consultations on the content and application of the *Handbook* will continue, and comments are welcome. Comments should be addressed to the Program Leader, Urban, Industry and Energy, Environment Department, World Bank, or to the Unit Head, Environment and Social Review, Environment Division, IFC, at the address given on the copyright page.

*Andreas Raczynski*
*Director*
*Technical and Environment Department*
*International Finance Corporation*

*Robert T. Watson*
*Director*
*Environment Department*
*The World Bank*

# Abbreviations, Acronyms, and Data Notes

ACM          Asbestos-containing materials
ADP          Air-dried pulp
AIJ          Activities Implemented Jointly (Kyoto Protocol)
AMD          Acid mine drainage
AOX          Adsorbable organic halides
BAT          Best available technology
BATNEEC      Best available technology not entailing excessive cost
BOD          Biochemical oxygen demand. In this *Handbook,* BOD is understood to refer to $BOD_5$, BOD measured over five days.
BOF          Basic oxygen furnace
BPT          Best practicable technology
CAC          Command and control
CDM          Clean development mechanism
CFC          Chlorofluorocarbon
CIP          Clean-in-place (methods)
COD          Chemical oxygen demand
CON          Control octane number
CP           Cleaner production
CSM          Continuous stack monitoring
CTC          Carbon tetrachloride
DALY         Disability-adjusted life year
DCF          Directed credit fund
DDT          Dichlorodiphenyltrichloroethane
DMT          Dimethyl terphthalate
DO           Dissolved oxygen
DRR          Dose-response relationship
DSS          Decision Support System for Integrated Pollution Control
EA           Environmental assessment
EAF          Electric arc furnace
ECF          Elemental chlorine-free (bleaching)
EIA          Environmental Impact Assessment
EMS          Environmental management system
EPI          Economic performance indicator
ESCO         Energy service company
ESP          Electrostatic precipitators
ETF          Earmarked tax fund
EU           European Union
FBC          Fluidized-bed combustion
FCC          Fluid catalytic cracking
FGD          Flue gas desulfurization

| FGR | Flue gas recirculation |
| FGT | Flue gas treatment |
| GEF | Global Environment Facility |
| GF | Green fund |
| GHG | Greenhouse gas |
| GIS | Geographic information system |
| GJ | Gigajoule |
| GW | Gigawatt |
| GWP | Global-warming potential |
| HCFC | Hydrochlorofluorocarbon |
| IARC | International Agency for Cancer Research |
| IBRD | International Bank for Reconstruction and Development |
| IDA | International Development Association |
| IFC | International Finance Corporation |
| IPCC | Intergovernmental Panel on Climate Change |
| IPPS | Industrial Pollution Projection System |
| IRIS | Integrated Risk Information System |
| ISIC | International Standard Industrial Classification |
| ISO | International Organization for Standardization |
| ISC | Industrial Source Complex (USEPA model) |
| kWh | Kilowatt-hours |
| LCA | Life cycle analysis |
| LEA | Low-excess-air (firing) |
| LIDAR | Light detection and ranging (system) |
| LPG | Liquefied petroleum gas |
| MCF | Methyl chloroform |
| MCP | Marginal production cost |
| MIGA | Multilateral Investment Guarantee Agency |
| MON | Motor octane number |
| MOS | Metal oxide semiconductor (technology) |
| MSC | Marginal social cost |
| MTBE | Methylterbutylether |
| MWe | Megawatts of electricity |
| NAPAP | National Acid Precipitation Assessment Program |
| NGO | Nongovernmental organization |
| $NO_2$ | Nitrogen dioxide |
| $NO_x$ | Nitrogen oxide |
| NPK | Nitrogen, phosphorus, potassium (fertilizer) |
| NSPS | New source performance standard |
| OD | Operational Directive |
| ODP | Ozone depletion potential |
| ODS | Ozone-depleting substance |
| OECD | Organisation for Economic Co-operation and Development |
| OFA | Overfire air |
| OTC | Over-the-counter (medicines) |
| PAH | Polynuclear aromatic hydrocarbons |
| PAHO | Pan American Health Organization |
| PBR | Polybutadiene rubber |
| PCB | Polychlorinated biphenyl |
| PFA | Pulverized fly ash |
| PFC | Perfluorocarbon |

| | |
|---|---|
| PIC | Product of incomplete combustion |
| $PM_{10}$ | Particulate matter 10 microns or less in aerodynamic diameter |
| POM | Prescription-only medicine |
| ppb | Parts per billion |
| ppm | Parts per million |
| PRTR | Pollutant Release and Transfer Registry |
| RON | Research octane number |
| RRAD | Respiratory-related restricted activity day |
| SBR | Styrene butadiene rubber |
| SCR | Selective catalytic reduction |
| SMEs | Small and medium-size enterprises |
| SMT | Surface mount technology |
| SNCR | Selective noncatalytic reduction |
| $SO_2$ | Sulfur dioxide |
| $SO_x$ | Sulfur oxide |
| SPM | Suspended particulate matter |
| SSP | Single phosphate |
| TCLP | Toxic characteristic leachate procedure |
| TCF | Total chlorine-free (bleaching) |
| TEL | Tetraethyl lead |
| TEWI | Total equivalent warming impact |
| TFP | Total factor productivity |
| tpd | (Metric) tons per day |
| TML | Tetramethyl lead |
| TOR | Terms of reference |
| TRI | Toxic Release Inventory |
| TRS | Total reduced sulfur |
| TSS | Total suspended solids |
| TSP | Total suspended particulates; triple phosphate |
| UNEP | United Nations Environment Programme |
| UNFCCC | United Nations Framework Convention on Climate Change |
| UNIDO | United Nations Industrial Development Organization |
| USAID | U.S. Agency for Environmental Development |
| USEPA | U.S. Environmental Protection Agency |
| VOC | Volatile organic compound |
| VOSL | Value of statistical life |
| WAD | Weak acid dissociable |
| WHO | World Health Organization |
| WQO | Water quality objective |

The references and sources of information provided at the end of chapters and guidelines are not intended to be comprehensive. Unless otherwise specified, the source of all tables is the World Bank Group.

# PART I

---

# OVERVIEW

# Pollution Management: Key Policy Lessons

*Progress toward bringing about a cleaner environment has relied on a philosophy of pollution control. This has involved sometimes costly measures and controversial political decisions. As a result, developing countries, poor communities, and financially constrained enterprises have often argued that the environment is an expensive luxury that diverts resources from more productive uses. This perspective is giving way to a new paradigm stating that neglecting the environment can impose high economic and even financial costs, while many environmental benefits can in fact be achieved at low cost. For this to work, however, we need to better understand what motivates those responsible for pollution and their responses to different regulations, incentives, and other pressures. Moreover, we can no longer afford to view the environment as a technical issue to be addressed independently from overall municipal and industrial strategic decisionmaking. The new approach can be summed up by the expression: environmental management, not just pollution control.*

## Change the Emphasis

Environmental progress over the past 40 years has relied on a philosophy of *pollution control*. A wide range of control technologies has been developed, and it is now technically possible to greatly reduce or entirely eliminate discharges of the major pollutants. However, this approach is yielding decreasing benefits per unit of expenditure in the rich industrial countries, and the necessary preconditions for implementing pollution control measures do not exist in many developing countries. At the same time, some countries fear that pollution control is an expensive luxury that will divert resources from more productive uses.

The emphasis is shifting to *environmental management*, using a broad mix of incentives and pressures to achieve sustainable improvements. This involves:

- Definition of environmental policies in terms of goals rather than inputs
- More explicit consideration of and reference to priorities
- Greater decentralization, especially with respect to the implementation of policies
- Promotion of improved performance and management rather than just control of emissions

- Adoption of cost-effective strategies rather than specifying particular control measures.

This chapter summarizes the main issues that have emerged in the course of operational work throughout the world.

## Work with Agreed Priorities

*Start with clear goals and objectives, not mechanisms.* Governments need to set clear objectives for environmental issues, related to overall development and growth goals, before focusing on specific sector actions or institutional changes. These objectives are frequently set out in terms of human health, productive resources, and conservation of ecosystems.

*An effective environmental strategy requires clear priorities.*

In many countries, the task of improving environmental performance on the ground is unnecessarily complicated by a reluctance to define environmental priorities and to articulate clear strategies that address them. Often, this reflects a lack of political commitment to environmental policies. Yet effective environmental management depends on making choices. These choices form the basis for developing targets that can be understood and assessed by communities and the public as well as by specialists. Without such an effort, the policy process is likely to be captured by special interest groups, whether these be committed to narrow environmental goals or to industrial growth without regard for its consequences.

*Agree on priorities.*
Dirty air (especially *fine particulates* resulting from incomplete combustion) and *lack of clean drinking water* are among the most important problems. It is easy to tell whether policies affecting these issues have been effective, and it is possible to gain considerable political capital from addressing them. Decisionmakers should therefore aim to set concrete goals that mean something to the public and politicians and then focus their attention on achieving real progress. This strategy will succeed only if progress toward meeting the goals is regularly monitored and the strategy is revised in response.

*First do those things that are a high priority and that are also inexpensive and easily implemented.*
Environmental policies often affect problems and people in unforeseen ways. Problems are often claimed to be critical even though they have little impact on human health or on sensitive ecosystems. Conversely, serious issues (e.g., dust pollution) may go unnoticed.

Problems that are relatively easy to solve but have large demonstrable benefits (e.g., removing lead from gasoline, switching home heating from coal to gas) are sometimes ignored in favor of concentrating on complex problems that require very large amounts of resources to address (e.g., nuclear cleanup). Some of the thinking on these issues is influenced by the priorities of industrial countries that have already solved many of the "simpler" problems with which developing countries still have to grapple.

*Cooperative approaches are essential.*
Adversarial systems of environmental management typically do not work well over a sustained period. Developing and implementing effective environmental strategies requires cooperation between enterprises and other polluters, regional and local authorities, and national agencies. Environmental authorities must, at a minimum,

ensure the acquiescence and understanding of most of those whom they seek to regulate, whether in the private or the public sector. A carrot-and-stick approach will still be necessary, but the carrot may be the opportunity to participate in critical decisions, rather than ill-directed financial assistance. Similarly, penalties for poor environmental performance may be expanded to include public exposure and social stigma, as well as financial levies.

*Information is power; share it.*
In many countries, formal regulations are difficult to implement, yet there is public demand for a cleaner environment and for more responsible behavior on the part of enterprises. Several countries are therefore experimenting with schemes to make the environmental behavior of enterprises public.

The evidence is very encouraging, suggesting as it does that enterprises value their public image and are willing to take steps to preserve it. The lesson: an informed public (or regulator) can achieve much through informal pressures.

*Set realistic standards.*
Strict standards, per se, often do not lead to a cleaner environment. In some cases, initial compliance deteriorates—for example, pollution control equipment is installed but is subsequently poorly maintained or is bypassed. In many cases, there is no enforcement culture, and the strict standards are ignored altogether.

Where new projects are being developed, the key to sound environmental performance lies in a comprehensive environmental assessment (EA) that must be carried out before any project design work is started and that should be based on close collaboration with local authorities and the community. The EA identifies the relevant emission levels and other measures necessary to ensure that the proposed project does not cause significant environmental harm. To the extent that the EA represents a genuine effort to reach a broadly accepted plan of action, the subsequent environmental performance can be expected to be far better than if the project is simply required to meet independently established strict standards.

Where existing facilities are to be rehabilitated, an environmental audit will provide the necessary information on which to base cost-effective measures to significantly upgrade environmental performance.

## Devolve Responsibility

*Delegate responsibility downward as far as possible.*
The division of responsibility for environmental policy and regulation will depend on historical, social, and legal factors. Just as environmental authorities should not attempt to micromanage the decisions of individual enterprises and plants, national agencies should focus on the broad framework of priorities and instruments while devolving responsibility for detailed strategy and regulation to regional and local bodies wherever possible. This may be frustrating at times, but lack of local political or administrative commitment will sabotage policies imposed from above as much as would resistance from those who have to comply with them.

The overall legal and institutional framework should cover legislation that establishes specialized regional agencies such as water basin authorities or that gives national or subnational agencies powers to inspect premises, collect data, and impose various penalties. The lack of such a legislative framework has caused serious problems in countries where provinces or states have attempted to introduce discharge fees to recover the costs of dealing with water pollution and to provide an incentive for polluters to reduce their discharges.

*Think strategically at the level of the river basin or airshed.*
Where there are few significant sources of pollution in a river basin or airshed, it is fairly easy to reach agreements with the polluters to improve their performance. Where the river basin or airshed encompasses a large metropolitan area with numerous sources, a range of instruments should be applied, tailored to the capacity of the various implementing agencies. First, there should be a clear understanding of the contribution of different sources to water or air quality and of the options at each source that would lead to cost-effective overall improvement in quality. (See Box 1 for a checklist of the kinds of questions that might be asked.) Market-based instru-

**Box 1. Strategic Choices for Cost-Effective Municipal Wastewater Investments: A Sample Checklist**

- Have measures been taken to reduce domestic and industrial water consumption?
- Has industrial wastewater been pretreated?
- Is it possible to reuse or recycle water?
- Can the proposed investment be analyzed in a river basin context? If so, have the merits of this investment been compared with the benefits from different kinds of investments in other parts of the river basin? Note that a least-cost strategy for achieving improved ambient water quality may involve different (or no) technologies at different locations.
- Has the most cost-effective technology been used to achieve the desired improvement in ambient water quality?
- Has an economic analysis been done to assess the benefits (in terms of ambient water quality) that could be achieved by phasing in investments over, say, 10 or more years?

ments are useful but should be kept as simple as possible.

It may also be useful to allow enterprises to negotiate with each other to agree on cost-effective measures for achieving quality improvements in a given watershed or airshed. Appropriate solutions will vary from case to case and will often involve lengthy negotiations. The key to success is to keep the solutions as simple as possible, and to ensure transparency and accountability on the part of all those involved. In poor countries or communities, the need to devolve responsibility to the local level may sometimes be even more important than in wealthier communities. Experience shows that local communities are willing and able to organize effectively to provide basic urban services (a reliable drinking water supply, basic sanitation, solid waste collection, and so on) at affordable cost and in a sustainable manner, if municipalities or higher-level government authorities provide appropriate incentives.

*Set goals and objectives at a national level, but allow local flexibility in implementation.*
The notion of a "level playing field" within a country has a very strong intuitive appeal to both

environmental policymakers and those whom they regulate. Yet common sense tells us that any attempt to enforce uniform environmental policies throughout large, diverse countries will be doomed to failure. Indeed, the whole point of decentralization is to permit different policy responses to differences in priorities and problems. The dilemma is usually resolved by establishing a default or minimum set of incentives, standards, and other interventions. Default requirements apply wherever subnational authorities do not introduce explicit amendments, which may, subject to certain restrictions, be either stricter or more relaxed than the defaults. Minimum requirements imply that no subnational authority is permitted to adopt less demanding policies—although, in practice, such variation may occur as a result of differences in enforcement behavior. The extent of such default or minimum requirements varies greatly across countries, but everywhere they tend to include measures for dealing with the most sensitive environmental issues. In all countries, it will be the responsibility of national authorities to propose and broker agreements on the extent and nature of such core requirements.

## Adapt Solutions to Circumstances

*Identify the target group: is it the top third or the bottom third?*
The reality that good management is a necessary condition for good environmental performance poses a dilemma in devising environmental policies. One option is to focus on raising the standards of the best third of all polluters, hoping that the laggards will gradually improve by learning from the example of their peers. This strategy is most likely to be effective when competition and social pressure provide a stimulus for improvements in operational as well as environmental performance. Even then, progress tends to be limited for the worst third of plants, and the only solution may be to force them out of business.

The alternative option of setting minimum emission standards and concentrating on plants that fail to meet them tends to lead to an adversarial style of regulation. Often, this undermines attempts to encourage the better plants to improve their performance. Few agencies have the resources or political support to enforce emis-

sion standards strictly for more than a limited number of plants at a time, especially if frequent monitoring of operational performance is required. As a result, reducing emissions from the worst plants may be a lengthy process with much backsliding.

*Define targets, not solutions, with an emphasis on operational practices and good housekeeping.*
At the level of enterprises and plants, the emphasis must shift to environmental performance viewed as one dimension of overall operational efficiency and quality management. The objective should be the consistent attainment of targets and, over time, the progressive reduction of emissions that are linked to important indicators of environmental quality. The focus of attention needs to be more on operational practices, good housekeeping, and the training of workers than on the technological and design specifications of pollution controls.

*Make full use of compliance agreements as an essential tool in dealing with large polluters.*
The achievement of environmental targets may start with the installation of new controls at the sources responsible for the most damaging emissions. This is accompanied by arrangements to monitor the effective operation of controls and to assess their impact on the critical indicators of environmental quality. Even such a straightforward scenario, however, allows ample scope for difficulties, ranging from disagreements about who should bear the costs to how the results of monitoring should be interpreted.

More typically, it will be necessary to negotiate with many sources, each of which—even with good will—will have many reasons to delay or modify the strategy proposed. The outcome will be some balance between (a) a bottom-up consensual approach in which agreements about targets for each source are laboriously reached on an individual or a collective basis (as in Japan or the Netherlands) and (b) a top-down approach based on some combination of emissions standards and economic incentives.

*Use yardstick competition to improve environmental performance over time.*
The nature of the relationship between environmental agencies and those regulated may mean

that the best approach is a combination of minimum requirements and market incentives. In such cases, it is critical that the minimum requirements be adjusted regularly (as part of a transparent permit system) to reflect the average performance of enterprises, rather than being determined by technical criteria. The goal would be a system of regulation based on yardstick competition, which has the desirable property of encouraging a continuous search for cost-effective improvements while penalizing laggards, perhaps heavily.

*Prevention is often less expensive than after-the-fact measures.*
For the same environmental benefits, retrofitting existing plant has been found to be three to five times as expensive as up-front measures. The latter include implementing appropriate technologies at the outset, applying simple yet effective maintenance, and setting up monitoring systems to ensure good performance and management.

## Promote Good Management

*Internalize environmental management.*
Significant and lasting environmental improvements will not come until the objectives and requirements of environmental protection are internalized in the behavior of polluters, whether these be enterprises, organizations, or individuals.

*Rely on incentives—both financial and social—wherever possible.*
Pollution control policies have relied heavily on technological standards. Even where these standards are effective, they tend to be an expensive way of meeting environmental goals. Market incentives that reward good environmental management offer an alternative strategy, but they may be resisted on grounds of fairness and because of uncertainty about the level of reduction of total emissions. In practice, any differences between policies based on standards and those based on incentives are not large for particular industries or sources. The real advantage of relying on incentives lies in their flexibility and cost savings when emissions from many industries and sources have to be reduced. Incentives need not be financial; the provision of information and

public participation can have a significant impact on the behavior of some polluters.

*Recognize that "win-win" options are not costless when management is the critical constraint.*
The adoption of "win-win" options such as cleaner production techniques, waste minimization, and energy efficiency seems to offer the prospect of environmental improvement at little or no cost. Yet diffusion of such practices is often frustratingly slow, and the resulting benefits are modest. The problem, once again, is one of management capacity. The enterprises best placed to adopt and benefit from many "win-win" opportunities are likely to be among those that already have the best environmental performance. The same management constraints and weaknesses that lead to poor performance mean that the costs of innovation are likely to be relatively high and the benefits low for laggards.

*Improved management is the best "win-win" option, especially for small and medium-size enterprises.*
It is helpful to think in terms of two categories of enterprise:

- *Large enterprises* that tend to produce differentiated products, possess ample management and technical skills, enjoy access to world as well as domestic markets, and have a time horizon for their business decisions of at least five years. Because the quality of their products is often a central aspect of their competitive strategy, these enterprises are concerned to build up and maintain a reputation for reliability and high standards. Achieving and maintaining such a reputation means that managers are used to focusing on the good housekeeping aspects of production that are characteristic of many "win-win" opportunities. Of necessity, they have learned and adopted some or all of the precepts of good management outlined above. Thus, good environmental performance simply becomes another dimension of the continuous process of implementing efficiency and quality improvements that is required to compete on quality of output as well as on price.
- *Small and medium-size enterprises* that typically produce undifferentiated products and services for local or domestic markets, with very

limited management and technical resources, short time horizons, and little experience of how to upgrade the quality and efficiency of their production. Simple survival may be their primary concern, so that they tend to be risk averse when it comes to changing their operating methods. While the quality of their output may influence their customers, they tend to compete primarily on price. The painstaking process of building up a reputation for high quality is usually beyond both their resources and their time horizon. Few of the conditions that promote the adoption of good management practices apply, and the firms' environmental performance will reflect the general weaknesses of their management and operational practice.

The contrasting circumstances of the enterprises in the two groups highlight the fact that what may appear to be a clear "win-win" opportunity to an outsider may prompt very different responses from different enterprises. Still, it should not be assumed that even the most sophisticated firms in the first group will easily or rapidly adopt many "win-win" opportunities. For many, the economic gains may simply be too small to justify the bother, unless there are other incentives. Improved management capacity in small and medium-size enterprises will yield substantial benefits, and assistance toward this end will result in financial and environmental rewards—provided that assistance does not simply compensate for poor management actions in the past.

In other words, technical solutions to improve efficiency and environmental performance should come as a result of management decisions, not be a substitute for them. This implies that subsidies to promote cleaner production—in the form of grants for hardware or of centers which provide technical advice—will rarely achieve their intended purpose. However, demonstration projects that serve as concrete examples may provide useful lessons for enterprises that do not want to be the first to try new approaches.

*Recognize that privatization or corporatization is often the best and only solution to the environmental problems of state-owned enterprises.*
Experience suggests that the environmental performance of state-owned enterprises is often worse than that of privately operated enterprises or, at least, of state-owned enterprises operated on a commercially independent basis. Rectifying this situation depends on fundamental changes in incentives and on the resolution of conflicting objectives among those responsible for supervising such enterprises. Privatization (or at least full corporatization) is almost always the best and often the only way of addressing the problems. Nonetheless, privatization is no panacea.

Careful consideration must be given to the environmental obligations to be met by privatized enterprises, especially where these enterprises are responsible for providing environmental services. The most important requirement is that a clear plan for achieving environmental objectives in the most cost-effective manner (e.g., in a river basin context) must be a required part of the bidding process prior to privatization. The successful bidder must then also be given the responsibility for making all the long-term infrastructure decisions necessary to meet the environmental objectives agreed at the outset.

## Reward Good Behavior? Penalize Bad Behavior?

*Money is often not the limiting factor.*
Our understanding of what is required to improve the environmental behavior of utilities and enterprises is changing. It had been generally assumed that violations of regulations occur because of lack of resources to invest in pollution control. Increasingly, it is accepted that reality is more complicated. Often, investments to comply with regulations are often made, but controls are then switched off or bypassed, or poor plant management negates whatever pollution control measures may have been put in place. The question is, therefore, whether improvements in environmental performance really depend on investments in pollution control.

To what extent should pollution abatement be subsidized? Are lines of credit an effective mechanism for reducing pollution? Who should finance investments by public authorities? Experience with a broad range of projects throughout the world suggests the following answers.

In general, governments should not subsidize investments in pollution abatement by profitable enterprises. The "polluter pays" principle is clearly applicable, and the incentive effects of such subsidies are almost wholly undesirable. Any exceptions to this broad precept must rest on the existence of unusual and very specific external benefits. Lack of commitment or of effective regulatory oversight merely strengthens the case for not providing subsidies, since it implies that the resources will almost certainly be wasted.

*Improve financial performance and operational management.*
Unprofitable state-owned enterprises face many problems of more importance (to their managements) than their environmental performance. The best way of solving their environmental problems is through improvements in their financial performance and operational management. Subsidies, low-interest credits, and any other assistance will do nothing to change this harsh reality and will just be throwing good money after bad. The advice to such enterprises must be to straighten out their overall performance and then focus on environmental concerns, which will already be lessened because of the benefits of better operational practices.

Lines of credit for industrial pollution abatement are rarely an effective way of promoting better pollution management. The beneficiaries tend to be large enterprises with access to other sources of credit. For such recipients, finance is not the critical constraint in implementing effective measures to reduce pollution. Small and medium-size enterprises may face more serious financial constraints, but these pale by comparison with the problems caused by lack of commitment to good environmental performance and by limited managerial or technical capacity. It is better to allocate resources to outreach, training, and technical assistance activities than to provide privileged access to finance. There are circumstances in which a targeted (unsubsidized) line of credit may be a useful and justifiable complement to a broad action program implementing a package of measures that includes real incentives and effective regulatory intervention. However, most general lines of credit simply represent the triumph of hope over experience.

Users of the services provided by public utilities should be expected to pay prices that are sufficient to cover any investment costs involved. It may be sensible and efficient for such agencies to draw on a general public investment pool, but the objective should be to ensure that they have individual access to financial markets as high-quality borrowers. Investments in pollution controls should be financed either by borrowing or by the use of depreciation funds, not out of current revenues from taxes or service charges. If utilities find that they may be unable to recoup the borrowing costs by increasing service charges, there is a question as to whether the investments are really justified.

*Close down or privatize industrial dinosaurs; don't use environmental concerns as an excuse for restructuring.*
The argument for subsidies appears especially strong for industrial dinosaurs, handicapped by an inheritance of outdated capital equipment, excess labor, and poor operational practices. However, such subsidies are likely to be misdirected to investment in new equipment, whereas improvements in operational performance and good housekeeping would bring about efficiency as well as environmental gains. The remedy for both the economic and the environmental problems of such plants is either privatization or closure. Environmental concerns should not be used as an excuse to defer or divert necessary measures to implement appropriate actions, nor should the enterprises be exempt from the regular requirements of environmental policies.

*Set requirements for old plants that reflect their economic life.*
To the extent that exceptions are made to this general rule, the implicit payback period for any expenditures, taking account of both economic and environmental benefits, should be very short—not more than two years. This criterion will minimize the danger of financing redundant or wasteful measures to achieve goals that might be better met in some other way. Providing finance for projects that produce such rapid and large benefits should not delay any move to privatize the enterprise, and little will be lost if a decision is made to close all or parts of the plants concerned.

## Box 2. Management of Industrial Pollution: Suggestions for Enterprises, Governments, and External Donors

### Enterprises
- Good environmental practice is just good management; environmental problems are often a symptom of inefficiency and waste of resources.
- Focus on plant housekeeping, maintenance, and management. Would you sit on your plant floor? If not, why not, and what can you do about it?
- Involve your staff and workers. Environmental problems are often occupational health problems. Define clear goals, provide training, and monitor performance.
- Focus on those environmental investments that can be financed out of cash flow. This ensures that environmental management is seen as part of the overall operating costs of the enterprise.

### Governments
- Identify critical problems, and focus political, human, and financial resources on priorities. This will ensure that the greatest impact will be made on the most important problems.
- Get the external incentives for enterprises right. Decisions on taxes and the like may be more important than environmental regulations. Don't neglect pollution charges. Ministries of finance should think of taxes as a way of changing behavior, not just generating revenues. Get all ministries to follow consistent policies.

- Be realistic in drawing up environmental regulations. Pure coercion has not worked and will not work. Negotiate realistic targets with industries and plants; then insist that these targets be met. Allow adequate time for compliance.
- Strengthen environmental agencies; develop their technical and monitoring capabilities; encourage them to understand industries. Provide advice as well as enforce permits. Decentralize responsibility to regional authorities wherever possible.

### External donors
- Focus on those issues where well-directed efforts can accelerate change. Broad environmental progress will come largely as a result of economic change.
- Massive new investment may not be the solution; it may add to the problem. The pursuit of investment projects may distract management attention from smaller but practical improvements and goals. Investment projects should be the reward for better management, not an incentive to attempt to bring it about.
- Avoid soft loans to enterprises (as distinguished from national governments). Apply strict economic criteria in assessing projects. Grants may have a role where there are large external benefits that cannot be achieved by other means.
- Ensure that consultant studies and technical assistance have clear objectives and are directed toward specific needs of enterprises or governments.

*Recognize the need for reasonable transition arrangements.* Concerns about fairness are valid, but only if a fair outcome is seen as one that imposes uniform obligations—emission reductions or control technologies—on all sources. Any focus on environmental management must emphasize opportunities rather than obligations. Initial differences in capital equipment, age of plant, and the like that give rise to different opportunities decay as managers respond to the new policy framework. Thus, fairness only requires adequate transitional arrangements, not a permanent commitment to inappropriate policy instruments.

## Mainstream Environmental Concerns

The broad concepts of sustainable development are now universally accepted. In practical terms, the challenge is to find ways to integrate pollution prevention and abatement into the ways that cities are run, enterprises are managed, and people lead their daily lives. The emphasis must now be on making environmental management and performance part of the basic criteria by which the success of any operation or process is measured. A number of practical suggestions are summarized in Box 2.

# PART II

IMPLEMENTING POLICIES IN PRACTICE

Basic Principles

Setting Priorities

Air Quality Management

Water Quality Management

Industrial Pollution Management

Financing Environment

Global and Transboundary Issues

# Indicators of Pollution Management

*The definition and selection of environmental performance indicators is still at an early stage, but the use of indicators is increasing, both for tracking trends in pollution and other environmental issues on a large scale (national or regional) and for monitoring Bank projects. This chapter provides a framework to assist in the selection of appropriate indicators for pollution projects and discusses the issues that must be considered. It provides examples of commonly used indicators of air and water pollution.*

World Bank involvement in pollution control and urban environment projects forms a significant share of a growing environmental portfolio (61% of a lending portfolio that has almost doubled since 1992). As investments in this area grow, it becomes increasingly important to develop quantitative measures of the effect of such investments on the environment, in this case air and water. There is therefore a heightened need to use environmental performance indicators (EPIs) for monitoring the success of investments in meeting the stated objective of pollution management.

## Environmental Performance Indicators

An indicator is "something that provides a clue to a matter of larger significance or makes perceptible a trend or phenomenon that is not immediately detectable" (Hammond et al.1995). An indicator's main defining characteristic is that it quantifies and simplifies information in a manner that promotes the understanding of environmental problems by both decisionmakers and the public. Above all, an indicator must be practical and realistic, given the many constraints faced by those implementing and monitoring projects.

EPIs can help quantify impacts and monitor progress. The goals are to assess how project activities affect the *direction* of change in environmental performance and to measure the *magnitude* of that change. Indicators that allow a quantitative evaluation of project impacts are particularly useful, since they provide more information than just whether the project is improving or degrading the environment.

Information on the magnitude of a benefit is required to determine whether it is worth the resources being expended to achieve it. Similarly, information on the magnitude of adverse impacts might indicate whether the harm is justified, given the other benefits of the activity or project in question.

## Indicator Typology

In the past, monitoring of Bank projects focused on *inputs* (resources provided under the project) and *outputs* (the immediate goods or services provided by the project). Input indicators can be specified in terms of overall funds earmarked, specific tasks to be funded, and funding agencies. Output indicators relate to specific actions taken (such as electrostatic precipitators installed, rehabilitation of the water supply network, introduction of substances with low or no ozone-depleting potential, and switching of the fuel used in power plants); these would evolve from the design phase of the project. In addition to often being unduly rigid, such a project-centric approach focuses attention too narrowly on the process of implementing projects rather than on the results. Increasingly, it is being realized that the ultimate assessment of the performance of a pollution-related project should be based on its immediate and longer-term effects on parameters such as air and water quality. The emphasis is therefore moving toward the definition of *outcome indicators* (to measure the immediate results of the project) and *impact indicators* (to monitor the longer-term results). The *input* and *output* indicators relate more to project process; the *outcome* and *impact* indicators relate to the overall effect on the environmental resource, such as the quality of an airshed or a water body.

For example, a loan to control dust emissions from cement plants might specify the following indicators:

- *Input* (project-specific resources): financial ($X million); technical assistance
- *Output* (goods and services produced): number of electrostatic precipitators and fabric filter systems installed
- *Outcome* (immediate results): reduced emissions of particulate matter
- *Impact* (longer-term results): reductions in ambient concentrations of particulate matter; fewer health problems from respiratory diseases.

Outcome and impact indicators should form an integral part of assessing the success of an environment sector project. Formulating effective outcome and impact indicators, however, remains a major challenge.

## Framework

Considerable work has been done to come up with a coherent framework within which to assess the positive or negative effect of human activity on the environment. In a conceptualization by the Organisation for Economic Co-operation and Development (OECD 1994), three aspects of the environmental problem are distinguished: the *pressure* that causes the problem (for example, emissions of sulfur dioxide, $SO_2$); the resulting *state* of the environment (for example, ambient concentrations of sulfur dioxide in the air); and the *response* to the problem (for example, regulations requiring the use of low-sulfur coal to reduce emissions and ambient levels of sulfur dioxide). The pressure and state indicators measure project outcomes and impacts, respectively.

The pressure variable describes the underlying cause of the problem. The pressure may be an existing problem (for example, soil erosion in cultivated uplands or air pollution from buses), or it may be the result of a new project or investment (for example, air pollution from a new ther-

mal power plant, or loss of a mangrove forest because of port development). Whatever the cause, pressures affect the state of the environment and then may elicit responses to address these issues.

The state variable usually describes some physical, measurable characteristic of the environment. Ambient pollution levels of air or water are common state variables used in analyzing pollution (for example, particulate concentrations in air or biochemical oxygen demand in water bodies). For natural or renewable resources, other measures are used: the extent of forest cover, the area under protected status, the size of an animal population, or grazing density. Most EPIs relate to easily measured state variables.

The response variables are those policies, investments, or other actions that are introduced to solve the problem. Bank projects that have important environmental components can be thought of as responses to environmental problems. Such projects can affect the state either directly, by way of ex-post cleanup activities, or indirectly, by acting on the pressures (for example, by providing alternative income sources for farmers who would otherwise clear forests). In some cases, projects also seek to improve responses to environmental problems, for example, by increasing institutional capacity to monitor environmental problems and enforce environmental laws. Because Bank projects are themselves considered to be responses to environmental problems, the following discussion focuses on the use of pressure and state indicators to monitor project outcomes and impacts.

The relevant question is: what immediate and long-term impacts will the project have on causal factors (pressures) and the condition (state) of the environmental problem? It is important to look at immediate outcomes that reduce pressures, as well as at the longer term impact—otherwise the project may be incorrectly blamed (or credited) for a worsening of (or improvement in) the state of the environmental resource.

## Choosing Environmental Performance Indicators

Choosing appropriate EPIs is a difficult task. No universal set of indicators exists that would be equally applicable in all cases. The diversity of environmental problems, of the contexts in which they arise, and of the possible solutions to them is simply too great. This section discusses how task managers might proceed to select EPIs for their projects and the factors that must be borne in mind when doing so. Given the limited experience in this field, the discussion is necessarily preliminary and is likely to be revised on the basis of lessons derived from actually applying EPIs.

### Link to Project Objectives

The process of selecting EPIs must necessarily start from a precise understanding of the environmental problems being addressed and of project objectives. Vague or overly broad objectives such as "reducing erosion" or "protecting biodiversity" are of little assistance in selecting EPIs and may well indicate that the project or component itself is not very well thought out. The appropriate responses will differ depending on whether, for example, erosion is caused by deforestation or by inappropriate farming practices, and so will the EPIs. Likewise, it makes a difference whether erosion is a concern because of sedimentation in downstream reservoirs or because it undermines agricultural productivity. Again, the EPI best suited to the specific situation should be chosen. Where the environmental consequence is not an explicit project objective but a by-product of project activities, the environmental assessment (EA) process can aid in understanding the possible impacts and hence in selecting the appropriate EPI.

### Pressure versus State Indicators

The goal of EPIs is to monitor and evaluate environmental impacts arising from Bank-supported activities. This implies a need to measure two dimensions of the environmental problem: the state of the environment and any changes in that state, and the contribution—direct or indirect— that the project is making to those changes. Indicators of both pressure and state are therefore typically required to properly evaluate project impact. Indicators of pressure alone are often insufficient because the link between a given pressure and the consequent effect on the state of the environment may be ambiguous or of unknown magnitude.

An important factor in the design or assessment of a project is to determine as accurately as possible the relationship between the project and the overall state that is of concern. For example, airshed modeling may be required to quantify the relationship between a particular point source and ambient air quality.

### Level of Measurement

Indicators of state and pressure can both be measured at various levels. The objective of quantifying project benefits (or costs) will be aided if indicators are selected as close to the project objective as possible. This is particularly true when the environmental function of concern plays an important economic function (air quality as an input into health; water quality as an input into agriculture, fish production, or human consumption; soil quality as an input into agricultural production). For example, in the case of land degradation, indicators of achievable yield are more useful than indicators of soil depth. Well-chosen indicators would speak directly to the problem of concern and, in most cases, would give direct measures of project benefits (if the project is alleviating problems) or costs (if the project is causing them). The further the chosen indicator is from the economic end point, the more difficult it will be to evaluate the returns to the project.

### Spatial and Temporal Coverage

Careful thought needs to be given to the appropriate spatial and temporal coverage of EPIs. Project activities might have an impact beyond the area in which the project is active. The affected area may not coincide with the national territory, making national-level measures inappropriate. (Where feasible, however, it is highly desirable that project-level indicators be comparable to national-level indicators.) There may also be lags before project effects are felt. Changes in the long-term status of biodiversity, for example, often only manifest themselves over time scales much longer than those of typical Bank projects.

*Feasibility and Cost*

To be effective as an aid to decisionmaking, EPIs must be limited in number and should highlight essential factors concisely. They must also be practical and realistic in terms of the costs involved. This may lead to tradeoffs between the information content of various indicators and the cost of collecting them. These tradeoffs will obviously vary across technologies and will depend heavily on institutional capacity. Certain indicators that are extremely simple or inexpensive to collect may be inadequate for various reasons. The case of air pollution provides an example of the tradeoffs that must often be made in selecting EPIs. Ideally, the project's impact on morbidity and mortality would be measured, since reducing these indicators is generally the intended result. Morbidity and mortality themselves can be measured, but establishing a clear link between them and either ambient pollution levels (a state indicator) or any given source of emissions (a pressure indicator) remains extremely difficult, despite recent progress in this area (Ostro 1994). The only feasible solution in most such situations is to fall back on indicators of ambient concentrations or, if the source has been established as contributing significantly to total pollution, of emissions.

*Interpreting EPIs*

Once an indicator has been selected and measured, it must still be interpreted. Emphasis has increasingly shifted toward performance indicators that measure changes relative to a goal established by environmental policy. Such an explicit reference to goals is important to put the project's impact in perspective. Once the project is under way, the emphasis is usually on variations in the indicator over time. A positive change in a state indicator or a diminution of a pressure indicator is usually considered an indication of success, as long as it can be shown that it is not the result of nonproject factors or random effects. (It may be necessary to establish baseline levels for preproject conditions and follow up with measurements over extended periods to ascertain trends with confidence.) The appropriate comparison, however, is generally not with the preproject situation but with the counterfactual situation: what would have happened in the absence of the project? An increase in a pressure indicator could still be considered evidence of success if the pressure would have increased even faster without the project. In some cases, control groups can be used to measure conditions in areas not affected by the project; in others, statistical techniques are needed to estimate what would have happened without the project.

## Air Pollution

A wide variety of airborne pollutants are of concern from the point of view of health and environmental impacts. A number of site-specific studies have examined pollution risks, and although results vary, there are some important consistent findings. Health problems have typically been associated with airborne *particulates*, measures of which include total suspended particulates (TSP) and particulate matter of 10 microns or less in diameter ($PM_{10}$, the more damaging, smaller particles), and with ambient *lead*. Damage to structures, forests, and agricultural crops tend to be primarily linked with sulfur dioxide and with ground-level ozone.

Even though the ultimate objective of a project might be to mitigate damage to human health, monitoring such effects directly is extremely difficult because of substantial uncertainties about the exposure of different population groups to pollutants, their response to different levels of exposure, and the cumulative nature of damage. It is common, therefore, in gauging a project's impact, to fall back on monitoring indicators of ambient concentrations or of emissions, depending on the project's potential contribution to correcting the overall problem. The most commonly used indicators of air pollution emissions and concentrations are listed in Table 1. These indicators may need to be supplemented by additional EPIs, depending on local conditions.

## Water Pollution

Industrial and agricultural chemicals and organic pollutants from agro-based industries are significant source of surface water and groundwater pollution. Acidification of surface waters from air pollution is a more recent phenomenon and is a threat to aquatic life.

Understanding of the impact of water quality on human health and aquatic life has improved enormously in recent years. Two broad measures of water quality have come to be widely used (see Table 1): oxygen levels or demands in the water, and concentration of heavy metals. A measure of pollutant concentrations could be regarded as a pressure when measured in a stream that feeds into a lake or as a state when measured in the water body fed by the stream. Used together, these indicators provide a rough but useful picture of the overall health of the water body and of the threats to it.

The procedures required in measuring water quality indicators are problem specific and are generally well understood. Sampling methods differ depending on whether the water body of interest is, for example, a lake or a stream. Timing of measurements is often an issue, since concentrations can vary substantially as the flow varies; a given pressure may cause few problems when flow is at its peak but may have a major impact at times of low flow.

## Global Environmental Problems

Measuring the impact of projects on global environmental problems such as climate change or damage to stratospheric ozone poses significant problems of scale. No single project is likely to have any measurable impact on these problems. Measuring the state of the problem, therefore, does not generally fall within the scope of project-level monitoring, but determining the effect of a project on pressures is feasible.

### Climate Change

Climate change is linked to a number of important effects on the global life support system. Sea-level rise and shifts in primary agricultural production are among the most dramatic potential impacts. Although monitoring global climatic effects is impractical at the project level, emis-

**Table 1. Selected Environmental Performance Indicators for Air and Water Pollution and for Global Environmental Problems**

| Problem | Pressure indicators | State indicators | Comments |
|---|---|---|---|
| Air pollution | Emissions<br>Particulates<br>Sulfur dioxide<br>Lead | Ambient concentrations<br>Particulates<br>Sulfur dioxide<br>Lead | The same indicators can serve as measures of pressure or state, depending on where they are measured—at the smokestack or in the ambient air. |
| Water pollution | Discharges of industrial wastes<br>Biochemical oxygen demand (BOD)<br>Chemical oxygen demand (COD)<br>Heavy metals | Concentrations of pollutants in water bodies<br>Biochemical oxygen demand (BOD)<br>Chemical oxygen demand (COD)<br>Heavy metals | See comment on air pollution. |
| Global environmental problems | Climate change<br>Emissions of greenhouse gases (carbon dioxide, methane)<br>Stratospheric ozone<br>Emissions of ozone-depleting substances (chloroflurocarbons; halons; hydrochloro-fluorocarbons | | Measuring the impact of specific projects on a global problem is unrealistic. |

## Table 2. Matrix of Representative Environmental Performance Indicators

| Environment sector | Outcome or pressure (measures the immediate outcome) | Impact or state (measures the long-term environmental impact) | Comments |
|---|---|---|---|
| Forestry | Rate of deforestation<br>Per capita wood consumption<br>Incentives for forest clearing | Deforestation<br>Area of forest<br>Preservation of intact forest areas<br>Area of roadless forest<br>Forest fragmentation index<br>Watershed protection<br>Proportion of watershed with appropriate cover | The appropriate state indicators depend on the objective; pressure indicators are often similar across objectives, but the appropriate resolution changes (for example, to a focus on particular watersheds). |
| Biodiversity | Encroachment into natural habitats<br>Legal and illegal hunting offtakes<br>Upstream pollution sources | Area of natural habitat<br>Habitat fragmentation index<br>Proportion of habitat adjoining incompatible land uses<br>Population status of selected indicator organisms<br>Changes in the biogeochemistry of soils and waterways | Special attention needs to be devoted to identifying and monitoring the state of critical natural habitats |
| Land quality | Nutrient removal in excess of fertilizer applications and natural regeneration<br>Erosion rates | Nutrient level (of nitrogen, phosphorus, potassium, and other nutrients, depending on the specific crops being grown)<br>Soil depth<br>Organic matter content<br>Total factor productivity (TFP) | Appropriate indicators are very site specific. |
| Air pollution | Emissions of:<br>Particulates (TSP or $PM_{10}$)<br>Sulfur dioxide<br>Lead | Ambient concentrations of:<br>Particulates (TSP or $PM_{10}$)<br>Sulfur dioxide<br>Lead | The same indicators can serve as measures of pressure or of state, depending on where they are measured. |
| Water pollution | Discharges of human and industrial wastes<br>Fecal coliform counts<br>Biochemical oxygen demand (BOD)<br>Chemical oxygen demand (COD)<br>Heavy metals | Concentrations of pollutants in water bodies<br>Fecal coliform counts<br>Biological oxygen demand (BOD)<br>Chemical oxygen demand (COD)<br>Heavy metals | The same indicators can serve as measures of pressure or of state, depending on where they are measured. |
| Global environmental problems | Climate change<br>Emissions of greenhouse gases (carbon dioxide, methane)<br>Stratospheric ozone<br>Emissions of ozone-depleting substances (CFCs, halons, etc.) | | Measuring the impact of specific projects on a global problem is unrealistic. |
| Institutional capacity | | Existence of environmental laws and agencies<br>Active nongovernmental organizations (NGOs)<br>Number of trained staff in environmental agencies<br>Number of laboratory facilities | |

*Note*: This table provides *examples* of EPIs used in the major categories of environmental problems that are normally encountered in Bank work; it is not meant to be exhaustive. Project effects are grouped according to whether they are primarily pressure indicators (equivalent to the project-linked outcome measures) or measures of change in the overall state (equivalent to impact indicators). Since input and output indicators are already measured by Bank projects, they are not listed in the matrix below. Examples of such indicators are best provided with a specific project in mind. See Table 3 for examples of input and output indicators for the Lithuania Siauliai Environment Project.

**Table 3. Use of EPIs in the Lithuania Siauliai Environment Project**

| Objectives | Input (resources provided for project activities) | Output (goods and services produced by the project; details to be determined at "detailed design" phase) | Outcome (direct outcomes of project activities) | Risks | Impact |
|---|---|---|---|---|---|
| Reduce pollutant loads from the Siauliai area into the Upper Lielupe river basin | IBRD loan (US$6.20 million)<br>Bilateral grants (US$8.54 million)<br>Government (US$7.6 million)<br>Municipal (US$0.4 million)<br><br>All funds will be utilized for procurement of equipment, works, consultants, and technical assistance (training). | Rehabilitated sewer network<br>Rehabilitated wastewater treatment plant<br>New wastewater treatment plant<br>Pollution control measures at pig farms<br>Pollution control measures for agricultural runoff | Amount of treated wastewater increased from 40,000 cubic meters per day (m³/d) to 50,000 m³/d.<br>Pollution level reduced at the treatment plants' outlets and at other locations<br>*At mouth of Lielupe River*<br>Nitrogen reduced from 250 metric tons per year (t/y) to 18 t/y<br>Phosphorus reduced from 56 t/y to 15 t/y<br>*At wastewater treatment plant*<br>BOD reduced from 1000 t/y to 200 t/y<br>Suspended solids reduced from 1,000 t/y to200 t/y<br>Nitrogen reduced from 500 t/y to 360 t/y<br>Phosphorus reduced from 75 t/y to20 t/y<br>Pollution levels from agricultural pilot sites and pig farms reduced at selected points downstream (baseline to be determined). | Problems with availability of local funding | Lower health care costs (by X%)<br>Increased tourism revenues (by Y%)<br>Increased international political goodwill (measured through...)<br><br>(Baselines to be determined) |
| Improve the quality, reliability, and cost of water supply and wastewater services in Siauliai | | Rehabilitated equipment<br>New equipment<br>Restructured water utility<br>Trained people | Improved drinking water quality<br>Decreased iron content<br>Softer, potable water<br>Reduced number of breaks and trouble calls on:<br>Water supply and distribution system<br>Wastewater collection and conveyance system (baseline to be determined)<br>Adequate operating ratio (< 85%)<br>Adequate working ratio (< 70%) for the water utility | Outcome dependent on ability to adjust tariffs<br>Revenue collection difficulties<br>Political difficulties with organizational restructuring (staff reduction)<br>Potential coordination difficulties between concerned parties | |
| Improve regional and local environmental quality monitoring and enforcement system in the Upper Lielupe river basin | | Monitoring and laboratory equipment<br>Other equipment<br>Trained people<br>Management plans for industrial pollution reduction and sludge<br>Emergency management plan | Regular and accurate monitoring of water quality<br>Regular enforcement visits at pollution sources (quantified definitions to be determined when drafting management plans) | | |

sions of greenhouse gases (GHGs) give an indication of the pressures being generated. The most commonly used indicator in this area is some measure of carbon emissions (or other gases that contribute to global warming) or a measure of the percentage reduction in carbon emissions from some base scenario. When multiple GHGs are involved, the global-warming potential can be used as a weighting factor.

### Stratospheric Ozone

The ozone layer blocks ultraviolet radiation that is harmful to humans and all living things. The degradation of the ozone layer is precipitated by ozone-depleting substances (ODSs) such as chlorofluorocarbons (CFCs) and halons. Here too, monitoring global effects is impractical, so work focuses on measuring changes in pressure resulting from project activities. The consumption and hence the emissions of ODSs can be used as a measure of the pressures being generated by economic agents. At the national level, production, net of exports and with imports added, can be taken as a proxy for the country's contribution to the problem. At the project level, the project's contribution to national production and consumption can be used as a proxy.

### Health Dimensions

Climate change and ozone depletion have numerous health repercussions that are only beginning to be understood in a manner that allows for preventive measures. For example, climate change can directly cause injury and death related to temperature extremes, storms, floods, and forest and brush fires. Climate change can also have a number of indirect effects that collectively cause even more serious health problems, such as an increase in malaria due to a spread of mosquito habitat, malnutrition due to desertification and droughts, aggravation of diarrheas linked to water pollution and of respiratory diseases linked to air pollution, and mental and physical stress caused by storms and floods. The Intergovernmental Panel on Climate Change (IPCC) has concluded that the overall health effects of climate change and ozone depletion are likely to be wide ranging and

negative and that developing countries will be hardest hit and most constrained in finding options to prevent or adapt to changes.

Table 2 provides several examples of pressure indicators for global environmental problems; no state indicators are provided, since it is unrealistic to hope to link any specific project with changes in the state of global problems. Additional details on climate change and ozone depletion problems can be found in recent publications of the World Bank's Global Coordination Division (World Bank 1995a, 1995b).

### Examples

Practical implementation of pollution indicators in World Bank projects is just beginning. One example that presents a complete set of proposed indicators is the Lithuania Siauliai Environment Project (see Table 3).

### References and Sources

Adriaanse, Albert. 1993. Environmental Policy Performance Indicators. The Hague: Ministry of Housing, Physical Planning and the Environment.

Hammond, Allen L., A. Adriaanse, E. Rodenburg, D. Bryant, and R. Woodward. 1995. Environmental Indicators: A Systematic Approach to Measuring and Reporting on Environmental Policy Performance in the Context of Sustainable Development. Washington, D.C.: World Resources Institute.

Hettige, Hemamala, Paul Martin, Manjula Singh, and David Wheeler. 1995. "The Industrial Pollution Project System." Policy Research Working Paper 1431. World Bank, Policy Research Department, Washington, D.C.

IPCC (Intergovernmental Panel on Climate Change). 1994. The Radiative Forcing of Climate Change. Report of IPCC Working Group 1. Geneva: World Meteorological Organization and United Nations Environment Programme.

OECD (Organisation for Economic Co-operation and Development). 1994. Environmental Indicators. Paris.

Ostro, Bart. 1994. "Estimating the Health Effects of Air Pollutants: A Method with an Application to Jakarta." Policy Research Working Paper 1301. World Bank, Policy Research Department, Washington, D.C.

World Bank. 1993a. "Operational Directive 4.01: Environmental Assessment." *World Bank Operational Manual.* Washington, D.C.

————. 1993b. *Portfolio Management: Next Steps—A Program of Action.* Washington, D.C.

————. 1994. "Operational Directive 10.04: Economic Evaluation of Investment Operations." *World Bank Operational Manual.* Washington, D.C.

————. 1995a. "The Decision Support System for Industrial Pollution Control." Draft. Environment Department, Washington, D.C.

————. 1995b. *Monitoring Environmental Progress: A Report on Work in Progress.* Washington, D.C.

————. 1995c. "Monitoring and Evaluation Guidelines for ODS Phaseout Investment Projects." Draft. Environment Department, Global Coordination Division, Washington, D.C.

————. 1995d. "Monitoring and Evaluation Guidelines for GEF Global Warming Investment Projects." Draft. Environment Department, Global Coordination Division, Washington, D.C.

# The Environmental Assessment Process

The Pollution Prevention and Abatement Handbook *is intended to be used principally as input to the World Bank Group's environmental assessment (EA) processes. This chapter outlines the key features of the EA procedure for World Bank projects. The International Finance Corporation (IFC) and the Multilateral Investment Guarantee Agency (MIGA) follow the same overall policies but have somewhat different environmental analysis and review procedures. (For details, contact IFC's or MIGA's Environmental Unit.)*

In recent years, environmentally sustainable development has become one of the most important challenges facing development institutions such as the World Bank. Accordingly, the Bank has introduced a variety of instruments into its lending and advisory activities. Environmental assessment (EA) is one of the most important of these tools.

The purpose of EA is to enhance projects by helping prevent, minimize, mitigate, or compensate for any adverse environmental and social impacts. Development institutions and many developing countries have introduced EA requirements and regulations into their development activities. Their experience to date shows that EAs often do provide these benefits.

## EA at the World Bank

In 1989, the Bank adopted Operational Directive (OD) 4.00, "Annex A: Environmental Assessment." EA became standard procedure for Bank-financed investment projects. In 1991 the directive was amended as OD 4.01. It is in the process of conversion to an Operational Policy, OP 4.01. EA is designed to be a flexible process that makes environmental considerations an integral part of project preparation and allows environmental issues to be addressed in a timely and cost-effective way during project preparation and implementation.

The primary responsibility for the EA process lies with the borrower. the Bank's role is to advise the borrower throughout the process, to con-

firm that practice and quality are consistent with EA requirements, and to ensure that the process feeds effectively into project preparation and implementation.

*Stage 1: Screening*

To decide the nature and extent of the EA to be carried out, the process begins with screening at the time a project is identified. The project team determines the nature and magnitude of the proposed project's potential environmental and social impacts and assigns the project to one of three environmental categories.

*Category A:* a full EA is required. Category A projects are those expected to have "adverse impacts that may be sensitive, irreversible, and diverse" (OD 4.01), with attributes such as direct pollutant discharges large enough to cause degradation of air, water, or soil; large-scale physical disturbance of the site or surroundings; extraction, consumption, or conversion of substantial amounts of forest and other natural resources; measurable modification of hydrologic cycles; use of hazardous materials in more than incidental quantities; and involuntary displacement of people and other significant social disturbances.

*Category B:* although a full EA is not required, some environmental analysis is necessary. Category B projects have impacts that are "less significant . . ., not as sensitive, numerous, major or diverse. Few, if any of these impacts are irreversible, and remedial measures can be more easily designed" (OD 4.01). Typical Category B projects entail rehabilitation, maintenance, or upgrading rather than new construction.

*Category C:* no EA or other environmental analysis is required. Category C projects entail negligible or minimal direct disturbance to the physical setting. Typical Category C projects focus on education, family planning, health, and human resource development.

Projects with multiple components are classified according to the component with the most significant adverse impact; if there is a Category A component, the project as a whole is classified as A.

Between October 1989 and May 1995, more than 1,000 projects subject to the requirements of the OD on Environmental Assessment were presented to the World Bank's Board of Directors. The breakdown of these projects by category is shown in the table below; the breakdown by sector is shown in Table 1.

| Project category | Number of projects | Percentage of total |
|---|---|---|
| A | 104 | 10 |
| B | 418 | 41 |
| C | 498 | 49 |

*Stage 2: Scoping and Development of Terms of Reference*

Once a project is categorized, a scoping process is undertaken to identify key issues and develop the terms of reference (TOR) for the EA. At this stage, it is essential to identify more precisely the likely environmental impacts and to define the project's area of influence. As part of this process, information about the project and its likely environmental effects is disseminated to local affected communities and nongovernmental organizations (NGOs), followed by consultations with representatives of these groups. The main purpose of these consultations is to focus the EA on issues of concern at the local level.

*Stage 3: Preparing the Environmental Assessment Report*

When a project is classified as Category A, a full-scale environmental assessment (EA) is normally undertaken, resulting in an EA report. Category B projects are subject to a more limited EA, the nature and scope of which are determined case by case (see Figure 1). The main components of a full EA report are the following:

*Executive summary.* A concise discussion of the significant findings of the EA and recommended actions in the project.

*Policy, legal and administrative framework.* Discussion of the policy, legal, and administrative framework within which the EA is prepared. The environmental requirements of any cofinanciers should be explained.

*Project description.* A concise description of the project's geographic, ecological, social, and temporal context, including any offsite investments that may be required by the project, such as dedicated pipelines, access roads, power plants,

**Table 1. IBRD Category A Projects by Sector, Fiscal 1991–95**

| Sector | 1991 | 1992 | 1993 | 1994 | 1995 | Total |
|---|---|---|---|---|---|---|
| Agriculture | 2 | 1 | 3 | 7 | 5 | 18 |
| Energy and power | 6 | 14 | 10 | 9 | 8 | 47 |
| Industry | 2 | 1 | 0 | 0 | 1 | 4 |
| Mining | 0 | 0 | 0 | 1 | 0 | 1 |
| Tourism | 0 | 0 | 1 | 0 | 0 | 1 |
| Transport | 2 | 2 | 3 | 4 | 5 | 16 |
| Urban | 0 | 0 | 0 | 4 | 4 | 8 |
| Water and sanitation | 0 | 2 | 2 | 0 | 5 | 9 |
| Total | 12 | 20 | 19 | 25 | 28 | 104 |

*Note:* IBRD, International Bank for Reconstruction and Development. IBRD and the International Development Association (IDA) make up the World Bank.

## Figure 1.  The Environmental Assessment Process

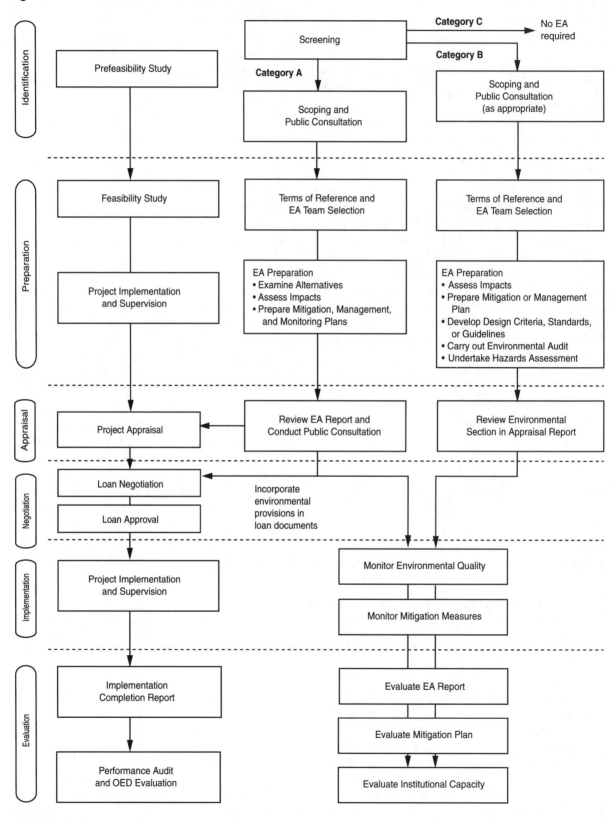

*Note:* OED, World Bank Operations Evaluation Department.

water supply, housing, and raw material and product storage.

*Baseline data.* For EA purposes, include an assessment of the study area's dimensions and a description of relevant physical, biological, and socioeconomic conditions, including any changes anticipated before the project begins, and current and proposed development activities within the project area, even if not directly connected with the project.

*Impact assessment.* Includes identification and assessment of the positive and negative impacts likely to result from the proposed project. Mitigation measures and any residual negative impacts that cannot be mitigated should be identified. Opportunities for environmental enhancement should be explored. The extent and quality of available data, key gaps in data, and uncertainties associated with predictions should be identified or estimated. Topics that do not require further attention should be specified.

*Analysis of alternatives.* Assesses investment alternatives from an environmental perspective. This is a key purpose of EA work and the more proactive side of EA—enhancing the design of a project through consideration of alternatives, as opposed to the more defensive task of reducing the adverse impacts of a given design. The Bank's Operational Directive on Environmental Assessment calls for the systematic comparison of the proposed alternatives for investment design, site, technology, and operations in terms of their potential environmental impacts, capital and recurrent costs, suitability under local conditions, and institutional, training, and monitoring requirements. For each alternative, the environmental costs and benefits should be quantified to the extent possible, economic values should be attached where feasible, and the basis for the selected alternative should be stated.

*Mitigation or management plan.* The set of measures to be taken during implementation and operation to eliminate or offset adverse environmental impacts or reduce them to acceptable levels. The plan identifies feasible, cost-effective measures and estimates their potential environmental impacts, capital and recurrent costs, and institutional, training, and monitoring requirements. The plan should provide details on proposed work programs and schedules to help ensure that the proposed environmental actions

are in phase with construction and other project activities throughout implementation. It should consider compensatory measures if mitigation measures are not feasible or cost-effective.

*Environmental monitoring plan.* Specifies the type of monitoring, who will do it, how much it will cost, and what other inputs, such as training, are necessary.

*Public consultation.* Recognized as key to identifying environmental impacts and designing mitigation measures. The Bank's policy requires consultation with affected groups and local NGOs during at least two stages of the EA process: (a) at the scoping stage, shortly after the EA category has been assigned, and (b) once a draft EA report has been prepared. Consultation throughout EA preparation is also generally encouraged, particularly for projects that affect people's livelihood and for community-based projects. In projects with major social components, such as those requiring involuntary resettlement or affecting indigenous people, the consultation process should involve active public participation in the EA and project development process, and the social and environmental issues should be closely linked.

*Stage 4: EA Review and Project Appraisal*

Once the draft EA report is complete, the borrower submits it to the Bank for review by environmental specialists. If it is found satisfactory, the Bank project team is authorized to proceed to appraisal of the project. On the appraisal mission, Bank staff members review the Environmental Impact Assessment's (EIA's) procedural and substantive elements with the borrower, resolve any outstanding issues, assess the adequacy of the institutions responsible for environmental management in light of the EIA's findings, ensure that the mitigation plan is adequately budgeted, and determine whether the EIA's recommendations are properly addressed in project design and economic analysis.

*Stage 5: Project Implementation*

The borrower is responsible for implementing the project according to the agreements derived from the EA process. The Bank supervises the implementation of environmental aspects as part of overall project supervision, using environmental specialists as necessary.

## Guidance and Best Practice Development and Dissemination

The World Bank's three-volume *Environmental Assessment Sourcebook* (World Bank 1991) is an important source of EA information for Bank staff and borrowers. A digital version has recently become available on-line and on diskette. The printed version is available in Chinese, English, Russian, and Spanish and will soon be available in Arabic. In addition, the *Sourcebook* is being expanded incrementally in the form of EA Sourcebook Updates in a looseleaf format. Updates issued to date include:

- "The World Bank and Environmental Assessment: An Overview"
- "Environmental Screening"
- "Geographic Information Systems for Environmental Assessment and Review"
- "Sectoral Environmental Assessment"
- "Public Involvement in Environmental Assessment: Requirements, Opportunities, and Issues"
- "Privatization and Environmental Assessment: Issues and Approaches"
- "Coastal Zone Management and Environmental Assessment"
- "Cultural Heritage in Environmental Assessment"
- "Implementing Geographic Information Systems in Environmental Assessment"
- "International Agreements on Environment and Natural Resources: Reference and Appendix in EA"
- "Environmental Auditing."

Other Bank units, such as the regional environment divisions and the Transport, Water, and Urban Development Department and the Industry and Energy Department, are also active developers of guidance and "good practice" in the EA area. For example, an EA handbook for the roads sector was recently completed, and a digital environmental manual is being finalized for the power sector.

## Reference

World Bank. 1991. *Environmental Assessment Sourcebook.* Washington, D.C.

> Vol. 1: *Policies, Procedures, and Cross-Sectoral Issues.* World Bank Technical Paper 139.
> Vol. 2: *Sectoral Guidelines.* World Bank Technical Paper 140.
> Vol. 3: *Guidelines for Environmental Assessment of Energy and Industry Projects.* World Bank Technical Paper 154.

# Types of Environmental Standards

*Different kinds of environmental standards can serve quite different purposes in environmental policy, as discussed in this chapter.*

## Ambient Standards

Ambient standards set maximum allowable levels of a pollutant in the receiving medium (air, water, or soil). Ambient standards can offer a simple method of establishing priorities, since areas (or stream lengths) that comply with the relevant ambient standards are considered to require no further intervention, while other areas may be ranked by the extent to which concentrations exceed the ambient standards. Setting ambient standards requires an explicit agreement on the environmental quality objectives that are desired and the costs that society is willing to accept to meet those objectives. However, because ambient standards can be set at different levels for different locations, it is possible to use them to protect valuable ecosystems in a way that would not be possible by using emissions standards.[1]

It has been usual to establish an ambient standard for a pollutant by referring to the health effects of different levels of exposure, although some countries are moving toward ambient standards aiming to protect natural ecosystems. Historically, ambient standards in the industrial market economies have been continually tightened in the light of medical evidence on the impact of certain pollutants and in response to increased demand for better environmental quality. In particular, as reductions are achieved in the levels of simple pollutants such as biochemical oxygen demand (BOD), the focus has moved to the control of less obvious but more persistent pollutants such as heavy metals, polychlorinated biphenyls (PCBs), and the like, which are accumulative and essentially not biodegradable.

## Emissions Standards

Emissions standards set maximum amounts of a pollutant that may be given off by a plant or other source. They have typically been expressed as concentrations, although there is increasing use of load-based standards, which reflect more directly the overall objective of reducing the total load on the environment. Emissions standards may be established in terms of what can be achieved with available technology or in terms of the impacts of the emissions on the ambient environment.

Technology-based standards are based on knowledge of what can be achieved with current equipment and practices. A wide range of principles has been used, including "best available technology" (BAT), "best practicable technology" (BPT), and "best available technology not entailing excessive cost" (BATNEEC). All these approaches are open to interpretation and are related to establishing what are the highest levels of equipment and performance that can reasonably be demanded from industrial plants.

Alternatively, emissions standards can be established by estimating the discharges that are compatible with ensuring that receiving areas around the plant meet the ambient standards defined for the pollutant. This, however, requires considerable information on both the sources and the ambient environment and varies from area to area.

New source performance standards (NSPSs) are specific emissions standards in which the standard is applied only to new plants. They represent a special form of grandfathering, since emissions from existing plants are treated differently from those from new plants. Where NSPSs are significantly stricter than standards imposed on existing plants and are therefore costly, they may have the effect of prolonging the economic life of existing plants—subject, of course, to the influence of other economic and technological factors. On the other hand, it is easier for new plants to adopt cleaner processes and to incorporate treatment requirements in the initial design. Therefore, the costs of well-designed NSPSs need not be excessive.

**Note**

1. An example of this differentiation is the setting of "critical loads" for acidic depositions in various areas of Europe and Asia. Critical loads are a specific application of an ambient standard designed to protect vulnerable ecosystems from the damage caused by acid rain. They are a quantitative estimate of an exposure to one or more pollutants below which significant harmful effects on specified sensitive elements of the environment do not occur, according to present knowledge. Critical loads illustrate that it may be desirable to set joint ambient standards for several pollutants that interact or reinforce each other. Another example is the joint ambient standard for particulates and sulfur dioxide that has been adopted by the European Union.

# Principles of Waste Avoidance and Utilization

*The minimization of wastes requiring disposal is increasingly important as available disposal options become more and more constrained, and particularly as more substances enter every-day use that are not readily decomposed in the natural environment and that can present long-term hazards. This chapter sets out some basic principles for waste minimization in industrial processes, where "minimization" is taken to include avoidance of the generation of wastes, when practical, and the productive utilization of any wastes that are generated.*

In some rural or nonindustrialized areas, wastes are typically organic or inert and do not pose major disposal problems, particularly since they are often utilized for animal food or other purposes. However, as the level of industrialization increases, or even simply as a result of growing access to packaged and consumer goods, waste disposal becomes an increasing problem in virtually all societies. The problems are typically associated with nonbiodegradable or bioaccumulative substances such as waste pesticides, solvents, heavy metals, and chemical sludges. These are often production wastes, but they can also arise from inappropriate application (pesticides) or poor consumer behavior (waste motor oils). The development and widespread use of new substances such as plastics and the products that they have made possible have improved the standard of living for millions, but they have also introduced new threats to the environment, as typified by the histories of DDT and polychlorinated biphenyls (PCBs).

The long-term solution to the problem of persistent or hazardous wastes must lie in efforts to find alternatives to the hazardous substances. In the meantime, high priority should be given to minimizing the use of resources and reducing the discharge of wastes.

## Precautionary Approaches

The need to avoid or minimize the release of complex organic or inorganic substances into the environment is all the greater because of un-certainty about their effects on human health and the natural environment and the very high costs of retrofitting or cleanup. At the same time a realistic attitude must be maintained regarding developing countries. Much industrial and product design is based on industrial country practice, and almost all of the fundamental science on which regulation is based has been carried out in the more advanced economies. Although there will be some opportunities to leapfrog to more sophisticated systems, the priority in developing countries should be to ensure that policymakers and regulators are up-to-date and informed and avoid repeating fundamental mistakes made in the course of industrialization elsewhere.

A particular challenge for developing countries is to take advantage of affordable and productive technologies from industrial countries without allowing the importation of outdated or outlawed equipment or substances. Technologies and materials science are changing rapidly, but so are the sources of information. Environmental agencies in developing countries that do not have the resources to carry out their own research can find much of the necessary information publicly available, although an investment of time and resources will frequently be needed to find the appropriate answers.

## Definitions

*Waste minimization* is one of a number of related terms and concepts that, despite having similar overall goals and often being used interchangeably, may differ significantly in basic principles and in emphasis. In this *Handbook, waste* is used to refer to a material from a manufacturing process that has no value to the manufacturer and that has to be disposed of in some manner. (Waste of energy, an important related issue, is addressed elsewhere.)

*Avoidance* refers to actions by the producer to avoid generating the waste. *Utilization* includes the range of actions that make the waste a useful input to other processes, eliminating the need for disposal. Waste minimization thus comprises both avoidance and utilization. Processes that reduce the toxicity or potentially harmful impacts of a waste can in some cases be regarded as minimization, although in other circumstances such changes represent treatment before disposal.

Although the terminology used may vary, a number of important activities can be distinguished. *Reuse* refers to the repeated use of a "waste" material in a process (often after some treatment or makeup). *Recycling* refers to the use by one producer of a waste generated by another. *Recovery* is the extraction from a waste of some components that have value in other uses.

## Hierarchy of Approaches

Waste avoidance and utilization can be seen as part of a broader hierarchy of approaches to achieving sustainable development. At the highest level are approaches that seek to satisfy human needs and requirements in ways that do not waste resources or generate harmful by-products or residuals. These approaches include changing consumer behavior and reexamining the range and character of the products and services produced. At a slightly lower level are efforts to redesign products and services and to raise consumers' awareness about the impacts of their decisions. Application of techniques such as life cycle analysis (LCA) is part of the difficult analysis of the overall impacts of products and services on the environment. Such approaches are at present adopted mainly by the more advanced organizations in industrial countries.

More directly relevant to industrial activity in developing countries are approaches focused on improvements in production processes. These approaches include cleaner production, pollution prevention, and waste minimization, all of which are related, to a greater or lesser degree, to better management, improvements in production processes, substitution of hazardous inputs, reuse and recycling of wastes, and so on.

The next step, which should be minimized but is not to be neglected, is treatment and proper disposal of wastes. The lowest level in the hierarchy, and the one that all the other levels strive to eliminate, is remediation of the impacts of wastes discharged to the environment. Cleanup is costlier than prevention.

## Policy and Regulatory Framework

A clear and effective governmental framework for waste management is necessary. Such a framework should include the delegation of relevant powers to the lower levels of government that are typically responsible for implementation. It should be based on a clear and broadly accepted long-term policy and should include a predictable and flexible regulatory regime and targeted economic incentives. At the same time, programs should be put in place to increase awareness and education, with the long-term objective of changing the behavior of manufacturers and consumers in the direction of minimizing waste generation.

## Producers and Consumers

Efforts must be made to involve both producers and consumers in waste minimization and utilization. Producers can improve their performance through both management changes and technological improvement; some producers in industrial countries are now making serious efforts to examine the impacts not only of their production processes but also of the products themselves. LCA is still an evolving tool, but it does focus attention on the overall impact of the production, use, and disposal of products.

Consumers in some of the wealthier countries are moving toward a greater awareness about the need for waste reduction, as shown by participation in recycling schemes and some demand for environmentally friendly products. However, progress is often slow, and there is a need for ongoing education and awareness, as well as careful analysis of options and incentives. In developing countries, the demand for resources often leads to significant recycling of materials such as glass, metals, and plastics. These recycling systems have important social and economic consequences at the local level, and their "improvement" must be approached with care.

## Complexity

Waste management efforts are linked closely with income levels. There is a broad progression from recycling of most materials in the poorest societies, through increasing consumerism—often with little concern for waste problems—in low- and middle-income countries, to the environmental activism of some rich countries. The appropriate waste avoidance and utilization strategy for any situation must take into account the level of the economy, the capabilities of government at different levels, and the environmental circumstances. As with any other environmental strategy, there is a need for public involvement and political support in the identification of priorities and the implementation of the necessary enabling measures.

# Efficient Use of Energy

*Efficient use of energy is one of the main strategic measures not only for the conservation of fossil energy resources but also for abatement of air pollution and the slowing down of anthropogenic climate change. Accordingly, economic and technical measures to reduce specific energy demand should be priorities across all sectors of an economy. Many opportunities exist for improving efficiency, but progress has been disappointingly slow in many cases. This chapter identifies some of the key areas where improvements are possible and describes the World Bank Group's support for energy efficiency, drawing heavily on the recent strategy paper "Fuel for Thought."*

The term *efficient use of energy* includes all the technical and economical measures aimed at reducing the specific energy demand of a production system or economic sector. Although implementation of energy-saving techniques may require initial investments, short-term financial returns can often be achieved through lower fuel costs due to the reduced energy demand.

Improving the use of energy is a issue in virtually all sectors of an economy, but the focus here is on the power sector and the industrial sector, which have the highest primary energy demand and thus the highest potential for energy savings.

## Growth in Energy Use

Energy is vital to economic development in developing countries. Poverty will not be reduced without greater use of modern forms of energy. Assuming that energy demand in developing countries grows by 2.6% per year (a likely figure, given current trends; see World Energy Council 1995), their total consumption of energy will be double the level of total consumption in industrial countries by 2050. Even then, each person in the developing countries will be using, on average, a mere quarter of the energy consumed by each inhabitant of the industrial world. As they seek to improve their standards of living, developing countries have the opportunity to do things differently from what has happened in the past. The challenge is to break the link between economic growth and energy consumption by pursuing efficient production processes and reducing waste and, at the same time, to break the link between energy consumption and pollution by relying more on renewables and by using fossil fuels more efficiently.

According to World Energy Council projections, fossil fuels will still account for almost two thirds of primary energy even decades from now. Some long-term scenarios (for example, by Shell International and the Intergovernmental Panel on Climate Change, IPCC) postulate a rapidly increasing share of renewable technologies—solar, wind, geothermal, and modern biomass, as well as the more traditional hydroelectric. Under these scenarios, with appropriate policies and new technological developments, renewables could reach up to 50% of the total by the middle of the twenty-first century. However, even in fairly optimistic scenarios, carbon emissions from burning fossil fuels (in the form of carbon dioxide) are predicted to increase dramatically. Industrial countries are responsible for the bulk of the buildup of heat-trapping gases currently in the atmosphere, and only they have made firm commitments to cut their emissions at the Conference of the Parties to the United Nations Framework Convention on Climate Change in Kyoto in December 1997. Yet emissions from developing countries are already growing rapidly, and by early in the next century they are expected to exceed those of industrial countries. The fundamental question is how to reconcile economic growth, primarily fueled by coal, oil, and gas, with protection of the environment.

## The Approach of the World Bank Group

The guiding principles for the Bank's work in energy efficiency have been set out in a number of policy papers (e.g., World Bank 1993a, 1993b) and the strategy paper "Fuel for Thought" (World Bank 1998). Among them are these:

- The World Bank Group will not invest in a country's energy sector unless that country shows a commitment to improving efficiency, whether by restructuring the sector or by reforming its policies.
- It will support competition, private sector investment, and sound regulation of the energy sector.
- It will promote energy efficiency both on the supply side and on the demand side and will integrate energy pricing with environmental policies.
- It will help to improve access to modern forms of energy for the 2 billion people in rural areas who must rely on traditional forms of energy such as fuelwood and agricultural waste.

A recent internal Bank study indicates that market-based restructuring of the energy sector is already yielding financial and operational efficiency rewards in some developing countries. However, the study concluded that much more time than initially estimated is needed in other countries to implement the necessary reforms. It also found that there was not yet much evidence of the environmental impact of reforms, and the evidence of much progress on energy efficiency— on either the supply side or the demand side—is still thin.

## Supply-Side Efficiency

Power industries in developing countries often lose more than 20% of their electricity to theft or inefficiency. One way to stop this is to encourage either private-sector participation (as in Côte d'Ivoire) or complete privatization (as in Argentina and Chile, where losses are now at an acceptable level of 10–12%). However, many projects that were aimed in part at cutting electricity losses in publicly owned utilities have achieved much less than hoped, indicating that the Bank and its borrowers need to increase substantially their efforts in this area.

There is huge scope for reducing energy losses in countries that use district heating systems, and the Bank has achieved successes in this area. The World Bank recently assisted a project to rehabilitate district heating in major Polish cities, and the improvements there are remarkable: 15–20% of energy has been saved; government subsidies—once 80% of cost—have been eliminated; and emissions of pollutants have fallen by 15–20%.

## Demand-Side Management

*Bank Involvement*

Bank lending for industrial energy conservation has had mixed success. Over 70% of the projects reviewed did not meet their objectives fully. The barriers included lack of interest by consumers, lack of credit, and—most notably—a low level of commitment on the part of the borrower. Those project that did succeed were mostly in East European countries, where access to foreign exchange after the collapse of communism allowed firms to buy new, more efficient machinery. End-use energy efficiency programs in the electric power sector and in other sectors such as industry and district heating are still in early stages, but currently, more than 20 projects include energy efficiency measures. Much of this assistance is for projects outside the energy sector—for example, retrofitting apartment blocks in Russia. Projects are currently under way in Thailand, and major operations are planned in Brazil and China; these will include establishment of energy service companies (ESCOs).

In the area of energy efficiency, the International Finance Corporation (IFC) has invested in numerous projects that improve the efficiency of industrial energy use through the rehabilitation and upgrading of plants in energy-intensive sectors such as cement, chemicals, and pulp and paper. In addition to these process improvements, the IFC has invested more directly in energy efficiency through several different types of projects:

improvements in transmission and distribution equipment owned by private electric utilities; manufacturing of goods such as efficient light bulbs and insulation material; profit-oriented ESCOs that upgrade equipment and change processes to reduce energy consumption in client companies; and financial intermediaries with credit facilities targeted at improvements in energy efficiency. The IFC is actively pursuing further investments in this area. (For an overview of the IFC's strategy in the energy sector, see Box 1.)

## Power Sector Opportunities

### Greater Efficiency in Conventional Power Plants

Between 35% and 40% of total annual primary energy demand in the industrialized countries is used in power plants to generate electricity or heat. As a result, between 25% and 33% of total annual carbon dioxide emissions arise from power plants. These figures underline the importance of efficient use of energy in the energy supply sector.

Various technical measures are available for increasing the efficiency of generation of electricity and heat in existing and new conventional fossil-fuel-fired power plants. Replacement or further optimization of main process items may be an option; for example, replacement of steam turbines in several power plants in the former East Germany after reunification resulted in an overall system efficiency increase of about 1.7 percentage points. Other measures include lowering condenser pressure, optimizing the feedwater preheat system, utilizing waste heat, and using ultracritical steam cycle conditions. The total system efficiencies that can be attained by taking advantage of current developments in power plant technology can be about 43% for hard-coal-fired plants, 41% for lignite-fired plants, and 56% for gas-fired combined-cycle plants.

Since combustion of fossil fuels contributes greatly to emissions of carbon dioxide—the most important greenhouse gas—fuel switching has to be regarded as a major option for the reduction of carbon dioxide emissions.

### Cogeneration

Use of cogeneration plants, which produce both electricity and heat, can reduce overall energy consumption by 10–30%, in comparison with separate generation of electricity and heat. Cogeneration plants are based on currently available standard technologies, and thus no technical risks are involved. However, reasonable and cost-effective utilization of this technology is only feasible if the heat can be supplied to a district heating network or to a nearby industrial plant where it can be used for process heating purposes.

---

### Box 1. The IFC's Strategy

In view of the increasing commercial viability of renewable energy technologies, and in anticipation of potential changes in how the market values environmental externalities such as emissions of greenhouse gases, the IFC is actively investigating—and in certain cases financing—environmentally friendly energy projects. In approaching newer technologies, the IFC seeks out projects that fall into two basic categories:

- Ventures that appear to be commercially viable from the IFC's perspective but that are still perceived as too risky by private sector investors or lenders
- Ventures that the IFC and the private sector consider to be close to, but not quite at, commercial viability.

The IFC's efforts reflect a commitment by the corporation's senior management to expand investments in this area and to help accelerate market acceptance of environmentally sustainable energy projects. The IFC is considering renewable energy projects ranging from those that are often competitive with conventional energy sources (e.g., small-scale hydroelectric, biomass, and wind) to those that usually require some level of concessional assistance, such as solar photovoltaics. The IFC is also assessing various types of energy efficiency projects, including energy service companies (ESCOs), transmission and distribution improvements, and industrial upgrades. The IFC has identified a large potential market in this sector but has also noted many barriers (small project size, lack of collateral, and so on).

*Emerging Power Plant Technologies*

New energy technologies are being developed, such as integrated gasification combined-cycle power plants, pressurized pulverized-coal-firing technology, humid air turbines, and fuel cells. Some of these technologies, although they are capable of efficiencies well in advance of current technology and show greatly reduced emissions, are yet not in a mature state of development. Currently, several large integrated gasification combined-cycle demonstration projects are being assessed, but it is too early to rely on these approaches as technically and economically viable alternatives to conventional plants.

## Industrial Power and Heat Utilization

Industrial production processes often show a high specific energy demand. Industry is estimated to account for between 25% and 35% of total final energy consumption. Although great progress has been made in the rational use of energy in the industrial sector during the last two decades, improvements in cost-effective energy utilization have not nearly been exhausted. This holds true for new plants as well as for existing plants. Improvement in energy end-use efficiency offers the largest opportunity of all alternatives for meeting the energy requirements of a growing world economy.

It is impossible to list all the measures that have been implemented or that show promise for further improvements in special industrial branches. Many of the technical options for energy saving require only small investments and are easy to implement. In several cases, even simple organizational changes bring about considerable energy savings, yielding not only environmental benefits but also financial returns. Energy-saving measures often show very short payback times, especially in industrial applications. However, as in the case of cleaner production approaches, it is often difficult to generate management interest in and support for the identification and implementation of energy-saving measures. Without such support, success is almost always limited.

*Energy Audits and Efficiency Planning*

The first step in identifying energy-saving potential within an industrial plant is to carry out an energy audit, taking into account the specific conditions at the plant and the local conditions at the production site. This energy audit is required to determine the scope of the energy efficiency project, to achieve a broad view of all the equipment installed at the production site, and to establish a consistent methodology of evaluation. Preparation of an improved energy utilization scheme starts with an inventory of the equipment, its energy demand, and the flow of energy through the plant. Electrical energy and heat should be recorded separately, and the time dependence of the energy demand should be taken into account. A few key areas can be identified on which to focus conservation efforts.

- Electricity production typically requires three times as much primary energy as direct heat use. Therefore, electricity should only be used if it cannot be replaced by other, more direct energy sources.

- The chemical energy contained in fuels should be utilized as efficiently as possible. When combustion processes are used to meet the energy demand of a process or an industrial plant, high combustion efficiencies should be achieved by utilizing as much as possible of the thermal energy contained in the flue gases, by minimizing heat losses (through use of insulation), and by recovering the thermal energy contained in combustion by-products such as ashes and slag.

- Special attention should be given to separation processes for recovering and purifying products, which account for up to 40% of the total energy demand of chemical processes. Energy savings of 10–40% can be achieved through heat integration of the reboiler and the condenser of distillation columns, by using heat pumps or water compression systems. In several applications, it may also be possible to replace the common but very energy-intensive distillation process with advanced separation processes, such as membrane processes, that show a significantly reduced energy demand.

## Residential Sector

There is a huge potential for energy savings in the residential sector. Energy can be saved by increasing the thermal integrity of buildings or by using energy-saving lighting such as fluorescent lamps. Because people's behavior is so important for residential energy consumption, information campaigns and demand-side management measures are the most important options for reducing energy consumption in the residential sector.

## Capturing the Easy Opportunities

The first step in breaking the energy-environment link is to capture the opportunities for reaping environmental benefits through economically attractive solutions at no additional cost. These opportunities include, at the very least, energy sector reform and restructuring, improvements in energy efficiency on the supply and demand sides, and a switch to less polluting energy sources (see Box 2). Such "win-win" measures can go a long way toward reducing local environmental degradation, but they will not be sufficient. The objective must be for all countries to integrate local environmental and social externality costs into energy pricing and investment decisions so that the polluter pays for the additional costs of environmental protection and pollution abatement.

## The Global Dimension

The Bank accepts the IPCC's conclusion that emissions of greenhouse gases from human activities are affecting the global climate. It also believes that the consequences of climate change will disproportionately affect both poor people and poor countries. The World Bank Group has an important role to play in helping to avert climate change, and it will assist its clients in meeting their obligations under the United Nations Framework Convention on Climate Change (UNFCCC). Under the 1997 Kyoto Protocol, some client countries with economies in transition have obligations to reduce emissions of greenhouse gases. Other clients—developing nations—have obligations to measure and monitor GHG emissions within their countries but do not have to reduce emissions yet. In the case of developing country clients, the World Bank Group will seek additional resources to ensure that they do not bear the additional costs of adopting climate-friendly technologies and policies and that their

---

### Box 2. "Win-Win" Opportunities

#### On the Demand Side
- Improved customer billing and metering (electricity, gas, district heating) to link prices and the rational use of energy
- Industrial boiler tune-ups
- Temperature and lighting controls
- Replacement of motors and lights
- Cogeneration of electricity from waste heat
- Reduction of energy losses through building codes
- Optimization of water pumping through time-of-day tariffs, metering, and replacement of pumps
- Streamlining regulatory requirements

#### On the Supply Side
- Promotion of competition and private investment within a sound regulatory framework
- Cleanup of oil and gas leaks
- Improvements in coal mining and production
- Rehabilitation of power plants and district heating systems; loss reduction programs in transmission and distribution
- Fuel switching to natural gas
- Large hydroelectric projects, under the right conditions
- Gas trade (liquefied natural gas, pipelines) and power trade
- Wind power, photovoltaics, and small hydroelectric installations

#### Obstacles to "Win-Win" Strategies
- Lack of information or interest among consumers about potential and techniques
- Lack of access to financing
- Small absolute returns that make efficiency measures less interesting for firms than big projects ·
- Legal constraints (e.g., tenants may not be allowed to improve building structures)
- High real or perceived risk
- Weak institutions and high transaction costs
- Inconsistent or ineffectual monitoring of energy savings over the lifetime of the investment

goals for national economic development and environmental quality are not compromised.

## Additional Resources

The Bank has established a Thematic Group on Energy Efficiency that can be contacted through the Knowledge Manager for the Energy, Mining, and Telecommunications Department (IEN) or through the Bank's Website (www.worldbank.org).

## References

World Energy Council. 1995. *Global Energy Perspectives to 2050 and Beyond: Mid-Range Current Trends Forecast of Energy Demand.* London.

World Bank. 1993a. *The World Bank's Role in the Electric Power Sector: Policies for Effective Institutional, Regulatory, and Financial Reform.* A World Bank Policy Paper. Washington, D.C.

———. 1993b. *Energy Efficiency and Conservation in the Developing World: The World Bank's Role.* A World Bank Policy Paper. Washington, D.C.

———. 1998. "Fuel for Thought: A New Environmental Strategy for the Energy Sector." Draft. Available on-line (www.esd.worldbank.org/cc/eestrat.html).

# Monitoring Environmental Quality

*In order to determine the effectiveness of actions to improve environmental quality, it is necessary to be able to measure relevant environmental parameters at a level of detail accurate enough to distinguish the anticipated changes. Because the establishment and maintenance of monitoring systems is time consuming and expensive, the scale of such systems needs to be kept to a realistic minimum, and the greatest possible use must be made of the data collected. Experience with monitoring systems in World Bank projects has been mixed, but a number of key factors can be identified, including clear objectives, quality control, and sustainability.*

## Monitoring in World Bank Projects

Monitoring of environmental quality is often included in World Bank projects to aid understanding of the state of the ambient environment or to monitor the emissions and impacts of specific discharges. Although monitoring is usually only a small component (except in technical assistance projects), it is often important in measuring and evaluating the outcomes of a project. Feedback on the success of these components has been limited to date, but this is changing as more emphasis is placed on monitoring the impacts of projects. However, comments in a number of World Bank reports indicate that the information available on the environment is often incomplete or unreliable (see Box 1). While technical consultants can advise on the design of systems, ensuring the long-term effectiveness and performance of such systems is much more difficult.

---

**Box 1. Insights from a Sample of Bank Reports**

*The systems are often not providing useful data.*
- "Data and information systems (physical, technical, socioeconomic, etc.) relating to water resources in terms of quantity, quality, accessibility, and use are generally inadequate throughout the region" (African Water Resources project).
- "With adequate information, setting priorities is not difficult, requiring only a comparison of benefits and costs. But environmental data are generally incomplete, so uncertainty about costs and benefits is high" ("Study of East Asia's Environment").
- "In most parts of the country there is no basis upon which to make informed decisions about ambient environmental conditions. Filling the gaps is a precondition for an assessment of pollution costs in these areas" (Argentina Pollution Study).

*A number of causes have been identified.*
- "Reduction of budgetary support; lack of understanding of the economic importance of the data; and [technical assistance] programs which are unsustainable because the outputs have not been of use to decisionmakers and therefore programs are not funded" (Sub-Saharan Africa Hydrological Assessment).
- "High turnover rates [of high quality trained technicians] have been a major problem . . . and have contributed to the intermittent operation of a sophisticated network of . . . monitoring stations built with [donor] financing." (Thailand Country Report).
- "The old system of central planning and control has left a legacy of inefficiency and mismanagement resulting from unreliable basic information; narrow segregation of responsibility; poor information dissemination and analysis; incomplete accountability for performance and results; and in certain cases, deliberate misreporting of environmental data" (former Soviet Union).

---

The most important steps in establishing or upgrading an environmental monitoring system are to agree on the objectives of the system and to design the system to address these objectives. A monitoring system should be designed to provide practical management or scientific information. Better information will improve environmental decisionmaking, up to a point. At the same time, collecting data, maintaining a database, and carrying out appropriate analyses are costly in terms of both human and financial resources. It is therefore important to focus resources and priorities on those areas where the information is most needed and most useful.

Monitoring is always included in the preparation and design of major projects that may have a direct environmental impact, such as power stations and sewage treatment plants. There are other examples in the portfolio in which specific support has been given to monitoring components (see Box 2). In these more focused cases, success with monitoring has typically been greater.

## Ambient Data and Emissions Data

The conceptual model underlying most pollution management is that emissions of pollutants lead to changes in ambient levels, which in turn control the impacts on health and environment. The ultimate concern is the impacts, but in practice, data on ambient pollution are often used to provide information on background conditions and as a basis for policy setting. In the design and control of a specific project, it is usual to work with emissions data because they are strongly related to the pollution sources and because they are more easily measured and managed at a specific site. The emissions requirements, however, must be related to estimates of the overall impact on ambient levels and, ultimately, on the environment.

The links between emissions, ambient levels, and impacts need to be well understood when a monitoring system is being designed because an error in the assumed relationships can lead to wasteful or counterproductive policies and actions.

## Ambient Monitoring

Ambient monitoring is carried out for a variety of reasons, including assessment of environmental problems and evaluation of interventions. The initial design of a program is usually based on the available (but often unreliable) data on existing conditions or sometimes on simple models based on emissions estimates. In any case, the program should have the flexibility to be adjusted in the light of initial results.

The choice of parameters should be based on the sources in the area and on the receptors and impacts of concern. In practice, it is usually worthwhile to measure a basic set of parameters (see Table 1), plus any other indicators of special concern. The monitoring plan should set out the rationale for selecting the number and location of monitoring stations, the monitoring frequency, and the sampling methods and should include a quality control plan. The design of monitoring systems should not be overly ambitious: even in the United States and the countries of the European Union, the management information available from large-scale monitoring systems is less than might be hoped. Such experience reinforces

---

### Box 2. Examples from the Portfolio

- *Shanghai Environment Project.* Water quality monitoring was a significant part of this project, which had as a key objective the relocation of the water supply system intake to a point in the river where industrial pollution was a minimum threat to the supply. A sophisticated satellite and geographic information system (GIS) was provided to track urbanization in the catchment area.
- *Lake Victoria Environmental Management Programme.* A major objective of this project, which covered the three major lake countries of Kenya, Tanzania, and Uganda, was to collect and share the data necessary to understand the dynamics of the lake system.
- *Bolivia Environment, Industry, and Mining Project.* Detailed sampling and analysis of a mining area were carried out with bilateral (Swedish) assistance, separately from the Bank project but as part of the same overall government program.
- *Brazil National Industrial Pollution Control Project.* This project, which focused on improving industrial pollution control in the city of São Paulo, included a component to strengthen the data management capabilities of the local agency.

**Table 1.  Air Sampling Methods**

| Method | Advantages | Disadvantages | Cost (U.S. dollars) |
|---|---|---|---|
| Passive samplers | Very low cost; very simple; useful for baseline and screening studies | Unproven for some pollutants; in general, provides only weekly or monthly averages | 2–4 per sample |
| Active samplers | Low cost; easy to operate; reliable operation and performance; yields historical data sequence | Daily averages; labor-intensive; laboratory analysis required | 2,000–4,000 per unit |
| Automatic analyzers | Proven; high performance; hourly data; on-line information and low direct costs | Complex; expensive; high skill required; high recurrent costs | 10,000–20,000 per analyzer |
| Remote sensors | Path or range resolved data; useful near sources and for measurements taken vertically through the atmosphere; multi-component measurements | Very complex and expensive; difficult to support, operate, calibrate, and validate; not always comparable with conventional analyzers | > 200,000 per sensor |

*Source:* GEMS/Air.

the benefits of beginning with a small, focused monitoring system and concentrating on answering key management questions.

A realistic set of monitoring parameters would normally include the following (the exact requirements will vary with specific circumstances).

*Ambient Air*

- Basic set: suspended particulate matter (preferably including fine particulate matter, $PM_{10}$ or $PM_{2.5}$), sulfur oxides, nitrogen oxides, and lead
- Other: ozone, volatile organic compounds (VOCs), and aerosol acid

*Ambient Water*

- Basic set: pH (indicating acidity or alkalinity); dissolved oxygen (DO); biochemical oxygen demand (BOD); suspended solids; and flow (if appropriate)
- Other: coliform bacteria, ammonia, nitrogen, phosphorus, chlorophyll, nitrates, and metals

To give an example, Singapore regularly monitors 6 key air pollutants ($PM_{10}$, sulfur dioxide, nitrogen oxides, ozone, carbon monoxide, and hydrocarbons) at about 15 main sites. It monitors 3 major water quality parameters (DO, BOD,

and suspended solids) at about 70 locations around the island.

**Emissions Monitoring**

Emissions monitoring is usually carried out to collect information for the design and operation of pollution control systems or for regulatory purposes. For operational purposes, a small number of parameters (or surrogates) may be measured on a regular or continuous basis. Sampling schedules for regulatory requirements are typically very specific.

Emissions monitoring should include measurement of flow rates, although a surrogate such as production rate is often used. Flow measurements are necessary to convert measurements of concentrations into estimates of pollutant loads. Continuous monitoring methods are now available for many of the most important air and water pollutants, but the value of the additional data obtained needs to be weighed against the cost and complexity of such systems.

An *environmental quality assessment* is essentially a baseline study, either for the examination of the impacts of a project (in a formal EA) or as a basis for the preparation or examination of policy options. In the more sophisticated type of assessment, cause-and-effect relationships are estimated so that the impacts of different interventions can be determined. In such an assessment, large amounts of useful data and analyses are often obtained, but the details are then frequently stored in a form or location that makes subsequent access difficult.

## Monitoring as a System

*Monitoring* usually refers to the tracking of trends over time. It must be regarded as a system comprising a number of elements, with the overall quality of the system controlled by the weakest segment.

*Sampling* refers to the collection of data that are representative of a system. In some cases, the data can be measured directly (temperature is an example), but often the representative sample has to be analyzed or tested to determine the value of individual parameters. Important questions are the design of the sampling scheme and the protocols for the collation, storage, and transport of samples. A wide range of national, international, and sector-specific standards for sampling and analysis exists.

*Analysis* of samples is a critical step; the value of the results of the monitoring depends greatly on the degree of confidence that can be assigned to the analysis. In many cases, a major issue is the capability and credibility of the laboratory system used for the analysis.

*Information management* refers to processing of the data obtained from the sampling system. This includes recording the data, analyzing it, and presenting the information in a form useful to decisionmakers and other stakeholders.

Box 3 describes an application of monitoring to a river system.

### Sampling

The choice of sampling methods should always be made on the basis of an evaluation of factors such as reliability, accuracy, ease of operation, and cost. Documentation from the GEMS/Air program provides an indication of the tradeoffs between simple (but often labor-intensive) methods and more sophisticated approaches.

### Analysis

The keyword for analytical systems is simplicity. The developing world is littered with sophisticated laboratories, funded by donors or projects, that are idle because of lack of funds for simple items such as glassware or purging gases or are highly unreliable—often because the laboratory buildings cannot be kept at constant temperature or free of dust and contaminants. The problems are commonly compounded by the lack of a national standards infrastructure to grade or certify the laboratories.

Experience has shown that an incremental approach is often best (see Box 4). Under such a plan, the capabilities and reliability of existing

---

**Box 3. Monitoring the Vistula River in Poland**

The Vistula River has been monitored since the 1970s, with the results being used to classify the state of the river. The basic monitoring program involved 35 stations on the main river and over 500 monitoring stations on the tributaries, which collected a standard set of samples. The samples were analyzed in 50 local laboratories across the country. Given the large amounts of data being collected, concerns arose as to the quality of the results. A new set of five key permanent monitoring stations has therefore been set up on the Vistula, together with a certified laboratory testing program, to provide a highly reliable set of baseline data.

---

**Box 4. Laboratory Upgrading**

Many World Bank projects have included a component to finance laboratory equipment for pollution monitoring and to train personnel. In the Poland Environment Management Project, a Polish-speaking external expert with many years of experience in managing laboratory systems was brought in to inventory existing facilities and optimize the use of existing equipment. A quality control system was introduced before decisions were made on the expansion of the laboratories and the purchase of new equipment. The laboratories were encouraged to operate as far as possible on a commercial basis and to broaden their client base beyond the state agencies that they had traditionally served. The project also included support for national standardization efforts, designed to increase the reliability of the overall laboratory system in the country.

laboratories are gradually strengthened and expanded. The main emphasis is on maximizing the use and productivity of existing systems and in implementing quality control systems before introducing new equipment or capabilities. External quality control, by national or international bodies, is critical for establishing the credibility and competitiveness of individual laboratories.

*Information Management*

*Definition and collection of data.* Decisions on the data required and their collection will be influenced by a range of factors. These include the existing data and their quality; local capabilities in sampling and analysis; the existing information infrastructure, such as the availability of remote-sensing data; the projected life of the monitoring system; and the costs of establishing and maintaining the data collection system. The costs of collecting and entering data can be many times those of the hardware and the initial training.

*Data-handling systems and information management.* The determination of institutional responsibilities for handling and managing information is frequently difficult. The pragmatic approach is to have the organization that needs the data do the initial collection (or contract for collection). The initial processing should be as simple and straightforward as possible, for example using spreadsheets or simple database software on a standard personal computer. Data should be stored in a format that is simple and convenient to exchange, once agreement on responsibilities has been reached.

More elaborate systems (often based on a geographic information system, GIS) need to be founded on institutional agreements regarding technical issues such as the georeferencing system) and exchange and interpretation of data. The installation of a number of GIS systems in different agencies or organizations is not necessarily inefficient, but care must be taken to avoid duplication and to ensure compatibility.

## Costs

The costs of a monitoring system include both capital costs and operating and maintenance costs. The capital costs of equipment can be estimated reasonably well, but operating costs are often highly dependent on local labor costs and the difficulties of obtaining spare parts.

A 1993 estimate of air pollution monitoring costs by the U.S. Environmental Protection Agency (USEPA) indicated an annualized figure of around US$26,000 for continuous monitoring of some key pollutants (see Table 2). These costs generally decrease as equipment is improved. In Germany in 1997, the average cost of these tests was about US$20,000.

Estimates for the establishment of pollution control laboratories in India in connection with a 1991 World Bank project were US$220,000 for a regional laboratory, US$140,000 for a mobile laboratory, US$140,000 for a continuous ambient air monitoring station, and US$11,000 for a continuous water monitoring station.

Estimates for a 1993 project in Ukraine included US$2.2 million for 16 stationary air quality monitoring stations (costing about US$140,000 each), US$1.3 million for 7 mobile ambient air quality monitoring stations (about US$190,000 each), and $1.9 million for 7 mobile emissions monitoring vans (about US$270,000 each). In addition, sample costs for measurement of deposition of toxic substances were estimated to be of the order of US$200–$500 per sample for polychlorinated aromatic hydrocarbons (PAHs), polychlorinated biphenyls (PCBs), and mercury.

As an example, a basic ambient air quality monitoring program for one large metropolitan area is based on 6 automatic monitoring stations around the city, each measuring sulfur dioxide, carbon monoxide, ozone, nitrogen oxides, and nonmethane hydrocarbons, and 16 manual moni-

### Table 2. Costs of Monitoring Selected Pollutants

| Pollutant | Monitoring period | Annualized cost (U.S. dollars) |
|---|---|---|
| Particulate matter (PM$_{10}$) | Continuous | 19,000 |
| Sulfur dioxide | Continuous | 26,000 |
| Nitrogen dioxide | Continuous | 27,000 |
| Lead | Daily | 20,000 |
| Ozone | Continuous | 26,000 |
| Carbon monoxide | Continuous | 26,000 |

*Source:* USEPA, 1993 data.

toring stations measuring particulates ($PM_{10}$) and sulfur dioxide. A composite air quality index is prepared and announced daily, and contingency plans are implemented when the index is very high. The performance of the system is audited twice a year by an internationally reputable laboratory. The annual cost of the system is estimated to be less than US$1 million.

## Sustainability

Given the costs in time and in human as well as financial resources, it is essential to establish responsibility for the collection of data and maintenance of the information system. Data collection is almost always the most costly component of a monitoring system, and it is unrealistic for an environmental agency or a national statistics office to attempt to collect large amounts of information. To minimize the operating costs of the monitoring group, collection should be the responsibility of the line agencies responsible for various functions such as water supply or transport. The coverage of the data may be less than desirable or optimal, but the system is far more likely to be sustainable in the long term.

It is essential that the environmental monitoring unit have an assured budget to sustain the effort. Reliance on donor funds for setup is acceptable, but the ongoing operations must be funded at a realistic level by the country. Examples of the practical budget problems that have been encountered include lack of fuel to drive project vehicles to sampling sites, inability to pay for long-distance phone calls to regional centers, and lack of an operating budget to pay for basic consumables such as glassware and distilled water.

Difficulties can arise when governments seek grant money for the development of new monitoring systems; such systems tend to be capital-intensive and overly sophisticated and therefore unsustainable in the long run. As awareness of these concerns grows, there is an increasing emphasis in project design on working within realistic institutional and budgetary constraints.

## Community Monitoring

Monitoring is usually thought of as technically complex, to be carried out by experts. However, there is increasing interest in developing simple

## Table 3. Basic Principles for Designing an Environmental Information System

| Principles | Practical concerns |
|---|---|
| Clear objectives | The system should be designed to support specific management objectives. There should be clear, easily understood questions that need to be answered. |
| Appropriateness | The level of sophistication of the sampling and analysis should match the skills and resources available, as well as the objectives. Achieving this may involve tradeoffs between extent of coverage, level of detail, and quality of the information generated. |
| Institutional support | The incentives for collection of data and maintenance of the systems must be clearly understood. Agreements must be made up front about the sharing of data and the publication of results. |
| Quality control | The level of accuracy required of the data must be appropriate to the use foreseen and must be explicit. A quality control system must be established, with sufficient outside involvement to ensure confidence in the results. |
| Flexibility | The system should be set up on the minimum scale necessary; it can be expanded when the benefits of better information become clear. There should be sufficient flexibility to adjust the system in the light of initial results. |
| Sustainability | The system must be designed in light of a realistic assessment of the long-term financial and human resources that are likely to be available. It is essential for sustainability to be able to demonstrate to decisionmakers that the system produces useful and relevant information. |

systems that can be adopted by communities to monitor their own local environment. These systems can be based on simple technologies (the equivalent of a strip of litmus paper) or can be more sophisticated and involve the training of local technicians in basic sampling and testing procedures. In either case, the involvement of the community in the design and implementation of the system is critical. Experience with these approaches is gradually developing and is likely to expand in Bank projects, with greater involve-

ment of communities and nongovernmental organizations.

## What Is a Minimum Data System?

A fundamental question should be asked: what is a minimum data system for a given situation? There is no simple answer, but Table 3 sets out a number of basic principles for the design of an environmental information system.

# Comparative Risk Assessment

*Comparative risk assessment provides a systematic way of looking at environmental problems that pose different types and degrees of health risk. It combines information on the inherent hazards of pollutants, exposure levels, and population characteristics to predict the resulting health effects. Using data from available sources, rapid, inexpensive comparative risk assessments can identify the most significant health problems. Together with consideration of costs, technical feasibility, and other factors, the results of comparative risk assessment can be used to set priorities for environmental management.*

Comparative risk assessment provides a general framework for evaluating environmental problems that affect human health.[1] Risk assessment does not have to be cumbersome or costly to provide useful insights. Rapid, inexpensive approaches can be considered risk assessment as long as certain basic concepts are included. There are four generally recognized steps in assessing human health risks, as described by the U.S. National Research Council:

- *Hazard identification* is the process of describing the inherent toxicity of a chemical on the basis of toxicological data from laboratory or epidemiologic studies.
- *Exposure assessment* combines data on the distribution and concentrations of pollution in the environment with information on behavior and physiology to estimate the amount, or dose, of a pollutant to which humans are exposed. Exposure is typically estimated by modeling the dispersion of emissions from a polluting source.
- *Dose-response assessment* relates the probability of a health effect to the dose of pollutant (see the Annex) It relies on statistical or biologically based models to describe this relationship, using either experimental animal data or epidemiologic studies. Estimated dose-response relationships (DRRs) are readily available for a large number of industrial chemicals and other types of pollutants and need not be derived separately for each individual country. However, relationships based on site-specific epidemiologic data are preferred, if available.
- *Risk characterization*, the final step in risk assessment, combines the exposure and dose-response assessments to calculate the health risk estimates, such as the number of people predicted to experience a particular disease, for the population of concern. Risk characterization also describes uncertainties in the calculations and provides other information to help interpret the results of the analysis.

Comparative risk assessment is a simplified, focused methodology for deriving reasonable findings from readily available data. It is used to provide understanding and guidance in the absence of detailed scientific studies and analysis.

## Issues in the Use of Risk Assessment

### Defining the Scope of the Analysis

An effective risk assessment must have a well-defined scope. The appropriate scope depends on the purpose of the analysis. For example, an evaluation of emissions from a particular industrial facility is likely to concentrate on the health effects on local population; a project to set national environmental priorities may include a broader range of issues, such as the effects of national policies on emissions of greenhouse gases and ozone-depleting substances.

The purpose of most comparative risk assessments is to identify the most important health risks from the point of view of the people affected. Although the options for mitigating risks may be evaluated on a sectoral basis, the initial analysis should consider all types and sources of environmental risk in making the ranking.

The analyst must choose the types of risks and populations to assess. These may include:

- Type and duration of health end point (acute or chronic, cancer or noncancer, occupational disease)
- Special target populations such as children, pregnant women, and asthmatics
- Ecological effects (for example, on populations, unique habitats, or biodiversity).

An assessment of a particular industrial project or sector typically begins with a description of the source of pollution. Models of the transport and potential transformation of the pollutants in the environment are used to estimate the concentration of contaminants in air, water, or soil. Concentrations in these media are used to estimate the human dose, which, combined with dose-response information, predicts the occurrence of disease.

For some pollutants, monitored data on concentrations in air or water may be available, obviating the need for modeling the transport and fate of the pollutant. In other cases, data on measures of pollutants in the human body, such as blood lead levels, or measures of characteristic clinical responses to exposures, such as elevations in blood enzyme levels, may be available. These may be used as a direct measure of exposure in the dose-response functions, rather than using estimated exposure rates.

*Complexity of Analysis*

Risk assessment does not necessarily require sophisticated techniques or extensive data collection. Reasonable, practical results can be derived using minimal available information on pollution and the populations exposed to it.

For example, in a study by the U.S. Agency for International Development (USAID 1994), an American team worked in Cairo for six weeks with Egyptian counterparts to refine the methodology to be used, identify sources, and collect data. The study relied on existing data without any additional environmental sampling or monitoring. Such rapid evaluations usually mean greater uncertainty in the results, but they are still useful for getting a general idea of the magnitude of problems associated with pollution sources and to demonstrate to decisionmakers that the problems posed by pollution are real and significant.

Comparative risk assessment is an important tool for helping to prioritize solutions to health problems by distinguishing *actual* risk from *potential* exposure. Its strength lies in its ability to compare and evaluate the effects of two or three pollutants or other hazards. Nonetheless, because these techniques emphasize pollution, they do not necessarily portray the complete range of environmental health problems. Thus, for example, vector-related diseases such as malaria, dengue fever, and schistosomiasis—all still very important in developing countries—would not necessarily be covered in an assessment. Additional public health inputs may therefore be required to gain a complete portrait of environmental health risks.

The results of rapid assessments are likely to be most valuable when they are used in a relative or comparative, rather than an absolute, way. The appropriate complexity of analysis will be influenced by a number of factors, including the likelihood that additional refinement would resolve the uncertainties in budgets, time constraints, availability of data, and use of the results.

*Quality of Data Required*

The quality and quantity of data needed to produce a meaningful analysis will depend on how much uncertainty the analyst is willing to accept. Ideally, high-quality local data for all parts of the analysis, including locally based epidemiology for the dose-response functions, would be available. The ideal will rarely, if ever, be the case. However, limited good data can be supplemented through techniques that fill data gaps with reasonable assumptions and extrapolations. For example, data on ambient concentrations of many chemicals are often unavailable, since monitoring is expensive and is likely to be directed at only a few constituents. In its place, emissions data can be used in conjunction with environmental modeling systems to estimate concentrations in the environment.

Two such systems developed within the World Bank are the Decision Support System and the Industrial Pollution Projection System. The USEPA has also developed and published emissions factors for air pollution sources; these include AP-42 (USEPA 1985) for "criteria" pollutants and Toxic Air Pollutant Emission Factors, or TAPEF.

*Adjustments for Site-Specific Conditions*

Many of the data sources and analytical techniques used in a risk assessment will, by necessity, be transferred from OECD contexts. It may be possible to adjust such data on the basis of a comparison of country-specific conditions with the conditions in the countries where the data were derived. For example, epidemiologic studies frequently use measures of ambient pollutant concentrations to represent personal exposure. To adjust the results of such studies, the analyst will consider how the relationship between ambient concentrations and personal exposures may differ in the country of interest.

## Examples of Comparative Risk Assessment

*In Industrial Countries*

Risk assessment has been used during the past decade in a number of OECD countries. In the United States, it has been used to set overall environmental priorities for the nation, to guide legislation, and to choose among regulatory approaches. Almost every environmental program within the USEPA now uses risk assessment to determine regulatory priorities, to perform cost-benefit analysis, or to target enforcement activities. Risk assessment has been used, for example, to decide which air pollutants to control, which pesticides to allow and which to ban, and to what degree contaminated hazardous waste sites should be cleaned up. In Western Europe, both the EU and individual countries are working to adjust risk assessment techniques for application within their contexts.

*In Developing Countries and Transition Economies*

Comparative risk assessment can help regions and countries allocate limited resources efficiently (see Table 1). For example, the method has been applied on a citywide basis in Bangkok and in Cairo to identify specific recommendations for targeted actions such as reducing lead in gasoline and managing traffic situations to decrease levels of particulate matter. The method was also applied in the Silesia region of the Czech Republic and Poland, where it was coupled with an effort to identify realistic, cost-effective solutions (USEPA 1992b, 1994).

Many of the comparative risk assessments performed in developing countries have examined urban areas that do not have significant industrial sources of pollution. These studies have identified a consistent set of priority problems: particulate air pollution and microbiological diseases caused by water and food contamination. These problems are likely to be of high concern in any rapidly developing area that lacks adequate municipal infrastructure and is experiencing a rise in industrial activity and traffic volume. Comparative risk assessments performed in such settings may direct resources to examining these problems first, although the specific conditions of each urban area may suggest additional priorities.

## Key Issues in Risk Characterization and Priority Setting

Risk assessment attempts to evaluate environmental problems using objective, scientifically based measures. Risk management considers not only the magnitude and severity of the health risks posed by pollution but also the costs and technical feasibility of abatement and the political will and institutional capacity to manage risks. By itself, it cannot establish environmental management priorities. It is the first of several steps in the process of setting priorities, structuring policies, and implementing strategies to deal with pollution.

The use of risk assessment in cost-benefit analysis and priority setting has typically meant the use of overall population risk measures, such

Table 1. Summary of Risk Assessment Projects in Developing Countries and Transition Economies

| Study location (reference) | Intent of study | Scope of problems examined | Notable features | Major findings |
|---|---|---|---|---|
| Bangkok (USAID 1990) | Comparative risk across a range of environmental problems | Air, and water pollution; solid and hazardous waste disposal; microbiological disease | Estimated incidence and severity index used to rank problems | Highest-priority problems: airborne particulate matter; lead; infectious disease |
| Bangkok follow-up (World Bank 1994) | Focus on air pollution from energy, transport and manufacturing sectors; identification of cost-effective risk reduction strategies | Primary reanalysis focus on air pollution, but other media examined | Included economic valuation component | Priority problems: particulate matter and lead; surface water pollution from microorganisms; congestion; air pollution control strategies for energy and road transport discussed |
| Cairo (USAID 1994) | Comparative risk across a range of environmental problems | Air and water pollution; solid and hazardous waste disposal; microbiological disease | Used estimated incidence and qualitative estimate of severity and probability to rank problems | Highest-priority problems: particulate matter; lead; food and water contamination leading to disease |
| Quito (USAID 1993a) | Comparative risk scoring across a broad range of environmental and health problems; other problems | Air and water pollution; solid waste; occupational disease; traffic | Used both quantitative risk assessment and health outcome data; performed site-specific ethnographic study; performed explicit scoring of problems based on probability and severity | Highest-priority problems: air pollution, and food contamination with microorganisms |
| Silesia region, Czech Republic and Poland (USEPA, 1992b, 1994) | Identification of actions to reduce risk and improve environmental management capabilities in a coal- and steel-producing region | Air, food, water, and solid waste; occupational disease; ecological risks for water pollution | Examined ecological as well as human health risks; used two dimensions—severity and scale—to characterize risk | High risks from particulate matter and toxic air pollution (coke oven emissions); food contamination with PCBs; high occupational risks; severe risks to aquatic life |
| URBAIR projects: Mumbai, Jakarta, Manila (Shah and Nagpal 1997a, 1997b, 1997d) | Estimate the health and economic impacts of air pollution resulting from continued urban growth | Air pollution only | Estimated health effects using monitoring data and U.S.-based concentration-response functions; some studies include explicit monetization of health effects | All studies found significant effects of air pollution (thousands of deaths, tens to hundreds of thousands of cases of illness) |

48

as the number of cases of disease predicted, as the preferred risk descriptor. But there may be other important measures, such as levels of individual risk, the distribution of risks across the general population and highly exposed subpopulations, identification of special at-risk populations, and consideration of the relative severity of the effects characterized.

Vital to the interpretation of risk assessments is the identification of major sources of uncertainty. Open, frank description of the uncertainties in the analysis enhances its credibility and provides a context in which the results should be viewed.

**Resources Required**

The scale and cost of some risk assessments that have been conducted demonstrate that the practical application of standard techniques of risk assessment can enhance project design without being overly resource-intensive.

USAID (1993b) presents a typical schedule for conducting an environmental health analysis. The example suggests a project lasting four to six months, from project planning through the final report. The schedule assumes a full-scale analysis of many types of problems; the actual time required may be less for site-specific projects,

where a narrower set of likely pollution problems can be identified. (See Table 2 for some recent examples.)

The types of consultants needed for a risk assessment will depend on the data available and the problems to be assessed. If industrial pollution sources are the focus, the project may need environmental scientists or engineers familiar with predicting the fate of emissions in the environment. The exposure assessment, dose-response, and risk characterization steps typically require individuals with training in risk assessment, toxicology, or epidemiology. The task manager may also want specialists familiar with the particular country's governmental and social structure to facilitate the collection of data from diverse sources.

**Some Sources of Data**

*Environmental Quality Data*

The most important sources of environmental quality data are local and regional. When local data are not available, other sources may provide limited information. For example, some international organizations maintain environmental quality data for certain pollutants: the United Nations Environment Programme (UNEP) Glo-

**Table 2. Time and Resource Requirements of Some Recent Studies**

| Location (reference) | Time required | Approximate resources (U.S. dollars) | Notes |
|---|---|---|---|
| Bangkok (USAID 1990) | Approximately 3 weeks on the ground; a few months total to prepare report | On the order of 60,000–70,000 | |
| Bangkok follow-up (World Bank 1994) | Four to 5 person-weeks for risk assessment portion (20 person-weeks for entire report) | 25,000 for risk assessment; 100,000 for entire report | Covered risk assessment, cost-effectiveness analysis, and development of policy framework |
| Cairo (USAID 1994) | Six weeks on the ground | "Moderate cost" | |
| Quito (USAID 1993a) | Five to 6 months, with local consultants on the ground in advance; shorter time in country | Approximately 200,000 | Included health risk assessment, environmental health survey, and ethnographic survey |
| URBAIR projects (Shah, Nagpal, and Brandon 1997; Shah and Nagpal 1997a, 1997b, 1997c, 1997d) | | | Covered only air problems |

bal Environmental Monitoring Network System is an example of such a source. Other organizations may have collected environmental quality data for specific purposes, such as USAID environmental action plans and World Bank country reports on environmental management. The World Resources Institute compiles environmental data from a variety of sources for its annual *World Resources* report.

### Human Health and Ecological Toxicity Data

International organizations are good sources of information on hazard evaluations of chemicals, including environmental standards and, for some pollutants, dose-response evaluations. The World Health Organization (WHO) develops guidelines for acceptable concentrations in environmental media based on protection of human health. Often, the background documents supporting these guidelines can provide further information on chemical hazards. The International Agency for Research on Cancer (IARC) supplies data on the carcinogenic effects of pollutants.

Since risk assessment is widely practiced in the United States, the USEPA is an important source of information on toxicological information and evaluation methods. The agency maintains a centralized, on-line database, the Integrated Risk Information System (IRIS), containing toxicological information on over 600 chemicals, which can be easily accessed by risk assessment practitioners. Other USEPA documents, such as the scientific documents that support standards for the criteria pollutants ($PM_{10}$, sulfur dioxide, lead, ozone, nitrogen oxides, and carbon monoxide), contain substantial reviews and evaluations of the literature on these major air pollutants.

A recent World Bank report (Ostro 1994) summarizes much of this same information, with additional discussion of its applicability to developing countries. In particular, it reviews health effects studies commonly used in assessing risk from particulate matter and ozone exposure. The studies were performed primarily in North America and Europe, and many of them are time-series studies that focus on short-term (e.g., daily) changes in morbidity and mortality in response to short-term changes in pollution concentrations. A peer review of Ostro pointed out the difficulties of extrapolating these results to developing countries, due to differences in the populations and exposures considered. The peer reviewers expressed concern that the time-series studies capture primarily the acute effects of air pollution on mortality. Short-term fluctuations in mortality due to air pollution episodes may largely reflect the hastening (by days or weeks) of the deaths of diseased individuals in the population. If so, this component of overall mortality results in fewer life-years lost and may be of less significance to public health than the chronic effects of long-term exposure to air pollution in otherwise healthy individuals.

Two recent cohort studies, Dockery et al. (1993) and Pope et al. (1995), have reported a significant and dramatic association between mortality in the study cohorts and long-term exposure to airborne particulate matter. Because such studies better reflect the morbidity and mortality effects of interest, using the results of chronic effects studies in comparative risk assessment is preferred, when they are available.

### Factors for Human Exposure Assessment

Exposure assessment requires the integration of environmental quality data with an estimate of the rate of human contact with contaminated media. This stage of risk assessment should rely heavily on local data, since it allows an assessment of how particular local conditions and cultural practices affect risk potential. Local data on food consumption patterns, indoor-outdoor activity patterns, types of housing, prevalence of health conditions, and so on can all be important to the assessment process. These data can be obtained from local health department and social service ministries, environmental ministries, NGOs, or sociological investigations conducted as part of the analysis.

## Annex. Dose-Response Functions and the Health Impacts of Air Pollution

Few would question that too much air pollution is a bad thing. Not only does air pollution reduce visibility and destroy the aesthetic beauty of our surroundings; it has been generally recognized as a health hazard. The question is not whether air pollution should be controlled but, rather, how much should be spent to control it. To answer this question it is necessary to estimate the reductions in health damages that are likely to occur if air pollution is reduced.

Dose-response functions measure the relationship between exposure to pollution and specific health outcomes. By regressing a specific measure of health on a measure of pollution exposure while controlling for other factors, the role of pollution in causing the health effect can be estimated. This estimate can then be used to predict the health improvement corresponding to a decrease in exposure. In short, dose-response functions translate changes in air quality into changes in health.

Both humans and animals have been the subjects of studies that examine the effects of air pollution exposure on health. This annex discusses only epidemiologic studies—those based on human populations.

*Exposure to Air Pollution*

Exposure to air pollution is usually measured in terms of ambient levels of pollutants. Not surprisingly, the pollutants included in the epidemiologic literature are limited by the availability of data. Those commonly monitored by environmental authorities can be divided into four categories:

- Sulfur oxides, nitrogen oxides, and particulates generated by burning fossil fuels
- Photochemical oxidants (e.g., ozone) created by the interaction of motor vehicle emissions (hydrocarbons, nitrogen oxides, and the like) in the atmosphere
- Other pollutants generated by mobile sources (e.g., carbon monoxide and lead)
- Miscellaneous pollutants (e.g., cadmium and lead) generated by localized point sources such as smelters and manufacturing plants.

*Health Outcomes*

Health outcomes are usually precisely defined. They are often expressed as a measure of breathing capacity, such as forced expiratory volume (FEV), forced vital capacity (FVC), or forced expiratory flow (FEF). However, respiratory symptoms such as cough, phlegm, and throat irritation, the incidence of respiratory disease,

including bronchitis and pneumonia, and mortality rates are studied as well. Table A.1 shows some health effects associated with selected common pollutants.

To date, most studies have examined the effects of acute (short-term) exposure to pollution. This should not be interpreted to mean that long-term exposure has no effect on health. Long-term exposure to low levels of pollution has been shown to affect an individual's tolerance of short-term exposure to high levels of pollutants. Furthermore, questions have been raised concerning the relationship between long-term exposure and the incidence of cancer and heart disease. Unfortunately, long-term exposure is often difficult to measure due to the high immigration rates in some urban populations.

*Confounding Factors*

A good study will attempt to control for confounding factors that may contribute to an individual's likelihood of experiencing the health outcome in question. However, these factors are often not easy to control for and can weaken the results of the research.

For instance, although individuals may be affected by a combination of pollutants, the presence of other pollutants may not be incorporated into the study due to the limited availability of pollution data. Other confounding factors include temperature, humidity, physical activity, smoking habits, occupational exposure to pollutants, dietary factors, availability and quality of

**Table A.1. Health Effects of Common Air Pollutants**

| Pollutant | Health effect |
|---|---|
| Particulate matter; sulfur dioxide | Decreased lung function; increased respiratory morbidity among susceptible adults and children; increased mortality among the elderly and the chronically ill |
| Ozone | Eye, nose, and throat irritation; chest tightness; cough; shortness of breath; pain on inspiration |
| Nitrogen oxides | Increased risk of respiratory disease in children under 12 years old |
| Lead | Impaired neurological development; high blood pressure |

medical care, and age. The age structure of the population is especially important because children and the elderly are more susceptible to respiratory infection.

*Applying the Dose-Response Function*

Calculating the total health impact of a proposed pollution control program is relatively easy once the dose-response functions have been estimated. The dose-response equation given below is taken from Evans et al. (1984), which summarizes the results of numerous cross-sectional analyses. The equation relates excess mortality to total suspended particulates (TSP).

$$\text{Excess mortality} = 0.45 \times \rho TSP \times POP$$

where *POP* is the size of the exposed population and $\rho TSP$ is the magnitude of the proposed change in pollution measured in micrograms per cubic meter ($\mu g/m^3$). Excess mortality is expressed as the age-adjusted mortality rate per 100,000 persons.

Ideally, the total life-years saved as a result of an environmental improvement would be measured. This can be done only when the dose-response function is estimated separately for different age groups—which, unfortunately, seldom occurs.

Recently, dose-response functions estimated for one country have been applied to populations lacking their own epidemiologic studies in order to estimate the effects of exposure to air pollution. Although this practice, referred to as "benefits transfer," does provide a rough estimate of the adverse health effects caused by pollution in these previously unstudied countries, it should be applied with caution. Without further testing, there is no reason to believe that the dose-response relationship calculated for one area will be exactly the same as that for another. Differences in the composition of air pollution, in the age distribution of the population, in access to and quality of medical care, in baseline health, and in education and other behavioral and socioeconomic variables may cause variations in the response to air pollution exposure.

In an effort to estimate the health effects of air pollution in Latin America, where few epidemiologic studies have been done to obtain dose-response functions, Romieu, Weitzenfeld, and Finkelman (1990) applied to a hypothetical population dose-response functions for TSP found in the literature (see Table A.2). The hypothetical population was similar in size and age distribution to the sum of all "high-risk" Latin American cities. The assumption used was that among the total population of 81 million people, 14.5 million would be exposed to a very high level of TSP (250 $\mu g/m^3$), 23.5 million would be exposed to a high level of TSP (150 $\mu g/m^3$), and 43 million would be exposed to a moderate level of TSP (100 $\mu g/m^3$). Table A.2 shows the health impacts attributable to TSP levels above the WHO guideline value of 75 $\mu g/m^3$. For instance, over 24,000 deaths, representing 6% of annual mortality, would be avoided if TSP levels were reduced to 75 $\mu g/m^3$.

## Note

1. The term *risk assessment* is used in a wide variety of contexts and meanings. Here, comparative risk assessment refers to an analytical approach to estimating the key environmental health risks faced by a population group. The approach does not address ecosystem impacts, which should be considered separately.

**Table A.2.  Health Effects of Selected Annual Mean TSP Levels in a Hypothetical Population**

| Excess number | Micrograms per cubic meter | | | |
| --- | --- | --- | --- | --- |
| | 250 | 150 | 100 | Total |
| Mortality (thousands per year) | 11.5 | 7.9 | 4.9 | 24.3 |
| Chronic cough in children (millions per year) | 1.1 | 0.76 | 0.47 | 2.3 |
| Respiratory-related restricted activity days (RRAD) in adults (millions of days per year) | 32.0 | 21.0 | 12.0 | 65.0 |
| Chronic bronchitis in the elderly (thousands) | 50.0 | 33.0 | 22.0 | 105.0 |

*Source:* Romieu, Weitzenfeld, and Finkelman 1990.

## References and Sources

Dockery, D., C. A. Pope, X. Xiping, J. Spengler, J. Ware, M. Fay, B. Ferris, and F. Speizer. 1993. "An Association between Air Pollution and Mortality in Six U.S. Cities." *New England Journal of Medicine* 329(24): 1753–59.

Evans, J. S., et al. 1984. "Cross-Sectional Mortality Studies and Air Pollution Risk Assessment." *Environmental International* 10: 55–83.

Ostro, Bart. 1994. "Estimating Health Effects of Air Pollution: A Methodology with an Application to Jakarta." Policy Research Working Paper 1301. World Bank, Policy Research Department, Washington, D.C.

Pope, C. A., M. Thun, M. Namboodiri, D. Dockery, J. Evans, F. Speizer, and C. Heath. 1995. "Particulate Air Pollution as a Predictor of Mortality in a Prospective Study of U.S. Adults." *American Journal of Respiratory and Critical Care Medicine* 151: 669–74.

Romieu, Isabelle, Henryk Weitzenfeld, and Jacobo Finkelman. 1990. "Urban Air Pollution in Latin American and the Caribbean: Health Perspectives." *World Health Statistical Quarterly* 43(3): 153–67.

Schwartz, Joel. 1991/92. "Particulate Air Pollution and Daily Mortality: A Synthesis." *Public Health Reviews* 19: 39–60.

Shah, Jitendra J., Tanvi Nagpal, and Carter J. Brandon, eds. 1997. *Urban Air Quality Management Strategy in Asia: Guidebook.* World Bank, Washington, D.C.

Shah, Jitendra J., and Tanvi Nagpal, eds. 1997a.*Urban Air Quality Management Strategy in Asia: Greater Mumbai Report.* World Bank Technical Paper 381. Washington, D.C.

———. 1997b. *Urban Air Quality Management Strategy in Asia: Jakarta Report.* World Bank Technical Paper 379. Washington, D.C.

———. 1997c. *Urban Air Quality Management Strategy in Asia: Kathmandu Valley Report.* World Bank Technical Paper 378. Washington, D.C.

———. 1997d. *Urban Air Quality Management Strat-egy in Asia: Metro Manila Report.* World Bank Technical Paper 380. Washington, D.C.

USAID (U.S. Agency for International Development). 1990. "Ranking Environmental Health Risks in Bangkok, Thailand." Prepared for USAID Office of Housing and Urban Programs under Contract PDC-1008-I-00-9066-00. Washington, D.C.

———. 1993a. "Environmental Health Assessment: A Case Study Conducted in the City of Quito and the County of Pedro Moncayo, Pichincha Province, Ecuador." Environmental Health Division, Office of Nutrition and Health, Washington, D.C.

———. 1993b. "Environmental Health Assessment: An Integrated Methodology for Rating Environmental Health Problems." Environmental Health Division, Office of Nutrition and Health, Washington, D.C.

———. 1994. "Comparing Environmental Health Risks in Cairo, Egypt." USAID Project 398-0365. Washington D.C.

USEPA (U.S. Environmental Protection Agency). 1985. "Compilation of Air Pollution Emissions Factors." Office of Air Quality Planning and Standards, Washington, D.C.

———. 1992a. "Framework for Ecological Risk Assessment." EPA/630/R-92/001. Prepared by the Risk Assessment Forum. Washington, D.C.

———. 1992b. "Project Silesia: Comparative Risk Screening Analysis." Prepared for the Technical Workgroup, Ostrava (former Czechoslovakia), and USEPA by IEC, Inc., and Sullivan Environmental Consulting. Washington, D.C.

———. 1994. "Project Silesia: Comparative Risk Screening Analysis." Prepared for the Technical Workgroup, Katowice, Poland, and USEPA by IEC, Inc., and Sullivan Environmental Consulting. Washington, D.C.

World Bank. 1994. "Thailand: Mitigating Pollution and Congestion Impacts in a High-Growth Economy." Country Economic Report. Report 11770-TH. East Asia and Pacific Region, Country Operations Division, Country Department I, Washington, D.C.

# Economic Analysis of Environmental Externalities

*In order to perform economic analysis of pollution prevention and abatement measures, estimates of the potential benefits from controlling pollution, as well as the better-known costs of new equipment or processes, are needed. This chapter discusses the economic analysis of environmental externalities, using a wide range of valuation techniques.*

Pollutants produced by industrial activities—solid wastes, toxic wastes, and substances that cause air and water pollution—may impose costs on society and individuals. The identification and quantification of these pollutants and the assessment of their monetary and nonmonetary impacts are important elements in a broader economic analysis of the benefits and costs of various production alternatives. Information on the costs of pollution is also important in helping decide what level of pollution control is economically justified.

The effects of pollution can generally be classified into four major categories: health impacts, direct and indirect effects on productivity, effects on the ecosystem, and aesthetic effects. All these are commonly encountered examples of *economic externalities* of industrial production activity, that is, the externality occurs because the individual or resource affected is not part of the enterprise's decisionmaking process. For example, a factory may emit soot that dirties surrounding buildings, increasing maintenance costs. The higher maintenance costs are a direct result of the factory's use of a resource—air—that from the plant's point of view is free but that has a cost to society. The same analogy applies to health impacts linked to air pollution. Sometimes a project makes certain groups better off, but the nature of the benefits is such that the project entity cannot extract a monetary payment for them. A sewerage and water supply project, for example, may not only improve water quality and yield direct health benefits but may also produce benefits from decreased pollution of coastal areas, in turn increasing recreational use and property values. Such externalities are real costs and benefits attributable to the project and should be included in the economic analysis as project costs or benefits.

Conceptually, the externalities problem is quite simple. Consider Figure 1, where *MPC* is the marginal production cost of a good (e.g., power produced by a coal-fired boiler), as perceived by the project entity. Suppose that the process produces a negative externality—for example, it emits soot that increases the maintenance costs of adjacent buildings. Because the production process also produces an externality, the marginal social cost is higher and is given by the line *MSC*. For any given level of output, $q^*$, the total cost of producing that level of output is given by the area under the curve. The difference between the areas under the two curves gives the difference between the private and the social costs. The financial costs of the project will not include the costs of the externality, and hence an evaluation of the project based on *MPC* will understate the social costs of the project and overstate its net benefits. In principle, to account for the externality, one simply works with social rather than private costs. In practice, the measurement difficulties are tremendous because often the shape of the *MSC* curve, and hence its relationship to the *MPC* curve, are unknown. Also, it is not always feasible to trace and measure all external effects. Nevertheless, an attempt should always be made to identify them and, if they appear significant, to measure them. When externalities

**Figure 1.  Private and Social Costs**

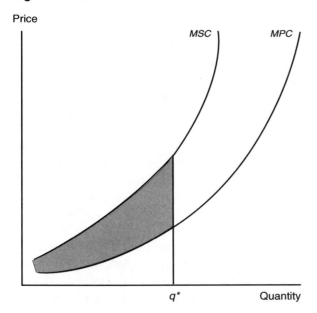

cannot be quantified, they should be discussed qualitatively.

In some cases, it is helpful to "internalize" externalities by considering a package of closely related activities as one project—that is, to draw the "project boundary" to include them. For example, in the case of the soot-emitting factory, the externality could be internalized by treating the factory and the neighboring buildings as if they belonged to the project entity. The additional maintenance costs then become part of the maintenance costs of the project entity. If the factory pays for the additional maintenance costs, or if the factory is forced to install a stack that does not emit soot, the externality again becomes internalized. In these cases, the formerly external cost becomes an internal cost that is reflected in the accounts of the factory.

### Environmental Externalities

Environmental externalities are a particular form of externalities that good economic analysis should take into account. Environmental externalities are identified as part of the environmental assessment. They are quantified where possible and are included in the economic analysis as project costs (e.g., increased illness, or reduced productivity of nearby farmlands) or benefits (such as reduction in pollu-

tion of coastal areas). A monetary value is assigned to the costs and benefits, and they are entered into the cash flow tables just as any other costs and benefits.

### Project Boundaries and Time Horizon

Analysts must make two major decisions when assessing environmental impacts. First, they must decide how far to look for environmental impacts—that is, they must determine the *boundary of the economic analysis.* When the internal benefits and costs of a project are assessed, the boundaries of the analysis are clear: if the benefits accrue to the project entity or if the costs are borne by the project entity, they enter into the analysis. When attempting to assess the externalities of a project to determine its impact on society, the boundaries become blurred. Identifying externalities implies expanding the conceptual and physical boundaries of the analysis. An oil-palm mill will generate wastewater that will adversely affect downstream uses of water—drinking, irrigation, and fishing. Other impacts on the environment may be more distant or more difficult to identify: the effects of emissions from a power plant on creation of acid rain, for example. How far to expand the boundaries is a matter of judgment and depends on the individual project.

The second decision concerns the *time horizon.* Like the project's physical boundaries, its time horizon becomes blurred when moving from financial to economic analysis. A project's environmental impact may not last as long as the project, or it may outlive it. If the environmental impact is shorter-lived than the expected economic life of the project, the effects can be included in the standard economic analysis. If, however, the effects are expected to last beyond the lifetime of the project, the time horizon must be extended. This can be done in two ways: by extending the cash flow analysis a number of years, or by adding to the last year of the project the capitalized value of the part of the environmental impact that extends beyond the project's life. The latter technique treats the environmental impact much as one would treat a capital good whose life extends beyond the project's lifetime, by giving it a "salvage value."

## Valuation of Environmental Impacts

The first step in assessing the costs or benefits of environmental impacts is to determine the relationship between the project and the environmental impact, that is, to determine a relationship such as that depicted in Figure 2. This *Handbook* provides detailed information on the likely environmental impacts of many classes of industrial activities. The second step is to assign a monetary value to the environmental impact. These two steps are equivalent to determining the shape of the *MSC* curve shown in Figure 1 and its relationship to the *MPC* curve. For example, suppose an objective of the project is to reduce air pollution, perhaps through installation of scrubbers at the industrial facility or by replacing an old bus or taxi fleet with new, less polluting vehicles. First, the impact of the project on air quality, as measured by some physical characteristic, is determined. Second, the monetary value of the improvement in air quality is assessed. In most cases, it is not necessary to estimate the entire cost curve; it suffices to identify the cost (or benefit) of an externality at a given level of activity. That is, it is enough to estimate the difference between the private and the social cost for a given level of activity.

In some cases, the market value of the externality is not readily available. There might also

### Figure 2.  Environmental Damage as a Function of Activity Level

Level of activity

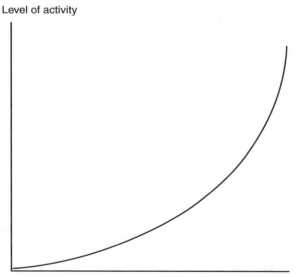

Environmental impact

be instances where neither the market value nor the functional relationship between the level of the activity and the environmental impact is known. Arriving at a monetary estimate of impacts in such cases is very difficult. A number of functional relationships that relate the level of activity to the degree of physical damage (or benefit) have been developed for various environmental impacts. Environmental damages include changes in production (e.g., of crops or fisheries affected by polluted water), changes in health, damage to infrastructure due to air or water pollution, and even loss of aesthetic benefits or recreational opportunities. Various methods are available for valuing environmental externalities.

The choice of valuation technique depends on the impact to be valued, the data and time available for the analysis, financial resources, and the social and cultural setting within which the valuation exercise is to be carried out. Some valuation approaches are more robust, and more likely to be applied, than are others. Figure 3 presents a menu of the more commonly used valuation approaches.

Although "objective" techniques rely on observable environmental changes, use market prices, and are more "concrete" and easier to present to decisionmakers, subjectively based techniques (especially those using surrogate markets and hypothetical markets) are increasingly accepted for decisionmaking. These subjective methods offer the only practical way of measuring certain categories of environmentally related benefits and costs. For example, suppose one wishes to measure the recreational benefits from preventing damage to a marine park or a pristine forest area. Under the travel-cost approach, the time and cost of travel are used to develop estimates of the value of the park to its users. Under the various survey-based contingent valuation methods, users are asked to state the value they place on the "park experience," permitting an estimate to be made of consumer's surplus associated with park use. Both are fairly robust techniques if carefully applied.

It is important to remember that the simplest techniques are usually the most useful. In most Bank projects, the most useful valuation techniques will be those that rely on actual changes in production, on replacement costs or preventive expenditures, or on information about im-

**Figure 3. A Simple Valuation Flowchart**

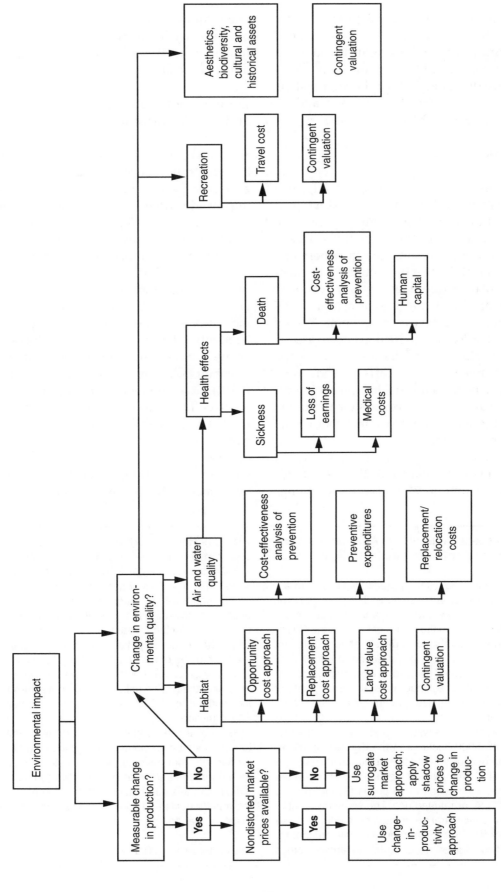

*Source:* Adapted from Dixon and Böjo in Dixon and others 1994.

pacts on human health (cost of illness). All these deal with physical changes that can be valued using market prices, and all are included in the objectively based set of techniques. These approaches are discussed in the following section. (For more detailed information on these and the other techniques, see Dixon et al. 1994.)

### Loss in Productivity

A project may raise or lower the productivity of another system. In these cases the valuation is fairly straightforward. For example, in Fiji conversion of a coastal wetland to an industrial site resulted in lower catches in a coastal fishery that was partly dependent on the wetland. The monetary value of the reduced catch was an economic externality attributable to the industrial development project and hence an economic cost of the project. The loss in production had an assessable market value. Because the lower production was accompanied by lower costs of production, the change in net benefits yielded the net impact of the externality. Box 1 illustrates the use of the change-in-production approach in a geothermal project in the Philippines.

In some cases, the impact of the project is not on the level of production but on the costs of production or consumption. For example, buildings

may require more frequent painting as a result of emission of pollutants by a nearby factory. The higher maintenance costs should be included as a cost of the factory in the economic analysis.

### Dose-Response Relationships and Health Outcomes

Some investment projects yield important health benefits from reduced mortality and morbidity; examples are an increased potable water supply, improved sewage collection and treatment, and reduction of vehicular pollution. Some investments however, may have unintended but important negative impacts on health. For example, expanded industrial production or new thermal power plants produce important economic benefits but also result in some undesirable environmental externalities. These health impacts should be identified and incorporated in the economic analysis, either qualitatively or quantitatively.

For air pollution, a dose-response relationship (DRR) is commonly used to link changes in ambient pollution levels to health outcomes. The DRR is a statistically estimated relationship between levels of certain pollutants in the air and different health outcomes—illness, lost workdays, and so on. Although the DRR approach was developed in the United States and Europe, there

---

### Box 1.  Assessing Disposal Alternatives for Geothermal Wastewater in the Philippines

The change-in-production approach was used to assess the impacts of various means of disposing of toxic geothermal wastewater from a geothermal power development project on the island of Leyte in the Philippines. The analysis considered seven different disposal options, including reinjection of geothermal wastewater, untreated disposal in local rivers, and use of ocean outfalls. It estimated the economic costs of these options for irrigated rice production and an offshore fishery.

Pollution of surface water would prevent its use for irrigation of 4,000 hectares in the dry season. Rainfed crop production would continue during the wet season, but with lower average yields. The net return per hectare was estimated at 346 pesos (P) for irrigated rice and P324 for rain-fed rice. The economic cost of the loss of agricultural production on 4,000 hectares would therefore be the difference between the net return from two irrigated crops (4,000 hectares × 2 crops

× P346/hectare = P 2,768,000) and the net return from one crop of unirrigated rice (4,000 hectares × 1 crop × P324/hectare = P1,296,000). The difference represents an annual loss of about P1.47 million.

The change-in-production approach was also applied to a coastal fishery. Various disposal options that did not include treatment of wastewater would cause heavy-metal pollution of coastal waters and lead to closing of the coastal fishery. The cost of this loss was calculated by multiplying the value of the annual catch (P39.4 million) by the net return to fishing, estimated at 29%, for an annual loss valued at P11.4 million.

Both of these annual costs were then capitalized to represent the economic damage to rice and fishery production from environmental pollution. Other environmental costs were also calculated (some qualitatively), and this information was used to help assess the total benefits and costs of the various wastewater disposal management alternatives.

*Source:* Balagot and Grandstaff 1994.

---

**Box 2.  Using Dose-Response Relationships to Estimate Health Outcomes in Jakarta**

This case study illustrates the use of dose-response relationships (DRRs) to estimate the health impacts of reducing air pollution. The health impact can be estimated by the following relationship:

$$dH_i = b_i \times POP_i \times dA$$

where $dH_i$ stands for the change in population risk of health effect $i$; $b_i$ for the slope from the dose-response curve for health impact $i$; $POP_i$ for the population at risk of health effect $i$; and $dA$ for the change in ambient air pollutant under consideration.

Foreign dose-response functions were applied to local conditions in Jakarta to assess the benefits of reducing airborne pollution to meet both Indonesian standards and the more stringent WHO standards. The estimated numbers of lives saved and illnesses avoided per year in the population of 8.2 million are shown below.

| Health effect | Medium estimate |
|---|---|
| Premature mortality (deaths) | 1,200 |
| Hospital admissions | 2,000 |
| Emergency-room visits | 40,600 |
| Restricted-activity days | 6,330,000 |
| Lower-respiratory illness (cases) | 104,000 |
| Asthma attacks (cases) | 464,000 |
| Respiratory symptoms (cases) | 31,000,000 |
| Chronic bronchitis (cases) | 9,600 |

*Source:* Ostro 1994.

---

is increasing acceptance of its transferability to other countries. Recent Bank work in Jakarta (Ostro 1994) and Chile (Ostro et al. 1995) illustrate what can be done (see Box 2).

Whereas everyone breathes the same air in a location, actual exposure to polluted water is the key variable in determining whether a person becomes ill. Individuals can "self-insure" themselves from the effects of contaminated water by, for example, boiling their water or using bottled water. Epidemiologic studies are therefore usually required in order to estimate the impacts of changes in water quality on health outcomes. Such studies take into account the important social and economic factors that determine the links between contaminated water and illness and death.

Once the impacts on health have been identified, they can be quantified in physical terms and, where feasible, assigned a monetary value. Sickness is much easier than death to measure in economic terms. For illness, it is possible to estimate, for example, the costs of medical treatment and hospitalization (doctors' visits, medicine, hospital costs, and lost work time). It is more difficult to estimate the "cost" of pain and suffering to the sick individual, relatives, and others. The measured costs of illness based on direct expenditures (or their appropriate shadow prices) are a minimum estimate of the true costs of illness and, in turn, of the potential benefits from preventing morbidity.

For death, we do not have an equivalent, equally applicable valuation approach. Various methods are used in practice: estimation of willingness to pay to avoid premature death, wage differential approaches, and, although not economically sound, a "human capital" approach that estimates the present value of the future earnings of an individual that would be lost due to premature mortality. The difficulty arises when one compares estimates for different countries, especially countries with very different income levels. For example, a common value for a "statistical life" in the United States s now US$3 million–$5 million or more, as determined by income levels and willingness to pay to avoid premature death (see Box 3).

Clearly this same value cannot be applied directly to another country with a per capita income one twentieth the size of the U.S. economy. Yet, deflating the U.S. value by the relative difference in income levels also ignores important dimensions, including purchasing power parity. In the absence of careful national studies of the value of a statistical life, it is often best to present mortality data in terms of the number of lives lost or saved rather than in terms of dollar value.

## Measuring Intangibles

One of the most difficult valuation areas is measuring subtle or dramatic changes in ecosystems, destruction of nonsubstitutable goods (such as biodiversity), effects on historical or cultural sites, and recreational benefits. Although these considerations are seemingly distant from this

## Box 3.  Use of Statistical Techniques for Valuing Life

The use of loss of earnings to value the cost associated with premature mortality is referred to as the human capital approach. It is similar to the change-in-production approach in that it is based on a damage function relating pollution to production, except that in this case the loss in productivity of human beings is measured. In essence, this method is an ex-post, exogenous valuation of the life of a particular individual using as an approximation the present value of the lost (gross or net) market earnings of the deceased.

This approach has many shortcomings. By reducing the value of life to the present value of an individual's income stream, the human capital approach to the valuation of life suggests that the lives of those with high earnings are worth more than the lives of those with low earnings. As a direct consequence, the lives of residents of rich countries would be rated as more valuable than the lives of people in poor countries. Narrowly applied, the human capital approach implies that the lives of subsistence workers, the unemployed, and retirees have a low or zero value and that the lives of the underemployed have a very low value. The very young are also valued low, since their future discounted earnings are often offset by education and other costs incurred before they entered the labor force. Furthermore, the approach ignores substitution possibilities that people may make in the form of preventive health care, and it excludes nonmarket values such as pain and suffering.

At best, this method provides a first-order, lower-bound estimate of the lost production associated with a particular life. However, the current consensus is that the societal value of reducing risk of death cannot be based on such an estimate. Although most economists do not favor using this method for policy analysis purposes, it is often used to establish ex-post values for court settlements related to the death of a particular individual.

An alternative method of valuing reductions in risk of death—the wage differential approach—uses information on the "wage premium" commonly paid to individuals with risky jobs (e.g., coal miners and steel construction workers) to impute a value for an individual's implicit valuation of a statistical death. This value is found by dividing the wage premium by the increased chance of death; for example, a US$100 per year premium to undertake a job with a chance of accidental death of 1 in 10,000 is equivalent to a value of US$1 million for a statistical death. Information on self-insurance and other measures also gives an indication of an individual's willingness to pay to avoid premature death.

In many cases, a project's impact on the environment is not apparent, but the market value of the externality is assessable, albeit sometimes indirectly. For example, property values decrease with the proximity of houses to a highway. The increased noise from traffic creates a project externality that should be included in assessing the costs of the highway. The exact relationship between the highway and the noise level may be unknown, but the value of quiet surroundings can be assessed indirectly. For example, information from another neighborhood may be used to compare the value of houses that are close to a highway with the value of houses farther away, controlling for differences in other characteristics of the properties.

---

*Handbook*'s main concern, industrial pollution, in many cases an important benefit from controlling pollution may be the protection or enhancement of a recreational site or important natural habitat. It is possible, although difficult, to estimate economic values for, say, the consumer's surplus of visitors to parks and protected areas, by using the travel cost approach or conducting contingent valuation studies. Recent work in East Africa is incorporating the results of such studies in the analysis of projects (see Box 4). Intangible benefits often include important environmental benefits that are secondary to the primary benefits produced by a project. Air pollution control projects in Santiago and Mexico City, for example, will yield primary benefits from reduced health effects and reductions in

damage to buildings, equipment, and other capital goods as a result of pollution. Cleaner air will also improve visibility—an important but unpriced benefit. Ideally, the visibility benefits should also be entered into the economic analysis. Because of data and measurement difficulties, however, these measures are usually entered into the analysis only qualitatively.

## Preventing and Mitigating Environmental Impacts

Sometimes a project can go ahead only if the implementing agency takes measures to prevent or mitigate its environmental impact. If the impact is completely prevented, the costs of prevention are taken into consideration in the

## Box 4. Valuing Consumer Surplus of International Tourists in Madagascar

This example presents an application of the travel cost and contingent valuation methods for estimating some of the benefits associated with the creation of a new park in Madagascar. A strong point of the study is that it used questionnaires based on two different valuation techniques to estimate consumer surplus and compared the estimated results.

Questionnaires were prepared and administered to visitors to the small Perinet Forest Reserve adjacent to the proposed Mantadia National Park. Visitors tended to be well off and well educated, with, on average, annual income of $59,156 and 15 years of education. The average stay in Madagascar was 27 days. Data from the visitor survey, supplemented with data from tour operators, was used in an econometric analysis that employed the travel cost approach. To estimate demand by international tourists, traditional travel cost models have to be reformulated because people who travel to a country like Madagascar engage in a variety of activities, of which the visit to the proposed national park would be only one. The travel cost model was then used to predict the benefits to tourists (the increase in consumer surplus) under the assumption that the new national park would result in a 10% increase in the quality of local guides, educational materials, and facilities for interpreting natural areas in Madagascar. The estimation indicated an average increase in willingness to pay per trip of $24 per tourist. If 3,900 foreign tourists visit the new park—a conservative assumption that uses the same number as currently visit the Perinet Reserve—the annual "benefit" to foreign tourists would be $93 600.

The contingent valuation method was used to estimate directly the value of the proposed park to foreign tourists. Visitors to the Perinet Forest Reserve were provided with information about the new park. Using a discrete choice format, they were asked how much more they would have been willing to pay for their trip to Madagascar if in the new national park (a) they saw twice as many lemurs, and (b) they saw the same number of lemurs as on their current visit. Since most of these visitors are expected to visit Madagascar only once, their response represents a one-time, lump-sum payment they are willing to make in order to have the park available. Mean willingness to pay for the park (conditional on seeing the same number of lemurs) was $65. Assuming current visitation patterns, the total annual willingness-to-pay for the park would be $253,500.

The information from these two estimates could be used to help design policies to capture part of this willingness to pay and compensate nearby villagers for income lost when the establishment of the park prevents their traditional activities within the park.

*Source:* Kramer 1993; Kramer et al. 1993.

---

economic and financial analysis of the project. If a factory is required to install equipment to *eliminate* air pollution, there is no environmental impact. If the factory is merely required to *mitigate* the environmental impact, the cost of the mitigating action is a direct and identifiable cost of the project, but the value of the residual environmental impact also needs to be considered in the costs of the project. If a dam reduces fish catch downstream, despite mitigating measures, the reduction of the catch is still a cost of the project. Care however, must be taken to avoid double counting. If the favored solution to an environmental impact is to let the damage occur, tax the culprit, and then repair the damage, the cost of the project should include the environmental cost only once—as the cost of repairing the environmental damage or as the tax (if the tax is exactly equal to the cost of repairing the environment), but not both.

## References and Sources

Balagot, B., and S. Grandstaff. 1994. "Tongonan Geothermal Power Plant: Leyte, Philippines." Case Study 5 in Dixon et al. (1994).

Dixon, John A., and Paul B. Sherman. 1990. *Economics of Protected Areas: A New Look at Benefits and Costs.* Washington, D.C." Island Press.

Dixon, John A., Louise F. Scura, Richard A. Carpenter, and Paul B. Sherman. 1994. *Economic Analysis of Environmental Impacts.* London: Earthscan Publications.

Kramer, Randall A. 1993. "Tropical Forest Protection in Madagascar." Paper presented at Williams College, Williamstown, Mass.

Kramer, R. A., Mohan Munasinghe, N. Sharma, E. Mercer, and P. Shyamsundar. 1993. "Valuation of Biophysical Resources in Madagascar." In Mohan Munasinghe, ed., *Environmental Economics and Sustainable Development.* World Bank Environment Paper 3. Washington, D.C.

Ostro, Bart. 1994. "Estimating the Health Effects of Air Pollution: A Methodology with an Application to Jakarta." Policy Research Working Paper 1301. World Bank, Policy Research Department, Washington, D.C.

Ostro, Bart, José Miguel Sanchez, Carlos Aranda, and Gunnar S. Eskeland. 1995. "Air Pollution and Mortality: Results from Santiago, Chile." Policy Research Working Paper 1453. World Bank, Policy Research Department, Washington, D.C.

# The Effects of Pollution on Health: The Economic Toll

*Measuring and valuing the health impacts of pollution are very complex, and available methods of economic analysis are often rudimentary. In recent years, however, considerable progress has been made, especially in respect to air pollution. This chapter summarizes the latest findings and outlines some basic approaches that can be applied in the economic analysis of Bank projects and sector studies. It should be noted that some uncertainty remains, and great care must be taken in the application of these methods.*

Investments in air pollution control in Mexico City alone are likely to total more than US$4.7 billion over the next five years. Even modest water and sewerage projects cost hundreds of millions of dollars. Health improvements are often cited as the major justification for such investments. Consequently, one of the more troublesome problems, both practical and ethical, facing policymakers is that of valuing the health impacts of pollution. While some argue that it is not possible (or morally ethical) to place monetary values on sickness or death, in many situations governments have to make choices about health interventions or investments. Should available funds go to air pollution reduction, or would they be better spent on water supply and sanitation? Or should priority be given to education and health care, or to some other pressing concerns? Putting a value (even if it is underestimated) on morbidity and mortality due to pollution can be a powerful tool for demonstrating the costs of inaction.

The problems of valuing the health impacts of pollution are twofold. The first difficulty is with the actual identification and measurement of health impacts. The second is that once impacts have been determined, it is often necessary to estimate monetary values for the associated morbidity (illness) and mortality (death).

## Measuring the Health Impacts of Pollution

The health impacts of air and water pollution are well recognized. Air pollution affects human health in a variety of ways, from itchy eyes and chest discomfort, to chronic bronchitis and asthma attacks, to premature death. There is ample evidence that inadequate water supply and sanitation can have a significant impact on the incidence of mortality and morbidity associated with diarrhea, intestinal nematodes, and other diseases.

The most accurate way of measuring the health impacts of air pollution or of lack of access to clean water and sanitation in a given area is to conduct epidemiologic studies for that area that establish dose-response relationships (DRRs) linking environmental variables with observable health effects. However, given the time and cost involved in such studies, as well as likely problems with data availability, it may often be the case that DRRs established in other locations will have to be used instead. This chapter summarizes recent progress in quantifying air pollution dose-response functions and addresses major problems in applying these functions to other situations. In the case of water pollution, establishing DRRs is more complicated and far less advanced, since it is not ambient water quality per se that affects health but access to clean drinking water and adequate sanitation, along with the household's level of income and education. Box 1 describes an approach adopted in a recent study of pollution problems in Brazil.

## Air Pollution Dose-Response Studies

Dose-response functions correlate mortality and morbidity outcomes for susceptible population groups with the ambient concentrations of a given air pollutant. Most have focused on the mortality effects of exposure to particulates. Chronic exposure to particulates can lead to premature death by exacerbating respiratory illness, pulmonary disease, and cardiovascular disease. Acute exposure (short-term peaks in the levels of particulates) can increase the chance that a person in a weakened state or an especially susceptible person will die. Detailed studies completed in recent years conclusively indicate that fine particulates (usually measured as $PM_{2.5}$) are responsible for most of the excess mortality and morbidity associated with high levels of exposure to particulate matter. (See Airborne Particulate Matter in Part III of this *Handbook*.)

Although a single study that finds a statistically significant association between a health effect and a specific air pollutant does not prove causality, the inference of causation is strengthened if epidemiologic results are duplicated across several studies, if a range of effects is found for a given pollutant, and if these results are supported by human clinical and animal toxicology literature. An approach for reducing the uncertainty associated with individual studies is to use meta-analytical techniques that, on the basis of the statistical pooling and aggregating of results from several studies, produce a "best estimate" in which more confidence may be placed.

The reported epidemiologic studies involve two principal study designs: time-series and cross-sectional. The more common time-series studies correlate daily variations in air pollution

---

## Box 1. Health Benefits of Water Supply and Sanitation in Brazil: A New Approach

Few studies have attempted to use epidemiologic data on water-related diseases as the basis for setting priorities in expanding water and sanitation services. A recent World Bank study in Brazil drew on a detailed epidemiologic study of the impact of water and sanitation on infant and under-five mortality to estimate the net benefits of improvements in water and sanitation.

The analysis was carried out using a sample of 1,533 municipalities in four states—Minas Gerais, Pernambuco, Rio de Janeiro, and São Paulo—that represent the full range of incomes and living conditions in Brazil today. The main independent variables used in the analysis were average income of head of household, percentage of population living in urban areas, percentage of females age 5 or older who are illiterate, percentage of urban population served by piped drinking water, and percentage of total population served by sewers or septic tanks. The analysis established that the coefficients for the variables characterizing income per person, the level of female education, and access to piped water and sanitation are highly significant and negative. The coefficient on the level of urbanization turned out to be very significant and positive; infant and under-five mortality rates are higher in urban than in rural areas if other factors are held constant. The relative importance of water and sanitation can be illustrated by the impact on mortality rates of 10-percentage-point increases in water and sanitation variables, as shown below.

| | Impact of water and sanitation on mortality rates | |
| --- | --- | --- |
| | Infant mortality | Under-five mortality |
| Change (reduction) per 10-percentage-point rise in: | | |
| Urban access to piped water | 0.8 | 0.25 |
| Urban access to sewers | 0.6 | 0.15 |
| Average mortality rate | 39.4 | 8.8 |

The health benefits that would be generated by expanding urban water and sewerage services are large. The analysis shows that in the four states sampled, it should be possible to avoid nearly 3,000 deaths of babies and young children each year and so reduce the burden of disease by nearly 220,000 disability-adjusted life years (DALYs). The largest impact would be achieved by ensuring that the entire urban population has access to piped water, at an average cost of US$1,560 per DALY. The average cost per DALY saved by expanding urban sewers is much higher, US$2,440, but it is still well below a reasonable estimate of willingness to pay to save a DALY in Brazil. Even if the value of statistical life (VOSL) were set at only US$1 million for the United States, this would imply an average willingness to pay per DALY saved for Brazil of about US$5,500 in 1991, well above the annualized costs per DALY saved by expanding water supplies and sewers for all but a small number of municipalities.

*Source:* World Bank 1997.

with variation in daily mortality in a given city and measure, primarily, the effects of acute exposure to air pollution. The advantage of these studies is that they do not have to control for a large number of confounding factors, since the population characteristics (age, smoking, occupational exposure, health habits, and so on) are basically unchanged. On the basis of meta-analysis of acute mortality studies that measure the ambient levels of particulates of less than 10 microns in aerodynamic diameter ($PM_{10}$), estimates of average percentage change in total mortality per 10 microgram per cubic meter ($mg/m^3$) change in $PM_{10}$ range from 0.74 (Maddison 1997) to 1.23 (Ostro 1996).[1]

A cross-sectional analysis compares differences in health outcomes across several locations at a selected point or period of time and, in principle, allows the capture of both acute and chronic effects of air pollution. Two types of cross-sectional long-term exposure studies can be distinguished. The first type is a retrospective (ecological) cross-sectional study design that correlates variations in air pollution levels with mortality rates across various locations at a single point in time. Such studies have consistently found measurably higher mortality rates in cities with higher average levels of particulate matter in the United States. A common concern about these studies is whether potential omitted and confounding variables have been adequately controlled.

A second type involves a prospective cohort design in which a population sample is selected and followed over time in each location. These studies use individual-level data, allowing other health risk factors to be better taken into account. Two such studies conducted to date (Dockery et al. 1993; Pope et al. 1995), both in the United States, reported a statistically significant correlation between exposure to particulate matter, measured as $PM_{10}$ or $PM_{2.5}$, and mortality, which was considerably higher by comparison with acute mortality studies. (Pope et al. 1995 found a 4.2 percent change in all-cause mortality per 10 $mg/m^3$ change in $PM_{10}$.) Prospective cohort studies have potentially greater value for public health and environmental policies and for estimating dose-response functions that can be applied elsewhere. However, these studies are most expensive, so their replication is difficult.

Since cohort studies are few and cross-sectional studies are less reliable, the question remains, how can long-term exposure to particulates be factored into results based on acute exposure mortality studies that seem to provide lower-bound estimates for the health effects of air pollution?

In addition to mortality counts, dose-response functions can also be derived for many lesser health impacts, for example, respiratory hospital admissions, emergency room visits, bed disability days, restricted activity days, minor restricted activity days, asthma attacks, acute respiratory symptoms, chronic bronchitis, lower respiratory illness, and so on. The principal results from meta-analyses of available studies for a number of key air pollutants ($PM_{10}$, sulfur dioxide, nitrogen dioxide, and ozone) are summarized in Table A.1.

## Valuation of Health Impacts

Several methods have been used in various studies to value the health costs associated with environmental pollution. These methods can be grouped in two broad categories. The first includes methods that measure only the loss of direct income (lost wages and additional expenditures). These measures do not include inconvenience, suffering, losses in leisure, and other less-tangible impacts to individual and family well-being and may seriously underestimate or completely ignore the health costs of people who are not members of the labor force. Therefore, they indicate only the lower bound of the social costs and understate the total costs to individuals. The second category includes approaches that attempt to capture individuals' willingness to pay to avoid or reduce the risk of death or ill health. The principal techniques are summarized in Table 1 and discussed below.

### Lower Bound of the Social Costs Estimates

*The human capital approach,* which places a value on a premature death, is the easiest but perhaps the least accurate and most ethically troubling method of valuing health impacts. It considers individuals as units of human capital that produce goods and services for society. Just as the

## Table 1. Valuation Methods for the Health Effects of Pollution

| Valuation method | Example |
|---|---|
| Human capital | Earnings forgone due to premature death as a result of exposure to air or water pollution |
| Cost of illness | Lost workdays, plus out-of-pocket costs (medical and other), due to health effects of pollution |
| Preventive or mitigative expenditure | Purchase of bottled water to avert health effects of polluted water<br>Installation of air conditioners to avert air pollution in the residence |
| Wage differential | Value of reduction of risk to health implicit in the difference in otherwise similar occupations |
| Contingent valuation | Direct questioning to provide a value for a potential change in air quality or health |

useful life of man-made capital can be calculated on the basis of the discounted stream of future production, the human capital theory assumes that the value of each unit of human capital is equivalent to the present value of the future output, in the form of earnings, that might have been generated had the individual not died prematurely.

The values calculated are very dependent on the age of death and on income, skill level, and country of residence. (Both the very young and the old would have low values when the human capital approach is used; see Table 2.) For example, in Mexico each life lost due to exposure to TSP pollution was valued at US$75,000, using the human capital approach, whereas in Brazil, the cost of premature death was estimated at US$7,700 for São Paulo in 1989 and at US$25,000 for Cubatao in 1988. The big difference between São Paulo and Cubatao was accounted for by the difference in average age at which exposed people died.

## Table 2. Human Capital and Mortality Cost by Age, United States

| Age group (years) | Life years lost | Mortality cost (1992 U.S. dollars) |
|---|---|---|
| Under 5 | 75 | 502,421 |
| 5–14 | 68 | 671,889 |
| 15–24 | 57 | 873,096 |
| 25–44 | 42 | 785,580 |
| 45–64 | 25 | 278,350 |
| 65 and older | 10 | 22,977 |

Note: The cost estimates are based on life expectancy at the time of death and include labor-force participation rates, average earnings, the value of homemaking services, and a 6% discount rate.
Source: Institute for Health and Aging.

Even taking only this minimal estimation of the cost of deaths, the economic benefits of investments that prevent the health effects of pollution are often apparent. For example, the minimal estimate of the "worth" of the life of a child outweighs the costs of a major immunization program.

*The cost of illness approach* applies to morbidity and is consistent with the human capital approach. The direct cost of morbidity can be divided into two categories: medical expenditure for treating illness (a large portion of the costs of hospital admissions and emergency room visits) and lost wages during days spent in bed, days missed from work, and other days when activities are significantly restricted due to illness.

For example, in Mexico in 1990, cases of nonlethal diarrhea were estimated to number 3,360,000. The costs of treatment and laboratory analysis alone came to US$30 million, or about US$9.00 per person. (This figure represents less than 1% of the estimated costs for deaths from similar causes.)

Under the *preventive expenditures approach*, tentative inferences about the minimum amount people are willing to pay to reduce health risks are made on the basis of the amounts people living in polluted areas spend on averting measures. For example, expenditures on bottled water can be used to infer the minimum value people are willing to pay to avoid waterborne diseases.

### Willingness-to-Pay Approaches

If people's preferences are a valid basis on which to make judgments concerning changes in human well-being, it follows that changes in human mortality and morbidity should be valued according to what individuals are willing to pay for (or are willing to accept as compensation for) the changes in health status or the risks that they face. This is not the same as valuing an actual life and should not be interpreted as such. Instead, it involves valuing ex-ante changes in the level of risk people face and then aggregating those changes. Since the exact identity of those at risk is unknown, valuing ex-ante changes in the level of risk is the appropriate policy context.

The *wage differential approach* uses differences in wage rates to measure the compensation people require for (perceived) differences in the chance of dying or falling ill from occupational hazards. Recent wage differential studies in the United States have produced estimates of the value of statistical life (VOSL) in the range of US$1.9 million–$10.7 million (1990 dollars).

The *contingent valuation approach* uses survey information to determine what people are prepared to pay to reduce the likelihood of premature death or of certain diseases. Contingent valuation studies have produced slightly lower estimates of US$1.2 million–$9.7 million (1990 dollars) per statistical life.

A question often asked is how a difference in the age distribution of those involved in willingness-to-pay studies and those primarily affected by pollution would affect the VOSL estimates. Wage differential studies measure compensation for risk of instantaneous death for people of about 40 years old and thus value approximately 35 years of life (Viscusi 1993). Because death from air pollution reduces life years by less than 35 years, on average, labor market estimates should be adjusted accordingly. For instance, the relative numbers of people over 65 and people under 65 who will die prematurely from air pollution in the United States (estimated at 85% of the over-65 group), coupled with some evidence of a lower willingness to pay for that group (about 75% of mean willingness to pay), implies that the respective VOSL should be adjusted downward by 20%.

The concept of disability-adjusted life years (DALYs) provides a standard measure of the burden of disease (World Bank 1993; Murray and Lopez 1996). DALYs combine life years lost due to premature death and fractions of years of healthy life lost as a result of illness or disability.

A weighting function that incorporates discounting is used for years of life lost at each age to reflect the different social weights that are usually given to illness and premature mortality at different ages. Thus, it is possible to link the VOSL obtained from wage differential and contingent valuation studies with the corresponding number of DALYs lost and so estimate the implicit value per DALY, as well as adjust the respective VOSL according to an average number of DALYs lost in a specific study. DALYs can also serve as an independent aggregate measure of health benefits (losses) in cost-effectiveness analysis of pollution control policies and options.

Although the valuation of morbidity is very important to cost-benefit analysis of air pollution control programs and to many other areas of economic activity, relevant studies are much more limited in scope and are based entirely within the United States. The main findings are shown in Table A.2.[2]

### How Can These Methods Be Used in Developing Countries?

How appropriate is it to transfer the results from dose-response studies of air pollution in industrial countries into the context of developing countries? Three issues warrant careful attention:

- *Measures of particulate matter.* To obtain reliable results when applying dose-response functions derived in other countries, it is essential to use epidemiologic studies based on $PM_{10}$ or $PM_{2.5}$ in combination with $PM_{10}$ or $PM_{2.5}$ measurements for the country in question.
- *Disease-specific mortality profile.* If the distribution of deaths by cause differs significantly between the country of interest and the countries where dose-response studies were done, it may be necessary to use dose-response functions for disease-specific mortality or to adjust for the difference to improve the accuracy of the projections. For instance, exposure to particulates affects primarily respiratory and cardiovascular deaths, which account for half of all deaths in the United States. In Delhi, fewer than 20% of all deaths are attributable to these causes. Therefore, even identical reactions by susceptible groups of population in Delhi and the United States to the change in the levels of

particulates would result in a lower total mortality in Delhi (Cropper and Simon 1996).

- The *age pattern of deaths from air pollution causes.* The age profile of those affected by air pollution may be very different in developing and industrial countries. Whereas peak effects were observed among people age 65 and older in the United States (Schwartz and Dockery 1992), in Delhi, peak effects occur in the 15–44 age group, implying that more life years are lost there as a result of a death associated with air pollution (Cropper et al. 1997).

The need to adjust the social costs of mortality and morbidity for income levels in different countries is obvious. In the United States, for example, VOSL estimates are typically 5 to 10 times higher than the value of forgone earnings. If people in other countries were equally risk averse, it would be appropriate to multiply the value of forgone earnings by the same factor. It is plausible to assume, however, that risk aversion varies with living standards and that the value of a statistical life in developing countries is a smaller multiple of forgone earnings than in the United States. Unfortunately, the literature on the income elasticity of willingness to pay for reducing the risk of insults to health is extremely limited, and empirical analyses in industrial countries do not lend sufficient support to this assumption (Maddison, et al. 1997). Until further research is conducted, one possible approach is simply to adjust an average U.S. value for the income difference between countries. For a conservative

estimate of the VOSL in a developing country, a lower-bound U.S. value, adjusted for the income difference, can be used.

Application of this approach to valuing a variety of health effects of exposure to particulate matter in China produced estimates of the total health costs of urban air pollution countrywide of about US$27 billion–$32 billion. Estimates of the costs attributable to mortality were US$11billion–$15 billion. It is important to stress that, under a number of assumptions on dose-response levels and base costs for these health effects drawn from different studies, the social costs of morbidity consistently appeared to be as significant as those of mortality.

The approaches to measuring the physical impact and health costs of pollution outlined above represent the cutting edge of research in this area. Although carefully scrutinized in the light of the best available evidence from toxicological, epidemiologic, and economic work, these approaches are inevitably surrounded by some degree of uncertainty and controversy. They are presented to respond to the need of Bank staff and consultants to strengthen the economic analysis of pollution control projects and policies and to help in advising policymakers on the necessary level of targets and interventions. Application of these approaches to a specific context of any particular project or study requires careful interpretation, and the limitations of the analysis should be fully understood before making conclusions and recommendations on its basis.

## Annex. Measuring and Valuing the Morbidity Effects of Air Pollution

### Table A.1. Morbidity Effects for Key Air Pollutants

| Health effects | $PM_{10}$ (per ug/m³) | $SO_2$ (per ug/m³) | $NO_2$ | 1-hour ozone (per ppm) |
|---|---|---|---|---|
| Respiratory hospital admissions per 100,000 population | 1.2 (Ostro 1994) 0.294 (Maddison 1997) | 0.201 (Maddison 1997) | 0.165 per ug/m³ (Maddison 1997) | 0.77 (Ostro 1994) 0.429 (Maddison 1997) |
| Asthma attacks per 100,000 asthmatics | 3,260 (Ostro 1994) 6,499 (Maddison 1997) | | | 6,800 (Ostro 1994) 7,356 (Maddison 1997) |
| Emergency room visits per 100,000 population | 23.54 (Ostro 1994; Maddison 1997) | | | |
| Restricted activity days per 100,000 adults | 5,750 (Ostro 1994; Maddison 1997) | | | |
| Lower-respiratory illnesses per 100,000 children | 169 (Ostro 1994; Maddison 1997) | | | |
| Respiratory symptoms per 100,000 adults | 18,300 (Ostro 1994; Maddison 1997) | | | 5,475 (Ostro 1994; Maddison 1997) |
| Chronic bronchitis per 100,000 adults | 6.12 (Ostro 1994; Maddison 1997) | | | |
| Cough days per 100,000 children | | 1.81 (Ostro 1994; Maddison 1997) | | |
| Chest discomfort days per 100,000 adults | | 1,000 (Ostro 1994; Maddison 1997) | 1,000 per ppm (Ostro 1994) | |
| Minor restricted activity days per 100,000 adults | | | | 3,400 (Ostro 1994; Maddison 1997) |
| Eye irritation per 100,000 adults | | | | 2,660 (Ostro 1994; Maddison 1997) |

*Note:* ppm, part per million; $PM_{10}$, particulate matter 10 microns or less in aerodynamic diameter; $SO_2$, sulfur dioxide; $NO_2$, nitrogen dioxide.

**Table A.2. The Social Costs of Morbidity**

| Morbidity effect | Study | Duration (days) | Valuation type | Value per case (1993 U.S. dollars) |
|---|---|---|---|---|
| Respiratory hospital admissions | Cropper and Krupnick 1989 | 9.5 | Cost of illness | 7,248 |
| Emergency-room visits | Rowe et al. 1986 | 1 | Cost of illness | 242 |
| Severe chronic bronchitis | Viscusi et al. 1991 | 15,596 | Willingness to pay | 1,030,000 |
| Bad asthma days | Rowe and Chestnut 1985 | 9.5 | Willingness to pay | 578 |
| Cough day | Tolley et al. 1986 | 1 | Willingness to pay | 35 |
| Eye irritation | Tolley et al. 1986 | 1 | Willingness to pay | 38 |

## Notes

1. Only estimates based on studies using $PM_{10}$ are cited here, because $PM_{10}$ is a better proxy for fine particulates than other measures (e.g., TSP; black smoke, or BS) employed in a variety of studies. A number of estimates have been produced across studies that use different measures of particulate matter. In producing these estimates, TSP is usually converted to $PM_{10}$, using a factor of 0.55, and BS and COH are considered equal to $PM_{10}$. These estimates are less reliable, however, because variations in the levels of TSP or other measures of particulates may be quite different from those for $PM_{10}$ and even more different for $PM_{2.5}$. As more studies using $PM_{2.5}$ become available, the analysis will have to focus on those studies.

2, A potentially useful approach is to integrate the health status index literature with the willingness-to-pay morbidity valuation literature. The health status index literature attempts to measure perceptions of well-being on a cardinal scale from 0 (death) to 1 (perfect health). Once the relationship between the health status index and willingness to pay is found, willingness to pay can be predicted for any condition (which can be described using the health status index), even conditions for which no valuation experiments are available. This approach has been taken in TER (1996) and Maddison et al. (1997).

## References and Sources

Cropper, Maureen L., and Alan J. Krupnick. 1989. "Social Costs of Chronic Heart and Lung Disease." Resources for the Future, Washington, D.C.

Cropper, Maureen, and Nathalie Simon. 1996. "Valuing the Health Effects of Air Pollution." DEC Notes 7. World Bank, Washington, D.C.

Cropper, Maureen L., Nathalie B. Simon, Anna Alberini, and P. K. Sharma. 1997. "The Health Effects of Air Pollution in Delhi, India." Policy Research Working Paper 1860. World Bank, Development Economics Research Group, Washington, D.C.

Dockery, Douglas W., C. A. Pope, X. Xiping, J. Spengler, J. Ware, M. Fay, B. Ferris, and F. Speizer. 1993. "An Association between Air Pollution and Mortality in Six U.S. Cities." New England Journal of Medicine 329(24): 1753–59.

Esrey, S.A., et al. 1993. "Effects of Improved Water Supply and Sanitation on Ascariasis, Diarrhoea, Dracunculiasis, Hookworm Infection, Schistosomiasis, and Trachoma." Bulletin of the World Health Organization 69(5): 609–21.

Maddison, D. 1997. "A Meta-analysis of Air Pollution Epidemiological Studies." Centre for Social and Economic Research on the Global Environment. London: University College London and University of East Anglia.

Maddison, D., et al. 1997. "Air Pollution and the Social Costs of Fuels." World Bank, Environment Department, Washington, D.C.

Margulis, S. 1991. "Back of the Envelope Estimates of Environmental Damage Costs in Mexico." Latin American Region Discussion Paper. World Bank, Washington, D.C.

Mitchell, R. C., and R. T. Carson. 1989. "Using Surveys to Value Public Goods: The Contingent Valuation Method." Resources for the Future, Washington, D.C.

Murray, Christopher J. L., and Alan D. Lopez, eds. 1996. The Global Burden of Disease. The Global Burden of Disease and Injury Series, 1. Harvard School of Public Health. Cambridge, Mass.: Harvard University Press.

Ostro, Bart. 1994. "Estimating the Health Effects of Air Pollution: A Method with an Application to Jakarta." Policy Research Working Paper 1301. World Bank, Policy Research Department, Washington, D.C.

————. 1996. "A Methodology for Estimating Air Pollution Health Effects." WHO/EHG/96. Geneva, World Health Organization.

Pope, C.A., M., Thun, M. Namboodiri, D. Dockery, J. Evans, F. Speizer, and C. Heath. 1995. "Particulate Air Pollution as a Predictor of Mortality in a Prospective Study of U.S. Adults." *American Journal of Respiratory and Critical Care Medicine* 151: 669–74.

Rowe, R., and V. Chestnut. 1985. "Oxidants and Asthmatics in Los Angeles: A Benefits Analysis." U.S. Environmental Protection Agency, Washington D.C.

Rowe, R., et al. 1986. "The Benefits of Air Pollution Control in California." Energy and Resource Consultants Inc., Boulder, Colo.

Schwartz, Joel, and Douglas Dockery. 1992. "Increased Mortality in Philadelphia Associated with Daily Air Pollution Concentrations." *American Review of Respiratory Disease* 145: 600–604.

TER. 1996. "Valuing Morbidity: An Integration of the Willingness to Pay and Health Status Index Literatures." Durham, N.C.

Tolley, George, et al. 1986. "Valuation of Reductions in Human Health Symptoms and Risk." In *Contingent Valuation Study of Light Symptoms and Angina.* Washington, D.C.: U.S. Environmental Protection Agency.

Viscusi, W. Kip. 1993. "The Value of Risks to Life and Health." *Journal of Economic Literature* 31: 1912–46.

Viscusi, W. Kip, et al. 1991. "Pricing Health Risks: Survey Assessments of Risk-Risk and Dollar-Risk Tradeoffs." *Journal of Environmental Economics and Management* 21(1): 32–51.

World Bank. 1993. *World Development Report 1993: Investing in Health.* New York: Oxford University Press.

————. 1997. "Brazil: Managing Pollution Problems —The Brown Environmental Agenda." Washington, D.C.

# Public Involvement in Pollution Management

*Formal public involvement at the scoping and draft review stages is part of the environmental assessment (EA) process and is usually required for industrial projects. The wider use of participatory approaches in World Bank pollution management projects is still evolving. Public involvement in setting priorities for pollution management is not yet common, although there is evidence that an informed public has an influence on reducing pollution. In the development of projects with a pollution management component, emphasis should be placed on improving consultation between government, industry, and the public.*

## Value of Public Involvement

Public participation, in a broad sense, is becoming part of Bank activities in many areas, including sector work, as well as projects. Participatory approaches have been most widely used in rural development projects, but there is increasing involvement of local communities in the design and implementation of urban and rural water and sanitation programs. A study of rural water supply projects concluded that the effectiveness of participation was the single most important determinant of overall quality of implementation (Narayan 1994).

Recent OECD annual Evaluation Results have concluded that beneficiary participation in preparation enhances the sustainability of projects. In response to concerns of task managers, it was noted that although participation typically added 10-15% staff-weeks to preparation time in the design phase, much of the additional cost was covered by outside funding sources. Furthermore, the longer preparation time was typically offset by speedy negotiation and quick loan effectiveness.

Bank experience with public involvement in pollution management is still limited, but this is changing. In addition to involving those directly affected by a program or project, public involvement can help build an informed constituency to influence priority setting in pollution management and support for enforcement. It may also be a way to reach and educate small-scale industry.

Public involvement is a way of ensuring that the project is relevant to local needs and responds to local concerns. It can improve the overall quality and success of a project and should be endorsed by task managers as an integral part of project identification and design.

## Public Involvement

### Levels of Public Involvement

Public involvement can be defined as a social communication process whereby individual citizens, NGOs, the private sector, and other interested parties participate with government at various levels in decisionmaking. The *World Bank Participation Sourcebook* (World Bank 1996) presents experience on projects, lessons learned, and methods of participation. There are several broad levels of public involvement:

- *Information dissemination* is a one-way flow, usually involving disclosure of information about a proposed project to interested parties.
- *Consultation* is a two-way information exchange between stakeholders; decisionmaking authority remains with the promoter but other groups provide feedback on decisions.
- *Participation* is a process through which stakeholders influence and share control over development initiatives and the decisions and resources that affect them. There are several

types of participation: *joint assessment* and *collaboration* both involve partnership in design and implementation, while *empowerment* puts decisionmaking responsibility and resources in the hands of the stakeholders directly involved in the project.

In practice, in industrial projects, the emphasis has normally been on information dissemination and consultation (for example in the EA process for a new facility). Formal, structured exercises in participation are less common but may occur, for example, in environmental audits or in industrial monitoring activities.

### Identifying Stakeholders

The key to successful participation is the effective involvement of all the main stakeholders. The *World Bank Participation Sourcebook* defines stakeholders as "those affected by the outcome—negatively or positively—or those who can affect the outcome of a proposed intervention."

Stakeholder identification is essential to the process of public involvement. The task manager, the project sponsor, or the government can prepare an initial list of stakeholders, and others will usually come forward or be identified through the public involvement process. Stakeholders fall into four broad groups:

- The borrower or project sponsor
- Beneficiaries of the project
- Other groups affected by the project
- Other interested parties (for example, NGOs and other donors).

Social assessment procedures may be necessary for systematic stakeholder identification and participation (see World Bank 1995).

### Impacts of Information

An informed and active public can have a significant impact on the performance of industry. Detailed studies by the Bank in Indonesia and elsewhere have shown that industries in areas where there is an educated and informed population are less polluting than their counterparts elsewhere. Clearly a number of reasons underlie this difference, but the impact of public opinion is a key factor.

The same concept underlies the U.S. requirements for publication of the Toxic Release Inventory. Focusing public attention on the wastes being generated in facilities has prompted significant reductions in the actual levels in subsequent years. Recent developments in the EU on the release of pollution information are designed to have similar impacts. In the Asia and Pacific region, the Australian government and the OECD are promoting the development of Pollutant Release and Transfer Registers (PRTR) for countries in the area.

### Involvement with Specific Industrial Projects

#### New Plants

Public consultation is required as part of the scoping and review of the draft EA for major new industrial projects (those ranked as Category A). For Category B projects, the formal requirements for consultation are less well defined, but the benefits of early consultation should be considered.

The focus of the formal consultation has typically been those people directly affected, usually because of resettlement concerns (OD 4.30) or impacts on indigenous peoples (OD 4.20). In some cases, issues may be raised concerning pollution and health impacts, and this input provides information for resettlement planners.

A project that involved a wide range of organizations was the preparation of a waste management program in the Caribbean. By contrast, preliminary consultations on an oil project in Central Asia could not identify any NGOs outside the government system and had to rely on appointed local officials to provide input.

#### Upgrading Old Plants

In some cases where a highly polluting industry is also a major local employer, public concerns have led to a "jobs versus pollution" debate on the options (remediation or shutdown).

For example, a USAID technical assistance project in Romania has involved extensive consultation and discussion. There, a major copper smelter and refinery is the main source of environmental health risks in surrounding towns. Working groups have been established on a number of issues of high concern (for example, blood lead levels). The groups included representatives from the smelter, local government agencies, medical researchers, and organizations such as the local kindergarten. The groups are working to develop and implement work plans for short-term actions to improve local conditions.

In a Bank project in Algeria, local NGOs from the communities surrounding a major steel plant were brought into a health assessment process to identify the local impacts of the plant. These groups have been active in discussions on realistic options for upgrading the productivity and environmental performance of the plant.

The design of a pollution abatement project in Egypt promotes the involvement of NGOs (including the influential professional associations) and the media, in order to build public expectation and pressure for the adoption of good environmental and safety practices by the industries in the project area.

In many cases, environmental audits are carried out to provide data that can inform the debate. The solutions have typically involved closure of certain processes and upgrading of others. Worker representatives should be involved in such discussions.

### Community Relations Programs

It is increasingly common practice in industrial countries for major facilities to develop a formal community relations program. To date, experience with these approaches in Bank work has been limited. A project in Central Europe (funded by another development bank) that involved upgrading of a large metal smelter included a specific component for the establishment of a community group to track progress of the upgrading. An independent technical consultant was appointed as the liaison between the project and the community.

One broad possible community role is that of a "watchdog" over the performance of the particular enterprise, an attitude sometimes known as environmental vigilance. This is preferably done as part of a structured community involvement program developed by the enterprise, but it can also be done separately. Typically, a com-

munity-based group regularly monitors the pollution performance of the plant, disseminates the information gathered, and provides feedback to the plant and the relevant authorities. Monitoring in this context could mean simple visual observation, basic testing of effluents, or participation in a more formal regular sampling and testing program. Participation of community groups and NGOs in the preparation of projects (as is beginning to happen) clearly provides a basis for longer-term involvement.

### Involvement in Priority Setting

In the past, priorities for pollution management have typically been set by "experts" from specialist government agencies or by outside consultants. An example from Calcutta (see Box 1) demonstrates the increasing recognition of the shortcomings of this attitude. There is growing understanding that priority setting must involve all the parties (that is, all the stakeholders) affected by the issues. Newer approaches have been based on various forms of community involvement, through existing political structures and ad hoc consultations. Comparative risk assessment methods (see the chapter on this topic) have been used to present information on pollution impacts in a structured and informed way and, in some approaches, as the basis for community awareness raising and education.

For example, in Nizhnii Tagil in the Urals region of Russia, an American NGO is applying a community action model to concerns about the impacts of the many sources of industrial pollution. As a result of the intervention, a broad-based committee has been appointed by the city to identify and address the most urgent pollution problems. The committee is carrying out a comparative risk assessment of the many toxic air pollutants that have been identified, and local specialists are developing a prioritized risk reduction strategy.

### Community Monitoring

#### Approaches

Community monitoring is not a new concept: concern for environmental issues has been a grass-roots issue in many countries. The new aspect of community monitoring is to extend interest in the environment from the educated elite to the broader population directly affected by pollution and other issues. Community monitoring is also a logical progression of the change of emphasis in environmental management, from source control alone to achieving real ambient improvements.

The advantages of involving the community in monitoring can include a clearer view of priorities, cost-effective extension of the database, and mobilization of local support for necessary preventive and remedial actions. In particular, a focus on the health and economic impacts of pollution at the local level can allow assistance to be targeted at critical problems, with the active support of those directly affected. For example, studies by USAID in periurban neighborhoods of Quito identified a number of health risks, such as food poisoning, gastrointestinal diseases, and bronchial infections (from dust in the dry season), that required quite different solutions from those proposed for dealing with perceived citywide problems.

*Techniques*

The introduction of community monitoring or environmental vigilance approaches requires the availability of simple and reliable testing methods that can be used by local communities. For example, the use of litmus paper strips may be sufficient to monitor the acidity of wastewater discharges from a plant. More sophisticated systems can be developed; in Canada, a number of members of a native-peoples community were trained in simple laboratory methods, allowing them to monitor and control the quality of the local water supply. This Canadian community is now providing advice to a Chilean Indian community on such methods.

Community monitoring methods can span a wide range of technologies. A number of NGOs are working on the development of simple kits using locally available materials. Commercial suppliers in developed countries offer several basic testing systems that can measure a wide range of parameters for, typically US$0.5–$2.0 per test for each parameter. At a slightly more expensive level, robust portable monitors are available for a number of key environmental parameters. Once purchased, these instruments are reliable and simple to use.

The availability of technology is only a part of any monitoring system. Regular and reliable sampling and good analysis and reporting are also essential. Sustaining local interest in monitoring over a long period can be a difficult task; experience is lacking on this question.

## Policy Work: Lessons from the Urban Sector

Many industrial pollution problems have an urban connection, and most urban pollution problems have an industrial component. Urban environmental priority setting is frequently closely related to industrial issues, and the findings on public participation emerging from urban studies are very relevant to management of industrial pollution.

The Urban Management Programme has concluded that "one of the main contributions to environmental degradation is the lack of public awareness of the problems and low participation in efforts to improve the urban environment."[1] In particular:

- A fundamental problem is lack of effective public information and education; a public educated in environmental issues and possible alternatives is in a position to apply pressure. Opportunities to influence and participate in decisionmaking are also crucial.

- There is a need to build public pressure and political will. In the absence of public pressure, decisionmakers will choose options that offer the highest short-to-medium-term benefits. This is a particular problem where decision-makers may have a vested interest in promoting new industrial development, for example.

Through participation, the people affected (especially the disadvantaged) can influence policy and management decisions. Participation should continue over the life cycle of a project or program. However, "urban environmental improvement cannot be initiated or sustained without constituencies that demand a better quality of life." In most developing-country cities, there is already a powerful constituency for the environment among the upper class; the challenge is to build a constituency among the urban poor.

## Outline of a Participatory Process

The following general practice pointers are used to guide the participatory process and to keep the necessary time and cost to a minimum.

- Start the participatory process as early as possible in the project design.
- Ensure government support for a participatory approach.
- Identify and then involve the stakeholders.
- Involve intermediary NGOs that have local credibility.
- Identify and involve responsive individuals or agencies in the government.
- Build community capacity to make decisions and to convey information back and forth.
- Make a particular effort to understand the concerns of the poor, who are often not well represented.
- Facilitate participation by women, who may not be represented in the formal structures.
- Consider institutional or regulatory measures to support participation.

## Procurement Issues

Early experience with projects with a high level of community participation demonstrated a number of problems related to procurement, contracting, and disbursement when dealing with small and often rather unstructured organizations (Bartone et. al. 1994). These issues are still being resolved, but the key point is that they need to be addressed early in the preparation process. One recommendation is that an implementation manual be prepared for the particular circumstances, setting out clear and simple contractual practices that would be acceptable under the project.

## Support to Task Managers

The Social Policy and Resettlement Division of the World Bank's Environment Department (ENVSP) has prepared a series of Dissemination Notes and other documents on participation and can provide advice to task managers. There is also an increasing number of social policy specialists in the regions who can assist with project design and implementation.

## Note

1. The Urban Management Programme is jointly sponsored by the World Bank, the United Nations Development Programme (UNDP), and the United Nations Centre for Human Settlement (Habitat).

## References and Sources

Bartone, Carl, Janis Bernstein, Josef Leitmann, and Jochen Eigen. 1994. *Toward Environmental Strategies for Cities: Policy Considerations for Urban Environmental Management in Developing Countries*. Urban Management Programme Series Paper 18. Washington, D.C.: World Bank.

Biswas, K. 1995. *The Urban Age*, pp. 6–7. World Bank, Transport, Water, and Urban Development Department, Washington, D.C.

Gopal, Gita, and Alexandre Marc. 1994. *World Bank–Financed Projects with Community Participation: Procurement and Disbursement Issues*. World Bank Discussion Paper 265. Washington, D.C.

Narayan, Deepa. 1994. *The Contribution of People's Participation: Evidence from 121 Rural Water Supply Projects*. Environmentally Sustainable Development Occasional Paper 1. Washington, D.C.: World Bank.

World Bank. 1993.: "EA Sourcebook Update No.5. Public Involvement in Environmental Assessment: Requirements, Opportunities and Issues." Environment Department, Washington, D.C.

—————. 1994. "The World Bank and Participation." Operations Policy Department, Washington, D.C.

—————. 1995. "Dissemination Note No. 35." Environment Department, Washington, D.C.

—————. 1996. *World Bank Participation Sourcebook.* Washington, D.C.

# Analytical Support for Cost-Effective Pollution Control

*Analytical tools have been developed by the World Bank Group to estimate rapidly the extent and impacts of pollution in a given situation and to support decisions on pollution management. These tools help decisionmakers overcome the frequent lack of data concerning emissions from different sources, their impact on ambient quality, and mitigation alternatives.*

## Decision Support System for Integrated Pollution Control (DSS)

*What Is the DSS?*

The Decision Support System for Integrated Pollution Control (DSS), developed by the World Bank in collaboration with the World Health Organization (WHO) and the Pan American Health Organization (PAHO), allows a rapid assessment of the pollution situation in a specific geographic location, such as a metropolitan area or water basin. The DSS is designed to assist in the analysis of alternative pollution control strategies and policy options. It is a personal computer software program and database that has been developed from the approach and parameters provided in the 1989 WHO working document on management and control of the environment. The DDS generates estimated pollution loads in a study area by applying emissions factors to data on economic activities. This load data can then be further processed to estimate areawide concentrations or to examine the impacts and costs of selected pollution control measures. Full details of the system, the basic assumptions, and the base parameters are given in the manual that accompanies the software.

The following databases are included, compiled by medium of discharge:

- Pollution-intensive technological processes across all sectors of economic activity, including mining, manufacturing industries, energy, transport, and municipal sectors, grouped ac-

cording to the United Nations International Standard Industrial Classification (ISIC) at the four-digit level
- Principal control options available for each process, including "good housekeeping" and waste prevention programs
- Emissions factors associated with these processes and "process-control option" combinations
- Normalized costs and parameters for control technologies
- Health guidelines for air and water pollutants, where applicable.

Editing and calibration features of the software allow adjustment of the default data to local conditions when actual information is available.

Computation modules enable the user to estimate:

- Air, water, and solid waste emissions, based on an inventory of economic activities for a given location
- Ambient concentrations of air and water pollutants, obtained by using simple (screening) dispersion models with minimum meteorological and hydrological data
- Total costs of control options, derived by using standardized engineering-type cost functions
- Long-run marginal cost schedules for achieving a certain level of emissions reduction (or decline in ambient concentration) for a chosen pollutant.

*What Are the Uses of the DSS?*

The DSS can be used by Bank staff, environmental agencies, pollution engineers, economists, and policy analysts for the following tasks:

- Obtaining information on typical emissions factors and control costs (at a generalized level)
- Managing data on economic and industrial activity and related pollution loads
- Estimating impacts and analyzing options
- Conducting training in pollution economics and management.

Each task is discussed in detail below.

*Information.* The DSS database can provide information on pollutants, emissions factors, technological processes, control options, and unit costs that can be independently applied in other models or studies or can serve as a point of reference. However, the range and variability of the parameters included is frequently large, and the database should be validated or adjusted for local conditions wherever possible.

*Data management.* The DSS helps to estimate pollution conditions in the absence of monitored data on emissions and ambient concentrations and permits identification of the major pollution sources. It can also help to highlight gaps in the existing system of data collection by providing a framework for organizing the information-gathering process systematically and presenting the information in a convenient format as a table, chart, or map. The system requires a detailed inventory of industries in a given area, including data on key inputs and outputs in physical units and the types of existing pollution controls. This type of data is often more readily available than actual pollutant emissions or concentrations.

When such an inventory is not possible within the limited time and resources available, the Industrial Pollution Projection System (IPPS), which has less demanding data requirements, can be used to estimate pollution loads from manufacturing industries for a number of air and water pollutants. The IPPS is described in greater detail below.

*Analytical tool.* The DSS is designed to help develop a cost-effective pollution control strategy across various pollution sources for a given area and identify priority investments in specific

industries and in the municipal sector. The system supports integrated approaches to airshed management and wastewater treatment by capturing and evaluating the effect of all kinds of sources on pollution load and ambient quality. The computer-driven analysis of pollution sources and abatement options highlights variations in marginal costs of abatement across industries and other sources. It defines the control levels and associated investments that should be adopted for different industries to achieve a desired pollution abatement target (in terms of either emissions reduction or concentration decline of a particular pollutant) at least cost for the area as a whole. Specifically, the system estimates the amount of pollution that can be reduced without costly investments, just by improving management, operation, and maintenance. The software can also be used to support the selection of alternative locations for new industries or industrial zones, as well as for urban development and expanding municipal services. It can estimate the possible effects of different policies on the pollution situation and the associated costs of compliance with environmental regulations in each proposed location.

As a first step in analyzing pollution control policies, such as policies setting environmental standards or applying economic instruments, the DDS can be used to:

- Estimate the costs of attaining proposed emissions standards or ambient standards in an area
- Estimate the impact on ambient quality of proposed emissions standards or technological standards
- Allocate emissions limits across pollution sources in an area in a cost-effective way
- Estimate the incentive level of an emissions charge rate needed to achieve a certain environmental target in the area or watershed (using long-run marginal cost schedules)

*Educational tool.* The DSS helps to make key issues and causal links in pollution management transparent. It can demonstrate the comparative effect on pollution load and ambient quality of a number of factors that can be affected by sectoral and environmental policies. It can promote public participation and consensus building by informing various stakeholders about the key pollution problems, major pollution sources, and principal mitigation measures in the area.

In applying the DSS, it is important to remember that the system is a rapid and rough assessment tool that can only indicate where problems are likely to occur, the relative significance of different pollution sources, and the order of magnitude of the costs and effects associated with alternative pollution control strategies. Its main advantage is in helping to create a comprehensive picture of the pollution problems in an area and to focus further analysis on specific priorities.

### Implementing the DSS System

The DSS software runs under Windows and can be closely linked to Microsoft Excel. The database is established using Access software but can be manipulated directly through the DSS system. The minimum data for starting the system are industrial output or input for major industries (at the four-digit ISIC level), together with basic information on municipal services and traffic.

From this minimum information, the system can estimate emissions loads, using the default coefficients. The estimates can be improved with further knowledge on the levels of industrial pollution control and local emissions factors, which can be used to refine the default values. The system also includes simple air and water dispersion models that can offer estimates of pollutant concentrations if basic geographic data are provided.

In addition, the system can generate total and marginal costs for the reduction of pollution loads. These costs are also based on default values; the results can be refined by introducing locally specific economic data.

The system database covers 150 industry processes and other polluting activities and 30 air and water pollutants, as well as solid wastes. An expanded database covering about 1,500 activities and over 300 pollutants is also available.

### Industrial Pollution Projection System

The Industrial Pollution Projection System (IPPS) is a modeling system that uses manufacturing industry or trade data to generate profiles of industrial pollution for countries, regions, or urban areas. Most developing countries have little or no reliable information about their own emissions, but many of them have relatively detailed industry survey information on employment, value added, or output. IPPS converts any of these measures of manufacturing activity into estimates of the associated pollution output.

The IPPS initially combined extensive U.S. databases on manufacturing activity (Census Bureau data) and industrial emissions (USEPA data) to produce sectoral measures of "pollution intensity"—the level of emissions per unit of manufacturing activity. Pollution intensities have been developed for seven criteria air pollutants, two key water-pollution indicators, and several total indices of toxic pollution. The high level of sectoral detail in the U.S. databases and the great diversity of U.S. industry make it possible to match IPPS data with the industrial profile of virtually any country, but the data are being refined on the basis of information from other countries.

The IPPS exploits the fact that levels of industrial pollution are closely related to the scale and sectoral composition of industrial activity and to the level of control. The system is easy to use, in conjunction with macroeconomic or sectoral projections at various spatial levels, to trace the potential environmental implications of industrial growth and for rough screening of current industrial emissions when more specific information is not available.

The outcomes of the IPPC should be used primarily for estimating a *relative* change in emissions according to different scenarios of industrial activity rather than for drawing conclusions about absolute levels of industrial emissions.

### Compatibility of the DDS and the IPPS

The DDS and the IPPS are broadly compatible because they operate at different levels of aggregated data. The IPPS can be used to quickly assess the relative magnitude of emissions from different industries in cases where the application of DSS is constrained by lack of data on inputs and outputs in physical units. However, since the IPPS is limited to manufacturing industries, it has to be supplemented with other assessment tools when analyzing the pollution situation in urban areas. Where local industrial, municipal, and transport data are available or can be collected, the DSS provides a greater capability for estimating loads and concentrations and analyzing control strategies.

**Additional Resources**

*DSS*
Urban, Industry, and Energy Team
Environment Department
World Bank
Washington, D.C.

*IPPS*
Environment, Infrastructure, and Agriculture Division
Policy Research Department
World Bank
Washington, D.C.

or check the environmental section on the World Bank Group's Website (www.worldbank.org).

# Airshed Models

*Modeling may be necessary to estimate the changes in ambient air quality—both local and at a distance—caused by a particular set of emissions. Modeling can be appropriate for new plants and for modifications to existing plants. This chapter provides guidance on some models that may be useful in the context of typical World Bank Group projects.*

Air quality is an issue of increasing concern in many countries. Projects that introduce new sources of emissions or are designed to reduce emissions require careful analysis to quantify the effects as far as possible. For many sources, this will typically require mathematical modeling of the changes in ambient concentrations that result from the new emissions. The few widely used models are reviewed in this chapter.

Air quality modeling can be a complex task, and the objectives need to be clear. The costs of a study can range from US$10,000 to US$500,000, depending on the complexity of the situation and the level of detail required; in many cases, costs are at the lower end of this scale. The simplest approach uses a point source dispersion model to estimate the ground-level concentrations of the pollutants of interest at some distance (typically from hundreds of meters to tens of kilometers) from a point source. More complicated models allow the examination of multiple sources, including area (nonpoint) sources. For an area containing a number of point and nonpoint sources, an air quality model can be constructed that includes all of the sources in the area. In practice, such models are rare because of the costs of development and the data required to make the model a realistic tool.

This chapter examines the application of the most commonly used air quality dispersion models for assessing the impact on air quality of key pollutants—sulfur dioxide ($SO_2$), nitrogen oxides ($NO_x$), and particulates—emitted from point sources.[1] Far-field dispersion and acid rain deposition are governed by different principles and utilize different types of models, which are discussed elsewhere in this *Handbook*.

Although thermal power plants are often singled out as major polluting sources, nearly all industrial facilities, especially those with short stacks, have the potential to cause localized areas of unacceptable air quality. In addition, urban areas can act as diffuse sources of air pollution, particularly where poor-quality fuels are burned in household stoves. Cases of multiple point sources or area sources (or both) can often be modeled by using simplifying assumptions or by integrating the impacts of individual sources.

## Use of Near-Field Dispersion Models

Typically, dispersion models have been used in developing countries only in isolated cases where air pollution had been recognized as a serious problem (e.g., Mae Moh, Thailand, and Krakow, Poland). However, with increasing pollution problems and more emphasis on air quality standards in developing countries, dispersion models are expected to be used more extensively in the future for sector- and project-level environmental assessments, as well as for assistance in establishing specific emissions requirements.

As a general guide, it is suggested that a basic analysis of possible impacts on ambient concentrations be carried out on installations that have the potential to emit annually more than 500 metric tons of sulfur dioxide or nitrogen oxides, or 50 metric tons of particulate matter or any hazardous air pollutant. In many cases, simple calculations based on loads and air volumes may be sufficient to provide an order-of-magnitude estimate. However, the use of formal models should be considered for any project involving large new plant or significant modifications. For major sources, the modeling should include the planned source or sources, as well as existing sources in the same general area—within a radius of 10 to 15 kilometers (km)—so that the cumulative effect of all the facilities on local air quality can be assessed. In some cases, building-wake effects are important (for example, where release points such as stacks and vents are less than 2.5 times the height of nearby buildings), and more detailed modeling may be appropriate.

The models described in this document pertain to "near-field" (less than 50 km from the point source) dispersion of sulfur dioxide, nitrogen oxides, and particulates. Such models estimate the ground-level concentration of pollutants in the air, which is then compared with ambient air quality standards or guidelines.[2] Other models that address photochemical smog are not described in detail here.

## Factors Affecting Dispersion of Pollutants

The dispersion and ground-level concentration of pollutants are determined by a complex interaction of the physical characteristics of the plant stack or other emission points, the physical and chemical characteristics of the pollutants, the meteorological conditions at or near the site, and the topographical conditions of the surrounding areas.

In general, three different calculations are needed to estimate the time-averaged concentration of pollutants at a location downwind from a plant:

- The plume rise above the stack must be established (effective stack height).
- The dispersion of the pollutants between the source and the downwind locations of interest must be mathematically modeled on the basis of atmospheric conditions.
- The time-averaged concentration at ground level must be determined.

Key factors that affect these calculations, and therefore the selection of dispersion models, are:

- *Topography.* The area surrounding the plant is characterized either as flat to gently rolling terrain or complex terrain (having downwind locations with elevations greater than stack height).
- *Land use.* Whether the surrounding area is urban or rural is important because urban areas typically have large structures and heat sources that affect the dispersion of pollutants. In addition, the density of the population affects the numbers potentially impacted.
- *Pollutant properties.* Physical and chemical properties of the pollutants influence their transport. For modeling sulfur dioxide within 5 to 10 km of a source, no chemical transformations are assumed to occur. Beyond this distance, an exponential decay function may be useful. Most nitrogen oxide is emitted as nitric oxide (NO), but in a matter of minutes, depending on the availability of ozone, it becomes nitrogen dioxide. The deposition of particulates is a function of particle size and travel time.
- *Source configuration.* The height and temperature of the discharge and proximity to structures affect dispersion. Effective plume height is the physical height of the stack adjusted for factors that raise the plume (as a result of buoyancy or momentum) or lower it (as a result of downwash or deflection).
- *Multiple sources.* All dispersion models assume that the concentrations at any one target site are the arithmetic sum of concentrations from each of the sources being examined. Note that it is the effects that are summed, not the emissions rates or stack parameters.
- *Time scale of exposure.* The recommended models make calculations for the basic time period of one hour. Concentrations for longer time periods, such as 8 hours or 24 hours, are the arithmetic averages of the hourly concentrations of those time periods. Annual averages are computed by averaging hourly concentrations for a full year or by using models that use a frequency distribution of meteorological events to compute an annual average. The recom-

mended models have the necessary "book-keeping" incorporated into the processing or available as postprocessor routines.

## Selecting an Appropriate Model

Model selection requires matching the key characteristics of the site and the requirements of the evaluation with the capabilities of the model. Normally, expert advice is required in making a selection. As a general principle, modeling should always begin with the simplest form possible, moving to more complex approaches only where their necessity and value can be demonstrated. At the most basic level, a crude mass balance can indicate whether a new source is likely to pose a problem. Alternatively, a simple screening model, as described below, can provide a realistic estimate of the order of magnitude of the impacts of a source. Situations involving multiple sources or varying terrain may require a more sophisticated effort involving site-specific data collection and more complex models.

In some cases, more than one model may be required. For example, modeling of gaseous emissions and particulates in the Mae Moh Valley, Thailand, required the use of one model for the valley floor, where the terrain is flat, and another for the mountains that surround the valley on three sides (KBN Engineering and Applied Sciences, Inc. 1989).

## Commonly Used Models

### Screening Models

The preliminary scoping of the magnitude of the air pollution problem can be accomplished by the use of screening models designed to determine quickly and easily the impacts from a single source. If it is obvious that several sources are contributing to concentrations, screening is not appropriate. A useful screening model is SCREEN3 (EPA 450/4-9-006, Modeling Guideline, and EPA 454/R-92-019, Screening Procedures for Stationary Sources). This approach requires no site-specific meteorological input, as calculations are made for a spectrum of possible combinations of wind speed and atmospheric stability (using Pasquill classes). Concentrations at the downwind point of maximum impact, as

well as at other specified distances, are determined. No consideration of wind direction is required because the output represents the concentrations directly downwind. (This model is designed for average North American conditions; care should be taken in using it under different climatic conditions.)

Options in the model allow for the effects of a single dominant building and for terrain differences between the source and the receptors. To refine the estimates in complex terrain, a more sophisticated screening model is available in CTSCREEN, derived from CTDMPLUS (see below).

Although only a single source (stack) is considered, multiple nearby sources can be screened by using the sum of the emissions rates from the sources as the emissions rate for this single stack. This will yield an overestimate, since the effects of geographic separation of the sources or the points of maximum concentration will not have been included. Scaling factors to estimate concentrations for longer time averages (3 hours, 8 hours, 24 hours, and even one year) are included in the user's guide.

If the concentrations determined by using a screening model are within the relevant guidelines, no additional modeling should be necessary. If concentrations exceed the guidelines, more refined modeling should be done. Since the simplifying assumptions made in the screening model tend to overestimate impacts, refined modeling nearly always yields somewhat lower estimates of concentration.

Screening is straightforward and does not require difficult decisions as to the relevance and representativeness of meteorological data. It may be carried out by competent local specialists, perhaps with some expert assistance.

### Refined Models

More refined modeling of near-field dispersion can be carried out with one of several simple Gaussian plume models. These models predict the dispersion patterns of nonreactive pollutants such as sulfur dioxide, nitrogen oxides, and particulates within 50 km of the emissions source and are generally expected to produce results within a factor of 2 of the measured values. Most such dispersion models are similar in design and performance and do not attempt to account for complex situations such as long-range transport and highly reactive chemical emissions.

What distinguishes the various models is their capability to handle different settings. Some of the models (such as ISC3 and CTDMPLUS, described below) are characterized as *"preferred models"* by organizations such as the USEPA because they meet certain minimum technical criteria, have undergone field testing and have had extensive peer review. This does not make the nonpreferred models less suitable for an application, but it does mean there is a documented experience base for the preferred models, which may add more credibility to the analysis or eliminate the need for model validation. Two of the most commonly used models for assessment of pollutant dispersion are from the USEPA.

- The ISC3 (Industrial Source Complex) model is used for point (stack), area, and volume sources in flat or complex terrain. The complex terrain analysis does not employ a sophisticated algorithm. There are two versions: ISCST3, for averaging periods of 24 hours or less, and ISCLT3, for averaging periods of 30 days or longer.
- The CTDMPLUS (Complex Terrain Dispersion) model is for use in complex terrain. A screening version of this model, CTSCREEN, provides estimates if only one or two stacks affect high terrain.

Other commonly used models are:

- UK-ADMS, the United Kingdom Meteorological Office Atmospheric Dispersion Modeling System

- PARADE, developed by Electricite de France
- PLUME 5, developed by Pacific Gas & Electric Co., San Ramon, Calif., and applicable to both urban and rural areas with complex terrain
- The German TA Luft procedures.

Table 1 provides the key characteristics of the commonly used air quality dispersion models. More details on these, as well as on other dispersion models (e.g., ERTAQ, COMPTER, MPSDM, MTDDIS, MULTIMAX, LONGZ, SHORTZ, SCSTER, 3141 and 4141), are provided in USEPA (1993).

These models have been developed and used mainly in industrial countries, but they are suitable for developing countries, as demonstrated by their use in, for example, the projects in Mae Moh, Krakow, and Sri Lanka mentioned below. However, they may require some adaptation to or calibration for topography and weather patterns that are not common in industrial countries. For example, dispersion models have not been subject to a comparison of model calculations of existing sources with monitored air quality data in tropical weather conditions.

### ISC3 and CTDMPLUS Models

The Industrial Source Complex (ISC) model is a steady-state Gaussian plume model used to assess pollutant concentrations from a wide variety of industrial sources. It accounts for settling and dry deposition of particulates; wake effects stemming from building obstruction; plume rise as a function of downwind distance; and multiple but separate point, area, and volume

### Table 1. Key Characteristics of Commonly Used Dispersion Models

| | Terrain | | | | Pollutant | | Source configuration | | | Time scale | |
| | Flat/ gently rolling | Com- plex/ rough | Land use | | $So_x$/ $No_x$ | Parti- culate | Point | Ele- vated point | Mul- tiple point | Short- term exposure | Long- term exposure |
| | | | Urban | Rural | | | | | | | |
|---|---|---|---|---|---|---|---|---|---|---|---|
| SCREEN3 | Yes | Yes | Yes | Yes | Yes | Yes | Yes | Yes | No | Yes | No |
| ISCLT | Yes | Yes | Yes | Yes | Yes | Yes | Yes | Yes | Yes | Yes | Yes |
| ISCST | Yes | Yes | Yes | Yes | Yes | Yes | Yes | Yes | Yes | Yes | No[a] |
| PLUME5 | Yes | Yes | Yes | Yes | Yes | No | Yes | Yes | Yes | Yes | Yes |
| CTDMPLUS | No | Yes | No | Yes | Yes | Yes | Yes | Yes | Yes | Yes | No |

*Note:* All of the above models except PLUME 5 are available through NTIS, Springfield, Va. 22161. PLUME 5 is available through Pacific Gas and Electric Co, San Ramon, Calif.
a. "Yes," if all hours for the time period are averaged (e.g. 8,760 hours in a 365-day year).

sources. It has the ability to analyze concentrations in any type of terrain, and it can estimate hourly to annual pollutant concentrations. This model is recommended for both urban and rural areas.

An earlier version of the ISC model has been used in a number of World Bank projects such as Mae Moh, Thailand (KBN Engineering and Applied Sciences, Inc. 1990), Krakow, Poland (Adamson et al. 1996), and Sri Lanka (Meier and Munasinghe 1994).

Several private firms offer enhanced versions of the EPA models (see, for example, Scholze 1990). The enhancements include user-friendly data input, the capability of easily plotting the output, custom output summaries, and technical support. Some of these firms offer training in the use of models, both in the United States and overseas.

Addresses for obtaining further information on the USEPA and German models are given at the end of this chapter.

*Other Models*

In addition to the above-mentioned models, there are models that are not used widely but that may be the most suitable for specific locations because they have been developed by local institutions and have taken into account local requirements. For example, a World Bank study in Krakow, Poland (Adamson et al. 1996) utilized a model developed by the Warsaw University of Technology.

For a facility within 200 km of an urban center that has a smog problem, one may wish to examine the effects of photochemical reactions between volatile organic compounds (VOCs) and nitrogen oxides, if the new source contributes more than 1–2% to the total emissions of these compounds in the airshed. This analysis requires an enormous amount of data, takes highly skilled modeling personnel, and is generally quite expensive. Commonly used models for such an assessment are the USEPA Urban Air Quality Model (UAM) and the Regional Oxidant Model (ROM).

**Use of Refined Models**

Models such as ISCST3 are more sophisticated in their structure and capabilities than the simple screening models, but they can be applied in a basic manner when the necessary data are difficult to obtain or in order to determine the value of collecting further data. For example, in a complex airshed with several sources and differing meteorological conditions, it may be appropriate to calculate the impacts of each major source individually, using simplified meteorology for that source. The impacts from all the sources can then be summed, producing estimates that are not as precise as a multisource model but that may give a reasonable indication of the overall impact.

In complex situations, significant effort and professional judgment are often necessary for estimation of the emissions inventory (defining all the sources to be included), for collection of local meteorological data, and for selection of the specific combinations of conditions to be modeled. For example, in an industrial city, it may be appropriate to group the sources into different types, such as major sources, smaller industrial or municipal sources, and indeterminate residential emissions. Identification of sources and estimation of the emissions inventory for use in the model would be significant tasks. For the major sources, site-specific details should be obtained. Smaller industrial sources might be handled by aggregating them into groups or by defining typical characteristics. Residential sources would have to be partitioned in accordance with some estimates of population density or housing type. Efforts would have to be made to understand the local meteorology in some detail, addressing variability across the area, patterns of inversions, and perhaps day/night variations to reflect patterns of residential emissions.

Credible modeling in such complex situations requires significant effort and resources. Collection and interpretation of the data required as input can take a large part of the overall resources—perhaps 50% or more.

**Data Requirements**

The data requirements of dispersion models fall into three categories:

- *Source data*, including location of stacks and other sources (coordinates), physical stack height and inside diameter, stack exit gas velocity and temperature, and pollutant release rate. The latter is usually given as the time-weighted average (per 1 hour, 24 hours, or year).

Some dispersion models may require additional inputs such as point source elevation, building dimensions (e.g., average building width and space between buildings), particle size distribution with corresponding settling velocities, and surface reflection coefficients.

- *Meteorological data* are required for predicting the transport, dispersion, and depletion of the pollutants. Most models accept hourly surface weather data that include the hourly Pasquill stability class, wind direction and speed, air temperature, and mixing height. Ideally, a year of meteorological data would be available. In cases where some long-term data are available in the region (typically, readings taken at an airport), shorter-term local observations may allow the long-term records to be transferred to the site under examination. Where appropriate, a local meteorological station can be established (estimated cost, about US$30,000–$40,000 for setup and one year of operation of one automated site).
- *Receptor data*, meaning identification *of* all key receptors (e.g., areas of high population or expected maximum ground-level concentration). Usually, receptors are specified by their coordinates and elevation.

Values of input parameters can be determined by direct measurement, sampling, or estimates based on sound engineering principles. The literature may provide data or empirical correlations that can be used for estimating dispersion model inputs.

## Interpretation of Results

The results of dispersion modeling are typically maps showing the concentration of the considered pollutants (usually sulfur dioxide, nitrogen oxides, and particulates) throughout the immediate area surrounding the facility. The map consists of the computed concentrations at each site and a plot of the isopleths (lines of constant concentrations). Since plotting results in "smoothing," the actual computed data should be evaluated. The maps need to be evaluated (typi-

cally by an expert) to compare them with local ambient air quality standards and identify "hot spots"—areas where pollutant concentration is above desirable levels.

It should be emphasized that mathematical modeling of complex atmospheric processes involves a significant level of uncertainty, which can be made worse when data are lacking or unreliable. Model results must therefore be treated with care when using them in formal decision-making. The presentation of results should normally include a discussion of the probable variability and the confidence limits.

For decisionmakers, the results need to be summarized in a clear, understandable way. Table A.1, which sets out the key findings from a modeling study of a proposed power plant, is an example of such a presentation.

## Resource Requirements for Dispersion Studies

Information on screening models is generally readily available. The costs of acquiring the model, some training, and the actual study should be less than US$10,000. Local consultants can rapidly acquire skill with the screening models. Where refined modeling is required, the necessary skill level increases sharply.

Air quality monitoring and model validation can have significant costs. In the United States, air quality analysis costs for power plants have ranged from US$100,000 to US$2 million. The lower end of this range corresponds to the case of readily available meteorological data and flat terrain in a rural area. The high end of the range includes ambient air quality monitoring costs and, in some cases, the cost of demonstrating the inappropriateness of a model approved by the regulatory agency or of validating a model not approved by the regulatory agency. Although these costs are based on experience from industrial countries, costs in other countries are expected to be similar. Some cost reductions could be achieved by maximizing the utilization of local consultants, particularly if the local consultant has the opportunity to carry out four or five such projects annually. Unless there is frequent use of dispersion modeling, it may not be worthwhile to acquire the skill because of the rapid changes in the models themselves and in the com-

Annex. Example of Summary Output from an Airshed Model

## Table A.1. Air Pollution Characteristics of a Proposed Thermal Power Plant

A. AIR QUALITY PROJECTIONS
*(all units are μg/m3)*

| Reference values | World Bank guidelines | National standards | Monitoring point 1 | Monitoring point 2 | Monitoring point 3 | Monitoring point 4 |
|---|---|---|---|---|---|---|
| Annual average | | | | | | |
| Daily maximum | | | | | | |
| Annual maximum | | | | | | |
| **Background levels** | | | *Monitoring point 1* | *Monitoring point 2* | *Monitoring point 3* | *Monitoring point 4* |
| Annual average | | | | | | |
| Daily maximum | | | | | | |
| Annual maximum | | | | | | |
| **Design coal: background plus two 600 MW units** | | | *Monitoring point 1* | *Monitoring point 2* | *Monitoring point 3* | *Monitoring point 4* |
| Annual average | | | | | | |
| Daily maximum | | | | | | |
| Annual maximum | | | | | | |
| **Design coal: background plus four 600 MW units** | | | *Monitoring point 1* | *Monitoring point 2* | *Monitoring point 3* | *Monitoring point 4* |
| Annual average | | | | | | |
| Daily maximum | | | | | | |
| Annual maximum | | | | | | |
| **Check coal: background plus two 600 MW units** | | | *Monitoring point 1* | *Monitoring point 2* | *Monitoring point 3* | *Monitoring point 4* |
| Annual average | | | | | | |
| Daily maximum | | | | | | |
| Annual maximum | | | | | | |
| **Check coal: background plus four 600 MW units** | | | *Monitoring point 1* | *Monitoring point 2* | *Monitoring point 3* | *Monitoring point 4* |
| Annual average | | | | | | |
| Daily maximum | | | | | | |
| Annual maximum | | | | | | |

B. ASSUMPTIONS

1. Sulfur content
   Design value: 0.31%
   Check value: 0.92%

2. Ash content
   Design value: 15.5%
   Check value: 28.4%

3. Stack height

4. ESP efficiency

C. PROJECTED EMISSIONS

| | | World Bank guidelines | National standards | Two 600 MW units | Four 600 MW units |
|---|---|---|---|---|---|
| $SO_2$ (tons/day) | Design | | | | |
| | Check | | | | |
| TSP (mg/m³) | Design | | | | |
| | Check | | | | |
| $NO_x$ (ng/J) | Design | | | | |
| | Check | | | | |

*Note:* $SO_2$, sulfur dioxide; TSP, total suspended particulates; $NO_x$, nitrogen oxides; MW, megawatt; ESP, electrostatic precipitator; mg/m³, milligrams per cubic meter; ng/J, nanograms per joule.

89

puter technology needed to effectively use the models.

## When Should the Modeling Be Done?

Dispersion modeling should be part of the initial environmental assessment for a power project, for example. It is recommended that the dispersion modeling be carried out early in project preparation (e.g., as part of the feasibility study) before the plant location and the detailed design have been finalized.

## Additional Resources: For Further Information on the Models

- USEPA (U.S. Environmental Protection Agency). "ISC Dispersion Model User's Guide: Volumes 1 and 2. " EPA 454/B-95-003, a, b, and c. Office of Air Quality Planning and Standards, Research Triangle Park, N.C.
- USEPA. "CTDMPLUS Model User's Guide." EPA 600/8-89/041. "Terrain Processor." EPA 600/8-88/003. Office of Air Quality Planning and Standards, Research Triangle Park, N.C.

All USEPA models are available from the EPA SCRAM bulletin board free of charge.
  Tel: 919/541-5742
  e-mail: TTNBBS.RTPNC.EPA.GOV
In addition all EPA models are available for a fee from the National Technical Information Service (NTIS), Springfield, Va. 22161.

- Germany, Federal Ministry for the Environment, Nature Conservation, and Nuclear Safety. 1992. "Manual of Ambient Air Quality Control in Germany." Berlin.
- Germany, Federal Ministry for the Environment, Nature Conservation, and Nuclear Safety. 1992. "Air Pollution Control: Manual of Continuous Emission Monitoring." Berlin.

## Notes

1. *Dispersion* refers to the movement of parcels of gases, whether vertically or horizontally, and their simultaneous dilution in the air.

2. *Standards* pertain to the environmental requirements of the country or the local authority; *guidelines* are practices suggested by organizations such as WHO and the World Bank.

## References and Sources

Adamson, Sebron, Robin Bates, Robert Laslett, and Alberto Pototschnig. 1996. *Energy Use, Air Pollution, and Environmental Policy in Krakow: Can Economic Incentives Really Help?* World Bank Technical Paper 308. Washington, D.C.

Electric Power Research Institute. 1986. "Estimating the Cost of Uncertainty in Air Quality Modeling." EA-4707. Palo Alto, Calif.

KBN Engineering and Applied Sciences, Inc. 1989. "Mae Moh Air Quality Update: Units 1–11." Prepared for the Survey and Ecology Department of the Electricity Generating Authority of Thailand. Bangkok.

KBN Engineering and Applied Sciences, Inc. 1990. "Sulfur Dioxide Air Quality Impact Analysis for Mae Moh: Units 1–13." Prepared for the Survey and Ecology Department of the Electricity Generating Authority of Thailand. Bangkok.

Meier, Peter, and Mohan Munasinghe. 1994. *"Incorporating Environmental Concerns into Power Sector Decisionmaking: A Case Study of Sri Lanka.* World Bank Environment Paper 6. Washington, D.C.

Scholze, R. H. 1990. "Dispersion Modeling Using Personal Computers." *Atmospheric Environment* 24A(8): 2051–57.

USEPA (U.S. Environmental Protection Agency). 1993. "Selection Criteria for Mathematical Models Used in Exposure Assessments: Atmospheric Dispersion Models." EPA/600/8-91/038. Washington, D.C.

# Removal of Lead from Gasoline

*Human exposure to lead is a major environmental health hazard, a large part of which is attributed to the use of lead in gasoline. Experience has shown that significant reduction of present and future human exposure to lead can be achieved cost-effectively by removing lead from gasoline. This chapter provides guidance on implementation of programs to phase out lead from gasoline.*

## Impacts and Sources of Exposure to Lead

Lead is a highly toxic heavy metal that adversely affects the nervous, blood-forming, cardiovascular, renal, and reproductive systems. Of most concern are its effects on the nervous system of young children—reduced intelligence, attention deficit, and behavioral abnormalities—and its contribution to cardiovascular disease in adults. Such impacts occur even at low levels of exposure; there is no known lower threshold.

Human exposure to lead can be attributed to four types of sources: vehicular, when lead additives are used in gasoline; industrial emissions, largely from the mining, smelting, and processing of lead and lead-containing metal ores; waste disposal and processing of lead-containing substances through such means as incineration; and use of lead-containing products such as water pipes and solder, food-can solder, ceramic glazes, paint pigment, and batteries. Many of the uses of lead (for example, in paint) have been banned by most countries. As a result, vehicular traffic is often the largest source of human exposure, accounting for as much as 90% of all atmospheric lead emissions in many urban areas. A close connection has been discovered between the use of lead in gasoline and human health impacts (USEPA 1985). In addition to the immediate health exposures through inhalation, lead also accumulates in the soil, causing long-term exposure.

## Rationale of Removing Lead from Gasoline

Since the 1930s, alkyl-lead compounds have been widely used to improve auto engine performance by increasing the resistance of the internal combustion engine to early ignition (measured by the octane rating of gasoline). The use of lead additives allowed car manufacturers to produce larger and more powerful engines, leading to rapid growth in the use and emission of lead from vehicular sources. Two major factors have brought about a decline in the use of lead in gasoline since the 1970s:

- The introduction of catalytic converters, designed to reduce tailpipe emissions of various pollutants, which required the introduction of unleaded gasoline to protect the converters.
- The recognition that health impacts occur even at low exposure levels, which induced measures to reduce the lead content of gasoline to minimize health impacts.

Because the social benefits of phasing out lead largely outweigh the costs, policies should facilitate the reduction of lead from gasoline in addition to and beyond the demands of changing car technology.

## Worldwide Experience with Phasing Out Lead from Gasoline

Phase-out of lead is in different stages around the world. Argentina, Austria, Bermuda, Brazil,

Canada, Colombia, Costa Rica, Denmark, El Salvador, Finland, Germany, Guatemala, Honduras, Hong Kong (China), Japan, Nicaragua, the Slovak Republic, Sweden, Thailand, and the United States, among others, have completed a total phase-out. In some countries, such as the United States, the phase-out was initially driven by the desire to protect catalytic converters. In others (for example, EU member countries), the regulation of lead levels in gasoline preceded the widespread use of catalytic converters. Brazil and Colombia, among others, have introduced alternative fuels such as alcohol. Many developing countries, however, still use alarmingly high concentrations of lead in gasoline and have not yet introduced unleaded gasoline (see Table 1).

## Technical Issues

*Refinery Capacity to Produce Unleaded Gasoline*

Gasoline-importing countries have greater flexibility in phasing out the use of lead in gasoline than do countries where domestic oil-refining capacity determines the options and cost of adjustment. Experience shows that the modifications required in refinery processes to reduce lead may be quite modest, depending on such factors as refinery complexity (more complex refineries adjust more easily), spare octane capacity, and the octane requirement of the car fleet. The additional cost of producing unleaded gasoline rarely exceeds US$0.01–$0.02 per liter of gasoline. The potential adverse

## Table 1. Worldwide Use of Lead in Gasoline

| Maximum allowed lead in gasoline | Market share of unleaded gasoline (%) | | |
|---|---|---|---|
| | *Low (0–30)* | *Medium (30–70)* | *High (70–100)* |
| Low (< 0.15 g/l) | Cyprus, Greece, Ireland, Israel, Italy, Malaysia, Philippines, Poland, Portugal, Spain, Turkey | Belgium, Brunei, France, Hungary, Iceland, Luxembourg, Norway, Singapore, Switzerland, Taiwan (China), United Kingdom | Argentina, Austria, Bermuda, Brazil, Canada, Colombia, Costa Rica, Denmark, El Salvador, Finland, Germany, Guatemala, Honduras, Hong Kong (China), Japan, Netherlands, Nicaragua, Slovak Republic, Sweden, Thailand, United States |
| Medium (0.15–0.40 g/l) | Bahrain, Côte d'Ivoire, Egypt, Iran, Jordan, Kenya, Laos, Mauritania, Mauritius, Namibia, Paraguay, Qatar, Russian Federation, Saudi Arabia, Sri Lanka, South Africa, United Arab Emirates, Uruguay, Vietnam | Australia, Ecuador, Mexico | |
| High (> 0.40 g/l) | Algeria, Angola, Bangladesh, Benin, Botswana, Burkina Faso, Burundi, Cameroon, Chad, China, Cuba, Ethiopia, Gabon, Ghana, India, Jamaica, Kuwait, Lebanon, Liberia, Libya, Madagascar, Malawi, Mali, New Zealand, Niger, Nigeria, Oman, Pakistan, Panama, Peru, Romania, Senegal, Syria, Venezuela, Yemen, Zimbabwe | | |

*Note:* Table is based on 1993–95 data; g/l, grams per liter.
*Source:* Lovei 1996.

environmental impacts of certain refinery processes should restrict the choice of technologies for replacing lead. Specifically, an increase in the aromatic (benzene) content of gasoline should be avoided by relying on isomerization, alkylation, and the use of oxygenates such as methyl-tertiary butyl ether (MTBE) to replace the octane-enhancing capacity of lead.

### The Impact of Unleaded Gasoline on Cars Designed to Use Leaded Gasoline

Besides enhancing engine performance, lead lubricates the exhaust valves. In the past, this characteristic allowed car manufacturers to use soft, low-grade metals in the engine valves. The lubricating function of lead has become unnecessary in the new generation of cars; as most car manufacturers began using hard metals in valves during the last two decades. However, a significant share of the car fleets in many developing and transition economies may still consist of old cars with soft valves. The recession of these soft valves (especially the valve seats) caused by unleaded gasoline has been seen as an obstacle to the rapid phase-out of lead from gasoline in many countries. Tests and experience show, however, that (a) this problem is not as serious as is believed; (b) much lower lead concentrations than are found in most leaded gasolines still provide adequate protection to sensitive engines; (c) significant maintenance savings are associated with the switch from leaded to unleaded gasoline; and (d) valve seat recession can be avoided by adding lubricants to unleaded gasoline.

## Policy Issues

Since the social benefits of removing lead from gasoline are large and the technical obstacles are relatively easy to deal with, the key to successful lead phase-out programs is the introduction of proper government policies. Recognition of the lead problem and political commitment to tackle it play a decisive role in initiating phase-out. The main areas on which government policies should focus are discussed below.

### Public Awareness-Building and Education

Public awareness of the rationale of phasing out lead from gasoline plays an important role in changing consumer habits and demand. Public education should provide information on:

- The health impacts of lead
- The feasibility of using unleaded gasoline in various types of cars
- Recommended fueling practices
- Recommended maintenance requirements.

### Consensus Building

A lead phase-out program requires the participation of various stakeholders whose consensus in the support and implementation of the program is essential. National programs should be designed with the participation of the main stakeholders including:

- The ministries of energy, industry, transport, environment, health, and finance
- Interest groups such as associations of car manufacturers and oil refineries
- Consumer groups such as auto clubs
- NGOs.

### Fuel Specifications

Fuel specifications should provide clear requirements for scheduling the reduction and ultimate elimination of lead use in gasoline. To avoid the potential negative health impacts of certain refinery processes, fuel specifications should also limit the aromatics and benzene content of gasoline.

### Regulations for Implementation

Government regulations should facilitate the cost-effective adjustment of gasoline supply to changing demand and requirements. In countries where a large number of refineries exist, the optimal timing and speed of adjustment at each refinery is likely to vary. Incentive regulations, such as lead trading among refineries (implemented, for example, in the United States) allow for flexibility in the timing of compliance with changing fuel specifications.

## Price Policies

Gasoline prices should enable domestic refineries to adjust. Liberalized price and market policies allow refineries to generate sufficient resources and returns to finance such adjustment. Controlled gasoline prices, however, can facilitate such adjustment only if prices are set at least at the level of prevailing international market prices. Gasoline price subsidies should be eliminated to encourage rapid supply-side adjustment.

## Tax Policies

A tax rate that is higher for leaded than for unleaded gasoline is justified to reflect the social costs of negative health impacts caused by lead. Experience has shown that differentiated taxation which results in a 5–10% difference in favor of unleaded gasoline prices facilitates the rapid adjustment of consumer habits and demand. If revenue neutrality is an objective, the difference in tax rates will need to be adjusted over time as the market share of unleaded gasoline increases during the phase-out period.

## Environmental Policies

Air pollution causes serious health damage, especially in densely populated urban areas. Traffic is generally a large and growing contributor to these pollution problems. In many cases, the requirement to install catalytic converters is justified to reduce the damage. Such regulations facilitate the shift in gasoline demand toward unleaded gasoline brands.

## Import Policies

Import regulations and customs levied on imported cars on the basis of their age and environmental performance affect gasoline demand. Import policies should reflect the social cost of pollution generated by imported cars, using such proxies as presence of an emissions control de-

vice, typical emissions factors of the car model, and age of the vehicle.

## Promotion and Training

Governments can accelerate the adjustment of markets to the wider use of unleaded gasoline by encouraging promotion of unleaded gasoline and by supporting the training of technicians and car mechanics in the proper maintenance and adjustment of the various types of vehicles to enable use of unleaded gasoline.

## World Bank Experience

### Policies

World Bank studies have pointed out the danger of lead exposure in, for example, Indonesia, Mexico, Thailand, the Middle East, and Central and Eastern Europe. Evidence of the adverse health impacts of lead has led to government action to address the problem and, with the assistance of the Bank, to design and implement lead phase-out programs and supporting policies in a number of countries, including Bulgaria, Mexico, the Philippines, and Thailand. Experience in Thailand has shown that rapid lead phase-out is possible if the government sets clear deadlines, gasoline prices are liberalized, and refineries respond to market changes and regulations. The lead phase-out program was severely hampered in Mexico, where price policies and market liberalization efforts failed to support the adjustment of refineries and of consumer behavior.

### Implementation

The Bank has provided financial support for the restructuring of the Bangchak refinery in Thailand to enable the refinery to produce unleaded gasoline. The Bank's financing role has been largely catalytic, to attract the participation of commercial sources. As a result of government policies and rapid refinery adjustment, lead was completely phased out from gasoline by the end of 1995 in Thailand. A similar project, in preparation, will assist the main refinery in Bulgaria to improve its technical capacity to increase the production of unleaded gasoline.

## References and Sources

Hertzman, Clyde. 1995. *Environment and Health in Central and Eastern Europe: A Report for the Environmental Action Programme for Central and Eastern Europe.* Washington, D.C.: World Bank.

Hirshfeld, D., and J. Kolb. 1995. "Phasing Out Lead from Gasoline: Feasibility and Costs." Implementing the Environmental Action Programme for Central and Eastern Europe. World Bank, Environment Department, Washington, D.C.

Lovei, Magda. 1996. *Phasing Out Lead from Gasoline: World-Wide Experience and Policy Implications.* Environment Department Paper 40. Washington, D.C.: World Bank.

Nriagu, J. O. 1992. "The Rise and Fall of Leaded Gasoline." *Science of the Total Environment* 92: 13–28.

Octel. 1994. *Worldwide Gasoline Survey 1992–1993.* London: The Associated Octel Company Ltd.

USEPA (U.S. Environmental Protection Agency). 1985. *Costs and Benefits of Reducing Lead in Gasoline: Final Regulatory Impact Analysis.* EPA-230-05-85-006. Washington D.C.: Office of Policy Analysis.

# Urban Air Quality Management

*Poor air quality due to pollution is a serious environmental problem in most urban areas. The greatest burden of pollution is on human health. Urban air quality management requires an integrated approach that determines which are the most serious problems; identifies the measures that offer cost-effective and feasible solutions across a range of economic sectors and pollution sources, and builds a consensus among key stakeholders concerning environmental objectives, policies, implementation measures, and responsibilities.*

Rapid urbanization, motorization and economic growth contribute to a growing air pollution problem in most large developing urban centers. Comparative risk assessment and health studies have been carried out in a number of cities (e.g., Bangkok, Cairo, Mexico City, Quito, Santiago, and cities of Central and Eastern Europe). These studies indicate that the greatest damage to human health comes from exposure to fine suspended particulates—particulate matter with an aerodynamic diameter of less than 10 microns ($PM_{10}$ and smaller)—and to lead. Other pollutants of concern are sulfur dioxide ($SO_2$), to the extent it contributes to fine particulates and long-range environmental damage; ozone ($O_3$), mainly in warmer, sunny locations with unfavorable topographic conditions; volatile organic compounds (VOCs), some of which are known carcinogens; nitrogen oxides ($NO_x$), contributors to ozone formation; and carbon monoxide (CO), which is associated with global warming.

## Main Sources of Pollution

Anthropogenic air pollution originates from large stationary sources (industries, power plants, and municipal incinerators); small stationary sources (households and small commercial boilers); and mobile sources (traffic); see Figure 1. Many of these sources are closely related to the production and consumption of energy, especially fossil fuels. Besides power plants and industries,

domestic use of fossil fuels, especially heavy fuel oil, biomass, and brown coal, is a significant source of ambient particulates and sulfur dioxide, especially in temperate regions (e.g., in China and Eastern Europe). Traffic is a large contributor to both particulate and sulfur emissions in cities with frequent traffic congestion and with large, poorly maintained fleets of vehicles that use high-sulfur diesel fuel (e.g., in Asia). In cities where leaded gasoline is still used, traffic may contribute 80–90% of atmospheric lead concentrations. (Poorly controlled emissions from lead

### Figure 1. Sources of Particulate Emissions in Selected Cities

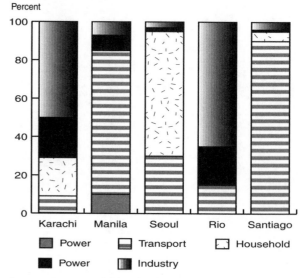

*Source:* UNEP and WHO 1992; World Bank 1996.

smelters could also be significant.) The roles of natural and anthropogenic sources are equally important in the formation of ground-level ozone. Natural sources, such as biogenic emissions from plants and trees, and traffic emissions are the largest sources of atmospheric VOC. Natural, mobile, and stationary combustion sources are significant contributors to nitrogen oxide concentrations. Motor vehicles are typically responsible for the greatest part of carbon monoxide emissions.

The impact of emissions on human exposures depends on the location and dispersion of pollution: large stationary sources, often located at a distance from most densely populated city centers, disperse into higher layers of the atmosphere, while households and traffic emit near ground levels in highly populated areas. As a result, mobile and small stationary sources contribute more to ambient urban pollutant concentrations, and the resulting health effects, than their share in total emissions loads indicates.

## Options for Reducing the Harmful Impacts of Pollution

Measures to mitigate the negative effects of pollution may focus on separating pollution sources and receptors, reducing the polluting activity, reducing its pollution characteristics, and controlling emissions with filtering devices. Not all of these alternatives are available for all pollutants. Changing the location of the pollution source may be an effective strategy for universally mixed

pollutants with only localized health effects, such as particulates. Urban planning, zoning, and other land use regulations can influence urban air quality through microlevel decisions. However, these measures are not effective for persistent pollutants such as heavy metals and for pollutants with significant regional and global impacts such as sulfur dioxide and carbon dioxide. Opportunities for applying alternative methods of emissions reduction also vary across pollution sources (Table 1).

The impact of emissions from large stationary sources can be reduced by choosing a location away from populated areas; using clean fuels such as gas and low-sulfur or low-ash coal; applying cleaner technologies such as fluidized-bed combustion and low-$NO_x$ burners; improving maintenance and housekeeping; and installing proper end-of-pipe control technologies such as electrostatic precipitators and baghouses.

The impacts of traffic-related emissions may be mitigated by diverting traffic away from heavily populated areas (for example, by building ring roads around cities or restricting downtown traffic); converting high-use vehicles to cleaner fuels (for example, converting buses to natural gas); improving vehicle maintenance; increasing the share of less polluting traffic modes; using more fuel-efficient vehicles; and installing catalytic control devices. Supply-side traffic management measures aimed at reducing congestion (for example, by improving road infrastructure) rarely lead to significant overall emissions reductions because they may simply increase traffic flows.

**Table 1. Most Effective Pollution Abatement Options at Key Sources**

| | Industry and energy | | | | | House-holds: Fuels | Traffic | | | | |
|---|---|---|---|---|---|---|---|---|---|---|---|
| | Location | Fuels | Mainte-nance | Clean tech-nology | End-of-pipe | | Location | Fuels | Mainte-nance | Clean tech-nology | End-of-pipe |
| $PM_{10}$ | x | x | x | x | x | x | x | x | x | x | |
| Lead | | x | | | x | | x | | | x | |
| $SO_2$ | | x | x | x | x | x | x | | x | x | |
| VOCs | | | | | | | x | | x | x | x |
| $NO_x$ | x | x | | x | | | x | | x | x | x |
| CO | | | | | | | x | | x | x | x |

*Note:* $PM_{10}$, particulate matter 10 microns or less in aerodynamic diameter; $SO_2$, sulfur dioxide; VOCs, volatile organic compounds; $NO_x$, nitrogen oxides; CO, carbon monoxide.

Emissions from households and other small stationary sources can be reduced most effectively through conversion to cleaner fuels.

## Policy Approaches and Instruments

### Setting Priorities

Because of the many sources of emissions in an airshed, pollution abatement focused on a single sector may lead to little improvement in air quality (see Box 1). Proper air quality management requires an integrated approach consisting of:

- Use of *monitoring and modeling* to establish an emissions inventory of key pollutants and emissions sources
- Use of *dispersion modeling* to determine the impacts of the emissions on ambient concentrations
- Use of *dose-response functions and valuation techniques* to estimate the impacts of the pollutants on human health
- Identification of *technically feasible abatement options* and calculation of their costs
- Estimation of the *impacts* of these abatement alternatives on ambient air quality and human health

- Determination of *priority measures* with high benefit-cost ratios.

An integrated approach requires coordination and consensus building across sectors and among affected stakeholders to agree on priorities and adaptable measures; agreement on acceptable benchmarks for environmental performance in individual sectors; introduction of policies and instruments to support implementation; and establishment of an implementation monitoring and enforcement mechanism cutting across sectors and authorities.

### Guidelines and Standards

WHO establishes guidelines for ambient pollutant concentrations at which the risk of adverse health impacts is considered negligible. (For certain pollutants with no threshold below which there are no observable effects, WHO provides exposure-effect information, illustrating the major health impacts of different levels of the pollutant.) In developing countries with heavily polluted areas, these guidelines may serve as long-term objectives; however, short-term actions should be guided by a careful analysis of the expected benefits and costs of pollution abatement

---

**Box 1. Setting Priorities: Three Examples**

*The sectoral approach in São Paulo: tackling the "wrong" sources of pollution.* Early World Bank projects to abate pollution did not attempt to address pollution problems in an integrated way. The São Paolo Industrial Pollution Control Project, for example, succeeded in reducing particulate emissions from industrial sources but ignored mobile sources, which were important contributors to pollution. As a consequence, the city's ambient dust levels did not improve.

*An integrated approach in Slovenia.* The government of Slovenia requested World Bank assistance to finance the installation of flue-gas desulfurization technology at a power plant to reduce ambient particulate and sulfur dioxide concentrations in neighboring cities. An analysis of the main pollution sources found, however, that the principal contributor to poor ambient air quality was the use of low-quality coal in households and small boilers, which could be effectively tackled by a coal-to-gas conversion program for small combustion sources. Under the Bank-financed Environment Project, an Air Pollution Abatement Fund was established to provide loans to households in eli-

gible municipalities that adopted smoke-reduction regulations.

*Integrated analysis of alternatives for reducing emissions in Santiago.* A Bank study (World Bank 1994) analyzed the costs and the impacts on ambient air quality of several strategies for controlling pollution in Santiago de Chile:

- Tightening emissions standards for light-duty vehicles
- Setting more stringent emissions limits for diesel buses and trucks
- Converting buses to natural gas
- Tightening emissions limits for large stationary sources
- Converting households to clean fuels.

The study found that, on an emitted-ton basis, reductions in particulates were more than 10 times more valuable, in terms of health benefits, than reductions in any other pollutant. Of the control options analyzed, measures to reduce emissions from fixed sources and gasoline vehicles had the highest benefit-cost ratios, followed by measures to reduce emissions from diesel trucks and buses.

measures. In practical terms, this leads to interim, achievable ambient quality objectives.

The analysis of good practices for management and pollution abatement, available technologies, and the expected impacts on emissions and ambient concentrations can provide minimum requirements for pollution abatement performance (or, alternatively, maximum emissions levels) in each sector. Requirements for pollution performance at individual sources, should, however, take into account local conditions and may focus on reductions at those sources that can carry out the reductions at the least cost. Allowing intersectoral and intercompany agreements within an airshed (the bubble concept) may be a more cost-effective way of achieving the required emissions reductions than less flexible approaches.

*Regulations and Incentive Instruments*

In the past, pollution management most often focused on the improvement of technologies and on the addition of end-of-pipe controls relying on uniform emissions or technological standards. The limitations of this approach have directed policymakers' attention to more flexible measures that rely on improved management and pollution prevention techniques, with an increased focus on the complex effects of pollution from a variety of sources on ambient air quality and human exposures (see Box 2).

Incentive-based policy instruments increase the price of pollution, encourage the search for cleaner operations, and influence the demand for polluting activities:

- *Direct-incentive policy instruments* such as emissions charges (or, alternatively, emissions permit trading) may be best applied to large stationary sources and to pollutants (such as $PM_{10}$, $SO_2$, and $NO_x$) for which the abatement cost varies across pollution sources and for which monitoring is feasible. The best examples are the acid rain trading program in the United States, which contributed to a significant reduction of the overall costs of reducing sulfur dioxide emissions from large stationary sources, and the nitrogen oxide emission charge on large combustion plants in Sweden.

> ### Box 2. "Good" and "Bad" Choices of Policy Instruments
>
> Fuel taxes have been effectively applied in many countries to increase demand for cleaner fuels. One of the best-known examples is the differentiated taxation of gasoline according to its lead content. This measure has contributed to a significant increase in the market share of unleaded gasoline in a large number of European and other countries.
>
> Other policy instruments have been less successful. For example, many big cities have experimented with placing various restrictions on traffic (for example, according to license plate number) to reduce air pollution from mobile sources. These programs did not fulfill policymakers' expectations of reducing overall emissions. In Mexico City, for example, the measures encouraged drivers to buy additional, typically more-polluting vehicles.

- *Indirect policy instruments* such as product charges, taxes, and deposit-refund systems are best applied to small and diffuse pollution sources that cannot be monitored easily; where the use and disposal of products are closely linked to their pollution effects; and where prices can influence producer and user behavior. Examples are fuel taxes and deposit-refund systems for batteries.

While incentive policy instruments offer potential cost savings and allow flexibility in responding to environmental requirements, the administrative costs of such measures may be high, or the feasibility of implementation may be low, requiring direct regulation. Prohibiting the use of highly toxic substances (such as lead in gasoline) and industrial processes (such as mercury cell chlor-alkali production) is a typical example.

### References and Sources

Eskeland, Gunnar S., and Shantayanan Devarajan. 1995. *Taxing Bads by Taxing Goods: Pollution Control with Presumptive Charges.* Directions in Development series. Washington, D.C.: World Bank.

OECD (Organisation for Economic Co-operation and Development). 1995. *Motor Vehicle Pollution: Reduction Strategies beyond 2010.* Paris.

UNEP (United Nations Environment Programme) and WHO (World Health Organization). 1992. *Urban Air*

*Pollution in Megacities of the World.* Oxford: Blackwell Publishers.

World Bank. 1994. "Chile: Managing Environmental Problems: Economic Analysis of Selected Issues." Report 13061-CH. Washington, D.C.

————. 1996. "Brazil: Managing Environmental Pollution in the State of Rio de Janeiro." Report 15488-BR. Washington, D.C.

# Water Quality Models

*In order to determine the impacts of a particular discharge on ambient water quality, it is usually necessary to model the diffusion and dispersion of the discharge in the relevant water body. The approach applies both to new discharges and to the upgrading of existing sources. This chapter provides guidance on models that may be applicable in the context of typical Bank projects.*

Mathematical models can be used to predict changes in ambient water quality due to changes in discharges of wastewater. In Bank work, the models are typically used to establish priorities for reduction of existing wastewater discharges or to predict the impacts of a proposed new discharge. Although a range of parameters may be of interest, a modeling exercise typically focuses on a few, such as dissolved oxygen, coliform bacteria, or nutrients.

Predicting the water quality impacts of a single discharge can often be done quickly and sufficiently accurately with a simple model. Regional water quality planning usually requires a model with a broader geographic scale, more data, and a more complex model structure.

## Model Classification

Water quality models are usually classified according to model complexity, type of receiving water, and the water quality parameters (dissolved oxygen, nutrients, etc.) that the model can predict.

The more complex the model is, the more difficult and expensive will be its application to a given situation. Model complexity is a function of four factors.

- *The number and type of water quality indicators.* In general, the more indicators that are included, the more complex the model will be. In addition, some indicators are more complicated to predict than others (see Table 1).

- *The level of spatial detail.* As the number of pollution sources and water quality monitoring points increase, so do the data required and the size of the model.
- *The level of temporal detail.* It is much easier to predict long-term static averages than short-term dynamic changes in water quality. Point estimates of water quality parameters are usually simpler than stochastic predictions of the probability distributions of those parameters.
- *The complexity of the water body* under analysis. Small lakes that "mix" completely are less complex than moderate-size rivers, which are less complex than large rivers, which are less complex than large lakes, estuaries, and coastal zones.

The level of detail required can vary tremendously across different management applications. At one extreme, managers may be interested in the long-term impact of a small industrial plant on dissolved oxygen in a small, well-mixed lake. This type of problem can be addressed with a simple spreadsheet and solved by a single analyst in a month or less. At the other extreme, if managers want to know the rate of change in heavy metal concentrations in the Black Sea that can be expected from industrial modernization in the lower Danube River, the task will probably require many person-years of effort with extremely complex models and may cost millions of dollars.

For indicators of aerobic status, such as biochemical oxygen demand (BOD), dissolved oxy-

**Table 1. Criteria for Classification of Water Quality Models**

| Criterion | Comment |
|---|---|
| Single-plant or regional focus | Simpler models can usually be used for single-plant "marginal" effects. More complex models are needed for regional analyses. |
| Static or dynamic | Static (constant) or time-varying outputs. |
| Stochastic or deterministic | Stochastic models present outputs as probability distributions; deterministic models are point-estimates. |
| Type of receiving water (river, lake, or estuary) | Small lakes and rivers are usually easier to model. Large lakes, estuaries, and large river systems are more complex. |
| Water quality parameters | |
| Dissolved oxygen | Usually decreases as discharge increases. Used as a water quality indicator in most water quality models. |
| Biochemical oxygen demand (BOD) | A measure of oxygen-reducing potential for waterborne discharges. Used in most water quality models. |
| Temperature | Often increased by discharges, especially from electric power plants. Relatively easy to model. |
| Ammonia nitrogen | Reduces dissolved oxygen concentrations and adds nitrate to water. Can be predicted by most water quality models. |
| Algal concentration | Increases with pollution, especially nitrates and phosphates. Predicted by moderately complex models. |
| Coliform bacteria | An indicator of contamination from sewage and animal waste |
| Nitrates | A nutrient for algal growth and a health hazard at very high concentrations in drinking water. Predicted by moderately complex models. |
| Phosphates | Nutrient for algal growth. Predicted by moderately complex models. |
| Toxic organic compounds | A wide variety of organic (carbon-based) compounds can affect aquatic life and may be directly hazardous to humans. Usually very difficult to model. |
| Heavy metals | Substances containing lead, mercury, cadmium, and other metals can cause both ecological and human health problems. Difficult to model in detail. |

gen, and temperature, simple, well-established models can be used to predict long-term average changes in rivers, streams, and moderate-size lakes. The behavior of these models is well understood and has been studied more intensively than have other parameters. Basic nutrient indicators such as ammonia, nitrate, and phosphate concentrations can also be predicted reasonably accurately, at least for simpler water bodies such as rivers and moderate-size lakes. Predicting algae concentrations accurately is somewhat more difficult but is commonly done in the United States and Europe, where eutrophication has become a concern in the past two decades. Toxic organic compounds and heavy metals are much more problematic. Although some of the models

reviewed below do include these materials, their behavior in the environment is still an area of active research.

Models can cover only a limited number of pollutants. In selecting parameters for the model, care should be taken to choose pollutants that are a concern in themselves and are also representative of the broader set of substances which cannot all be modeled in detail.

**Data Requirements**

As one might expect, the data requirements for different models increase with the complexity and scope of application. As shown in Table 2, all models require data on flows and water tem-

**Table 2. Data Requirements for Water Quality Models**

| Data requirements | Comment |
|---|---|
| Water flows | Needed by all water quality models. Average flows needed by simpler models; detailed, dynamic information needed for more complex models. |
| Temperatures | Average temperatures required for simple models; detailed time-series required for complex models. |
| Dissolved oxygen concentrations | Base-case concentrations required by all models predicting dissolved oxygen impacts of a management alternative. |
| Biochemical oxygen demand (BOD) | Base-case concentrations and loads required by all models predicting dissolved oxygen impacts of a management alternative. |
| Ammonia, nitrates, phosphates, organic compounds, heavy metals | Base-case concentrations and loads required by all models predicting ammonia, nitrate, and other impacts of a management alternative. |

peratures. Static, deterministic models require point estimates of these data and often use worst-case "design flow" estimates to capture the behavior of pollutants under the worst plausible circumstances. For most management purposes, the worst case will be high summer temperatures, which exacerbate problems with dissolved oxygen and algal growth, and low flows, which lead to high concentrations of BOD and other pollutants. Dynamic models will need time-series data on flows, temperatures, and other parameters.

In addition to hydraulic data, models require base-case concentrations of the water quality parameters of interest (dissolved oxygen, mercury, and so on). These are required both to calibrate the models to existing conditions and to provide a base against which to assess the effects of management alternatives. The models also need discharges or loads of the pollutants under consideration from the sources (e.g., industrial plants) being studied. The types and amounts of data needed for a given application are specific to the management question at hand.

**Examples of Water Quality Models**

Table 3 contains information on five representative water quality models, using the criteria in Table 1; Table 4 contains a textual description of each model. A large number of water quality models have been developed for particular watersheds, project-specific analyses, and other specialized purposes. In many cases, models are developed and used only once, for a particular

project. In other cases, models are available only as proprietary, commercial software packages.

The list of models in Table 3 is not intended to be exhaustive, and the inclusion of a model should not be viewed as an endorsement or recommendation by the World Bank. The models were selected because they have been applied in a wide variety of management analyses and because public domain versions of the software are readily available. The list should be viewed as a representative sample of models that might be applied to a particular management problem. Sources of additional information on the models discussed here and on comprehensive surveys of water quality modeling are given at the end of the chapter.

The models shown in Table 4 vary from simple analytical models suitable for approximating the effects on water quality of individual industrial plants (WQAM) to complex models that include a wide variety of pollutants and pollution sources (WASP). Of the five models, WASP is the only one that is potentially capable of handling all types of water bodies, management analyses, and water quality parameters under consideration. The others may well be sufficient for a problem where WASP's complexity is not needed.

It is extremely important to recognize that the models or software packages only provide a framework for the analyses. Data specific to the watershed, industrial plants, and management scenarios will need to be gathered on site to make any model operational. An economic analogue might be the use of input-output analysis of a

**Table 3. Water Quality Models for Management Analyses and Receiving Water Types**

| Management analysis | WQAM | QUAL2E | WASP | CE-QUAL-RIV1 | HEC-5Q |
|---|---|---|---|---|---|
| *Receiving waters* | | | | | |
| Rivers and streams | x | x | x | x | x |
| Lakes and reservoirs | x | x | x | | x |
| Estuaries and coastal areas | x | | x | | |
| Single-plant effects | x | x | x | x | x |
| Multiplant regional effects | | x | x | x | x |
| Static | x | x | x | | |
| Dynamic | | | x | x | x |
| Deterministic | x | x | x | x | x |
| Stochastic | | x | x | x | x |
| *Quality parameters* | | | | | |
| Dissolved oxygen | x | x | x | x | x |
| Biochemical oxygen demand (BOD) | x | x | x | x | x |
| Temperature | x | x | x | x | x |
| Ammonia nitrogen | x | x | x | x | x |
| Coliform bacteria | | x | x | x | |
| Algal concentrations | x | x | x | x | x |
| Nitrates | | x | x | x | x |
| Phosphates | | x | x | x | x |
| Toxic organic compounds | | | x | | |
| Heavy metals | | | x | | |
| Reference | Mills et al. 1985 | Brown and Barnwell 1987 | Ambrose, Wool, and Connolly 1988 | USACE 1990 | USACE 1986 |

regional economy. Although the framework (input-output tables arranged by economic sector, etc.) is the same regardless of the region or management question being analyzed, the data required will be specific to the problem at hand. To carry the analogy a bit further, both water quality and input-output models often require some customization when applied to localized problems. In the case of input-output models, particular economic sectors may be analyzed in more detail than others. Similarly, some water bodies and water quality constituents will receive more attention than others, depending on the problem at hand.

The next sections give three hypothetical examples of applications of various models and one actual case.

*Hypothetical Examples*

*1. Modernization of a petroleum refinery in a severely degraded river basin*
A Latin American government has applied for a loan to upgrade processing technology at a large oil refinery. The improvements are expected to decrease waterborne discharges of BOD and phenols by 50 percent. Use of a simple model (WQAM) shows that this reduction will slightly improve downstream dissolved oxygen levels. It also predicts that under the 10-year, 7-day design flow (the lowest flow for a 1-week period in 10 years), dissolved oxygen levels will increase from 2 parts per million (ppm) to 2.5 ppm. Although WQAM cannot analyze phenol concentrations, ambient levels are already very low because of a high dilution by flow in the river. Managers then use WQAM to assess the effects of added end-of-pipe treatment, which would increase dissolved oxygen levels from 2.5 ppm to 3.0 ppm. They concluded that further improvements will not significantly affect water quality because of high levels of discharge from other sources. The analysis takes 1 to 2 person-months, assuming that the requisite data on water flow and quality are readily available, and costs approximately US$10,000.

**Table 4. Descriptions of Selected Models**

| Model | Comment |
|---|---|
| WQAM | Set of methods or mathematical tools used for preliminary analysis of changes in water quality due to changes in loadings. Unlike the other examples, WQAM is not a computer model per se but a collection of simple methods and procedures. |
| QUAL2E | Steady-state model for simulating well-mixed rivers and streams. Commonly used for assessing the impact of changes in point-source discharges on water quality. Especially suited for analyzing the effects of nutrients on algal concentration and dissolved oxygen. Widely applied in the United States and elsewhere. |
| WASP | Flexible, compartmental modeling structure for analysis of a wide variety of pollutants in almost any type of water body. The most powerful and complex of the models discussed here, it also requires more data and expertise for successful application. Extensively applied to water quality assessments in rivers and streams. |
| CE-QUAL-RIV1 | Intended primarily for simulating the dynamics of highly unsteady stream flows, such as those occurring during flood events. Consists of a module for water quantity linked to one for water quality. Although the quantity module has seen numerous applications, the quality module is less widely applied than WQAM, QUAL2E, or WASP. |
| HEC-5Q | Developed primarily for analyzing water flows and water quality in reservoirs and associated downstream river reaches. It can perform detailed simulations of reservoir operations, such as regulating outflows through gates and turbines, and vertical temperature gradients in reservoirs. |

*2. New food-processing plant in a moderately polluted coastal estuary*

A new vegetable-canning plant is planned for a moderately polluted tropical estuary. Use of a simple model (WQAM) shows that the mill's discharges may have a significant effect on the estuary's dissolved oxygen and nutrient levels. If the plant is brought on line, dissolved oxygen would decrease from 4.5 ppm to 3 ppm, which could cause problems for aquatic life. Phosphorus concentrations could increase from 0.5 ppm to 2.0 ppm, which, according to local experts, could lead to algal blooms and affect the local fishery. Next, a more complex model (WASP) is used to obtain a more detailed assessment, and it too shows effects that are deemed unacceptable. Since the plant is new and is projected to have state-of-the-art pollution abatement equipment in place, it is found to be more cost-effective to improve water quality by upgrading a nearby municipal sewage treatment plant. Projected discharge reductions in the municipal plant are found to give acceptable water quality when analyzed with WASP. The analysis takes 10 to 12 person-months, assuming that the requisite data on water flow and quality are readily available, and costs approximately US$100,000.

*3. Regional water quality enhancement plan for a moderate-size river basin*

A Central European government has received a loan to perform long-term investment planning for industrial and municipal sewage treatment for a river basin of 20,000 square kilometers. The basin contains approximately 100 point sources, one quarter of which are industrial treatment plants. Increased user fees are expected to pay for primary sewage treatment for all municipalities within 10 years. In addition, increases in emissions fees should induce all industrial sources to install and operate primary sewage treatment plants within the same time frame. The central government has agreed that it will finance more advanced treatment facilities for a subset of municipalities out of general revenues. In addition, it will use the emissions fees levied on industrial dischargers to finance advanced treatment works for some sources. Because of a shortage of investment capital, the government wishes to get as much improvement in water quality per amount invested as possible.

The government has decided to focus its water quality control efforts on dissolved oxygen and nutrients. It plans to tackle toxic pollutants (a problem in some heavily industrialized areas) at a later date, when the economy is projected to improve. A survey of existing water quality data shows that dissolved oxygen is especially problematic downstream from two major cities and that nutrient concentrations are of particular concern just below an industrial complex. Because of the large number of pollution sources, a simple approach using WQAM is rejected, but a model as complex as WASP is thought to be too expensive to calibrate and run for such a large area. In any case, since the government is formulating a long-term investment plan, it believes that the dynamic information provided by WASP or HEC-5Q is not required. Therefore, the government plans to use QUAL2E to project the effects on water quality of different investment strategies.

QUAL2E can assess whether a particular combination of treatment plants will meet a set of water quality goals. In addition to a water quality model, a simple optimization model will also be required to assess which combination will meet the goals at least cost. The government decides on a simple spreadsheet model with a commercial optimization add-on. The results show that significant savings can be achieved, in comparison with a strategy that requires all plants to have the same level of treatment. Assuming that the requisite data on water flow and quality are readily available, the analysis takes 100 to 150 person-months and costs approximately US$1,000,000.

*A Real-Life Example: The Nitra River*

An example demonstrating the savings that can be identified by a modeling exercise is a study of the Nitra River, a tributary of the Danube River. Current dissolved oxygen levels could be raised to a minimum of 4 milligrams per liter (mg/l), at a cost of about US$13 million, by using a mix of treatment systems for the major different discharges. To raise this value to a minimum of 6 mg/l would cost about US$26 million, with higher treatment requirements for most of the discharges. To bring all the discharges up to EU standards would cost about US$65 million; dissolved oxygen levels would be about 7 mg/l, and nutrient levels in the river would also be reduced. Despite some uncertainty in the results because of data shortcomings, the study concluded that the results "strongly suggest that substantial cost savings are possible using a least-cost control policy."

## Management Objectives and Applications

A point often overlooked in the real-world application of water quality models is that they are a means of achieving a set of management objectives, not an end in themselves. In many cases, it may not be necessary to use a water quality model at all, even when it is known in advance that a project will affect water quality. Suppose that in hypothetical example 1 the local water quality was acceptable to local environmental authorities prior to upgrading the plant. Given that the plant upgrade will reduce discharges and so improve water quality, there is no need for model results that will assess the projected water quality improvement. To deal with the problem at hand, it may be enough to know that water quality will not become worse.

It should also be kept in mind that the motivations of project managers and those of water quality modelers may not be in concert. If environmental regulations focus on long-term averages for dissolved oxygen and BOD, there may be little, if any, need for advanced water quality modeling that can predict concentrations of heavy metals and toxic organic compounds. Water quality analysts, however, may be interested in performing complex analyses on metals and organic compounds because of the technical challenge.

Managers should remember that the accuracy of model projections is severely constrained by the quality and quantity of the available data used to calibrate and test the models. The hypothetical examples given above explicitly assume that these data are readily available, but this will often not be the case in practice. Although data on water quantity are often collected for larger water bodies, water quality information may be collected sporadically or not at all. This is especially true of information on algae and other biological indicators, heavy metals, and toxic organic compounds, since scientific interest in these data is relatively new.

Lack of data can create three problems. First, a model cannot be calibrated and tested until a monitoring system has been designed and operated for a considerable length of time. Second, water sample collection and analysis may be considerably more expensive than the modeling effort that it is designed to support. Finally, design of a monitoring system may fall prey to the same types of problems that can affect water quality modeling, including a lack of clear connections to management objectives and a tendency to excessive complexity.

Models are only an abstraction from the reality of a situation, and the improper use or misinterpretation of outputs from a model can lead to imprecise or incorrect results. Any conclusions reached on the basis of a model should therefore always be checked for realism and common sense.

In summary, managers should be cautious about underwriting the development and application of water quality models. They should be clear about their management goals, and model application should support those goals. In some settings, models may not be needed at all, while in others, simple models may suffice. Any model will require a substantial amount of supporting data, which may not be immediately available.

### Sources of Additional Information

Although many textbooks and journal articles have surveyed water quality model development and application, most surveys are not readily accessible to nonspecialists. Among the less technically oriented materials available, Wurbs (1995) provides an up-to-date survey of modeling techniques for water management, covering both quality and quantity, and contains a useful guide to software packages. Novotny and Capodaglio (1995) provide a survey of the concepts used in water quality modeling and an overview of available models. Thomann and Mueller (1987) and

Orlob (1982) are standard texts on the principles of water quality modeling.

### References and Sources

Ambrose, R. B., T. A. Wool, and J. P. Connolly. 1988. "WASP4, A Hydrodynamic and Water Quality Model...." PA/600/3-87/039. U.S. Environmental Protection Agency, Environmental Research Laboratory, Athens, Ga.

Brown, L. C., and T. O. Barnwell. 1987. "The Enhanced Stream Water Quality Models QUAL-2E and QUAL2E-UNCAS: Documentation and User Manual." EPA/600/3-87/007. U.S. Environmental Protection Agency, Environmental Research Laboratory, Athens, Ga.

Mills, W. B., et al. 1985. "Water Quality Assessment: A Screening Procedure for Toxic and Conventional Pollutants in Surface and Ground Water—Parts I and II." EPA/600/6-85-002 a, b. U.S. Environmental Protection Agency Environmental Research Laboratory, Athens, Ga.

Novotny, Vladimir, and Andrea Capodaglio. 1995. "Use of Water Quality Models." In Vladimir Novotny and László Somlyody, eds., *Remediation and Management of Degraded River Basins: With Emphasis on Central and Eastern Europe*. NATO (North Atlantic Treaty Organization) ASI Series. Berlin: Springer-Verlag.

Orlob, Gerald T., ed. 1982. *Mathematical Modeling of Water Quality*. Chichester, U.K.: Wiley Interscience/ International Institute for Applied Systems Analysis.

Thomann, Robert V., and John A. Mueller. 1987. *Principles of Surface Water Quality Modeling and Control*. New York: Harper and Row.

USACE (U.S. Army Corps of Engineers). 1986. "HEC-5 Simulation of Flood Control and Conservation Systems, Appendix on Water Quality Analysis." USACE Hydrologic Engineering Center.

USACE. 1990. "CE-QUAL-RIV1: A Dynamic, One-Dimensional (Longitudinal) Water Quality Model for Streams...." Instruction Report E-90-1. U.S. Army Engineer Waterway Experiment Station, Vicksburg, Miss.

Wurbs, Ralph A. 1995. *Water Management Models: A Guide to Software*. Englewood Cliffs, N.J.: Prentice-Hall.

# Integrated Wastewater Management

*Appropriate wastewater management within an overall water resources management program is essential for responsible use of the environment and affordable provision of services. Such management programs are best developed at a river basin or subcatchment level. An approach is outlined for developing a wastewater strategy and an implementation plan for a river basin.*

## Integrated Management

The World Bank promotes a systematic approach to water resources management, incorporating water resources planning and management issues into policy discussions at the national level. Water quality protection and appropriate wastewater management are two essential elements in an integrated scheme.

The overall goal of water quality management is to protect the resource. Formal management normally becomes necessary when there are increasing and competing demands on the resource and when uncontrolled access or certain uses are likely to cause (or have already caused) unacceptable deterioration in water quality. The development of a realistic and practical management plan requires discussion, consultation, and negotiation, involving not just government and municipal agencies but also industrialists, local communities, NGOs, and representatives of nonpoint sources such as agriculture and transport. In many cases, the plan should be regarded as a process rather than a single document or agreement.

There are, unfortunately, numerous examples worldwide of poor wastewater planning and management—of poorly targeted government investments that addressed low-priority problems or tackled problems piecemeal and ineffectively. As a consequence, predicted benefits were not achieved, funds were diverted from other possible investments, and more cost-effective measures may have been neglected because of perceived administrative or political problems.

Failure of investment projects to achieve the design goals is often blamed on lack of institutional capacity or on financial weaknesses. A frequent cause, however, may be an insistence on inappropriate technologies and a failure to take into account the socioeconomic circumstances in which the plant must operate.

## Basic Principles

In order to protect the quality of a water body, it is necessary to address the problems on at least the same scale as the water body itself, whether a lake, a river, or a coastal ecosystem. A focus on individual discharges without an understanding of the broader context is likely to lead to inefficient and often costly interventions. Comprehensive water resources management, of which wastewater management is one component, should be based on several broad principles:

- Water can be considered an economic good. (This is a basic principle of the World Bank's water resources policy; see World Bank 1993.)
- Water management must recognize the social aspects of water uses and therefore must involve the stakeholders at all levels.
- Maintenance of ecosystems is a legitimate goal of water management.
- The institutional framework and legal framework must be as broad as the physical water system.

## Wastewater Management Approaches

A wide variety of wastewater management approaches are practiced throughout the world but they can be classified into three broad categories:

Decentralized local action
Coordinated regional action
Uniform national standards systems.

The first is essentially the project-by-project approach, driven by individual initiatives. While it may solve local problems, it is often inefficient and is not capable of dealing with widespread problems or large systems. It is typically the first stage of development in wastewater control but cannot be considered a desirable long-term approach.

The second approach appears to be the most attractive, in principle, because it can lead to comprehensive, cost-effective programs. However, although a regional or river basin approach is used in a number of European countries, it is by no means the norm in the industrial world.

The uniform national standards approach is the system currently used in the United States and was essentially the model underlying the EU approach. (Recent legislation, however, is moving toward an approach that allows more basin-level flexibility.) The national standards approach has the advantages of simplicity and uniformity of application.

In broad terms, the existing models that should be considered by developing countries are the uniform standards approach and the river basin approach.

### Uniform Standards Approach

The standards-based approach is currently used in both the United States and the EU countries, but there are concerns in both areas about high costs, and questions have been raised concerning the efficiency of the overall system in meeting water quality goals.

The uniform standards system used in the United States since 1972 has achieved significant improvements in levels of wastewater treatment but at a cost higher than for alternative approaches. (It is noteworthy that, for a decade, federal subsidies provided much of the capital investment in municipal wastewater treatment.) Earlier legislation had established a system under which states set water quality standards for different bodies of water and then set limits on discharges at loads consistent with the quality standards. This approach was found to be unworkable, primarily because of the difficulties of apportioning total allowable loads among dischargers and of determining responsibility for breaches of water quality standards. The EU has adopted uniform wastewater treatment requirements without regard to local conditions, except for imposition of stricter requirements in "sensitive areas." As the costs of implementing this policy—never seriously considered during preparation of the legislation—become clearer, opposition to the high charges and state subsidies required to finance the required works is increasing. The practical consequence of the high costs is delay in compliance with the requirements.

### River Basin Approaches

The EU approach is, in fact, a departure from the river basin approach that was widely used in national systems in Western Europe. Germany, France, Spain, and the United Kingdom all have river basin authorities of one kind or another. All have systems of fees and charges that provide financing, to a greater or lesser degree, for wastewater investments. Those systems are now changing to come into compliance with EU requirements. Nevertheless, they still have some flexibility within their own areas of authority.

Such flexibility to set appropriate local standards within some national framework provides the possibility of setting priorities and realistic targets consistent with available resources. However, the implementation of a river basin approach requires a level of institutional sophistication that may take time to develop. Therefore, practical systems are often a mixture of basin management and standards.

In practice, a *combined approach* may be best, using both control of pollution at source through emissions limits and environmental quality standards for individual pollutants.

## Options for Developing Countries

Many developing countries have established uniform national discharge standards, but these are often ignored. Whatever may be the chosen long-term system for a country, in most cases lack of financial and institutional resources will impose a cost-minimizing, priority-setting approach in the short to medium term, and this must be carried out on a water body basis.

### Practical Framework

In many developing countries, inadequate wastewater control and rapidly growing populations have led to deterioration of natural water systems, public health impacts, and increased economic costs, as well as broader losses of environmental benefits. The development of a solution requires numerous decisions on the area to be served, the technology to be used, the location and standard of discharge, and the allocation of the cost burden. Solutions must be sought on the same scale as the problems, typically on the scale of a river basin or a lake catchment.

Although it would be desirable to have a fully objective method for comparing and ranking alternative upgrading programs, there are difficulties in valuing the environmental impacts of wastewater discharges. More important, perhaps, the distribution of costs and benefits will vary with different programs, and a process approach is required to reach a consensus among the parties involved.

The framework suggested here is a practical approach that quantifies the issues wherever possible but allows for identification of alternatives, followed by discussion and selection of a preferred option. Because no approach will be perfect, there must be mechanisms for monitoring, review, and adjustment over time.

The key steps are to:

- Establish a lead organization and involve stakeholders
- Identify broad goals
- Define specific, measurable objectives
- Formulate and assess possible strategies
- Select the preferred strategy, and then implement and monitor it.

### Lead Organization

For progress to be made, there must be general acceptance of the importance of the problem, and there must be an organization or agency that takes the lead in the process. Ideally, this would be an existing river basin agency, but in practice, the problems may have arisen because there is no such body.

The lead organization must have access to all the relevant ministries and agencies and must have enough influence to ensure the involvement of key private sector stakeholders. It must also be sufficiently persuasive to promote discussion and consensus among the many parties involved. It does not have to have all the powers and functions necessary for implementation, and in fact it may be better for it to be given only technical and coordination functions, as this will reduce concern that it is driving a particular agenda. However, it must have sufficient support at all government levels and with other stakeholders so that all the relevant bodies cooperate in the planning process and are held to the agreements reached.

### Goals

Broad agreement must be reached on the overall goals of a water resources strategy or of a wastewater management program. These goals can include social concerns (improving public health conditions or extending services to groups that are presently outside the system); economic issues such as reducing costs of water supply, protecting fisheries, or encouraging development; and environmental goals such as protecting or restoring certain ecosystems.

All these goals are important, and they will conflict to some extent. None can be given absolute priority over the others. The aim of planning is to find the strategy that allows significant progress toward achievement of all the goals.

### Measurable Objectives

The agreed goals must be translated into specific, measurable objectives so that different strategies can be developed and assessed. This is an iterative process that may also include staging the objectives to reach a realistic program.

Depending on the scope of the planning process, the objectives could include coverage of municipal services, specific levels of service for water and sanitation customers, protection and provision of treated water, and the like. For the purposes of this discussion, however, the focus is on water quality objectives.

*Water Quality Objectives*

Management of water quality should focus on the ambient state of the water. Typically, the first step is to develop water quality objectives (WQOs) that define target values for key ambient quality parameters. These numerical WQOs can then be used to evaluate existing conditions; as a basis for the establishment of load limits for inputs to the water body (if this approach is adopted); and as a yardstick against which to measure changes over time.

The concept underlying WQOs is that of the beneficial uses of the water body (be it a river, lake, coastal zone, or whatever.) These uses represent the ways in which the community would like to make use of the water body. They include ecological uses such as preservation of species in the wild and fish breeding, as well as more direct uses such as drinking water. The clearest example of such uses is the goal set down in U.S. legislation of making surface waters "fishable and swimmable." In practice, most systems adopt four to six main uses for which clear numerical parameters can be agreed on.

A typical set of uses (in more or less descending order of water quality) would be:

- Source of potable water
- Maintenance of fishery ecosystems
- Agricultural uses (irrigation and livestock)
- Amenity and conservation.

These uses are sometimes also presented as a classification, with Class I (potable water, in this example) typically having the highest standards and with the lowest category representing those waters that fail to meet even the lowest of the desired uses. For each of these classes, a set of basic numerical parameters can be defined, often focusing on key factors such

as dissolved oxygen levels and nutrients (see the Annex).

Given an agreed classification, an initial step is usually to map the basin into classes or uses based on estimates of current water quality. From this baseline, the broad goals can be translated into desired beneficial uses for all the waters of the basin. The key point of debate will be the realistic long-term achievement of high-level uses for areas that are now very polluted. (The return of salmon to the formerly very heavily polluted Thames River in London is often quoted as an example of what can be achieved with consistent effort over a long period.) Once a first set of quantified goals has been prepared, the critical step is to develop an improvement strategy that specifies the costs of and constraints on achieving the goals. This should be the beginning of an iterative process aimed at reaching agreement on short- to medium-term goals that can be achieved with the resources to be made available.

*Strategy Formulation*

A management strategy is a set of decisions, policies, regulations, infrastructure investments, and other activities that, if implemented, is expected to reach the selected goals. A wastewater management strategy would typically include controls on industrial and nonpoint sources (including standards, charges, and other instruments), development of reuse, redefinition of municipal sewer catchment boundaries, upgraded treatment, relocation of discharge points, changes in regulated water flows, and a range of other actions.

Strategy formulation should include the preparation of a number of dissimilar options that are all relatively cost-effective but that may depend on nonquantifiable factors such as the degree of industrial discharge realistically attainable within the time frame or given different distributions of the cost burden through taxes and charges. A key variable will be the rate of progress that can be achieved at different levels of resource availability. All reasonable configurations of technologies, regulations, and system components should be included, with realistic costs assigned to each configuration.

The stakeholders need to be involved both in the determination of the options to be analyzed in detail and in the selection of the preferred strategy. (Documents available from the World Bank Group offer advice on public involvement in environmental assessment and similar projects.) The development of the strategy should involve, where necessary, the examination of existing institutions, regulations, and fiscal constraints to determine the benefits and costs of possible changes in these constraints. Achievement of significant progress may require changes in some of the existing systems. The arguments for such changes must be made clearly and persuasively.

The outcome of the process should be the selection of a preferred strategy that is acceptable to all the key stakeholders and that sets out clearly the actions to be taken, the resources required, and the legal and administrative responsibilities for each action.

*Implementation*

The agreed strategy should include an implementation schedule covering not only the adoption of standards, regulations, and policies and the construction of new facilities but also the generation of long-term political and financial support for the operation and maintenance of the old and new systems.

*Monitoring*

The design of the strategy must include the capability to monitor its implementation. Monitoring should cover the progress of both the implementation of the agreed strategy and improvements in the overall condition of the environment as the strategy is put in place. A successful monitoring program requires time, money, and appropriate expertise. The location of the responsibility for monitoring has to be given careful consideration so as to achieve an independent review while taking advantage of existing operational expertise.

The strategy should include formal reviews of progress as implementation proceeds, to allow for adjustment in response to changing circumstances or improved information. A high-level advisory group can be a good mechanism for providing such reviews.

## Resources

The preparation of a comprehensive river basin strategy can require significant time and resources. However, the first steps—acceptance of the need for a comprehensive approach, designation of a lead agency, and identification of broad goals—require breadth of vision and political commitment more than financial resources.

The level of detail in the analytical work required to define the objectives and to evaluate the strategies will depend on the complexity of the river basin and of its problems. In some cases, a simple model using estimated loads from a few critical sources may be adequate. For large, complex water bodies the exercise can cost hundreds of thousands of dollars. (For further information see the chapters on Water Quality Models and Optimizing Wastewater Treatment.)

Normally, specialist modelers (consultants or academics) need to be involved. It is important, however, that the analytical work be used a tool for the development of the strategy rather than as an end in itself.

## Annex. Some Examples of Classification Systems

*Chile* has a national system of classification of waters that covers surface water, groundwater, and coastal waters. Surface waters are generally divided into three categories:

- 1C. Noncontact recreation; propagation and maintenance of aquatic life; fishing; agriculture and any other uses not given a higher classification
- 1B. Contact recreation and all uses under 1C
- 1A. Source of water for drinking, cooking, food processing and all uses under 1B.

There are two exceptional categories:

- 1EB. Uses beyond 1A—water for which an exceptionally high quality is desired
- 1EM. Uses below 1C, describing waters that fail to reach the basic classification.

*Poland* generally uses three classes for surface water:

- III. Industrial water supply and irrigation
- II. Water for animals, recreation, and water sports
- I. Potable water and support of salmonoid fishes.

*China* has a similar classification but with five classes.

In each case, a number of key parameters such as biochemical oxygen demand (BOD), dissolved oxygen, and nutrients are used to define the classes. The values used are broadly similar but can vary. Care must be taken in making comparisons, particularly in relation to the conditions under which the parameters are measured. For example, in Poland, the parameters are set in relation to mean-low flows, rather than average flows.

## Reference

World Bank. 1993. *Water Resources Management*. World Bank Policy Paper. Washington, D.C.

# Optimizing Wastewater Treatment

*Growing volumes of industrial and municipal wastewater are being discharged to surface waters. The treatment provided is frequently inadequate to protect the desired uses of the receiving waters. Limited institutional capacity and financial resources make for difficult choices as governments try to optimize their investments in municipal systems and establish practical requirements for industrial wastewater treatment. This chapter presents a framework for making coherent decisions on the level of wastewater treatment.*

In many urban situations, both the municipal sewage system and industrial wastewater treatment are inadequate. A municipal sewage network may be in place, but coverage is usually incomplete, and the level of treatment provided is inadequate. Even where reasonable treatment facilities exist, poor maintenance and operation often result in failure to meet design effluent levels. In such circumstances, management of industrial wastewater discharges is also frequently poor, with uncontrolled discharges of untreated effluent to surface waters (through often drainage or stormwater channels) or to the sewer system. The result is high levels of water pollution. It is not uncommon for streams or water bodies to be almost or completely anaerobic and heavily polluted with organic compounds, pathogens, and heavy metals.

## Objectives

There are several objectives that must be addressed in such a situation:

- The collection and removal of domestic and municipal wastewater to protect public health and to improve the immediate environment (particularly important where inadequate disposal is resulting in groundwater pollution)
- The establishment of an effective industrial pollution control system to reduce the loads and impacts of industrial discharges
- Provision of municipal and industrial treatment as necessary to protect the environment at the points of final discharge

- Efficient and cost-effective achievement of all these goals within the relevant social and political constraints.

## Public and Private Involvement

The basic responsibility for municipal sewage lies with the government (at the appropriate level, preferably local). Industrial wastewater treatment is fundamentally the responsibility of the enterprise but in practice has to be driven by government action. The challenge for the government is to use the whole range of options and instruments available to achieve the objectives outlined above, combining physical and operational improvements in the municipal infrastructure with the controls and incentives necessary to induce improvements in the industrial sector. This chapter focuses on the management of industrial wastewater within this broader context.

## Focus on Water Bodies

From the environmental (as distinguished from the sanitation) point of view, the focus must be on the receiving water bodies. The problems are typically diffuse, with hundreds or thousands of small discharges and with the problems concentrated to some extent where particularly polluted streams or poorly treated effluents discharge to major water bodies. Upgrading or extension of the wastewater collection system may reduce this diffuse pollution but may produce major point discharges that must receive adequate treatment.

A wastewater strategy must therefore be based on a water quality plan for all the receiving waters in the catchment, usually on the basis of water quality objectives.

## Water Quality Objectives

It is necessary to have explicit medium- to long-term objectives for the quality of water in the various water bodies in the catchment under consideration. These objectives are often based on defined beneficial uses for the water bodies, typically including about a half dozen uses such as source of water supply, agricultural use, fisheries protection, and so on. A set of key numerical parameters can be defined for each use, and the water quality objectives can be developed in terms of uses for different sections of the water bodies and a strategy for achieving those standards. (See the related chapter on Integrated Wastewater Management.) The objectives then provide clearly defined goals for protection or improvement of each section of the system.

## Development of the Strategy

### Load Estimation

The first step in developing a wastewater strategy is to estimate the overall loads in the catchment over the time scale being considered, which is typically about 20 years. This will require, in addition to information on population growth and densities, estimates of industrial activity and of projected changes in industrial and population patterns.

In some cases, direct observations of industrial pollution loads are available, but more often, estimates are based on statistical information on economic activity (sectors, employment, turnover, and so on), using various coefficients for the unit loads of pollution. Overall planning requires estimates of both domestic and industrial loads on a geographic basis and over the time period under consideration. The estimates need to be developed for key parameters such as suspended solids, oxygen demand, nutrients, organic materials, and heavy metals, depending on the particular characteristics of the catchment and receiving waters.

### Determination of the Reductions Necessary

Once load estimates are available, it is possible to determine the reductions in present and future loads needed to achieve the water quality objectives. In simple cases, a mass balance may suffice, but often it will be necessary to carry out water quality modeling (see the chapter on Water Quality Models).

The objective of the modeling is to estimate the impacts of the increasing loads on water quality and to identify where load reductions are required in order to achieve the water quality objectives. The sophistication required in the modeling will depend on conditions. In some cases, a simple one-dimensional model of oxygen depletion will be acceptable; in other cases, complex models will have to be developed to address water circulation and the degradation and interaction of several pollutants.

### Development of Options for Load Reduction

After the desired degree of reduction in pollutant loads has been estimated, the next step is to develop options for achieving that reduction. If the most significant pollutants are those associated with industrial effluents—for example, complex organic compounds or heavy metals—the control efforts will clearly be concentrated on the industrial discharges. Often, however, oxygen depletion and nutrients are the critical issues, and the causes are typically a mixture of municipal and industrial sources. Then it is necessary to control both types of sources.

The costs of cleaning up a major industrialized urban area can be massive. The estimated costs of water pollution control in Shanghai in 1986 were US$1.4 billion. Preliminary estimates show that the Buenos Aires sewerage authority faces an investment program of nearly US$1 billion over the next decade. Clearly, such programs require decades for implementation, making it important to tackle them in an organized and cost-effective manner.

## Components of an Urban Wastewater Program

An urban wastewater program comprises several distinct but interlocking components. Municipal system improvement is almost always a central feature, but the emphasis given to the industrial wastewater control component depends greatly on the extent of the industrial contribution to the overall problem, the types and sizes of industries involved, and the costs of enforcement and implementation. In some cases, or for some pollutants, small or nonpoint sources may be a significant problem, and one that is typically difficult to tackle.

## Municipal System Upgrading

There are normally two imperatives behind municipal system upgrading:

- Expansion of the coverage and quality of sewerage provision
- Reduction of the impacts of final disposal of treatment plant effluents.

Detailed treatment of expansion of the coverage of the service is beyond the scope of this chapter. It should be noted, however, that because of limited funds, sewerage authorities often have to make tradeoffs between expanded coverage and higher levels of treatment, with consequent implications for the quality of the receiving water.

The impacts of final disposal depend, obviously, on the discharge location. In many cases, an existing system configuration more or less limits the choice of the discharge site, and therefore the emphasis is on improving the level of treatment provided.

## Levels of Treatment

Municipal wastewater systems are normally designed to treat influents that are essentially domestic in nature. Such systems are ineffective in removing some industrial pollutants and may even be damaged by them.

Design of municipal wastewater treatment is a sophisticated operation. In general terms, however, there are three major types of process, in ascending order of removal effectiveness (and cost): physical, sometimes assisted by chemicals; biological; and "advanced," which includes further chemical or biological stages, filtration, or combinations of these methods. These

systems can achieve high levels of removal of organic material and of suspended solids. The advanced systems can also remove nutrients to a high degree.

Municipal systems do not cope well with high concentrations of complex organic chemicals such as solvents and hydrocarbons or of heavy metals. The removal efficiencies are low, and biological treatment systems can be poisoned if incoming levels are too high. Other wastewater treatment processes that can be tailored to deal with such industrial effluents are available. Because of the limitations of municipal systems, and to protect the physical infrastructure and workers, it is normal practice to require pretreatment of industrial effluents that are discharged to a sewer system.

## Control of Industrial Effluents

Treatment systems for industrial effluents can be designed to provide any required level of pollutant removal, although at increasing cost and sometimes with a resultant wastewater treatment sludge that presents its own disposal problems. Where effluent treatment costs are high, waste minimization programs become very worthwhile.

The degree of industrial effluent treatment required is established, in theory at least, in relation to relevant ambient quality or effluent standards. In practice, control of industrial effluents is frequently poor, and industry may be a major contributor to the overall pollution load.

Where practical controls exist, industry is typically faced with two choices: direct discharge to surface waters (licensed groundwater discharge is rare), or discharge to the sewer system, if one is available. Effluent standards will apply to both options. Sewer regulations will require pretreatment to remove toxic substances, but effluents that can be treated by normal municipal systems will be accepted, at a charge. Direct discharge standards will depend on the character and objectives of the receiving water but would normally be expected to be more stringent than sewer standards.

Because of economies of scale, sewer discharge of simple wastes such as BOD is often cheaper than industrial onsite treatment. However, there are often problems with the capacity of the municipal treatment system and with implementing correct charging procedures, and so this option may not always be available.

Clearly, where regulations are inadequate or enforcement is lax, there is a financial incentive for industry to avoid treating the effluents.

*Optimizing the Program*

Once the basic information on water quality, municipal and industrial loads and trends, and estimated control costs is available, it is possible to begin to optimize a wastewater management program.

A key decision variable is the time scale over which the required upgrading is to be implemented. The costs of major treatment systems are so high that upgrading almost always has to be staged. Moreover, high urban growth rates mean that significant investment is often required just to maintain present levels of service to the growing population. Implementation of effective industrial pollution control programs takes time, and a realistic approach to projecting load reductions must be adopted.

An iterative planning process is therefore required that examines a number of options for the scale and rate of wastewater treatment improvement, balancing the costs of the program against the time needed to achieve the water quality objectives. This process should involve an appropriate level of public discussion so that a practical program can be developed that will have the broad public and political support necessary for implementation.

**Benefits and Costs**

A set of agreed water quality objectives (WQOs) that has been adopted by the government can be taken as reflecting the value of improving the receiving water quality, assuming that it is based on evaluation of the economic benefits of the improved uses of the water resources and on the outcome of a public priority-setting process.

The major components of a wastewater management plan, which typically compete for investment funds, are:

- Upgrading of *sewer systems* in existing urban areas to remove pollution from neighborhoods

and to reduce uncontrolled discharges to local watercourses and groundwater
- Upgrading of *municipal treatment systems* to reduce the impacts of the effluent discharges on the receiving waters
- Introduction of a system to identify and regulate *discharges from industry*
- Reduction of *current industrial pollution loads* through recycling, improved waste management, onsite treatment, or connection to sewer systems
- Adequate provision of sewerage and treatment for *new urban development*
- Effective control of effluent discharges from projected *new industrial development*
- Development of programs to quantify and tackle *nonpoint sources* of pollution, including combined sewer overflows.

Both the overall costs of these components and the distribution of costs must be taken into account in arriving at an estimate of the most cost-effective investments for achieving WQOs. In effect, a marginal cost curve can be developed for the water quality improvements, although there are always many uncertainties in the estimates.

Two practical problems have to be resolved in preparing realistic options: the actual costs of pollutant removal for each component and the impact of such removal on water quality.

*Unit Costs of Pollutant Reduction*

Each of the components outlined above will have a different effective cost of pollutant reduction, and the distribution of the burden of the costs will usually be different. For example, for BOD, which is usually one of the main parameters, the following general conclusions can be drawn.

*Upgrading sewer systems* can greatly reduce local pollution loads but will increase the loads at the treatment plant. It is reasonable and realistic to set domestic charge levels to cover at least this component of sewerage, since it provides direct benefits to households. Thus, it should be possible to cover investment costs out of increased revenue.

*Upgrading municipal treatment* addresses what is often the single largest point source of BOD in a system, and the costs of removal can be calculated quite accurately. Sludge handling and disposal costs can be a significant element and must be included in the estimates. BOD removal normally entails increasing marginal costs in moving from primary to secondary systems and on to advanced systems. The costs of treatment should, in principle, be borne by the system users (the polluters pay). It is often politically difficult, however, to raise surcharges enough to cover the higher treatment levels because the users do not see the benefits directly. In many projects, some component of the treatment costs is borne directly by the government.

*Introducing industrial pollution controls* is used to achieve reductions in industrial effluent discharges. To do this, a regulatory and permitting system has to be in place, whether it is based on standards or on charges. The cost of putting a system in place or reinforcing it is part of the investments that are necessary (but not sufficient) to achieve reductions in industrial discharges of BOD or other pollutants. The design of the system should specifically address how effective it can be in actually achieving certain levels of reductions. This effectiveness depends on a number of factors, but the number and size of polluters is clearly a key one: it is much quicker and more cost-effective to deal with a small number of large firms than with many different small ones.

*Reducing industrial loads* can often be done at little or no net cost to industry, even for significant reductions (see the chapter on Implementing Cleaner Production), but there are often transaction costs that are typically borne by the government. Estimates can be made of, for example, the volume of BOD generated by industrial sources and the costs of reduction, if an inventory of sources is available. Clear priority should be given to ways of inducing waste minimization as a first step in reducing overall loads.

In principle, the costs of treating BOD loads from industrial sources should be no more than the costs of municipal treatment because industry can, in the ideal case, choose to use the municipal sewers and pay the costs. Given the waste minimization opportunities that typically exist in industry, the marginal costs of pollution reduction should be no higher than the costs in the municipal system.

*New urban developments* should be provided with sewerage and treatment systems adequate for meeting the necessary discharge require-ments. The costs should be borne by the users. In practice, however, fringe developments are often expensive to service and are occupied by poorer (often illegal) households. Projections of development should therefore include realistic estimates of the extent and net cost of control of expanding urban areas.

*New industrial development* presents a much easier task in enforcing effluent standards than does retrofitting older plants. The net cost of controlling new pollution loads can therefore be expected to be less. In this context, it is important, in setting water quality objectives, to take into account the growth of urban and industrial activity so that realistic discharge requirements can be placed on new projects.

*Nonpoint sources* account for a significant load of many pollutants, including BOD but particularly nutrients. This category typically includes runoff from urban and agricultural land but can be broadened to include small polluted urban drains and streams, where the precise sources of the pollution are too small and numerous to be readily identified. The costs of controlling these sources are typically high. Unfortunately, the loads may be also high, so that it is difficult to achieve water quality objectives by dealing with point sources only. It is therefore important to try to address the extent and control the costs of nonpoint sources.

From detailed analysis of the sources and the costs, it is possible to estimate marginal reduction costs for the major types and locations of pollutant loads. These load reductions must then be translated into real water quality improvements.

## Optimizing Load Reduction

Most large water catchments are not uniform and fully mixed, and therefore not all load reductions will have the same impact on final water quality. In most cases, too, the WQOs vary across the catchment. It is therefore necessary to estimate (usually using a water quality model) the improvements that can be obtained with different levels and locations of load reduction. For some pollutants, such as heavy metals, the number and location of sources may be sufficiently limited that such modeling is not required.

The model makes it possible to identify, to an acceptable level of uncertainty, the most cost-effective investments for achieving the desired WQOs. Once an initial estimate has been prepared, one can examine the implications of adopting more or less ambitious objectives. On this basis it is possible to carry out an informed process of discussion and agree on a water quality plan and a wastewater management strategy and program.

The approach outlined here is standard when the problem is presented and tackled as a water quality management issue. Unfortunately, in sector projects, such as municipal services, industrial upgrading, and pollution reduction projects, the tradeoffs between the different water pollution sources are sometimes not recognized.

To illustrate: a major study of the impacts of the Vistula River in Poland on pollution of the Baltic Sea identified a wide range of regulatory and institutional measures and possible investments (Baltic Sea Environment Programme 1992). Priority investments were identified by a screening process, taking into account the size of the load, the cost-effectiveness of the actions, and the impacts of different types of pollution. Two perspectives were used to evaluate cost effectiveness: regional benefits at the level of the Baltic Sea, and benefits to the local population and environment directly affected. Most of the actions identified were cost- effective at both levels, but the priority ranking on cost-effectiveness differed. For example, the cost of reducing loads on the Baltic Sea varied from 8 European currency units per kilogram (ECU/kg) for the most cost-effective plant to 21 ECU/kg for the project ranked ninth. The recommended priority investments were based on a balance of local and regional rankings.

## Monitoring and Feedback

A major improvement program addressing a complex natural system will have uncertainties in the initial analysis and design. Sensitivity analysis will indicate which assumptions are critical, and these should be reviewed and checked. However, the most critical management issue is to monitor the desired outcome (the ambient water quality) and to compare it with the projections used in the design. Any major variations from the design predictions will then be identified, and appropriate adjustments can be made.

The value of detailed information and analysis is demonstrated by two examples, both containing complexities that were identified early in the process and were taken into account in the detailed design.

Modeling of oxygen levels in the highly polluted Huangpo River at *Shanghai* demonstrated that oxygen depletion would be a problem, even after high levels of treatment of wastewater discharges. The treated wastes would have had very long detention times in the tidal section and would have continued to degrade and remove oxygen. The conclusion was that costly high levels of treatment would not result in correspondingly high levels of water quality improvement.

Detailed modeling of Guanabara Bay, *Rio de Janeiro,* uncovered the apparently perverse result that high levels of wastewater treatment could, in the short term, cause deterioration in overall water quality. Cleaner water would promote algal blooms, because of excess nutrients, leading to severe water quality problems. The recommended approach assigned a higher priority to nutrient reduction than had originally been proposed.

## Reference

Baltic Sea Environment Programme. 1992. "Prefeasibility Study of the Vistula River and the Baltic Coast of Poland." Copenhagen, Stockholm, and Warsaw.

# Developing a Culture of Industrial Environmental Compliance

*Efforts to reduce industrial pollution in developing countries have focused on developing environmental institutions and legal frameworks, largely by establishing command-and-control regulations and market- based incentives. Overall, however, formal regulation alone has not proved very effective in reducing industrial pollution in these countries. Although there is no substitute for an environmental regulatory regime, there is a need to focus on incentives for action by industry. Several innovative approaches are now emerging as effective ways to improve environmental compliance. These include pollution inventories, information on enterprise performance, cleaner production, environmental management systems, negotiated agreements, and government-industry partnerships. International experience, although still limited, suggests that industrializing countries may have much to gain from these approaches in developing a culture that fosters improved industrial environmental compliance and overall environmental performance.*

In recent years, industrializing countries have devoted much attention to developing and strengthening environmental institutions and regulatory frameworks to reduce industrial pollution. Many governments have established national environmental agencies and have adopted standards and regulations similar to those of industrial countries. Although much can be learned from the experience of countries with more mature environmental programs, simply importing systems developed elsewhere has often not been effective. Similarly, some countries have experimented with market-based instruments to encourage compliance, but this approach has not been applied to the extent anticipated.

Effective environmental regulations must first reflect their own context and be compatible with the administrative capabilities of regulatory agencies. Regulations meant for industrial countries are inherently unenforceable in developing countries, where institutional capabilities are weak. The success of environmental regulations also depends on a culture of compliance that is the result of a country's legal traditions, the maturity of its institutions, the available resources, and the capacity and support of citizens and the private sector. Compliance does not automatically happen when requirements are legislated

and issued; rather, it is achieved as a result of targeted efforts that encourage behavioral changes on the part of polluters.

Several mechanisms are now emerging as effective ways to improve environmental compliance in countries that lack the necessary institutional capabilities for formal regulation. Rather than being alternatives to environmental regulation, these approaches provide pathways for achieving environmental goals within a legal framework by developing a culture of compliance. Although experience with these approaches is still limited, industrializing countries may have much to gain by adopting them (see Table 1).

## Pollution Inventories

Pollution inventories can accelerate environmental compliance by providing an information base for understanding pollution problems, identifying priority actions, making informed decisions, and identifying opportunities for waste minimization and cleaner production.

On the facility level, a pollution inventory is a comprehensive, accurate, and current accounting of specific pollutant discharges. On the government level, it is a database of reliable,

**Table 1. Mechanisms for Developing a Culture of Industrial Environmental Compliance**

| Mechanism | Requirements | Impact |
|---|---|---|
| Pollution inventories | Industry and government monitoring and dissemination of data on ambient environment and pollution loads | Inventories provide stakeholders with an environmental information base for understanding pollution problems better and for making informed decisions. |
| Information on enterprise performance | Industry monitoring of pollution loads; communications strategy for disseminating information | Collection and dissemination of environmental information can result in (a) an informed constituency that can effectively demand improvement from firms with poor performance and (b) open discussions with communities that can reduce mistrust. |
| Cleaner production techniques | For government: regulation and real natural resource pricing<br>For industry: commitment from management | Improvements in industrial processes and management reduce the volume of pollution generated, increase production efficiencies, and cut overall operating costs. |
| Environmental management systems | International trade and market pressures; commitment from management | Impacts of industry facilities are managed by a process of continuous environmental improvements that are regularly monitored, measured, and reported. |
| Supplier chain impacts | International trade and market pressures; concern of large firms with reputation and quality of products | Large firms work with smaller ones to provide advice and mentoring on developing environmental management systems and improving overall environmental performance. |
| Negotiated agreements and government-industry partnerships | Flexible government structures; political stability; trust between government and industry; persuasion and social pressures | Mechanism for consensus building among major stakeholders facilitates commitment to achieving clearly defined environmental goals. |

regularly updated, aggregated, and publicly available information quantifying industrial releases of specific pollutants. The OECD has developed a common framework for a pollution inventory, the Pollutant Release and Transfer Register (PRTR).

In the Netherlands, an emissions inventory is used to track pollution reduction targets under national environmental goals to determine whether covenants between firms and regulators are being implemented. In the United Kingdom and Denmark, data reported in pollution inventories cover substances included in the permitting process. The baseline information about the pollution burden provided by the inventory is increasingly being used by firms in the United States and Europe to set internal environmental goals, often in connection with industry standards, including environmental management systems.

Similar approaches are now being adopted by industrializing countries. For example, Querétaro State, Mexico, is using a PRTR to identity priorities and develop a state-level environmental strategy that complies with existing federal regulations. The Czech Republic has developed a PRTR, and Colombia, India, and the Philippines are working on pilots. (See the chapter on Pollutant Release and Transfer Registers.)

**Information on Enterprise Performance**

The collection and dissemination of environmental information are essential to building an informed constituency that will support the changes necessary to achieve environmental improvement. Disclosure of actual performance information allows the relevant public to monitor progress (or lack of it) and develop informed positions; it also strengthens confidence in company statements about compliance and improvements. An informed public can achieve much through informal pressure, and progressive firms are finding that open discussions with their communities can reduce mistrust.

Under the Community Right-to-Know Act, the United States publishes an annual Toxic Releases Inventory (TRI) based on mandated reporting and disclosure of specific toxic chemical releases and transfers by industrial facilities. It is up to local governments or community groups to assess the performance of firms in their vicinity and to act on this information through public appeals, negotiations, or citizen suits. When TRI data were first released, the ensuing pressure led many firms to announce goals for reducing significant amounts of pollution, and many met these goals.

Although few developing countries have such far-reaching right-to-know legislation, in Indonesia and the Philippines, public pressure stemming from release of environmental information has led to similar improvements in industrial behavior. Under Indonesia's PROPER program and the Philippines' Ecowatch program, firms are graded on the basis of their environmental performance, ratings are made public, and facilities are held accountable. Similarly, in Korba, India, newspapers publish daily levels of ambient particulate and effluent discharges by two thermal power plants and an aluminum plant. A committee of citizens, constituted by the local administration, can inspect these plants at any time. As a result of such awareness raising, ambient particulate levels have dropped significantly, and discharges into the river no longer go unnoticed.

## Cleaner Production

Cleaner production (CP) techniques offer improvements in industrial processes and management that can reduce the volume of pollution generated, increase production efficiencies, and reduce operating costs. Industry most often uses this approach in response to external pressures, including government regulation and the costs of natural resources and of pollution management (e.g., water charges and costs of treating wastes).

In China, the World Bank is collaborating with the UNEP to establish a CP Center that will provide local expertise to evaluate CP options for companies. Studies carried out under the project identified several areas of major savings. Similar work, supported by donors and international organizations, has been done in Chile, India, the Philippines, Poland, and Tunisia. Unfortunately, in many cases, only a few of the recommendations have been put into practice. Such limited success emphasizes the importance of motivating, involving, and obtaining commitment from senior management. (See the chapter on Implementing Cleaner Production.)

## Environmental Management Systems

Environmental management systems (EMSs) are logical complements to cleaner production techniques. They help firms establish a structured process of continuous environmental improvements that are monitored, measured, and reported. Management commitment to improving performance, as well as strong existing managerial and measurement capacities, are prerequisites for a successful EMS.

In a world of increasing free trade, much attention has been focused on internationally coordinated specifications for EMS under the ISO 14001 standard issued by the International Organization for Standardization (ISO). A key component of the ISO 14001 standard is that it identifies the elements of an EMS that can be independently audited and certified. However, obtaining certification can involve significant costs, and there are issues relating to the international acceptance of national certification. The use of ISO 14001 certification to replace statutory reporting is a topic of considerable interest.

While it is clear that EMS is not a substitute for a regulatory framework, there may be cases where the monitoring and reporting systems of a well-managed firm might substitute for some statutory inspections, audits, and reports. However, the extent to which a government can rely on the capabilities and commitment of a firm to self-monitor its environmental performance needs to be determined. While a number of practical issues have to be sorted out with ISO 14001, EMS can be used as a mechanism for achieving improvements in environmental performance and for supporting the trade prospects of good performers. (See the chapter on Environmental Management Systems and ISO 14000.)

## The Supplier Chain Relationship

The power of the supply chain can be an effective mechanism for promoting improved environmental performance. Large firms serving international markets will most often be driven to improve their performance. Small firms that serve as local suppliers do not experience the same external pressures. Recently, however, multinationals are asking for better performance from their suppliers. Large firms (buyers) are often better able to negotiate lower prices from suppliers as a result of efficiencies and cost savings. In addition, most large firms are willing to work with their suppliers in a mentoring relationship to improve environmental performance in order to receive better-quality products and maintain their reputation in the international marketplace.

B&Q, the United Kingdom's largest hardware and garden center retailer, developed a system for grading each of its suppliers on its environmental performance. B&Q set realistic targets that did not alienate suppliers by being too tough and that led to improvements in a large number of companies. Most suppliers perceived the program as an opportunity to improve their own businesses. Production efficiencies enabled B&Q to negotiate better prices from its suppliers, resulting in actual cost savings. Similarly, the Swedish automobile manufacturer Volvo selects its suppliers in part on the basis of information obtained from pollution inventories and corporate environmental reporting. U.S. apparel manufacturers in Asia are serving as mentors to their suppliers and providing advice to foster improved environmental performance, better-quality products, and an enhanced reputation and image.

## Negotiated Agreements and Government-Industry Partnerships

Building a consensus among a range of stakeholders is a prerequisite for achieving successful environmental compliance. Although not a substitute for a regulatory regime, negotiated agreements offer a way for government and industry to take concrete steps toward pollution management while the details of regulations are still evolving. Such agreements give industry and communities a voice in determining specific pol-

lution reduction targets and offer firms flexibility as to how to comply with targets.

In Japan, pollution control agreements between industry and local governments were the forerunner of national environmental policy. Now that national regulations have been established, pollution control agreements continue to be used as a means by which local governments can achieve higher goals. In the Netherlands, negotiated agreements are used to implement national environmental policy goals. Major economic sectors, represented by trade unions, design strategies to meet environmental goals set by government and industry. Commitments are implemented through legal covenants, and conventional laws and regulations are used to back up covenants if industry fails to meet its commitments.

Indonesia has used pollution control agreements to clean up severely polluted waterways by persuading a large number of firms to commit to cutting pollution loads by specific amounts in an agreed time frame. Riverside villages in Bangladesh have also successfully pursued negotiated agreements with upstream polluters that include requirements for monetary compensation and first-stage effluent treatment of industrial discharges. In Brazil, the state governments of Rio de Janeiro, Espíritu Santo, and Minas Gerais are using partnerships with industry under which the governments rely on self-enforcement by industry through environmental auditing programs to achieve pollution targets.

## Determining What Will Work Where

The mechanisms discussed above are to a large extent interrelated. The fact that relationships exist among them underscores their common purpose—to develop a culture of compliance and a constituency for pollution management. We have noted how firms can use pollution inventories to pressure their suppliers to make changes. Pollution inventories are also useful tools for setting firms' internal environmental policies, identifying opportunities for cleaner production, and developing environmental management systems. At the same time, the public availability of environmental information is an important mechanism for developing a constituency for pollution management through negotiated agreements.

The challenge lies in determining which tool, or which combination of tools, can be most effective in a given situation.

## The World Bank's Role

Currently, the World Bank and its clients are beginning to experiment with these approaches. Indonesia and the Philippines are receiving World Bank assistance in developing pollution inventories to rate and publicly disclose facilities' environmental performance. In Mexico, the World Bank is supporting efforts to develop ISO 14001 approaches and transfer them from large companies to their suppliers. These efforts use the supply chain to drive improved environmental performance as part of a joint effort with government regulators, who are examining how the new systems may lead to a streamlining of the licensing system. In Argentina, the Bank is supporting efforts to negotiate agreements between industrial facilities and regulators. Innovative approaches to pollution management, including pollution inventories, dissemination of information on enterprise performance, cleaner production, and EMSs, are being introduced to achieve agreed environment objectives.

All these applications are concentrated in projects with primarily environmental objectives, but the mechanisms can also be useful in other projects that focus on industrial performance, including privatization, industrial reform, energy, and mining projects. For example, pollution inventories can provide baseline environmental information that is essential in evaluating the environmental liabilities of state-owned enterprises that are being privatized. Similarly, application of cleaner production techniques and EMSs can reveal cost-saving opportunities in industrial restructuring.

# Environmental Audits in Industrial Projects

*An environmental audit is a process for assessing the nature and extent of environmental concerns at an existing facility–an industrial plant, an abandoned site, a mine area, or any other site where industrial pollution problems are identified or anticipated. It is used to provide data on the extent of pollution in an industrial area, to quantify the scale of pollution at a particular site, or to examine the causes and potential remedies of problems at a facility. This chapter provides guidance on the uses of environmental audits in industrial pollution management and on the scope of a typical audit.*

## Types of Environmental Audit

The term *environmental audit* covers a wide range of activities based on formal evaluation of an organization's or a facility's performance in relation to environmental objectives. There are many different definitions reflecting different emphases and objectives, but the critical elements are that the audit should be objective, systematic and based on defined criteria. (For a broader discussion of environmental audits, see the World Bank's Environmental Assessment Sourcebook Update series.) Several broad categories of audit can be defined (see Box 1), but this chapter focuses on the use of environmental audits in World Bank industrial pollution management activities. In these cases, the principal objective is to collect factual information about the extent and causes of pollution at a site or facility and possible remedial actions. In some IFC projects, a project-specific environmental audit is used as part of the formal environmental analysis and review process, and particular requirements apply. (For details, contact the Environment Division at the IFC.) Clearly, it is important that the scope and objectives of an audit be clearly defined.

## Use of Site Audits

A site audit is often the first step in obtaining a quantitative understanding of pollution problems. In many cases, the audit allows an evalua-

---

**Box 1. Types of Environmental Audit**

Several types of environmental audit can be distinguished, although with considerable overlap:

- *Site audit:* assesses onsite conditions and the extent of contamination problems
- *Liability audit:* requested by potential purchasers or by financial institutions when considering investment or acquisition
- *Compliance audit:* addresses compliance with company policies and regulatory requirements
- *Management system audit:* reviews both technical and organizational aspects, usually within the context of corporate environmental strategy
- *Waste minimization or pollution prevention audit:* examines production and waste management systems to identify improvements

---

tion to be made of priorities and of the extent and cost of control and remediation measures. This information then shapes all remediation actions and investments. Some examples of the use of site audits in Bank projects are given in Box 2.

## Role in Environmental Assessment

An environmental audit can, in certain circumstances, meet most of the World Bank's or the IFC's environmental assessment requirements for a Category B project. (A project in which

---

### Box 2. Uses of Site Audits in Bank Projects

- In *Bulgaria*, an audit provided information on the extent and severity of contamination at a metal smelter.
- In *Bolivia*, audits were used to define environmental issues and provide a basis for discussions with potential investors in the mining and hydrocarbons sectors.
- In *Algeria*, audits were carried out on several major industries in the preparation of an industrial pollution management project.
- In *Estonia*, the IFC's preparation for investment in a cement plant included a detailed audit that provided the basis for an environmental management plan.

---

significant retrofitting or upgrading of industrial plant is being considered would normally be classified as Category B). For such a project, an environmental audit should be carried out as part of the preparation for the upgrading, and this audit can provide the main documentation necessary for the environmental assessment. (All other relevant requirements of OP 4.01 must also be taken into consideration, particularly in relation to consultation, which is not usually part of the audit.)

## Scope and Level of Detail

In an industrial context, the overall objective is to understand the scale and sources of the pollution problems at a facility or in a defined area and to set out the options available for dealing with those problems. There is often a staged process of investigation in which each stage is narrower in scope but more detailed than the preceding one.

An initial assessment can be relatively quick, drawing on readily available sources, including site interviews, and providing an overview of the actual or suspected sources of pollutants and the extent of their impact. This overview can be carried out during project definition or as a scoping stage and provides a basis for further detailed investigations or for defining priorities for action.

A useful function of the initial assessment is to describe data availability and needs and to indicate where site sampling and monitoring might be cost-effective.

### Extent of Coverage

A key difference between a plant environmental audit and a full site audit is that the coverage of the audit should be wide enough to include the areas affected by the plant so that the benefits of improvements in operations can be estimated. Detail may be lacking, but it is important to indicate the extent of offsite impacts, where these occur.

### Full Audit

A full site audit is detailed, requiring careful site inspections (perhaps including sampling and testing) and review of past and present production processes, as well as pollution emissions and control measures. The audit should also clarify the legal and regulatory framework, licensing agreements, corporate policies, and management structures and priorities that affect the environmental performance of the plant.

In many cases, relevant technical and environmental standards for performance may be ill defined or may not exist, and professional judgments will have to be made as to the appropriate benchmarks. However, it is essential that the standards or emissions limits proposed for the plant be clearly defined and that the rationale for their selection be given. If full new plant requirements appear unachievable with the current plant, the audit should address what might be acceptable as realistic interim requirements.

### Recommendations for Action

The audit should provide a list of recommended actions, in terms of increasing cost-effectiveness in addressing the critical environmental issues. This list should include interim and long-term targets and a timetable for achieving them, together with an indication of the investments and other resources (human, information, and so on) that would be required.

## Scale and Cost

The scale and cost of site audits can vary widely, depending, above all, on the extent of field data collection required. A scoping study can be carried out in a couple of days by one or two people, with cooperation from site personnel. A full site audit of a typical industrial plant can be carried out within one to two months, of which perhaps one week is spent on the main fieldwork, usually followed by a shorter visit to verify initial findings. Using a typical team comprising local technical staff and a small number of international specialists, budget costs would be of the order of US$30,000–$50,000. For a large plant, especially where the area involved is extensive or where there is need for a program of sampling and testing, the costs can rise to US$200,000–$400,000. Where the objectives are limited and local expertise is available, a reasonable audit can be carried out for much smaller amounts. It is therefore critical that the objectives and requirements of the audit be clearly stated and justified.

## Terms of Reference

The terms of reference (TOR) will be site-specific, but the examples given in Box 3 illustrate what might be included in a comprehensive TOR. Examples of formats for reporting that have been required are shown in Box 4.

## Points of Procedure

The following points relate to the procedures for the execution of an audit.

- *Selection of auditors.* Various forms of certification of environmental auditors are under discussion in different countries, but, in general, no formal qualifications or registration should be required for carrying out a site audit.

Although many of the skills required for a site assessment are general environmental or engineering skills, it is important that the audit team contain personnel with detailed knowledge of the specific industry being addressed. Selection of auditors should follow the normal procedures for consultants. Arrangements should be made to

---

### Box 3. Example: TOR for a Mining Area Site Audit

- Overall objective
- Specific objectives
- General scope of work
- Baseline data
- Principal sources of contamination
- Area of impact
- Technical approach
- Work plan
- Prevention, control, and mitigation
- Recommended priority actions
- Environmental management plan
- Site-specific scope of work (by site)
- Laboratory services
- Norms and standards
- Pre-bid site visits
- Client contacts and counterparts
- Facilities provided by the client
- Reporting and deliverables

---

### Box 4. Examples of Audit Report Contents Required in the TOR

*For an IFC project*

- Executive summary
- Project description
- Regulatory setting
- Audit procedure
- Mitigation
- Costs and schedule
- Annexes

*Russian Federation Environmental Management Project*

- Executive summary
- Introduction
- The site
- Review of environmental management
- Survey of compliance with environmental laws, regulations, and company policies
- Conclusions and recommendations
- Recommendations for further investigation
- Appendices
- Photolog
- Supporting documentation

allow bidders to become familiar with the site before the tender closure date.

- *Briefing and terms of reference.* It is essential that the consultants selected have a clear understanding of the objectives of the work, especially if it is to become part of the overall environmental assessment for the project. The TOR therefore need to be as specific as possible.
- *Preparation phase.* An *audit plan* should be prepared describing the information required, the site visit schedule, and the site personnel to be involved or interviewed.

A *protocol* may be prepared defining the specific information that will be sought during the site visit. The protocol should be provided to the enterprise well in advance of the visit.

Available file information on the facility should be obtained and reviewed before the visit, and the audit plan should then be refined, if necessary.

- *Execution of the audit.* Active cooperation of the plant owners and managers is essential for a good result and should be secured in advance. Good coordination reduces delays and costs. Therefore site visits, interviews, and any sampling should be organized as early as possible. The site inspection should be carefully documented, to support the findings and recommendations and to provide a reference for future audits.

- *Review of findings.* It is important that the management in place be allowed to comment on the findings and recommendations of the audit.

## Other Issues

If the environmental audit is to form part of the environmental assessment process required under OP 4.01, the documents must be made available as part of the public consultation. To avoid disclosure problems, the audit report may have to be written in such a way as to provide the necessary environmental information without disclosing commercially confidential information. In such a case, the task manager must be satisfied that the public report provides sufficient detail to satisfy the EA requirements.

## Reference and Source

UNEP (United Nations Environment Programme) and UNIDO (United Nations Industrial Development Organization). 1991. "Audit and Reduction Manual for Industrial Emissions and Wastes." UNEP, Paris, and UNIDO, Vienna.

World Bank. 1995. "Environmental Auditing." Environmental Assessment Sourcebook Update 11. Environment Department, Washington, D.C.

# Environmental Management Systems and ISO 14000

*Environmental management systems (EMSs) such as ISO 14000 are seen as mechanisms for achieving improvements in environmental performance and for supporting the trade prospects of "clean" firms. The potential advantages of EMSs are clear, but the adoption of ISO 14000 is very recent, and practical issues are emerging, among them the need for an emphasis on performance improvement and for simplification of certification; the potential for regulatory streamlining; and the trade consequences. This chapter outlines the key elements of an EMS and discusses these issues.*

## The Benefits of an EMS

An environmental management system (EMS) is a structured program of continuous environmental improvement that follows procedures drawn from established business management practices (see Box 1). The concept is straightforward, and the principles can be easily applied, given the necessary support. There has been increasing interest in the potential value of EMS approaches, of which the recently released ISO 14000 series is the most widely known.

The first steps in the control of industrial pollution have been the creation of the necessary regulatory framework and the specification and design of control equipment to reduce emissions. These efforts have been broadly successful in improving the performance of many polluters, but in other cases, investments in pollution equipment are wasted because the equipment is not operated properly. Attention, in the World Bank and elsewhere, is turning to support of regulatory and end-of-pipe approaches through incentives, production efficiencies, and management improvements—a range of measures often grouped under the broad banner of cleaner production and ecoefficiency.

The potential benefits of ecoefficiency are unequivocal: good operational practices, supported by committed management, can achieve considerable improvements in environmental performance at low cost and can get the maximum benefits from investments in hardware. Without management and worker support, the best equipment can be useless. The challenge is to achieve long-lasting improvements in performance, and EMS is seen as one of the key tools in achieving this.

An important related issue, in a context of increasingly free trade, is the concern that environmental performance may become an important commercial factor, either as a positive attribute or as a potential trade barrier. The implementation of an EMS, and particularly of the ISO 14000 system, is seen as a way to demonstrate an acceptable level of environmental commitment.

A good EMS allows an enterprise to understand and track its environmental performance. It provides a framework for implementing improvements that may be desirable for financial or other corporate reasons or that may be required to meet regulatory requirements. Ideally, it is built on an existing quality management system.

## ISO 14000 and Other Standards

If an EMS were adopted purely as an internal management tool, the details of the system and its structure would not be important. However, the EMS is becoming more and more a matter of interest to people outside the management of the enterprise—to workers, regulators, local residents, commercial partners, bankers and insurers, and the general public. In this context, the EMS is no longer an internal system and becomes a mechanism for communicating the enterprise's performance to outside parties, and some level

---

**Box 1. What Is an EMS?**

An EMS can be described as a program of continuous environmental improvement that follows a defined sequence of steps drawn from established project management practice and routinely applied in business management. In simple terms these steps are as follows:

- Review the environmental consequences of the operations.
- Define a set of policies and objectives for environmental performance.
- Establish an action plan to achieve the objectives.
- Monitor performance against these objectives.
- Report the results appropriately.
- Review the system and the outcomes and strive for continuous improvement.

Not every system will present these steps in exactly the same way, but the basic principles are clear and easily understandable.

The ISO 14000 series is a series of standards for different aspects of environmental management. A number of these standards relating to environmental management systems have been adopted formally by the members of the ISO, while others are in different stages of preparation.

The standards that have been adopted are (as of early 1997):

**1SO 14001-1996** Environmental management systems: specification with guidance for use
**ISO 14004-1996** Environmental management systems: general guidelines on principles, systems, and supporting techniques
**ISO 14010-1996** Guidelines for environmental auditing: general principles of environmental auditing
**ISO 14011-1996** Guidelines for environmental auditing: audit procedures; auditing of environmental management systems.
**ISO 14012-1996** Guidelines for environmental auditing: qualification criteria for environmental auditors

Standards currently available as draft international standards:

**ISO 14021** Environmental labels and declarations: self-declaration environmental claims; guidelines and definition and usage of terms.
**ISO 14040** Environmental management: life cycle assessment; principles and framework
**ISO 14050** Environmental management: vocabulary

More than half a dozen others in this series have been drafted and are under discussion.

---

of standardization and common understanding is required.

The best-known common framework for EMS is the ISO 14000 series. This series is based on the overall approach and broad success of the quality management standards prepared and issued as the ISO 9000 series. ISO 14000 consists of a series of standards covering ecolabeling and life cycle assessment (LCA), as well as EMS (see Box 1). The documents formally adopted (by the end of 1996) as international standards are those covering EMS: ISO 14001 and ISO 14004.[1]

There are two other major EMS standards: the British BS 7750, which was one of the first broadly accepted systems and has been adopted by a number of other countries, and EMAS, the European Eco-Management and Audit Scheme. A process of harmonization has been under way to ensure reciprocal acceptability of these systems with ISO 14001. BS 7750 and EMAS are, however, broader in their requirements than ISO 14000. In particular, EMAS includes requirements for continued improvement of performance and for communication with the public, which are not part of ISO 14001.

Within the ISO system, ISO 14001 sets out the basic structure for an EMS, while ISO 14004 provides guidance. The crucial feature of the ISO 14001 standard is that it identifies the elements of a system which can be independently audited and certified. The issue of certification underlies much of the discussion about environmental management systems. The presentation in these standards is clear and concise and provides a framework that can be used as the starting point for a simple system for a small company or a highly detailed one for a multinational enterprise.

Compliance with ISO 14001 does not by itself automatically ensure that an enterprise will actually achieve improved environmental performance. The standard requires that there be an environmental policy that "includes a commitment to continual improvement and pollution prevention" and "a commitment to comply with relevant environmental legislation and regulations." It also requires that the enterprise establish procedures for taking corrective and preventive action in cases of nonconformance. It may seem to be splitting hairs to say that these requirements for a policy and procedures would not result in improved performance, but the issue becomes one of following the spirit and not just the letter of the standard. The desirable approach would be for management to make a commitment to specific environment performance improvements within a defined period and then use ISO 14000 as the mechanism for demonstrating that it is complying with that commitment. As a manager for a multinational firm observed, "Having a certificate doesn't mean that you have a clean company. The bad guys who pollute today will still do it, and they'll have a certificate."

It should be noted that ISO 14000 standards are voluntary. "Adoption" by a country normally means that the national standards organization has said that the ISO version is the EMS standard that is recognized. It does not imply any formal requirement that companies adopt such a standard.

## Issues to be Resolved

EMS is clearly a good concept and is supported in principle by the World Bank and by environmental agencies and organizations everywhere. At the same time, there are costs associated with implementation—particularly in enterprise time and effort, more than direct out-of-pocket costs—and a number of issues need to be addressed in making decisions about the type and level of system to be adopted.

## Commitment to Performance Improvements

The direct benefits to an enterprise of implementing an EMS usually come from savings through cleaner production and waste minimization approaches. (An order of magnitude estimate is that about 50% of the pollution generated in a typical "uncontrolled" plant can be prevented, with minimal investment, by adopting simple and cheap process improvements.) Even in industrial countries, increased discharge fees and waste disposal charges provide incentives for cost-effective pollution reduction—which, incidentally, demonstrates the importance of an appropriate framework of regulations and incentives to drive the performance improvements. The major impact of the introduction of an EMS can be the identification of waste minimization and cleaner production possibilities.

Management and worker commitment to improving performance is essential. The process of introducing the EMS can be a catalyst for generating support for environmental performance improvements, including the simple changes that make up "good housekeeping," and also for making the best use of existing pollution control equipment. Just as important, the development of good management systems is one of the best hopes for sustaining the improvements that can be achieved when attention is focused on environmental performance.

A concern often expressed about the ISO 14001 system is the lack of a clear commitment to improvements in actual environmental performance. The whole EMS approach is designed to improve performance, but critics of the rush to implement ISO 14001 argue that the standard can be misused. It is not yet clear how valid this point is, and its resolution will depend on how the overall approach is used in trade and regulatory areas. However, there is a legitimate concern that some may view ISO 14000 as an end rather than a means.

Given the current stage of development of auditing and certification systems, it may be possible in some places to obtain (or claim) certification with a minimum level of real environmental improvement. From the World Bank's point of view, it is essential that enterprises demonstrate serious good-faith efforts to achieve the performance goals underlying an environmental management system, if certification is to have any real meaning. An acceptable system must comply with the spirit of the EMS, not just the minimum formal requirements.

## Certification

ISO 14001 sets out a system that can be audited and certified. In many cases, it is the issue of certification that is critical or controversial and is at the heart of the discussion about the trade implications. Certification means that a qualified body (an "accredited certifier") has inspected the EMS system that has been put in place and has made a formal declaration that the system is consistent with the requirements of ISO 14001.

The standard allows for "self-certification," a declaration by an enterprise that it conforms to ISO 14001. There is considerable skepticism as to whether this approach would be widely accepted, especially when certification has legal or commercial consequences. At the same time, obtaining certification can entail significant costs, and there are issues relating to the international acceptance of national certification that may make it particularly difficult for companies in some countries to achieve credible certification at a reasonable cost. For firms concerned about having certification that carries real credibility, the costs of bringing in international auditors are typically quite high, partly because the number of internationally recognized firms of certifiers is limited at present.[2]

The issue of accreditation of certifiers is becoming increasingly important as the demand increases. Countries that have adopted ISO 14001 as a national standard can accredit qualified companies as certifiers, and this will satisfy national legal or contractual requirements. However, the fundamental purpose of ISO is to achieve consistency internationally. If certificates from certain countries or agencies are not fully accepted or are regarded as "second class," the goal will not have been achieved. It is probable that the international marketplace will eventually put a real commercial value on high-quality certificates, but this level of sophistication and discrimination has not yet been achieved. It is essential to the ultimate success of the whole system that there be a mechanism to ensure that certification in any one country has credibility and acceptability elsewhere.

The ISO has outlined procedures for accreditation and certification (Guides 61 and 62), and a formal body, QSAR, has been established to operationalize the process. At the same time, a number of established national accreditation bodies heavily involved in ISO have set up the informal International Accreditation Forum (IAF) to examine mechanisms for achieving international reciprocity through multilateral agreements (MLAs). However, these systems are in the early stages, and many enterprises continue to use the established international certifiers, even at additional cost, because of lack of confidence in the acceptability of local certifiers.

Given the variability in the design of individual EMS and the substantial costs of the ISO 14000 certification process, there is a growing tendency for large companies that are implementing EMS approaches to pause before taking this last step. After implementing an EMS and confirming that the enterprise is broadly in conformance with ISO 14001, it is becoming routine to carry out a "gap analysis" to determine exactly what further actions would be required to achieve certification and to examine the benefits and costs of bringing in third-party certifiers.

## Reducing the Cost of Regulation

A question commonly raised is the extent to which an EMS can reduce the costs of regulation, in terms of both the overall government enforcement effort and the costs of compliance of the individual enterprise. The use of ISO 14001 certification to replace some statutory reporting requirements is a topic of considerable discussion in a number of countries, particularly those where regulatory requirements are extensive enough to be a real burden on industry. It is now clear that an EMS is not a substitute for a regulatory framework, but the monitoring and reporting systems of a well-managed enterprise might substitute for some of the statutory inspections, audits, and reports normally required under government regulations. The issue is when and how the government can trust the capabilities and commitment of an enterprise to self-monitor its environmental performance and whether some formal EMS and certification system, such as ISO 14000, would provide the mechanism to convince regulators that scarce government resources would be better used elsewhere in pursuing less cooperative organizations.

This approach is attractive, but there are a number of hurdles to clear before it can be put into place on a widespread basis. Reaching agreement on such matters is proving to be a more difficult and complex task than might at first be assumed. Some of the difficulties are legal (lack of flexibility in regulations or the need to ensure that voluntary reports are not unreasonably used to prosecute enterprises that are making good-faith efforts to improve), but often they relate to the necessary level of confidence on both sides that the other parties are genuine in their efforts. Pilot programs being tested in a number of U.S. states will provide essential feedback on these issues. The World Bank is currently supporting a pathfinding exercise in Mexico, looking at implementation of EMS and how it might dovetail with a streamlining of the licensing system. There are clear benefits all around in making such partnerships work, but it will be some time before clear, workable models are available.

## Disclosure of Information and External Relations

There is considerable evidence that an informed public has a strong influence on the environmental performance of industrial enterprises, through a variety of mechanisms that include market forces, social pressures, and support for improved regulatory controls. ISO 14000 does not include specific requirements for the disclosure or publication of environmental performance measures or audit results, but other EMS models do have some such requirements. The World Bank strongly supports disclosure of actual performance information because this allows the relevant public to monitor progress (or the lack of it) and to take informed positions on issues related to plant performance. It also allows much higher confidence in company statements about compliance and improvements.

There is a growing interest on the part of commercial banks and insurance companies in environmental risk (in a purely business sense). Such organizations are considering whether EMS certification (typically EMAS, in Europe) demonstrates that a firm has real control over its environmental risk and potential liability. It is possible that certification may lead to commercial benefits, such as lower insurance rates, in certain high-risk sectors.

Public release of the main environmental information from an EMS can also be used as a central component of a community relations program, although this goes beyond the basic concept of an EMS.

## Trade Implications

Statements have been made to the effect that before long, ISO 14000 certification will be an essential passport for developing countries wishing to trade with the industrial nations. Such statements, in this extreme form, are speculative and almost certainly incorrect. It is, however, unclear to what extent ISO 14001 might become a barrier

to trade, in direct contradiction to the basic objectives of the ISO, or, alternatively, might provide a competitive edge for certified firms. The trade implications are of concern to many countries, and the World Trade Organization is beginning to consider some of the issues under its mandate on technical barriers to trade. In this context, a distinction needs to be made between product standards, such as the ecolabeling and LCA standards under ISO 14000, and production process standards such as ISO 14001; the impacts are likely to be different.

In many cases in developing countries, the environmental pressures come through the supplier chain—the ongoing relationship between a major company (often a multinational) and its smaller national suppliers. The sensitivity of multinationals to pressures regarding their performance on environmental and other issues is causing them to look for better performance from the suppliers. This relationship is typically a cooperative one in which large companies work with smaller ones to achieve better performance in such areas as quality and price. The multinationals may ask their suppliers to achieve and demonstrate environmental performance improvements, but there is no evidence that unreasonable targets or time scales are being applied. Where ISO 14001 certification is an ultimate aim, certification is seen as a long-term objective rather than a short-term requirement.

Even if ISO 14001 is not likely to be a contractual constraint in the foreseeable future, environmental performance is increasingly becoming a factor in commercial transactions, and companies looking to establish a presence in the international marketplace are considering whether a "green badge" would be an advantage to them. In practice, it is often marketing rather than environmental concerns that drive the ISO certification process.

## Application to Small and Medium-Size Enterprises

Most of the development and application of EMS has taken place in large companies. The use of such systems in small and medium-size enterprises (SMEs) has been limited—although it is in this segment of industry that some of the largest benefits might be anticipated, because of the difficulty of regulating large numbers of small firms and the potential efficiency improvements that are believed to exist. In practice, however, the characteristics of the typical SME make the adoption of EMS difficult: most SMEs do not have a formal management structure, they lack technically trained personnel, and they are subject to severe short-term pressures on cash flow.

Anecdotal evidence indicates that an EMS cannot be used to drive improved performance in a poorly organized SME. Targeted training in management and quality control can improve overall performance, including its environmental aspects, and can provide a basis for more specific EMS development. Many firms can reap significant benefits from introducing quality management concepts, even where they are not aiming at formal certification. Any steps in this direction should be encouraged.

## Practicalities in Establishing an EMS

An EMS, as normally envisaged, builds on existing production and quality management systems. Where such systems are weak or ineffective, as is often the case in enterprises that have poor environmental performance, a better management framework has to be established before focusing on the details of the EMS. The costs of establishing an EMS will therefore obviously depend on the starting point in terms of both management systems and environmental performance. The ecoefficiency savings can, in some cases, pay for the costs of establishing the EMS, particularly if most of the planning and organizational work is carried out in-house. However, a poor performer will very likely have to invest in production upgrading or pollution control in order to meet environmental requirements, and these costs can be significant.

A full EMS can be complex and can require an appreciable commitment of operational resources. However, the final system can be reached reasonably through a series of discrete steps, starting from a basic, simple procedure and becoming more comprehensive and sophisticated as capabilities and resources allow. In this way, even a small enterprise can begin to put in place the basic elements of an ISO 14001 system and can develop them at an appropriate pace. Once the basic EMS is in place, it is possible to carry out a gap analysis and to make a balanced judgment on the costs and benefits of seeking certification.

A related issue is the coverage of the EMS. Certification is normally for specific sites or facilities. A large enterprise may have a number of different sites and production facilities and may choose to seek certification only for a subset of the sites.

## Role of Governments

Although ISO 14000 is a set of voluntary standards that individual companies may or may not choose to adopt, governments can clearly have a role in providing information, establishing the necessary framework and infrastructure, and, in some cases, helping companies to develop the basic capabilities to adopt ISO 14000. There are two particular areas in which government action would be useful: (a) providing information on the sectors and markets where ISO 14001 certification is a significant issue and assisting sector organizations to develop appropriate responses, and (b) helping to establish a certification framework, based on strengthening national standards organizations and encouraging competitive private sector provision of auditing and certification services. At present, the World Bank is having discussions with a number of countries about how assistance could be provided with these issues.

Governments should see EMS approaches as part of a broad environmental strategy that includes regulatory systems, appropriate financial incentives, and encouragement of improved industrial performance. Such encouragement can really only be effective where there is cooperation at the government level between the relevant departments, including industry and trade, as well as environment. There is a growing interest in integrating environmental management issues into productivity or competitiveness centers designed to promote SME performance, but little information exists on experience to date.

## Will It Perform?

The spectacular blossoming of interest in ISO 14000 should lead to increased understanding of the benefits of better environmental management and greater awareness of environmental performance as a factor in succeeding in increasingly competitive markets. At the same time, this standard is not a magic wand that will achieve environmental improvements where regulation and enforcement are ineffective or that can open markets where competition is strong. The standard provides a framework on which to build better performance, greater efficiency, and a competitive image. With serious commitment and effort from the organization, implementing a system such as ISO 14001 can yield solid benefits.

## Additional Resources

For details on ISO standards, contact national standards organizations or the International Organization for Standardization:

ISO Central Secretariat
1, rue de Varambe
Case postale 56
CH-1211 Geneva 20
Switzerland
Tel: +41 22 749 0111, fax: +41 22 734 1079

A training kit in EMS, prepared by a group of international organizations, is available from the UNEP (address on p. 143):

UNEP/ICC/FIDIC. 1995. "Environmental Management System Training Resource Kit." Version 1.0.

## Notes

1. ISO standards are available through the national standards organizations in most countries. For example, the ISO 14000 series is available through the American National Standards Institute (ANSI) at costs ranging between US$27 and US$78 for the formal standards and, typically, US$30 each for the drafts.

2. It is not possible to be precise, but costs typically start in the tens of thousands of dollars for any but the smallest sites.

# Implementing Cleaner Production

*Cleaner production (CP) should be an essential part of any comprehensive pollution management system, at the enterprise or the national level. Significant reductions in pollution loads can often be obtained at little cost, and efficient use of resources and reduction in wastage in industrial production are clearly preferable to reliance on end-of-pipe treatment. Some firms— the "dynamic" ones that are responsive to external changes—will adopt CP readily in order to gain competitive advantage. By contrast, static firms—often small, traditional businesses or inflexible state-owned enterprises—require targeted intervention to persuade them to take advantage of the benefits of CP. In many cases, it may be worthwhile to combine promotion of CP with the adoption of an environmental management system (EMS).*

Cleaner production (CP) minimizes the use of resources and reduces the wastes discharged to the environment. In many cases, the adoption of CP improvements can reduce or even eliminate the need for end-of-pipe investments and can therefore provide both financial and economic net benefits (see Box 1). As a rough guide, 20–30% reductions in pollution can often be achieved with no capital investment required, and a further 20% or more reduction can be obtained with investments that have a payback time of only months.

CP is also attractive because of concerns about the lack of effectiveness of end-of-pipe solutions: there are numerous examples of poor operation and maintenance of treatment plants, with resulting failure of the system to achieve its objectives.[1]

CP and related approaches will be increasingly important in environmental management in the future. However, changes will require effort and will be gradual. CP should therefore be seen as part of an overall approach, not as a "costless" alternative to a comprehensive set of environmental polices and regulations.

The introduction of CP is an ongoing process: as resource prices and disposal costs continue to rise, new opportunities arise for pollution prevention and reductions in treatment costs. For this reason, CP can be linked closely with environmental management systems.

## Definitions

The term *cleaner production* has came into general use through the efforts of the UNEP Cleaner Production Program, established in 1989. A number of related terms are also used, including low- or no-waste technologies; waste minimization (India); waste and emissions prevention (Netherlands); source reduction (United States); ecoefficiency (World Business Council on Sustainable Development) and environmentally sound technology (United Nations Council on Sustainable Development). All these terms essentially refer to the same concept of integrating pollution reduction into the production process and even the design of the product.

## Reluctant Implementation

Despite the increasing and often very focused promotional efforts, there is anecdotal evidence that the practical implementation of cleaner production recommendations fell short of the level anticipated in the early years of promotion, although it is believed that the situation is improving. There is no accepted way to measure the overall impact of CP programs, but typical figures suggested by people in the field indicate that 15–20% of the identified measures were put into practice within a reasonable time after the

## Box 1. Examples of Cleaner Production

### China

At the request of China's National Environmental Protection Agency (NEPA), a US$6 million cleaner production component was included in the World Bank's Environmental Technical Assistance Project, approved in 1993. The UNEP Cleaner Production Programme assisted in the design and implementation of the component, which included studies in 18 companies, the training of a cadre of local experts, and the preparation of a Chinese cleaner production manual. A large distillery was one of the plants involved; a first assessment of the bottling plant identified good housekeeping options that cost less than US$2,000 and resulted in savings of over US$70,000. This initial success was followed by detailed studies of the alcohol plant that resulted in a number of equipment optimizations (carried out during a maintenance shutdown), producing nearly US$700,000 in savings. Three technology replacement options were also identified, costing up to US$500,000 and with paybacks of one and a half to four and a half years.

### Tunisia

A study of a battery manufacturer employing 200 people identified 19 actions, of which the first 7 changes alone offered potential savings of nearly US$750,000 in the first year, with no capital investment required.

### Chile

An assessment of a large textile mill employing nearly 300 people identified potential reductions in water and energy use and improvements in the control of sus- pended solids. Three specific investments were recommended, at a total cost of US $11 million and with payback periods of 14–24 months.

### India

In 1993, a CP demonstration project targeting SMEs was initiated by UNIDO, in cooperation with the Indian National Productivity Council and other industry associations. This DESIRE project focused on three sectors: agro-based pulp and paper, textile dying and printing, and pesticides formulation. Results for one of the pulp and paper plants demonstrate the types of savings possible. In a plant producing 36 tons of paper per day, a combination of process and equipment modifications and some new technology was identified that improved the product and the operating conditions for a capital investment of US$25,000, with a payback period of less than three months.

### Poland

A Polish CP Program has developed from a 1991 NGO training program, organized by engineering federations and supported by the Norwegian government, to a national government-sponsored movement, with a formal charter, that has produced 400 trained, certified experts. The CP improvements that have been implemented are now in the hundreds, and formalization of the CP center and its funding are in progress.

### Other Countries

Since 1990, the World Environment Center's Industrial Waste Minimization Program, funded by USAID, has implemented 52 projects in 18 companies, producing over US$8 million in savings with a total investment of about US$1.5 million and a payback period typically less than six months.

completion of the audits or investigations. This figure is increasing as experience is gained in designing programs and overcoming barriers to implementation. For example, in focused, sustained programs, it appears to be possible to obtain implementation of 30–50% of recommended measures, representing more or less the full set of no- or low-cost improvements.[2]

## Promotion of CP

Pollution prevention has been around for some time (Dow Chemical's 3P program in the United States is now 20 years old). Over this period, vari- ous industry and governmental efforts have been made in the United States and Europe. The emphasis in developing countries has been on providing access to the necessary technical expertise to identify CP opportunities, principally through the establishment of Cleaner Production Centers. Several major initiatives are under way, supported by the UNEP, UNIDO, and bilateral agencies.

## World Bank Experience

Experience within the World Bank has been increasing, with the focus on assisting country governments to promote and develop the use of CP in industry. Prevention of industrial pollution was included in the Metropolitan Environmental Improvement Program (MEIP) in the cities of Beijing, Manila, and Mumbai. The first major project was in China, and a significant program has been completed in the Philippines. CP elements are now increasingly being included in a number of World Bank industrial and environmental projects (for example, in Bolivia, India, Mexico, and Tunisia).

## Critical Success Factors

Two major issues have to be addressed in developing an effective CP program.

- *External incentives.* An appropriate government policy and regulatory framework must be in place to provide effective incentives for firms to adopt cleaner production.
- *Response of the firms.* In many cases, firms are slow or incapable of responding to the incentives, and it may be appropriate to assist the firms to adjust. The approaches adopted will vary considerably, depending on the characteristics of the sector and of the firms involved.

It must be emphasized that CP is only one of a number of possible components of a government industry and environment strategy, and it is only one of the approaches that an enterprise can adopt to improve its environmental and financial performance.

## Appropriate Government Framework

A number of key characteristics of the government framework required for the promotion of CP have been identified:

- A broad macroeconomic context that sets real resource prices, encourages investment in new technology, and supports an orientation toward export markets, thus providing strong incentives
- A predictable and flexible regulatory regime under which predictability will encourage investment in pollution management and flexibility will allow enterprises to adopt the most cost-effective solutions

- A credible enforcement system to provide backbone for the regulations
- Targeted measures to assist enterprises in adopting cleaner production.

## Enterprise Characteristics

Firms respond in different ways to the incentives provided by the government and by the market. It is possible to suggest two extreme types of firm that have different characteristics and require different approaches.

At one end of the spectrum are enterprises that are operating in a highly differentiated market in which product quality is important. Such firms focus on quality, product improvement, and brand and company image. They typically have high-quality management, are responsive to external changes, and concentrate on revenue enhancement. These firms can be characterized as *dynamic*, in a literal sense, because their processes and methods have to evolve continually if the enterprises are to maintain their position in competitive markets.

At the other end of the spectrum are firms that can be characterized as *static* because their processes and markets change very slowly. Included in this category are small firms that are price takers in a mature industry. They use traditional and relatively simple production methods, focus on cost minimization, are often undercapitalized, and lack depth in management. This group includes many of the traditional polluting sectors such as electroplating and tanning.

Large state-owned enterprises (SOEs), especially in heavy industry, can also often be characterized as static. They typically operate in monopolistic markets, and their management is frequently extremely bureaucratic. A classic example of failure to take advantage of CP opportunities is provided by a major state-owned chemical plant in Sub-Saharan Africa, as described in Box 2.

The approaches required to introduce and disseminate new processes are very different in dynamic and in static firms. Information and incentives will be most effective in the dynamic enterprises. Static enterprises require a blunter approach because the management is typically much less responsive to incentives.

## Box 2. Lost Opportunities Stemming from Sluggish Management

An audit of a large state-owned chemical plant—a possible candidate for privatization—in Sub-Saharan Africa identified a number of cost-effective options, including one that involved recovery of incompletely processed raw material which had been dumped as waste. This option alone was estimated to generate US$60 million in savings for an investment of about US$4 million—a startling figure. However, because of lack of internal incentives for management, the option was never taken up. It was later discovered that the same plant had a track record of poor management and that previous attempts to upgrade the operations had ended in shambles.

## Encouraging Dynamic Firms

Dynamic firms are keen to introduce environmentally sound technology where this gives them a competitive edge, either because of reduced regulatory costs or because of better positioning in the marketplace. They typically have an aggressive management that seeks to improve production performance and has both the motivation and the skills to take advantage of new techniques. They respond to opportunities for technology transfer and management upgrading using approaches such as total quality management (TQM) and environmental management systems. The requirement on the government side is to provide incentives, information, and examples, such as demonstration projects or centers of excellence.

## State-Owned Enterprises

Many, although by no means all, SOEs are static, in the sense used here. They are inefficient, as a result of lack of competition and of hard budget constraints and because management priorities rarely include efficient use of resources. Such enterprises are typically significant polluters, with large opportunities for CP gains.

Restructuring or privatization of such SOEs should include audits to identify CP opportunities. Experience demonstrates, however, that new management attitudes are essential if advantage is to be taken of the potential savings.

## Sector-Based Approach for Other Static Industries

A number of industrial subsectors are dominated by small, static, highly polluting firms that are difficult to regulate because of the informal nature of the firms or the social consequences of enforcing pollution control. CP methods have obvious attractions in dealing with such firms, but the firms are very slow to respond to the apparent benefits.

There are several possible reasons for this poor response:

- Pollution may be a low priority for overstretched management.
- CP opportunities may be crowded out by other projects with more immediate returns.
- Adequately skilled and motivated personnel may be lacking.
- Obtaining finance from internal or external sources may be difficult.

In such cases, the government needs to intervene in a focused way, normally with the objective of solving a particular pollution problem. A number of steps in designing and implementing the intervention can be set out.

### Select the Sector Carefully

The sector should be one that is economically important, especially in terms of future development, and that presents a serious environmental problem. There must be a sufficient level of existing public concern and political will to make changes.

### Build Consensus and Support

All the players—environment and industry ministries, industrial associations (including suppliers and subcontractors), union or labor organizations, and relevant civic and environmental groups—must be involved. Table 1 lists key players and what their roles could be.

It is crucial that the private sector be involved in the process in the early stages because of the

**Table 1. Possible Roles and Responsibilities for Cleaner Production**

| Responsible agency | Upgrading existing industry | Influencing future investment toward cleaner production |
|---|---|---|
| Environment ministry | Establish environmental objectives; design regulations; negotiate sector agreements. | Establish clear framework of long-term environmental objectives and requirements. |
| Industry ministry | Mobilize sectors and identify necessary resources. | Identify and promote appropriate technology; support improvements in management. |
| Finance ministry | Review resource pricing and incentives; support discharge fees and similar instruments. | Consider environmental objectives in designing fiscal instruments for industrial promotion. |
| Local government | Negotiate site-specific agreements that address environment, employment, and local concerns within a sector framework. | Ensure that infrastructure exists that encourages cleaner industry (waste disposal and recycling, educated work force, etc.). |
| Broadly based business organizations | Accept and promote the concepts of cleaner production; support sector initiatives; encourage involvement of financial institutions; sponsor management improvement. | Identify and build links with relevant overseas organizations and firms; advise business on suitability of incoming technologies; promote development of indigenous firms to provide services in CP. |
| Sector associations | Accept and promote concepts of CP and cooperate in identification of technologies that are locally relevant to the sector. | Provide advice and support for the adoption of appropriate new technologies and management approaches. |
| Trade unions | Assist in identification of issues and opportunities: upgrade work-force skills. | Promote continued training of work force in necessary skills and attitudes. |
| Academic institutions | Provide independent advice; conduct research on local problems. | Develop technical and management skills to drive local initiatives in clean technology. |
| Suppliers | Provide advice on alternative equipment and materials. | Develop cleaner alternatives. |
| NGOs | Transmit local community viewpoints and priorities; assist in monitoring progress; reach firms and groups that are outside the structured industry associations. | Mobilize public support for improvements and new techniques; encourage informed wider debate on issues and options. |
| World Bank and other multilateral financial institutions | Assist in designing and planning schemes; provide technical assistance and access to funding. | Assist in developing industrial policy and promoting transfer of information and technologies; facilitate dialogue between public and private sectors. |

direct impacts on industry and because of the potential role that the private sector can play in initiating and developing process and operational changes to achieve CP goals. It is important to aim for high-level commitment from industry, as well-intentioned operatives at the bottom of the management system have limited influence.

It is also essential to involve the work force in the program. The distinction between the working environment and the general environment is becoming less relevant, and improvement in one often brings benefits to both (Box 3).

*Set Clear Objectives*

In order to concentrate efforts and to pave the way for the important short-term successes that can establish the credibility of a program, the focus should be on a small number of specific technical objectives that are relevant, feasible, and measurable.

**Box 3. Philippines**

The Metro Manila Clean Technology Initiative involved pollution management assessments and technology-matching missions in six sectors. The missions brought small groups of industry representatives and local regulators to the United States, where they visited companies, regulators, and university centers to discuss regulatory approaches, technology choices, and management issues. This exposure to all sides of the difficult issues was very productive for the visitors, and the experience was disseminated through industry seminars following participants' return to Manila. Investment opportunities identified in the sectors are being implemented through financing from a number of sources.

*Establish Incentives*

Appropriate external incentives must be established. It may be necessary to raise resource prices and to ensure that the threat of enforcement of disposal requirements is credible.

*Design Interventions to Assist Industry to Adjust*

The following is an initial set of interventions that have the potential to achieve results.

- *Research, analyze, and publicize the options.* In this way provide a menu of choices that can be adopted according to specific enterprise or local requirements.
- *Provide technical assistance* to help enterprises evaluate their situation. Although technical information may not be a sufficient condition for change, it is a necessary condition. Continued support should be given to programs aimed at improving technical capabilities and identifying opportunities.
- *Establish appropriate training opportunities* for management, workers, and regulators. Experience with training courses that bring regulators and industry together has demonstrated major benefits.
- *Improve access to financing.* Much more attention needs to be paid to issues of financing when examining technical options, at the enterprise or the sector level. This may require training both industry staff and financiers in

the preparation and analysis of project proposals.[3]
- Where appropriate, provide *start-up funds* to overcome the reluctance of traditional sources to finance CP. This is a good example of the possibilities for a narrowly defined, limited-life revolving fund with a specific objective of achieving commercial mainstreaming of this type of finance.
- Combine CP with the introduction of EMS.

*Monitor and Report*

The project should establish and publicize an agreed timetable for achieving measurable improvement, together with mechanisms for monitoring and reporting progress. A few simple numbers should be used as indicators of the success of the CP program and of the consequent environmental improvements.

**Financing Issues**

Financing constraints are often mentioned as a major barrier to adopting CP, although in practice this is rarely the fundamental problem. In many cases, major reductions in pollution can be achieved at little or no cost. To implement further improvements, some investment is required.

For projects requiring investment, the first source considered should be internal funds. If a comprehensive CP program has been prepared, it may be possible to use the cash flow from initial low-cost, quick-return measures to fund more expensive investments later.

Where external funding is required, the best approach is for the firm to use its normal bankers or financiers. This is usually the route taken by the more sophisticated and advanced firms. As with any other financing proposal, a thorough business plan for the introduction of cleaner production is needed, together with a realistic forecast of the benefit stream.

In countries where the banking system is not sophisticated or where credit is restricted, the use of environmental funds or lines of credits is frequently suggested as a mechanism for encouraging the introduction of CP. The issue of the appropriate design and functional criteria for such finance is a difficult one, but some broad comments can be made.

- Establishment of a successful fund is complex and time consuming and requires high-level involvement from environmental and industry authorities.
- Any subsidy or grant component is best used to assist in identification of opportunities and preparation of detailed proposals. Finance for the actual investments should be as close to commercial rates as possible, to avoid distorting investment decisions.
- The routine operation of the finance facilities can be contracted to commercial banks. Experience to date, however, has been poor, with the rate spread available and the volume of business often insufficient to ensure serious involvement by the banks.
- The main obstacle in finance appears to be not lack of funds but rather the difficulty in turning engineering reports into financial proposals. Overcoming this shortcoming will require assistance to enterprises in learning how to prepare proposals and training of bankers to be more receptive to requests for environmental funding.
- Care must be taken so that the availability of finance does not attract relatively high-cost CP proposals and distract the enterprise management from mundane but more cost-effective housekeeping and management changes;
- In many cases, the initial sums required are often small, perhaps a few thousand dollars. Very simple procedures must apply to such loans if the transaction costs are not to be prohibitive. There is a need to develop mechanisms that will allow financiers to accept greater risk with such small loans, perhaps through unusual endorsement procedures or by developing a portfolio approach that will absorb the inevitable nonperforming loans.

## The Broader Context

As noted, CP is only one element in improving industrial environmental performance. Nevertheless, developing and implementing a CP program can be an effective context for developing environmental awareness and building the necessary skills to undertake a wider range of environmental improvements. For this reason, a government strategy for CP should be more ambitious than simply achieving a minimum number of CP projects. At the very least, a CP campaign can be used as a starting point for identifying and monitoring environmental problems, for developing the technical analysis and the business plans required, and for building confidence between the government, enterprises, and bankers.

## Governments' Role in Promotion

The development of capability in industrial management at a national level should be supported, together with the capacity of the government to influence the direction of technology cooperation. CP is essentially a subset of good management practices and perhaps is best supported in this broader context.

## World Bank Involvement

The World Bank can support the objectives of cleaner production in a number of ways:

- It can continue to stress the need to achieve real economic levels of resource prices, including fees and charges.
- Good practices in ecoefficiency, in its many aspects, should be required in projects funded directly by the World Bank.
- The development of capability in industrial management at a national level should be supported, together with the capacity of the government to influence the direction of technology cooperation.
- Assistance might be provided to specific local or national CP initiatives and organizations, through their use as specialist consultants or by assisting such organizations to become self-supporting.
- The World Bank may have a particular role in assisting in the increased productivity and environmental performance of the small-scale and informal sectors, where adoption of improved methods is often very uneven and where the social issues are especially important.
- The World Bank can provide funding for CP projects, but its greatest contribution might be in the design of such funds and in environ-

mental awareness raising and training for the commercial banks and other financial intermediaries.

- Information exchange and networking are critical. The World Bank may help, but it is not obvious that it should take the lead.

## Additional Resources

A wide range of activities is under way, and it is not possible to provide a comprehensive list. Much of the basic work has been carried out by international and bilateral agencies, which should be the first point of reference for further information. For example:

- A joint UNEP/UNIDO program is establishing National Cleaner Production Centers (NCPC) to provide a focal point for CP efforts. Centers are being set up in China, the Czech Republic, India, Indonesia, Mexico, the Slovak Republic, Tanzania, and Zimbabwe, and several others are under negotiation.
- The EP3 Program, funded by USAID, has set up local operations providing technical assistance and carrying out audits in Chile, Egypt, and Tunisia. Other initiatives have been proposed, for example, in Bolivia.
- Bilateral donors are financing a range of CP efforts, including waste minimization audits and provision of technical assistance. For example the Norwegian and U.S. governments are supporting a major program in Central Europe.
- Efforts under the Basel Convention on Control of Transboundary Movement of Hazard-

ous Wastes include the establishment of regional centers in Central America that would provide advice, particularly related to waste minimization.

- The UNEP Industry and Environment office in Paris has been the leader in the promotion of CP. It publishes a Cleaner Production newsletter and a range of related documents. The address is:

  UNEP IE
  Tour Mirabeau
  39-43 quai Andre Citroen
  75739 Paris CEDEX 15, France
  Telephone: 33-1-44-37-14-50
  Fax: 33-1-44-37-14-54

- World Bank work on CP in Asia has been coordinated through the CP unit in the Asia Technical Department. General advice on the implementation of CP can be obtained from the Environment Department through the Technology and Pollution Policy Unit.

## Notes

1. Reported figures for the textile industry in one South American country indicate that 38% of the plants have treatment systems installed but that more than half of these were not operating properly, reducing the effective share of plants with treatment to about 17%.

2. Examples include the Dutch PROGRES project, the World Bank China CP project, and Norwegian/USAID programs in Central and Eastern Europe.

3. It is notable that the Norwegian CP program in Poland is reported to have put 20% of its effort into economic and financial training rather than technical analysis.

# Management of Hazardous Wastes

*Managing hazardous wastes is a growing concern in many countries. The long-term impacts and costs of improper disposal can be very high, and the emphasis must be on prevention. A comprehensive management system should include (a) policies, institutions, and effective regulations and (b) adequate and acceptable disposal facilities, either public or private. This chapter outlines the key elements of such a system.*

Improper disposal of hazardous wastes is an increasing problem in many developing countries. Typically, but not ideally, the first stages of pollution control focus on discharges into air and water, leaving a wide range of other materials that are poorly controlled. These materials include substances that pose serious threats to public health and the environment and that are considered hazardous under almost any definition. Examples include sludges from chemical plants, clinical wastes, contaminated oils, and metal-bearing wastes. Materials of particular concern are those that do not degrade quickly in the environment, such as metals and persistent chemicals, and that can pose a threat for long periods into the future.

Proper management and disposal of hazardous wastes is expensive, and therefore illegal dumping is common in many areas. The consequences include not only environmental degradation but also the undermining of legitimate waste management systems. Control of dumping is thus a key issue to be considered when designing and implementing regulations.

The World Bank can assist governments in designing and implementing hazardous waste management systems and in the provision of appropriate treatment and disposal facilities, often with the involvement of the private sector.

## Scale of the Problem

### Definitions

Hazardous waste can be defined in a number of ways including:

- Hazardous characteristics (e.g., toxicity and flammability)
- Certain toxic components (e.g., PCBs and arsenic)
- Types of materials (e.g., organic solvents and explosives)
- Processes from which hazardous wastes originate, such as refining and clinical work
- Specific waste streams such as chemical wastewater treatment sludges.

Defining hazardous waste is difficult, but the establishment of a proper management framework in developing countries should not be delayed by debates about what constitutes a hazardous waste. Pragmatic working definitions can be adopted initially and refined as the system is developed.

Many countries adopt an inclusive approach that specifies which wastes are to be considered hazardous for regulatory purposes. Clearly, there have to be procedures for granting exceptions and for adding and deleting wastes.

### Estimates

Although for planning purposes it is necessary to estimate the total volume of waste produced, one should avoid putting too much effort into trying to refine numbers. Estimates are inherently unreliable, for several reasons. To begin with, recorded data on waste quantities are almost never available, and quantities have to be estimated on some basis such as number of firms, value of output, or number of employees. The coefficients for such estimates are very unreliable, and the resulting figures can vary by an order of magnitude. Even where estimated quantities are available, definitional questions can have a major impact. For example, wastes from mining or materials processing can often be a major portion of the total, and their reclassification can have a significant effect on the estimates of total "hazardous" wastes.

A related planning problem is the highly elastic nature of waste generation. Once real disposal costs are imposed on the generators through regulatory effort the reductions in waste quantities can be dramatic. Experience has shown that wastes delivered to treatment facilities have, in some cases, been only one third of the design estimates of wastes generated. This drop is ascribed to a combination of waste reduction and evasion of the regulatory system.

For practical purposes, estimates of quantities should be based on a relatively narrow definition, perhaps in terms of specific industries or process streams, and realistic allowance should be made for the effects of waste minimization.

## Policy and Regulation

Hazardous wastes are by their nature a threat to public health and the environment and therefore need to be regulated under the full force of the law. However, management of hazardous wastes is complex, and regulations must be developed within the context of a comprehensive policy that covers the responsibilities of different parties, methods for defining hazardous wastes, incentives to reduce quantities, education of waste generators and the public, the establishment of approved facilities (with particular concern for criteria for siting), and systems for controlling and monitoring the movement and disposal of hazardous wastes. Legislation on hazardous wastes should be coordinated with other related topics such as management of hazardous materials and industrial health and safety.

The establishment of a hazardous waste management system is often complicated by a "chicken and egg" problem: legislation may require disposal in approved facilities, but such facilities are expensive and will usually not be established until legislation and enforcement have demonstrated the scale of the "market" for proper disposal. In the initial stages, therefore,

industry may be in the position of having no realistic options for compliance with the law. Government policy must therefore address the problems of phasing in the new regulations, by assisting in the provision of some acceptable facilities or by licensing interim solutions.

## Basel Convention

There have been a number of cases of export of hazardous wastes from countries with strict regulations to those without similar controls, resulting in serious pollution problems in the receiving countries. This trade in hazardous wastes is now controlled under the Basel Convention (the Global Convention on the Control of Transboundary Movement of Hazardous Wastes, adopted at Basel in 1989). The convention also promotes the development of sound national management of hazardous wastes as a prerequisite for the control of transboundary movement.

## Components of a Management System

*Prevention*

Ideally, the generation of hazardous wastes should be avoided altogether. It is clear from experience in industrial countries with strong controls on hazardous wastes that it is possible to eliminate certain wastes and make major reductions in others. This is achieved by imposing the real costs of disposal on the generators, at which point the incentives for cleaner production and waste minimization become very strong. Where the production of the hazardous waste cannot be eliminated, action should be taken to reduce the hazardous characteristics by treatment or immobilization.

*Responsibility for Wastes*

Unfortunately, proper treatment and disposal is costly, while illegal dumping is very cheap and therefore profitable for illegal waste haulers. An effective control system is essential both to protect the environment from illegal dumping and to internalize the disposal costs to waste generators in an equitable way. The basic principle underlying control systems is that waste generators should be responsible for the final disposal of their wastes in an acceptable manner.

In practical terms, three different actors have to be considered in waste management: the generator, the disposal facility, and the transporter of the wastes between the first two. The law will normally put the responsibility on the generator, but there must be a system that allows the government to monitor the movement of wastes from the generator to approved disposal. Such a system normally consists of a number of elements. These include placing formal responsibility on the generator to prove its compliance with disposal requirements, licensing waste haulers and disposal facilities, and establishing a manifest system to track the movement of wastes.

In the design of a manifest system, care must be taken to provide sufficient control without generating excessive administrative or regulatory effort. The basic principle is that each load of waste is accompanied by a multicopy document that identifies the characteristics of the waste, the approved disposal facility, and the responsible companies or individuals. Copies of the manifest are held, at a minimum, by the generator and the disposal facility. The manifest can provide valuable information to the authorities about patterns and trends in waste generation and disposal and make possible confirmation of compliance with regulations.

### Storage of Hazardous Wastes

A hazardous waste management system should include regulations governing the storage of hazardous wastes at the generator's site or at any other transfer or disposal facility. In the absence of approved (or affordable) disposal options, it is common for generators or transporters to store wastes as a stopgap measure, but this approach can result in neglected piles of deteriorating wastes that pose significant hazards. It is not acceptable to allow generators to stockpile wastes over an extended period of time as a way of avoiding disposal problems.

### Treatment and Disposal Facilities

Hazardous waste facilities frequently comprise storage, recovery, and treatment stages, as well as final disposal. This allows the facility to take advantage of economies of scale and of opportunities to blend different waste streams and to recover some materials, particularly oils and solvents. Such a facility can be complex and needs proper management and supervision. Potential operators need to demonstrate the necessary technical, financial, and managerial capabilities before a license to operate is issued. Any discharges from the site to air or water need to be very closely controlled and monitored.

Final disposal is almost always incineration or landfill. (Since incineration generates an ash, which is normally landfilled, it is sometimes considered a treatment step rather than final disposal, but this distinction is not often important.)

### Incineration

Incineration involves the thermal destruction of gaseous, liquid, or solid wastes. Thermal oxidation converts complex organics into simple compounds, greatly reduces waste volumes, and can recover the heat content of wastes. Incineration requires relatively high temperatures (typically above 1,000°C), normally requires control of flue gases, and generates small quantities of ash or slag.

Hazardous waste incineration normally takes place in purpose-built facilities whose high capital and operating costs require significant throughputs for economic viability—typically, more than 10,000 metric tons a year. This required scale limits their feasibility in many newly industrializing countries.

Incineration is an accepted form of disposal for certain wastes in industrial countries, where careful gas cleaning and monitoring are required. Similar systems can be suitable for developing countries if adequate attention is given to the management and monitoring aspects.

Successful incineration requires good design and careful operation. The key operational characteristics are temperature, residence time, and turbulence in the combustion chamber, all of which affect the efficiency of destruction. A poor installation can emit particulates, acidic gases, unburned wastes, and trace quantities of hazardous organic by-products. Some wastes, such as PCBs, require careful control to ensure, for example, that minimum temperatures are maintained.

Selected wastes can be incinerated in high-temperature process plants such as cement kilns. However, the waste stream must be limited to those wastes for which full destruction can be ensured and no unacceptable residues are emitted.

### Landfills

The final disposal for many hazardous wastes or their treated residues is controlled land disposal. However, a properly located, engineered, and operated hazardous waste landfill is a major facility, not to be confused with the uncontrolled or open dumping that frequently occurs. Such controlled or "secure" landfilling should be used only for the minimal quantities of remaining wastes after all possible reduction and treatment have been carried out.

The main environmental threat of a landfill is water pollution. A landfill should be sited where the geological and hydrological characteristics are least likely to allow impacts on groundwater or surface water.

A well-designed, secure landfill is normally divided into a number of cells to allow for better control of operations and to allow segregation of incompatible wastes. The landfill is lined, often with a double or even triple lining, and has leachate collection facilities and groundwater monitoring systems. The design should include provisions for the closure and long-term monitoring of the site. Operation of the landfill should include requirements for pretreatment and containment of wastes, control and recording of the burial of different waste types, planning and preparation for spills and accidents, and regular monitoring of the surrounding environment.

The joint disposal of domestic and certain selected industrial wastes in a properly designed and operated municipal landfill may be acceptable as an interim measure or where investigations have demonstrated that the wastes involved are compatible. (For example, waste motor oils or some sludges may be acceptable.) However, such joint disposal should be carefully controlled with regard to the type and quantities of industrial wastes and should not be used as a cheap alternative to proper management of these wastes.

## Development of a Hazardous Waste Management Plan

The key steps in a systematic approach to developing a national hazardous waste management plan can be summarized as follows. (For further details, see Batstone, Smith, and Wilson 1989.)

- Define the scope.
- Define the objectives and constraints.
- Formulate the key questions to be addressed.
- Collect the necessary information.
- Prepare a technical assessment of appropriate available technologies.
- Review the existing situation and develop a short list of critical problems and the technical options.
- Prepare a number of alternative management plans, based on the preferred technical options.
- Conduct review, discussion, and feedback.
- Make decisions and carry out implementation and regular monitoring and adjustment.

## Economic Justification of Hazardous Waste Management Programs

Given the amount of public attention focused on hazardous wastes, it is surprising how little is known about the nature and scope of the risks involved. While the *potential* risks to public health from exposure may be significant, not much is known about the *actual* risks to public health. There is a significant lack of epidemiologic dose-response data linking the level of exposure to various toxins in the ambient environment with human health impacts. The lack of solid data on risks will continue to limit our understanding of the benefits of hazardous waste regulation. Very few studies or formal risk assessments have been conducted in the vicinity of abandoned or currently operating facilities. In addition, examples of significant and direct health impacts from hazardous wastes are limited (examples are Minimata disease, Itai-itai, and pesticide poisonings). While the risks to human health are difficult to calculate, some damages can be more clearly associated with hazardous wastes, such as the loss of value in contaminated land and the loss of productive water supply aquifers.

Uncertainty about risks causes uncertainty about regulatory benefits. The current limited knowledge of the chronic health effects of low exposure to many hazardous wastes makes it virtually impossible to estimate the benefits of reducing the impacts. One economic justification of a hazardous waste management program is the benefits in terms of future cleanup costs avoided. However, given the uncertainty about the location and extent of future damage and about the rules for the level of cleanup that might be required, the estimation of benefits is extremely uncertain. In fact, numbers from the U.S. experience show that benefits in these cases are more often low than high. It is difficult to compare hazardous wastes with other environmental problems for which it is easier to estimate benefits in terms of overall reduction of risk to public health.

An economics-based approach to managing hazardous wastes takes advantage of incentives to reduce risks while balancing the costs and benefits of doing so. One way of achieving this is to tailor requirements to reflect the wide variations in the risks of different waste types, disposal sites, and exposure conditions (rather than regulating facilities at the same level), and concentrating resources on the worst risks first.

### Siting: A Critical Issue

The location of a hazardous waste facility requires careful consideration of a wide range of technical, economic, and social factors. It is often a controversial process because of local opposition. Many schemes have been delayed or abandoned because of difficulties in obtaining an acceptable site. The government obviously has a role in leading the siting process and ensuring that clear information is provided, that there is a process for taking local concerns into account, and that realistic commitments are made about control and monitoring of operations. An environmental assessment will normally be required, depending on the type, scale, and location of facility being proposed.

### Financing and Funding

Proper management, treatment, and disposal of hazardous wastes are costly; and there are strong incentives for generators and transporters to avoid paying the real costs. In practice, it has normally been difficult to implement a realistic system of charges for hazardous wastes without a strong enforcement regime, which is itself rare. The consequence is that it is almost impossible, especially in the early stages of a new system, to generate an adequate revenue stream to cover the costs of the necessary facilities. In the absence of a reliable revenue stream, it is difficult to finance the capital investment required. The lack of an effective system for imposing costs on generators also undermines any financial incentive to adopt waste reduction measures. International experience indicates that integrated hazardous waste treatment facilities are typically not commercially viable except in well-regulated industrial countries.

Without a credible government-driven market for hazardous waste management infrastructure, it is difficult to expect investment by industry or the financial sector in this area. In this case, a transition period of blended incentives ("carrots") and disincentives ("sticks") can be used, as has been the case in many OECD countries and, more recently, in Asia. Subsidized seed capital and targeted credit, for a limited period of time, can help ease the adjustment of industries to a tighter regulatory environment as they face one-time adjustment costs and can strengthen the environmental services industry's ability to provide services for hazardous waste management.

### Role of the Private Sector

The overall design and implementation of a hazardous waste management program is normally a government function, but the private sector can play a major role in the provision and operation of the necessary facilities. Transport of wastes is nearly always a private sector function, although careful control and licensing by the relevant authorities may be required.

The design, construction, and operation of treatment and disposal facilities are frequently carried out by the private sector. However, particularly in the early stages of a hazardous waste management program, government involvement may be required in the siting and initial development of key facilities. In most cases, some practical demonstration of government commitment to regulation of waste generators and haulers may be required to convince the private sector to invest in major facilities.

## Remediation

A national or regional hazardous waste management plan should identify existing hazardous waste dumps, illegal sites, and areas contaminated by toxic or hazardous materials. However, the costs of remediation can be high, and careful assessments of the benefits should be carried out before any commitments are made to spend public funds on cleanup.

Experience with high cleanup standards in the United States and the Netherlands has shown that the result can be very costly projects without correspondingly high benefits. An alternative approach is to design cleanup to meet the requirements for realistic subsequent land uses.

## Scale and Costs of Facilities

Some indicative values can be given for the scale and cost of typical facilities.

The construction costs for a secure hazardous waste landfill will obviously depend on the size, but a facility capable of accepting 100,000 metric tons (t) per year would probably cost US$3 million–$8 million for initial construction. The planning, siting, and permitting processes can add 10–20% to this cost.

The economic minimum size for an integrated facility (treatment, incineration, and landfill) is probably of the order of 20,000–40,000t/year capacity. Such a facility would cost US$20 million–$50 million to construct (say US$1,000–$1,500 per metric ton capacity) and would require revenues of perhaps US$500–$1,000/t for profitable operation. In practice, such facilities are not usually commercially successful outside well-regulated industrial countries. For example, Hong Kong (China) has developed a successful large, high-

technology facility, but it operates at a low level of cost recovery.

More successful approaches are based on simpler facilities to deal with a somewhat limited range of wastes. One such site with a stabilization system and secure landfill, together with the facilities for burning waste oil in a cement plant, is reported to have cost US$20 million for a total capacity of 70,000t/y (about US$300 per metric ton capacity).

## A Road Map

Development of a hazardous waste management system is a complex and time-consuming task, but experience suggests a number of steps:

- There must be the political will to impose the costs on the generators, through enforcement or other persuasive mechanisms.
- Start by dealing with the simpler problems for which there are well-established technical solutions
- Address the siting problem early—it is very difficult for the private sector to obtain sites without government involvement in the selection process. Where possible, use existing sites, as long as they are technically and environmentally acceptable.
- Be skeptical about projections of quantities; design a flexible system. Support waste reduction and recycling efforts.
- Focus on prevention of dumping; remediation of contaminated sites is usually a second priority.

## Reference and Sources

Basel Convention. 1994. "Framework Document on the Preparation of Technical Guidelines for the Environmentally Sound Management of Wastes Subject to the Basel Convention." Document 94/005. Secretariat of the Basel Convention, Geneva.

Batstone, Roger, James E. Smith, and David Wilson, eds. 1989. *The Safe Disposal of Hazardous Wastes: The Special Needs and Problems of Developing Countries.* World Bank Technical Paper 93. 3 vols. Washington, D.C.

IMO (International Maritime Organization). 1995. "Global Waste Survey: Final Report." Draft. London.

UNEP (United Nations Environment Programme). 1992. "Hazardous Waste Policies and Strategies: A Training Manual." UNEP Industry and Environment Programme, Technical Report 10. Paris. (Also available in French and Spanish.)

WHO (World Health Organization). 1983. "Management of Hazardous Waste: Policy Guidelines and Code of Practice." Regional Publications, European Series 14. WHO Regional Office for Europe, Copenhagen.

# Pollutant Release and Transfer Registers

*A Pollutant Release and Transfer Register (PRTR) is a tool that can augment government efforts to achieve integrated environmental management and promote pollution prevention. PRTRs are part of a new cooperative approach to environmental management involving governments, industry, and the public. All three groups can use the information generated in a PRTR to improve efficiencies, monitor environmental policy, initiate cleaner production, and reduce waste. Although this approach is now being implemented in several industrial countries, the relative novelty of PRTR means that the uses and benefits of these programs in developing countries are still unfolding.[1]*

A PRTR is an environmental database or inventory of potentially harmful releases to air, water, and soil, as well as of wastes transported to treatment and disposal sites. Facilities releasing one or more of the substances must report periodically on what was released, the quantities involved, and to which environmental media. Some PRTR systems include estimates of diffuse releases, such as those from transport and agriculture. Most national schemes make PRTR data available to all interested parties.

Several OECD members have established or are developing a PRTR system: Australia, Canada, the Czech Republic, France, the Netherlands, Mexico, Switzerland, the United Kingdom, and the United States. One of the earliest and best-known systems is the U.S. Toxic Release Inventory (TRI), which in 1993 included more than 23,000 industries. In September 1996, the European Union approved an amendment to the Integrated Pollution Control Directive requiring all member states to implement a pollutant emissions register. Each PRTR system is developed according to national (sometimes regional and local) goals and objectives, and no two systems are the same, even though many features are similar. Each PRTR responds to the conditions and priorities within the specific country. The design and operation therefore differ, but there are many commonalties between national PRTR systems.

## What Are the Benefits of a PRTR?

Establishing a PRTR can lead to a number of benefits. However, it is important to note that governments, the private sector, and the public derive different benefits and uses from a PRTR system, and these depend strongly on the goals, objectives, design, and operation of the specific system.

Among the possible benefits are the following:

- A PRTR allows governments to develop environment strategies and identify priorities by providing baseline information about the pollution burden.
- It allows governments to monitor progress on achieving pollution or chemical reduction objectives and to identify trends over time.
- It helps firms identify material loss and stimulates more efficient use of chemical substances.
- It allows more informed participation of the public in environmental decisionmaking by providing the public with information about hazardous chemicals and potential risks in their communities.
- It can help identify priority areas for the introduction of technologies for cleaner production and provide indicators for monitoring the success of such approaches.
- It can provide information to help in planning for possible emergencies.

- It provides a template for environmental reporting under EMSs such as ISO 14000. (If industries have already implemented auditing, monitoring, and reporting systems this will greatly facilitate their ability to do PRTR work cost-effectively.)
- It complements active industry programs such as responsible care.
- It offers companies the opportunity to lead by example; providing release and transfer information can change the public's image of a company and its response to the company's activities and allow workers and the public to be informed about the pollutant releases in their local environment.

It is important to bear in mind that the benefits achieved through PRTR do involve costs. As might be expected, the costs are highest at the outset, when the reporting facilities must identify what data to report; the government needs to collect, collate, organize and disseminate data; and the public accesses the outputs of the PRTR system.

Experience of OECD member countries with operating PRTR systems indicates that the costs to government and reporting firms are incurred during the first and second reporting cycles. After this initial outlay, costs for collecting, reporting, and collating the information drop considerably.

## Developing a PRTR System

### Guidance Manual for Governments

Under the auspices of the International Programme for Chemical Safety, the UN organization with responsibility for the development of PRTRs, the OECD developed a guidance manual for governments wishing to implement a PRTR system. A series of workshops attended by representatives from governments, industry, and NGOs culminated in the development of a manual setting forth basic principles for developing a PRTR and presenting a set of options for implementing an effective system. The next section highlights key aspects of the guidance manual.

### Basic Principles

Several basic principles underpin the establishment of an effective system. Governments wishing to implement a PRTR need to review and address each principle in the context of their own circumstances in order to develop a practical national PRTR system.

### Use of Data

The PRTR data should be used to promote prevention of pollution at the source, e.g., by encouraging the implementation of cleaner technologies.

National governments should use PRTR data to evaluate the progress of environmental polices and to assess the extent to which national environmental goals are being or can be achieved.

### Affected and Interested Parties

In devising a PRTR system, or when modifying existing systems, governments should consult affected and interested parties to develop a set of goals and objectives for the system, and to identify potential benefits, and to estimate the costs to firms that will have to report, to governments, and to society as a whole.

The results of the PRTR should be made accessible to all affected and interested parties on a timely and regular basis.

### PRTR System Characteristics

- PRTR systems should cover a realistic number of those substances that may be harmful to humans or to the environment into which the substances are released or transferred.
- PRTR systems should involve both the public and private sectors, as appropriate. A PRTR should include those facilities or activities that might release or transfer substances of interest and, if appropriate, should also include diffuse sources.
- To reduce duplicative reporting, PRTR systems should be integrated to the degree practicable with existing information sources such as licenses or operating permits.

- Both voluntary and mandatory reporting mechanisms for providing PRTR inputs should be considered with a view as to how best to meet national goals and objectives.
- The comprehensiveness of any PRTR in helping to meet environmental policy goals should be taken into account. For example, whether to include releases from diffuse sources ought to be determined by national conditions and the need for such data.
- Any PRTR system should undergo regular evaluation and have the flexibility to be altered by governments in response to the evaluations or to the changing needs of affected and interested parties.
- The data handling and management capabilities of the systems should allow for verification of data entries and outputs and be capable of identifying the geographic distribution of releases and transfers.
- PRTR systems should allow, as far as possible, for comparison of information and cooperation with other national PRTR data systems and for consideration of possible harmonization with similar international data bases.
- The entire process of the establishment, implementation, and operation of the PRTR system should be transparent, objective, and consultative.
- PRTR data are valuable to the general public only if they are interpreted and presented in a way that is understandable for nonspecialists.

## PRTR Design

A PRTR is an incremental process. Before embarking on the detailed design of a system, it is important to review national policy goals and objectives and then coordinate local and regional needs. As goals and objectives are developed, governments should ensure that the system is compatible with other key data systems in operation (e.g., a global information system, or GIS, that could help meet the primary objective of the PRTR). There are several key components to designing a PRTR, as listed in Box 1.

During the preparation of the OECD's PRTR guidance manual, a common set of data elements emerged that can be seen as the building blocks

---

**Box 1. Key Steps in the Design of a PRTR**

- Establish clear goals and objectives.
- Consult with interested and affected parties (stakeholders).
- Develop a list of potentially hazardous pollutants or chemicals.
- Define the scope of the system (who must report, to whom, how often, and so on).
- Define what will be reported (e.g., which pollutants or chemicals, point or diffuse sources, data to specify the location and type of facility, etc.).
- Analyze existing reporting requirements to identify how they can be used to attain PRTR objectives.
- Determine how claims of confidentiality will be handled.
- Develop data verification methods.
- Define resource needs for the program.
- Define a program review system that will allow updates and modifications to the system as it grows and advances.
- Formulate an information dissemination strategy.

---

**Box 2. Common Set of Data Elements**

- Name and address of reporting facility (and mailing address if different)
- Grid reference or latitude and longitude of reporting facility
- Activity identifier—e.g., Standard Industrial Classification (SIC) or four-digit International Standard Industrial Classification (ISIC) code
- Chemical name and identifier for each substance covered
- Amount released and amount transferred, in agreed units
- Time period covered by the report
- Claim for confidentiality for any of the data provided

---

for a national PRTR information system. These elements are listed in Box 2.

## The Case of Small and Medium-Size Enterprises

Frequently, SMEs make up 80–90% of all industrial establishments in a country. For example, in the European Union over 90% of all firms have fewer than 50 employees. Many SME operations are releasing large amounts of potentially hazardous pollutants into the environment as a result of their daily operations.

Countries with operating PRTR systems have developed different methods of handling SMEs at different levels. For example, Canada and the United States both have a reporting threshold: firms with 10 full-time employees or more must report PRTR data. In addition, there are thresholds for quantities of toxic chemicals released. The United Kingdom requires SMEs to report if they fall into a specific process or production category. These countries use a much simpler form for reporting of releases and transfers by SMEs, i.e., requiring coverage of only a subset of substances.

Whether or not SMEs are required to report, the inclusion of SME figures is important for establishing a national profile of potentially harmful releases and transfers. If it is decided that SMEs are not required to report, estimates of SME releases should be included in the PRTR to provide a better representation of the national situation.

## Future Work by the OECD

During 1997, the OECD Secretariat collected information on the costs to industry of reporting under different PRTR schemes. The OECD will be conducting a study of reporting firms to find out whether and to what extent a PRTR has affected pollution prevention or promoted cleaner technologies; to identify the costs of reporting under different PRTR regimes; and to analyze the role of a PRTR within the context of the EMS ISO 14000. Following the first phase of the study, in 1997, the OECD in 1998 held an international PRTR conference for governments, industry, NGOs, academics, and experts from around the world. The preliminary results of the 1997 study were one of the topics of the conference.

## Note

1. This chapter is based on a discussion paper prepared by the Environment Directorate of the OECD.

## Sources

Commission for Environmental Cooperation. 1996. "Putting the Pieces Together: The Status of Pollutant Release and Transfer Registers in North America." Quebec, Canada. Also available in Spanish and French (Web address: http://www.cec.org).

OECD (Organisation for Economic Co-operation and Development). 1996. "Pollutant Release and Transfer Registers: Guidance Manual for Governments." Paris.

# Environmental Funds

*Environmental funds are increasingly popular environmental financing mechanisms in developing and transition economies. The failure of governments to tackle environmental problems by putting in place incentive policies, environmental regulations, and enforcement mechanisms, as well as failures of the financial and capital markets to provide access to financing at reasonable terms, are typically the underlying reasons why special environmental financing mechanisms are established. Environmental funds, however, often only postpone rather than solve these problems, and they may contribute to existing distortions. This chapter provides guidance on approaches to dealing with environmental funds.*

## Main Categories and Characteristics of Environmental Funds

Environmental funds are earmarked financing mechanisms that may support a variety of environmental expenditures. Three main categories of environmental funds can be distinguished: earmarked tax funds (ETFs), directed credit funds (DCFs), and green funds (GFs).[1] Some examples of environmental funds are shown in Table 1.

### Earmarked Tax Funds

ETFs are created by governments that designate environmental taxes, charges, and other, mainly environment-related levies for special funds. Several countries (e.g., Poland and Russia) have attempted to set up a charge system to compensate for environmental damage and create incentives to change polluter behavior. In reality, however, charges are rarely high enough to significantly influence behavior. ETFs are extensively used in transition economies, where they have a broad range of environmental financing objectives, including nature and biodiversity conservation; environmental education and awareness building; environmental research and institution building; and public and private pollution abatement. Public and commercial financing functions are mixed in the operation of ETFs that typically provide grants and soft loans. They are usually set up as extrabudgetary funds functioning as part of the environment ministry or strongly influenced by it. ETFs often lack transparency, and the participation and influence of the main stakeholders in decision-making are limited.

### Directed Credit Funds

DCFs may be established as financial intermediaries by either donor organizations such as the World Bank or national governments. They are designed to finance small commercial or municipal pollution abatement projects by avoiding the transaction cost of direct financing.[2] DCFs typically operate on a revolving basis, often for a predetermined time period corresponding, for example, to the disbursement period of donor lending. They are commercial institutions with strong development goals aimed at correcting certain market, administrative, and regulatory failures. Donor lending is sometimes supplemented by the recipient government or other sources in order to soften onlending terms through grant elements, technical assistance, or better-than-market interest rates.

### Green Funds

GFs are typically capitalized at the initiative of external donors by one-time donor contributions or debt-for-nature swaps to finance expenditures

## Table 1. Examples of Environmental Funds

| *Example* | *Revenues* | *Main expenditures* | *Beneficiaries* | *Disbursement* |
|---|---|---|---|---|
| *Earmarked tax funds* | | | | |
| Hungary: Central Environmental Protection Fund | Fuel tax; product charges; traffic transit fee; pollution fines; EU PHARE grant | Air pollution abatement; waste management; water pollution control; public awareness building | Public transport companies; municipalities; industrial enterprises; research institutes | Grants; low-interest loans |
| Poland: National Fund for Environmental Protection and Water Management | Air and water pollution charges; water use and waste charges | Air and water pollution abatement; soil protection; environmental monitoring and education | Industrial enterprises, municipal companies, universities | Soft loans; loan guarantees, grants |
| Russia: Federal Environmental Fund | Pollution charges, fines | Pollution control; environmental R&D; institution building | Municipal companies; industrial enterprises; research institutes | Grants |
| *Directed credit funds* | | | | |
| China: Tianjin Industrial Pollution Control Fund | IDA credit; pollution charges | Waste reduction and recovery; pollution prevention (cleaner technology) | Industrial enterprises | Market-rate loans plus grant (10–30%) |
| Russia: Pollution Abatement Facility | IBRD loan | Waste recovery | Public and private industrial enterprises | IBRD rate plus 400 basis points |
| Slovenia: Eco-Fund | Budget allocation; IBRD loan | Urban pollution abatement | Households; cooperatives; commercial and industrial enterprises; municipalities | London interbank offered rate (LIBOR) plus 200 basis points |
| *Green funds* | | | | |
| Bolivia: FONAMA | Debt-for-nature swaps by international NGOs; foreign government contributions | Support to protected areas in nature conservation | Local communities; NGOs | Grants |
| Colombia: ECOFONDO | Debt-for-nature swaps; NGOs; foreign governments | Nature protection; environmental education; integrated watershed management | NGOs; local groups | Grants |

in nature and biodiversity protection, most often providing grants to cover the recurrent costs of operating national parks and small community-based programs.[3] The willingness of industrial countries to contribute to GFs is strengthened by the benefits of investment in nature conservation that accrue outside the boundaries of countries where such investments are undertaken. A popular form of GFs is trust funds that utilize only the revenues of invested funds, leaving the principal intact. Many GFs have successfully pooled revenues from various donor sources. In some cases, domestic sources, such as royalties and ecotourism revenues, also accrue to the fund. The design of GFs usually requires transparency of spending and decisionmaking and the participation of the main stakeholders such as NGOs and community groups.

## Conceptual Issues

Environmental funds are financing mechanisms established to solve the problem of "insufficient funding" for environmental projects. Although dysfunctional and underdeveloped financial and capital markets, unsolved collateral issues, high transaction costs, and insufficient information often limit access to financing in developing and transition economies, such constraints are not unique to environmental investments. Financial system weaknesses affect all investments in the economy, but the key financial constraints on environmental investments are typically on the demand side. Some of these constraints are:

- The failure of governments to tackle environmental problems by putting into place proper incentive policies, environmental regulations and enforcement
- Low political priority attached to the environment in government budgeting
- Uncertainties about environmental regulations and the low perceived likelihood of serious penalties for violating regulations
- Limited knowledge and expertise available to municipalities, local groups, and enterprises for identifying solutions to environmental problems, using alternative funding sources, and preparing projects for financing
- Sluggish response of polluters to incentives as a result of the dominance of the public sector
- Slow change in traditional enterprise decision-making, capital budgeting, and accounting practices that traditionally exclude environmental considerations.

## Key Lessons from Practical Experience

Raising awareness of environmental problems has been one of the main benefits of environmental funds. Donors have used their financial leverage successfully during the establishment of several green funds, for example, by requiring matching funds and government commitment to policy reform. ETFs have facilitated the introduction of environmental taxes, establishing the framework for incentive environmental policies

and raising enterprise awareness of environmental costs.

Environmental funds are generally better suited to addressing "green" (nature and biodiversity protection) than "brown" (pollution abatement) issues. The use of public funds to finance environmental expenditures is justified when benefits cannot be allocated to private economic agents or public financing is more efficient than private. Most green environmental expenditures fall into this category because of their global and transgenerational benefits. By contrast, pollution is a negative externality that can be tackled most effectively by making polluters internalize the social costs of pollution. The use of public funds to support pollution abatement should therefore be temporary, targeted to areas where it can accelerate environmental improvements and the adjustment of behavior to changing environmental regulations.

Because of the fundamental differences in the nature of various categories of environmental funds, they do not mix easily. Donors, for example, have not considered most ETFs suitable channels for their financial resources. The World Bank decided to capitalize new DCFs in several countries (e.g., China and Russia) despite existing ETFs. There are many reasons for such incompatibility, including: conceptual problems in using earmarked tax revenues for primarily commercial lending; lack of financial and banking expertise in ETFs; a too broadly defined mandate of ETFs; lack of transparency and accountability in the operation of ETFs; and limited willingness of ETFs to accommodate donor requirements.

Financing through environmental funds will be effective only if the underlying reasons for the environmental problems are simultaneously tackled at the policy level. Most environmental problems are the result of regulatory and market failures such as price subsidies for energy and fertilizers, underpriced natural resources, undefined property rights, and the failure of environmental regulations and enforcement to force the internalization of the social costs caused by environmental damage. Without policy reform to accompany the operation of environmental funds, environmental problems re-create themselves, and environmental funds postpone the introduction of sustainable solutions.

Without strengthened environmental regulations and enforcement, environmental funds send the wrong messages and contribute to existing distortions. Subsidies to remedy environmental problems and to provide public environmental services may reward and attract environmentally damaging practices, lead to postponement of environmental improvements in expectation of support, and crowd out commercial financing. Only a carrot-and-stick approach that simultaneously rewards improved practices and strengthens environmental policies, regulation, and enforcement can ensure the positive role of environmental funds.

Environmental funds can more effectively contribute to finding sustainable solutions to environmental problems if attention is paid to building self-financing capacities and tackling the causes of financial constraints. Environmental funds should therefore focus on eliminating such constraints as lack of information about alternative ways to achieve environmental improvements, limited access to commercial financing, and lack of cost recovery.

Without a clear spending strategy and eligibility and project selection criteria based on cost-effective solutions to environmental priorities, the allocation of financial resources becomes suboptimal and wasteful. Environmental funds should therefore have links to the environmental policymaking body to obtain guidance for spending priorities.

Transparency and accountability in the operation of environmental funds are essential for avoiding ad-hoc political influence and mismanagement of public funds. Mechanisms for the participation of the main stakeholders in the decisionmaking of environmental funds not only contribute to the transparency of fund operations but also build local capacity to identify and implement environmental projects. Capacity-building has been especially strongly emphasized and successfully carried out by green funds.

## Checklist for World Bank Projects

Before agreeing to a government request to use World Bank resources to support an existing environmental fund or set up a new one, it is rec-ommended that World Bank staff consider policy issues, design issues, onlending criteria, and measures to be avoided.

### Policy Issues

- Examine or identify the environmental priorities of the borrowing country.
- Identify steps and measurable indicators of strengthened environmental policies.

### Design Issues

- Evaluate the pros and cons of direct versus intermediary lending alternatives.
- If intermediary lending is justified because of the high transaction cost of reaching a large number of small borrowers, assess the following choices of intermediaries: the banking sector; an existing environmental fund; and a new environmental fund. The default should be onlending through the banking sector rather than establishing new institutions and full-blown environmental funds. For environmental funds designed to address pollution abatement, establish a schedule for phasing out the environmental fund tied to monitorable improvements in environmental regulations and enforcement.
- Onlending is best introduced on a pilot basis, and a thorough economic analysis of the impacts should be carried out after the initial phase of operation.

### Onlending Criteria

- Define clear criteria for project selection based on environmental priorities.
- Instead of softening the financing conditions of onlending, give preference to assistance in eliminating the main constraints on financing. Possible areas for support include financing environmental audits to identify low-cost solutions to environmental problems and alternatives for improving environmental performance; providing technical assistance in appraising and preparing loan applications for environmental projects; and disseminating information about available technologies and best practices.

- If softening the final credit terms of subprojects becomes necessary to target existing pollution sources, credit-plus-grant schemes are usually preferable to subsidized interest rates because of transparency and other considerations.
- Financial performance indicators should be at least as strict as indicators used in commercial lending.
- Eligibility for grants has to be linked to noninternalized environmental benefits expected from subprojects.
- Clear and measurable environmental performance indicators have to be agreed on, and grants should be converted to credit at market terms if a borrower does not comply with these indicators.
- Grant allocation should be transparent, and the people and institution in charge of the grant facility should be held accountable for the proper handling of funds. The participation of NGOs or community groups in the design of the program and in the monitoring of implementation is highly desirable.

*To Be Avoided*

- Setting up an onlending program with soft credit terms for pollution abatement when significant improvement in environmental regulations and enforcement cannot be expected or enterprise management is nonresponsive
- Financing pollution abatement projects at soft terms without clear objectives for environmental quality improvements and strong links of subproject financing to these improvements.

## Notes

1. The term *environmental fund* is also used to denote investment funds that specialize in environmentally friendly industries and services. This chapter does not deal with this type of funds.

2. In a broader sense, social funds also belong to this category insofar as they finance basic environmental services such as waste disposal and sanitation. Although social funds often have environment-related expenditures, their primary objectives are to alleviate poverty and provide a social safety net targeting the poor.

3. Debt-for-nature swaps are debt-conversion programs in which either an international NGO purchases commercial debt of a developing country on the secondary market at a discount, or official debt is forgiven by lender governments in exchange for the debtor country's commitment to spend an equal or agreed amount on nature protection. Commercial debt-for-nature swaps typically establish green funds; environmental funds created by official debt-for-nature swaps have broader environmental objectives.

## Sources

Lovei, Magda. 1995. *Financing Pollution Abatement: Theory and Practice.* World Bank Environment Department Paper 28. Washington, D.C.

Mikitin, K. 1994. "Issues and Options in the Design of GEF-Supported Trust Funds for Biodiversity Conservation." World Bank, Environment Department, Washington, D.C.

OECD (Organisation for Economic Co-operation and Development). 1995. *Environmental Funds in Economies in Transition.* Paris.

Spergel, B. 1993. "Trust Funds for Conservation." Draft. World Wildlife Fund, Washington, D.C.

# Pollution Charges: Lessons from Implementation

*Pollution charges are becoming an increasingly popular instrument for environmental policy. Currently, they are widely applied in OECD countries, they play a key role among environmental policy instruments in most transition economies, and they are being introduced in developing countries, particularly in Latin America and East Asia. Many recent World Bank environmental projects propose using pollution charges. Economic instruments have a theoretical advantage over uniform command-and-control (CAC) regulations because of their greater flexibility and cost-effectiveness. However, the performance of poorly designed pollution charge programs may not demonstrate measurable economic and environmental benefits. This chapter provides some guidance on setting charges and designing an effective program.*

Pollution charges exist in various forms, as described in Box 1. They can be imposed on emissions or products; they can be levied as a fee for service or as a fine for noncompliance; and they can be collected as separate payment or as part of a broader levy, such as a locally defined water use tariff or national energy tax.

Pollution charges can be levied on actual source emissions (*direct* emissions charge), estimated emissions (*presumptive* emissions charge), or products whose use or disposal is linked to pollution (*product* charge or tax). While the direct charge is most straightforward, the difficulty of systematically measuring discharges limits its possible application and may give a comparative advantage to indirect instruments, such as fuel taxes or water charges. Indirect pollution charges assume a certain connection between the tax base and the amount of pollution. The problem with these charges is that if the connection is not straight or strong enough, the incentive signals may be distorted or insufficient.

The design of pollution charge programs entails many compromises between the advantages and shortcomings of direct and indirect instruments. For example, indirect charges based on fuel use or water consumption can very closely approximate the direct pollution charge when supplemented with rebates according to actual source emissions.

Whereas the theoretical advantage of pollution charges is in their incentive impact, it is their revenue-raising function that often makes this instrument appealing to environmental policymakers. At the same time, it may require changes in legislation to allow additional taxes that may then give rise to political opposition. In this situation, user charges (payments for services rendered) or earmarking of charges for specific environmental expenditure often becomes more politically acceptable.

## Summary of Implementation

User and product charges are most common in OECD countries. Most of the charges (apart from tax differentiation) are introduced to raise revenue. Where an incentive impact was intended, there is little evidence of actual incentive effects of emissions and product charges (except for Sweden). This is partly because of a lack of systematic evaluation and partly because when the charge is applied in conjunction with other policy instruments, the data on incentive impacts are inconclusive. A number of pollution charge programs were operated on a temporary basis and were subsequently modified or abolished. Overall, the OECD approach was to incorporate the costs of pollution into water charges and fuel taxes as a way of charging for emissions.

---

**Box 1. Typology of Pollution Charges**

Pollution charges fall into several major categories.

*Emission, or effluent, charges* are charges on emissions to the environment (air, water, or soil). In principle, they are based on the quantity and toxicity of discharged pollutants. In practice, emissions charges can be levied on:

- Actual source emissions that are directly metered, for example, Sweden's nitrogen oxide ($NO_x$) charge
- A proxy of source emissions that may be derived from prespecified technical characteristics or from input quantities that correlate with emissions. For instance, water consumption commonly serves as a proxy for wastewater emissions.
- Discharge sources in the form of a flat rate, commonly applied to households and small firms for municipal waste and wastewater charges.

*User charges*—payments for the costs of collective or public treatment of effluents—are one form of emissions charges. They may be based on the amount or quality of effluent treated, on water usage, or on uniform tariffs.

*Product charges* are charges or taxes on products that are polluting in the manufacturing, consumption, or disposal phase. These charges can be based on some characteristics of the product (e.g., a charge on sulfur content in mineral oil in Norway and Sweden) or on the product itself (mineral oil charge in a number of OECD countries).

In practice, product charges may take the form of *tax differentiation* that creates more favorable market conditions for "cleaner" products and less favorable conditions for polluting products. Because tax differentiation is meant primarily as an incentive, it usually operates in a fiscally neutral manner. Other product charges can be designed to be revenue raising as well.

*Administrative charges,* such as control and authorization fees and payments for administrative services (licensing, registering, etc.), are not considered here.

*Sources:* OECD 1991; Opschoor et al. 1994.

---

In developing countries and transition economies, emissions and effluent charges are the most common economic instruments used in environmental policy. However, in most of the cases where charges have been implemented so far, they were set at very low levels and, although intended to provide an incentive, had little impact on the behavior of polluters. Furthermore, because these charges have often not been systematically enforced, their revenue-raising capabilities have been limited. One exception is Poland, where the revenues have been significant and where some incentive effects have been achieved.

**Lessons Learned: What Works and When**

Economic instruments can make environmental policies based on CAC regulations more cost-effective (Tietenberg 1992). Yet poorly designed pollution charge programs may not achieve tangible results. The evidence from cross-country experience emerging in recent years, although not yet sufficient for a complete analysis and comprehensive conclusions, allows for a number of recommendations on how to design an effective pollution charge program for various types of charges (see Box 2 for examples of successful programs).[1]

*Emissions Charges in Practice: Key Observations*

In theory, emissions charges, set at the level of marginal environmental damage or abatement costs, are the best way to internalize the social costs of pollution and change the behavior of economic agents (Baumol and Oates 1988). The realities of implementation, however, impose significant constraints on the effective use of this instrument.

*Emissions charges are more effective when they are set at a high level* for a limited number of pollutants and sources rather than at a low level for a great number of pollutants and sources. Charges can be increased gradually, with rate increases scheduled in advance, to allow industries to make timely adjustments. The ultimate level of charges should be sufficient to provide an incentive for a targeted level of pollution abatement in an area or watershed over a designated period of time.

Low emissions charges, which are introduced with the primary purpose of raising funds, have not proved to have a comparative advantage in relation to other charges or taxes, given the higher

---

**Box 2.  Examples of Application: What Works, and Why**

*Example 1: Water Pollution Charge in the Netherlands.* The rate of the Dutch water pollution charge is determined by the revenue required for sewage treatment and for maintaining and improving water quality in general. The charge is implemented by the water boards—self-governing bodies of surface water users responsible for water management. The charge is based on biochemical oxygen demand (BOD) and (in most cases) heavy metal pollution. It is levied on all direct and indirect discharges. Households and small firms pay a fixed amount. According to the research done on this issue, there has been an incentive effect for large firms that are actually metered, including the agricultural sector, especially livestock production.

*Why does it work?*

- The level of the charge is rather high and is aimed at providing full cost recovery of sewage treatment.
- The charge base is directly linked to pollution load (for large firms).
- The charge program is decentralized and transparent for water users.

*Example 2: Sulfur Tax in Sweden.* The Swedish tax is levied on the sulfur content of diesel fuel and heating oil that exceeds a threshold of 0.1%. The tax, which is a product charge, approximates an emissions charge and is repayable if a taxpayer can demonstrate an actual reduction of emissions of sulfur oxides. An official evaluation indicates that the sulfur content of oil decreased nearly 30% between 1990 and 1992 as a result of the tax and that emissions from burning coal and peat also considerably decreased. The tax promoted cleaning flue gases to a larger degree than before, but emissions have also been reduced by substituting among fossil fuels. The carbon dioxide tax provides an additional incentive for substitution. Administrative costs are somewhat less than 1% of revenue.

*Why does it work?*

- The tax level is high.
- A transparent rebate scheme strengthens the incentive effect of the tax.
- The design of the program provides for easy implementation and low administrative costs. The burden of proving the actual emissions level is imposed on polluters.

*Source:* Opschoor et al. 1994.

---

administrative complexity and costs. This is especially relevant for air emissions.

Emissions charges can be effectively applied to a very limited number of standard pollutants that are (a) emitted by many various sources with different costs of abatement, (b) controlled by commonly available technologies, and (c) relatively easy to measure by conventional methods. The examples are, for water, biochemical oxygen demand (BOD) and phosphates and, for air, total suspended particulates (TSP), sulfur oxides ($SO_x$), and nitrogen oxides ($NO_x$). Carbon dioxide ($CO_2$), which is affected by a change in fuel rather than a change in burning technology, is more suitable for a product charge, i.e., a carbon tax on fuel.

*Emissions charges can be effectively applied to a relatively limited number of the most significant sources* (except for user charges, which are applicable to all sources). Criteria for selecting sources include (a) feasibility of systematic monitoring or inspection, (b) potential for technical innovation, and (c) financial viability (ability to respond

by adopting new technologies or improving operation and maintenance).

A good example is *air emissions charges*, which are most suited for large stationary sources. For instance, the Swedish $NO_x$ charge and the French air pollution charge are levied on a limited category of burning installations with capacity over 10 megawatts (MW) and 20 MW, respectively. In the case of significant air pollution from diffuse sources such as vehicles or households using coal for space heating, product charges (for example, taxes on gasoline or heating fuel) may be a good proxy.

*Upper-bound presumptive charges that are adjusted for those polluters that demonstrate a lower level of actual emissions can moderate monitoring and enforcement problems.* Under this scheme, polluters are motivated to monitor and report their emissions, while an implementing agency supervises self-reporting with random inspections and stiff penalties for false emissions reports.

*Emissions charges achieved the best results when implemented as part of broader pollution control programs with clear ambient quality or emissions reduc-*

*tion targets.* Examples include effluent charges in France, Germany, and the Netherlands, an oil palm charge in Malaysia, and an $NO_x$ charge in Sweden. In most of these cases, charges were introduced to facilitate and speed up compliance with preannounced stricter emissions and effluent standards.

The qualities of emissions charges described above do not allow a strong case to be made for their unquestionable superiority over other possible environmental regulations of large sources. In principle, location- and source-specific emissions limits may be as cost-effective and provide similar flexibility to polluters. In this case, the choice between charges or limits (or their combination) for controlling large sources should mainly depend on the administrative feasibility of and political support for a particular program in each country.

The real advantage of pollution charges emerges when they can be used to control various sources, including a large number of small sources, where other policies and instruments are not applicable or are very expensive. Water charges and product taxes appear to have this advantage.

### Pollution Control with Water and User Charges

*A careful approach is required when designing effluent charges that would apply to small industries and households,* especially in developing countries where environmental objectives compete with the needs of industrial growth and poverty alleviation. Air emissions charges are typically not applicable to these two groups, but water effluent charges are. Households generate a very significant input to water pollution in urban areas. A user charge for municipal or collective wastewater treatment with differentiated tariffs for industries and households is one instrument in these cases. Where water usage is metered, a water charge itself may provide an incentive to reduce water use and the corresponding pollution. In addition, a pollution surcharge may be added to the regular water charge for those polluters that discharge more than an average amount within a given group of users. However, the distribution effect on large-size, low-income households has to be assessed and mitigated.

*User charges can be used to recover the costs of municipal or collective treatment plants and are appropriate in all cases where such treatment takes place.* The basic principles of designing an effective economic instrument of this type are as follows:

- There should be a differentiated approach to setting tariffs for industry, other big consumers, and households.
- Charges are based on pollution load or water usage where possible. This is especially relevant for industry and other big consumers.
- Tariffs are set at the level (on average) that provides full recovery of investment and operating costs.
- Full cost recovery is warranted only if the size of the public or collective treatment plant and the level of treatment adopted are defined on the basis of an extended economic analysis as part of optimizing wastewater treatment strategy in a watershed.

### Use of Product Charges and Fuel Taxes

Product charges are most widely imposed on fuels, as a proxy for an air pollution charge, and on products that can be recycled or that need to be safely disposed of. Unlike air emissions charges, fuel taxes can be used to control diffuse sources and are relatively easy to collect, given the possibility of using existing administrative and fiscal channels.

A product charge is the preferred instrument when:

- There is a strong connection between the use (or disposal) of the product and the amount of pollution, as in the case of fuel taxes.
- Pollution occurs at the consumption or disposal phase and is generated by a great number of small sources (e.g., gasoline engines and batteries).
- Pollution occurs at the manufacturing or power-generating phase and the discharge of the targeted pollutant depends on input characteristics rather than on abatement or process technology, as in the case of carbon taxes or, to some extent, sulfur taxes.

*Earmarking of Revenues*

If revenues from charges are earmarked for environmental expenditures, it is important to have a coherent, transparent, and accountable allocation system with clear financing objectives and priorities. One example is user charges for wastewater treatment or, in a broader context, effluent and user charges implemented by a basin organization to support a well-defined water quality improvement program. A fiscally neutral charge-rebate scheme such as the Swedish $NO_x$ charge is another example of a transparent earmarked program that facilitates the incentive effect of the charge. All revenues from the Swedish charge, imposed on actual $NO_x$ emissions of large power and heat producers, are rebated back to these producers on the basis of their final energy output. The incentive effect has been very significant. The charge-rebate scheme can also be implemented through the general budget.

## Recommended Steps in Designing a Pollution Charge Program

*Analyze the scope and impact of pollution and identify targeted areas and watersheds.* Cross-country experience shows that *emissions charges* are more widely applied to effluents than to air emissions, largely because of monitoring difficulties. Applying these charges to solid waste is least common, and user charges are most appropriate. The situation is reversed for product charges, which are most widely used to control air pollution and waste disposal. While effluent charges, especially user charges, tend to be a long-term instrument in environmental policy, air pollution charges are in many cases more appropriate as a temporary program to tackle a particular problem.

*Identify medium-specific priority pollutants that are of major concern in terms of ambient quality and health and environmental damage.* Sensitivity to abatement technologies, variation in abatement costs, availability of measuring and sampling techniques, correspondence between product use and discharge, and environmental impact of a certain pollutant are factors that determine the applicability and design of an economic instrument (see Table 1).

*Identify the major sources of pollution.* Different approaches are needed to deal with different categories of polluters, such as industries, utilities, vehicles, and households (see Table 1).

*Pay attention to the scope of pollution.* The spatial level of the pollution problem—local, subnational, national, regional, or global—affects approaches toward setting the charges and the related range of institutions and stakeholders involved. Pollution charges, and economic incentives in general, have an advantage where there is homogeneous pollution extending over a broad area. Decentralized pollution charge programs focusing on certain watersheds or saturated airsheds benefit from a simpler institutional arrangement, better accountability, and transparency for stakeholders. In these cases, establishing watershed agencies and air quality councils responsible for media-specific management in targeted areas, including pollution charge programs, is generally recommended. When the impacts of pollution are heavily localized or very harmful, pollution charges may be used only if combined with direct site-oriented regulations, such as requirements to install best controls, zoning, relocation, or a ban on highly toxic products.

*Scrutinize administrative costs.* Pollution charges, especially emissions charges, may reduce the costs of compliance for industries, but they increase administrative costs for the implementing agency, compared with command and control (CAC) regulations. When designing a specific pollution charge program, the costs associated with its implementation should be explicitly estimated and included in the comparative analysis of alternative policy instruments that can tackle the environmental problem. A special financial framework should be established that keeps the program accountable. Any measures to lower administrative costs by, for example, using existing fiscal channels to collect revenues or shifting the responsibility of systematic monitoring to polluters, should be taken to the greatest extent possible.

*Examine the existing fiscal system in the targeted area with respect to targeted pollution sources and try to identify pollution charge programs that would best fit into this system, so that administrative and en-*

**Table 1. Pollution Charges Typically Recommended for Different Pollutants and Sources**

| Source | Air pollutant | | | | Water pollutant | | |
|---|---|---|---|---|---|---|---|
| | Particu- lates | Sulfur oxides | Carbon dioxide | Lead | BOD | Phosphates | Metals |
| **Vehicles** | | | | | | | |
| Gasoline | | | Fuel tax | Fuel tax | | | |
| Diesel | Fuel tax | Fuel tax | Fuel tax | | | | |
| **Households and small enterprises** | Fuel tax | Fuel tax | Fuel tax | | User charge based on water use or flat rate | | |
| **Power and heat utilities** | Emissions charge or limit | Fuel tax or emissions charge | Fuel tax | | | | |
| **Industry** | | | | | | | |
| General | (Presumptive) emis- sions charges or limits | | Fuel tax | Emissions limits (plus charge) | | | |
| Connected to collective waste- water treatment plant | | | | | User charge (plus pollu- tion surcharge) based on water use; user charge based on pollutant load | | Emissions limits (plus charge) |
| Not connected to collective wastewater treatment plant | | | | | Effluent charge based on load or presumptive effluent charge based on water use | | Emissions limits (plus charge) |

*forcement costs are minimized.* If the fiscal system is undergoing or will undergo reform in the relevant sectors (e.g., introducing water charges, modifying energy taxes, etc.), "mainstream" the pollution charges into the broader reform process. That is, try to design pollution charges in such a way as to allow the sharing of institutional capacities and collection mechanisms with other new or modified fiscal instruments.

## Implementation Sequence Generally Recommended for Developing Countries

*Water pollution.* Start with locally imposed user charges, paying special attention to the distribution effects on small consumers and the metering of large industries, which ought to be charged on the basis of water usage or pollution load. Examine and assess institutional and legal options for introducing presumptive effluent charges (preferably based on water usage) for other significant sources that are not connected to public treatment plants.

*Air pollution.* Examine the possibilities of using existing fiscal channels for product charges. Consider designing, for specific pollution problems, focused programs that could be fiscally neutral (tax differentiation or charge-rebate schemes) Assess the changes that would be required in legislation, and give preference to programs that do not require major changes.

## Implementation: Other Important Lessons and Considerations

One of the key lessons is that pollution charges have little chance to be successful unless a certain macroeconomic and environmental policy framework is in place (see Box 3).

### Necessary Macroeconomic Conditions

*Competitive market.* In noncompetitive markets, the effects of pollution charges are reduced, since polluters, which operate either under "soft budget constraints" or as monopoly providers, can

---

**Box 3. Examples of Implementation Problems: Macroeconomic Aspects**

*Estonia.* Emissions charges were introduced in the centrally planned economy in the 1980s. Incentive effects were difficult to achieve even after independence and the course toward a market economy in the early 1990s, due to soft budget constraints for many enterprises that carried over their monopolistic status from the old regime. In addition, charges were constantly eroded by high inflation that made their real level very low. This situation was typical for many transition economies that were applying emissions charges in the early stage of economic reform.

*Poland.* Emissions charges were introduced in the 1970s, with the intention of influencing the behavior of polluters. Although the charge rates were increased several times during the central planning era, the effects were counterbalanced by the lack of financial motivation of economic actors, mainly state-owned enterprises. After the transition to a market economy started, the incentive effect of the charges, whose level was considerably increased and linked to an official inflation index, became far more significant.

*Sources:* Opschoor et al. 1994; Lovei 1995.

---

pass on costs to consumers with no pressure to look for alternative solutions.

*Well-developed market of environmental services offering alternative options.* Various control or cleaner technologies (in the case of emissions charges) and product or fuel substitutes with "cleaner" characteristics (in the case of product charges) should be easily available to polluters—a condition that is often missing in the domestic markets of developing countries and transition economies.

*General economic and political stability,* contributing to the effectiveness of pollution charges. An unstable situation works against economic incentives in environmental policy. First, it focuses decisionmaking on short-term goals and implies a higher discount rate of future savings as a result of pollution abatement investments. Second, it is usually accompanied by inflation that erodes charges unless an automatic revaluation mechanism is built in.

---

*Key Environmental Policy Issues*

In a country where environmental regulations are not enforced and environmental agencies are weak, economic instruments are not of much help either. Introducing pollution charges should go along with improving the overall environmental policy framework and strengthening the institutional capacities of environmental agencies. The following issues should be carefully considered before a pollution charge program is implemented (see Boxes 4 and 5 for examples of problems in this area).

*Legal basis.* Legislation should be carefully examined and brought into harmony with the implementation of pollution charges.

*Political commitment.* The support of the entire government is important for any innovative policy program.

*Consensus among stakeholders.* There is an increasing recognition that consensus among

---

**Box 4. Implementation Problems: Lack of Legal and Political Support**

*Argentina.* In 1980, Argentina attempted to introduce a discharge fee for industrial effluents. The tariff included a fee for discharges within the maximum allowable level and a much higher penalty for discharges above the maximum allowable threshold. There were provisions for increasing the level of fees gradually over 10 years, up to the level of treatment costs, and for granting transitory waivers for up to 2 years where enterprises were in the process of implementing abatement measures. In practice, the fees were never applied on a wide basis, and the system was modified in 1989 to lower the level of fees and to revise the penalties. Environmental groups sued the government on the grounds that the fee system amounted to a license to pollute beyond legal limits. The court declared the decree that introduced the fees unconstitutional, and the issue remains confused in legal terms. It appears that the court regarded the fee as exceeding the powers of the national government to levy taxes and concluded that it could not be justified as payment for a service.

*Source:* von Amsberg 1995.

**Box 5. Implementation Problems: Lack of Institutional and Enforcement Capacity**

*Russia.* The national emissions charge system introduced in 1991 is a combination of emissions charges and noncompliance penalties allocated in a network of earmarked environmental funds. The system is similar to those in many other newly independent states. The charges, which are set at a very low level, are levied on over 300 air and water pollutants and a large number of stationary sources. Available capacities of reliable monitoring and inspection fall well short of what is needed. There is neither a special staff training program nor a special implementation program. Although the central body of the environment ministry formally governs the program, including guidelines to calculate fees and set the permitted levels of discharges, negotiated agreements between polluters and local authorities determine the collection of the charges. The common practice is to waive the fees on the amount enterprises invest in pollution control or to exempt from payment polluters experiencing financial problems, using contradictions in the legislation. Currently, collection rates are low, and no coherent approach to spending revenues exists.

*Source:* NAPA 1994.

major stakeholders, such as environmental agencies, industries on which pollution charges are imposed, and communities exposed to pollution, plays a decisive role in implementing environmental policies. Public awareness and participation, including pressure on governments through NGOs, can be a powerful enforcement tool.

*Institutional capacity of the implementing agency.* The failure to build an adequate institutional capacity is one of the main constraints on implementing pollution charges. The staffing and structure of the implementing agency have to differ significantly from those of agencies operating CAC instruments. Where environmental problems have been successfully managed by CAC regulations, it may be worthwhile first applying an economic instrument to new problems not yet tackled by traditional CAC methods. In a developing country without a strong tradition of CAC regulations and well-established environmental institutions, or in a country undergoing a radical change in government structure, it may be politically easier to incorporate pollution

charges into the system of environmental management than in industrial countries.

Evidence from a number of countries suggests that a lack of previous experience with well-enforced and effective CAC regulations leads to a dangerous underestimation of the need for strong institutional support when designing pollution charge programs. An adequate capacity for monitoring or inspection, as well as extensive and systematic training of staff involved in implementing a new instrument, should be built into the design of the charges.

*Enforcement.* Enforcement ability is the Achilles' heel of many existing pollution charge programs. Various factors weaken this ability, including (a) contradictions in the legal system; (b) a lack of expertise in or motivation for collecting charges, often exacerbated by a general problem of underreporting and undercollecting of taxes; and (c) insufficient capacity to monitor discharges. In developing countries, ensuring adequate monitoring faces additional challenges not only because of a lack of testing equipment and trained personnel but also because of a lack of measurement and sampling standards that makes comparison of collected data difficult. Enforcement needs not only a clear legal basis and technical expertise but also broad political support. In this respect, commitment of the government, consensus among stakeholders, and public participation are important inputs to improving enforcement practices.

*Systematic program evaluation.* Currently, most economic instruments worldwide are administered without systematic measurement of their performance, either through self-examination or through external oversight. Evaluation that focuses on clear-cut objectives and final outcomes, i.e., measurable effects on the environmental impact of targeted economic activities, provides the feedback that is necessary for the long-term success of pollution charge programs.

**Note**

1. The description in this section draws on analysis in Eskeland and Jimenez (1991); OECD (1991); NAPA (1994); Opschoor et al. (1994); Lovei (1995); and von Amsberg (1995).

# References

Baumol, William J., and Wallace E. Oates. 1988. *The Theory of Environmental Policy.* Cambridge, U.K.: Cambridge University Press.

Eskeland, Gunnar S., and Emmanuel Jimenez. 1991. "Choosing Policy Instruments for Pollution Control." Policy Research Working Paper 624. World Bank, Policy Research Department, Washington, D.C.

Lovei, Magda. 1995. *Financing Pollution Abatement: Theory and Practice.* Environment Department Paper 28. Washington, D.C.: World Bank.

NAPA (National Acid Precipitation Assessment Program). 1994. *Environment Goes to the Market: Implementation of Economic Incentives for Pollution Control.* Washington, D.C.

OECD (Organisation for Economic Co-operation and Development). 1989. *Economic Instruments for Environmental Protection.* Paris.

————. 1991. *Environmental Policy: How to Apply Economic Instruments.* Paris.

Opschoor, J. B., et al. 1994. *Managing the Environment: The Role of Economic Instruments.* Paris.

Tietenberg, Tom. 1992. *Environmental and Natural Resource Economics.* New York: Harper Collins.

von Amsberg, Joachim. 1995. "Selected Experience with the Use of Economic Instruments for Pollution Control in Non-OECD Countries." July. World Bank, Environment Department, Washington, D.C.

# Greenhouse Gas Abatement and Climate Change

*The World Bank Group supports a number of efforts to help its client countries reduce emissions of greenhouse gases through measures such as promoting energy efficiency and increasing the use of renewable energy.*

In 1995, the Intergovernmental Panel on Climate Change (IPCC), a panel of experts assembled by the United Nations, concluded after detailed scientific reviews that "the balance of evidence suggests a discernible human influence on global climate." This human influence on climate comes from emissions of three greenhouse gases in particular—carbon dioxide ($CO_2$), methane ($CH_4$), and nitrous oxide ($N_2O$). Such gases act like a blanket around the Earth, trapping heat emitted from the Earth's surface. Overall, about 80% of greenhouse gas (GHG) emissions from human activities are related to the production and use of energy—and particularly the burning of fossil fuels. The bulk of the remaining 20% is associated with agriculture and changes in land use, such as deforestation.

The objective of the UN Framework Convention on Climate Change (UNFCCC) is to achieve "stabilization of greenhouse gas concentrations in the atmosphere at a level that would prevent dangerous anthropogenic interference with the climate system." The Convention is founded on the principle of "common but differentiated responsibilities." Commonality refers to the need of all nations to assume responsibility for the protection of the global atmosphere and the recognition that developing country GHG emissions will exceed those from the industrial nations within the coming generations. Differentiation is predicated on the scientific fact that the industrial countries are responsible for the bulk of the present atmospheric stock of GHGs, and the realization that developing countries are least able to bear the costs of GHG mitigation and are most vulnerable to climate change effects.

The Kyoto Protocol to the UNFCCC was adopted on December 11, 1997, and, if it enters into force, will result in binding emissions reduction limitations for 39 industrial countries and transition economies listed in Annex B to the Protocol. These parties agreed to ensure that their aggregate GHG emissions do not exceed their assigned amounts, "with a view to reducing their overall emissions by at least 5.2% below 1990 levels in the commitment period 2008 to 2012."

The Kyoto Protocol also contains provisions allowing various elements of flexibility for Annex B countries in meeting their obligations. These include the ability to trade carbon reductions among countries ("emissions trading") and to jointly implement projects that can lead to carbon reductions on a project basis by reducing emissions or improving sinks ("Joint Implementation"). Emissions trading can take place only among Annex B parties. Joint implementation involving non-Annex B (i.e., developing country) parties can take place under the Clean Development Mechanism (CDM), with crediting being allowed after 2000.

## Commitments of Bank Borrower Countries

The World Bank's borrower countries that are parties to the Convention and may sign the Kyoto Protocol can be broadly classified in three categories: (a) transition economies in Eastern Europe and the former Soviet Union that are listed in Annex I of the UNFCCC and in Annex B of the Kyoto Protocol, (b) developing countries, and (c) least developed countries. A further distinction is made for those developing countries that are particularly vulnerable to the impacts of climate change. The operational implications of this categorization are highlighted in Table 1.

The Convention and the Protocol do not impose mandatory emissions restrictions on developing countries and least developed countries, whereas they call on industrial-country parties to limit their anthropogenic emissions of greenhouse gases. However, developing countries and least developed countries do have obligations to measure and monitor emissions within their countries.

### Principles of World Bank Group Assistance

The World Bank's role is to help finance sustainable development. In fulfilling this role, the Bank has a substantial capacity to assist its client countries in implementing their commitments under international conventions. In the case of the UNFCCC and the Kyoto Protocol, the World Bank will ensure that its activities are consistent with these conventions and will actively support its member countries in building capacity and undertaking investments for their implementation. Global environmental externalities can be recognized at the project level and, increasingly, in economic and sector work and in national environmental action plans. Where appropriate, country assistance strategies also include global environmental issues.

### Sustainable Development, Equity, and Consistency with the UNFCCC and the Kyoto Protocol

Defining which policies and investments are "consistent" with the Convention is difficult, especially regarding developing countries. It is universally recognized that the energy needs of developing countries are enormous, that increased energy consumption and economic growth will be essential if the living standards of the poor are to be raised, that without accelerated development in many countries domestic environmental degradation will worsen, and that the current threat from anthropogenic climate change is caused much more by affluent countries than by the poorer nations. For all these reasons, the Convention and the Protocol make it clear that continued growth of energy and use of fossil fuels in developing countries is consistent with the stipulations of the Convention and the Protocol. But guidance from the parties as to when and how such growth must be moderated in order to maintain this consistency will only evolve over time.

There is significant potential in Bank client countries for efficiency gains, substitution of lower carbon fuels such as natural gas, and the application of renewable energy technologies. Emissions factors for various fuels are presented in Table 2.

There are also critical shortages of conventional energy supplies and, in many countries,

### Table 1. Differentiated UNFCCC and Kyoto Protocol Commitments of World Bank Clients

| World Bank client category | Timetable for initial national communication | Description of mitigation policies and measures | Limitation of year 2000 emissions to 1990 levels | Financing for climate change mitigation |
|---|---|---|---|---|
| Transition economies | Within 6 months of entry into force; flexibility granted | Detailed, with net GHG emissions projections | By 0-8%, but with flexibility and optional base year | GEF; bilaterals and multilaterals; Joint Implementation |
| Developing countries | Within 3 years of entry into force of the UNFCCC (by 1997) | General | No | GEF grant and concessional; bilaterals and multilaterals; CDM |
| Least developed countries | At country discretion | General | No | GEF grant and concessional; bilaterals and multilaterals; CDM |

Note: GEF, Global Environment Facility; CDM, clean development mechanism.
Source: UNFCCC; Kyoto Protocol; GEF Legal Instrument; World Bank staff estimates.

## Table 2. Emissions Factors for Utility and Industrial Combustion Systems
(*grams per gigajoule energy input*)

| Source | Emissions factor | | | | |
|---|---|---|---|---|---|
| | Carbon dioxide (CO₂) | Carbon monoxide (CO) | Methane (CH₄) | Nitrogen dioxide (NO₂) | Nitrous oxide (N₂O) |
| *Utility application* | | | | | |
| Natural gas boilers | 56,100 | 19 | 0.1 | 267 | — |
| Gas turbine, combined cycle | 56,100 | 32 | 6.1 | 187 | — |
| Gas turbine, simple cycle | 56,100 | 32 | 5.9 | 188 | — |
| Residual oil boilers | 77,350 | 15 | 0.7 | 201 | — |
| Distillate oil boilers | 74,050 | 15 | 0.03 | 68 | — |
| Municipal solid waste (mass feed) | — | 98 | — | 140 | — |
| Coal, spreader stoker | 94,600 | 121 | 0.7 | 326 | 0.8 |
| Coal, fluidized bed | 94,600 | — | 0.6 | 255 | — |
| Coal, pulverized | 94,600 | 14 | 0.6 | 857 | 0.8 |
| Coal, tangentially fired | 94,600 | 14 | 0.6 | 330 | 0.8 |
| Coal, pulverized, wall fired | 94,600 | 14 | 0.6 | 461 | 0.8 |
| Wood-fired boilers[a] | 26,260 | 1,473 | 18 | 112 | — |
| *Industrial application* | | | | | |
| Coal-fired boilers | 94,600 | 93 | 2.4 | 329 | — |
| Residual-fired boilers | 77,350 | 15 | 2.9 | 161 | — |
| Natural gas–fired boilers | 56,100 | 17 | 1.4 | 67 | — |
| Wood-fired boilers[a] | 26,260 | 1,504 | 15 | 115 | — |
| Bagasse/agricultural waste boilers | — | 1,706 | — | 88 | — |
| Municipal solid waste, mass burn | — | 96 | — | 140 | — |
| Municipal solid waste, small modular | — | 19 | — | 139 | — |

— Not available.

*Note:* The table is based on fuel energy input rather than output; that is, it does not take account of combustion efficiency. Values are based on lower heating value, converted from original data in higher heating value using OECD/IEA assumptions (lower heating value is 10% below the higher heating value for natural gas; 5% for coal and oil); CO₂ values for coal represent an average value of subbituminous through anthracite.

a. Values for wood-fired boilers derived separately; not reported in IPCC.

*Source:* World Bank 1994a.

major shortcomings in energy policies. The World Bank's energy sector strategy encourages the adoption of appropriate energy pricing and institutional reform, which are prerequisites for improving both supply-side and demand-side efficiency and for more rapid adoption of no- and low-carbon-emitting energy sources. The strategy also recognizes the need to support commercial energy development as part of economic development and as a substitute for environmentally damaging dung and fuelwood consumption. The World Bank also considers within its investment operations cost-effective mitigative measures that would greatly reduce a country's vulnerability to climate change, particularly in the infrastructure and agricultural sectors.

Concerning climate change and the forestry sector, the scientific literature suggests that a significant fraction of total CO₂ releases from all sources is caused by tropical deforestation and burning. In addition, accelerated utilization of temperate and boreal forests contributes to rising global net emissions. The World Bank believes that measures for forest resource conservation, sustainable use, and enhancement could be an important part of many of its borrowers' climate change mitigation plans. These strategic directions provide potential synergies with the principles of the Convention on Biological Diversity. Carbon sink protection and enhancement actions are also in accord with the World Bank's support for the forest sector, as summarized in its 1991 forest policy paper (World Bank 1991). The policy gives high priority to combating deforestation and maintaining areas of forest intact.

## Strategic Elements

The strategic elements of the World Bank Group's assistance for mitigating climate change include:

- Promoting and capturing "win-win" policy and investment opportunities and, at the same time, identifying, analyzing, and clarifying tradeoffs between socioeconomic and global environmental objectives
- Supporting implementation of client countries' Convention and Protocol commitments as expressed in, inter alia, their national climate change plans and strategies
- Supporting clients who are parties to the agreements in integrating climate change considerations (including both GHG abatement and climate change adaptation) into development policy and planning
- Leveraging and maximizing the impact of resources available by virtue of the World Bank Group's role as implementing agency of the Global Environment Facility (GEF) and as a mobilizer of bilateral and private sector financing
- Integrating GEF financing with regular development finance and private sector resources for promoting transfer of no- and low-carbon energy, industry, and transport technologies
- Assisting in the development of a global market for carbon emissions offsets and credits that will help cut the costs of averting climate change.

## World Bank Support for the Objectives of the Convention and the Protocol

The Convention and the Protocol recognize the complexity of the climate change problem by prescribing a broad range of policies and measures in the energy, transport, industry, agriculture, forestry, and waste management sectors. Especially relevant to the realization of the objectives of the Convention and the Protocol are three focal areas of World Bank assistance: energy efficiency, renewable energy, and mainstreaming of global environmental concerns.

### Energy Efficiency

Macroeconomic and structural reforms are a centerpiece of World Bank advice to many of its client countries and will contribute a large fraction of future carbon and other GHG savings. A wide range of studies indicates that macroeconomic policies that effect structural change and promote efficient resource allocation are the single most important source of GHG emissions savings. The following examples help demonstrate this point.

First, energy subsidies add to the potential for climate change. Many countries, in both the industrial and the developing world, subsidize the use of fossil fuels. A World Bank study has shown that such subsidies are substantial for some countries and reach as much as 10% of gross domestic product (GDP). Worldwide fossil fuel subsidies are in excess of US$210 billion a year, or 20–25% of the value of global fossil fuel consumption at world prices. Phasing out subsidies would save scarce public resources and, at the same time, reduce GHG emissions. The study estimates that removal of fossil fuel subsidies would reduce global carbon emissions by almost 7%—in some countries, by more than 20%, assuming no change in world fuel prices.

Second, evidence is growing that changes in economic structure affect the future path of GHG emissions more than any other factor. A joint study by the China National Environmental Protection Agency, China's State Planning Commission, the UNDP, and the World Bank (UNDP 1994) emphasizes the importance of structural change for energy intensity, energy demand, and the associated GHG emissions reductions. The study isolates the factors that are responsible for reducing the energy intensity of the Chinese economy below the level that would be reached with static production technologies.

The study shows that only 21% of the total expected decline in energy intensity results from technical efficiency gains at the project level such as industrial modernization, improvement in industrial equipment, and energy conservation. The remaining 79% is the consequence of different types of structural change at the sectoral and subsectoral levels. The most important change is the shift in the product mix within subsectors, which contributes 37% of the total decline. This change represents movement up the product quality ladder and a shift into higher value added products, mainly in the chemical, machinery, building materials, and light industry sectors. The findings indicate the enormous effects that structural changes have on energy intensity and, consequently, on energy consumption and associated $CO_2$ emissions. Macroeconomic and other policies can therefore have a larger impact on GHG emissions than any explicit mitigation option at the project level.

This finding is consistent with recent research in OECD countries. An extensive ongoing study at the Lawrence Berkeley Laboratory analyzed the impacts of various factors on $CO_2$ emissions in manufacturing industries in major OECD economies. Structural change within the manufacturing sector since 1973 has reduced $CO_2$ emissions in that sector by about 20% in Germany, Japan, and the United States. What is more striking is that reductions in energy intensity cut emissions by 25–35% in these and most other OECD countries. Without this evolution of both structure and intensity, $CO_2$ emissions from manufacturing in the early 1990s would have been twice their actual level.

### Renewable Energy

Renewable energy is a growing focus of World Bank/GEF projects. Studies by the World Bank point out the insufficiency of energy efficiency measures alone and the massive shift to renewable energy required if the IPCC-prescribed stabilization of atmospheric $CO_2$ concentrations is to be achieved.

A small number of renewable energy forms have emerged as the most promising in the immediate term. *Biomass-based applications*, such as direct combustion of wood residues in the forest product industries, industrial-scale methane generation from animal and distillery wastes, and so on, have long been used commercially in many countries. New techniques such as fluidized-bed combustion systems and modern gasification systems, especially when combined with high efficiency gas turbines, are likely to expand these applications considerably.

For large, grid-connected power applications, *windfarms* and *solar thermal conversion*, particularly with use of parabolic trough technology, have made important technical and economic progress in the last decade due, in large part, to valuable operational experience acquired in California. Depending on the available wind regime, some windfarm installations can already be competitive with fossil-fuel alternatives. Solar thermal schemes are still relatively more costly, but the cost differential can be reduced by properly configuring the solar field with a combined-cycle/gas-turbine set that obviates the need for energy storage. *Photovoltaic (PV) cell* costs have dropped from about US$50 per peak watt in the mid-1970s to less than US$5 per peak watt today, considerably expanding opportunities for practical use of PV power, particularly for rural applications such as lighting, water pumping, battery charging, and vaccine refrigeration. Further cost reductions can extend PV use in the future for peak-shaving purposes in urban areas.

### Mainstreaming Global Environmental Concerns

The successful pursuit of environmentally sustainable development at the national level will ultimately depend on the protection of the global commons, including the atmosphere. The commons are being degraded because decisions taken at the country level on use of natural resources for national economic development do not adequately reflect the global impacts of the actions. Agricultural, industrial, energy, transport, and other national sector development strategies and programs generally fail to consider the impact of the emissions of greenhouse gases on climate change. Hence, local and global optima for resource utilization diverge.

The principal challenge for sustainable use of the global commons, therefore, is to bring about the internalization of global environmental externalities in national economic and sector development policies and programs, as well as in local management of natural resources. This challenge breaks down into two main elements:

- Countries should be informed about options and encouraged to pursue actions that are in their own best interest and will also help to capture global environmental benefits. Policies and measures for energy efficiency, for example, typically reduce fuel consumption, $SO_2$, $NO_x$, and particulate emissions, and carbon emissions. Thus, up to a point, global and domestic benefits are produced jointly.

- Reflecting global environmental externalities in national decisionmaking will frequently require going beyond "no regrets" actions of the type referred to above. In Convention and GEF terminology, this is the case when the additional domestic costs of addressing the global externality exceed the extra domestic benefits and the host country incurs "incremental costs." This would, for example, be the case when reduction of carbon emissions from burning fossil fuel requires going beyond the level dictated by national economic efficiency. The GEF has been established to help countries meet the incremental costs of capturing additional global environmental benefits, that is, in effect, to make available the "global premium" on national environmental management.

The World Bank has initiated support to bring the global environmental dimension into its regular economic and sector work program as it relates to sector development strategies, and in later stages, into strategic planning of environmental management (e.g., in national environmental action plans). Complementary efforts are under way to apply greenhouse gas accounting techniques at the individual investment level, where global externality impacts serve as an input to the environmental scoping process and affect project choice.

## References and Sources

Anderson, Dennis, and Kulsum Ahmed. 1995. *The Case for Solar Energy Investments*. World Bank Technical Paper 279. Washington, D.C.

Asian Development Bank. 1992. *Environmental Considerations in Energy Development*. Manila.

ICC (Information Unit on Climate Change, United Nations Environment Programme and World Meteorological Organization). 1992. *United Nations Framework Convention on Climate Change*. Geneva: United Nations Environment Programme.

UNDP (United Nations Development Programme). 1994. *China: Issues and Options in Greenhouse Gas Emissions Control. A* summary report prepared by a joint team from the National Environmental Protection Agency of China, the State Planning Commission of China, the United Nations Development Programme, and the World Bank. World Bank, East Asia and Pacific Regional Office, China and Mongolia Department, Industry and Energy Division. Washington, D.C.

World Bank. 1991. *The Forest Sector.* A World Bank Policy Paper. Washington, D.C.

————. 1994a. "Greenhouse Gas Abatement Investment Project Monitoring and Evaluation Guidelines." Environment Department, Global Environment Coordination, Washington, D.C.

————. 1994b. Greenhouse Gas Assessment Methodology." Environment Department, Global Environment Coordination Division, Washington, D.C.

————. 1994c. OP 10.04, "Economic Evaluation of Investment Operations." *World Bank Operational Manual: Operational Policies.* Washington, D.C.

————. 1995a. "The World Bank and the UN Framework Convention on Climate Change." Environment Department Papers, Climate Change Series 8. Environment Department, Washington, D.C.

————. 1995b. "Joint Implementation of Climate Change Measures." Environment Department Papers, Climate Change Series 5. Environment Department, Washington, D.C.

# Least-Cost Approaches to Reducing Acid Emissions

*The costs of meeting sulfur emissions targets can be high. It is essential, therefore, that countries adopt policies which minimize the net economic and social costs of reducing emissions to the agreed target levels and maximize the overlap between measures designed to reduce acidifying emissions and those addressing other forms of air pollution. This chapter discusses alternative approaches to reducing acid emissions cost-effectively, identifies possible mechanisms for international assistance, and describes the health and ecological damages caused by acid emissions and acid rain.*

Considerable work has been undertaken on the comparison of alternative mechanisms for meeting given emissions targets. Among the *market-based* systems are emissions charges and tradable permits. Possible *regulatory* systems range from the imposition of uniform emissions standards to the negotiation of plant-specific emissions permits. All raise practical problems of implementation, as well as issues of designing a system of incentives that induces emitters to reduce their emissions in the most efficient, i.e., least-cost, manner.

The use of geographic differentiation in charges or emissions standards, to take account of the fact that emissions from sources in one region may be more damaging than those from sources elsewhere in the country, adds a further layer of complication. However, introducing a spatial element may be essential in any system if the basic objective of reducing the damage caused by acid rain—as represented by exceedances of deposition rates over critical loadings—is to be met at an acceptable total cost.

It is possible to identify combinations of actions that may be used to reduce emissions of sulfur and nitrogen oxides at least cost, subject to constraints on monitoring and institutional feasibility. The list of possible actions includes energy conservation, the use of low-sulfur fuels, fuel switching, changes in levels or patterns of equipment operation, installation of controls to mitigate or eliminate emissions, and changes in combustion or other technologies. These actions may be mandated by specific regulations or may be adopted in response to economic or other incentives such as differentiated fuel taxes, pollution charges, permit trading, and investment subsidies. For large stationary emissions sources, a considerable range of alternative actions can be considered, but small or area sources, including households and small industrial and commercial boilers, should not be neglected, although they cannot be treated at the same level of detail.

## Sample Terms of Reference for a Study

- Prepare a countrywide database of large stationary sources of sulfur and nitrogen oxide emissions, with information on location, current emissions, and options for controlling emissions (including modifying combustion processes, switching to alternative fuels, and fitting abatement equipment).
- Collect data on the marginal and average costs of fuel use and operation for the alternative methods of reducing emissions for a sample of sources and generalize to the full range of stationary sources in the country database.
- Where applicable, investigate the impact of economic and regulatory instruments on the merit order for operating power stations to meet a given load curve and level of aggregate electricity demand in each country.
- Examine evidence on the "local" damage to human health, ecosystems, economic productivity, and amenity caused by air pollutants in

the areas surrounding emissions sources. Use this evidence to prepare approximate estimates of the benefits of reducing such air pollution in order to estimate the net cost of adopting alternative measures to reduce emissions of sulfur dioxide ($SO_2$) and nitrogen oxides ($NO_x$), from both large and small sources.

- Compare the total and marginal costs of meeting different targets for reducing emissions using different policy instruments, allowing for the "local" benefits of improving ambient air quality near the emissions sources. The comparisons should take account of the feasibility and costs of monitoring and enforcing the different systems of control.
- Investigate the scope for introducing regional differentiation to take account of the greater damage caused by depositions from some sources than from others. This analysis should be extended to take account of the benefits of reducing concentrations of particulates in the neighborhood of the sources as a result of the control measures and changes in utilization induced by the alternative instruments.
- Examine the institutional and administrative aspects of using alternative regulatory and economic instruments to reduce acidifying emissions, with particular attention to requirements for monitoring and enforcement.

In identifying the least-cost strategies for reducing emissions in each country, considerable attention should be paid to the administrative or regulatory issues that arise in implementing the alternative actions. Whatever the theoretical advantages or disadvantages of different instruments of environmental policy, it is crucial to base the analysis on a realistic assessment of the costs and performance, in practice, of the various mechanisms available.

## Transboundary versus Local Effects

The analysis should assess the net costs of implementing each alternative action after allowing for the associated health and other benefits to the country. For example, the net economic cost of switching households and small boilers from burning coal to gas may be small or even negative because this change will also reduce the population's exposure to high levels of particulates or sulfur dioxide and thus lower the health damage caused by such pollution. Such a study can identify the net costs of actions to reduce sulfur emissions as a basis for agreements between countries or for donor assistance designed to meet emissions reduction targets. In the future, Activities Implemented Jointly (AIJ) arrangements, as provided for in the Kyoto Protocol, might be one way of developing more cost-effective strategies.

## Environmental Damage from Acid Emissions

### Health Impacts

Sulfur dioxide is an irritant that, in high concentrations, can cause acute respiratory problems. In conjunction with high levels of exposure to particulates, it is implicated in the excess mortality observed during severe smogs, and it worsens the morbidity associated with chronic respiratory problems.

Sulfur dioxide also reacts with other substances in the atmosphere to form sulfate aerosols that may have an important health impact. Moreover, sulfate aerosols can be transported long distances through the atmosphere before deposition occurs.

Exposure to high levels of nitrogen oxides can also worsen the health of those with pre-existing respiratory problems. It is, however, through its contribution to the generation of photochemical smog and ozone (another respiratory irritant that aggravates the condition of people with asthma and heart disease) that $NO_x$ emissions have their main effect on health.

### Other Impacts

High levels of $SO_2$ and $NO_x$ emissions can damage buildings and other structures because of relatively high concentrations of acid and of sulfur particles in rainfall. Much concern has been expressed about damage to cultural artifacts and especially historic buildings in cities in Eastern Europe. It is, however, difficult to disentangle this damage from that caused by poor maintenance and mistaken attempts at restoration in the past. While the scale of the damage to materials caused by acid emissions is uncertain, emissions undoubtedly give rise to amenity costs because they reduce visibility. The presence of sulfate and nitrate particles and of acid aerosols, as a result of either direct emissions or their secondary formation in the atmosphere, leads to light scattering. Furthermore, gaseous nitrogen dioxide absorbs light at the high end of the spectrum, giving the atmosphere a reddish-brown tinge. The result is a haze that may extend over a large region, or topographical features may concentrate the haze over a city.

*Acid Rain*

Depositions of sulfur and nitrogen, or "acid rain," are primarily associated with the long-distance transport of acid aerosols formed in the atmosphere from a mixture of dilute hydrochloric, nitric, and sulfuric acids, plus ammonium sulfate and nitrate. Rainfall gives rise to wet deposition, which rapidly infiltrates soils, groundwater, rivers, and lakes. Both dry and wet depositions may cause direct damage to trees and other vegetation by affecting their plant chemistry and pathology. Acidification of soils leads to leaching of plant nutrients and to mobilization of aluminum that would otherwise be bound up in rocks and mineral particles. Excessive levels of aluminum damage roots, reduce the capacity of plants to take up necessary trace elements such as calcium and magnesium, and interfere with water transport within trees, which increases their sensitivity to drought. Acidification of rivers and lakes can result in drastic changes in their ecosystems, including the complete loss of fish stocks.

The dose-response relationships between acidic emissions and damage to forests, crops, and lakes are complex and are still poorly understood. Recent evidence suggests that nitrogen compounds may be more damaging to ecosystems than sulfur compounds. Rainwater has not become significantly more acidic in Central Europe over the last 50 years, but the area covered by highly acid rainfall has increased greatly. Evidence from Germany and other western European countries suggests that forest loss may be linked to the long-term effects of acid depositions but that other (often site-specific) stress factors are also involved.

The nature of the damage to ecosystems caused by acid rain means that it is necessary to distinguish between the "stock" and "flow" aspects of the problem. Long-term acidification of soils is a "stock" problem that cannot be quickly reversed by reducing the level of current depositions, although applications of lime and nutrients and changes in silvicultural practices may mitigate its consequences. At the same time, it is possible to define "critical loads" representing the maximum "flow" of acid depositions that can be absorbed by specific soil types without provoking a tendency to acidification. These critical loads define a measure of long-run sustainability that can be used in setting the ultimate goals of environmental policy. However, in setting priorities for short-term actions, countries must also consider how much immediate measures to reduce acid emissions will affect the amount of damage that will occur over the next few years.

## Conclusions

The implication is that short-term priorities should focus on the local, health-related, damage caused by acid emissions, while damage to ecosystems should be the basis for a longer-term reduction in emissions from those sources and regions that have contributed most to acidification in the past. Any measures to alleviate the local damage caused by sulfur dioxide and other emissions should be consistent with achieving a declining trend in emissions, which would not, for example, be the case with a policy of constructing tall stacks to extend the area over which acid emissions are deposited.

# PART III

## PROJECT GUIDELINES

PRINCIPLES OF INDUSTRIAL POLLUTION
    MANAGEMENT
MONITORING
SUMMARY OF AIR EMISSION AND EFFLUENT
    DISCHARGE REQUIREMENTS
POLLUTANTS
POLLUTANT CONTROL TECHNOLOGIES
INDUSTRY SECTOR GUIDELINES

# Principles of Industrial Pollution Management

## A New Approach

In the 10 years since the World Bank Group produced its first set of *Environmental Guidelines*, there has been an important shift in the way in which environmental agencies and the Bank Group approach the problem of minimizing the environmental damage caused by industrial development. In the past, guidelines and legislation tended to focus on achieving acceptable pollution concentrations in different media, and it was logical to rely on end-of-pipe controls and "external" treatment of pollution. Moreover, since environmental concerns were seen as distinct from industrial ("productive") processes, environmental legislation steered well clear of interfering in industrial production decisions.

This approach has achieved significant reductions in pollution, but the costs have sometimes been high, and performance has not always been consistent. Thus, it has become clear that another approach is required, especially in countries experiencing rapid economic and industrial growth, if progress in preventing industrial pollution is to continue. The new approach that is emerging incorporates the concepts of sustainable development and cleaner production, together with an emphasis on good management practices.

## Sustainable Development

The World Bank Group recognizes and promotes the concept of sustainable development, in which growth and environmental protection are compatible. Within this framework, it is important to avoid or reduce the discharge of pollutants and to minimize their impact on human health and the environment. The *precautionary principle* is a fundamental guiding principle of this *Handbook*: whenever possible, projects should seek approaches that avoid additional burdens on the environment, especially where the outcome is uncertain and potentially irreversible. One way of applying the precautionary principle is by implementing cleaner production.

### Cleaner Production and Pollution Prevention

Pollution prevention is preferable to reliance on end-of-pipe pollution controls. The Bank Group encourages the adoption of cleaner production approaches, which go beyond pollution prevention. Cleaner production encompasses production processes and management procedures that entail less use of resources than conventional technologies and also generate less waste and smaller amounts of toxic or other harmful substances. It emphasizes the human and organizational dimensions of environmental management, including good plant operation to avoid deliberate or accidental discharges.

Industries striving toward environmental excellence now also consider how environmentally friendly the final product is. Thus, a petroleum refinery would not only address the emissions caused by the refining process itself but would also change its processes to discontinue the use of lead as an additive to boost octane in gasoline, because of the well-known serious health effects of lead. Today, cleaner production aims to include everything from the drawing board to final disposal or reuse of the product.

### Treatment and Disposal

Cleaner production and pollution prevention can reduce the quantities of waste and eliminate some pollutants, but treatment and disposal of remaining wastes are required. Appropriate treatment systems must be designed and installed to achieve acceptable emissions levels. The systems must then be operated and maintained to attain the required reductions in pollutants. The transfer of pollutants from one medium to another (e.g., from effluent to sludges) may simplify but does not solve the disposal problems of an industry. An integrated approach should be adopted toward management of pollutants to ensure that the overall treatment and disposal solution is the most appropriate.

Monitoring of control devices, treatment plant performance, and emissions is an integral part of the operation of the system. The information gathered from monitoring should be utilized to achieve and maintain system performance.

### Good Management

The Bank Group promotes good management and operating practices such as maintaining and operating production processes and pollution control devices according to design specifications. It encourages the continual improvement of processes, the installation of controls, and the monitoring of performance.

In support of this emphasis on pollution prevention, the new approach also stresses the human and organizational dimensions of environmental management that are required to develop sound plant management and operational practices and the need for a regulatory and resource pricing framework that provides incentives for continuous improvements in environmental performance. In its economic and sector work, the Bank Group assesses the role of prices, taxes, and other instruments to ensure that there are incentives to apply such measures.

### Environmental Regulations

The World Bank encourages its country borrowers to develop (a) appropriate permitting procedures to encourage pollution prevention and to decide on applicable emissions limits and (b) sound and enforceable ambient environmental standards. It supports the strengthening of appropriate institutions and the training of staff to identify pollution prevention and cleaner production options and to monitor and enforce compliance with permit conditions and environmental standards. Some of these responsibilities might be carried out by the private sector as a way of ensuring the long-term sustainability of its investments.

## Guidelines

### Purpose

The *Pollution Prevention and Abatement Handbook* has been prepared to assist Bank Group staff and consultants, other financial institutions, and borrowers in ensuring that industrial projects achieve adequate environmental performance. To protect human health and the environment, Bank Group–financed industrial projects must comply with pollution prevention and abatement measures acceptable to the Bank Group. The *Handbook* describes measures that the Bank Group would consider acceptable for the purposes of deciding on Bank Group financing. It must be applied in conjunction with other Bank Group requirements, in particular those on environmental assessment, EA (see "Using the Guidelines," below).

### Scope

The principal focus of Part III of this *Handbook* is on industrial pollution. However, from the point of view of environmental impacts, the sources of pollution are often very hard to distinguish, particularly in urban areas. Indeed, in many cases, the key issue is to understand the relative contributions of point and nonpoint sources, urban and industrial sources, large polluters and small and medium-size enterprises.

### Underlying Principles

The *Handbook* is based on good industrial practices. The cleaner production and waste minimization guidelines cannot cover all possible processes and products, but they do indicate typical levels of performance that are achievable in a well-designed and well-managed plant. The Bank Group supports continuing improvement in industrial efficiency and encourages enterprises to achieve better performance than the *Handbook* recommends.

Minimizing waste reduces not only the demand for resources but also the scale of final treatment required. However, in most cases there will also be a need for pollution control measures to supplement cleaner production efforts. The relevant treatment requirements and the emissions levels given in the *Handbook* are based on good practice; they are intended to be maintained in the long term using the skills and resources normally available in industry in the countries in which the Bank Group operates.

The *Handbook* also stresses the need for good management and for adequate operating and monitoring resources to ensure that a plant's proper environmental performance is maintained, documented, and reviewed as a matter of course. Good pollution management habits should be developed so that good performance becomes routine. Each plant should also put in place measures to minimize accidental releases (such as spills) and emergency response procedures to manage such events.

Design and implementation of industrial projects to minimize the use of resources must include energy conservation measures. Energy efficiency is frequently indistinguishable from environmental efficiency. Whenever possible, both issues should be addressed together.

*Process of Preparation*

The preparation of the *Handbook* has been a long and cooperative process, drawing on a wide range of expertise and experience both inside and outside the World Bank Group.

The sections in Part III were circulated for comment, initially to a small number of specialists and later to a wider audience of interested parties. The guidelines related to thermal power plants were discussed at a two-day meeting of an international panel of experts at the World Health Organization in Geneva. The review and comment process had to balance breadth of review with the time and resources required for the preparation of each document.

The documents in Part III are intentionally short. Their aim is to emphasize the key points that should be addressed in the preparation of a project involving the particular sector. They are not intended to be comprehensive guides to the technologies of the sector.

## Using the Guidelines

Normal Bank Group procedures for analysis of industrial projects include (a) an appropriate EA that takes into account relevant national legislation and (b) an economic analysis that includes an assessment of the costs and benefits of the alternative environmental measures available for new or existing plant, evaluating reductions in exposure and improvements in ambient conditions compared with the situation without such environmental measures. On the basis of these analyses, site-specific requirements related to the local conditions and resources available are established (e.g., emissions limits and special operating procedures) to ensure that human health is protected and environmental benefits are optimized. Depending on the circumstances, these site-specific requirements will be as strict as, or stricter than, those set out in the *Handbook*. In rare instances, the EA may show that less-strict site-specific requirements would be acceptable. If these are adopted, the project documentation would be expected to provide detailed justification for the measures chosen.

The site-specific requirements determine the level and type of pollution abatement measures required for a particular project. These depend on (a) the impact of the pollutants from that plant on the overall ambient pollution level; (b) the environmental and health damage caused by pollutants relative to the costs of reducing emissions levels; and (c) the most cost-effective options for reducing the ambient level of pollution, for example, through an approach that takes into account systemwide technical and institutional solutions within a river basin, an airshed, or a power grid.

*Projects Involving New Plant*

An EA for a new industrial project should not only determine the environmental impact of the project but should also identify alternative options for achieving the project objectives at equal or lower cost, taking into account environmental cost. Among the options to be considered are policy and institutional measures and comprehensive approaches to airshed and watershed management, including use of alternative sources of energy. Some of these alternatives will apply only to projects initiated by governments, but many will also apply to private sector investors who will find it in their best interest to conduct EAs that consider the broadest reasonable range of alternatives. Early investments in a sound EA often pay off in smoother project implementation.

When a project involves adding new plant in an area where there are already plants in operation, the EA should examine a range of alternative ways of reducing the exposure of people and the environment to harmful pollution by taking into account the contribution of other pollution sources. If the EA indicates that there will be no significant deterioration in ambient conditions, the plant should comply, at a minimum, with the measures set out in the *Handbook*.

If the EA indicates that there may be a significant deterioration in ambient conditions, several possibilities should be examined: (a) the new project simply complies with the measures recommended in the *Handbook*; (b) the Bank Group may require the application to the plant of additional measures on the basis of site-specific conditions; or (c) the Bank Group may require, as a condition for providing financing, that further measures be taken to address other sources within the project area of influence, where this is a more cost-effective approach to reducing the overall impacts. This option may call for the assistance of the World Bank Group in facilitating negotiations between various government institutions or between the government and the private sector.

### Projects Involving Existing Plant

For any Bank Group–financed industrial project involving significant modifications to an existing facility, the Bank Group requires that the facility undergo an environmental audit as the basis for appropriate project design. The report should (a) assess past and current releases to land, air, surface water, and groundwater; (b) identify good housekeeping and good maintenance practices, process modifications, and end-of-pipe measures that can improve the environmental

performance of the facility; and (c) recommend site-specific targets and a timetable for achieving them.

The economic prospects of an existing industrial plant should define the type of expenditure to be made to reduce pollution. Plants with a longer expected economic life are required to focus to a greater extent on process improvements to reduce their pollution emissions and should be held to standards that approach those of a new plant. Plants with a shorter economic life should make management improvements and should reduce emissions of the most damaging pollutants by implementing other cost-effective measures for which the benefits achieved within the anticipated economic life of the plant exceed the costs involved. With technical justification and government approval, such plants may be held to less strict standards if there is a clear commitment to close the plant within an agreed time period and to avoid or clean up any hazardous materials and soil or groundwater contamination that pose an immediate threat or a persistent risk to human health and the environment

The Bank Group encourages governments to undertake a process of negotiation between plant owners and management, on the one hand, and local regulators, on the other. The success of cleaner production or industrial pollution abatement measures depends crucially on an agreement with plant managers regarding the management and process modifications that are required, after considering the different options available to achieve environmental objectives.

For each plant, a detailed public schedule should be worked out that refers to the industry's specific pollution performance over time and includes agreements on (a) *initial compliance*, involving management improvements and installation of certain equipment, and (b) *continuing compliance* based on the results of environmental monitoring, which is normally carried out by the enterprises themselves and verified independently.

### Industry-Specific Guidelines

The industry-specific sections provide information on pollution prevention measures and emissions requirements. The *pollution reduction targets* and pollution emissions levels provided cannot be applied rigidly to every project, but they should be achieved wherever possible. Where they cannot be achieved, the reasons for nonperformance should be explained in detail.

Specific *emissions guidelines* are intended to be measurable with the expertise and equipment normally available within the industry or to the relevant regulatory and enforcement body. The intention of the *Handbook* is to present realistic performance levels to which industry will be held rather than nominal targets that enterprises do not take seriously. Where appropriate, the Bank Group may assist in developing local capabilities for monitoring and interpreting results.

New projects should meet the *maximum emissions levels* contained in the sector-specific guidelines unless the site-specific environmental analysis recommends stricter controls or provides a justification for a variance from the guidelines contained in the *Handbook*. The Bank Group requires a site-specific environmental analysis for all projects that may affect the environment. The analysis should take into account local conditions and national legislation.

The *Handbook* is intended to apply to both the design and monitoring of projects. The emissions guidelines are typically stated as concentrations, which are normally more easily measured than loads. However, the objective is to reduce the overall loads discharged to the environment. Any process or operating procedure that uses dilution or similar approaches to circumvent the objective of reducing pollutant loads is unacceptable.

Project design should include consideration of the equipment and personnel requirements for the operation and monitoring of pollution prevention and abatement measures. Basic sampling and laboratory facilities should be included as project components, if necessary.

Avoidance of damage to human health is a principal objective of the guidelines. However, the guidelines focus on industrial sources and do not necessarily reflect all the potential exposures to pollutants. For example, in dealing with pesticides and fertilizers, there are potentially serious exposures that are not addressed here and that could be far more important than those related to manufacturing and waste disposal. These include exposures of children playing in recently sprayed fields or with large containers (drums), repackaging of wholesale quantities for individual consumption, contamination of the food chain, and so on. Similarly, for lead, the individual industry guideline does not address factors such as removal of existing environmental lead (which can circulate for up to 30 years), nor does it deal with various nonfuel sources of lead that may be more important locally but are often not monitored. Thus, compliance with emissions standards at individual sources can give a false sense of security by creating the impression that the overall problem has been addressed. The appropriate watchword is, "Environmental management, not just pollution control."

## Application of the Guidelines

Technical and managerial circumstances and constraints will continue to change, and further experience will be gained as regulatory and pollution management systems are implemented. This *Handbook* can be used as a basic point of reference, but users must constantly be aware of new developments and change and must apply the advice provided here in the light of conditions that pertain at a given time and place.

The next document in Part III is a discussion on monitoring of pollutants, followed by a summary table of requirements for air emissions and effluent discharges as presented in the *Handbook*. The remainder of Part III presents material on specific pollutants, brief descriptions of control technologies for pollutants of special importance, guidelines for specific industries, and a document on general environmental guidelines. A glossary of terms follows Part III.

# Monitoring

## Objectives

Pollutants of concern for the environment must be monitored to obtain reliable information on the quality of ambient air and media. Such information is a necessary part of any environmental management system, whether in the private or the public sector. It provides a basis for informed decisionmaking and the development of environmental management strategies. To ensure that decisions are made on a sound basis, it is essential to be confident that the measurements reflect the existing situation; in other words, the data must be of clearly defined and documented quality. Hence, quality assurance and quality control are important. The way in which samples are taken and analyzed is as important as the results of the measurement (analysis) itself. A quality assurance system should include institutional as well as technical aspects.

Environmental releases from major industrial sources are monitored as part of the overall monitoring of sources of the pollutants of concern within an airshed or water basin. The objectives of monitoring systems also include process optimization, auditing, and compliance with regulatory requirements such as emissions standards.

### Methodology

Monitoring plans are designed and implemented for collecting data on ambient air and water quality and on releases of pollutants of concern from major point sources. The elements of a monitoring plan normally include selection of the parameters of concern; the method of collection and handling of samples (specifying the location, the frequency, type, and quantity of samples, and sampling equipment); sample analysis (or, alter-

natively, on-line monitoring); and a format for reporting the results.

Ambient levels of pollutants such as heavy metals are measured in air, water, and soil, along with other parameters, at specified locations and frequencies and using specified equipment and methods. The objective is to collect and analyze representative samples to produce data for use in the environmental management system. To ensure acceptable ambient levels, concentrations of pollutants in the environment are predicted, using models and information on emissions from some of the major pollution sources, and are then monitored (that is, verified by actual observation). Corrective action, follows, when necessary.

### Ambient Air Quality

Although, in theory, all pollutants should be monitored, in practice, only the significant pollutants are monitored, at best. Usually, monitoring is limited to some key pollutants such as suspended particulate matter (SPM). A good air quality management system usually reviews the probable emissions sources and the environmental receptors in the area of concern and then selects the pollutants to be monitored. One such pollutant is particulate matter of less than 10 microns in aerodynamic diameter ($PM_{10}$). (Some modern air quality monitoring systems are being developed to monitor $PM_{2.5}$ and $PM_1$, that is, particulates of sizes less than 2.5 microns and 1 micron, respectively.) Other pollutants normally monitored include sulfur oxides, ozone, and nitrogen oxides. In some places, other priority pollutants may be included in ambient air monitoring: examples are volatile organics such as benzene and vinyl chloride, polynuclear aromatic hydrocarbons (PAHs), dioxins, furans, asbestos, inorganics, and arsenic, cadmium, lead, mercury, nickel, and other heavy metals.

Locations of monitoring stations are determined on the basis of the receptors in the airshed. A network of monitoring stations is usually established to estimate the exposure levels. Normally, a monitoring station is also set up to measure background concentrations in cases where the resultant ambient levels of a particular source or sources are to be computed. The quality assurance plan should include the rationale for selecting the number and location of monitoring stations, the monitoring frequency, the equipment, and the method of sample collection. Monitoring may be continuous or may be done for short durations of, say, 1 hour, 8 hours, or 24 hours to determine the maximum and average for the set period.

Table 1 presents examples of the common ambient air monitoring systems used for some pollutants of concern.

*Water Quality*

Water quality management usually involves monitoring of key pollutants that serve as indicators of acceptability for a specific use. For example, there may be restrictions on pollutant levels for water used in irrigation and stricter restrictions for water destined for human con-

sumption. Further information on these issues is provided in the Water Quality Management chapters of this *Handbook* and in Jorgensen and Vollenweider (1988); World Bank (1993); Le Moigne et al. (1994); and Lee and Dinar (1995). Table 2 lists some pollutants of concern and methods of monitoring them.

On the basis of the nature of the water body (canal, river, lake, or sea) and its uses, the quality assurance plan establishes the number and locations of monitoring stations to estimate exposure levels, including exposure of aquatic ecosystems.

Typically, monitoring of water quality for human consumption includes measurements of fecal coliform; toxic organics such as benzene, trichloroethane, tetrachloroethene, chlorophenols, and pesticides; polynuclear aromatics such as benzo(a)pyrene, carbon tetrachloride, polychlorinated biphenyls (PCBs), dioxins, and furans; oil and grease; pH; toxic metals, including arsenic, cadmium, chromium, copper, lead, and mercury; and cyanides, as well as color, taste, odor, turbidity, and hardness (see WHO 1984). The quality of data obtained from analyzing collected samples or from continuous monitors should at least be of a level at which the cost-effectiveness of sampling and monitoring techniques is balanced with the adverse consequences of erroneous data.

## Table 1. Examples of Ambient Air Monitoring Systems

| Parameter | Sampling or monitoring system |
| --- | --- |
| $SPM/PM_{10}$ | ISO/TR7708/DP 4222 (measurement of atmospheric deposit; horizontal deposit gauge method) ISO/DP 10473 (measurement of the mass of particulate matter on a filter medium; beta ray absorption); ISO/DIS 9835 (determination of a black smoke index) 40 CFR, Part 50, Appendix J (for $PM_{10}$); Appendix B (for SPM) |
| Sulfur dioxide | ISO 4219/4221; 40 CFR, Part 50, Appendix A (pararosaniline method) |
| Nitrogen dioxide | ISO 6768, 7996; 40 CFR, Part 50, Appendix F (gas phase chemiluminescence method); Salzman automatic colorimeter (method used in Japan) |
| Ozone | 40 CFR, Part 50, Appendix D; measurement of photochemical oxidants using the neutral buffered automatic potassium iodide colorimetric method; used in Japan |
| Lead | ISO/DIS 9855; 40 CFR, Part 50, Appendix G (extraction with nitric and hydrochloric acids and analysis by atomic absorption spectrometry) |
| Asbestos | ISO/DIS 10312/VDI 3492 (fibers counted using scanning electron microscope) |

*Note:* SPM, suspended particulate matter; CFR, United States, *Code of Federal Regulations;* ISO, International Organization for Standardization.

## Table 2. Examples of Monitoring Systems for Water Bodies and Liquid Effluents

| Parameter | Sampling or monitoring system |
|---|---|
| *General* | |
| PH | pH meter<br>ISO (1980–91), Water Quality Standards<br>APHA, ASTM, BS, DIN, SCA |
| BOD | Determine dissolved oxygen concentration in the test solution before and after incubation (APHA, ASTM, BS, DIN, ISO, SCA); 40 CFR, Part 136; USEPA Method 405.1 |
| COD | Digest with potassium dichromate in strong acid solution with silver sulfate as catalyst after sample homogenization (APHA, ASTM, BS, DIN, ISO, SCA);  40 CFR, Part 136; USEPA Method 410.1 |
| AOX | USEPA Method 1650 (titrimetric) |
| TSS | Filtration<br>40 CFR, Part 136; USEPA Method 160.2; APHA, BS, DIN, ISO, SCA |
| Total dissolved solids (TDS) | Pretreatment with membrane filtration, followed by evaporation APHA, BS, DIN, ISO, SCA |
| Phenol | Extract with MIBK, followed by GC analysis<br>USEPA Methods 420.1, 420.2 |
| Sulfide | React with dimethlphenylenediamine and ferric chloride in acid solution to form methylene blue; USEPA Methods 376.1, 376.2 |
| Oil and grease | Extract with light petroleum, evaporate solvent, and measure weight<br>USEPA Method 413.1 |
| *Organic compounds* | |
| Total organic carbon | UV oxidation followed by infrared analysis<br>USEPA Method 415.1; APHA, ASTM, DIN, ISO, SCA |
| Organics | 40 CFR, Part 136.3 (GC, GC/MS, HPLC, ASTM D4657-87) |
| PAHs | Gas chromatography with flame ionization detection |
| Pesticides | Gas chromatography; 40 CFR, Part 136.3, Table 1-D. |
| *Inorganic substances* | |
| General reference | 40 CFR, Part 136.3, Table 1-B. |
| *Metals* | |
| Arsenic | Atomic absorption spectroscopy; APHA, ASTM, SCA |
| Cadmium | Atomic absorption spectrometry; APHA, ASTM, BS, DIN, ISO, SCA<br>Inductively coupled plasma emission spectrometry; ASTM, DIN, SCA |
| Chromium | Atomic absorption spectrometry; APHA, ASTM, BS, DIN, ISO, SCA<br>Inductively coupled plasma emission spectrometry; ASTM, DIN, SCA |
| Lead | Atomic absorption spectrometry; APHA, ASTM, BS, DIN, ISO, SCA<br>Inductively coupled plasma emission spectrometry; ASTM, DIN, SCA |
| Mercury | Flameless atomic absorption spectrometry; APHA, ASTM, BS, DIN, ISO, SCA |
| Nickel | Atomic absorption spectrometry; APHA, ASTM, DIN, SCA<br>Inductively coupled plasma emission spectrometry; ASTM, DIN, SCA |
| Zinc | Atomic absorption spectrometry; APHA, ASTM, BSI, DIN, ISO, SCA |

*Note:* See UNEP, Technical Report 27, for details. APHA, American Public Health Administration, *Standard Methods for the Examination of Water and Wastewater;* ASTM, American Society for Testing and Materials Standards, *Annual,* vols. 11.01, 11.02; BS, British Standards Institute, *Water Quality,* BS-6068; CFR, United States, *Code of Federal Regulations;* DIN, German Industrial Standard Methods for the Examination of Water, Wastewater and Sludge, DIN 38404–09; ISO, International Organization for Standardization, *Water Quality Standard Method;* SCA, Standing Committee of Analysts, U.K. Department of the Environment, *Methods for the Examination of Waters and Associated Materials.*

*Point-Source Releases*

Releases, including fugitive air emissions, are usually monitored to provide feedback to pollution prevention and control systems and to guide the necessary corrective action. Although releases from transport, households, and other sources are also monitored, this chapter deals solely with industrial sources. The chapter does not cover fugitive emissions; the empirical methods required for monitoring fugitive emissions are addressed in such sources as Bounicore and Davis (1992) and USEPA, *Compilation of Air Pollutant Emission Factors* (AP-42).

*Air*

Monitoring of air emissions from point sources usually involves monitoring pollutant concentra-

tions. The flow rate of stack gases and their temperature are among the basic parameters usually monitored, along with the level of pollutants present (see Table 3). (In extractive systems, a sample of stack gases is drawn.) The major pollutants monitored in stack gases include particulate matter; sulfur oxides and, in some cases, hydrogen sulfide and total reduced sulfur compounds; nitrogen oxides; carbon monoxide and. in some cases, carbon dioxide; halogens or halides (such as chlorine or hydrogen chloride); volatile organic compounds; and toxic materials, including metals. The parameters are selected on the basis of knowledge of the process and the associated environmental issues of concern, as described in the guidelines for the specific industry sector.

Monitoring methods for stack emissions specify locations, frequency, and equipment; the

**Table 3. Examples of Air Emissions Monitoring Systems**

| Parameter | Sampling and analytical methods |
|---|---|
| Stack gases | Extractive methods using pitot tubes; 40 CFR, Part 60, Appendix A, Methods 1–4; BS 1756:1977, Part 2 |
| $PM_{10}$/ TSP | In situ nondispersive infrared spectrophotometry and extractive gravimetric; ISO 9096; ISO/TC 146/SCI/WG1N16(1994); 40 CFR, Part 60, Appendix A, Methods 5, 5A, 17; BS 3405:1983 VDI 2066, Parts 1, 2 |
| Sulfur oxides | Extractive nondispersive infrared spectrophotometry; ISO 8178; 40 CFR, Part 60, Appendix A, Method 6; BS 1756:1977, Part 4; VDI 2462, Parts 1–7 |
| Nitrogen oxides | Extractive fluorescence; ISO 8178; 40 CFR, Part 60, Appendix A, Method 7, 7A–7E; VDI 2456 Parts 1–7 |
| VOCs | Extractive flame ionization; 40 CFR, Part 60, Appendix A, Method 18; VDI 3493, Part 1 |
| Total hydrocarbons | Extractive nondispersive infrared spectrophotometry; 40 CFR, Part 60, Appendix A, Methods 25, 25A, 25 B; VDI 2460 (Parts 1–3), 2466 (Part 1), 3481 (Parts 1, 2), 2457 (Parts 1–7) |
| Carbon monoxide | Extractive nondispersive infrared spectrophotometry; 40 CFR, Part 60, Appendix A, Methods 10, 10A, 10B; VDI 2459, Part 6 |
| Chlorine/hydrogen chloride | Extractive nondispersive infrared spectrophotometry; VDI 3488, Parts 1 and 2; VDI 3480, Part 1 |
| Hydrogen sulfide | Extractive electrochemical analysis; VDI 3486, Parts 1–3 |

*Note:* Metals are usually analyzed by the methods outlined in Table 2. BS, British Standards Institute; CFR, United States, *Code of Federal Regulations*; ISO, International Organization for Standardization, *Method for the Gravimetric Determination of Concentration and Mass Flow Rate of Particulate Material in Gas-Carrying Ducts* (Geneva 1994); VDI, Germany, Federal Minister for the Environment, Nature Conservation and Nuclear Safety, *Air Pollution Control Manual for Continuous Emission Monitoring* (Bonn, 1992).

method of collecting, handling, and analyzing samples; and the method of reporting validated results. The sampling points should be at least 8 pipe diameters downstream and 2 pipe diameters upstream of any obstruction or change in flow direction. (For details, see United States, 40 CFR, Part 60, Appendix A; UNEP and UNIDO 1996.) Ports should normally be installed so as to extend at least 5 to 20 centimeters from the exterior of the stack. If the sum of stack inside diameter and port length is less than 3 meters, a minimum of two ports at 90° to each other is needed. In other cases, at least four ports 90° apart are needed. It is important to prevent the sampling process itself from causing changes in concentrations, and several criteria are specified to ensure the representativeness of the sample. Sampling points should be chosen to avoid the possibility of reverse flow, which might affect the validity of samples.

*Liquid Effluents*

Monitoring of liquid effluents is performed to meet the objectives of environmental management systems. The priorities of the water quality management are used as a guide in setting up the monitoring program. It is important to know the discharge load levels that will not compromise the sustainability of the aquatic system. The liquid effluent monitoring system normally includes selection of the sampling location; parameters to be measured; type of samples to be collected and frequency of measurement; equipment to be used; method of preserving and analyzing the sample; and data reporting and validation, including quality assurance and quality control.

To obtain representative samples, the samples should be taken where liquids are turbulent and well mixed. Sampling points should be located at least 25 pipe diameters downstream of disturbances such as places where streams join, to ensure that mixing is complete and the sample is representative. Sampling at or near boundaries of pipes, tanks, or lagoons where stagnant or otherwise unrepresentative conditions exist should be avoided.

The parameters for each process or effluent stream to be monitored and the frequency of monitoring are described in the guidelines for specific industrial sectors. Sampling may be performed after each stage, to assess its performance, or at the inlet and the outlet of a treatment train. Fluctuations in the process may necessitate more frequent monitoring if some parameter is expected to reach levels of concern. The number of samples required should be such that at least a 95% confidence level can be attained. The types of samples can be discrete (spot, snap, or grab) or composite. Discrete samples are usually taken when concentrations of individual samples are of greater interest than are averages, as may be the case with compliance monitoring. Composite samples are prepared by mixing a series of discrete samples to get a representative sample over a period of time and for different locations. Sampling quantities should be sufficient for performing analysis and subsequent quality assurance and quality control; as a general rule, the sample should be at least 500 milliliters. Sample containers are selected to minimize contamination of samples or leakages of volatiles, if present.

The instruments used include pH meters, ion-selective electrodes, redox potential measurement devices, conductivity meters, dissolved-oxygen meters, turbidity meters, colorimeters and spectrophotometers (infrared and ultraviolet), ultraviolet fluorescence, chemiluminescence, flame ionization detector, atomic absorption spectroscope (for metals), flame photometer, electrochemical cell, and photo-ionization detector. The analytical methods to be used are presented in Table 2.

*Solid Wastes*

The objectives of monitoring solid wastes are to determine the acceptable treatment, storage, transport, and disposal methods that can be used and to obtain information on production processes. Accuracy, the time needed for analysis, and monitoring cost are considered when determining the data to be obtained from monitoring solid waste streams. Representative samples are collected by methods such as moving a cutter through dry flowing material or collecting wet materials from sampling ports in a pipeline. The sampling frequency and the parameters to be analyzed are specified in the guidelines for specific industrial sectors. Analytical methods for solid wastes are provided in USEPA (1986).

Wastes that may leach toxics such as heavy metals are analyzed for their leachability by methods such as toxic characteristic leachate procedure, or TCLP (see United States, 40 CFR, Part 261, Appendix).

Monitoring of some process parameters is essential for processes that are prone to accidental releases. Typically, alarms are set to go off when a selected parameter (an indicator of a potential accidental release) exceeds a predetermined level. For example, the pressure of the polymerization reactor in a high-density polyethylene plant is used to warn of the imminent release of process ingredients to the atmosphere. Similarly, monitoring of oil in liquid effluents in a petroleum refinery can warn operators of possible leakage of oil from storage tanks or process areas to the effluent system when unusually high amounts of oil are detected.

*Surrogate Monitoring*

In some cases, alternative schemes, termed *surrogate monitoring,* are developed that cost-effectively achieve the objectives of environmental monitoring systems and, in some cases, even the objectives of process optimization. Monitoring of some key parameters reliably indicates the performance of the operating and pollution control systems. The validity of such a scheme is then established by performing a series of tests (say, three tests for each case of worse operating conditions) at regular intervals, usually at least once a year. For example, among the parameters needed to measure the performance of a power generation process are fuel feed rates, including the feed rates of ash and sulfur, in addition to heat content; steam pressure; steam production rate; temperature inside the combustion chamber (at the nearest feasible location of the probe to the burner or combustion zone); air feed rate; flue gas flow rate; minimum power supply to the electrostatic precipitator or minimum pressure drop across the baghouse; carbon monoxide level in the flue gases; and oxygen level in the flue gases (representing the excess oxygen level). Similarly, for aerobic biological treatment systems, the minimum power supply for the aeration equipment per unit of wastewater treated at maximum inlet BOD loads, validated by actual tests of the inlet and outlet streams, may be a

useful indicator of the treatment effectiveness of the system. The monitoring data of some of the key monitoring parameters need to be verified by alternate means to ensure some level of confidence in the monitored results. For example, the flowmeter readings can be verified by taking tank dips to check the results obtained from the flowmeter.

## Quality Assurance and Quality Control

Quality assurance means developing a system of activities to ensure that measurements meet defined standards of quality with a stated level of confidence. Development of a plan for quality assurance includes defining monitoring objectives, the quality control procedures to be followed, and quality assessment. Monitoring objectives are defined and are then used to arrive at data quality objectives, including accuracy, precision, completeness, representativeness, and comparability.

Quality assurance includes designing a network, selecting sampling or monitoring sites, selecting instruments and designing the sampling system, and developing a training schedule.

Quality control includes preparing protocols (including standard operating procedures and record keeping) for site operation and equipment maintenance; preparing protocols for equipment calibration; preparing site visit schedules; and preparing protocols for data inspection, review, validation, and usage. Quality assessment includes developing a schedule for audits and reports.

Typical monitoring objectives include establishing a sound scientific basis for policy development; determining compliance with statutory criteria; assessing population and ecosystem exposure and risk; providing public information; identifying pollution sources as a part of air and water quality management systems; and evaluating long-term trends.

## References and Sources

Bounicore, Anthony J., and Wayne T. Davis, eds. 1992. *Air Pollution Engineering Manual.* New York: Van Nostrand Reinhold.

Germany, Federal Minister for the Environment, Nature Conservation and Nuclear Safety. 1992. *Air*

*Pollution Control Manual for Continuous Emission Monitoring.* Bonn.

Jorgensen, S. E., and R. A. Vollenweider, eds. 1988. *Guidelines of Lake Management.* Vols. 1–5. United Nations Environment Programme and International Lake Environment Committee.

Lee, Donna J., and Ariel Dinar. 1995. "Review of Integrated Approaches to River Basin Planning, Development, and Management." Policy Research Working Paper 1446. World Bank, Agricultural and Natural Resources Department, Agricultural Policies Division. Washington, D.C.

Le Moigne, Guy, Ashok Subramanian, Mei Xie, and Sandra Giltner, eds. 1994. *A Guide to the Formulation of Water Resources Strategy.* World Bank Technical Paper 263. Washington, D.C.

Lioy, Paul J., and Mary Jean Lioy, eds. 1983. *Air Sampling Instruments for Evaluation of Atmospheric Contaminants.* Cincinnati, Ohio: American Conference of Governmental Industrial Hygienists.

UNEP (United Nations Environment Programme) and UNIDO (United Nations Industrial Development Organization). 1996. *Monitoring Industrial Emissions and Wastes.* Technical Report 27. Paris.

UNEP (United Nations Environment Programme) and WHO (World Health Organization). 1994. *Earthwatch, Global Environment Monitoring System (GEMS), GEMS/AIR Methodology Review Handbook Series.* Vols. 1, 2, and 3. Nairobi: UNEP; Geneva: WHO.

United Nations Statistical Commission and Economic Commission for Europe. 1984. *Statistics of Air Quality Models: Some Methods.* Conference of European Statisticians Statistical Standards and Studies 36. New York.

United States. CFR (*Code of Federal Regulations*). Washington, D.C.: Government Printing Office.

USEPA (United States Environmental Protection Agency). 1973. *Handbook for Monitoring Industrial Wastewater.* Washington, D.C.

————. 1982. *Air Quality Criteria for Particulate Matter and Sulfur Oxides.* Vols. I, II, and III. EPA-600/8-82-029a, b, and c. Research Triangle Park, N.C.

————. 1986. *Test Methods for Evaluating Solid Wastes.* SW-846. Washington, D.C.

————. 1993. *Guidance for Estimating Ambient Air Monitoring Costs for Criteria Pollutants and Selected Air Toxic Pollutants.* EPA-454/R-93-042. Research Triangle Park, N.C.: Office of Air Quality Planning and Standards.

WHO (World Health Organization). 1977. *GEMS: Global Environmental Monitoring System, Air Monitoring Program Design for Urban and Industrial Areas.* WHO Offset Publication 33. Geneva: United Nations Environment Programme, World Health Organization, and World Meteorological Organization.

————. 1979. "Sulfur Oxides and Suspended Particulate matter." *Environmental Health Criteria* 8. Geneva.

————. 1984. *Guidelines for Drinking Water Quality.* Geneva.

————. 1987. *Air Quality Guidelines for Europe.* European Series 23. Copenhagen: WHO Regional Office for Europe.

World Bank. 1991. "Staff Appraisal Report: India's Industrial Pollution Control Project." Report 9347-IN. Asia Technical Department, Industry and Finance Division, Washington, D.C.

————. 1993. *Water Resources Management.* World Bank Policy Paper. Washington, D.C.

————. 1997. "Environmental Monitoring Systems." Draft Technical Background Document. Environment Department, Washington, D.C.

# Summary of Air Emission and Effluent Discharge Requirements Presented in the Industry Guidelines

## Terms Used in the following Tables 1–3

| | |
|---|---|
| ADP | Air-dried pulp |
| Ag | Silver |
| AOX | Adsorbable organic halides |
| As | Arsenic |
| BOD | Biochemical oxygen demand (understood as BOD measured over five days, $BOD_5$) |
| Cd | Cadmium |
| Cl | Chlorine |
| CN | Cyanide |
| Co | Cobalt |
| CO | Carbon monoxide |
| COD | Chemical oxygen demand |
| $Cr^{+6}$ | Hexavalent chromium |
| Cr, total | Total chromium |
| CTMP | Chemical, thermal, mechanical process for producing pulp |
| Cu | Copper |
| F | Fluorine |
| Fe | Iron |
| g/mm Btu | Grams per million British thermal units |
| GJ | Gigajoule |
| HC | Hydrocarbons |
| HCl | Hydrogen chloride/hydrochloric acid |
| HF | Hydrogen fluoride/hydrofluoric acid |
| Hg | Mercury |
| $H_2S$ | Hydrogen sulfide |
| Kg | Kilogram |
| kg/t | Kilograms per metric ton |
| mg/l | Milligrams per liter |
| mg/m³ | Micrograms per cubic meter |
| Mg/Nm³ | Milligrams per normal cubic meter |
| MPN/100 ml | Coliform count expressed as most probable number per 100 milliliters |
| MWe | Megawatts of electricity |
| N | Nitrogen |
| Ng/J | Nanograms per joule |
| $NH_3$ | Ammonia |
| $NH_4$ | Ammonium nitrogen |
| Ni | Nickel |
| $NO_3$ | Nitrate nitrogen |
| $NO_x$ | Nitrogen oxides |
| O&G | Oil and grease |
| P | Phosphorus |
| PAH | Polynuclear aromatic hydrocarbons |
| Pb | Lead |
| pH | Measure of acidity/alkalinity |
| PM | Particulate matter |
| $PM_{2.5}$ | Particulate matter with aerodynamic diameter less than 2.5 microns |
| $PM_{10}$ | Particulate matter with aerodynamic diameter less than 10 microns |
| ppm | Parts per million |
| S | Sulfur |
| Sb | Antimony |
| Se | Selenium |
| Sn | Tin |
| $SO_2$ | Sulfur dioxide |
| $SO_x$ | Sulfur oxides |
| t | Metric ton |
| TCE | Trichloroethylene |
| Temp. increase | Temperature increase at the edge of the zone where initial mixing and dilution take place; where the zone is not defined, 100 meters from the point of discharge is used |
| tpd/MWe | Metric tons per day per megawatt of electricity |
| TSS | Total suspended solids |
| V | Vanadium |
| VOCs | Volatile organic compounds |
| WAD | Weak acid dissociable cyanide |
| Zn | Zinc |

**Table 1. Air Emission Requirements: Parameters and Maximum Values**

(mg/Nm³, unless otherwise specified)

| Guideline | PM | SO$_x$ | NO$_x$ | Other; comments |
|---|---|---|---|---|
| Aluminum manufacturing | 30 | | | Total F: 2; HF: 1; VOCs: 20 |
| Base metal and iron ore mining | | | | |
| Breweries | | | | |
| Cement manufacturing | 50 | 400 | 600 | |
| Chlor-alkali industry | | | | Cl: 3 |
| Coal mining and production | 50 | | | |
| Coke manufacturing | 50 | 1,000 (SO$_2$) | | Benzene: 5 (leaks); VOCs: 20; sulfur recovery at least 97% (preferably over 99%) |
| Copper smelting | * | | | PM: smelters, 20, other sources, 50; As: 0.5; Cd: 0.05; Cu: 1; Pb: 0.2; Hg: 0.05 |
| Dairy industry | | | | Odor: acceptable to neighbors |
| Dye manufacturing | 50 | | | Cl: 10; VOCs: 20 |
| Electronics manufacturing | | | | VOCs: 20; phosphine: 1; arsine: 1; HF: 5; HCl: 10 |
| Electroplating industry | | | | VOCs: 90% recovery |
| Foundries | * | | | PM: 20 where toxic metals are present, 50 in other cases |
| Fruit and vegetable processing | | | | |
| General environmental guidelines | * | 2,000 (SO$_2$) | Coal: 750 (260 ng/J or 365 ppm) Oil: 460 (130 ng/J or 225 ppm) Gas: 320 (86 ng/J or 155 ppm) | PM: 50 for ≥ 50 MWe; 100 < 50MWe; dioxins: 2,3,7,8-TCSS equivalent): maximum of 1 ng/Nm³ |
| Glass manufacturing | * | Oil fired: 1,800 Gas fired: 700 | 1,000 (up to 2,000 depending on technology and if justified in the EA) | PM: 50 (20 where toxic metals are present); Pb + Cd: 5; heavy metals (other, total): 5; As: 1; F: 5; HCl: 50 |
| Industrial estates | * | 2,000 | Solid fuels: 750 (260 ng/J or 365 ppm); Liquid fuels: 460 (130 ng/J or 225 ppm); Gaseous fuels: 320 (86 ng/J or 155 ppm) | PM: 50 (> 10 GJ/hr), 150 (< 10 GJ/hr); H$_2$S: 15 |
| Iron and steel manufacturing | 50 | 500 (sintering) | 750 (260 ng/J or 365 ppm) | F: 5 |
| Lead and zinc smelting | 20 | 400 (SO$_2$) | | As: 0.1; Cd: 0.05; Cu: 0.5; Hg: 0.05; Pb: 0.5; Zn: 1 |
| Meat processing and rendering | * | | | PM: 150 for smokehouses with a carbon content of less than 50; odor: minimize impacts on residents |
| Mini steel mills | * | 2,000 | 750 | PM: 20 where toxic metals are present, 50 in other cases |
| Mixed fertilizer plants | 50 | | 500 (nitrophosphate unit) 70 (mixed acid unit) | NH$_3$: 50; F: 5 |

| Industry | | | | Other; comments |
|---|---|---|---|---|
| Nitrogenous fertilizer plants | 50 | | 300 | $NH_3$: 50; urea: 50 |
| Oil and gas development (onshore) | | 1,000 | Oil: 460 (130 ng/J or 225 ppm)<br>Gas: 320 (86 ng/J or 155 ppm) | VOCs: 20; $H_2S$: 30; odor: not offensive at receptor end ($H_2S$ at the property boundary should be less than 5 $\mu g/m^3$) |
| Pesticides formulation | * | | | PM: 20 (5 where very toxic compounds are present); VOCs: 20; Cl: 5 |
| Pesticides manufacturing | * | | | PM: 20 (5 where very toxic compounds are present); VOCs: 20; Cl: 5 |
| Petrochemicals manufacturing | 20 | 500 | 300 | HCl: 10; benzene: 5 (emissions), 0.1 ppb (plant fence); 1,2-dichloroethane: 5 (emissions), 1.0 ppb (plant fence); vinyl chloride: 5 (emissions), 0.4 ppb (plant fence); $NH_3$: 15 |
| Petroleum refining | 50 | 150 (sulfur recovery units)<br>500 (combustion units) | 460 (130 ng/J or 225 ppm) | $H_2S$: 15; Ni + V: 2 |
| Pharmaceutical manufacturing | 20 | 460 (130 ng/J or 225 ppm) | | Active ingredients (each): 0.15; Class A compounds (total): 20; Class B compounds (total): 80; benzene, vinyl chloride, dichloroethane (each): 5; F: 5 |
| Phosphate fertilizer plants | 50 | Sulfuric acid plant:<br>$SO_2$: 2 kg/t acid<br>$SO_3$: 0.15 kg/t acid | | |
| Printing industry | * | | | VOCs: 20; Cl: 10 |
| Pulp and paper mills | * | | 2 kg/t ADP | PM: 100 (recovery furnace); $H_2S$: 15 (lime kilns); S (total): 1.5 kg/ton ADP (sulfite mills), 1.0 kg/ton ADP (kraft and other) |
| Sugar manufacturing | * | 2,000 | Liquid fuels: 460 (130 ng/J or 225 ppm)<br>Solid fuels: 750 (260 ng/J or 365 ppm) | PM: 100 (150 mg/$Nm^3$ for small mills with less than 8.7 MW heat input to the boiler); odor: acceptable to residents |
| Tanning and leather finishing | | | | Odor: acceptable to neighbors<br>VOC: 20 |
| Textiles industry | | | | |
| Thermal power, new plants | 50* | 0.2 tpd/MWe (to 500 MWe)<br>0.1 tpd/MWe (incr. over 500 MWe)<br>Not to exceed 2,000 mg/$Nm^3$ in flue gases<br>Not to exceed 500 tpd | For thermal power plants:<br>Coal: 750 (260 ng/J or 365 ppm);<br>Oil: 460 (130 ng/J or 225 ppm);<br>Gas: 320 (86 ng/J or 155 ppm)<br>For combustion turbine units:<br>Gas: 125<br>Diesel fuel (No. 2 oil): 165<br>Fuel oil (No. 6 and other): 300 | Less than 50 MWe: PM 100; for coal with less than 10% volatile matter, $NO_x$ is 1,500 mg/$Nm^3$ |
| Thermal power, rehabilitation of existing plants | 100* | | | In rare cases, 150 mg/$Nm^3$ PM is acceptable |
| Vegetable oil processing | 50 | | | Odor: acceptable to neighbors<br>VOCs: 20 |
| Wood preserving industry | | | | |

* See column headed "Other; comments."

# Table 2. Effluent Discharge Requirements: Parameters and Maximum Values, Miscellaneous Parameters

*(mg/l, except pH and as otherwise specified)*

| Guideline | pH | BOD₅ | COD | TSS | O&G | Phenol | CN⁻ | N | P | F | Cl | Coli-form | Temp. Increase | Other; comments |
|---|---|---|---|---|---|---|---|---|---|---|---|---|---|---|
| Aluminum manufacturing | 6–9 | | 150 | 50 | | | | | | 20 | | | ≤3°C | HC: 5 |
| Base metal and iron ore mining | 6–9 | | 150 | 50 | 10 | | Free: 0.1 WAD: 0.5 Total: 1.0 | | | | | | | |
| Breweries | 6–9 | 50 | 250 | 50 | 10 | | | NH₄: 10 | 5 | | | | ≤3°C | |
| Cement manufacturing | 6–9 | | | 50 | | | | | | | | | ≤3°C | |
| Chlor-alkali industry | 6–9 | | 150 | 20 | | | | | | | 0.2 | | | AOX: 0.5; sulfite: 1.0 TSS: 35 (monthly average) |
| Coal mining and production | 6–9 | | | 50 | 10 | | | | | | | | | |
| Coke manufacturing | | 30 | 150 | 50 | 10 | 0.5 | Total: 0.2 | Total: 10 | | | | | ≤3°C | Benzene: 0.05; dibenz(a,h)anthracene: 0.05; benzo(a)pyrene: 0.05 |
| Copper smelting | 6–9 | | | 50 | | | | | | | | | ≤3°C | |
| Dairy industry | 6–9 | 50 | 250 | 50 | 10 | | | Total: 10 | 2 | | | 400 MPN/100 ml | ≤3°C | |
| Dye manufacturing | 6–9 | 30 | 150 | 50 | 10 | 0.5 | | | | | | | | Total organic (each), e.g., benzidine: 0.05; AOX: 1 mg/l |
| Electronics manufacturing | 6–9 | 50 | | * | 10 | | Free: 0.1 Total: 1 | NH₃: 10 | 5 | 20 | | | | TSS: 50 (maximum), 20 (monthly average); chlorocarbons and hydrochlorocarbons (total): 0.5 |
| Electroplating industry | 7–10 | | | 25 | 10 | | Free: 0.2 | | 5 | 20 | | | | Trichloroethylene and trichloroethane (each): 0.05 |
| Foundries | 6–9 | | | 50 | 10 | | | | | | | | | |
| Fruit and vegetable processing | 6–9 | 50 | 250 | 50 | 10 | | | Total: 10 | 5 | | | | ≤3°C | |
| General environmental guidelines | 6–9 | 50 | 250 | 50 | 10 | 0.5 | Total: 1 Free: 0.1 | NH₃: 10 | 2 | 20 | 0.2 | 400 MPN/100 ml | ≤3°C | Sulfide: 1.0 |
| Glass manufacturing | 6–9 | | 250 | 50 | 10 | | | | | | | | | |
| Industrial estates | 6–9 | 50 | 250 | 50* | 10 | 0.5 | | | | | | | ≤3°C | TSS: 20 mg/l where toxic metals are present at significant levels; sulfide: 1; AOX: 1; benzene: 0.05; benzo(a)pyrene: 0.05 |

| Industry | pH | BOD | COD | TSS | Oil and grease | Phenols | Cyanide | Ammonia / Total N | | Coliform | Temperature increase | Other parameters |
|---|---|---|---|---|---|---|---|---|---|---|---|---|
| Iron and steel manufacturing | 6–9 | | 250 | 50 | 10 | 0.5 | Free: 0.1; Total: 1 | | | | ≤3° C | |
| Lead and zinc smelting | 6–9 | | 50 | 20 | | | | | | | ≤3° C | |
| Meat processing and rendering | 6–9 | 50 | 250 | 50 | 10 | | | Total: 10 | | 400 MPN/100 ml | ≤3° C | |
| Mini steel mills | 6–9 | | | 50 | 10 | | | | 5 | | ≤3° C | |
| Mixed fertilizer plants | 6–9 | | | 50 | | | | NH$_4$: 10 | 5 | | | |
| Nickel smelting and refining | 6–9 | | | 50 | | | | | | | ≤3° C | |
| Nitrogenous fertilizer plants | 6–9 | | | 50 | | | | NH$_3$: 10; Urea: 1 | 20 | | ≤3° C | |
| Oil and gas development (onshore) | 6–9 | | | 50 | 20* | 1 | | | | | ≤3° C | O&G: up to 40 mg/l is acceptable for facilities producing < 10,000 tpd.; sulfide: 1 |
| Pesticides formulation | 6–9 | | 150 | 20 | 10 | | | | | | | TSS: 20, monthly average must not exceed 50 mg/l at any time; AOX: 1; organochlorines: 0.05; nitroorganics: 0.05; pyrethroids: 0.05; phenoxy compounds: 0.05; active ingredients (each): 0.05 |
| Pesticides manufacturing | 6–9 | 30 | 150 | 10 | 10 | 0.5 | | | | | | AOX: 1; active ingredients (each): 0.05; BOD test to be done only when no toxics to microorganisms are present |
| Petrochemicals manufacturing | 6–9 | 30 | 150 | 30 | 10 | 0.5 | | Total: 10 | | | ≤3° C | Benzene: 0.05; vinyl chloride: 0.05; sulfide: 1 |
| Petroleum refining | 6–9 | 30 | 150 | 30 | 10 | 0.5 | | Total: 10 | | | ≤3° C | Benzene: 0.05; benzo(a)pyrene: 0.05; sulfide: 1 |
| Pharmaceutical manufacturing | 6–9 | 30* | 150 | 10 | 10 | 0.5 | | | | | | AOX: 1; active ingredients (each): 0.05; BOD test to be done only when no toxics to microorganisms are present |

*(Table continues on the following page.)*

**Table 2.** *(continued)*

| Guideline | pH | $BOD_5$ | COD | TSS | O&G | Phenol | $CN^-$ | N | P | F | Cl | Coliform | Temp. Increase | Other; comments |
|---|---|---|---|---|---|---|---|---|---|---|---|---|---|---|
| Phosphate fertilizer plants | 6–9 | | | 50 | | | | | 5 | 20 | | | | |
| Printing industry | 6.5–10 | 30 | 150 | 50 | 10 | | | | | | | | | |
| Pulp and paper mills | 6–9 | | * | | | | | 0.4 kg/t | 0.05 kg/t | | | | ≤ 3° C | COD: kraft and CTMP, 300 mg/l, 15 kg/t; sulfite, 700 mg/l, 40 kg/t; mechanical and recycled fiber, 10 mg/l, 5 kg/t; paper mills, 250 mg/l; AOX: 40 mg/l, 2 kg/t for new mills (target is 4 mg/l. 0.2 kg/t); 40 mg/l, 2 kg/t for retrofits (target is 8 mg/l, 0.4 kg/t); 4 mg/l for paper mills |
| Sugar manufacturing | 6–9 | 50 | 250 | 50 | 10 | | | $NH_4$: 10 | 2 | | | 400 MPN/ 100 ml | ≤ 3° C | |
| Tanning and leather finishing | 6–9 | 50 | 250 | 50 | 10 | 0.5 | | $NH_4$: 10 | 2 | | | 400 MPN/ 100 ml | | Sulfide: 1 |
| Textiles industry | 6–9 | 50 | 250 | 50 | 10 | | | | | | | | ≤ 3° C | AOX: 8; pesticides (each): 0.05; sulfide: 1 |
| Thermal power | 6–9 | | | 50 | 10 | | | | | | Total residual: 0.2* | | ≤ 3° C | Chlorine shocking: maximum value is 2 mg/l for up to 2 hours, not to be repeated more frequently than once in 24 hours, with a 24-hour average of 0.2 mg/l |
| Vegetable oil processing | 6–9 | 50 | 250 | 50 | 10 | | | Total: 10 | | | | | | |
| Wood preserving industry | 6–9 | 50 | 150 | 50 | 10 | 0.5 | | | | 20 | | | ≤ 3° C | PAHs (each): 0.05; pesticides (each): 0.05; dioxins/furans (sum of all): 0.0005 |

* See column headed "Other; comments."

198

## Table 3. Effluent Discharge Requirements: Parameters and Maximum Values, Metals

(mg/l, unless otherwise specified)

| Guideline | Ag | Al | As | Cd | $Cr^{+6}$ | Total Cr | Cu | Fe | Hg | Ni | Pb | Sn | Zn | Total metals | Other; comments |
|---|---|---|---|---|---|---|---|---|---|---|---|---|---|---|---|
| Aluminum manufacturing | | 0.2 | | | | | | | | | | | | | |
| Base metal and iron ore mining | | | 0.1 | 0.1 | 0.1 | | 0.5 | 3.5 | 0.01 | 0.5 | 0.2 | | 2 | 10 | |
| Breweries | | | | | | | | | | | | | | | |
| Cement manufacturing | | | | | | | | | | | | | | | |
| Chlor-alkali industry | | | | | | | | | | | | | | | |
| Coal mining and production | | | | | | | | 3.5 | | | | | | 10 | |
| Coke manufacturing | | | | | | | | | | | | | | | |
| Copper smelting | | | 0.1 | 0.1 | | | 0.5 | 3.5 | 0.01 | | 0.1 | | 1 | 10 | |
| Dairy industry | | | | | | | | | | | | | | | |
| Dye manufacturing | | | | | 0.1 | | 0.5 | | | | | | 2 | | |
| Electronics manufacturing | | | 0.1 | 0.1 | 0.1 | | 0.5 | | 0.01 | 0.5 | 0.1 | 2 | | 10 | |
| Electroplating industry | 0.5 | | 0.1 | 0.1 | 0.1 | 0.5 | 0.5 | | 0.01 | 0.5 | 0.2 | | 2 | 10 | |
| Foundries | | | | | | | 0.5 | | | | | | 2 | | |
| Fruit and vegetable processing | | | | | | | | | | | | | | | |
| General manufacturing | 0.5 | | 0.1 | 0.1 | 0.1 | 0.5 | | 3.5 | 0.01 | 0.5 | 0.1 | | 2 | 10 | Se: 0.1 |
| Glass manufacturing | | | | | | | | | | | 0.1 | | | 10 | |
| Industrial estates | | | | 0.1 | 0.1 | 0.5 | 0.5 | | | 0.5 | 0.1 | | 2 | | |
| Iron and steel manufacturing | | | | 0.1 | | 0.5 | | | 0.01 | | 0.2 | | 2 | | |
| Lead and zinc smelting | | | 0.1 | 0.1 | | 0.5 | 0.5 | 3.5 | 0.01 | | 0.1 | | 2 | 5 | |
| Meat processing and rendering | | | | | | | | | | | | | | | |
| Mini steel mills | | | | 0.1 | 0.1 | 0.5 | 0.5 | | | 0.5 | 0.1 | | | | |
| Mixed fertilizer plants | | | | 0.1 | | | | | | | | | | 10 | |
| Nickel smelting and refining | | | | | | | | 3.5 | | 0.5 | | | | 10 | |
| Nitrogenous fertilizer plants | | | | | | | | | | | | | | | |
| Oil and gas development (onshore) | | | | | | | | | | | | | | See com-ments | Total toxic metals (antimony, arsenic, beryllium, cadmium, chromium, copper, lead, mercury, nickel, selenium, silver, thallium, vanadium, zinc): 5 |
| Pesticides formulation | | | 0.1 | | 0.1 | | 0.5 | | 0.01 | | | | | | |
| Pesticides manufacturing | | | 0.1 | | 0.1 | | 0.5 | | 0.01 | | | | | | |
| Petrochemicals manufacturing | | | | 0.1 | 0.1 | | 0.5 | | | | | | | | |

(Table continues on the following page.)

# Table 3. (continued)

| Guideline | Ag | Al | As | Cd | Cr+6 | Cr (Total) | Cu | Fe | Hg | Ni | Pb | Sn | Zn | Total metals | Other; comments |
|---|---|---|---|---|---|---|---|---|---|---|---|---|---|---|---|
| Petroleum refining | | | | | 0.1 | 0.5 | | | | | 0.1 | | | | |
| Pharmaceutical manufacturing | | | 0.1 | 0.1 | 0.1 | | | | 0.01 | | | | | | |
| Phosphate fertilizer plants | | | | 0.1 | | | | | | | | | | | |
| Printing industry | 0.5 | | | 0.1 | 0.1 | 0.5 | 0.5 | 0.5 | | | | | | 2 | |
| Pulp and paper mills | | | | | | | | | | | | | | | |
| Sugar manufacturing | | | | | | | | | | | | | | | |
| Tanning and leather finishing | | | | | 0.1 | 0.5 | | | | | | | | | |
| Textiles industry | | | | | | 0.5 | 0.5 | | | 0.5 | | | 2 | | |
| Thermal power | | | | | | 0.5 | 0.5 | 1 | | | | | 1 | | Co: 0.5 |
| Vegetable oil processing | | | | | | | | | | | | | | | |
| Wood preserving industry | | | 0.1 | 0.1 | 0.1 | 0.5 | 0.5 | | | | | | | | |

# Airborne Particulate Matter

Airborne particulate matter, which includes dust, dirt, soot, smoke, and liquid droplets emitted into the air, is small enough to be suspended in the atmosphere. Airborne particulates may be a complex mixture of organic and inorganic substances. They can be characterized by their physical attributes, which influence their transport and deposition, and their chemical composition, which influences their effect on health.

The physical attributes of airborne particulates include mass concentration and size distribution. Ambient levels of mass concentration are measured in micrograms per cubic meter (mg/m³); size attributes are usually measured in aerodynamic diameter. Particulate matter (PM) exceeding 2.5 microns (mm) in aerodynamic diameter is generally defined as coarse particles, while particles smaller than 2.5 mm (PM$_{2.5}$) are called fine particles. The acid component of particulate matter, and most of its mutagenic activity, are generally contained in fine particles, although some coarse acid droplets are also present in fog. Samples taken in the United States showed that about 30% of particulate matter was in the fine fraction (Stern et al. 1984).

Particles interact with various substances in the air to form organic or inorganic chemical compounds. The most common combinations of fine particles are those with sulfates. In the United States, sulfate ions account for about 40% of fine particulates and may also be present in concentrations exceeding 10 micrograms per normal cubic meter, mg/Nm³ (USEPA 1982b). The smaller particles contain the secondarily formed aerosols, combustion particles, and recondensed organic and metal vapors. The carbonaceous component of fine particles—products of incomplete combustion—contains both elemental carbon (graphite and soot) and nonvolatile or- ganic carbon (hydrocarbons emitted in combustion exhaust, and secondary organic compounds formed by photochemistry). These species may be the most abundant fine particles after sulfates. Additionally, atmospheric reactions of nitrogen oxides produce nitric acid vapor (HNO$_3$) that may accumulate as nitrate particles in both fine and coarse forms. The most common combination of coarse particles consists of oxides of silicon, aluminum, calcium, and iron.

## Terms and Sampling Techniques

Several terms are used to describe particulates. Generally, these terms are associated with the sampling method:

*Total suspended particulates (TSP)* includes particles of various sizes. Some proportion of TSP consists of particles too large to enter the human respiratory tract; therefore, TSP is not a good indicator of health-related exposure. TSP is measured by a high-volume gravimetric sampler that collects suspended particles on a glass-fiber filter. The upper limit for TSP is 45 mm in diameter in the United States and up to 160 μm in Europe.

TSP sampling and TSP-based standards were used in the United States until 1987. Several countries in Central and Eastern Europe, Latin America, and Asia still monitor and set standards based on measurements of TSP. As monitoring methods and data analysis have become more sophisticated, the focus of attention has gradually shifted to fine particulates. Recent evidence shows that fine particulates, which can reach the thoracic regions of the respiratory tract, or lower, are responsible for most of the excess mortality and morbidity associated with high levels of exposure to particulates. Most sophisticated studies suggest that fine particulates are the sole factor accounting for this health damage, while exposure to coarse particulates has little or no independent effect.

The particles most likely to cause adverse health effects are the *fine particulates* $PM_{10}$ and $PM_{2.5}$—particles smaller than 10 mm and 2.5 mm in aerodynamic diameter, respectively. They are sampled using (a) a high-volume sampler with a size-selective inlet using a quartz filter or (b) a dichotomous sampler that operates at a slower flow rate, separating on a Teflon filter particles smaller than 2.5 mm and sizes between 2.5 mm and 10 mm. No generally accepted conversion method exists between TSP and $PM_{10}$, which may constitute between 40% and 70% of TSP (USEPA1982b).

In 1987, the USEPA switched its air quality standards from TSP to $PM_{10}$. $PM_{10}$ standards have also been adopted in, for example, Brazil, Japan, and the Philippines. In light of the emerging evidence on the health impacts of fine particulates, the USEPA has proposed that U.S. ambient standards for airborne particulates be defined in fine particulates.

*Black smoke (BS)* is a particulate measure that typically contains at least 50% respirable particulates smaller than 4.5 mm in aerodynamic diameter, sampled by the British smokeshade (BS) method. The reflectance of light is measured by the darkness of the stain caused by particulates on a white filter paper. The result of BS sampling depends on the density of the stain and the optical properties of the particulates. Because the method is based on reflectance from elemental carbon, its use is recommended in areas where coal smoke from domestic fires is the dominant component of ambient particulates (WHO and UNEP 1992). After reviewing the available data, Ostro (1994) concluded that BS is roughly equivalent to $PM_{10}$. However, there is no precise equivalence of the black smoke measurements with other methods. The BS measure is most widely used in Great Britain and elsewhere in Europe.

## Sources of Particulates

Some particulates come from natural sources such as evaporated sea spray, windborne pollen, dust, and volcanic or other geothermal eruptions. Particulates from natural sources tend to be coarse. Almost all fine particulates are generated as a result of combustion processes, including the burning of fossil fuels for steam generation, heating and household cooking, agricultural field burning, diesel-fueled engine combustion, and various industrial processes. Emissions from these anthropogenic sources tend to be in fine fractions. However, some industrial and other processes that produce large amounts of dust, such as cement manufacturing, mining, stone crushing, and flour milling, tend to generate particles larger than 1 mm and mostly larger than 2.5 mm. In cold and temperate parts of the world, domestic coal burning has been a major contributor to the particulate content of urban air. Traffic-related emissions may make a substantial contribution to the concentration of suspended particulates in areas close to traffic. Some agroindustrial processes and road traffic represent additional anthropogenic sources of mostly coarse particulate emissions.

The largest stationary sources of particulate emissions include fossil-fuel-based thermal power plants, metallurgical processes, and cement manufacturing. The physical and chemical composition of particulate emissions is determined by the nature of pollution sources. Most particles emitted by anthropogenic sources are less than 2.5 mm in diameter and include a larger variety of toxic elements than particles emitted by natural sources. Fossil fuel combustion generates metal and sulfur particulate emissions, depending on the chemical composition of the fuel used. The USEPA (1982b) estimates that more than 90% of fine particulates emitted from stationary combustion sources are combined with sulfur dioxide ($SO_2$). Sulfates, however, do not necessarily form the largest fraction of fine particulates. In locations such as Bangkok, Chongqing (China), and São Paulo (Brazil), organic carbon compounds account for a larger fraction of fine particulates, reflecting the role of emissions from diesel and two-stroke vehicles or of smoke from burning coal and charcoal. Although sulfates represent a significant share (30–40%) of fine particulates in these cases, care is required before making general assertions about the relationship between sulfates and fine particulates, since the sources and species characteristics of fine particulates may vary significantly across locations. Combustion devices may emit particulates comprised of products of incomplete combustion (PICs, which may include toxic organics) and toxic metals, which are present in the fuel and in some cases may also be carcinogenic. Particulates emitted by thermal power generation may contain lead, mercury, and other heavy metals. The melting, pouring, and torch-cutting procedures of metallurgy emit metal particulates containing lead, cadmium, and nickel. Particles emitted by the cement industry are largely stone or clay-based particulates that may contain toxic metals such as lead.

## Impacts of Exposure

### Human Health Effects

The respiratory system is the major route of entry for airborne particulates. The deposition of particulates in different parts of the human respiratory system depends on particle size, shape, density, and individual breathing patterns (mouth or nose breathing). The effect on the human organism is also influenced by the chemical composition of the particles, the duration of exposure, and individual susceptibility. While all particles smaller than 10 mm in diameter can reach the human lungs, the retention rate is largest for the finer particles.

Products of incomplete combustion, which form a significant portion of the fine particulates, may enter deep into the lungs. PICs contribute significantly to health impacts associated with fine particulates.

Clinical, epidemiologic, and toxicological sources are used to estimate the mortality and morbidity effects of short- and long-term exposure to various particulate concentration levels. Several studies have found statistically significant relationships between high short-term ambient particulate concentrations and excess mortality in London and elsewhere. The estimated 4,000 excess deaths in the London metropolitan area in December 1952 were associated with BS measurements equivalent to a 4,000 mg/m³ maximum daily average ambient concentration of particulates (Schwartz and Dockery 1992b). Schwartz (1993b) has also found a significant association between daily average $PM_{10}$ concentrations and mortality at concentrations below the current U.S. standard of 150 mg/m³ for short-term $PM_{10}$ concentrations.

Population-based cross-sectional and longitudinal studies (see, for example, Lipfert 1984; Dockery et al. 1993) have found an association between long-term exposure and mortality. Using 14-to-16-year studies in six U.S. cities, and controlling for individual risk factors, including age, sex, smoking, body-mass index, and occupational exposure, Dockery et al. (1993) found a significant connection between particulate air pollution and excess mortality at average annual $PM_{10}$ concentrations as low as 18 mg/m³, well below the current U.S. ambient standard of 50 mg/m³. Studies on the effect of particulates on human health summarized by Ostro (1994) suggest an increase in human mortality rates ranging from 0.3% to 1.6% for each 10 mg/m³ increase in average annual $PM_{10}$ concentrations.

A study conducted on over a half million people in 151 U.S. metropolitan areas during 1982–89 by Pope et al. (1995) found that death rates in the areas most polluted with fine particulates were 17% higher than in the least polluted areas, as a result of a 31% higher rate of death from heart and lung disease, even when most cities complied with the U.S. federal standards for particulate pollution. Cities with average pollution that complied with federal standards still had about a 5% higher death rate than the cleanest cities.

In addition, relationships between morbidity and short- and long-term exposure to particulate matter have been found in a number of studies. Schwartz et al. (1993) found a significant increase in emergency room visits among people under the age of 65 in areas with daily average $PM_{10}$ concentrations that were less than 70% of the U.S. air quality standard of 150 mg/m³. Several studies carried out in Canada, Germany, Switzerland, and the United States have found an association between respiratory symptoms and exposure to long-term ambient particulate concentrations of about 30–35 mg/m³, without any evidence of a threshold level below which health effects do not occur. (For a summary, see Schwartz 1991/92.) Kane (1994) demonstrated an association between mineral dusts such as silica or asbestos fibers accumulating in the lungs and a characteristic spectrum of diseases. Recently, the potential carcinogenic effect of certain dust compounds has been analyzed, and in some cases (for example, for silica dust), limited evidence of carcinogenic effects has been found (see Ulm 1994).

Recent epidemiologic evidence (for example, Schwartz 1991/92; Schwartz and Dockery 1992b; Ostro 1994) suggests that there may be no safe threshold for fine particulate matter and that the effects are linearly related to concentration.

*Other Effects*

Vegetation exposed to wet and dry deposition of particulates may be injured when particulates are combined with other pollutants. Coarse particles, such as dust, directly deposited on leaf surfaces can reduce gas exchange and photosynthesis, leading to reduced plant growth. Heavy metals that may be present in particulates, when deposited on soil, inhibit the process in soil that makes nutrients available to plants. This, combined with the effects of particulates on leaves, may contribute to reduction of plant growth and yields. In addition, particulates contribute to the soiling and erosion of buildings, materials, and paint, leading to increased cleaning and maintenance costs and to loss of utility.

Particulate emissions have their greatest impact on terrestrial ecosystems in the vicinity of emissions sources. Ecological alterations may be the result of particulate emissions that include toxic elements. Furthermore, the presence of fine particulates may cause light scattering, or atmospheric haze, reducing visibility and adversely affecting transport safety, property values, and aesthetics.

## Ambient Standards and Guidelines

The most frequently used reference guidelines for ambient particulate concentration are those of WHO, the EU, and the USEPA. These guidelines are based on clinical, toxicological, and epidemiologic evidence and were established by determining the concentrations with the lowest observed adverse effect (implicitly accepting the notion that a lower threshold exists under which no adverse human health effects can be detected), adjusted by an arbitrary margin of safety factor to allow for uncertainties in extrapolation from animals to humans and from small groups of humans to larger populations.[1] The WHO guidelines are based on health considerations alone;

the EU and USEPA standards also reflect the technological feasibility of meeting the standards. In the EU, a prolonged consultation and legislative decisionmaking process took into account the environmental conditions and the economic and social development of the various regions and countries and acknowledged a phased approach to compliance. A potential tradeoff was also recognized in the guidelines for the combined effects of sulfur dioxide and particulate matter (see European Community 1992).

## Conclusions

The main objective of air quality guidelines and standards is the protection of human health. Since fine particulates ($PM_{10}$) are more likely to cause adverse health effects than coarse particulates, guidelines and standards referring to fine particulate concentrations are preferred to those referring to TSP, which includes coarse particulate concentrations.

Scientific studies provide ample evidence of the relationship between exposure to short-term and long-term ambient particulate concentrations and human mortality and morbidity effects. However, the dose-response mechanism is not yet fully understood. Furthermore, according to WHO (1987), there is no safe threshold level below which health damage does not occur. Therefore, policymakers may have to consider acceptable risk rather than try to achieve absolute safety when setting ambient particulate concentration standards. Furthermore, ambient guidelines can become an effective part of the environmental management system only if implementation is feasible and the enforcement of other policy instruments ensures their attainment. Consideration should therefore be given to the technical feasibility and the costs of attainment.

Another difficulty is that airborne particulates are rarely homogeneous: They vary greatly in size and shape, and their chemical composition is determined by factors specific to the source and location of the emissions. The combined effects and interactions of various substances mixed with particulates have not yet been established (except for sulfur dioxide), but they are believed to be significant, especially where long-term exposure occurs. Measurement techniques and their reliability may vary across regions and countries, and so may other factors, such as diet, lifestyle, and physical fitness, that influence the human health effects of exposure to particulates.

## Recommendations

In the long term, countries should seek to ensure that ambient exposure to particulates, especially to $PM_{10}$, do not exceed the WHO recommended guidelines (see Table 1). In the interim, countries should set ambient standards for total particulates, $PM_{10}$, or both that take into account (a) the benefits to human health of reducing exposure to particulates; (b) the concentration levels achievable by pollution prevention and control measures; and (c) the costs involved in meeting the standards. In adopting new ambient air quality standards, countries should set appropriate phase-in periods during which districts or municipalities that do not meet the new standards are expected to come into compliance and will be assisted to attain the standards. Where there are large differences between the costs and benefits of meeting air quality standards, it may be

appropriate to establish area-specific ambient standards case by case.

Prior to carrying out an environmental assessment, a trigger value for annual average concentrations of $PM_{10}$ should be agreed on by the country and the World Bank. Countries may wish to adopt EU, USEPA, or WHO guidelines or standards as their trigger values. The trigger value should be equal to or lower than the country's ambient standard. The trigger value is not an ambient air quality standard but simply a threshold. If, as a result of the project, the trigger value is predicted to be exceeded in the area affected by the project, the EA assessment should seek mitigation alternatives on a regional or sectoral basis. In the absence of an agreed value, the World Bank Group will classify an airshed as moderately degraded if the annual average concentration levels of particulates are above 50 mg/m³ or if the 98th percentile of 24-hour mean values over a one-year period is estimated to exceed 150 mg/m³ of $PM_{10}$. In areas where $PM_{10}$ measurements do not exist, the value of 80 mg/m³ for TSP will be used. Airsheds will be classified as having poor air quality with respect to particulate mat-

## Table 1. Reference Standards and Guidelines for Average Ambient Particulate Concentration
*(micrograms per cubic meter)*

| Standard or guideline | Long-term (annual) | | | Short-term (24 hours) | | |
|---|---|---|---|---|---|---|
| | $PM_{10}$ | BS | TSP | $PM_{10}$ | BS | TSP |
| EU limit values | | 80[a] | 150[b] | | 250[c] | 300[d] |
| EU guide values | | 40–60[a] | | | 100–150[e] | |
| USEPA primary and secondary standards | 50[f] | | | 150[g] | | |
| WHO guidelines[h] | | 40–60 | 60–90 | | 100–150 | 150–230 |
| WHO guidelines for Europe[g] | 50 | | 70[i] | 125 | 120 | |

*Notes:* PM10, particulate matter less than 10 microns in aerodynamic diameter; BS, black smoke (converted to µg/Nm³ measure); TSP, total suspended particulates.
a. Median of daily mean values.
b. Arithmetic mean of daily mean values.
c. 98th percentile of all daily mean values throughout the year.
d. 95th percentile of all daily mean values throughout the year.
e. Daily mean values.
f. Arithmetic mean.
g. Guideline values for combined exposure to sulfur dioxide and particulates.
h. Not to be exceeded for more than one day per year.
i. Guideline for thoracic particles. According to International Organization for Standardization standard ISO-TP, thoracic particle measurements are roughly equivalent to the sampling characteristics for particulate matter with a 50% cutoff point at 10 mm diameter. Values are to be regarded as tentative at this time, being based on a single study that also involved sulfur dioxide exposure.
*Sources:* European Community 1992 (EU); United States, CFR (USEPA); WHO 1979 (WHO guidelines); WHO 1987 (WHO guidelines for Europe).

ter if the annual mean value of $PM_{10}$ is greater than 100 mg/m³ or if the 95th percentile of 24-hour mean values of $PM_{10}$ over a period of one year is estimated to exceed 150 mg/m³.

Good practice in airshed management should encompass the establishment of an emergency response plan during industrial plant operation. It is recommended that this plan be put into effect when levels of air pollution exceed one or more of the emergency trigger values (determined for short-term concentrations of sulfur dioxide, nitrogen oxides, particulates, and ozone). The recommended emergency trigger value for $PM_{10}$ is 150 mg/m³ for 24-hour average concentrations. Where $PM_{10}$ measurements do not exist, the value of 300 mg/m³ for TSP is recommended.

## Note

1. Adverse effect is defined as "any effect resulting in functional impairment and/or pathological lesions that may affect the performance of the whole organism or which contributed to a reduced ability to respond to an additional challenge" (see USEPA 1980).

## References and Sources

Dockery, D., C. A. Pope, X. Xiping, J. Spengler, J. Ware, M. Fay, B. Ferris, and F. Speizer. 1993. "An Association between Air Pollution and Mortality in Six U.S. Cities." *New England Journal of Medicine* 329(24): 1753–59.

European Community. 1992. *European Community Deskbook.* Washington, D.C.: Environmental Law Institute.

Kane, A. B. 1994. "Particle- and Fiber-induced Lesions: An Overview." In D. L. Dungworth, J. C. Mauderly, and G. Oberdorfer, eds., *Toxic and Carcinogenic Effects of Solid Particles in the Respiratory Tract..* Washington, D.C: International Life Sciences Institute.

Lipfert, F. W. 1984. "Air Pollution and Mortality: Specification Searches Using SMSA-Based Data." *Journal of Environmental Economics and Management* 11: 208–43.

Ostro, Bart. 1994. "Estimating the Health Effects of Air Pollutants: A Method with an Application to Jakarta." Policy Research Working Paper 1301. World Bank, Policy Research Department, Washington, D.C.

Pope, C. A., M. Thun, M. Namboodiri, D. Dockery, J. Evans, F. Speizer, and C. Heath. 1995. "Particulate Air Pollution as a Predictor of Mortality in a Prospective Study of U.S. Adults." *American Journal of Respiratory and Critical Care Medicine* 151: 669–74.

Schwartz, Joel. 1991/92. "Particulate Air Pollution and Daily Mortality: A Synthesis." *Public Health Reviews* 19: 39–60.

———. 1993a. "Particulate Air Pollution and Chronic Respiratory Disease." *Environmental Research* 62: 7–13.

———. 1993b. "Air Pollution and Daily Mortality in Birmingham, Alabama." *American Journal of Epidemiology* 137(10).

Schwartz, Joel, and D. W. Dockery. 1992a. "Increased Mortality in Philadelphia Associated with Daily Air Pollution Concentrations." *American Review of Respiratory Disease* 145: 600–604.

———. 1992b. "Particulate Air Pollution and Daily Mortality in Steubenville, Ohio." *American Review of Respiratory Disease* 135(1).

Schwartz, Joel, et al. 1993. "Particulate Air Pollution and Hospital Emergency Room Visits for Asthma in Seattle." *American Review of Respiratory Disease* 147: 826–31.

Stern, Arthur C., et al. 1984. *Fundamentals of Air Pollution.* Orlando, Fla.: Academic Press.

Ulm, K. 1994. "Epidemiology of Chronic Dust Exposure." In D. L. Dungworth, J. C. Mauderly, and G. Oberdorfer, eds., *Toxic Carcinogenic Effects of Solid Particles in the Respiratory Tract.* Washington, D.C: International Life Sciences Institute.

United States. CFR (*Code of Federal Regulations*). Washington, D.C.: Government Printing Office.

USEPA (United States Environmental Protection Agency). 1980. "Guidelines and Methodology Used in the Preparation of Health Effect Assessment Chapters of the Consent Decree Water Quality Criteria." *Federal Register* 45: 79347–57.

———. 1982a. *Air Quality Criteria for Particulate Matter and Sulfur Oxides.* Vol. I. EPA-600/8-82-029a. Research Triangle Park, N.C.

———. 1982b. *Second Addendum to Air Quality Criteria for Particulate Matter and Sulfur Oxides (1982): Assessment of Newly Available Health Effects Information.* Research Triangle Park, N.C.

———. 1990. *Review of the National Ambient Air Quality Standard for Particulate Matter: Assessment of Scientific and Technical Information.* Research Triangle Park, N.C.

WHO (World Health Organization). 1979. "Sulfur Oxides and Suspended Particulate Matter." *Environmental Health Criteria 8.* Geneva.

————. 1987. *Air Quality Guidelines for Europe.* Copenhagen: WHO Regional Office for Europe.

WHO (World Health Organization) and UNEP (United Nations Environment Programme). 1992. *Urban Air Pollution in Megacities of the World.* Cambridge, Mass.: Blackwell Reference.

# Arsenic

Arsenic is a metalloid that is distributed widely in the earth's crust. Pure arsenic is rarely found in the environment. More commonly, it bonds with various elements such as oxygen, sulfur, and chlorine to form inorganic arsenic compounds and with carbon and hydrogen to form organic arsenic compounds. The water-soluble trivalent and pentavalent oxidation states of inorganic arsenic are the most toxic arsenic compounds. Atmospheric arsenic exists primarily in inorganic form and is absorbed by particulate matter, while soluble arsenate and arsenite salts are the most typical forms in water. Atmospheric arsenic deposits to the soil, and is then absorbed by plants, leached to groundwater and surface water, and taken up by plants and animals.

Airborne concentrations of arsenic range from a few nanograms per cubic meter ($ng/m^3$) to a few tenths of a microgram per cubic meter ($\mu g/m^3$), but concentrations may exceed $1\ \mu g/m^3$ near stationary sources of emissions (Bencko 1987). A few micrograms per liter ($mg/l$) of arsenic are normally found in drinking water. In some locations, however, concentrations may exceed 1 milligram per liter ($mg/l$); see WHO (1981). Uncontaminated soil typically contains about 7 micrograms per gram ($mg/g$) arsenic, on average, but levels in the range of 100–2,500 $mg/g$ have been detected near stationary sources, and up to 700 $mg/g$ in agricultural soils treated with arsenic-containing pesticides (WHO 1987). High concentrations of arsenic, mainly fat-soluble or water-soluble organoarsenic compounds, have been observed in seafood (WHO 1981).

## Sources and Uses

Arsenic occurs widely in the natural environment. The highest mineral concentrations can be found as arsenides of copper, lead, silver, and gold, but high levels may also be found in some coal. The principal natural sources of arsenic in the atmosphere are volcanic activity and, to a lesser degree, low-temperature volatilization.

White arsenic (arsenic trioxide), a by-product of roasting sulfide ores, is the basis for manufacturing all arsenicals. The main uses of arsenicals, as components of pesticides and herbicides, have been banned in many countries. Arsenicals are also used in leather pigments. Chromated copper, sodium, and zinc arsenates are used in antifungal wood preservatives, and in some places, arsanilic acid is added to farm animal feed as a growth stimulant. Metallic arsenic is used in electronics and as a metal alloy, and sodium arsenite has been included in drugs for treating leukemia and other diseases. Arsenic is also used in lead crystal glass manufacturing, contributing to atmospheric emissions and the generation of highly toxic wastes.

The greatest part of anthropogenic arsenic emissions originates from stationary sources, including copper smelting (about 50%), combustion of coal, especially low-grade brown coal (about 20%), and other nonferrous metal industries (around 10%). The drying of concentrates in mining operations also contributes to atmospheric emissions of arsenic. The contribution of agriculture to anthropogenic arsenic releases, through the use of arsenicals as pesticides and herbicides and through the burning of vegetation and of wood treated with arsenic-containing preservatives, is estimated at around 20% (Chilvers and Peterson 1987). The largest contributors of arsenic in terrestrial waters are landfills, mines, pit heaps, wastewater from smelters, and arsenic-containing wood preservatives (Bencko 1987). Some iron and steel plants that use iron pyrites from metal mines, as well as other industries, such as sulfuric acid plants, that use pyrite as a source of sulfur for production, could be substantial sources of arsenic pollution of both air and water.

## Health Impacts of Exposure

Ingestion is the main route of exposure to arsenic for the general population. Arsenic can have both acute and chronic toxic effects on humans. It affects many organ systems including the respiratory, gastrointestinal, cardiovascular, nervous, and hematopoietic systems. When ingested in dissolved form, both inorganic and organic soluble arsenic compounds are readily absorbed from the gastrointestinal tract; less soluble forms have lower absorption rates.

Short-term acute poisoning cases involving the daily ingestion of 1.3–3.6 mg arsenic by children in Japan resulted in acute renal damage, disturbed heart function, and death (WHO 1981). Chronic exposure leads to accumulation of arsenic in the bone, muscle, and skin and, to a smaller degree, in the liver and the kidneys. Mild chronic poisoning causes fatigue and loss of energy. More severe symptoms include peripheral vascular disorders ("blackfoot disease"), gastrointestinal problems, kidney degeneration, liver dysfunction, bone marrow injury, and severe neuralgic pain. Such symptoms have been reported in populations consuming water with 500–1,000 mg/l arsenic content. Chronic exposure also results in dermatological disorders such as palm and sole hyperkeratosis, allergic contact dermatitis, and cancerous lesions (Bencko 1987). Long-term consumption of drinking water with arsenic concentrations exceeding 200 mg/l has been connected with the prevalence of skin cancer (Tseng

et al. 1968). Further studies (cited by Wildavsky and Schleicher 1995) have failed to demonstrate a relationship at lower levels of exposure, which may indicate the existence of a lower threshold level for carcinogenic impacts of ingested arsenic.

Inhalation is a less significant pathway for arsenic exposure for the general population, although smokers are constantly exposed to some arsenic due to the natural arsenic content of tobacco leaf and the effect of arsenate insecticide treatment used by tobacco plantations.[1] There are some indications that smoking may exacerbate the effects of exposure to airborne arsenic. About 30% of inhaled arsenic is absorbed by the human body. Acute inhalation of inorganic arsenic compounds can result in local damage to the respiratory system, including perforation of the nasal septum. Increased mortality from cardiovascular diseases and lung cancer was associated with exposure of smelter workers to high levels of airborne arsenic. It is estimated that $1 \mu g/m^3$ arsenic in the air can be associated with a 0.003 lifetime risk of developing cancer (WHO 1987). The carcinogenic potential of inorganic arsenic is considered the key criterion in assessing the hazard from both environmental and occupational exposures.

Ingested organic arsenic compounds have no proven health effects even at relatively high concentrations.

## Ambient Standards and Guidelines

Ambient standards and guidelines for arsenic are aimed at protecting the population, livestock, and other organisms from exposure to ambient arsenic. Table 1 presents EU, USEPA, and WHO reference standards and guidelines for ambient levels of arsenic in water. To protect health, stan-

## Table 1. Reference Standards and Guidelines for Ambient Levels of Arsenic in Water

*(micrograms per liter)*

| Use | EU limit values | EU guide values | USEPA standard | WHO guide values |
|---|---|---|---|---|
| Drinking water | 50 | | 50 | 10 |
| Surface water intended for drinking | | | | |
| Before normal treatment | 50 | 10 | | |
| Before intensive treatment | 100 | 50 | | |

*Sources:* Drinking water: CEC 1980 (EU); United States, CFR, vol. 21, no. 52 (USEPA); WHO 1993. Surface water: CEC 1975 (EU).

dards for acceptable arsenic concentrations in ambient water focus on water intended for drinking. Since various treatment methods achieve different levels of purification, allowable concentrations before treatment may differ depending on the impact of treatment on drinking water. No reference ambient standards or guidelines have been set for atmospheric arsenic concentrations.

## Conclusions

Considering differences in diets, habits, and the pathways through which arsenic may affect human health, as well as the complex biological cycle of arsenic, regulation through ambient standards may not be the best tool for protecting populations from the adverse health effects of exposure to environmental arsenic. Policymakers should adopt a complex approach to the abatement of arsenic exposure, emphasizing preventive measures and considering location-specific factors and the effects of the global cycle of arsenic across environmental media.

## Recommendations

Stationary sources that contribute to the increase of arsenic in the environment should not exceed the arsenic emissions referred to in the relevant industry section of this *Handbook*. These emissions are normally achievable through good industrial practices.

In addition, the impacts of new sources on ambient concentrations of arsenic should be considered. When the use of certain fuels or industrial processes results in emissions that contribute to a significant increase in ambient arsenic concentrations, or in areas where the natural occurrence of arsenic is very high, the environmental assessment should ensure that arsenic emissions are properly abated, taking into consideration alternative fuels, technologies, and control measures. Intermittent monitoring of the surrounding water bodies, soil, and plants should ensure that arsenic concentrations do not impose an increased health threat to the population in the vicinity of the industrial plant.

## Note

1. According to certain estimates (WHO 1987), about 6 mg of arsenic may be inhaled per pack of cigarettes smoked, of which about 2 mg would be retained in the lungs.

## References and Sources

Bencko, Vladimir. 1987. "Arsenic." In Lawrence Fishbein, Arthur Furst, and Myron A. Mehlman, eds. *Genotoxic and Carcinogenic Metals: Environmental and Occupational Occurrence and Exposure.* Advances in Modern Environmental Toxicology, vol. 11. Princeton, N.J.: Princeton Scientific Publishing.

CEC (Commission of the European Communities). 1975. *Official Journal of the European Communities* 195. Luxembourg.

————. 1980. *Official Journal of the European Communities* 229. Luxembourg.

Chilvers, D. C., and P. J. Peterson. 1987. "Global Cycling of Arsenic." In T. C. Hutchinson and K. M. Meema, eds., *Lead, Mercury, Cadmium and Arsenic in the Environment.* Scientific Committee on Problems of the Environment (SCOPE) 31. New York: John Wiley & Sons.

Hutton, M. 1987. "Human Health Concerns of Lead, Mercury, Cadmium and Arsenic." In T. C. Hutchinson and K. M. Meema, eds., *Lead, Mercury, Cadmium and Arsenic in the Environment.* Scientific Committee on Problems of the Environment (SCOPE) 31. New York: John Wiley & Sons.

Roychowdhury, Mahendra. 1982. "Health Hazards of Toxic Metals in Industry." *American Society of Safety Engineers* (November).

Tseng, W. P., et al. 1968. "Prevalence of Skin Cancer in an Endemic Area of Chronic Arsenicism in Taiwan." *Journal of the National Cancer Institute* 40: 453–63.

United States. CFR (*Code of Federal Regulations*). Washington, D.C.: Government Printing Office.

USEPA (United States Environmental Protection Agency). 1984. *Health Assessment Document for Inorganic Arsenic.* Final Report: EPA/600-8-33-021F. Washington, D.C.: Office of Health and Environmental Assessment.

WHO (World Health Organization). 1971. *International Standards for Drinking Water,* vol. 3. Geneva.

—————. 1981. "Arsenic." *Environmental Health Criteria,* no. 18. Geneva.

—————. 1987. *Air Quality Guidelines for Europe.* Copenhagen.

—————. 1993. *Guidelines for Drinking Water Quality.* Vol. 1: *Recommendations.* 2d ed. Geneva.

Wildavsky, Aaron, and D. Schleicher. 1995. "How Does Science Matter?" In Aaron Wildavsky, ed., *But Is It True? A Citizen's Guide to Environmental Health and Safety Issues.* Cambridge, Mass.: Harvard University Press.

# Cadmium

Cadmium is a relatively rare soft metal that occurs in the natural environment typically in association with zinc ores and, to a lesser extent, with lead and copper ores. Some inorganic cadmium compounds are soluble in water, while cadmium oxide and cadmium sulfide are almost insoluble. In the air, cadmium vapor is rapidly oxidized. Wet and dry deposition transfers cadmium from the ambient air to soil, where it is absorbed by plants and enters the food chain. This process may be influenced by acidification that increases the availability of cadmium in soil.

Atmospheric levels of cadmium range up to 5 nanograms per cubic meter ($ng/m^3$) in rural areas, from 0.005 to 0.015 micrograms per cubic meter ($\mu/m^3$) in urban areas, and up to 0.06 $\mu g/m^3$ in industrial areas (WHO 1992). Concentrations may reach 0.3 $\mu g/m^3$ weekly mean values near metal smelters (WHO 1987). Atmospheric cadmium is generally associated with particulate matter of respirable size. Fresh water typically contain levels of cadmium below 1 microgram per liter ($\mu g/l$), but concentrations up to 10 $\mu g/l$ may occur on rare occasions due to environmental disturbances such as acid rain. Concentration in nonpolluted agricultural soils varies between 0.01 and 0.7 micrograms per gram ($\mu g/g$); see WHO 1975).

Food contains cadmium as a result of uptake from the soil by plants and bioaccumulation in terrestrial and aquatic animals. The highest concentrations of cadmium are found in shellfish (over 1 $\mu g/g$) and in the liver and kidneys of farm animals (0.1–1 $\mu g/g$); see Kazantzis (1987).

## Sources and Uses

Cadmium is emitted into the atmosphere from natural sources, mainly volcanic activities, and from anthropogenic sources. Metal production (drying of zinc concentrates and roasting, smelting, and refining of ores) is the largest source of anthropogenic atmospheric cadmium emissions, followed by waste incineration and by other sources, including the production of nickel-cadmium batteries, fossil fuel combustion, and generation of dust by industrial processes such as cement manufacturing (Kazantzis 1987).

The largest contributors to the contamination of water are mines (mine water, concentrate processing water, and leakages from mine tailings); process water from smelters; phosphate mining and related fertilizer production; and electroplating wastes.

The largest sources of cadmium in landfills are smelters, iron and steel plants, electroplating wastes, and battery production. Mine tailings generated as the result of zinc mining also have the potential to transfer cadmium to the ambient environment.

Cadmium is mainly used as an anticorrosion coating in electroplating, as an alloying metal in solders, as a stabilizer in plastics (organic cadmium), as a pigment, and as a component of nickel-cadmium batteries. Cadmium production may use by-products and wastes from the primary production of zinc.

## Health Impacts of Exposure

Ingestion via food, especially plant-based foodstuffs, is the major route by which cadmium enters the human body from the environment. Average human daily intake of cadmium from food has been estimated at around 10–50 $\mu g$. This may increase to several hundred micrograms per day in polluted areas. The intake of cadmium through inhalation is generally less than half that via ingestion, while daily intake from drinking water ranges from below 1 µg to over 10 µg (WHO 1987). The kidney, especially the renal tract, is the critical organ of intoxication after exposure to cadmium. Excretion is slow, and renal accumulation of cadmium may result in irreversible impairment in the reabsorption capacity of renal tubules.

Only a small proportion (5–10%) of ingested cadmium is absorbed by humans (FAO and WHO, 1972), and large variations exist among individuals. Severe renal dysfunction and damage to the bone structure, a syndrome termed itai-itai disease, have been associated with long-term exposure to cadmium in food (mainly rice) and water in Japan. WHO (1987) estimated that long-term daily ingestion of 200 µg of cadmium via food can be connected with 10% prevalence of adverse health effects. Deficiencies of iron, zinc, and calcium in the human body generally facilitate cadmium absorption. Since most crops, with the exception of rice, contain zinc that inhibits the uptake of cadmium by animals and humans, there is no scientific proof that populations in general are at risk of cadmium exposure via the food chain (Chaney et al. 1995).

Less than 50% of inhaled cadmium is absorbed from the lungs. Acute and chronic exposure to cadmium dust and fumes, occurring mainly under working conditions, can result in cadmium poisoning. Acute respiratory effects can be expected at cadmium fume concentrations above 1 mg/m³. Chronic effects occur at exposures to 20 µg/m³ cadmium concentrations after about 20 years. Because of the cadmium content of tobacco, heavy smokers have elevated absorption of airborne cadmium. Cigarettes containing 0.5–3 mg cadmium per gram of tobacco can result in up to 3 mg daily cadmium absorption via the lungs, assuming a 25% absorption factor (WHO 1987). Considering various sources of exposure and applying a safety factor, WHO (1987) estimated that 0.2 µg/m³ was a safe level of atmospheric cadmium concentrations with regard to renal effects through inhalation.

Animal studies have yielded sufficient evidence of the carcinogenicity of cadmium in animals (IARC 1976). Limited evidence of human carcinogenicity is also available in studies (reviewed in WHO 1992a, b) linking long-term occupational exposure to cadmium to increased occurrence of prostate and lung cancer cases. USEPA (1985) estimated the incremental cancer risk from continuous lifetime exposure to 1 µg/m³ concentrations to be 0.0018.

## Ambient Standards and Guidelines

Ambient environmental standards and guidelines are meant to protect human health and natural resources by limiting exposure. Table 1 presents EU, USEPA, and WHO reference standards and guidelines. The WHO ambient air quality guidelines take into account the impact of atmospheric cadmium on deposition and accumulation in soil used for agricultural production and set different acceptable levels in urban and rural areas. Ambient water quality guidelines focus on drinking water and other water resources intended for drinking, to protect human health.

## Conclusion

Because of the indirect route of exposure to cadmium through the food chain, the accumulation of cadmium without natural degradation, and incomplete understanding of the relationship between emissions into the different media and

**Table 1. Reference Standards and Guidelines for Ambient Levels of Cadmium in Air and Water**

| Medium | EU limit values | EU guide values | USEPA standard | WHO guide values |
|---|---|---|---|---|
| Air (milligrams per cubic meter) | | | | |
| Not to be exceeded in rural areas | | | | 0.001–0.005 |
| Not to be exceeded in urban areas | | | | 0.01–0.02 |
| Drinking water and surface water intended for drinking (milligrams per liter) | 5 | 1 | 10 | 3 |

*Sources:* Air: WHO 1987. Water: CEC 1975, 1980 (EU limit and EU guide); United States, CFR, vol. 21, no. 52 (USEPA); WHO 1993.

long-term environmental and biological impacts, ambient environmental standards may not be the best tools for protecting human health from the effects of exposure to environmental cadmium. Targeted policy intervention should concentrate on areas where populations may be at high risk due to multiple sources of exposure and the uptake of cadmium without the accompanying uptake of zinc, and due to nutritional deficiencies in iron and zinc.

## Recommendations

Stationary sources that contribute to the increase of cadmium in the environment should not exceed the cadmium emissions referred to in the relevant industry section of this *Handbook*. These emissions are normally achievable through good industrial practices.

In addition, the impacts of new sources on ambient concentrations of cadmium should be considered. When the use of certain fuels results in emissions that contribute to a significant increase in ambient cadmium concentrations, or in areas where agricultural crops affected by such emissions are a main dietary source of the population, the environmental assessment should ensure that cadmium emissions are properly abated, taking into consideration alternative fuels, technologies, and control measures. Intermittent monitoring of the surrounding soil and plants should ensure that cadmium concentrations do not pose an increased health threat to the population in the vicinity of the industrial plant.

## References and Sources

CEC (Commission of the European Communities). 1975. *Official Journal of the European Communities* 194. Luxembourg.

———. 1980. *Official Journal of the European Communities* L229. Luxembourg.

Chaney, L. Rufus, et al. 1995. "A New Paradigm for Soil Cadmium Risk to Humans." Paper presented at the OECD Cadmium Workshop in Stockholm, Sweden, October 15–22. Organisation for Economic Co-operation and Development, Paris.

FAO (Food and Agriculture Organization of the United Nations) and WHO (World Health Organization). 1972. *Evaluation of Certain Food Additives and the Contaminants Mercury, Lead, and Cadmium.* 16th report of the Joint FAO/WHO Expert Committee on Food Additives. Geneva: World Health Organization.

Huppes, Gjalt. 1993. *Macro-Environmental Policy: Principles and Design.* Amsterdam: Elsevier.

IARC (International Agency for Research on Cancer). 1987. "Cadmium and Cadmium Compounds." In *Overall Evaluations of Carcinogenicity: An Updating of IARC Monographs.* Vols. 1–42. Lyon, France.

Kazantzis, G. 1987. "Cadmium." In Lawrence Fishbein, Arthur Furst, and Myron A. Mehlman, eds., *Genotoxic and Carcinogenic Metals: Environmental and Occupational Occurrence and Exposure.* Advances in Modern Environmental Toxicology, vol. 11. Princeton, N.J.: Princeton Scientific Publishing Co.

Krishna Murti, C. R., et al. 1987. "Group Report: Cadmium." In T. C. Hutchinson and K. M. Meema, eds., *Lead, Mercury, Cadmium, and Arsenic in the Environment.* Scientific Committee on Problems of the Environment (SCOPE) 31. New York: John Wiley & Sons.

United States. CFR (*Code of Federal Regulations*). Washington, D.C.: Government Printing Office.

USEPA (United States Environmental Protection Agency). 1985. *Updated Mutagenicity and Carcinogenicity Assessment of Cadmium. Addendum to the Health Assessment Document of Cadmium.* May 1981. EPA-600/8-83-025F. Washington, D.C.

WHO (World Health Organization). 1971. *International Standards for Drinking Water*, vol. 3. 3d ed. Geneva.

———. 1975. "Environmental Hazards of Heavy Metals: Summary Evaluation of Lead, Cadmium and Mercury." *Environmental Health Criteria* 20. Geneva.

———. 1987. *Air Quality Guidelines.* Copenhagen: WHO Regional Office for Europe.

———. 1992a. "Cadmium." *Environmental Health Criteria* 134. Geneva.

———. 1992b. "Cadmium: Environmental Aspects." *Environmental Health Criteria* 135. Geneva.

———. 1993. *Guidelines for Drinking Water Quality.* Vol. 1: *Recommendations.* 2d ed. Geneva.

Yamagata, N. 1970. *Cadmium Pollution in Perspective.* Koshu Eiseiin Kenkyi Hokuku (Institute of Public Health, Tokyo) 19(1): 1–27.

# Lead

Lead is a gray-white, soft metal with a low melting point, a high resistance to corrosion, and poor electrical conducting capabilities. It is highly toxic. In addition to its highly concentrated ores, lead is naturally available in all environmental media in small concentrations. From the atmosphere, lead is transferred to soil, water, and vegetation by dry and wet deposition. A significant part of lead particles from emissions sources is of submicron size and can be transported over large distances. Larger lead particles settle more rapidly and closer to the source. Lead in soil binds hard, with a half-life of several hundred years. New depositions, primarily atmospheric, therefore contribute to increased concentrations. Atmospheric deposition is the largest source of lead in surface water, as well. Only limited amounts are transported to water from soil. Terrestrial and aquatic plants show a strong capability to bioaccumulate lead from water and soil in industrially contaminated environments (WHO 1989). Lead can also be taken up by grazing animals, thus entering the terrestrial food chain.

Natural atmospheric lead concentrations are estimated to be in the range of 0.00005 micrograms per cubic meter ($\mu g/m^3$). Urban concentrations are around 0.5 $\mu g/m^3$, and annual average concentrations may reach 3 $\mu g/m^3$ or more in cities with heavy traffic (WHO 1987).

## Sources and Uses

Mining, smelting, and processing of lead and lead-containing metal ores generate the greatest part of lead emissions from stationary sources. In addition, the combustion of lead-containing wastes and fossil fuels in incinerators, power plants, industries, and households releases lead into the atmosphere. Airborne ambient lead concentrations reaching over 100 $\mu g/m^3$ have occasionally been reported in the vicinity of uncontrolled stationary sources, decreasing considerably with distance from the source due to the deposition of larger lead particles.

As a result of the extensive use of alkyl-lead compounds as fuel additives, vehicular traffic is the largest source of atmospheric lead in many urban areas, accounting for as much as 90% of all lead emissions into the atmosphere (Brunekreef 1986). High concentrations of lead in urban air have been attributed to vehicular emissions in various countries (Lovei and Levy 1997). Traffic-generated lead aerosols are mostly of the submicron size; they can penetrate deeply into the lungs after inhalation, and they are transported and dispersed over large distances (Brunekreef 1986). With the phase-out of leaded gasoline, the relative contribution of traffic to environmental lead concentrations is changing.

Due to its special physical characteristics, lead has been used in a variety of products. Water distribution systems frequently contain lead pipes or lead solder, contaminating drinking water. Lead carbonate ("white lead") was highly popular as a base for oil paints before its use was banned in most countries in the first half of the twentieth century. Lead-based paint and dust contaminated by such paint still represent significant sources of human exposure in several countries. Lead-acid batteries contribute to the contamination of all environmental media during their production, disposal, and incineration. Lead compounds may be also used as stabilizers in plastics. Other lead-based products include food-can solder, ceramic glazes, crystal glassware, lead-jacketed cables, ammunition, and cosmetics.

## Health Impacts of Exposure

The main pathways of lead to humans are ingestion and inhalation. Children up to about six years of age constitute the population group at the highest risk from lead exposure through ingestion: their developing nervous systems are susceptible to lead-induced disruptions; their intake of food is relatively high for their body weight; they are exposed to high intake from dust, dirt, soil, and lead-containing paint due to their hand-to-mouth behavior; and their absorption through the gut is very efficient. (According to WHO 1987, the proportion of lead absorbed from the gastrointestinal tract is four to five times higher in children than in adults.) The main sources of lead exposure of children are dust and dirt; the role of dissolved lead in water supply systems, lead-based paint, and other sources varies across locations. The contribution of drinking water to exposure is highest in infants under one year of age and children under five years of age. Lack of essential trace elements such as iron, calcium, and zinc and poor nourishment may increase the absorption of lead by the human body.

Inhalation poses the highest risk of exposure to environmental lead in adults. Inhaled airborne lead represents a relatively small part of the body burden in children, but in adults it ranges from 15 to 70%. About 30–50% of lead inhaled with particles is retained in the respiratory system and absorbed into the body (WHO 1987). In addition to environmental exposure, alcohol consumption and tobacco smoking have been shown to contribute to human exposure to lead. On the basis of a review of epidemiologic studies, Brunekreef (1986) concluded that a 0.1 μg/m³ change in the ambient air concentration of lead was associated with a change in blood lead level—the best indicator of exposure—of 0.3 to 0.5 micrograms per decaliter (μg/dl).

Lead affects several organs of the human body, including the nervous system, the blood-forming system, the kidneys, and the cardiovascular and reproductive systems. Of most concern are the adverse effects of lead on the nervous system of young children: reducing intelligence and causing attention deficit, hyperactivity, and behavioral abnormalities. These effects occur at relatively low blood lead levels without a known lower threshold (Schwartz 1994). Many of these symptoms can be captured by standardized intelligence tests. Various studies have found a highly significant association between lead exposure and the measured intelligence quotient (IQ) of school-age children (Needleman et al. 1979; Bellinger et al. 1992). Reviews of studies concluded that a 10 μg/dl increase in blood lead can be associated with a 2–2.5 point decrease in IQ (CDC 1991; WHO 1995). The negative impact of lead exposure is generally stronger on verbal IQ than on performance IQ. (WHO 1995)

Prenatal exposure to lead was demonstrated to produce toxic effects in the human fetus, including reduced birth weight, disturbed mental development, spontaneous abortion, and premature birth. Such risks were significantly greater at blood lead levels of 15 μg/dl and more (WHO 1995).

High lead concentrations, generally due to occupational exposure or accidents, result in encephalopathy, a life-threatening condition at blood lead levels of 100 to 120 μg/dl in adults and 80 to 100 μg/dl in children (ATSDR 1990). An acute form of damage to the gastrointestinal tract known as "lead colic" is also associated with high lead levels. The hematological effects of lead exposure are attributed to the interruption of biosynthesis of heme by lead, severely inhibiting the metabolic pathway and resulting in reduced output of hemoglobin. Reduced heme synthesis has been associated with blood levels over 20 μg/dl in adults and starting from below 10 μg/dl in children (WHO 1987).

Several studies (Schwartz 1988, 1995; Pocock et al. 1988, Hu et al. 1996; Kim et al. 1996) have shown that increased blood pressure and hypertension in adults are also related to elevated blood lead levels, even at lower levels of exposure, increasing the risk of cardiovascular diseases (Pirkle et al. 1985).

## Ambient Standards and Guidelines

Ambient standards and guidelines are aimed at protecting human health. Table 1 includes EU, USEPA, and WHO reference standards and guidelines for ambient levels of lead in air and water.

**Table 1. Reference Standards and Guidelines for Mean Ambient Lead Concentrations in Air and Water**

| Medium | EU limit values | USEPA standard | WHO guide values |
|---|---|---|---|
| Air (micrograms per cubic meter) | 2 | 1.5 | 0.5–1.0[b] |
| Drinking water and surface water intended for drinking (micrograms per liter) | 10 | 50 | 10 |

a. Maximum arithmetic mean over a calendar quarter.
b. Annual mean.
*Sources:* Air: CEC 1982 (EU), United States, 40 CFR, Part 532 (USEPA); WHO 1987. Water: CEC 1980 (EU); USEPA 1987; WHO 1993.

## Conclusions

People are exposed to lead from a variety of sources and in a variety of ways, and ambient guidelines and standards for individual media may not provide sufficient protection. A comprehensive approach and strategy is therefore necessary to protect human health. Ambient environmental quality guidelines and standards should be only the starting point for such a strategy. Environmental monitoring of ambient concentrations in soil, air, and drinking water should help to identify highly polluted areas and high-risk population groups. This step should be followed by targeted biological screening and policy intervention. Such an approach should be the core of a comprehensive policy intervention that deals with lead exposure from all sources.

## Recommendations

Stationary sources that contribute to the increase of lead in the environment should not exceed the lead emissions referred to in the relevant industry section of this *Handbook*. These emissions are normally achievable through good industrial practices.

In addition, the impacts of new stationary sources on ambient concentrations of lead should be considered. When the use of certain processes results in emissions that contribute to a signifi-cant increase in ambient lead concentrations, or in areas where significant background concentrations exist, the environmental assessment should ensure that lead emissions are properly abated, taking into consideration alternative technologies and control measures. Intermittent monitoring of ambient air, water, and soil should ensure that lead concentrations do not impose an increased health threat to the population in the vicinity of the industrial plant.

## References and Sources

ATSDR (Agency for Toxic Substances and Disease Registry). 1990. *Toxicological Profile for Lead.* Washington, D.C.: United States Public Health Service in collaboration with United States Environmental Protection Agency.

Bellinger, D., et al. 1992. "Low-Level Lead Exposure, Intelligence, and Academic Achievement: A Long Term Follow-up Study." *Pediatrics.*

Brunekreef, B. 1986. *Childhood Exposure to Environmental Lead.* MARC Report 34. London: Monitoring and Assessment Research Centre, King's College, University of London.

CDC (Centers for Disease Control). 1991. *Strategic Plan for the Elimination of Childhood Lead Poisoning.* Washington, D.C.: U.S. Department of Health and Human Services.

CEC (Commission of the European Communities). 1975. *Official Journal of the European Communities* 194(26). Luxembourg.

———. 1980. *Official Journal of the European Communities* 229(11). Luxembourg.

———. 1982. *Official Journal of he European Communities* 378(15). Luxembourg

Hayes, Edward B., et al. 1994. "Long-Term Trends in Blood Lead Levels among Children in Chicago: Relationship to Air Lead Levels." *Pediatrics* 93(2).

Hu, H., et al. 1996. "The Relationship of Bone and Blood Lead to Hypertension." *Journal of the American Medical Association* 27(15): 1171–76.

Kim, R., et al. 1996. "A Longitudinal Study of Low-Level Lead Exposure and Impairment of Renal Function." *Journal of the American Medical Association* 275(15): 1177–81.

Lovei, Magda, and B. S. Levy. 1997. "Lead Exposure and Health in Central and Eastern Europe: Evidence from Hungary, Poland and Bulgaria." In Magda

Lovei, ed., *Phasing Out Lead from Gasoline in Central and Eastern Europe: Health Issues, Feasibility, and Policies.* Washington, D.C.: World Bank.

National Research Council, Committee on Measuring Lead in Critical Populations. 1993. *Measuring Lead Exposure in Infants, Children, and Other Sensitive Populations.* Washington, D.C.: National Academy Press.

Needleman, H. L., et al. 1979. "Deficits in Psychologic and Classroom Performance in Children with Elevated Dentine Lead Levels." *New England Journal of Medicine* 300: 584–695.

Pirkle, J. L., et al. 1985. "The Relationship between Blood Lead Levels and Blood Pressure and U.S. Cardiovascular Risk Implications." *American Journal of Epidemiology* 121: 246–58.

Pocock, S. J., et al. 1988. "The Relationship between Blood Lead, Blood Pressure, Stroke and Health Attacks in Middle-Aged British Men." *Environmental Health Perspectives* 78.

Schlag, R. D. 1987. "Lead." In Lawrence Fishbein, Arthur Furst, and Myron A. Mehlman, eds., *Genotoxic and Carcinogenic Metals: Environmental and Occupational Occurrence and Exposure.* Advances in Modern Environmental Toxicology, vol. 11. Princeton, N.J.: Princeton Scientific Publishing Co.

Schwartz, Joel. 1988. "The Relationship between Blood Lead and Blood Pressure in the NHANES II Survey." *Environmental Health Perspectives* 78.

————. 1994. "Low Level Lead Exposure and Children's IQ: A Meta Analysis and Search for a Threshold." *Environmental Research* 65(1): 42–-55.

————. 1995. "Lead, Blood Pressure and Cardiovascular Disease in Men." *Archives of Environmental Health* 50(1): 31–37.

United States. CFR (*Code of Federal Regulations*). Washington, D.C.: Government Printing Office.

USEPA (United States Environmental Protection Agency). 1986. *Reducing Lead in Drinking Water: A Benefits Analysis.* EPA-230-09-86-019. Washington, D.C.: Office of Policy, Planning and Evaluation.

————. 1987. *Quality Criteria for Water 1986.* EPA 440/5-86-001. Washington, D.C.: Office of Water Regulations and Standards.

WHO (World Health Organization). 1987. *Air Quality Guidelines for Europe.* Copenhagen: WHO Regional Office for Europe.

————. 1993. *Guidelines for Drinking Water Quality,* vol. 1, no. 15: *Recommendations.* 2d ed. Geneva.

————. 1995. *Inorganic Lead.* International Programme on Chemical Safety. Geneva.

# Mercury

Mercury is a toxic heavy metal that can be found in cinnabar (red sulfide) and other ores containing compounds of zinc, tin, and copper; in rocks such as limestone, sandstone, calcareous shales, and basalt; and in fossil fuels such as coal. Mercury is present in trace amounts in all environmental media. The bulk of global atmospheric mercury is elemental mercury in vapor form. From the atmosphere, mercury elements are removed through precipitation, resulting in deposition to water bodies, the soil, and vegetation. The ultimate depository of mercury is the sediment of oceans, seas, and lakes, where inorganic mercury is readily transformed into highly toxic organic methylmercury through bacterial synthesis and other enzymic and nonenzymic processes. Organic mercury rapidly accumulates in the aquatic biota and biomagnifies upward through the aquatic food chain, attaining its highest concentrations in fish, especially in large predatory species, where it often exceeds 2.0 micrograms per gram ($\mu g/g$), and in such species as dolphins, reaching 10 $\mu g/g$. Average levels of 0.07–0.17 $\mu g/g$ mercury are found in fish, largely (over 70%) in the form of organic methylmercury (OECD 1974).

Atmospheric mercury concentrations range from a few nanograms per cubic meter ($ng/m^3$) to 0.05 micrograms per cubic meter ($\mu g/m^3$), averaging 0.002 $\mu g/m^3$. Near stationary sources such as mines, however, concentrations may reach 0.6–1.5 $\mu g/m^3$ (WHO 1987). Typical concentrations of mercury in water bodies range from below 0.001 to 0.003 micrograms per liter ($\mu g/l$); see Fan (1987). Normal levels in soil range from 0.05 to 0.08 $\mu g/g$. Mercury tends to bond strongly to particulate matter in fresh water, largely in inorganic mercuric form. Mercury concentrations in soil normally do not exceed 0.1 $\mu g/g$. Total human daily intake of all forms of mercury from all sources has been estimated at between 5 and 80 $\mu g$ (Fan 1987).

## Sources and Uses

The natural emissions of mercury, mainly a result of the degassing of the Earth's crust and evaporation from water bodies, are two to four times larger than those from anthropogenic sources (Hutchinson and Meema 1987). About half of the atmospheric mercury generated by anthropogenic sources can be attributed to fossil fuel combustion (EPRI 1991). Emissions from fossil fuel combustion vary according to the mercury content of the fuel (Watson 1979).[1] Mercury levels in coal tend to be one to four orders of magnitude greater than those in fuel oil and natural gas. Waste incineration and the mining and smelting of ores are also important contributors to anthropogenic air pollution. Additional sources include mercury-cell chlor-alkali production and coke ovens. The accumulation, processing, and incineration of mercury-containing waste (for example, batteries and various industrial wastes such as scrubber sludge) contribute to mercury contamination of all environmental media.

The main use of mercury has been as a cathode in the electrolysis of sodium chloride solution to produce caustic soda, which is used by various industries. The mercury-cell chlor-alkali industry has been the largest anthropogenic discharger of mercury to water bodies. The use of liquid metallic mercury in the extraction of gold also contributes to the contamination of rivers.

The use of mercury in caustic soda production is being gradually phased out and replaced with membrane technology. The agricultural use of organic mercury in pesticides and fungicides has been banned in many countries to prevent human exposure. Agricultural applications are of particular concern because of the extreme toxicity of the mercury compounds used, the limited control over dispersed use and exposure, and the potential for misuse that could contribute to direct poisoning through the diet. Uses of mercury in electric switches, batteries, thermal sensing instruments, cosmetics, pharmaceuticals and dental preparations have been similarly decreasing.

## Health Impacts of Exposure

The main human health hazard of mercury has been associated with exposure to highly toxic organic methylmercury through food, primarily through the ingestion of aquatic organisms, mainly fish. Methylmercury in the human diet is almost completely absorbed into the bloodstream and distributed to all tissues, the main accumulation taking place in the brain, liver, and kidneys.

Methylmercury poisoning affects the central nervous system and the areas associated with the sensory, visual, auditory, and coordinating functions. Increasing doses result in paresthesia, ataxia, visual changes, dysarthria, hearing defects, loss of speech, coma, and death. The effects of methylmercury poisoning are, in most cases, irreversible because of the destruction of neuronal cells. Methylmercury shows significant and efficient transplacental transfer and contributes to severe disruptions in the development of the child's brain. Thus, prenatal life is more sensitive to methylmercury exposure than adult life. Not enough evidence exists, however, to establish a no-observed-effect or a dose-response function. According to WHO (1990), daily intake of 3–7 micrograms per kilogram ($\mu$g/kg) body weight can be connected to an incidence of paresthesia of about 5%. Human intake of mercury through drinking water is generally low, representing only a fraction of the amount of methylmercury intake through diet (WHO 1987). The main form of mercury in drinking water is inorganic mercuric mercury with low (7–10%) absorption rates (WHO 1991) and very low penetration rates to the brain and fetus. The lethal oral dose of metallic and other inorganic mercury compounds for humans is estimated at 1–4 grams (USEPA 1980).

Atmospheric mercury, largely in vapor form, poses a less significant health risk to the general population than exposure to more toxic organic mercury compounds through the diet. About 80% of inhaled vapor is retained and absorbed in the bloodstream. In addition to direct exposure, the indirect impacts of atmospheric mercury on human health through deposition in lakes and rivers are of concern.

## Ambient Standards and Guidelines

Ambient standards and guidelines for mercury in the environment are aimed at protecting human health and aquatic life. Ambient criteria for waterborne mercury concentrations attempt to take into account the complex effects of bioaccumulation of mercury and average dietary habits, using calculations of mercury concentrations in edible fish species. However, the possibility of deposition and accumulation makes it difficult to establish guide values that allow for postdeposition impacts. Table 1 presents EU, USEPA, and WHO reference standards and guidelines for ambient levels of mercury.

## Conclusion

Because of the indirect route of the primary human exposure, the multiple and indirect sources of exposure, varying dietary habits of exposed population groups, and inadequate understanding of the accumulation, transformation, and complex effects of bioaccumulation of mercury in the environment, ambient standards and guidelines for individual environmental media are only a starting point for a comprehensive pollution management approach that considers the multiple sources of exposure, special dietary habits, and site-specific conditions.

## Recommendations

Stationary sources that contribute to the increase of mercury in the environment should not exceed the mercury emissions referred to in the relevant industry section of this *Handbook*. These emissions are normally achievable through good industrial practices.

In addition, the impacts of new sources on ambient concentrations of mercury should be considered. When the use of certain fuels results in mercury emissions that contribute to a signifi-

## Table 1. Reference Standards and Guidelines for Ambient Levels of Mercury

| Medium | EU limit values | EU guide values | USEPA standard | WHO guide values |
|---|---|---|---|---|
| Water (micrograms per liter) | | | | |
| Fresh water | 1[a] | 0.5[a] | 0.19 | |
| Estuary coastal water | | | 0.11 | |
| Marine water | | | 0.14 | |
| Drinking water | 1[a] | 0.5[a] | 2 | 1 |
| Air (micrograms per cubic meter) | | | | —[b] |

a. Arithmetic mean of results obtained over a year. EU, 1992 Council Directive 76/464/EEC.
b. Annual average indoor mercury concentration guideline of 1 mg/m³ was recommended. No ambient air quality guideline was established.
*Sources:* Water: European Union (EU) 1992, Council Directive 76/464/EEC; USEPA 1980; WHO 1976, 1993.

cant increase in ambient mercury concentrations, or in areas where fish is the main dietary source from waters affected by mercury emissions, the environmental assessment should ensure that mercury emissions are properly abated, taking into consideration alternative technologies and control measures. Intermittent monitoring of the surrounding water bodies and fish should ensure that mercury concentrations do not impose an increased health threat.

## Notes

1. Mercury emission coefficients have been estimated at 1,760 kilograms (kg) per $10^{15}$ British thermal unit (Btu) for oil and 7,560 kg per $10^{15}$ Btu for high-mercury utility and industrial coal.. The average emission coefficient for coal was estimated to be 3,000 kg per $10^{15}$ Btu.

## References and Sources

European Community. 1992. *European Community Deskbook.* Washington, D.C.: Environmental Law Institute.

EPRI (Electric Power Research Institute). 1991. "Mercury in the Environment." *EPRI Journal* (December).

Fan, Anna M. 1987. "Mercury." In Lawrence Fishbein, Arthur Furst, and Myron A. Mehlman, eds., *Genotoxic and Carcinogenic Metals: Environmental and Occupational Occurrence and Exposure.* Advances in Modern Environmental Toxicology, vol. 11. Princeton, N.J.: Princeton Scientific Publishing.

Hutchinson, T. C., and K. M. Meema. 1987. *Lead, Mercury, Cadmium, and Arsenic in the Environment.* Scientific Committee on Problems of the Environment (SCOPE) 31. New York: John Wiley & Sons.

Lumb, A. J. 1995. *Mercury (A Review with Special Emphasis on Pollution Effects from Gold Mining).* Keyworth, Nottingham: British Geological Survey.

Marsh, D. O. 1987. "Dose-Response Relationships in Humans." In Christine U. Eccles and Zoltan Annau, eds., *The Toxicity of Methyl Mercury.* Baltimore, Md.: The John Hopkins University Press.

OECD (Organisation for Economic Co-operation and Development). 1974. *Mercury in the Environment.* Paris.

Piotrowski, J. K. 1980. *Health Effects of Methylmercury.* MARC Report 24. London: Monitoring and Assessment Research Centre, Chelsea College.

USEPA (United States Environmental Protection Agency). 1980. *Ambient Water Quality Criteria for Mercury.* EPA 440/5-80-058. Washington, D.C.: Office of Water Regulations and Standards.

————. 1984. *Health Effects Assessment for Mercury.* EPA-540/1-86-042. Washington, D.C.: Office of Emergency and Remedial Response.

————. 1993. *Locating and Estimating Air Emissions from Sources of Mercury and Mercury Compounds.* EPA-454/R-93-023. Research Triangle Park, N.C.: Office of Air Quality Planning and Standards.

Watson, W. D. Jr. 1979. "Economic Considerations in Controlling Mercury Pollution." In J. O. Nriagu, ed., *The Biochemistry of Mercury in the Environment.* Amsterdam: Elsevier.

WHO (World Health Organization). 1972. *Evaluation of Certain Food Additives and the Contaminants Mercury, Lead and Cadmium.* 16th Report of the Joint FAO/WHO Expert Committee on Food Additives. Technical Report Series 505. Geneva.

————. 1976. "Mercury." *Environmental Health Criteria* 1. Geneva.

————. 1987. *Air Quality Guidelines for Europe.* Copenhagen: WHO Regional Office for Europe.

————. 1989. "Mercury: Environmental Aspects.". *Environmental Health Criteria* 86. Geneva.

————. 1990. "Methylmercury." *Environmental Health Criteria* 101. Geneva.

————. 1991. "Inorganic Mercury." *Environmental Health Criteria* 118. Geneva.

————. 1993. *Guidelines for Drinking-Water Quality.* Vol. 1: *Recommendations.* 2d ed. Geneva.

# Nitrogen Oxides

Nitrogen oxides ($NO_x$) in the ambient air consist primarily of nitric oxide (NO) and nitrogen dioxide ($NO_2$). These two forms of gaseous nitrogen oxides are significant pollutants of the lower atmosphere. Another form, nitrous oxide ($N_2O$), is a greenhouse gas. At the point of discharge from man-made sources, nitric oxide, a colorless, tasteless gas, is the predominant form of nitrogen oxide. Nitric oxide is readily converted to the much more harmful nitrogen dioxide by chemical reaction with ozone present in the atmosphere. Nitrogen dioxide is a yellowish-orange to reddish-brown gas with a pungent, irritating odor, and it is a strong oxidant. A portion of nitrogen dioxide in the atmosphere is converted to nitric acid ($HNO_3$) and ammonium salts. Nitrate aerosol (acid aerosol) is removed from the atmosphere through wet or dry deposition processes similar to those that remove sulfate aerosol.

## Major Sources

Only about 10% of all $NO_x$ emissions come from anthropogenic sources (Godish 1991). The rest is produced naturally by anaerobic biological processes in soil and water, by lightning and volcanic activity, and by photochemical destruction of nitrogen compounds in the upper atmosphere. About 50% of emissions from anthropogenic sources comes from fossil-fuel-fired heat and electricity generating plants and slightly less from motor vehicles. Other sources include industrial boilers, incinerators, the manufacture of nitric acid and other nitrogenous chemicals, electric arc welding processes, the use of explosives in mining, and farm silos.

Worldwide annual emissions of anthropogenic nitrogen oxides are estimated at approximately 50 million metric tons (World Resources Institute 1994). The United States generates about 20 million metric tons of nitrogen oxides per year, about 40% of which is emitted from mobile sources. Of the 11 million to 12 million metric tons of nitrogen oxides that originate from stationary sources, about 30% is the result of fuel combustion in large industrial furnaces and 70% is from electric utility furnaces (Cooper and Alley 1986).

## Occurrence in Air and Routes of Exposure

Annual mean concentrations of nitrogen dioxide in urban areas throughout the world are in the range of 20–90 micrograms per cubic meter ($\mu g/m^3$). Maximum half-hour values and maximum 24-hour values of nitrogen dioxide can approach 850 $\mu g/m^3$ and 400 $\mu g/m^3$, respectively. Hourly averages near very busy roads often exceed 1,000 $\mu g/m^3$. Urban outdoor levels of nitrogen dioxide vary according to time of day, season, and meteorological conditions. Typically, urban concentrations peak during the morning and afternoon rush hours. Levels are also higher in winter in cold regions of the world than in other seasons because of the increased use of heating fuels. Finally, since the conversion of nitrogen dioxide from nitric oxide depends on solar intensity, concentrations are often greater on warm, sunny days. Nitrogen oxides decay rapidly as polluted air moves away from the source. Concentrations of nitrogen oxides in rural areas without major sources are typically close to background levels. However, nitrogen oxides can travel long distances in the upper atmosphere, contributing to elevated ozone levels and acidic depositions far from sources of emissions.

Concentrations of nitrogen dioxide in homes may considerably exceed outdoor levels and may therefore be more important for human health. Large sources of indoor nitrogen dioxide include cigarette smoke, gas-fired appliances, and space heaters. Nitrogen dioxide concentrations in kitchens with unvented gas appliances can exceed 200 $\mu g/m^3$ over a period of several days. Maximum 1-hour concentrations during cooking may reach 500–1,900 $\mu g/m^3$, and 1,000–2,000 $\mu g/m^3$ where a gas-fired water heater is also in use. Smoke from one cigarette may contain 150,000–225,000 $\mu g/m^3$ of nitric oxide and somewhat less nitrogen dioxide.

## Health and Environmental Impacts

### Health

Epidemiologic studies have rarely detected effects on children or adults from exposure to outdoor nitrogen dioxide. One study of nurses in Los Angeles found an association between exposure to nitrogen dioxide and increased phlegm production (Schwartz and Zegler 1990). Studies have indicated that the use of gas appliances for cooking may have a very small effect on the human respiratory system, especially for small children, but that the effect (if it exists) disappears as the children grow older (WHO 1987).

Available data from animal toxicological experiments rarely indicate effects of acute exposure to nitrogen dioxide concentrations of less than 1,880 $\mu g/m^3$ (WHO 1987). Asthmatics are likely to be the group most sensitive to exposure to nitrogen oxides. Two laboratories have reported reversible effects on pulmonary function of asthmatics exercising intermittently after 30 minutes of exposure to nitrogen dioxide concentrations as low as 560 $\mu g/m^3$ (WHO 1987). However, the health impact of the change in pulmonary function is unclear; the change of about 10% is within the range of physiological variation and is not necessarily adverse. At levels above 3,760 $\mu g/m^3$, normal subjects have demonstrated substantial changes in pulmonary function (WHO 1987).

Studies with animals have found that several weeks to months of exposure to nitrogen dioxide concentrations less than 1,880 $\mu g/m^3$ causes both reversible and irreversible lung effects and biochemical changes. Animals exposed to nitrogen dioxide levels as low as 940 $\mu g/m^3$ for six months may experience destruction of cilia, alveolar tissue disruption, obstruction of the respiratory bronchioles, and increased susceptibility to bacterial infection of the lungs (WHO 1987). Rats and rabbits exposed to higher levels experience more severe tissue damage, resembling emphysema.

The available data suggest that the physiological effects of nitrogen dioxide on humans and animals are due more to peak concentrations than to duration or to total dose.

### Materials

Nitrogen dioxide in reaction to textile dyes can cause fading or yellowing of fabrics. Exposure to nitrogen dioxide can also weaken fabrics or reduce their affinity for certain dyes. Industry has devoted considerable resources to developing textiles and dyes resistant to nitrogen oxide exposure (Canada 1987).

### Effects on Ecosystems

Nitrogen oxides are precursors of both acid precipitation and ozone, each of which is blamed for injury to plants. While nitric acid is responsible for only a smaller part of hydrogen ion ($H^+$) concentration in wet and dry acid depositions, the contribution of nitrogen oxide emissions to acid deposition could be more significant. It is nitrogen oxide that absorbs sunlight, initiating the photochemical processes that produce nitric acid. Approximately 90–95% of the nitrogen oxides emitted from power plants is nitric oxide; this slowly converts to nitrogen dioxide in the presence of ozone.

The extent and severity of the damage attributable to acid depositions is difficult to estimate, since impacts vary according to soil type, plant species, atmospheric conditions, insect populations, and other factors that are not well understood. Nitrates in precipitation may actually increase forest growth in areas with nitrogen-deficient soils. However, the fertilizing effect of nitrates (and sulfates) may be counterbalanced by the leaching of potassium, magnesium, calcium, and other nutrients from forest soils. There is little evidence that agricultural crops are being injured by exposures to nitrates in precipitation. The amount of nitrates in rainwater is almost always well below the levels applied as fertilizer (NAPAP 1990).

The most evident damage from acid depositions is to freshwater lake and stream ecosystems. Acid depositions can lower the pH of the water, with potentially serious consequences for fish, other animal, and plant life. Lakes in areas with soils containing only small amounts of calcium or magnesium carbonates that could help neutralize acidified rain are especially at risk. Few fish species can survive the sudden shifts in pH (and the effects of soluble substances) resulting from atmospheric depositions and runoff of contaminated waters; affected lakes may become completely devoid of fish life. Acidification also decreases the species variety and abundance of other animal and plant life. "Acid pulses" have been associated with the fish kills observed in sensitive watersheds during the spring meltdown of the snowpack. The atmospheric deposition of nitrogen oxides is a substantial source of nutrients that damage estuaries by causing algal blooms and anoxic conditions.

Emissions of nitrogen oxides are a precursor of ground-level ozone ($O_3$), which is potentially a more serious problem. Plant scientists blame tropospheric ozone for 90% of the injury to vegetation in North America. Ozone can travel long distances from the source and can contribute to elevated ozone concentrations even in rural areas. Since the meteorological and climatic conditions that favor the production of ozone—abundant sunshine—are also good for agriculture, ozone has the potential to cause large economic losses from reductions in crop yields.

Nitrogen dioxide affects visibility by absorbing short-wavelength blue light. Since only the longer wavelengths of light are visible to the eye, nitrogen dioxide appears yellowish to reddish-brown in color. Nitrogen oxides can also combine with photochemical oxidants to form smog.

## Ambient Standards and Guidelines

The main goal of almost all the major national and international air quality standards and guidelines produced over the last two decades has been to protect human health. Some countries have also produced guidelines and standards for nitrogen oxides to protect vegetation and sensitive ecosystems, such as wetlands. Table 1 presents EU, USEPA, and WHO reference standards and guidelines for ambient levels of nitrogen dioxide.

## Conclusions

The evidence suggests that exposure to short-term peak concentrations of nitrogen dioxide may damage health, especially of sensitive individuals such as asthmatics. For many individuals, the most significant sources of repetitive exposure to peak levels of nitrogen oxides come from residing in homes with gas cooking or heating appliances or from cigarette smoking. Long-term exposures to high levels of nitrogen dioxide (well above the highest ambient levels reported in urban areas in the United States) has been shown to lead to development of chronic lung injury and disease in animals. However, there is still considerable uncertainty regarding chronic health effects for humans from exposure to ambient nitrogen oxides (NAPAP 1991).

## Table 1. Reference Standards and Guidelines for Ambient Levels of Nitrogen Dioxide

*(milligrams per cubic meter)*

| Standard or guideline | Annual average | 24-hour average | 1-hour average |
|---|---|---|---|
| EU limit values (1985) | 200[a] | | |
| USEPA standards (1992) | 100[b] | | |
| WHO guidelines (1977) | | | 190–320[c] |
| WHO guidelines for Europe (1987) | | 150 | 400 |

a. 98th percentile calculated from the mean values per hour or per period of less than an hour taken throughout the year.
b. Arithmetic mean.
c. Not to be exceeded more than once a month. Only a short-term exposure limit has been suggested.
*Sources:* European Community 1985 (EU); United States 1992, 40 CFR, Part 60; WHO 1977, 1987.

## Recommendations

In the long term, countries should seek to ensure that ambient exposure to nitrogen dioxide does not exceed the WHO recommended guidelines. In the interim, countries should set ambient standards for nitrogen dioxide that take into account the benefits to human health and to sensitive ecosystems of reducing exposure to nitrogen dioxide; the concentration levels achievable by pollution prevention and control measures; and the costs involved in meeting the standards. In adopting new ambient air quality standards, countries should set appropriate phase-in periods during which districts or municipalities that do not meet the new standards are expected and will be assisted to attain these standards. Where there are large differences between the costs and benefits of meeting air quality standards, it may be appropriate to establish area-specific ambient standards case by case.

Prior to carrying out an environmental assessment (EA), a trigger value for the annual average concentrations of nitrogen oxides should be agreed on by the country and the World Bank Group. Countries may wish to adopt EU, USEPA, or WHO guidelines or standards as their trigger values. The trigger value should be equal to or lower than the country's ambient standard. The trigger value is not an ambient air quality standard but simply a threshold. If, as a result of the project, the trigger value is predicted to be exceeded in the area affected by the project, the EA should seek mitigation alternatives on a regional or sectoral basis. The World Bank Group will classify airsheds as moderately degraded if concentration levels are above $100~\mu g/m^3$ annual average or if the 98th percentile of 24-hour mean values over a period of one year is estimated to exceed $150~\mu g/m^3$ of nitrogen oxides. Airsheds will be classified as having poor air quality with respect to nitrogen dioxide if the 95th percentile of 24-hour mean values of nitrogen dioxide for the airshed over a period of one year is estimated to exceed $150~\mu g/m^3$.

Good practice in airshed management should encompass the establishment of an emergency response plan during industrial plant operation. It is recommended that this plan be put into effect when levels of air pollution exceed one or more of the emergency trigger values (determined for short-term concentrations of sulfur dioxide, nitrogen oxides, particulates, and ozone). The recommended emergency trigger value for nitrogen oxides is $150~\mu g/m^3$ for the 24-hour average concentrations.

## References and Sources

Canada, Federal-Provincial Advisory Committee on Air Quality. 1987. *Review of National Ambient Air Quality Objectives for Nitrogen Dioxide*. Ottawa: Environment Canada.

Cooper, C. David, and F. C. Alley. 1986. *Air Pollution Control: A Design Approach*. Prospect Heights, Ill.: Waveland Press.

European Community. 1985. Directive 85/203, March 7. Brussels.

Godish, Thad. 1991. *Air Quality*. Chelsea, Mich.: Lewis Publishers.

NAPAP (National Acid Precipitation Assessment Program). Various years, 1987–91. Washington, D.C.: Government Printing Office.

Ostro, Bart. 1994. "Estimating the Health Effects of Air Pollutants: A Method with an Application to Jakarta." Policy Research Working Paper 1301. World Bank, Policy Research Department, Washington, D.C.

Schwartz, Joel, and S. Zegler. 1990. "Passive Smoking, Air Pollution and Acute Respiratory Symptoms in a Diary Study of Student Nurses." *American Review of Respiratory Disease* 141: 62–67.

United States. CFR (*Code of Federal Regulations*). Washington, D.C.: Government Printing Office.

USEPA (United States Environmental Protection Agency). 1990. *National Air Quality and Emission Trends Report, 1990*. EPA-450/4-91-023. Research Triangle Park, N.C.

WHO (World Health Organization). 1977. "Oxides of Nitrogen." *Environmental Health Criteria* 4. Geneva.

————. 1987. *Air Quality Guidelines for Europe*. WHO Regional Publications, European Series 23. Copenhagen: WHO Regional Office for Europe.

World Resources Institute. 1994. *World Resources 1994–95: A Guide to the Global Environment*. New York: Oxford University Press.

# Ground-Level Ozone

Ozone ($O_3$) is a colorless, reactive oxidant gas that is a major constituent of atmospheric smog. Ground-level ozone is formed in the air by the photochemical reaction of sunlight and nitrogen oxides ($NO_x$), facilitated by a variety of volatile organic compounds (VOCs), which are photochemically reactive hydrocarbons. The relative importance of the various VOCs in the oxidation process depends on their chemical structure and reactivity. Ozone may be formed by the reaction of $NO_x$ and VOCs under the influence of sunlight hundreds of kilometers from the source of emissions.

Ozone concentrations are influenced by the intensity of solar radiation, the absolute concentrations of $NO_x$ and VOCs, and the ratio of $NO_x$ and VOCs. Diurnal and seasonal variations occur in response to changes in sunlight. In addition, ground-level ozone accumulation occurs when sea breezes cause circulation of air over an area or when temperature-induced air inversions trap the compounds that produce smog (Chilton and Sholtz 1989). Peak ground-level ozone concentrations are measured in the afternoon. Mean concentrations are generally highest during the summer. Peak concentrations of ground-level ozone rarely last longer than two to three hours (WHO 1979).

Registered average natural background concentrations of ground-level ozone are around 30–100 micrograms per cubic meter ($\mu g/m^3$). Short-term (one-hour) mean ambient concentrations in urban areas may exceed 300–800 $\mu g/m^3$ (WHO 1979).

## Main Sources

Both natural and anthropogenic sources contribute to the emission of ground-level ozone precursors, and the composition of emissions sources may show large variations across locations. VOCs occurring naturally due to emissions from trees and plants may account for as much as two thirds of ambient VOCs in some locations (USEPA 1986). Anaerobic biological processes, lightning, and volcanic activity are the main natural contributors to atmospheric $NO_x$, occasionally accounting for as much as 90% of all $NO_x$ emissions (Godish 1991).

Motor vehicles are the main anthropogenic sources of ground-level ozone precursors. Other anthropogenic sources of VOCs include emissions from the chemical and petroleum industries and from organic solvents in small stationary sources such as dry cleaners. Significant amounts of $NO_x$ originate from the combustion of fossil fuels in power plants, industrial processes, and home heaters.

## Health Impacts of Exposure

The main health concern of exposure to ambient ground-level ozone is its effect on the respiratory system, especially on lung function. Several factors influence these health impacts, including the concentrations of ground-level ozone in the atmosphere, the duration of exposure, average volume of air breathed per minute (ventilation rate), and the length of intervals between short-term exposures.

Most of the evidence on the health impacts of ground-level ozone comes from animal studies and controlled clinical studies of humans focusing on short-term acute exposure. Clinical studies have documented an association between short-term exposure to ground-level ozone at concentrations of 200–500 $\mu g/m^3$ and mild temporary eye and respiratory irritation as indicated by symptoms such as cough, throat dryness, eye and chest discomfort, thoracic pain, and headache (WHO 1979, 1987). Temporary decrements in pulmonary function have been found in children at hourly average ground-level ozone concentrations of 160–300 µg/m³. Similar impacts were observed after 2.5-hour exposure of heavily exercising adults and children to concentrations of 240 µg/m³ (WHO 1987). Lung function losses, however, have been reversible and relatively mild even at concentrations of 360 µg/m³, with a great variety of personal responses (Chilton and Sholtz 1989). Full recovery of respiratory functions normally occurs within 24 to 48 hours after exposure (WHO 1987).

Animal studies have also demonstrated an inflammatory response of the respiratory tract following exposure to ground-level ozone at 1,000 µg/m³ for four hours (WHO 1987). Although biochemical and morphological alterations in the red blood cells were found in several animal species after exposure to ground-level ozone concentrations of 400 µg/m³ for four hours (WHO 1987), no consistent changes have been demonstrated in humans, even at concentrations as high as 1,200 µg/m³ (USEPA 1986), and extrapolation of such impacts to humans has not been supported.

Exposure to elevated concentrations of ground-level ozone has been shown to reduce physical performance, since the increased ventilation rate during physical exercise increases the effects of exposure to ground-level ozone. There is no evidence that smokers, children, older people, asthmatics, or individuals with chronic obstructive lung disease are more responsive to ground-level ozone exposure than others. Ground-level ozone may, however, make the respiratory airways more responsive to other inhaled toxic substances and bacteria. In addition, a synergistic effect of ground-level ozone and sulfur dioxide has been found, indicating that sulfur dioxide potentiates the effects of ground level ozone (WHO 1979).

Besides short-term impacts, the potential for irreversible damage to the lungs from repeated exposure over a longer period of time has been a health concern. Some studies have found an association between accelerated loss of lung function over a longer period of time (five years) and high oxidant levels in the atmosphere (Detels et al. 1987). WHO (1987) pointed out that the length of the recovery period between successive episodes of high ground-level ozone concentrations

and the number of episodes in a season may be important factors in the nature and magnitude of health impacts, since prolonged acute exposure to ground level ozone concentrations of 240–360 µg/m³ resulted in progressively larger changes in respiratory function. However, a cross-sectional analysis based on large samples from multiple locations in the United States (Schwartz 1989) found no correlation between chronic ground-level ozone pollution and reduced lung function except for the highest 20% of ground-level ozone exposures, suggesting the possibility of a lower threshold for effects of chronic ground-level ozone exposure. No evidence has been found of an association between peak oxidant concentrations and daily mortality rates of the general population (WHO 1979).

## Other Impacts

Elevated ground-level ozone exposures affect agricultural crops and trees, especially slow-growing crops and long-lived trees. Ozone damages the leaves and needles of sensitive plants, causing visible alterations such as defoliation and change of leaf color. In North America, tropospheric ozone is blamed for about 90% of the damage to plants. Agricultural crops show reduced plant growth and decreased yield. According to the U.S. Office of Technology Assessment (OTA 1988), a 120 µg/m³ seasonal average of seven-hour mean ground-level ozone concentrations is likely to lead to reductions in crop yields in the range of 16–35% for cotton, 0.9–51% for wheat, 5.3–24% for soybeans, and 0.3–5.1% for corn. In addition to physiological damage, ground-level ozone may cause reduced resistance to fungi, bacteria, viruses, and insects, reducing growth and inhibiting yield and reproduction. These impacts on sensitive species may result in declines in agricultural crop quality and the reduction of biodiversity in natural ecosystems.

The impact of the exposure of plants to ground-level ozone depends not only on the duration and concentration of exposure but also on its frequency, the interval between exposures, the time of day and the season, site-specific conditions, and the developmental stage of plants. Furthermore, ground-level ozone is part of a complex relationship among several air pollutants and other factors such as climatic and meteorological conditions and nutrient balances. According to some studies, for example, the presence of sulfur dioxide may increase the sensitivity of plants to leaf injury by ground-level ozone (WHO 1987). Reinert and Heck (1982) point out that the presence of ground-level ozone may increase the growth-suppressing effects of nitrogen dioxide.

## Ambient Standards and Guidelines

Ambient standards and guidelines for ground-level ozone are aimed at protecting human health, sensitive ecosystems, and agricultural plants from the harmful effects of ground-level ozone. Table 1 presents USEPA, California, and WHO reference standards and guidelines for ambient ground-level ozone concentrations. Due to uncertainty about chronic effects and the lack of established dose-response function data, these standards and guidelines focus on short-term ground-level ozone concentrations.

## Conclusions

Evidence suggests that exposure to short-term peak concentrations of ground-level ozone damages human health but that these impacts are relatively mild and reversible at ground-level ozone levels exceeding current U.S. and WHO standards and guidelines. Although repeated exposure to peak concentrations may result in cumulative impacts on lung function, inhibiting recovery, no clear evidence for such chronic effects of ground-level ozone exists. The large

**Table 1. Reference Standards and Guidelines for Ambient Atmospheric Ozone Concentrations**
*(milligrams per cubic meter)*

| Standard or guideline | Short-term (1 hour) average | Medium-term (8 hour) average |
|---|---|---|
| USEPA | 2,35[a] | |
| State of California | 1,80[a] | |
| WHO (1979) | 100–200 | |
| WHO guidelines for Europe (1987) | 150–200 | 100–120 |

a. Value not to be exceeded more than once a year.
*Sources:* USEPA 1986; WHO 1979, 1987.

variety of sources and factors contributing to the formation of ground-level ozone, differences in the sensitivity and response of affected receptors, and variations in the costs and benefits of achieving certain air quality requirements for ground-level ozone may call for area-specific guide values.

Since ground-level ozone is formed by the photochemical reaction of nitrogen oxides and certain hydrocarbons, abatement strategies should focus not only on reduction of emissions of these substances but also on their ratio and balance. In areas where $NO_x$ concentrations are high relative to VOCs, the abatement of VOC emissions can reduce the formation of ground-level ozone, while reduction in nitrogen oxides may actually increase it. In areas where the relative concentration of VOCs is high compared with nitrogen oxides, ground-level ozone formation is "$NO_x$-limited," and $NO_x$ reductions work better than VOC abatement (OTA 1989).

## Recommendations

In the long term, countries should seek to ensure that ambient exposure to ground-level ozone does not exceed the guidelines recommended by WHO (see Table 1). In the interim, countries should set ambient standards for ground-level ozone that take into account the benefits to human health and to sensitive ecosystems of reducing exposure to ground-level ozone; the concentration levels achievable by pollution prevention and control measures; and the costs involved in meeting the standards. In adopting new ambient air quality standards, countries should set appropriate phase-in periods during which districts or municipalities that do not meet the new standards are expected and will be assisted to attain these standards. Where there are large differences in either the costs or the benefits of meeting air quality standards, it may be appropriate to establish area-specific ambient standards case by case.

Prior to carrying out an environmental assessment (EA), a trigger value for annual average concentrations of ground-level ozone should be agreed on by the country and the World Bank. Countries may wish to adopt EU, USEPA, or WHO guidelines or standards as their trigger values. The trigger value should be equal to or lower than the country's ambient standard. The trigger value is not an ambient air quality standard but simply a threshold. If, as a result of the project, the trigger value is predicted to be exceeded in the area affected by the project, the EA should seek mitigation alternatives on a regional or sectoral basis.

In addition, good practice in airshed management should encompass the establishment of an emergency response plan during industrial plant operation. It is recommended that this plan be put into effect when levels of air pollution exceed one or more of the emergency trigger values determined for short-term concentrations of sulfur dioxide, nitrogen oxides, particulates, and ground-level ozone. The recommended emergency trigger value for ground-level ozone is 150 $\mu g/m^3$ for one-hour average concentrations.

## References and Sources

Chilton, K., and A. Sholtz. 1989. *Battling Smog: A Plan for Action*. St. Louis, Mo.: Washington University, Center for the Study of American Business.

Detels, R., et al. 1987. "The UCLA Population Studies of Chronic Obstructive Respiratory Disease." *Chest* 92 (October): 594–603.

Godish, Thad. 1991. *Air Quality*. Chelsea, Mich.: Lewis Publishers.

Krupnik, A. J., et al. 1989. *Ambient Ozone and Acute Health Effects: Evidence from Daily Data*. Washington, D.C.: Resources for the Future.

OTA (U.S. Congress, Office of Technology Assessment). 1988. *Urban Ozone and the Clean Air Act: Problems and Proposals for Change*. Washington, D.C.: Government Printing Office.

————. 1989. *Catching Our Breath: Next Steps for Reducing Urban Ozone*. OTA-0-412. Washington, D.C.: Government Printing Office.

Reinert, R. A., and W. W. Heck. 1982. "Effects of Nitrogen Dioxide in Combination with Sulfur Dioxide and Ozone on Selected Crops." In T. Schneider and L. Grant, eds., *Air Pollution by Nitrogen Oxides*. Amsterdam: Elsevier Scientific.

Schwartz, Joel. 1989. "Lung Function and Chronic Exposure to Air Pollution: A Cross-Sectional Analysis of NHANES II." *Environmental Research* 50: 309–21.

USEPA (United States Environmental Protection Agency). 1986. *Air Quality Criteria for Ozone and Other Photochemical Oxidants*. Washington, D.C.

WHO (World Health Organization). 1979. "Photochemical Oxidants." *Environmental Health Criteria 7*. Geneva.

————. 1987. *Air Quality Guidelines for Europe*. Copenhagen: WHO Regional Office for Europe.

# Sulfur Oxides

Sulfur oxides (SO$_x$) are compounds of sulfur and oxygen molecules. Sulfur dioxide (SO$_2$) is the predominant form found in the lower atmosphere. It is a colorless gas that can be detected by taste and smell in the range of 1,000 to 3,000 micrograms per cubic meter ($\mu$g/m$^3$). At concentrations of 10,000 $\mu$g/m$^3$, it has a pungent, unpleasant odor. Sulfur dioxide dissolves readily in water present in the atmosphere to form sulfurous acid (H$_2$SO$_3$). About 30% of the sulfur dioxide in the atmosphere is converted to sulfate aerosol (acid aerosol), which is removed through wet or dry deposition processes. Sulfur trioxide (SO$_3$), another oxide of sulfur, is either emitted directly into the atmosphere or produced from sulfur dioxide and is rapidly converted to sulfuric acid (H$_2$SO$_4$).

## Major Sources

Most sulfur dioxide is produced by burning fuels containing sulfur or by roasting metal sulfide ores, although there are natural sources of sulfur dioxide (accounting for 35–65% of total sulfur dioxide emissions) such as volcanoes. Thermal power plants burning high-sulfur coal or heating oil are generally the main sources of anthropogenic sulfur dioxide emissions worldwide, followed by industrial boilers and nonferrous metal smelters. Emissions from domestic coal burning and from vehicles can also contribute to high local ambient concentrations of sulfur dioxide.

## Health and Environmental Impacts

Periodic episodes of very high concentrations of sulfur dioxide are believed to cause most of the health and vegetation damage attributable to sulfur emissions. Depending on wind, tempera-ture, humidity, and topography, sulfur dioxide can concentrate close to ground level. During the London fog of 1952, levels reached 3,500 $\mu$g/m$^3$ (averaged over 48 hours) in the center of the city and remained high for a period of 5 days. High levels have been recorded during temperature inversions in Central and Eastern Europe, in China, and in other localities.

### Health

Exposure to sulfur dioxide in the ambient air has been associated with reduced lung function, increased incidence of respiratory symptoms and diseases, irritation of the eyes, nose, and throat, and premature mortality. Children, the elderly, and those already suffering from respiratory ailments, such as asthmatics, are especially at risk. Health impacts appear to be linked especially to brief exposures to ambient concentrations above 1,000 $\mu$g/m$^3$ (acute exposures measured over 10 minutes). Some epidemiologic studies, however, have shown an association between relatively low annual mean levels and excess mortality. It is not clear whether long-term effects are related simply to annual mean values or to repeated exposures to peak values.

Health effects attributed to sulfur oxides are due to exposure to sulfur dioxide, sulfate aerosols, and sulfur dioxide adsorbed onto particulate matter. Alone, sulfur dioxide will dissolve in the watery fluids of the upper respiratory system and be absorbed into the bloodstream. Sulfur dioxide reacts with other substances in the atmosphere to form sulfate aerosols. Since most sulfate aerosols are part of PM$_{2.5}$ (fine particulate matter, with an aerodynamic diameter of less than 2.5 microns), they may have an important role in the health impacts associated with fine particulates. However, sulfate aerosols can be transported long distances through the atmosphere before deposition occurs. Average sulfate aerosol concentrations are about 40% of average fine particulate levels in regions where fuels with high sulfur content are commonly used. Sulfur dioxide adsorbed on particles can be carried deep into the pulmonary system. Therefore, reducing concentrations of particulate matter may also reduce the health impacts of sulfur dioxide. Acid aerosols affect respiratory and sensory functions.

*Environment*

Sulfur oxide emissions cause adverse impacts to vegetation, including forests and agricultural crops. Studies in the United States and elsewhere have shown that plants exposed to high ambient concentrations of sulfur dioxide may lose their foliage, become less productive, or die prematurely. Some species are much more sensitive to exposure than others. Plants in the immediate vicinity of emissions sources are more vulnerable. Studies have shown that the most sensitive species of plants begin to demonstrate visible signs of injury at concentrations of about 1,850 $\mu g/m^3$ for 1 hour, 500 $\mu g/m^3$ for 8 hours, and 40 $\mu g/m^3$ for the growing season (Smith 1981, cited in NAPAP 1990). In studies carried out in Canada, chronic effects on pine forest growth were prominent where concentrations of sulfur dioxide in air averaged 44 $\mu g/m^3$, the arithmetic mean for the total 10 year measurement period; the chronic effects were slight where annual concentrations of sulfur dioxide averaged 21 $\mu g/m^3$ (Canada 1987).

Trees and other plants exposed to wet and dry acid depositions at some distance from the source of emissions may also be injured. Impacts on forest ecosystems vary greatly according to soil type, plant species, atmospheric conditions, insect populations, and other factors that are not well understood.

Agricultural crops may also be injured by exposure to depositions. Alfalfa and rye grass are especially sensitive. It appears that leaf damage must be extensive before exposure affects the yields of most crops. It is possible that over the long-term, sulfur input to soils will affect yields (OECD 1981; NAPAP 1990). However, sulfur dioxide may not be the primary cause of plant injury, and other pollutants such as ozone may have a greater impact.

Acid depositions can damage freshwater lake and stream ecosystems by lowering the pH of the water. Lakes with low buffering capacity, which could help neutralize acid rain, are especially at risk. Few fish species can survive large shifts in pH, and affected lakes could become completely devoid of fish life. Acidification also decreases the species variety and abundance of other animal and plant life.

Sulfate aerosols, converted from sulfur dioxide in the atmosphere, can reduce visibility by scattering light. In combination with warm temperatures, abundant sunlight, high humidity, and reduced vertical mixing, such aerosols can contribute to haziness extending over large areas.

*Materials*

Sulfur dioxide emissions may affect building stone and ferrous and nonferrous metals. Sulfurous acid, formed from the reaction of sulfur dioxide with moisture, accelerates the corrosion of iron, steel, and zinc. Sulfur oxides react with copper to produce the green patina of copper sulfate on the surface of the copper. Acids in the form of gases, aerosols, or precipitation may chemically erode building materials such as marble, limestone, and dolomite. Of particular concern is the chemical erosion of historical monuments and works of art. Sulfurous and sulfuric acids formed from sulfur dioxide and sulfur trioxide when they react with moisture may also damage paper and leather.

## Ambient Standards and Guidelines

The main goal of almost all the major national and international standards and guidelines produced over the last two decades has been to protect human health. Early research appeared to indicate a threshold or "no-effects" level below which health impacts were negligible for even the most vulnerable groups, such as asthmatics and smokers. Standards were then set below this level to provide a margin of safety. The EU standards recognize the possibility that exposure to both sulfur dioxide and particulate matter may have an additive or synergistic effect on health. (This is also recognized by WHO.) The EU limit value for ambient sulfur dioxide therefore varies depending on the concentration of particulate

## Table 1. Reference Standards and Guidelines for Ambient Sulfur Dioxide Concentrations
*(milligrams per cubic meter)*

| Standard or guideline | Annual average | | Winter | | 24-hour | | 1-hour, sulfur dioxide |
|---|---|---|---|---|---|---|---|
| | Sulfur dioxide | Associated particulate levels | Sulfur dioxide | Associated particulate levels | Sulfur dioxide | Associated particulate levels | |
| EU limit values | 80[a] | > 40[b] | 130[c] | > 60[b] | 250[d] | > 150[b] | |
| | 120[a] | ≤ 40[b] | 180[c] | ≤ 60[b] | 350[d] | ≤ 150[b] | |
| | 80[a] | > 150[e] | 130[c] | > 200[e] | 250[d] | > 350[e] | |
| | 120[a] | ≤ 150[e] | 180[c] | ≤ 200[e] | 350[d] | ≤ 350[e] | |
| USEPA standards | 80[f] | | | | 365[g] | | |
| WHO guidelines | 40–60[f] | | | | 100–150[d] | | |
| WHO guidelines for Europe | 50[f] | | | | 125[d] | | 350 |
| ECE critical value | 10/20/30 | | 20/30 | | | | |

a. Median of daily values taken throughout the year. b. Black smoke method c. Median of daily values taken throughout the winter. d. 98th percentile of all daily values taken throughout the year; should not be exceeded more than 7 days a year. e. Gravimetric method. f. Arithmetic mean. g. Not to be exceeded more than once a year. *Sources:* European Community Directive 80/779 (July 5, 1980) and amending Directive 89/427 (July 14, 1989); USEPA 1990; WHO 1979, 1987.

matter in the ambient air. Table 1 summarizes key reference standards and guidelines for ambient SO₂ concentrations.

## Recommendations

In the long term, countries should seek to ensure that ambient exposure to sulfur dioxide does not exceed the guidelines recommended by WHO. In the interim, countries should set ambient standards for sulfur dioxide that take into account the benefits to human health and sensitive ecosystems of reducing exposure to sulfur dioxide; the concentration levels achievable by pollution prevention and control measures; and the costs involved in meeting the standards. In adopting new ambient air quality standards or guidelines, countries should set appropriate phase-in periods. Where large differences exist between the costs and the benefits of meeting air quality standards and guidelines, it may be appropriate to establish area-specific ambient standards case by case.

Prior to carrying out an environmental assessment (EA), a trigger value for the annual average concentrations of sulfur dioxide should be agreed on by the country and the World Bank.

Countries may wish to adopt EU, USEPA, or WHO guidelines or standards as their trigger values. The trigger value should be equal to or lower than the country's ambient standard. The trigger value is not an ambient air quality standard but simply a threshold. If, as a result of the project, the trigger value is predicted to be exceeded in the area affected by the project, the EA should seek mitigation alternatives on a regional or sectoral basis. In the absence of an agreed value, the World Bank Group will classify airsheds as moderately degraded if concentration levels are above 80 μg/m³ annual average or if the 98th percentile of 24-hour mean values over a period of one year is estimated to exceed 150 μg/m³. Airsheds will be classified as having poor air quality with respect to sulfur dioxide if either the annual mean value of sulfur dioxide is greater than 100 μg/m³ or the 95th percentile of 24-hour mean value for sulfur dioxide for the airshed over a period of one year is estimated to exceed 150 μg/m³.

In addition, good practice in airshed management should encompass the establishment of an emergency response plan during industrial plant operation. It is recommended that this plan be put into effect when levels of air pollution exceed one or more of the emergency trigger values (determined for short-term concentrations of sulfur dioxide, nitrogen oxides, particulates, and ozone). The recommended emergency trigger value for sulfur dioxide is 150 µg/m$^3$ for the 24-hour average concentrations.

## References and Sources

Canada, Federal-Provincial Advisory Committee on Air Quality. 1987. *Review of National Ambient Air Quality Objectives for Sulphur Dioxide: Desirable and Acceptable Levels.* Ottawa: Environment Canada.

CEC (Commission of the European Communities). 1992. *European Community Environment Legislation.* Brussels.

Dockery, Douglas W., C. A. Pope, X. Xiping, J. Spengler, J. Ware, M. Fay, B. Ferris, and F. Speizer. 1993. "An Association between Air Pollution and Mortality in Six U.S. Cities." *New England Journal of Medicine* 329(24): 1753–59.

Godish, Thad. 1991. *Air Quality.* Chelsea, Mich.: Lewis Publishers.

NAPAP (National Acid Precipitation Assessment Program). 1990. *Effects of Pollution on Vegetation.* Report 18. Washington, D.C.: Government Printing Office.

————. Various years,1987–91. Washington, D.C.: Government Printing Office.

OECD (Organisation for Economic Co-operation and Development ). 1981. *The Costs and Benefits of Sulphur Oxide Control.* Paris.

Ostro, Bart. 1994. "Estimating the Health Effects of Air Pollutants: A Method with an Application to Jakarta." Policy Research Working Paper 1301. World Bank, Policy Research Department, Washington, D.C.

USEPA (United States Environmental Protection Agency). 1982. *Air Quality Criteria for Particulate Matter and Sulfur Oxides.* EPA-600/8-82-029. December. Research Triangle Park, N.C.

————. 1986. *Second Addendum to Air Quality Criteria for Particulate Matter and Sulfur Oxides (1982).* EPA-600/8-86/020F. December. Research Triangle Park, N.C.

————. 1990. *Review of the National Ambient Air Quality Standard for Particulate Matter: Assessment of Scientific and Technical Information.* Research Triangle Park, N.C.

————. 1991. *National Air Quality and Emission Trends Report, 1990.* EPA-450/4-91-023. November. Research Triangle Park, N.C.

UN (United Nations) and ECE (Economic Commission for Europe). 1992. "Critical Levels of Air Pollutants for Europe." Background paper prepared for the UN/ECE workshop on critical levels. Egham, U.K., March 23–26, 1992. Air Quality Division, Department of Environment.

WHO (World Health Organization). 1979. "Sulfur Oxides and Suspended Particulate Matter." *Environmental Health Criteria* 8. Geneva.

————. 1987. *Air Quality Guidelines for Europe.* WHO Regional Publications, European Series 23. Copenhagen: WHO Regional Office for Europe.

WHO (World Health Organization) and UNEP (United Nations Environment Program) 1992. *Urban Air Pollution in the Megacities of the World.* Oxford: Blackwell Reference.

# Airborne Particulate Matter: Pollution Prevention and Control

Airborne particulate matter (PM) emissions can be minimized by pollution prevention and emission control measures. Prevention, which is frequently more cost-effective than control, should be emphasized. Special attention should be given to pollution abatement measures in areas where toxics associated with particulate emissions may pose a significant environmental risk.

## Approaches to Pollution Prevention

### Management

Measures such as improved process design, operation, maintenance, housekeeping, and other management practices can reduce emissions. By improving combustion efficiency, the amount of products of incomplete combustion (PICs), a component of particulate matter, can be significantly reduced. Proper fuel-firing practices and combustion zone configuration, along with an adequate amount of excess air, can achieve lower PICs.

### Choice of Fuel

Atmospheric particulate emissions can be reduced by choosing cleaner fuels. Natural gas used as fuel emits negligible amounts of particulate matter. Oil-based processes also emit significantly fewer particulates than coal-fired combustion processes. Low-ash fossil fuels contain less noncombustible, ash-forming mineral matter and thus generate lower levels of particulate emissions. Lighter distillate oil–based combustion results in lower levels of particulate emissions than heavier residual oils. However, the choice of fuel is usually influenced by economic as well as environmental considerations.

### Fuel Cleaning

Reduction of ash by fuel cleaning reduces the generation of PM emissions. Physical cleaning of coal through washing and beneficiation can reduce its ash and sulfur content, provided that care is taken in handling the large quantities of solid and liquid wastes that are generated by the cleaning process. An alternative to coal cleaning is the co-firing of coal with higher and lower ash content. In addition to reduced particulate emissions, low-ash coal also contributes to better boiler performance and reduced boiler maintenance costs and downtime, thereby recovering some of the coal cleaning costs. For example, for a project in East Asia, investment in coal cleaning had an internal rate of return of 26% (World Bank 1991).

### Choice of Technology and Processes

The use of more efficient technologies or process changes can reduce PIC emissions. Advanced coal combustion technologies such as coal gasification and fluidized-bed combustion are examples of cleaner processes that may lower PICs by approximately 10%. Enclosed coal crushers and grinders emit lower PM.

## Approaches to Emission Control

A variety of particulate removal technologies, with different physical and economic characteristics, are available.

*Inertial or impingement separators* rely on the inertial properties of the particles to separate them from the carrier gas stream. Inertial separators are primarily used for the collection of medium-size and coarse particles. They include settling chambers and centrifugal cyclones (straight-through, or the more frequently used reverse-flow cyclones). Cyclones are low-cost, low-maintenance centrifugal collectors that are typically used to remove particulates in the size range of 10–100 microns (mm); see Henderson-Sellers (1984). The fine-dust-removal efficiency of cyclones is typically below 70%, whereas electrostatic precipitators (ESPs) and baghouses can have removal efficiencies of 99.9% or more. Cyclones are therefore often used as a primary stage before other PM removal mechanisms. They typically cost about US$35 per cubic meter/minute flow rate (m³/min), or US$1 per cubic foot/minute (cu. ft/min); see Cooper and Alley (1986).

*Electrostatic precipitators (ESPs)* remove particles by using an electrostatic field to attract the particles onto the electrodes. Collection efficiencies for well-designed, well-operated, and well-maintained systems are typically in the order of 99.9% or more of the inlet dust loading. ESPs are especially efficient in collecting fine particulates and can also capture trace emissions of some toxic metals with an efficiency of 99% (Moore 1994). They are less sensitive to maximum temperatures than are fabric filters, and they operate with a very low pressure drop. Their consumption of electricity is similar to that of fabric filters (see Table 1). ESP performance is affected by fly-ash loading, the resistance of fly ash, and the sulfur content of the fuel. Lower sulfur concentrations in the flue gas can lead to a decrease in collection efficiency (Stultz and Kitto 1992). ESPs have been used for the recovery of process materials such as cement, as well as for pollution control. They typically add 1–2% to the capital cost. of a new industrial plant.

*Filters and dust collectors (baghouses)* collect dust by passing flue gases through a fabric that acts as a filter. The most commonly used is the bag filter, or baghouse. The various types of filter media include woven fabric, needled felt, plastic, ceramic, and metal (Croom 1993). The operating temperature of the baghouse gas influences the choice of fabric. Accumulated particles are removed by mechanical shaking, reversal of the gas flow, or a stream of high-pressure air. Fabric filters are efficient (99.9% removal) for both high and low concentrations of particles but are suitable only for dry and free-flowing particles.

Their efficiency in removing toxic metals such as arsenic, cadmium, chromium, lead, and nickel is greater than 99% (Moore 1994).[1] They also have the potential to enhance the capture of sulfur dioxide ($SO_2$) in installations downstream of sorbent injection and dry-scrubbing systems (Stultz and Kitto 1992). They typically add 1–2% to the capital cost of new power plants.

*Wet scrubbers* rely on a liquid spray to remove dust particles from a gas stream. They are primarily used to remove gaseous emissions, with particulate control a secondary function. The major types are venturi scrubbers, jet (fume) scrubbers, and spray towers or chambers. Venturi scrubbers consume large quantities of scrubbing liquid (such as water) and electric power and incur high pressure drops. Jet or fume scrubbers rely on the kinetic energy of the liquid stream. The typical removal efficiency of a jet or fume scrubber (for particles 10 mm or less) is lower than that of a venturi scrubber. Spray towers can handle larger gas flows with minimal pressure drop and are therefore often used as precoolers. Because wet scrubbers may contribute to corrosion, removal of water from the effluent gas of the scrubbers may be necessary. Another consideration is that wet scrubbing results in a liquid effluent. Wet-scrubbing technology is used where the contaminant cannot be removed easily in a dry form, soluble gases and wettable particles are present, and the contaminant will undergo some subsequent wet process (such as recovery, wet separation or settling, or neutralization). Gas flow rates range from 20 to 3,000 m³/min. Gas flow rates of approximately 2,000 m³/min. may have a corresponding pressure drop of 25 cm water column (Bounicore and Davis 1992).

## Equipment Selection

The selection of PM emissions control equipment is influenced by environmental, economic, and engineering factors:

*Environmental factors* include (a) the impact of control technology on ambient air quality; (b) the contribution of the pollution control system to the volume and characteristics of wastewater and solid waste generation; and (c) maximum allowable emissions requirements.

*Economic factors* include (a) the capital cost of the control technology; (b) the operating and maintenance costs of the technology; and (c) the expected lifetime and salvage value of the equipment.

*Engineering factors* include (a) contaminant characteristics such as physical and chemical properties—concentration, particulate shape, size distribution, chemical reactivity, corrosivity, abrasiveness, and toxicity; (b) gas stream characteristics such as volume flow rate, dust loading, temperature, pressure, humidity, composition, viscosity, density, reactivity, combustibility, corrosivity, and toxicity; and (c) design and performance characteristics of the control system such as pressure drop, reliability, dependability, compliance with utility and maintenance requirements, and temperature limitations, as well as size, weight, and fractional efficiency curves for particulates and mass transfer or contaminant destruction capability for gases or vapors.

Table 1 presents the principal advantages and disadvantages of the particulate control technologies discussed here. ESPs can handle very large volumetric flow rates at low pressure drops and can achieve very high efficiencies (99.9%). They are roughly equivalent in costs to fabric filters and are relatively inflexible to changes in process operating conditions. Wet scrubbers can also achieve high efficiencies and have the major advantage that some gaseous pollutants can be removed simultaneously with the particulates. However, they can only handle smaller gas flows (up to 3,000 m³/min), can be very costly to operate (owing to a high pressure drop), and produce a wet sludge that can present disposal problems (Cooper and Alley 1986). For a higher flue gas flow rate and greater than 99% removal of PM, ESPs and fabric filters are the equipment of choice, with very little difference in costs.

## Recommendations

For effective $PM_{10}$ control in industrial application, the use of ESPs or baghouses is recommended. They should be operated at their design efficiencies. In the absence of a specific emissions requirement, a maximum level of 50 milligrams per normal cubic meter (mg/Nm³) should be achieved.

For gases containing soluble toxics and where the gas flow rate is less than 3,000 m³/min, wet scrubbers may be used. Cyclones and mechanical separators should be used only as precleaning devices upstream of a baghouse or an ESP.

## Key Issues for Pollution Prevention and Control Planning

The principal methods for controlling the release of particulate matter are summarized here.

- Identify measures for improving operating and management practices.
- Consider alternative fuels such as gas instead of coal.
- Consider fuel-cleaning options such as coal washing, which can reduce ash content by up to 40%.
- Consider alternative production processes and technologies, such as fluidized bed combustion, that result in reduced PM emissions.
- Select optimal particulate removal devices such as ESPs and baghouses.

## Note

1. However, controlling emissions of many heavy metals, such as cadmium, lead, and mercury, that are present as trace elements in fuels is a difficult and largely unsolved problem.

## References and Sources

Bounicore, Anthony J., and Wayne T. Davis, eds. 1992. *Air Pollution Engineering Manual*. New York: Van Nostrand Reinhold.

Cooper, C. David, and F. C. Alley. 1986. *Air Pollution Control: A Design Approach*. Prospect Heights, Ill.: Waveland Press.

Croom, Miles L. 1993. "Effective Selection of Filter Dust." *Chemical Engineering* (July).

Hanly, J., and Petchonka, J. 1993. "Equipment Selection for Solid Gas Separation." *Chemical Engineering* (July).

Henderson-Sellers, B. 1984. *Pollution of Our Atmosphere*. Bristol: Adam Hilger.

Jechoutek, Karl G., S. Chattopadhya, R. Khan, F. Hill, and C. Wardell. 1992. "Steam Coal for Power and Industry." Industry and Energy Department Work-

## Table 1. Advantages and Disadvantages of Particulate Control Technologies

| Advantages | Disadvantages |
| --- | --- |
| *Inertial or impingement (cyclone) separators* | |
| • Low capital cost (approximately US$1/cu ft/min flow rate)<br>• Relative simplicity and few maintenance problems<br>• Relatively low operating pressure drop (for the degree of particulate removal obtained) in the range of approximately 5–15 cm (2–6 inches) water column<br>• Temperature and pressure limitations imposed only by the materials of construction used<br>• Dry collection and disposal<br>• Relatively small space requirements | • Relatively low overall particulate collection efficiencies, especially for particulate sizes below 10 mm<br>• Inability to handle sticky materials |
| *Wet scrubbers* | |
| • No secondary dust sources<br>• Relatively small space requirement<br>• Ability to collect gases, as well as particulates (especially "sticky" ones)<br>• Ability to handle high-temperature, high-humidity gas streams<br>• Low capital cost (if wastewater treatment system is not required)<br>• Insignificant pressure-drop concerns for processes where the gas stream is already at high pressure<br>• High collection efficiency of fine particulates (albeit at the expense of pressure drop) | • Potential water disposal/effluent treatment problem<br>• Corrosion problems (more severe than with dry systems)<br>• Potentially objectionable steam plume opacity or droplet entrainment<br>• Potentially high pressure drop—approximately 25 centimeters (10 inches) water column and horsepower requirements<br>• Potential problem of solid buildup at the wet-dry interface<br>• Relatively high maintenance costs |
| *Electrostatic precipitators* | |
| • Collection efficiencies of 99.9% or greater for coarse and fine particulates at relatively low energy consumption<br>• Dry collection and disposal of dust<br>• Low pressure drop—typically less than 1–2 cm (0.5 inch) water column<br>• Continuous operation with minimum maintenance<br>• Relatively low operation costs<br>• Operation capability at high temperatures (up to 700°C, or (1,300°F) and high pressure (up to 10 atmospheres. or 150 pounds per square inch, psi) or under vacuum<br>• Capability to handle relatively large gas-flow rates (on the order of 50,000 m³/min | • High capital cost—approximately US$160/square meter ($15/square foot) of plate area<br>• High sensitivity to fluctuations in gas stream conditions (flow rates, temperature, particulate and gas composition, and particulate loadings)<br>• Difficulties with the collection of particles with extremely high or low resistivity<br>• Relatively large space requirement for installation<br>• Explosion hazard when dealing with combustible gases or particulates<br>• Special precautionary requirements for safeguarding personnel from high voltage during ESP maintenance by de-energizing equipment before work commencement<br>• Production of ozone by the negatively charged electrodes during gas ionization<br>• Highly trained maintenance personnel required |
| *Fabric filter systems (baghouses)* | |
| • Very high collection efficiency (99.9%) for both coarse and fine particulates<br>• Relative insensitivity to gas stream fluctuations and large changes in inlet dust loadings (for continuously cleaned filters)<br>• Recirculation of filter outlet air<br>• Dry recovery of collected material for subsequent processing and disposal<br>• No corrosion problems<br>• Simple maintenance, flammable dust collection in the absence of high voltage<br>• High collection efficiency of submicron smoke and gaseous contaminants through the use of selected fibrous or granular filter aids<br>• Various configurations and dimensions of filter collectors<br>• Relatively simple operation | • Requirement of costly refractory mineral or metallic fabric at temperatures in excess of 290°C (550°F)<br>• Need for fabric treatment to remove collected dust and reduce seepage of certain dusts<br>• Relatively high maintenance requirements<br>• Explosion and fire hazard of certain dusts at concentration (~50 g/m³) in the presence of accidental spark or flame, and fabric fire hazard in case of readily oxidizable dust collection<br>• Shortened fabric life at elevated temperatures and in the presence of acid or alkaline particulate or gas constituents ·Potential crusty caking or plugging of the fabric, or need for special additives due to hygroscopic materials, moisture condensation, or tarry adhesive components<br>• Respiratory protection requirement for fabric replacement<br>• Medium pressure-drop requirements—typically in the range of 10–25 centimeters (4–10 inches) in water column |

*Source:* Adapted from Bounicore and Davis 1992.

ing Paper. Energy Series Paper No. 58. World Bank, Washington, D.C.

Moore, T. 1994. "Hazardous Air Pollutants: Measuring in Micrograms." *EPRI Journal* 19(1).

Stultz, S. C., and John B. Kitto, eds. 1992. *Steam: Its Generation and Use.* 40th ed. Barberton, Ohio: The Babcock & Wilcox Co.

Vatavuk, W. M. 1990. *Estimating Costs of Air Pollution Control.* Chelsea, Mich.: Lewis Publishers.

World Bank. 1991. "China: Efficiency and Environmental Impact of Coal Use." Report No. 8915-CHA. China Department, Industry and Energy Division, Washington, D.C.

# Removal of Lead from Gasoline: Technical Considerations

## The Effects of Lead in Gasoline

Refiners add tetraethyl lead (TEL) and tetra-methyl lead (TML) to gasoline to increase octane. In most situations, adding lead is the least expensive means of providing incremental octane to meet gasoline specifications. At sufficiently high levels, addition of lead can increase octane as much as 10 to 15 control octane numbers (Figure 1). Lead susceptibility (the gasoline's propensity to increase in octane with lead addition) is a function of the gasoline's composition and blending properties. In general, the higher a base gasoline's clear octane (before lead addition), the lower is its lead susceptibility. Lead addition is subject to decreasing returns to scale: each increment of lead added to a gasoline blend provides a smaller octane boost than the previous increment. Thus, the marginal cost of octane from lead addition increases as the lead level increases.

In addition to its octane benefit, TEL also provides engine lubrication benefits. Lead in gasoline prevents the wear of engine parts (valve seat recession) under severe driving conditions such as prolonged high speed, towing, and hilly terrain for vehicles—typically older models—manufactured with soft valve seats. Consequently, a mandate for lead removal is often accompanied by requirements for gasoline additives designed to prevent valve seat recession. Sodium-based additives, for example, can be blended into gasoline for this purpose.[1]

## Gasoline Octane Number

Octane number is a measure of a gasoline's propensity to knock (ignite prematurely, before the piston reaches the top of the stroke) in standard test engines. The higher a gasoline's octane is, the better is its antiknock performance. Gasolines have two octane ratings. The *research octane number* (RON) measures antiknock performance at low engine speeds; the *motor octane number* (MON) measures antiknock performance at high engine speeds. For any gasoline, RON is higher than MON, usually by 8 to 12 numbers. The difference between the two is called octane sensitivity. Most countries set specifications (minimum levels) for both RON and MON by gasoline grade. The United States, however, sets specifications for the *control octane number* (CON), the arithmetic average of RON and MON.

## Oil-Refining Processes

Oil refineries transform crude oils into numerous coproducts. Refined coproducts fall into four broad categories in the order of increasing spe-

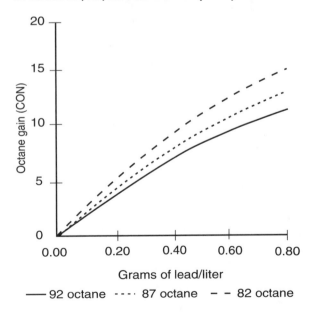

**Figure 1. Octane Improvement from Addition of Lead: 92, 87, and 82 Octane (CON) Gasolines**

Octane gain (CON) vs. Grams of lead/liter

— 92 octane  ···· 87 octane  – – 82 octane

cific gravity and decreasing volatility: liquefied petroleum gas (LPG) and refinery gases; gasoline; distillate (kerosene, jet fuel, diesel fuel, and heating oil); and residual oil (fuel oil, bunker oil, and asphalt). In virtually all situations, light products—gasoline and distillate—are the most valuable, and heavy products (residual oil) are the least valuable. The following main oil refining processes play key roles in gasoline production.

1. *Crude distillation* splits crude oil into discrete fractions suitable for further processing. It is the indispensable process in any refinery, the precursor for all others. Of the many crude fractions produced in the crude distillation unit, two, *light naphtha* and *medium to heavy naphtha*, are especially important in gasoline blending. Both are in the gasoline boiling range, and both have low octane, making them unattractive as gasoline blendstocks.

Light naphtha (boiling range, 15°–70°C) has three alternative dispositions: (a) direct blending to gasoline in small proportions; (b) direct blending in larger proportions (as present in the crude oil mix), with attendant addition of lead to the gasoline pool; or (c) upgrading by isomerization followed by blending.

Medium and heavy naphtha (boiling range, 160°–375°F) is the primary feed to catalytic reforming, the workhorse of the upgrading process.

2. *Conversion processes* convert heavy feeds into lighter materials for further processing or direct blending. *Fluid catalytic cracking* (FCC) is the most important conversion process. The FCC unit is the heart of a conversion refinery, the most important single determinant of the refinery's profit margin. The FCC unit converts heavy refinery streams, in the residual oil range, into a spectrum of lighter, more valuable refinery streams, including (a) a moderate-quality, high-octane gasoline blendstock (91–93 RON clear) called *FCC gasoline*; and (b) refinery gases, which may be sold or used as feed to alkylation and oxygenate production.

3. *Upgrading processes* improve the octane of crude fractions already in the gasoline boiling range.

*Catalytic reforming* is the most important and most universal upgrading process for gasoline manufacture. In most refineries, reforming is the primary source of additional octane. Reforming upgrades heavy naphtha (35–55 RON clear) to a prime gasoline blendstock, called *reformate*. The refiner can vary the octane level of reformate over a wide range (90–102 RON clear) by controlling the "severity" of the reformer, primarily by dropping pressure or increasing temperature, or both. No other refining process allows the refiner comparable control of blendstock octane. The combination of high-octane blendstock and operating flexibility usually makes reforming the process of choice for controlling octane level and producing incremental octane-barrels in response to lead phase-out. However, reformate is high in aromatics and benzene: the higher the reformer severity, the higher the aromatics and benzene content. (For example, increasing reformer severity from 90 to 100 RON increases the aromatics content of reformate by roughly 15 percentage points.)

*Isomerization* upgrades light naphtha (70–78 RON) to *isomerate*, a high-quality, moderate-octane blendstock (85–90 RON).

*Alkylation* combines light olefins (propylene, n-butenes, and isobutene), which are produced mainly by the FCC unit, and isobutane, coming from hydrocracking, FCC, reforming or straight-run, and NG processing, to form *alkylate*, a high-quality, high-octane blendstock (92–97 RON). Alkylation can be employed only in refineries with an FCC unit.

Polymerization converts light olefins (propylene and butenes) to form polygasoline, an olefinic, high-octane blendstock (97 RON). This process relies on the same olefin feeds as alkylation and can be employed only in refineries with an FCC unit. Polymerization increases the olefin content of gasoline;

- *Etherification processes* produce oxygenate blendstocks such as methylterbutylether (MTBE), ETBE, TAME and DIPE. Of these blendstocks, MTBE is the most widely used. It has exceptionally high octane (115 RON) and other desirable blending properties as well. In the refinery, MTBE is produced using purchased methanol and isobutene produced mainly by the FCC unit. As with alkylation, refinery-based etherification can be employed only in refineries with an FCC unit.

- *Blending* mixes blendstocks and additives to produce finished products that meet specifications. Merchant MTBE, for example, can be purchased on world oil markets. Because of its high octane, blending merchant MTBE is a common method of adding octane to gasoline without capital investment. Certain gasoline additives such as MMT and DurAlt are also known to increase gasoline octane.

## Refinery Categories

Refineries can be categorized into two main groups (see Table 1).

- *Skimming* refineries are relatively simple, comprising crude distillation, treating, upgrading (catalytic reforming in hydroskimming refineries only), and blending. Skimming refineries produce refined products in proportions determined mainly by the proportions of boiling-range fractions in the crude oil mix. For example, a skimming refinery's gasoline output can be no greater than the aggregate volume of the crude oil fractions in the gasoline boiling range (about 60°–400°F).
- *Conversion* refineries are relatively complex, comprising crude distillation, treating, upgrading (at least catalytic reforming and usually other processes as well), conversion (at least one conversion process and often more than one), and blending. Conversion refineries produce more light products and less heavy products than is indicated by the distribution of boiling range fractions in the crude oil mix. Some deep conversion refineries produce an all-light product slate containing no residual oil products. Conversion refineries shift the product slate toward light products by cracking (converting) heavy crude oil fractions into gasoline blendstocks, distillate blendstocks, and refinery gases. Conversion refineries offer more options for lead removal than skimming refineries.

## Technical Options for Replacing Lead in Gasoline

Various technical options are available for replacing lead when it is removed from a gasoline pool:

- Increasing the octane of reformate by increasing reformer severity (within the limits of sustainable operations). In some instances, achieving the necessary increase in reformer severity will call for revamping and modernizing the reformer.
- Increasing refinery production of high-octane blendstocks—FCC gasoline, reformate, isomerate, alkylate, polygasoline, and ethers (MTBE)—by increasing the utilization of existing process units and, if necessary, expanding or revamping existing process units or adding new units. As noted above, alkylate, polygasoline, and ethers can be produced only in conversion refineries. Increasing their production from existing units calls for increasing the output of the refinery's FCC unit;
- Reducing the volume of light naphtha in the gasoline pool, by (a) increasing the volume of light naphtha upgraded to isomerate; (b) increasing the volume of light naphtha sold to the petrochemical sector; or (c) reforming a part (the higher boiling range materials) of he light naphtha stream.
- Blending high-octane blendstocks, such as merchant MTBE, or octane enhancing additives, such as MMT—into the gasoline pool.
- Blending additional butanes into the gasoline pool. (This, however, will increase the volatility of gasoline.)

These technical options may be applied in any combination that is technically feasible in a given refinery. Each refinery has its own capital stock

## Table 1. Refinery Categories and Processes

| Process | Skimming | | Conversion | | |
| | Topping | Hydroskimming | Coking | Catalytic cracking | Deep conversion |
| --- | --- | --- | --- | --- | --- |
| Crude distillation | • | • | • | • | • |
| Treating | • | • | • | • | • |
| Blending | • | • | • | • | • |
| Upgrading | | • | • | •• | •• |
| Conversion | | | • | •• | ••• |
| Oxygenate production | | | | • | • |

and cost structure and faces a unique set of costs and technical requirements when it seeks to remove lead from its gasoline pool. Determining the optimal combination of technical options, therefore, calls for detailed refinery analysis.

## The Cost of Lead Phase-Out

The cost of lead phase-out depends on a number of factors, including: the initial lead concentration in gasoline, the processing capabilities of the refinery, planned refinery modernization or modification to meet evolving product demands, and limits on other gasoline properties (e.g., volatility, aromatics, and benzene).

The cost of lead removal is generally in the range of US$0.02–$0.03/liter of gasoline with initial lead levels of 0.6 g/liter or more and about US$ 0.01–$0.02/liter for initial lead levels of about 0.15 g/liter. Complex refineries with conversion capacity tend to have lower lead removal costs than do technically less-advanced refineries with limited process options. Refinery modernization, therefore, generally facilitates the phase-out of lead.

## Analysis of Lead Phase-Out

Analyzing lead phase-out alternatives can be carried out by a combination of detailed engineering analysis and refinery modeling. This approach exploits detailed information that engineers can develop regarding the refinery of interest and makes it possible to assess numerous alternatives for lead removal and their effects on refinery economics and gasoline quality. Refiners customarily rely on refinery models (linear programming models configured to represent their operations) to optimize refining and blending operations and as planning tools to assess the necessary changes in operations, the required process additions, and the blendstock or additive purchases needed to phase lead out of gasoline.

Modeling provides a quick and relatively inexpensive method of assessing the economic and technical aspects of lead reduction, such as: (a) alternative technical approaches for lead phase-out, including process upgrading, process additions, changes in operating procedures, and the use of purchased high-octane blendstocks or

additives; (b) cumulative refining costs; (c) investment requirements; (d) changes in gasoline composition; and (e) the potential costs and investment requirements of other constraints on refinery operations, such as limits on certain gasoline properties (e.g., aromatics content, benzene content, and volatility). Refinery analysis generally consists of the following steps:

- *Development of technical data on the refinery.* Actual process capacities and yields (and the potential for upgrading), crude oil slate, product slate, lead use, gasoline grade splits, prices for crude oil and refined products, and product specifications for the time period of interest are established.
- *Development of crude oil assays.* If not already incorporated in the refinery model, distillation curves for the crude oils processed by the refinery are constructed.
- *Adjustment of capital costs and required rates of return.* The costs of new process capacity are adjusted and incorporated in the refinery model, along with the rate of return used to annualize capital costs, to reflect the economic conditions faced by the refinery of interest.
- *Calibration of the refinery model.* The refinery model is configured so as to yield reasonable values for key measures of refinery operations: marginal refining costs at observed product volumes, marginal costs of meeting product specifications, gasoline blend recipes, lead use, and capacity utilization of various refining processes. The calibration case serves as the base for comparing the results of subsequent "lead reduction" cases. A well-calibrated refinery model increases confidence in the results of subsequent model runs.
- *Evaluation of various lead reduction cases for the projected product slate.* Once the refinery model is calibrated to represent baseline operations, further model runs are made to assess the feasibility and cost of progressively lower lead limits for gasoline. These model runs are designed to evaluate the effects of various approaches for reducing lead use on refinery operations, such as changes in operating severity, the addition of new process capacity (reforming, pen-hex isomerization, and so on), and the use of additives.

## Note

1. One such additive is Lubrizol's Powershield 8164. At the recommended concentration of 0.7 grams per liter (g/l), bulk blending of Lubrizol's additive in gasoline costs about US$0.003 per liter.

## Sources

ABT Associates, Inc. 1996. "Costs and Benefits of Removing Lead from Gasoline in Russia." Report prepared for the Office of Policy, Planning, and Evaluation, U.S. Environmental Protection Agency, Washington, D.C.

Chem Systems. 1994. "Study to Assess the Capability of the Bulgarian Refining Industry to Produce Unleaded Gasoline." Report prepared for the U.K. Know How Fund on Behalf of the World Bank, Washington, D.C.

Lefler, W. 1985. *Petroleum Refining for the Non-Technical Person*. Tulsa, Okla.: PennWell Publishing Co.

# Nitrogen Oxides: Pollution Prevention and Control

The first priority in designing a strategy to control nitrogen oxides is to protect human health. Human health impacts appear to be related to peak exposures to nitrogen oxides ($NO_x$). In addition to potentially damaging human health, nitrogen oxides are precursors to ozone ($O_3$) formation, which can harm human health and vegetation. Finally, nitrogen oxides contribute to acid deposition, which damages vegetation and aquatic ecosystems.

The extent to which $NO_x$ emissions harm human health depends on ground-level concentrations and the number of people exposed. Source location can affect these parameters. Gases emitted in areas with meteorological, climatological, and topographical features that favor dispersion will be less likely to concentrate near the ground. However, some meteorological conditions, such as inversion, may result in significantly higher ambient levels. Sources away from population centers will expose fewer people to harmful pollution. Plant siting is a critical feature in any air pollution management strategy. However, due to the dispersion of nitrogen oxides that may contribute to ozone formation and acid deposition far from the source, relying on plant siting alone is not a recommended strategy. The long-term objective must be to reduce total emissions.

Effective control of $NO_x$ emissions will require controls on both stationary sources and mobile transport sources. Each requires different strategies. This guideline focuses on control strategies for stationary sources (primarily fossil-fuel-fired electricity-generating plants).

## Limiting Emissions from Stationary Sources

Nitrogen oxides are produced in the combustion process by two different mechanisms: (a) burning the nitrogen in the fuel, primarily coal or heavy oil (fuel $NO_x$); and (b) high-temperature oxidation of the molecular nitrogen in the air used for combustion (thermal $NO_x$). Formation of fuel $NO_x$ depends on combustion conditions, such as oxygen concentration and mixing patterns, and on the nitrogen content of the fuel. Formation of thermal $NO_x$ depends on combustion temperature. Above 1,538°C (2,800°F), $NO_x$ formation rises exponentially with increasing temperature (Stultz and Kitto 1992). The relative contributions of fuel $NO_x$ and thermal $NO_x$ to emissions from a particular plant depend on the combustion conditions, the type of burner, and the type of fuel.

Approaches for controlling $NO_x$ from stationary sources can address fuel $NO_x$, thermal $NO_x$, or both. One way of controlling $NO_x$ emissions is to use low-nitrogen fuels. Another is to modify combustion conditions to generate less $NO_x$. Flue gas treatment techniques, such as selective catalytic reduction (SCR) processes, can remove $NO_x$.

### Choice of Fuel

Coals and residual fuel oils containing organically bound nitrogen contribute to over 50% of total emissions of $NO_x$, according to some estimates. The nitrogen content of U.S. coal ranges between 0.5% and 2% and that of residual fuel oil between 0.1% and 0.5%. In many circumstances, the most cost-effective means of reducing $NO_x$ emissions will be to use low-nitrogen fuels such as natural gas. Natural gas used as fuel can emit 60% less $NO_x$ than coal and virtually no particulate matter or sulfur oxides.

### Combustion Control

Combustion control may involve any of three strategies: (a) reducing peak temperatures in the combustion zone; (b) reducing the gas residence time in the high-temperature zone; and (c) reducing oxygen concentrations in the combustion zone. These changes in the combustion process can be achieved either through process modifications or by modifying operating conditions on existing furnaces. Process modifications include using specially designed low-$NO_x$ burners, reburning, combustion staging, gas recirculation, reduced air preheat and firing rates, water or steam injection, and low excess air (LEA) firing. These modifications are capable of reducing $NO_x$ emissions by 50 to 80%. The method of combustion control used depends on the type of boiler and the method of firing fuel.

### Process Modifications

New *low-$NO_x$ burners* are effective in reducing $NO_x$ emissions from both new power plants and existing plants that are being retrofitted. Low-$NO_x$ burners limit the formation of nitrogen oxides by controlling the mixing of fuel and air, in effect automating low-excess-air firing or staged combustion. Compared with older conventional burners, low-$NO_x$ burners reduce emissions of $NO_x$ by 40–60%. Because low-$NO_x$ burners are relatively inexpensive, power utilities have been quick to accept them; in fact, low-$NO_x$ burners are now a standard part of new designs. Capital costs for low-$NO_x$ burners with overfire air (OFA) range between US$20 and US$25 per kilowatt (Bounicore and Davis 1992; Kataoka, personal communication, 1994).

Unfortunately, low-$NO_x$ burners are not suitable for reducing $NO_x$ emissions from cyclone-fired boilers, which emit large quantities of $NO_x$, due to their high operating temperatures. Because combustion takes place outside the main furnace, the use of low-$NO_x$ burners is not suitable for these applications (Bounicore and Davis 1992). However, reburning technology can reduce $NO_x$ emissions.

*Reburning* is a technology used to reduce $NO_x$ emissions from cyclone furnaces and other selected applications. In reburning, 75–80% of the furnace fuel input is burned in the furnace with minimum excess air. The remaining fuel (gas, oil, or coal) is added to the furnace above the primary combustion zone. This secondary combustion zone is operated substoichiometrically to generate hydrocarbon radicals that reduce to nitrogen the nitrogen oxides that are formed. The combustion process is then completed by adding the balance of the combustion air through overfire air ports in a final burnout zone at the top of the furnace.

*Staged combustion (off-stoichiometric combustion)* burns the fuel in two or more steps. Staged combustion can be accomplished by firing some of the burners fuel-rich and the rest fuel-lean, by taking some of the burners out of service and allowing them only to admit air to the furnace, or by firing all the burners fuel-rich in the primary combustion zone and admitting the remaining air over the top of the flame zone (OFA); see Cooper and Alley 1986). Staged combustion techniques can reduce $NO_x$ emissions by 20–50%. Conventional OFA alone can reduce emissions of $NO_x$ by 30%, and advanced OFA has the potential of reducing them still further, although potential for corrosion and slagging exists. Capital costs for conventional and advanced OFA range between US$5 and $10 per kilowatt (Bounicore and Davis 1992).

*Flue gas recirculation (FGR)* is the rerouting of some of the flue gases back to the furnace. By using the flue gas from the economizer outlet, both the furnace air temperature and the furnace oxygen concentration can be reduced. However, in retrofits FGR can be very expensive. Flue gas recirculation is typically applied to oil- and gas-fired boilers and reduces $NO_x$ emissions by 20–50%. Modifications to the boiler in the form of ducting and an energy efficiency loss due to the power requirements of the recirculation fans can make the cost of this option higher than for some of the in-furnace $NO_x$ control methods.

*Reduced air preheat and reduced firing rates* lower peak temperatures in the combustion zone, thus reducing thermal $NO_x$. This strategy, however, carries a substantial energy penalty. Emissions of smoke and carbon monoxide need to be controlled, which reduces operational flexibility.

*Water or steam injection* reduces flame temperatures and thus thermal $NO_x$. Water injection is especially effective for gas turbines, reducing $NO_x$ emissions by about 80% at a water injection rate of 2%. For a gas turbine, the energy penalty is about 1%, but for a utility boiler it can be as high as 10%. For diesel-fired units, 25–35% reductions in $NO_x$ emissions can be achieved using water-fuel mixtures.

*Modifications in Operating Conditions*

*Low-excess-air firing (LEA)* is a simple, yet effective technique. Excess air is the amount of air in excess of what is theoretically needed to achieve 100% combustion. Before fuel prices rose, it was not uncommon to see furnaces operating with 50–100% excess air. Currently, it is possible to achieve full combustion for coal-fired units with less than 15–30% excess air. Studies have shown that reducing excess air from an average of 20% to an average of 14% can reduce emissions of NO$_x$ by an average of 19% (Cooper and Alley 1986).

Techniques involving low-excess-air firing, staged-combustion, and flue gas recirculation are effective in controlling both fuel NO$_x$ and thermal NO$_x$. The techniques *of* reduced air preheat and reduced firing rates (from normal operation) and water or steam injection are effective only in controlling thermal NO$_x$. These will therefore not be as effective for coal-fired units, since about 80% of the NO$_x$ emitted from these units is fuel NO$_x$.

*Flue Gas Treatment*

*Flue gas treatment (FGT)* is more effective in reducing NO$_x$ emissions than are combustion controls, although at higher cost. FGT is also useful where combustion controls are not applicable. Pollution prevention measures, such as using a high-pressure process in nitric acid plants, is more cost-effective in controlling NO$_x$ emissions. FGT technologies have been primarily developed and are most widely used in Japan and other OECD countries. The techniques can be classified as selective catalytic reduction, selective noncatalytic reduction, and adsorption.

*Selective catalytic reduction (SCR)* is currently the most developed and widely applied FGT technology. In the SCR process, ammonia is used as a reducing agent to convert NO$_x$ to nitrogen in the presence of a catalyst in a converter upstream of the air heater. The catalyst is usually a mixture of titanium dioxide, vanadium pentoxide, and tungsten trioxide (Bounicore and Davis 1992). SCR can remove 60–90% of NO$_x$ from flue gases. Unfortunately, the process is very expensive (US$40–$80/kilowatt), and the associated ammonia injection results in an ammonia slipstream in the exhaust. In addition, there are some concerns associated with anhydrous ammonia storage.

*Selective noncatalytic reduction (SNCR)* using ammonia- or urea-based compounds is still in the developmental stage. Early results indicate that SNCR systems can reduce NO$_x$ emissions by 30–70%. Capital costs for SNCR are expected to be much lower than for SCR processes, ranging between US$10 and US$20 per kilowatt (Bounicore and Davis 1992; Kataoka, 1992). Several dry *adsorption* techniques are available for simultaneous control of NO$_x$ and sulfur oxides (SO$_x$). One type of system uses activated carbon with ammonia (NH$_3$) injection to simultaneously reduce the NO$_x$ to nitrogen (N$_2$) and oxidize the SO$_2$ to sulfuric acid (H$_2$SO$_4$). If there is no sulfur in the fuel, the carbon acts as a catalyst for NO$_x$ reduction only. Another adsorption system uses a copper oxide catalyst that adsorbs sulfur dioxide to form copper sulfate. Both copper oxide and copper sulfate are reasonably good catalysts for the selective reduction of NO$_x$ with NH$_3$. This process, which has been installed on a 40-megawatt oil-fired boiler in Japan, can remove about 70% of NO$_x$ and 90% of SO$_x$ from flue gases (Cooper and Alley 1986).

## Applications of NO$_x$ Control Systems

For *coal-fired boilers* (which accounted for a major portion of all utility NO$_x$ emissions), the most widely applied control technologies involve combustion modifications, including low-excess-air firing, staged combustion, and use of low-NO$_x$ burners. For *oil-fired* boilers, the most widely applied techniques include flue gas recirculation, in addition to the techniques used for coal-fired units. For *gas-fired units*, which in any case emit 60% less NO$_x$ than coal-fired units, the primary control technologies include flue gas recirculation and combustion modifications. Finally, for *diesel plants*, the common technologies are water-steam injection, and SCR technology.

Table 1 summarizes the NO$_x$ reduction rates that are normally achieved through combustion modifications and flue gas treatment systems.

## Recommendations

The most cost-effective methods of reducing emissions of NO$_x$ are the use of low-NO$_x$ burners

**Table 1. NO$_x$ Removal Efficiencies for Combustion Modifications and Flue Gas Treatment**
*(percentage reduction in NO$_x$)*

| NO$_x$ reduction technique | Coal | Oil | Gas |
|---|---|---|---|
| *Combustion modification* | | | |
| Low-excess-air firing | 10–30 | 10–30 | 10–30 |
| Staged combustion | 20–50 | 20–50 | 20–50 |
| Flue gas recirculation | n.a. | 20–50 | 20–50 |
| Water/steam injection | n.a. | 10–50 | n.a. |
| Low-NO$_x$ burners | 30–40 | 30–40 | 30–40 |
| *Flue gas treatment* | | | |
| Selective catalytic reduction | 60–90 | 60–90 | 60–90 |
| Selective noncatalytic reduction | n.a. | 30–70 | 30–70 |

n.a.  Not applicable.

and the use of low nitrogen fuels such as natural gas. Natural gas has the added advantage of emitting almost no particulate matter or sulfur dioxide when used as fuel. Other cost-effective approaches to emissions control include combustion modifications. These can reduce NO$_x$ emissions by up to 50% at reasonable cost. Flue gas treatment systems can achieve greater emissions reductions, but at a much higher cost.

Table 2 shows applications of NO$_x$ abatement technologies.

## References and Sources

Bounicore, Anthony J., and Wayne T. Davis, eds. 1992. *Air Pollution Engineering Manual*. New York: Van Nostrand Reinhold.

Cooper, C. David, and F. C. Alley. 1986. *Air Pollution Control: A Design Approach*. Prospect Heights, Ill.: Waveland Press.

Godish, Thad. 1991. *Air Quality*. Chelsea, Mich.: Lewis Publishers.

Jechoutek, Karl G., S. Chattopadhya, R. Khan, F. Hill, and C. Wardell. 1992. "Steam Coal for Power and Industry." Industry and Energy Department Work-ing Paper. Energy Series Paper 58. World Bank, Washington, D.C.

Kataoka, S. 1992. "Coal Burning Plant and Emission Control Technologies." Technical Note. World Bank, China Country Department, Washington, D.C.

————. 1994. Personal communication.

OECD (Organisation for Economic Co-operation and Development). 1983. *Control Technology for Nitrogen Oxide Emissions from Stationary Sources*. Paris.

Stern, C., R. Boubel, D. Turner, and D. Fox. 1984. *Fundamentals of Air Pollution*. Orlando, Fla.: Academic Press.

Stultz, S. C., and John B. Kitto, eds. 1992. *Steam: Its Generation and Use*. 40th ed. Barberton, Ohio: The Babcock & Wilcox Co.

USEPA (United States Environmental Protection Agency). 1992. *Evaluation and Costing of NO$_x$ Controls for Existing Utility Boilers in the NESCAUM Region*. Washington, D.C.

————. 1986. "Compilation of Air Pollution Emission Factors. AP-42. (October 1992 version)." Washington, D.C.

Vatavuk, W. M. 1990. *Estimating Costs of Air Pollution Control*. Chelsea, Mich.: Lewis Publishers.

**Table 2. Applicability of NO$_x$ Abatement Technologies, by Type of Facility and by Technique**

| Technique | Boiler Large/medium | Boiler Small | Metal heating furnace | Petroleum heating furnace | Sintering furnace | Cement calcination furnace | Glass melting furnace | Coke oven | Waste incineration furnace | Nitric acid manufacture | Internal combustion engine | Gas turbine | Diesel |
|---|---|---|---|---|---|---|---|---|---|---|---|---|---|
| Low excess air | • | • | • | • | U | • | • | M | | | | | |
| Two-stage combustion (including off-stoichiometric combustion) | • | M | • | | | | | | | | | | |
| Flue gas recirculation | • | M | M | • | | U | | M | | | M | M | |
| Water/steam injection (including emulsion fuel) | M | U | U | M | | | | | | | M | M | M |
| Low-NO$_x$ burners | • | • | M | • | | | U | | | | | | |
| Selective catalytic reduction | M | | U | M | U | U | U | M | | M | U | U | M |
| Nonselective catalytic reduction | U | | | | | M | | | | M | | | |
| Noncatalytic reduction | M | | U | U | | | U | | | | | | |
| Wet-chemical scrubbing | M | | M | U | U | | | | U | M | | | |
| Other: change of temperature profile; nonsuspension preheater kiln | | | | | | • (Use pre-heaters and pre-calciners) | | | | • (Use high-pressure process) | | | |

*Notes:* • indicates high reliability; M, some points must be taken into account in the case of actual application; U, under study in a test plant.
*Source:* Adapted from OECD 1983 (verified as current).

249

# Ozone-Depleting Substances: Alternatives

Surrounding the earth at a height of about 25 kilometers is the stratosphere, rich in ozone, which prevents the sun's harmful ultraviolet (UV-B) rays from reaching the earth. UV-B rays have an adverse effect on all living organisms, including marine life, crops, animals and birds, and humans. In humans, UV-B is known to affect the immune system; to cause skin cancer, eye damage, and cataracts; and to increase susceptibility to infectious diseases such as malaria.

In 1974, it was hypothesized that chlorinated compounds were able to persist in the atmosphere long enough to reach the stratosphere, where solar radiation would break up the molecules and release chlorine atoms that would destroy the ozone. Mounting evidence and the discovery of the Antarctic ozone hole in 1985 led to the global program to control chlorofluorocarbons (CFCs) and other ozone-destroying chemicals. In addition to Antarctica, ozone loss is now present over New Zealand, Australia, southern Argentina and Chile, North America, Europe, and Russia.

The ozone-depleting chemicals or substances (ODSs) of concern are CFCs, halons, methyl chloroform (1,1,1,-trichloroethane; MCF), carbon tetrachloride (CTC), hydrochlorofluorocarbons (HCFCs), and methyl bromide. The ozone depletion potential (ODP) for these chemicals is shown in Table 1. CFC-11 was assigned an ODP of 1.0; all other chemicals have an ODP relative to that of CFC-11. An ODP higher than 1.0 means that the chemical has a greater ability than CFC-11 to destroy the ozone layer; an ODP lower than 1.0 means that the chemical's ability to destroy the ozone layer is less than that of CFC-11.

In September 1987, the Montreal Protocol on Substances That Deplete the Ozone Layer (the Protocol) was signed by 25 nations and the European Community. The Protocol was the first international environmental agreement, and its signing by so many nations represented a major accomplishment, and a major shift in the approach to handling global environmental problems. The Protocol called for a freeze on the production of halons and a requirement to reduce the production of CFCs by 50% by 1999. However, new scientific evidence surfaced after the entry into force of the Protocol, indicating that ozone depletion was more serious than originally thought. Accordingly, in 1990 (London), 1992 (Copenhagen), and 1995 (Vienna), amendments were made to the Protocol to regulate the phase-out of the original chemicals and the control and phase-out of additional chemicals.

**Table 1. Ozone Depletion Potential (ODP) of the Principal Ozone-Depleting Substances (ODSs)**

| ODS | ODP |
|---|---|
| CFC-11 | 1.0 |
| CFC-12 | 1.0 |
| CFC-113 | 0.8 |
| CFC-114 | 1.0 |
| CFC-115 | 0.6 |
| CFC-111, -112, -13, -211, -212, -213, -214, -215, -216, -217 | 1.0 |
| Halon 1211 | 3.0 |
| Halon 1301 | 10.0 |
| Halon 2402 | 6.0 |
| Carbon tetrachloride (CTC) | 1.1 |
| Methyl chloroform (MCF); 1,1,1-trichloroethane | 0.1 |
| HCFC-22 | 0.05 |
| HCFC-123 | 0.02 |
| HCFC-124 | 0.02 |
| HCFC-141b | 0.15 |
| HCFC-142b | 0.06 |
| HCFC-225ca | 0.01 |
| HCFC-225cb | 0.04 |
| Methyl bromide | 0.7 |

The principal provisions of the Montreal Protocol as it now stands are as follows:

- Production of CFCs, halons, methyl chloroform, and CTC ceased at the end of 1995 in industrial countries and will cease by 2010 in developing countries. Developing countries are defined in the Protocol as those that use less than 0.3 kilograms (kg) of ODS per capita per year. They are often called Article 5 countries in reference to the defining article in the Montreal Protocol.
- HCFCs, originally developed as a less harmful class of CFC alternatives, will be phased out by 2020 in industrial countries, with some provisions for servicing equipment to 2030. Developing countries are to freeze consumption by 2016 (base year 2015) and phase out use by 2040.
- Consumption and production of methyl bromide will end in 2005 in industrial countries (subject to phase-out stages and exemptions) and in 2015 in developing countries.

It was early recognized that undue hardships might be experienced by industry in developing countries as they implemented replacement technologies. Therefore, a fund was established under the Montreal Protocol to pay for incremental costs such as technical expertise and new technologies, processes, and equipment associated with the phase-out. The Multilateral Fund of the Montreal Protocol is managed by an executive committee consisting of delegates from seven developing countries and seven industrial countries. The following international organizations have been made Implementing Agencies of the Multilateral Fund for the purpose of helping governments and industries in developing countries with their programs to eliminate ODSs. (The roles outlined here are not intended to be exhaustive.)

- The *World Bank* assists developing countries with investment projects, country programs, workshops, training, and institutional strengthening.
- The *United Nations Environment Programme (UNEP)* has a clearinghouse function that includes information exchange, country programs, training, and workshops.
- The *United Nations Development Programme (UNDP)* is responsible for feasibility and preinvestment studies, training and workshops, demonstration projects, investment project design, and country programs.
- The *United Nations Industrial Development Organization (UNIDO)* implements small and medium-scale projects, feasibility studies at the plant level, technical assistance and training, and country programs.

## Uses of ODSs

In general, ODSs are most often used in the following applications:

- As propellants in aerosols (CFCs and HCFCs)
- In refrigeration, air conditioning, chillers, and other cooling equipment (CFCs and HCFCs)
- To extinguish fires (halons)
- In the manufacture of foams (CFCs and HCFCs)
- As solvents for cleaning printed circuit boards and precision parts and degreasing metal parts (CFCs, HCFCs, methyl chloroform, and CTC)
- In a variety of other areas, such as inks and coatings and medical applications (CFCs, HCFCs, methyl chloroform, and CTC)
- As a fumigant (methyl bromide).

## Alternative Technologies, Processes, and Chemicals

The following discussion provides a brief overview of the alternatives to ODSs that have been developed in various sectors. It is not intended to be an exhaustive listing of all alternatives, but it does summarize some proven alternatives and give an indication of future development trends. The selection of any alternative should be made with due consideration of other issues that could affect the final choice.

Identification, development, and commercialization of alternatives to ODSs are going on constantly. For this reason it is important to seek information on the latest alternatives from the World Bank's Global Environment Coordination Division. Technological updates are provided by the World Bank's Ozone Operations Resource Group, which is made up of experts in halons, solvents, aerosols, refrigerants, mobile air conditioning, foam blowing, and chemical production. For any alternative, consideration needs to be given to, for example, its compatibility with existing equipment, its health and safety aspects, its direct global-warming potential, whether it increases or decreases energy consumption, and the costs that may be incurred in eventual conversion to a non-ODS technology if an interim HCFC alternative is chosen. New ways of doing business may also develop in the course of review and selection of alternatives. For example, many electronics companies have now converted their manufacturing plants to "no-clean" technology. The benefits include elimination of circuit board cleaning after soldering, savings in chemical costs and waste disposal costs, savings in maintenance and energy consumption, improved product quality, and advances toward new technologies such as fluxless soldering. The selection of any alternative should not be made in isolation from the factors listed above.

*Flexible and Rigid Foams*

Zero-ODP alternatives are the substitutes of choice in many foam-manufacturing applications. However, the use of HCFCs is sometimes necessary in order to meet some product specifications. The viability of liquid hydrofluorocarbon (HFC) isomers in this industry remains to be proved, and hydrocarbon alternatives need to be better qualified, as well. The issues in these evaluations are safety (toxicity and flammability), environmental impact (generation of volatile organic compounds and global warming), product performance (insulating properties, conformity to fire codes, and the like), cost and availability, and regulatory requirements.

The next sections summarize the alternatives for specific products of the foam manufacturing sector. Because of the complexity of the industry and the variety of products, the alternatives have been listed briefly as short-term and long-term options, without an elaboration of the merits of each. Additional information is available in the 1995 UNEP Technical Options Report for this sector.

*Rigid polyurethane foams used in refrigerators and freezers.* Alternatives include hydrocarbons (pentane) and HCFC-141b; long-term alternatives include HFCs (-134a, -245, -356, -365). Vacuum panels may be used in the future.

*Rigid polyurethane for other appliances.* Alternatives include HCFC-141b, HCFC-22, blends of -22 and HCFC-142b, pentane, and carbon dioxide/water blowing. In the long term, the alternatives include HFCs.

*Rigid polyurethane used for boardstock and flexible-faced laminations.* Alternatives include HCFC-141b and pentane; in the long term, the use of HFCs should be developed.

*Sandwich panels of rigid polyurethane.* HCFC-141b, HCFC-22, blends of HCFC-22 and -141b, pentane, and HFC-134a are now used as alternatives to CFCs in this application. In the long term, HFCs and carbon dioxide/water will be the replacement technologies.

*Spray applications of rigid polyurethane.* Alternatives currently in use for spray applications include carbon dioxide/water and HCFC-141b. Long-term alternatives will be HFCs.

*Slabstock of rigid polyurethane.* Alternatives include HCFC-141b; long-term alternatives include HFCs and carbon dioxide/water. Pentane may also be used.

*Rigid polyurethane pipe construction.* CFCs in this application are being replaced by carbon dioxide/water, HCFC-22, blends of HCFC-22 and -142b, HCFC-141b, and pentanes. Long-term alternatives will include HFCs and carbon dioxide/water. For district central heating pipes, pentane and carbon dioxide/water are the preferred technologies.

*Polyurethane flexible slab.* Many alternatives now exist for flexible slab construction, including extended range polyols, carbon dioxide/water, softening agents, methylene chloride, acetone, increased density, HCFC-141b, pentane, and other alternative technologies such as accelerated cooling and variable pressure. The long term will probably see the use of injected carbon dioxide and alternative technologies.

*Molded flexible polyurethane.* The standard now is carbon dioxide/water blowing.

*Integral-skin polyurethane products.* The current alternatives for these products include HCFC-22, hydrocarbons, carbon dioxide/water, HFC-134a, pentanes, and HCFC-141b. The long-term alternate is expected to be carbon dioxide/water.

*Phenolic foams.* Phenolic foams can now be made using HCFC-141b, hydrocarbons, injected carbon dioxide, or HFC-152a instead of CFCs. In the long term, HFCs may be the predominant alternative.

*Extruded polystyrene sheet.* Alternatives currently include HCFC-22, hydrocarbons, injected carbon dioxide, and HFC-152a. In the long term, these same alternatives (except for HCFC-22) will be used, along with possible use of atmospheric gases.

*Extruded polystyrene boardstock.* HCFC-22 and -142b and injected carbon dioxide are the current alternatives. Long-term alternatives will be HFCs and injected carbon dioxide.

*Polyolefins.* Polyolefins are now manufactured using alternatives such as hydrocarbons, HCFC-22 and -142b, injected carbon dioxide, and HFC-152a. Hydrocarbons and injected carbon dioxide will be long-term alternatives.

### Refrigeration, Air Conditioning, and Heat Pumps

Refrigeration technology has also been rapidly evolving. Immediate replacements for many applications include hydrocarbons, HFCs, and HCFCs. Some of these will also be candidates for long-term replacement of the currently used CFCs. This section briefly describes the alternatives that are available for specific refrigeration, air conditioning, and heat pump applications.

*Domestic refrigeration.* Two refrigerant alternatives are predominant for the manufacture of new domestic refrigerators. HFC-134a has no ozone depletion potential and is nonflammable, but it has a high global-warming potential (GWP). HC-600a is flammable, has a zero ODP, and has a GWP approaching zero. Other alternatives for some applications include HFC-152a and binary and ternary blends of HCFCs and HFCs. Retrofitting alternatives may include HCFC/HFC blends, after CFCs are no longer available. However, the results obtained so far are still not satis-

factory. Neither HC-600a nor HFC-134a is considered an alternative for retrofitting domestic refrigeration appliances, but preliminary data indicate that a combination of the two may be a retrofit, or "servicing," candidate.

*Commercial refrigeration.* Alternatives to CFCs for new commercial refrigeration equipment include HCFCs (including HCFC mixtures) and HFCs and HFC mixtures. Retrofit of existing equipment is possible by using both HCFCs and HFCs, in conjunction with reduced charges and more efficient compressors. Hydrocarbons are, to a small extent, applied in hermetically sealed systems.

*Cold storage and food processing.* Although there has been a return to the use of ammonia for some cold storage facilities, there are safety issues, and some regulatory jurisdictions restrict its use. Other alternatives to CFCs in cold storage and large commercial food preservation facilities include HCFC-22 and HFC blends. Hydrocarbons and HCFC-22 will continue to be the favored alternatives until equipment using other alternatives is developed; ammonia will be used in selected applications.

*Industrial refrigeration.* New industrial refrigeration systems that are used by the chemical, petrochemical, pharmaceutical, oil and gas, and metallurgical industries, as well for industrial ice making and for sports and leisure facilities, can use ammonia and hydrocarbons as the refrigerant. Although the product base concerned is small, existing CFC equipment can be retrofitted to use HCFC-22, HFCs and HFC blends, and hydrocarbons.

*Air conditioning and heat pumps (air-cooled systems).* Equipment manufactured in this category generally uses HCFC-22 as the refrigerant. Alternatives under investigation include HFCs and HCs (propane). The most promising of these are the nonflammable, nontoxic HFC compounds, although there is more interest in propane in various regions. HCFs have been criticized for their global warming potential, but their total equivalent warming impact (TEWI), a measure that combines GWP and energy efficiency. is equal to or lower than that of the other alternatives.

*Air conditioning (water chillers).* HCFC-22 has been used in small chillers, and CFC-11 and -12 have been used in large chillers that employ centrifugal compressors. HFC blends are now beginning to be introduced to replace HCFC-22 in small chillers; HCFC-123 and HFC-134a are the preferred replacements for large units. Chillers that have used CFC-114 can be converted to use HCFC-124 or can be replaced by HFC-134a units.

*Transport refrigeration.* HCFC-22 and CFC-502 have been the refrigerants of choice for transport refrigeration units, although some applications are using ammonia as the refrigerant. The alternatives include various HFC blends.

*Automotive air conditioning.* The manufacturers of new automobiles have chosen HFC-134a as the fluid for air conditioning units, and retrofit kits are now available to allow older automobiles to convert to this alternative.

*Heat pumps (heating-only and heat recovery).* New heating-only heat pumps use HCFC-22, and this is expected to continue. HFC-134a is an alternative for retrofitting existing heat pumps, and investigation into the use of ammonia for large-capacity heat pumps is continuing. Other alternatives being explored include propane, other hydrocarbons, and hydrocarbon blends.

*Solvents, Coatings, Inks, and Adhesives*

There now exist alternatives or sufficient quantities of controlled substances for almost all applications of ozone-depleting solvents. Exceptions have been noted for certain laboratory and analytical uses and for manufacture of space shuttle rocket motors. HCFCs have not been adopted on a large scale as alternatives to CFC solvents. In the near term, however, they may be needed as transitional substances in some limited and unique applications. The UNEP Solvents Technical Options Committee does not recommend HCFC-141b as a replacement for methyl chloroform (1,1,1-trichloroethane) because its ODP is three times higher. Alternatives for specific uses of ozone-depleting solvents are described in this section.

*Electronics cleaning.* Experience has confirmed that for most uses in the electronics industry, ozone-depleting solvents can be replaced easily and, often, economically. A wide choice of alternatives exists. If technical specifications do not require postsolder cleaning, no-clean is the preferred technology. If cleaning is required, the use of water-soluble chemistry has generally proved to be reliable. Water-soluble chemistry is not, however, suitable for all applications.

*Precision cleaning.* Precision cleaning applications are defined as requiring a high level of cleanliness in order to maintain low-clearance or high-reliability components in working order. To meet exacting specifications, the alternatives that have been developed include solvent and nonsolvent applications. Solvent options include alcohols, aliphatic hydrocarbons, HCFCs and their blends, and aqueous and semiaqueous cleaners. Nonsolvent options include supercritical fluid cleaning (SCF), ultraviolet (UV)/ozone cleaning, pressurized gases, and plasma cleaning.

*Metal cleaning.* Oils and greases, particulate matter, and inorganic particles are removed from metal parts prior to subsequent processing steps such as further machining, electroplating, painting. Alternatives to ozone-depleting solvents that have been developed include solvent blends, aqueous cleaners, emulsion cleaners, mechanical cleaning, thermal vacuum deoiling, and no-clean alternatives.

*Dry cleaning.* Several solvents exist to replace the ozone-depleting solvents that have traditionally been used by the dry cleaning industry. Perchloroethylene has been used for over 30 years. Petroleum solvents, while flammable, can be safely used when appropriate safety precautions are taken. They include white spirit, Stoddard solvent, hydrocarbon solvents, isoparaffins, and n-paraffin. A number of HCFCs can also be used but should be considered only as transitional alternatives.

*Adhesives.* Methyl chloroform has been used extensively by the adhesives manufacturing industry because of its characteristics—it is nonflammable and quick drying, and it does not contribute to local air pollution—and its performance. One alternative for some applications is water-based adhesives. Other alternatives include hot melt adhesives; radiation-cured adhesives; high-solids adhesives; one-part epoxies, urethanes, and natural resins in powder form; moisture-cured adhesives; and reactive liquids.

*Coatings and inks.* Improvements have been made to water-based coatings, and these can be a substitute for ODS-based applications. Water-based coatings have been used in the following industries and manufacturing sectors: furniture, automotive electronics, aluminum siding, hardboard, metal containers, appliances, structural steel, and heavy equipment. Water-based inks are used successfully for flexographic and rotogravure laminates. High-solids coatings are now used for appliances, metal furniture, and a variety of construction equipment. Powder coatings are used for underground pipes, appliances, and automobiles. Ultraviolet light/electron beam (UV/EB) cured coatings and inks have been in limited use over the past 20 years, but their use is increasing. They are now used in flexographic inks and coatings, wood furniture and cabinets, and automotive applications.

*Aerosol solvent products.* Methyl chloroform is most often the solvent in aerosol applications, but some CFC-113 has also been used. Most of these applications can now be reformulated to avoid the use of ozone-depleting chemicals. With the exception of water, methylene chloride, and some HCFCs and non-ozone-depleting chlorinated solvents such as trichloroethylene and perchloroethylene, all of the alternatives to aerosol-applied solvents are more flammable than the solvents they replace. Alternative means of delivering the solvent can be considered.

*Other solvent uses of CFC-113, methyl chloroform, and carbon tetrachloride.* Specialized applications of ozone-depleting solvents include drying of components, film cleaning, fabric protection, manufacture of solid-fuel rockets, laboratory testing and analysis, process solvents, and semiconductor manufacture. Some of these applications have been granted an exemption under the Montreal Protocol, but it is the consensus of the experts on the UNEP Solvents Technical Options Committee that alternatives will be developed for all these specialized uses.

## Halons

*Halon hand-held extinguishers (containing 1211).* These can be replaced, in most applications, by multipurpose dry chemical extinguishers.

*Halon 1301 total flood systems.* New and existing alternatives are available for most halon 1301 total flood systems. These alternatives include zero-ODP halocarbons, inert gas mixtures, and new water-based technologies (e.g., water mist). The use of HCFCs and hydrobromofluorocarbons (HBFCs) as alternatives is not encouraged, and perfluorocarbons (PFCs) should not be used indiscriminately.

*Nonmedical Inhalants, Aerosols, Sterilants, and Carbon Tetrachloride Not Used as a Solvent*

*Nonmedical aerosol products.* A variety of alternatives to CFCs are used in nonmedical aerosol applications. Alternatives include hydrocarbons (HCs); dimethyl ether (DME); compressed gases such as carbon dioxide, nitrogen, and air; HCFC-142b and -22; HFC-134a -152a, and -227ea; and nonaerosol delivery means such as pump sprays, solid sticks, roll-ons, brushes, and the like. Because hydrocarbons, DME, and HFC-152a are flammable, there may be products in which they cannot be used. In a manufacturing plant where they are used for aerosol products, appropriate safety precautions will be required.

*Inhalant drug products.* Some medical aerosol products such as nasal preparations, local anesthetics, and antibiotics can be reformulated through the use of alternative propellants, mechanical pumps, and so on. However, finding suitable alternatives to the CFCs in metered dose inhalers (MDIs) used by asthma sufferers has been a challenge. Alternatives that have been developed and proven to date include dry powder inhalers and HFC-134a and -227.

*Sterilants.* A gas mixture of 88% CFC-12 and 12% ethylene oxide (EO) has been used by the medical community to sterilize equipment and parts. Replacement alternatives include steam sterilization; 100% EO; blends of carbon dioxide (10%) and EO (90%); formaldehyde; HCFC-124 (91.4%) and EO (8.6%); and other means such as gas plasma, chlorine dioxide, ozone, and radiation. Ethylene oxide is toxic, mutagenic, flammable, and explosive and is a suspected carcinogen. Its use must therefore be carefully controlled.

*Carbon tetrachloride (nonsolvent uses).* Carbon tetrachloride (CTC) has been used as a feedstock for the production of CFC-11 and –12. This application will cease with the closing of CFC production operations. CTC is also used as a feedstock and processing agent for some pharmaceuticals and agricultural chemicals and in the production of chlorinated rubber. The establishment of an alternative for each application will be found only through product-specific research.

## Methyl Bromide

Methyl bromide is used primarily as a fumigant. Only 3.2% of the global sale of more than 75,000 tons in 1992 was for nonfumigant purposes, as a feedstock for chemical synthesis. The greatest part was used to treat soil, to fumigate durables and perishables, and to fumigate structures and transport equipment. From a conservation perspective, technology exists to control the release of methyl bromide when treating soil and crops. Molecular sieves are shown to capture the methyl bromide that otherwise would have been lost to the atmosphere after batch fumigation and to regenerate the methyl bromide for use in subsequent batches. Alternatives to methyl bromide in each application area described below.

*Soil.* Chemical alternatives include 1,3-dichloropropene, dazomet, chloropicrin, metam sodium, and selective contact insecticides and herbicides. Nonchemical alternatives include crop rotation, organic amendments, steam, solar heating, biological control agents, cultural practices, and plant breeding.

*Commodities.* Chemical alternatives for crop fumigation include phosphine and carbonyl sulfide, as well as insecticides and rodenticides. Nonchemical alternatives include irradiation, controlled atmospheres utilizing nitrogen and carbon dioxide, and heat and cold.

*Structural.* Chemical alternatives include sulfuryl fluoride and phosphine, as well as contact insecticides and rodenticides. Nonchemical alternatives are the same as for commodity fumigation.

## Progress in Eliminating Ozone-Depleting Substances

Significant progress has been made in eliminating ozone-depleting substances since the entry into force of the Montreal Protocol in late 1987. For example, in the aerosol industry, the use of ODSs has been reduced from 300,000 metric tons (t) globally in 1986 to 180,000 t in 1989 to, it is estimated, less than 80,000 t in 1992. In the refrigeration sector, use of CFC refrigerants in industrial countries dropped from 862,000 t in 1986 to 302,000 t in 1993. Globally, CFC refrigerant use decreased from 1,133,000 t in 1986 to 643,000 t in 1992. To help in managing the phase-out of ODS refrigerants, a service industry has been established in most countries that captures and purifies ODSs during the servicing of equipment. The removed ODSs are then used to service the ongoing needs of ODS-containing refrigeration and cooling equipment until it has reached the end of its useful life. In the fire protection sector, the focus has been on establishing halon banks to recondition and store halon that has been removed from service and to make it available for maintaining other installations that require continued use of halon until suitable replacements are developed. The foam plastics industry has progressed from a global CFC use of 267,000 t in 1986 to 133,000 t in 1993—a reduction of 50%, in spite of a 45% increase in the size of the industry during the same period. The phase-out of ozone-depleting solvents is well advanced in industrial countries, and users are drawing on stockpiled solvents. In developing countries, CFC-113 use has been largely halted, and production facilities are shutting down. The use of methyl chloroform is no longer increasing in these countries. Countries such as Malaysia, Thailand, and Turkey have dramatically reduced solvent use.

It is important to note that the commercial supply chain has had a role to play in the speed of phase-out of ODSs. In many instances, customers have asked their suppliers to implement a phase-out program. These requests may originate because of labeling and tax legislation such as that implemented by the United States or because the customer has an environmental policy in place that commits it to encourage its suppliers to improve their environmental performance. Manufacturers also understand that the dwindling supply of ODSs causes price increases that will eventually make those products more expensive and less competitive.

# Sulfur Oxides: Pollution Prevention and Control

Traditionally, measures designed to reduce localized ground-level concentrations of sulfur oxides ($SO_x$) used high-level dispersion. Although these measures reduced localized health impacts, it is now realized that sulfur compounds travel long distances in the upper atmosphere and can cause damage far from the original source. Therefore the objective must be to reduce total emissions.

The extent to which $SO_x$ emissions harm human health depends primarily on ground-level ambient concentrations, the number of people exposed, and the duration of exposure. Source location can affect these parameters; thus, plant siting is a critical factor in any $SO_x$ management strategy.

The human health impacts of concern are short-term exposure to sulfur dioxide ($SO_2$) concentrations above 1,000 micrograms per cubic meter, measured as a 10-minute average. Priority therefore must be given to limiting exposures to peak concentrations. Industrial sources of sulfur oxides should have emergency management plans that can be implemented when concentrations reach predetermined levels. Emergency management plans may include actions such as using alternative low-sulfur fuels.

Traditionally, ground-level ambient concentrations of sulfur dioxide were reduced by emitting gases through tall stacks. Since this method does not address the problem of long-range transport and deposition of sulfur and merely disperses the pollutant, reliance on this strategy is no longer recommended. Stack height should be designed in accordance with good engineering practice (see, for example, United States, 40 CFR, Part 50, 100(ii).

## Approaches for Limiting Emissions

The principal approaches to controlling $SO_x$ emissions include use of low-sulfur fuel; reduction or removal of sulfur in the feed; use of appropriate combustion technologies; and emissions control technologies such as sorbent injection and flue gas desulfurization (FGD).

### Choice of Fuel

Since sulfur emissions are proportional to the sulfur content of the fuel, an effective means of reducing $SO_x$ emissions is to burn low-sulfur fuel such as natural gas, low-sulfur oil, or low-sulfur coal. Natural gas has the added advantage of emitting no particulate matter when burned.

### Fuel Cleaning

The most significant option for reducing the sulfur content of fuel is called beneficiation. Up to 70% of the sulfur in high-sulfur coal is in pyritic or mineral sulfate form, not chemically bonded to the coal. Coal beneficiation can remove 50% of pyritic sulfur and 20–30% of total sulfur. (It is not effective in removing organic sulfur.) Beneficiation also removes ash responsible for particulate emissions. This approach may in some cases be cost-effective in controlling emissions of sulfur oxides, but it may generate large quantities of solid waste and acid wastewaters that must be properly treated and disposed of.

Sulfur in oil can be removed through chemical desulfurization processes, but this is not a widely used commercial technology outside the petroleum industry.

### Selection of Technology and Modifications

Processes using fluidized-bed combustion (FBC) reduce air emissions of sulfur oxides. A lime or dolomite bed in the combustion chamber absorbs the sulfur oxides that are generated.

*Emissions Control Technologies*

The two major emissions control methods are sorbent injection and flue gas desulfurization:

- *Sorbent injection* involves adding an alkali compound to the coal combustion gases for reaction with the sulfur dioxide. Typical calcium sorbents include lime and variants of lime. Sodium-based compounds are also used. Sorbent injection processes remove 30–60% of sulfur oxide emissions.
- *Flue gas desulfurization* may be carried out using either of two basic FGD systems: regenerable and throwaway. Both methods may include wet or dry processes. Currently, more than 90% of utility FGD systems use a wet throwaway system process.

Throwaway systems use inexpensive scrubbing mediums that are cheaper to replace than to regenerate. Regenerable systems use expensive sorbents that are recovered by stripping sulfur oxides from the scrubbing medium. These produce useful by-products, including sulfur, sulfuric acid, and gypsum. Regenerable FGDs generally have higher capital costs than throwaway systems but lower waste disposal requirements and costs.

In wet FGD processes, flue gases are scrubbed in a liquid or liquid/solid slurry of lime or limestone. Wet processes are highly efficient and can achieve $SO_x$ removal of 90% or more. With dry scrubbing, solid sorbents capture the sulfur oxides. Dry systems have 70–90% sulfur oxide removal efficiencies and often have lower capital and operating costs, lower energy and water requirements, and lower maintenance requirements, in addition to which there is no need to handle sludge. However, the economics of the wet and dry (including "semidry" spray absorber) FGD processes vary considerably from site to site. Wet processes are available for producing gypsum as a by product.

Table 1 compares removal efficiencies and capital costs of systems for controlling $SO_x$ emissions.

## Monitoring

The three types of $SO_x$ monitoring systems are continuous stack monitoring, spot sampling, and

**Table 1. Comparison of $SO_x$ Emissions Control Systems**

| System | Percent $SO_x$ reduction | Capital cost ($/kilowatt) |
|---|---|---|
| Sorbent injection | 30–70 | 50–100 |
| Dry flue gas desulfurization | 70–90 | 80–170 |
| Wet flue gas sulfurization | >90 | 80–150 |

*Source:* Kataoka 1992.

surrogate monitoring. Continuous stack monitoring (CSM) involves sophisticated equipment that requires trained operators and careful maintenance. Spot sampling is performed by drawing gas samples from the stack at regular intervals. Surrogate monitoring uses operating parameters such as fuel sulfur content.

## Recommendations

The traditional method of $SO_x$ dispersion through high stacks is not recommended, since it does not reduce total $SO_x$ loads in the environment. Natural gas is the preferred fuel in areas where it is readily available and economical to use. Methods of reducing $SO_x$ generation, such as fuel cleaning systems and combustion modifications, should be examined. Implementation of these methods may avoid the need for FGD systems. Where possible and commercially feasible, preference should be given to dry $SO_x$ removal systems over wet systems.

## References and Sources

Cooper, C. David, and F. C. Alley. 1986. *Air Pollution Control: A Design Approach*. Prospect Heights, Ill.: Waveland Press.

Godish, Thad. 1991. *Air Quality*. Chelsea, Mich.: Lewis Publishers.

Kataoka, S. 1992. "Coal Burning Plant and Emission Control Technologies." Technical Note. World Bank, China Country Department, Washington, D.C.

Stern, C., R. Boubel, D. Turner, and D. Fox. 1984. *Fundamentals of Air Pollution*. Orlando, Fla: Academic Press.

Stultz, S. C., and John B. Kitto, eds. 1992. *Steam: Its Generation and Use*. 40th ed. Barberton, Ohio: The Babcock & Wilcox Co.

United States. CFR (*Code of Federal Regulations*). Washington, D.C.: Government Printing Office.

Vatavuk, W. 1990. *Estimating Costs of Air Pollution Control*. Chelsea, Mich.: Lewis Publishers.

World Bank. 1992. "Steam Coal for Power and Industry, Issues and Scenarios." Energy Series Working Paper No. 58. Industry and Energy Department. Washington, D.C.

# Aluminum Manufacturing

## Industry Description and Practices

The production of aluminum begins with the mining and beneficiation of bauxite. At the mine (usually of the surface type), bauxite ore is removed to a crusher. The crushed ore is then screened and stockpiled, ready for delivery to an alumina plant. In some cases, ore is upgraded by beneficiation (washing, size classification, and separation of liquids and solids) to remove unwanted materials such as clay and silica.

At the alumina plant, the bauxite ore is further crushed or ground to the correct particle size for efficient extraction of the alumina through digestion by hot sodium hydroxide liquor. After removal of "red mud" (the insoluble part of the bauxite) and fine solids from the process liquor, aluminum trihydrate crystals are precipitated and calcined in rotary kilns or fluidized bed calciners to produce alumina ($Al_2O_3$). Some alumina processes include a liquor purification step.

Primary aluminum is produced by the electrolytic reduction of the alumina. The alumina is dissolved in a molten bath of fluoride compounds (the electrolyte), and an electric current is passed through the bath, causing the alumina to dissociate to form liquid aluminum and oxygen. The oxygen reacts with carbon in the electrode to produce carbon dioxide and carbon monoxide. Molten aluminum collects in the bottom of the individual cells or pots and is removed under vacuum into tapping crucibles. There are two prominent technologies for aluminum smelting: prebake and Soderberg. This document focuses on the prebake technology, with its associated reduced air emissions and energy efficiencies.

Raw materials for secondary aluminum production are scrap, chips, and dross. Pretreatment of scrap by shredding, sieving, magnetic separation, drying, and so on is designed to remove undesirable substances that affect both aluminum quality and air emissions. The prevailing process for secondary aluminum production is smelting in rotary kilns under a salt cover. Salt slag can be processed and reutilized. Other processes (smelting in induction furnaces and hearth furnaces) need no or substantially less salt and are associated with lower energy demand, but they are only suitable for high-grade scrap. Depending on the desired application, additional refining may be necessary. For demagging (removal of magnesium from the melt), hazardous substances such as chlorine and hexachloroethane are often used, which may produce dioxins and dibenzofurans. Other, less hazardous methods, such as adding chlorine salts, are available. Because it is difficult to remove alloying elements such as copper and zinc from an aluminum melt, separate collection and separate reutilization of different grades of aluminum scrap are necessary. It should be noted that secondary aluminum production uses substantially less energy than primary production—less than 10–20 gigajoules per metric ton (GJ/t) of aluminum produced, compared with 164 GJ/t for primary production (mine to aluminum metal).

## Waste Characteristics

At the bauxite production facilities, dust is emitted to the atmosphere from dryers and materials-handling equipment, through vehicular movement, and from blasting. Although the dust is not hazardous, it can be a nuisance if containment systems are not in place, especially on the dryers and handling equipment. Other air emissions could include nitrogen oxides ($NO_x$), sulfur dioxide ($SO_2$), and other products of combustion from the bauxite dryers.

Ore washing and beneficiation may yield process wastewaters containing suspended solids. Runoff from precipitation may also contain suspended solids.

At the alumina plant, air emissions can include bauxite dust from handling and processing; limestone dust from limestone handling, burnt lime dust from conveyors and bins, alumina dust from materials handling, red mud dust and sodium salts from red mud stacks (impoundments), caustic aerosols from cooling towers, and products of combustion such as sulfur dioxide and nitrogen oxides from boilers, calciners, mobile equipment, and kilns. The calciners may also emit alumina dust and the kilns, burnt lime dust.

Although alumina plants do not normally discharge effluents, heavy rainfalls can result in surface runoff that exceeds what the plant can use in the process. The excess may require treatment.

The main solid waste from the alumina plant is red mud (as much as 2 tons of mud per ton of alumina produced), which contains oxides of alumina, silicon, iron, titanium, sodium, calcium, and other elements. The pH is 10–12. Disposal is to an impoundment.

Hazardous wastes from the alumina plant include spent sulfuric acid from descaling in tanks and pipes. Salt cake may be produced from liquor purification if this is practiced.

In the aluminum smelter, air emissions include alumina dust from handling facilities; coke dust from coke handling; gaseous and particulate fluorides; sulfur and carbon dioxides and various dusts from the electrolytic reduction cells; gaseous and particulate fluorides; sulfur dioxide; tar vapor and carbon particulates from the baking furnace; coke dust, tars, and polynuclear aromatic hydrocarbons (PAHs) from the green carbon and anode-forming plant; carbon dust from the rodding room; and fluxing emissions and carbon oxides from smelting, anode production, casting, and finishing. The electrolytic reduction cells (pot line) are the major source of the air emissions, with the gaseous and particulate fluorides being of prime concern. The anode effect associated with electrolysis also results in emissions of carbon tetrafluoride ($CF_4$) and carbon hexafluoride ($C_2F_6$), which are greenhouse gases, of concern because of their potential for global warming. Emissions numbers that have been reported for uncontrolled gases from smelters are 20–80 kilograms per ton of product (kg/t) for particulates, 6–12 kg/t for hydrogen fluoride, and 6–10 kg/t for fluoride particulates. Corresponding concentrations are 200–800 milligrams per cubic meter ($mg/m^3$); 60–120 $mg/m^3$; and 60–100 $mg/m^3$. These values are for a prebaked-technology plant built in 1983.

An aluminum smelter produces 40–60 kg of mixed solid wastes per ton of product, with spent cathodes (spent pot and cell linings) being the major fraction. The linings consist of 50% refractory material and 50% carbon. Over the useful life of the linings, the carbon becomes impregnated with aluminum and silicon oxides (averaging 16% of the carbon lining), fluorides (34% of the lining), and cyanide compounds (about 400 parts per million). Contaminant levels in the refractories portion of linings that have failed are generally low. Other by-products for disposal include skim, dross, fluxing slags, and road sweepings.

Atmospheric emissions from secondary aluminum melting include hydrogen chloride and fluorine compounds. Demagging may lead to emissions of chlorine, hexachloroethane, chlorinated benzenes, and dioxins and furans. Chlorinated compounds may also result from the melting of aluminum scrap that is coated with plastic. Salt slag processing emits hydrogen and methane. Solid wastes from the production of secondary aluminum include particulates, pot lining refractory material, and salt slag. Particulate emissions, possibly containing heavy metals, are also associated with secondary aluminum production.

## Pollution Prevention and Control

Pollution prevention is always preferred to the use of end-of-pipe pollution control facilities. Therefore every attempt should be made to incorporate cleaner production processes and facilities to limit, at source, the quantity of pollutants generated.

In the bauxite mine, where beneficiation and ore washing are practiced, a tailings slurry of 7–9% solids is produced for disposal. The preferred technology is to concentrate these tailings and dispose of them in the mined-out area. A concentration of 25–30% can be achieved through gravity settling in a tailings pond. The tailings can be further concentrated, using a thickener, to 30–50%, yielding a substantially volume-reduced slurry.

The alumina plant discharges red mud in a slurry of 25–30% solids, and this also presents an opportunity to reduce disposal volumes. Today's technology, in the form of high-efficiency deep thickeners, and large-diameter conventional thickeners, can produce a mud of 50–60% solids concentration. The lime used in the process forms insoluble solids that leave the plant along with the red mud. These lime-based solids can be minimized by recycling the lime used as a filtering aid to digestion to displace the fresh lime that is normally added at this point. Finally, effluent volume from the alumina plant can be minimized or eliminated by good design and operating practices: reducing the water added to the process, segregating condensates and recycling to the process, and using rainwater in the process.

Using the prebake technology rather than the Soderberg technology for aluminum smelting is a significant pollution prevention measure. In the smelter, computer controls and point feeding of aluminum oxide to the centerline of the cell help reduce emissions, including emissions of organic fluorides such as $CF_4$, which can be held at less than 0.1 kg/t aluminum. Energy consumption is typically 14 megawatt hours per ton (MWh/t) of aluminum, with prebake technology. (Soderberg technology uses 17.5 MWh/t.) Gas collection efficiencies for the prebake process is better than for the Soderberg process: 98% vs. 90%. Dry scrubber systems using aluminum oxide as the adsorbent for the cell gas permits the recycling of fluorides. The use of low-sulfur tars for baking anodes helps control $SO_2$ emissions. Spent pot linings are removed after they fail, typically because of cracking or heaving of the lining. The age of the pot linings can vary from 3 to 10 years. By improving the life of the lining through better construction and operating techniques, discharge of pollutants can be reduced. Note that part of the pot lining carbon can be recycled when the pots are relined.

Emissions of organic compounds from secondary aluminum production can be reduced by thoroughly removing coatings, paint, oils, greases, and the like from raw feed materials before they enter the melt process.

## Target Pollution Loads

Experience in Europe has shown that red mud produced at the alumina plant can be reduced from 2 t/t alumina to about 1 t/t alumina through implementation of good industrial practices.

## Treatment Technologies

At bauxite facilities, the major sources of dust emissions are the dryers, and emissions are controlled with electrostatic precipitators (ESPs) or baghouse dust collectors. Removal efficiencies of 99% are achievable. Dust from conveyors and material transfer points is controlled by hoods and enclosures. Dust from truck movement can be minimized by treating road surfaces and by ensuring that vehicles do not drop material as they travel. Dusting from stockpiled material can be minimized by the use of water sprays or by enclosure in a building.

At the alumina plant, pollution control for the various production and service areas is implemented as follows:

- *Bauxite and limestone handling and storage*: dust emissions are controlled by baghouses.
- *Lime kilns*: dust emissions are controlled by baghouse systems. Kiln fuels can be selected to reduce $SO_2$ emissions; however, this is not normally a problem, since most of the sulfur dioxide that is formed is absorbed in the kiln.
- *Calciners*: alumina dust losses are controlled by ESPs; $SO_2$ and $NO_x$ emissions are reduced to acceptable levels by contact with the alumina.
- *Red mud disposal:* the mud impoundment area must be lined with impervious clay prior to use to prevent leakage. Water spraying of the mud stack may be required to prevent fine dust from being blown off the stack. Longer-term treatment of the mud may include reclamation of the mud, neutralization, covering with topsoil, and planting with vegetation.

In the smelter, primary emissions from the reduction cells are controlled by collection and treatment using dry sorbent injection; fabric filters or electrostatic precipitators are used for controlling particulate matter. Primary emissions comprise 97.5% of total cell emissions; the balance consists of secondary emissions that escape into the potroom and leave the building through roof ventilators. Wet scrubbing of the primary emissions can also be used, but large volumes of toxic waste liquors will need to be treated or disposed of. Secondary emissions result from the periodic replacement of anodes and other operations; the fumes escape when the cell hood panels have been temporarily removed. While wet scrubbing can be used to control the release of secondary fumes, the high-volume, low-concentration gases offer low scrubbing efficiencies, have high capital and operating costs, and produce large volumes of liquid effluents for treatment. Wet scrubbing is seldom used for secondary fume control in the prebake process.

When anodes are baked on site, the dry scrubbing system using aluminum oxide as the adsorbent is used. It has the advantage of being free of waste products, and all enriched alumina and absorbed material are recycled directly to the reduction cells. Dry scrubbing may be combined with incineration for controlling emissions of tar and volatile organic compounds (VOCs) and to recover energy. Wet scrubbing can also be used but is not recommended, since a liquid effluent, high in fluorides and hydrocarbons, will require treatment and disposal.

Dry scrubber systems applied to the pot fumes and to the anode baking furnace result in the capture of 97% of all fluorides from the process.

The aluminum smelter solid wastes, in the form of spent pot lining, are disposed of in engineered landfills that feature clay or synthetic lining of disposal pits, provision of soil layers for covering and sealing, and control and treatment of any leachate. Treatment processes are available to reduce hazards associated with spent pot lining prior to disposal of the lining in a landfill. Other solid wastes such as bath skimmings are sold for recycling, while spalled refractories and other chemically stable materials are disposed of in landfill sites.

Modern smelters using good industrial practices are able to achieve the following in terms of pollutant loads (all values are expressed on an annualized basis): hydrogen fluoride, 0.2–0.4 kg/t; total fluoride, 0.3–0.6 kg/t; particulates, 1 kg/t; sulfur dioxide, 1 kg/t; and nitrogen oxides, 0.5 kg/t. $CF_4$ emissions should be less than 0.1 kg/t.

For secondary aluminum production, the principal treatment technology downstream of the melting furnace is dry sorbent injection using lime, followed by fabric filters. Waste gases from salt slag processing should be filtered as well. Waste gases from aluminum scrap pretreatment that contain organic compounds of concern may be treated by postcombustion.

## Emissions Guidelines

Emissions levels for the design and operation of each project must be established through the environmental assessment (EA) process on the basis of country legislation and the *Pollution Prevention and Abatement Handbook,* as applied to local conditions. The emissions levels selected must be justified in the EA and acceptable to the World Bank Group.

The guidelines given below present emissions levels normally acceptable to the World Bank Group in making decisions regarding provision of World Bank Group assistance. Any deviations from these levels must be described in the World Bank Group project documentation. The emissions levels given here can be consistently achieved by well-designed, well-operated, and well-maintained pollution control systems. The guidelines are expressed as concentrations to facilitate monitoring. Dilution of air emissions or effluents to achieve these guidelines is unacceptable.

All of the maximum levels should be achieved for at least 95% of the time that the plant or unit is operating, to be calculated as a proportion of annual operating hours.

*Air Emissions*

The air emissions levels presented in Table 1 should be achieved.

*Liquid Effluents*

If there is a process effluent from the aluminum

## Table 1. Air Emissions from Aluminum Smelting
*(milligrams per normal cubic meter)*

| Parameter | Maximum value |
|---|---|
| Particulate matter | 30 |
| Hydrogen fluoride | 1 |
| Total fluoride | 2 |
| VOCs | 20 |

## Table 2. Liquid Effluents from Aluminum Smelting
*(milligrams per liter, except pH and temperature)*

| Parameter | Maximum value |
|---|---|
| pH | 6–9 |
| TSS | 50 |
| Fluoride | 20 |
| Aluminum | 0.2 |
| COD | 150 |
| Hydrocarbons | 5 |
| Temperature increase | ≤ 3°C[a] |

*Note:* Effluent requirements are for direct discharge to surface waters.
a. The effluent should result in a temperature increase of no more than 3°C at the edge of the zone where initial mixing and dilution take place. Where the zone is not defined, use 100 meters from the point of discharge.

smelter, the effluent emissions levels presented in Table 2 should be achieved.

*Ambient Noise*

Noise abatement measures should achieve either the levels given below or a maximum increase in background levels of 3 decibels (measured on the A scale) [dB(A)]. Measurements are to be taken at noise receptors located outside the project property boundary.

| Receptor | Maximum allowable log equivalent (hourly measurements), in dB(A) | |
|---|---|---|
| | Day (07:00–22:00) | Night (22:00–07:00) |
| Residential, institutional, educational | 55 | 45 |
| Industrial, commercial | 70 | 70 |

## Monitoring and Reporting

Frequent sampling may be required during start-up and upset conditions. Once a record of consistent performance has been established, sampling for the parameters listed in this document should be as described below.

Air emissions should be monitored regularly for particulate matter and fluorides. Hydrocarbon emissions should be monitored annually on the anode plant and baking furnaces.

Liquid effluents should be monitored weekly for pH, total suspended solids, fluoride, and aluminum and at least monthly for other parameters.

Monitoring data should be analyzed and reviewed at regular intervals and compared with the operating standards so that any necessary corrective actions can be taken. Records of monitoring results should be kept in an acceptable format. The results should be reported to the responsible authorities and relevant parties, as required.

## Key Issues

The key production and control practices that will lead to compliance with emissions requirements are summarized here.

*Bauxite Production*

- Concentrate bauxite tailings prior to disposal.
- Control dust emissions at the bauxite mine and in the alumina plant by using ESPs and baghouses.

*Alumina Plant*

- Thicken and concentrate red mud in the alumina plant, using high-efficiency thickeners, and then dispose of it in engineered and managed stacks.

*Primary Aluminum Smelting*

- Give preference to the prebake process for smelting.
- Use computers to control the bath and limit anode effects.
- Incinerate baking furnace gases for energy recovery.

- Use dry scrubber systems with aluminum oxide absorbent for control of emissions from reduction cells and from anode bake ovens.
- Maximize the reuse of spent pot linings.
- Dispose of nonreusable spent pot linings in engineered landfills.

*Secondary Aluminum Production*

- Take advantage of processes for reusing salt slag.

## Sources

Bounicore, Anthony J., and Wayne T. Davis, eds. 1992. *Air Pollution Engineering Manual.* New York: Van Nostrand Reinhold.

Paris Commission. 1992. "Industrial Sectors: Best Available Technology—Primary Aluminium Industry."

World Bank. 1995. "Industrial Pollution Prevention and Abatement: Aluminum Smelting." Draft Technical Background Document. Environment Department, Washington, D.C.

# Base Metal and Iron Ore Mining

## Industry Description and Practices

This document addresses the mining of ores of base metals (copper, lead, nickel, and zinc) and of iron. The documents on Aluminum and on Coal Mining and Production also deal with mining activities.

The major phases in mine development are (a) exploration; (b) mine development; c) extraction (underground and open pit) and mine operation; (d) ore beneficiation; (e) storage and transport of ore; and (f) mine closure and reclamation. This document focuses on the development, operation, and closure phases.

## Waste Characteristics

The volume of solid waste generated, including tailings from processing, is one of the main pollution concerns in the mining industry. Removal of overburden to access the ore can pose major problems in storage and reclamation. The overburden (waste-to-ore) ratio for surface mining of metal ores generally ranges from 2:1 to 8:1, depending on local conditions. The ratio for solid wastes from underground mining is typically 0.2:1. Where concentration or other processing of the ore is done on site, the tailings generated also have to be managed. Ores with a low metal content, say, less than 0.4%, generate significant quantities of tailings.

In certain mines where ores have high sulfur content, drainage from mine workings and waste heaps can become highly acidic and can contain high concentrations of dissolved heavy metals. This acid mine drainage (AMD) can have a pH of 3 or lower; sulfate levels of 800–1,800 milligrams per liter (mg/l); copper levels up to 50 mg/l; iron levels up to 1,000 mg/l; lead levels up to 12 mg/l; zinc levels up to 1,700 mg/l; and cadmium levels of several milligrams per liter, depending on the contents of the ore. Effluent from tailings ponds may contain concentrations of chromium of several milligrams per liter. Base metal mining tailings decant may contain high concentrations of thiosalts. Chemicals used in flotation and other metal concentration processes could create toxicity problems when released in effluents.

Surface runoffs may also pose significant environmental problems through erosion and carryover of tailings and other mining residues. Explosives such as ammonium nitrate may be present in surface runoff. Transport of mined material and machinery maintenance and repair can lead to contamination of surface water.

Significant levels of dust, above 3 kilograms per ton (kg/t) of ore mined, and ranging from 0.003 to 27 kg/t, may be generated by extraction activities, crushing, ore beneficiation, transport and traffic, and wind-borne losses. Significant releases of dust containing metals, including mercury, may result from the drying of the ore concentrate. Fires may result from the oxidation of sulfide-bearing materials and can present a significant hazard.

## Pollution Prevention and Control

The critical factors in good environmental performance in mining are adequate planning and effective management and implementation. Responsibilities for the implementation and monitoring of environmental measures should be specifically assigned. Before mining begins, a mining plan and a mine closure and reclamation plan must be prepared and approved. These plans should be updated regularly as mining progresses.

*Development Plans*

Development plans define the sequence and nature of extraction operations and detail the methods to be used in closure and restoration. At a minimum, the plans must address the following:

- Removal, proper storage, and management of topsoil
- Early restoration of worked-out areas and of spoil heaps to minimize the extent of open areas
- Identification of potential areas for AMD generation, followed by planning for successive remediation of pyrites to reduce AMD generation
- A water management plan focusing on the effective use of mine water for operations (with recirculation of process water) and for postclosure
- Extraction methods in relation to subsidence and to surface use
- Development of restoration and vegetation methods that are appropriate to the specific site conditions
- Blasting methods that minimize noise and vibrations.

The development plan normally contains specific sections dealing with erosion and sediment control, tailings disposal, mine closure and site restoration, and operating measures. These are discussed next.

*Erosion and Sediment Control*

An erosion and sediment control plan should be prepared. It should include measures or methods, appropriate to the situation, for intercepting, diverting, or otherwise reducing stormwater runoff from exposed soil surfaces, tailings dams, and waste rock dumps. Both vegetative and nonvegetative soil stabilization measures should be an integral part of the erosion control plan. Sediment control structures (for example, detention and retention basins) should be provided to intercept and treat surface runoff prior to discharge. All erosion control and sediment containment facilities must receive proper maintenance during the life of the project.

*Tailings Disposal*

Tailings must be managed to optimize human safety and environmental protection. On-land tailings impoundment systems must be designed and constructed in accordance with internationally recognized engineering practices, local seismic conditions, and precipitation conditions (to accommodate surface run-on). The designs should address the structural integrity of the tailings dams or deposits even post-closure. On-land disposal systems should be designed to isolate acid leachate-generating material from oxidation and percolating water. Marine and riverine discharges are normally not acceptable and should be considered only when on-land disposal would pose an environmental risk and it can be demonstrated that such discharges will not have a significant adverse effect on downstream coastal or riverine resources. Riverine discharges are acceptable only when justified on the basis of an environmental analysis of the alternatives and the effects on aquatic resources and downstream users of riverine resources.

The design of the tailings management system must address postclosure issues such as the long-term geotechnical stability of the impoundment, the chemical stability of the tailings, long-term surface and groundwater management (including provisions for long-term spillway capacity requirements), and restoration.

*Mine Closure and Restoration Plan*

The closure and restoration plan should cover reclamation of tailings deposits, waste rock deposits, any open pit areas, sedimentation basins, and abandoned mine, mill, and camp sites. Mine reclamation plans should incorporate the following:

- Return of the land to conditions capable of supporting prior land use, equivalent uses, or other acceptable uses
- Elimination of significant adverse effects on adjacent water resources
- Use of waste rock for backfill and of topsoil (or other acceptable materials) for reclamation to the extent feasible

- Contouring of slopes to minimize erosion and runoff
- Planting of native species of vegetation and of other species that are environmentally acceptable, to prevent erosion and to encourage self-sustaining development of a productive ecosystem on the reclaimed land
- Postclosure management of AMD and tailings; reduction of AMD formation by sealing off pyrite-containing waste from oxidation and percolating water
- Budget and schedule for pre- and postclosure reclamation activities.
- Sealing or securing of all shaft openings and mine adits on closure of the mine.

Money should be reserved over the life of the mine to cover the costs associated with mine closure. The amount of money and the type of financing required will depend on a number of factors such as the projected life of the mine, the nature of the operations, the complexity of environmental issues, the financial and environmental management capacity of the borrower or project sponsor, and the jurisdiction in which the mine is located. The mine reclamation and closure plan, the timing of its submission, and financing of activities under the plan should be discussed and agreed on with the borrower or sponsor as early as possible.

*Operating Measures*

Other recommended pollution prevention measures include:

- Progressive backfilling to minimize land disturbances
- Use of dust control equipment on dryers and of pressure-air dryers instead of fuel-based drum dryers to dry concentrations.
- Use of covers or control devices for crushing and milling to avoid the generation of dust
- Minimization of AMD generation by reducing disturbed areas and isolating drainage systems
- Diversion of leachates from waste heaps to avoid contact with and contamination of surface water and groundwater
- Minimization of freshwater intake; recycling of tailings decant water and wastewater from

the concentration process to minimize contaminated discharges to the extent feasible
- Collection of leachates from tailings ponds and treatment before discharge, with sufficient residence time in the tailings pond to ensure thiosalt oxidation; provision of buffer capacity for the rainy season
- Use of ditches to divert surface runoff from tailing ponds
- Use of dust suppression measures (wetting work areas, roads, and storage piles; installing equipment covers; minimizing drop distances by using adjustable height conveyors; and using dust hoods and shields)
- Collection and recycling of waste oils and lubricants
- Prevention of spills of chemicals (including ammonium nitrate, if used in blasting operations)
- Provision of appropriate storage areas for chemicals and fuels
- Avoidance of the use of toxic floatation agents
- Control of noise through the use of berms and mufflers; control of noise and vibrations by means of sequenced blasting.

## Treatment Technologies

Filters for crushers, grinding mills, and dryers are used to control dust emissions.

AMD and wastewaters are typically dealt with by using physical-chemical treatment techniques such as neutralization, precipitation, flocculation, coagulation, settling, and filtration. In some cases, cyanide oxidation and ion exchange may also have to be performed. Chrome reduction may be needed for floatation water.

## Emissions Guidelines

Emissions levels for the design and operation of each project must be established through the environmental assessment (EA) process on the basis of country legislation and the *Pollution Prevention and Abatement Handbook,* as applied to local conditions. The emissions levels selected must be justified in the EA and acceptable to the World Bank Group.

The guidelines given below present emissions levels normally acceptable to the World Bank Group in making decisions regarding provision of World Bank Group assistance. Any deviations from these levels must be described in the World Bank Group project documentation. The emissions levels given here can be consistently achieved by well-designed, well-operated, and well-maintained pollution control systems.

The guidelines are expressed as concentrations, to facilitate monitoring. Dilution of air emissions or effluents to achieve these guidelines is unacceptable.

All of the maximum levels should be achieved for at least 95% of the time that the plant or unit is operating, to be calculated as a proportion of annual operating hours.

*Liquid Effluents*

Table 1 gives the effluent levels to be achieved during operation and after mine closure.

*Ambient Noise*

Noise abatement measures should achieve either the levels given below or a maximum increase in background levels of 3 decibels (measured on the A scale) [dB(A)]. Measurements are to be taken at noise receptors located outside the project property boundary.

| Receptor | Maximum allowable log equivalent (hourly measurements), in dB(A) | |
|---|---|---|
| | Day (07:00–22:00) | Night (22:00–07:00) |
| Residential, institutional, educational | 55 | 45 |
| Industrial, commercial | 70 | 70 |

## Monitoring and Reporting

Liquid effluents, including tailings dam outflows, should be monitored daily for pH and suspended solids. Metals and, when appropriate, thiosalts and floatation chemicals should be monitored on a monthly basis. If treatment is required to control soluble metals, metals and other parameters such as turbidity should be monitored more frequently. Frequent sampling may be required during start-up and upset conditions.

Monitoring data should be analyzed and reviewed at regular intervals and compared with the operating standards so that any necessary corrective actions can be taken. Records of monitoring results should be kept in an acceptable format. The results should be reported to the responsible authorities and relevant parties, as required.

## Key Issues

The key production and control practices that will lead to compliance with emissions requirements can be summarized as follows:

Develop a comprehensive environmental and mine management plan to include:

- Restoration and rehabilitation of disturbed areas
- Identification and management of AMD sources
- Water management for operations and postclosure conditions
- Management and sealing of tailings

### Table 1. Effluents from Base Metal and Iron Ore Mining

*(milligrams per liter, except for pH)*

| Parameter | Maximum value |
|---|---|
| pH | 6–9 |
| TSS | 50 |
| Oil and grease | 10 |
| Cyanide | 1.0 |
| Free | 0.1 |
| Weak acid dissociable (WAD) | 0.5 |
| COD | 150 |
| Arsenic | 0.1 |
| Cadmium | 0.1 |
| Chromium (hexavalent) | 0.1 |
| Copper | 0.5 |
| Iron | 3.5 |
| Lead | 0.2 |
| Mercury | 0.01 |
| Nickel | 0.5 |
| Zinc | 2 |
| Total metals | 10 |

Develop and implement a post-closure plan to include:

- Restoration of disturbed areas
- Long-term geotechnical and chemical stability of tailings
- Adequate spillway capacity for the tailings pond overflow
- Management of AMD, water drainage, and surface runoff

## Sources

UNEP (United Nations Environment Programme). 1991. "Environment Aspects of Selected Nonferrous Metals (Cu, Ni, Pb, Zn, Au) Ore Mining." Technical Report Series 5. Paris.

————. 1993. "Environmental Management of Nickel Production." Technical Report 15. Paris.

Warhurst, Alyson. 1994. *Environmental Degradation from Mining and Mineral Processing in Developing Countries: Corporate Responses and National Policies.* Paris: Organisation for Economic Co-operation and Development.

World Bank. 1996. "Pollution Prevention and Abatement: Base Metal and Iron Ore Mining. " Draft Technical Background Document. Environment Department, Washington, D.C.

# Breweries

## Industry Description and Practices

Beer is a fermented beverage with low alcohol content made from various types of grain. Barley predominates, but wheat, maize, and other grains can be used. The production steps include:

- *Malt production and handling:* grain delivery and cleaning; steeping of the grain in water to start germination; growth of rootlets and development of enzymes (which convert starch into maltose); kilning and polishing of the malt to remove rootlets; storage of the cleaned malt
- *Wort production:* grinding the malt to grist; mixing grist with water to produce a mash in the mash tun; heating of the mash to activate enzymes; separation of grist residues in the lauter tun to leave a liquid wort; boiling of the wort with hops; separation of the wort from the trub/hot break (precipitated residues), with the liquid part of the trub being returned to the lauter tub and the spent hops going to a collection vessel; and cooling of the wort
- *Beer production:* addition of yeast to cooled wort; fermentation; separation of spent yeast by filtration, centrifugation or settling; bottling or kegging.

Water consumption for breweries generally ranges 4–8 cubic meter per cubic meter ($m^3/m^3$) of beer produced. Water consumption for individual process stages, as reported for the German brewing industry, is shown in Table 1.

## Waste Characteristics

Breweries can achieve an effluent discharge of 3–5 $m^3/m^3$ of sold beer (exclusive of cooling waters). Untreated effluents typically contain suspended solids in the range 10–60 milligrams per liter (mg/l), biochemical oxygen demand (BOD) in the range 1,000–1,500 mg/l, chemical oxygen demand (COD) in the range 1,800–3,000 mg/l, and nitrogen in the range 30–100 mg/l. Phosphorus can also be present at concentrations of the order of 10–30 mg/l.

Effluents from individual process steps are variable. For example, bottle washing produces a large volume of effluent that, however, contains only a minor part of the total organics discharged from the brewery. Effluents from fermentation and filtering are high in organics and BOD but low in volume, accounting for about 3% of total wastewater volume but 97% of BOD. Effluent pH averages about 7 for the combined effluent but can fluctuate from 3 to 12 depending on the use of acid and alkaline cleaning agents. Effluent temperatures average about 30°C.

### Table 1. Water Consumption Reported for the German Brewing Industry

($m^3/m^3$ of sold beer; numbers in parentheses are ranges)

| Process step | Water consumption |
|---|---|
| Gyle (unfermented wort) to whirlpool | 2.0 (1.8– 2.2) |
| Wort cooling | 0.0 (0.0– 2.4) |
| Fermentation cellar and yeast treatment | 0.6 (0.5– 0.8) |
| Filter and pressure tank room | 0.3 (0.1– 0.5) |
| Storage cellar | 0.5 (0.3– 0.6) |
| Bottling (70% of beer produced) | 1.1 (0.9– 2.1) |
| Barrel filling (30% of beer produced) | 0.1 (0.1– 0.2) |
| Wastewater from cleaning of vehicles, sanitary use, etc. | 1.5 (1.0– 3.0) |
| Steam boiler | 0.2 (0.1– 0.3) |
| Air compressor | 0.3 (0.1– 0.5) |
| Total | 6.6 (4.9–12.6) |

*Note:* Numbers have been rounded.

Solid wastes for disposal include grit, weed seed, and grain of less than 2.2 millimeters in diameter, removed when grain is cleaned; spent grain and yeast; spent hops; broken bottles or bottles that cannot be recycled to the process; and cardboard and other solid wastes associated with the process, such as kieselguhr (diatomaceous earth used for clarifying).

Breweries do not discharge air pollutants, other than some odors.

## Pollution Prevention and Control

Pollution prevention and control are best practiced through effective management, maintenance, and housekeeping in a process that incorporates water conservation and recycling, energy conservation, and disposal of solid wastes as by-products. Some options that may be considered include:

- Clean-in-place (CIP) methods for decontaminating equipment
- High-pressure, low-volume hoses for equipment cleaning
- Recirculating systems on cooling water circuits
- Use of grit, weed seed, and discarded grain as chicken feed
- Use of spent grain as animal feed, either 80% wet, or dry after evaporation
- Disposal of wet hops by adding them to the spent grain
- Disposal of spent hop liquor by mixing with spent grain
- Use for livestock feed of spent yeast that is not reused
- Disposal of trub by adding it to spent grain
- Recovery of spilled beer, adding it to spent grain that is being dried through evaporation
- Filtration of bottom sediments from final fermentation tanks for use as animal feed
- Reduction of energy consumption through reuse of wort-cooling water as the process water for the next mash
- Collection of broken glass, bottles that cannot be used, and waste cardboard for recycling.

Consideration should be given to the use of non-phosphate-containing cleaning agents.

Breweries have a favorable steam-to-electricity ratio. Planning for cogeneration of electricity may be advantageous.

## Treatment Technologies

If the brewery does not discharge to a municipal sewer, primary and secondary treatment of the effluent is required. Primary treatment facilities may include pH adjustment, roughing screens, grit-settling chambers, and a clarifier. Choices of processes for removing BOD in a secondary treatment stage include anaerobic treatment followed by aerobic treatment and activated sludge systems.

Sludges from the clarifier are dewatered and disposed of through incineration or to an approved landfill.

Where the brewery is permitted to discharge to a municipal sewer, pretreatment may be required to meet municipal by-laws and to lessen the load on the municipal treatment plant. In some cases, sewer discharge fees imposed by the municipality on effluent volume and on the suspended and BOD loads may encourage the brewery to install its own treatment facility.

Modern plants using good industrial practices are able to achieve the following performance in terms of pollutant loads. Water conservation and recycling will allow water consumption to be kept to a minimum. A new brewery should target on achieving an effluent range of 3–5 m$^3$/m$^3$ beer produced. Provision for recycling liquors and reusing wash waters will help reduce the total volume of liquid effluent. A new brewery should set as a target the achievement of a treated effluent that has less than 0.3 kilograms (kg) of BOD/m$^3$ beer produced and 0.3 kg of suspended solids/m$^3$ beer produced (assuming discharge to receiving waters).

Odor emissions can be minimized if exhaust vapors are condensed before they are released to the atmosphere or if vapors are sent to the boiler and burned.

## Emissions Guidelines

Emissions levels for the design and operation of each project must be established through the environmental assessment (EA) process on the basis of country legislation and the *Pollution Prevention and Abatement Handbook,* as applied to local conditions. The emissions levels selected must be justified in the EA and acceptable to the World Bank Group.

The guidelines given below present emissions levels normally acceptable to the World Bank Group in making decisions regarding provision of World Bank Group assistance. Any deviations from these levels must be described in the World Bank Group project documentation. The emissions levels given here can be consistently achieved by well-designed, well-operated, and well-maintained pollution control systems.

The guidelines are expressed as concentrations to facilitate monitoring. Dilution of air emissions or effluents to achieve these guidelines is unacceptable.

All of the maximum levels should be achieved for at least 95% of the time that the plant or unit is operating, to be calculated as a proportion of annual operating hours.

*Liquid Effluents*

The effluent levels presented in Table 2 should be achieved.

*Ambient Noise*

Noise abatement measures should achieve either the levels given below or a maximum increase in background levels of 3 decibels (measured on the A scale) [dB(A)]. Measurements are to be taken at noise receptors located outside the project property boundary.

### Table 2. Effluents from Breweries

*(milligrams per liter, except for pH and temperature)*

| Parameter | Maximum value |
|---|---|
| pH | 6–9 |
| BOD | 50 |
| COD | 250 |
| TSS | 50 |
| Oil and grease | 10 |
| Ammonia nitrogen ($NH_4$–N) | 10 |
| Phosphorus | 5 |
| Temperature increase | $\leq 3°C$[a] |

*Note:* Effluent requirements are for direct discharge to surface waters.

a. The effluent should result in a temperature increase of no more than 3°C at the edge of the zone where initial mixing and dilution take place. Where the zone is not defined, use 100 meters from the point of discharge.

| Receptor | Maximum allowable log equivalent (hourly measurements), in dB(A) | |
|---|---|---|
| | Day (07:00–22:00) | Night (22:00–07:00) |
| Residential, institutional, educational | 55 | 45 |
| Industrial, commercial | 70 | 70 |

## Monitoring and Reporting

Monitoring of the final effluent for the parameters listed in this document should be carried out at least once per month, or more frequently if the flows vary significantly.

Monitoring data should be analyzed and reviewed at regular intervals and compared with the operating standards so that any necessary corrective actions can be taken. Records of monitoring results should be kept in an acceptable format. The results should be reported to the responsible authorities and relevant parties, as required.

## Key Issues

The key production and control practices that will lead to compliance with emissions requirements can be summarized as follows:

- Implement sound maintenance and housekeeping procedures.
- Minimize water consumption and effluent generation through recycling and reuse of process streams.
- Dispose of process solid wastes as by-products for animal feed.
- Send broken and rejected bottles and waste cardboard to recycling plants.
- Maintain effluent treatment facilities to operating design specifications.

## Source

World Bank, 1997. "Industrial Pollution Prevention and Abatement: Breweries." Draft Technical Background Document. Environment Department, Washington, D.C.

# Cement Manufacturing

## Industry Description and Practices

The preparation of cement involves mining; crushing, and grinding of raw materials (principally limestone and clay); calcining the materials in a rotary kiln; cooling the resulting clinker; mixing the clinker with gypsum; and milling, storing, and bagging the finished cement. The process generates a variety of wastes, including dust, which is captured and recycled to the process. The process is very energy-intensive, and there are strong incentives for energy conservation. Gases from clinker cooler are used as secondary combustion air. The dry process, using preheaters and precalciners, is both economically and environmentally preferable to the wet process because the energy consumption—200 joules per kilogram (J/kg)—is approximately half that for the wet process.

Certain solid waste products from other industries, such as pulverized fly ash (PFA) from power stations, slag, roasted pyrite residues, and foundry sand, can be used as additives in cement production.

## Waste Characteristics

The generation of fine particulates is inherent in the process, but most are recovered and recycled. Approximately 10–20% of the kiln feed can be suspended in the kiln exhaust gases, captured, and returned to the feed. Other sources of dust emissions include the clinker cooler, crushers, grinders, and materials-handling equipment. When the raw materials have high alkali or chloride content, a portion of the collected dust must be disposed of as solid waste, to avoid alkali buildup. Leaching of the dust to remove the alkali is rarely practiced. Grinding mill operations also result in particulate emissions. Other materials-handling operations, such as conveyors, result in fugitive emissions.

Ambient particulate levels (especially at sizes less than 10 microns) have been clearly demonstrated to be related to health impacts. Gases such as nitrogen oxides ($NO_x$) and sulfur oxides ($SO_x$) are formed from the combustion of the fuel (oil and coal) and oxidation of sulfur present in the raw materials, but the highly alkaline conditions in the kiln can absorb up to 90% of the sulfur oxides. Heavy metals may also be present in the raw materials and fuel used and are released in kiln gases. The principal aim of pollution control in this industry is to avoid increasing ambient levels of particulates by minimizing the loads emitted.

Cement kilns, with their high flame temperatures, are sometimes used to burn waste oils, solvents, and other organic wastes. These practices can result in the release of toxic metals and organics. Cement plants are not normally designed to burn wastes, but if such burning is contemplated, technical and environmental acceptability needs to be demonstrated. To avoid the formation of toxic chlorinated organics from the burning of organic wastes, air pollution control devices for such plants should not be operated in the temperature range of 230–400°C. (For further details, see United States1991.)

## Pollution Prevention and Control

The priority in the cement industry is to minimize the increases in ambient particulate levels by reducing the mass load emitted from the stacks, from fugitive emissions, and from other sources. Collection and recycling of dust in kiln gases is required to improve the efficiency of the operation and to reduce atmospheric emissions. Units that are well designed, well operated, and well maintained can normally achieve generation of less than 0.2 kilograms of dust per metric ton (kg/t) of clinker, using dust recovery systems. $NO_x$ emissions should be controlled by using proper kiln design, low-$NO_x$ burners, and an optimum level of excess air. $NO_x$ emissions from a dry kiln with preheater and precalciner are typically 1.5 kg/t of clinker, as against 4.5 kg/t for the wet process. The nitrogen oxide emissions can be reduced further, to 0.5 kg/t of clinker, by afterburning in a reducing atmosphere, and the energy of the gases can be recovered in a preheater/precalciner.

For control of fugitive particulate emissions, ventilation systems should be used in conjunction with hoods and enclosures covering transfer points and conveyors. Drop distances should be minimized by the use of adjustable conveyors. Dusty areas such as roads should be wetted down to reduce dust generation. Appropriate stormwater and runoff control systems should be provided to minimize the quantities of suspended material carried off site.

$SO_x$ emissions are best controlled by using low-sulfur fuels and raw materials. The absorption capacity of the cement must be assessed to determine the quantity of sulfur dioxide emitted, which may be up to about half the sulfur load on the kiln. Precalcining with low-$NO_x$ secondary firing can reduce nitrogen oxide emissions.

Alkaline dust removed from the kiln gases is normally disposed of as solid waste. When solid wastes such as pulverized fly ash are used with feedstock, appropriate steps must be taken to avoid environmental problems from contaminants or trace elements.

Stormwater systems and storage areas should be designed to minimize washoff of solids.

## Treatment Technologies

Mechanical systems such as cyclones trap the larger particulates in kiln gases and act as preconditioners for downstream collection devices. Electrostatic precipitators (ESPs) and fabric filter systems (baghouses) are the principal options for collection and control (achieving over 99% removal efficiency) of fine particulates. ESPs are sensitive to gas characteristics, such as temperature, and to variation in voltage; baghouses are generally regarded as more reliable. The overall costs of the two systems are similar. The choice of system will depend on flue gas characteristics and local considerations.

Both ESPs and baghouses can achieve high levels of particulate removal from the kiln gas stream, but good operation and maintenance are essential for achieving design specifications. Two significant types of control problem can occur: (a) complete failure (or automatic shutoff) of systems related to plant shutdown and start-up, power failures, and the like, leading to the emission of very high levels of particulates for short periods of time; and (b) a gradual decrease in the removal efficiency of the system over time because of poor maintenance or improper operation. The lime content of raw materials can be used to control sulfur oxides.

## Emissions Guidelines

Emissions levels for the design and operation of each project must be established through the environmental assessment (EA) process on the basis of country legislation and the *Pollution Prevention and Abatement Handbook,* as applied to local conditions. The emissions levels selected must be justified in the EA and acceptable to the World Bank Group.

The guidelines given below present emissions levels normally acceptable to the World Bank Group in making decisions regarding provision of World Bank Group assistance. Any deviations from these levels must be described in the World Bank Group project documentation. The emissions levels given here can be consistently achieved by well-designed, well-operated, and well-maintained pollution control systems.

The guidelines are expressed as concentrations to facilitate monitoring. Dilution of air emissions or effluents to achieve these guidelines is unacceptable.

All of the maximum levels should be achieved for at least 95% of the time that the plant or unit is operating, to be calculated as a proportion of annual operating hours.

## Air Emissions

A maximum emissions level of 50 milligrams per normal cubic meter (mg/Nm³), equivalent to a maximum of 0.2 kg/t of clinker, for particulates in stack gases under full-load conditions is to be achieved. This emissions level is based on values that are routinely achieved in well-run plants. Maximum emissions levels for sulfur oxides are 400 mg/Nm³; for nitrogen oxides, 600 mg/Nm³.

Management's capacity to maintain the necessary operational and maintenance standards should be carefully evaluated. If necessary, training for plant personnel should be provided under the project. The EA and the prefeasibility or feasibility study should examine the effects of fugitive and stack emissions (including dust, sulfur oxides, and nitrogen oxides) on ambient air quality and implement measures to maintain acceptable ambient air quality levels.

## Liquid Effluents

Normally, effluents requiring treatment originate from cooling operations or as stormwater. Treated effluent discharges should have a pH in the range of 6–9. Cooling water should preferably be recycled. If this is not economical, the effluent should not increase the temperature of the receiving waters at the edge of the mixing zone (or 100 meters, where the mixing zone is not defined) by more than 3° Celsius. If quantities of suspended solids in the effluent are high in relation to receiving waters, treatment may be required to reduce levels in the effluent to a maximum of 50 milligrams per liter (mg/l). Note that the effluent requirements are for direct discharge to surface waters.

## Ambient Noise

Noise abatement measures should achieve either the levels given below or a maximum increase in background levels of 3 decibels (measured on the A scale) [dB(A)]. Measurements are to be taken at noise receptors located outside the project property boundary.

| Receptor | Maximum allowable log equivalent (hourly measurements), in dB(A) | |
| --- | --- | --- |
| | Day (07:00–22:00) | Night (22:00–07:00) |
| Residential, institutional, educational | 55 | 45 |
| Industrial, commercial | 70 | 70 |

## Monitoring and Reporting

Frequent sampling may be required during start-up and upset conditions. Once a record of consistent performance has been established, sampling for the parameters listed in this document should be as described below.

Equipment for continuous monitoring of opacity levels (or particulates in the stack exhaust, whichever is cost-effective) should be installed. Measurement of the sulfur content of raw materials and fuel, and direct measurement of particulate, SO$_x$, and NO$_x$ levels at the plant boundary levels, should be carried out at least annually. When operational upsets occur, the opacity of kiln and clinker cooler exhaust gases should be measured directly and corrective actions taken to maintain the opacity level of the stack gases below 10% (or an equivalent measurement).

The pH and temperature of the wastewater effluent should be monitored on a continuous basis. Suspended solids should be measured monthly if treatment is provided.

Monitoring data should be analyzed and reviewed at regular intervals and compared with the operating standards so that any necessary corrective actions can be taken.

Records of monitoring results should be kept in an acceptable format. The results should be reported to the responsible authorities and relevant parties, as required.

## Key Issues

The key production and control practices that will lead to compliance with emissions guidelines can be summarized as follows:

Give preference to the dry process with preheaters and precalciners.

Adopt the following pollution prevention measures to minimize air emissions:

- Install equipment covers and filters for crushing, grinding, and milling operations.
- Use enclosed adjustable conveyors to minimize drop distances.
- Wet down intermediate and finished product storage piles.
- Use low-$NO_x$ burners with the optimum level of excess air.
- Use low sulfur fuels in the kiln.
- Operate control systems to achieve the required emissions levels.

Develop a strong unit or division to undertake environmental management responsibilities.

### References and Sources

Bounicore, Anthony J., and Wayne T. Davis, eds. 1992. *Air Pollution Engineering Manual.* New York: Van Nostrand Reinhold.

European Community. 1989. "Technical Note on Best Available Technologies Not Entailing Excessive Cost for the Manufacture of Cement." December 7. Paper presented to BAT Exchange of Information Committee, Brussels.

Fog, Mogens H., and Kishore L. Nadkarni. 1983. *Energy Efficiency and Fuel Substitution in the Cement Industry with Emphasis on Developing Countries.* World Bank Technical Paper 17. Washington, D.C.

Sittig, Marshall. 1975. *Pollution Control in the Asbestos, Cement, Glass, and Allied Mineral Industries.* Park Ridge, N.J.: Noyes Data Corporation.

United States. 1991. *Federal Register,* vol. 56, no. 35, February 21. Washington, D.C.: Government Printing Office.

World Bank. 1996. "Pollution Prevention and Abatement: Cement Manufacturing." Draft Technical Background Document. Environment Department, Washington, D.C.

# Chlor-Alkali Plants

## Industry Description and Practices

There are three basic processes for the manufacture of chlorine and caustic soda from brine: the mercury cell, the diaphragm cell, and the membrane cell. The membrane cell is the most modern and has economic and environmental advantages. The other two processes generate hazardous wastes containing mercury or asbestos.

In the membrane process, the chlorine (at the anode) and the hydrogen (at the cathode) are kept apart by a selective polymer membrane that allows the sodium ions to pass into the cathodic compartment and react with the hydroxyl ions to form caustic soda. The depleted brine is dechlorinated and recycled to the input stage. The membrane cell process is the preferred process for new plants. Diaphragm processes may be acceptable, in some circumstances, if nonasbestos diaphragms are used. The energy consumption in a membrane cell process is of the order of 2,200–2,500 kilowatt-hours per metric ton (kWh/t), as against 2,400–2,700 kWh/t of chlorine for a diaphragm cell process. *The World Bank does not finance mercury cell technology.*

## Waste Characteristics

The major waste stream from the process consists of brine muds—the sludges from the brine purification step—which may contain magnesium, calcium, iron, and other metal hydroxides, depending on the source and purity of the brines. The muds are normally filtered or settled, the supernatant is recycled, and the mud is dried and landfilled.

Chlorine is a highly toxic gas, and strict precautions are necessary to minimize risk to workers and possible releases during its handling.

Major sources of fugitive air emissions of chlorine and hydrogen are vents, seals, and transfer operations. Acid and caustic wastewaters are generated in both the process and the materials recovery stages.

## Pollution Prevention and Control

The following pollution prevention measures should be considered:

- Use metal rather than graphite anodes to reduce lead and chlorinated organics.
- Resaturate brine in closed vessels to reduce the generation of salt sprays.
- Use noncontact condensers to reduce the amount of process wastewater.
- Scrub chlorine tail gases to reduce chlorine discharges and to produce hypochlorite.
- Recycle condensates and waste process water to the brine system, if possible.
- Recycle brine wastes, if possible.

For the chlor-alkali industry, an emergency preparedness and response plan is required for potential uncontrolled chlorine and other releases. Carbon tetrachloride is sometimes used to scrub nitrogen trichloride (formed in the process) and to maintain its levels below 4% to avoid explosion. Substitutes for carbon tetrachloride may have to be used, as the use of carbon tetrachloride may be banned in the near future.

## Target Pollution Loads

Implementation of cleaner production processes and pollution prevention measures can yield both economic and environmental benefits. The production-related targets presented in Table 1 can be achieved by measures such as those described above. The numbers relate to

**Table 1. Target Levels per Unit of Production, Chlor-Alkali Industry**

*(maximum load/ton chlorine)*

| Parameter | Diaphragm process | Membrane process |
|---|---|---|
| Lead (kg) | 0.04 | — |
| Wastewater (cubic meters) | 1.6 | 0.1 |

— Not applicable.

the production processes before the addition of pollution control measures.

## Treatment Technologies

Caustic scrubber systems should be installed to control chlorine emissions from condensers and at storage and transfer points for liquid chlorine. Sulfuric acid used for drying chlorine should be neutralized before discharge.

Brine muds should be discharged to lined settling ponds (or the equivalent) to prevent contamination of soil and groundwater. Effluents should be controlled for pH by neutralization. Settling and filtration are performed to control total suspended solids. Dechlorination of wastewaters is performed using sulfur dioxide or bisulfite.

## Emissions Guidelines

Emissions levels for the design and operation of each project must be established through the environmental assessment (EA) process, on the basis of country legislation and the *Pollution Prevention and Abatement Handbook* as applied to local conditions. The emissions levels selected must be justified in the EA and acceptable to the World Bank Group.

The guidelines given below present emissions levels normally acceptable to the World Bank Group in making decisions regarding provision of World Bank Group assistance. Any deviations from these levels must be described in the World Bank Group project documentation. The emissions levels given here can be consistently

achieved by well-designed, well-operated, and well-maintained pollution control systems.

The guidelines are expressed as concentrations to facilitate monitoring. Dilution of air emissions or effluents to achieve these guidelines is unacceptable.

All of the maximum levels should be achieved for at least 95% of the time that the plant or unit is operating, to be calculated as a proportion of annual operating hours.

### Air Emissions

Chlorine concentration should be less than 3 milligrams per normal cubic meter ($mg/Nm^3$) for process areas, including chlorine liquefaction.

### Liquid Effluents

For membrane cell effluents, pH levels should be in the range 6–9.

For nonasbestos diaphragm plants, the effluents levels presented in Table 2 should be achieved. In some cases, bioassay testing of effluents may be desirable to ensure that effluent toxicity is at acceptable levels, say, toxicity to fish at a dilution factor of 2.

### Ambient Noise

Noise abatement measures should achieve either the levels given below or a maximum increase in background levels of 3 decibels (measured on the

**Table 2. Effluents from Nonasbestos Diaphragm Plants, Chlor-Alkali Industry**

*(milligrams per liter, except for pH)*

| Parameter | Maximum value |
|---|---|
| pH | 6–9 |
| TSS | 20 |
| COD | 150 |
| AOX | 0.5 |
| Sulfites | 1 |
| Chlorine | 0.2 |

*Note:* Effluent requirements are for direct discharge to surface waters.

A scale) [dB(A)]. Measurements are to be taken at noise receptors located outside the project property boundary.

| Receptor | Maximum allowable log equivalent (hourly measurements), in dB(A) | |
|---|---|---|
| | Day (07:00–22:00) | Night (22:00–07:00) |
| Residential, institutional, educational | 55 | 45 |
| Industrial, commercial | 70 | 70 |

## Monitoring and Reporting

Frequent sampling may be required during start-up and upset conditions. Once a record of consistent performance has been established, sampling for the parameters listed in this document should be as described below.

Daily monitoring for parameters other than pH (for effluents from the diaphragm process) is recommended. The pH in the liquid effluent should be monitored continuously. Chlorine monitors should be strategically located within the plant to detect chlorine releases or leaks on a continuous basis.

Monitoring data should be analyzed and reviewed at regular intervals and compared with the operating standards so that any necessary corrective actions can be taken. Records of monitoring results should be kept in an acceptable format. The results should be reported to the responsible authorities and relevant parties, as required.

## Key Issues

The key production and control practices that will lead to compliance with emissions guidelines can be summarized as follows.

Give preference to the membrane process.

Adopt the following pollution prevention measures to minimize emissions:

- Use metal instead of graphite anodes.
- Resaturate brine in closed vessels.
- Recycle brine wastes.
- Scrub chlorine from tail gases to produce hypochlorite.
- Provide lined settling ponds for brine muds.

## Sources

Arthur D. Little, Inc. 1975. *Assessment of Industrial Hazardous Waste Practices, Inorganic Chemicals Industry.* U.S. Environmental Protection Agency, Contract 68-01-2246. Washington, D.C.: USEPA.

Kirk, Raymond E., and Donald F. Othmer. 1980. *Kirk-Othmer Encyclopedia of Chemical Technology.* 3d ed. New York: John Wiley and Sons.

World Bank. 1996. "Pollution Prevention and Abatement: Chlor-Alkali Industry." Draft Technical Background Document. Environment Department, Washington, D.C.

# Coal Mining and Production

## Industry Description and Practices

Coal is one of the world's most plentiful energy resources, and its use is likely to quadruple by 2020. Coal occurs in a wide range of forms and qualities; but there are two broad categories: (a) hard coal, which includes coking coal, used to produce steel, and other bituminous and anthracite coals used for steam and power generation, and (b) brown coal (subbituminous and lignite), which is used mostly as onsite fuel. Coal has a wide range of moisture content (2–40%), sulfur content (0.2–8%), and ash content (5–40%). These can affect the value of the coal as a fuel and cause environmental problems in its use.

The depth, thickness, and configuration of the coal seams determine the mode of extraction. Shallow, flat coal deposits are mined by surface processes, which are generally less costly per ton of coal mined than underground mines of similar capacity. Strip mining is one of the most economical surface processes. Here removal of overburden and coal extraction proceed in parallel strips along the face of the coal deposit, with the spoil being deposited behind the operation in the previously mined areas. In open pit mining, thick seams (tens of meters) are mined by traditional quarrying techniques. Underground mining is used for deep seams. Underground mining methods vary according to the site conditions, but all involve the removal of seams followed by more or less controlled subsidence of the overlying strata.

Raw coal may be sold as mined or may be processed in a beneficiation/washing plant to remove noncombustible materials (up to 45% reduction in ash content) and inorganic sulfur (up to 25% reduction). Coal beneficiation is based on wet physical processes such as gravity separation and flotation. Beneficiation produces two waste streams: fine materials that are discharged as a slurry to a tailings impoundment, and coarse material (typically greater than 0.5 millimeters) that is hauled away as a solid waste.

## Waste Characteristics

The main impacts of surface mining are, in general, massive disturbances of large areas of land and possible disruption of surface and groundwater patterns. In some surface mines, the generation of acid mine drainage (AMD) is a major problem. Other significant impacts include fugitive dust and disposal of overburden and waste rock.

In underground mines, the surface disturbance is less obvious, but the extent of subsidence can be very large. Methane generation and release can also be a problem under certain geological conditions. If groundwater systems are disturbed, the possibility of serious pollution from highly saline or highly acidic water exists. Impacts may continue long after mining ceases.

Table 1 presents the levels of liquid effluents, solid waste, and dust generated by the major mining techniques.

Beneficiation plants produce large volumes of tailings and solid wastes. Storage and handling of coal generates dust at rates of as much as 3 kilograms per metric ton (kg/t) of coal mined, with the ambient dust concentration ranging from 10 to 300 micrograms per cubic meter ($\mu$g/m$^3$) above the background level at the mine site.

## Pollution Prevention and Control

Early planning and careful design of operations are the key to minimizing pollution associated with mining activities. Specific responsibilities should be assigned for the implementation and

## Table 1. Loads Per Unit of Coal Production, by Mining Technique

*(tons per 1,000 tons coal produced)*

| Waste characteristic | Surface mining | | Underground mining | |
|---|---|---|---|---|
| | Contour | Area | Conventional | Longwall |
| Liquid effluents | 0.24 | 1.2 | 1 | 1.6 |
| Solid waste | 10 | 10 | 3 | 5 |
| Dust | 0.1 | 0.06 | 0.006 | 0.01 |

*Note:* Local conditions will form the basis for choosing the appropriate mining method.
*Source:* Based on Edgar 1983.

monitoring of environmental measures. Before mining begins, a mining plan and a mine closure and restoration plan must be prepared and approved. These plans define the sequence and nature of extraction operations and detail the methods to be used in closure and restoration. The plans should be updated regularly (every 3 to 5 years) as mining progresses.

### Development Plan

The development plan defines the sequence and nature of extraction operations and describes in detail the methods to be used in closure and restoration. At a minimum, the plan must address the following:

- Removal and proper storage of topsoil.
- Early restoration of worked-out areas and of spoil heaps to minimize the extent of open areas.
- Diversion and management of surface and groundwater to minimize water pollution problems. Simple treatment to reduce the discharge of suspended solids may also be necessary. (Treatment of saline groundwater may be difficult.)
- Identification and management of areas with high potential for AMD generation.
- Minimization of AMD generation by reducing disturbed areas and isolating drainage streams from contact with sulfur-bearing materials.
- Preparation of a water management plan for operations and postclosure that includes minimization of liquid wastes by methods such as recycling water from the tailings wash plant.
- Minimization of spillage losses by proper design and operation of coal transport and transfer facilities.

- Reduction of dust by early revegetation and by good maintenance of roads and work areas. Specific dust suppression measures, such as minimizing drop distances, covering equipment, and wetting storage piles, may be required for coal handling and loading facilities. Release of dust from crushing and other coal processing and beneficiation operations should be controlled.
- Control of the release of chemicals (including floatation chemicals) used in beneficiation processes.
- Minimization of the effects of subsidence by careful extraction methods in relation to surface uses.
- Control of methane, a greenhouse gas, to less than 1% by volume, to minimize the risk of explosion in closed mines; recovery of methane where feasible. (When methane content is above 25% by volume, it normally should be recovered.)
- Development of restoration and revegetation methods appropriate to the specific site conditions.
- Proper storage and handling of fuel and chemicals used on site, to avoid spills.

### Mine Closure and Restoration Plan

The plan should include reclamation of open pits, waste piles, beneficiation tailings, sedimentation basins, and abandoned mine, mill, and camp sites. Mine reclamation plans should incorporate the following measures:

- Return of the land to conditions capable of supporting prior land use, equivalent uses, or other environmentally acceptable uses
- Use of overburden for backfill and of topsoil (or other plant growth medium) for reclamation

- Contouring of slopes to minimize erosion and runoff
- Planting of native vegetation to prevent erosion and encourage self-sustaining development of a productive ecosystem on the reclaimed land
- Management of postclosure AMD and beneficiation tailings
- Budgeting and scheduling of pre- and post-abandonment reclamation activities.

Upon mine closure, all shaft openings and mine adits should be sealed or secured.

There is a need to reserve money over the life of the mine to cover the costs associated with mine closure. The amount of money and the type of financing required will depend on a number of factors, such as the projected life of the mine, the nature of the operations, the complexity of environmental issues, the financial and environmental management capacity of the borrower or project sponsor, and the jurisdiction in which the mine is located. The mine reclamation and closure plan, the timing of its submission, and its financing should be discussed and agreed on with the borrower or sponsor as early as possible.

## Target Pollution Loads

Implementation of cleaner production processes and pollution prevention measures can provide both economic and environmental benefits. The loads presented in Table 1 can be used as a guide for pollution prevention purposes. The figures relate to each of the production processes before the addition of pollution control measures.

## Emissions Guidelines

Emissions levels for the design and operation of each project must be established through the environmental assessment (EA) process, on the basis of country legislation and the *Pollution Prevention and Abatement Handbook* as applied to local conditions. The emissions levels selected must be justified in the EA and acceptable to the World Bank Group.

The guidelines given below present emissions levels normally acceptable to the World Bank Group in making decisions regarding provision of World Bank Group assistance. Any deviations from these levels must be described in the World Bank Group project documentation. The emissions levels given here can be consistently achieved by well-designed, well-operated, and well-maintained pollution control systems.

The guidelines are expressed as concentrations to facilitate monitoring. Dilution of air emissions or effluents to achieve these guidelines is unacceptable.

All of the maximum levels should be achieved for at least 95% of the time that the plant or unit is operating, to be calculated as a proportion of annual operating hours.

### Air Emissions

Controls may be required on individual sources, such as ventilation exhausts, if they have a significant effect on ambient particulate levels. If coal crushers or dryers are used, fabric filters or other systems should be used to recover coal and reduce particulate emissions to levels below 50 milligrams per normal cubic meter ($mg/Nm^3$).

### Liquid Effluents

Settling ponds to catch stormwater and to reduce suspended solids should be provided for all effluent before discharge from the site.

Where treatment of AMD or other effluents is required, the effluent levels presented in Table 2 should be achieved during operation and after mine closure.

### Ambient Noise

Noise abatement measures should achieve either the levels given below or a maximum increase in

**Table 2. Acid Mine Drainage and Liquid Effluents from Coal Mining**
*(milligrams per liter, except for pH)*

| Parameter | Maximum value |
|---|---|
| pH | 6–9 |
| TSS[a] | 50 |
| Oil and grease | 10 |
| Iron | 3.5 |
| Total metals | 10 |

a. Monthly average, 35 milligrams per liter.

background levels of 3 decibels (measured on the A scale) [dB(A)]. Measurements are to be taken at noise receptors located outside the project property boundary.

| Receptor | Maximum allowable log equivalent (hourly measurements), in dB(A) | |
| | Day (07:00–22:00) | Night (22:00–07:00) |
| --- | --- | --- |
| Residential, institutional, educational | 55 | 45 |
| Industrial, commercial | 70 | 70 |

## Monitoring and Reporting

Frequent sampling may be required during start-up and upset conditions. All wastewater discharges from the operations should be monitored weekly for pH, total suspended solids, and oil and grease. A full analysis covering iron and other trace metals should be carried out quarterly. Where salinity is a potential problem, appropriate parameters (chloride, total dissolved solids, and conductivity) should be monitored.

Ambient air levels of particulate material, including $PM_{10}$, in and around mining operations should be measured quarterly. Methane levels should be monitored, where appropriate, at least annually even after mine closure.

## Key Issues

The key production and control practices that will lead to compliance with emissions guidelines can be summarized as follows.

Develop and implement a comprehensive environmental and mine management plan to include:

- Restoration and rehabilitation of disturbed areas
- Minimization of land subsidence
- Identification and management of AMD sources
- Water management for operations and postclosure conditions.
- Management and sealing of pyrite-containing piles to reduce AMD formation.

Develop and implement a post-closure plan to include:

- Restoration of disturbed areas
- Long-term geotechnical and geochemical stability of waste piles
- Restoration of acceptable long-term surface water and groundwater flow patterns.

## References and Sources

Edgar, T. F. 1983. *Coal Processing and Pollution Control.* Houston, Tex.: Gulf Publishing.

Hartman, Howard L., ed. 1992. *SME Engineering Handbook,* vol. 2. 2d ed. Littleton, Colo.: Society for Mining, Metallurgy, and Exploration.

World Bank. 1996. "Pollution Prevention and Abatement: Coal Mining." Draft Technical Background Document. Environment Department, Washington, D.C.

# Coke Manufacturing

## Industry Description and Practices

Coke and coke by-products, including coke oven gas, are produced by the pyrolysis (heating in the absence of air) of suitable grades of coal. The process also includes the processing of coke oven gas to remove tar, ammonia (usually recovered as ammonium sulfate), phenol, naphthalene, light oil, and sulfur before the gas is used as fuel for heating the ovens. This document covers the production of metallurgical coke and the associated by-products using intermittent horizontal retorts.

In the coke-making process, bituminous coal is fed (usually after processing operations to control the size and quality of the feed) into a series of ovens, which are sealed and heated at high temperatures in the absence of oxygen, typically in cycles lasting 14 to 36 hours. Volatile compounds that are driven off the coal are collected and processed to recover combustible gases and other by-products. The solid carbon remaining in the oven is coke. It is taken to the quench tower, where it is cooled with a water spray or by circulating an inert gas (nitrogen), a process known as dry quenching. The coke is screened and sent to a blast furnace or to storage.

Coke oven gas is cooled, and by-products are recovered. Flushing liquor, formed from the cooling of coke oven gas, and liquor from primary coolers contain tar and are sent to a tar decanter. An electrostatic precipitator is used to remove more tar from coke oven gas. The tar is then sent to storage. Ammonia liquor is also separated from the tar decanter and sent to wastewater treatment after ammonia recovery. Coke oven gas is further cooled in a final cooler. Naphthalene is removed in the separator on the final cooler. Light oil is then removed from the coke oven gas and is fractionated to recover benzene, toluene, and xylene. Some facilities may include an onsite tar distillation unit. The Claus process is normally used to recover sulfur from coke oven gas.

During the coke quenching, handling, and screening operation, coke breeze is produced. It is either reused on site (e.g., in the sinter plant) or sold off site as a by-product.

## Waste Characteristics

The coke oven is a major source of fugitive air emissions. The coking process emits particulate matter (PM); volatile organic compounds (VOCs); polynuclear aromatic hydrocarbons (PAHs); methane, at approximately 100 grams per metric ton (g/t) of coke; ammonia; carbon monoxide; hydrogen sulfide (50–80 g/t of coke from pushing operations); hydrogen cyanide; and sulfur oxides, $SO_x$ (releasing 30% of sulfur in the feed). Significant amount of VOCs may also be released in by-product recovery operations.

For every ton of coke produced, approximately 0.7 to 7.4 kilograms (kg) of PM, 2.9 kg of $SO_x$ (ranging from 0.2 to 6.5 kg), 1.4 kg of nitrogen oxides ($NO_x$), 0.1 kg of ammonia, and 3 kg of VOCs (including 2 kg of benzene) may be released into the atmosphere if there is no vapor recovery system. Coal-handling operations may account for about 10% of the particulate load. Coal charging, coke pushing, and quenching are major sources of dust emissions.

Wastewater is generated at an average rate ranging from 0.3 to 4 cubic meters ($m^3$) per ton of coke processed. Major wastewater streams are generated from the cooling of the coke oven gas and the processing of ammonia, tar, naphthalene, phenol, and light oil. Process wastewater may contain 10 milligrams per liter (mg/l) of benzene, 1,000 mg/l of biochemical oxygen demand (BOD) (4 kg/t of coke), 1,500–6,000 mg/l of chemical oxygen demand (COD), 200 mg/l of total suspended solids, and 150–2,000 mg/l of phenols (0.3–12 kg/t of coke). Wastewaters also contain PAHs at significant concentrations (up to 30 mg/l), ammonia (0.1–2 kg nitrogen/t of coke), and cyanides (0.1–0.6 kg/t of coke).

Coke production facilities generate process solid wastes other than coke breeze (which averages 1 kg/t of product). Most of the solid wastes contain hazardous components such as benzene and PAHs. Waste streams of concern include residues from coal tar recovery (typically 0.1 kg/t of coke), the tar decanter (0.2 kg/t of coke), tar storage (0.4 kg/t of coke), light oil processing (0.2 kg/t of coke), wastewater treatment (0.1 kg/t of coke), naphthalene collection and recovery (0.02 kg/t of coke), tar distillation (0.01 kg/t of coke), and sludges from biological treatment of wastewaters.

## Pollution Prevention and Control

Pollution prevention in coke making is focused on reducing coke oven emissions and developing cokeless iron- and steel-making techniques. The following pollution prevention and control measures should be considered.

### General

- Use cokeless iron- and steel-making processes, such as the direct reduction process, to eliminate the need to manufacture coke.
- Use beneficiation (preferably at the coal mine) and blending processes that improve the quality of coal feed to produce coke of desired quality and reduce emissions of sulfur oxides and other pollutants.
- Use enclosed conveyors and sieves for coal and coke handling. Use sprinklers and plastic emulsions to suppress dust formation. Provide windbreaks where feasible. Store materials in bunkers or warehouses. Reduce drop distances.
- Use and preheat high-grade coal to reduce coking time, increase throughput, reduce fuel consumption, and minimize thermal shock to refractory bricks.

### Coke Oven Emissions

- *Charging:* dust particles from coal charging should be evacuated by the use of jumper-pipe

systems and steam injection into the ascension pipe or controlled by fabric filters.
- *Coking:* use large ovens to increase batch size and reduce the number of chargings and pushings, thereby reducing the associated emissions. Reduce fluctuations in coking conditions, including temperature. Clean and seal coke oven openings to minimize emissions. Use mechanical cleaning devices (preferably automatic) for cleaning doors, door frames, and hole lids. Seal lids, using a slurry. Use low-leakage door construction, preferably with gas sealings.
- *Pushing:* emissions from coke pushing can be reduced by maintaining a sufficient coking time, thus avoiding "green push." Use sheds and enclosed cars, or consider use of traveling hoods. The gases released should be removed and passed through fabric filters.
- *Quenching:* where feasible, use dry instead of wet quenching. Filter all gases extracted from the dry quenching unit. If wet quenching, is used, provide interceptors (baffles) to remove coarse dust. When wastewater is used for quenching, the process transfers pollutants from the wastewater to the air, requiring subsequent removal. Reuse quench water.
- *Conveying and sieving:* enclose potential dust sources, and filter evacuated gases.

### By-Product Recovery

- Use vapor recovery systems to prevent air emissions from light oil processing, tar processing, naphthalene processing, and phenol and ammonia recovery processes.
- Segregate process water from cooling water.
- Reduce fixed ammonia content in ammonia liquor by using caustic soda and steam stripping.
- Recycle all process solid wastes, including tar decanter sludge, to the coke oven.
- Recover sulfur from coke oven gas. Recycle Claus tail gas into the coke oven gas system.

## Target Pollution loads

Implementation of cleaner production processes and pollution prevention measures can yield both economic and environmental benefits. The pro-

## Table 1. Air Emissions, Coke Manufacturing

*(kilograms per ton of coke produced)*

| Parameter | Maximum value |
|---|---|
| VOCs | 0.3 |
| Benzene | 0.1 |
| Particulate matter | 0.15 |
| Sulfur oxides | 0.5 |
| Nitrogen oxides | 0.6 |
| TSS | 50 |
| Oil and grease | 10 |
| Phenol | 0.5 |
| Benzene | 0.05 |
| Dibenz(a,h)anthracene | 0.05 |
| Benzo(a)pyrene | 0.05 |
| Cyanide (total) | 0.2 |
| Nitrogen (total) | 10 |
| Temperature increase | ≤ 3° C[a] |

*Note:* Effluent requirements are for direct discharge to surface waters.

a. The effluent should result in a temperature increase of no more than 3° C at the edge of the zone where initial mixing and dilution take place. Where the zone is not defined, use 100 meters from the point of discharge.

duction-related targets described below can be achieved by adopting good industrial practices.

### Air Emissions

Emissions should be reduced to the target levels presented in Table 1.

### Wastewater

The generation rate for wastewater should be less than 0.3 m³/t of coke.

### Solid and Hazardous Wastes

New coke plants should not generate more than 1 kg of process solid waste (excluding coke breeze and biosludges) per ton of coke.

## Treatment Technologies

### Air Emissions

Air emission control technologies include scrubbers (removal efficiency of 90%) and baghouses and electrostatic precipitators (ESPs), with re-

moval efficiencies of 99.9%. Baghouses are preferred over venturi scrubbers for controlling particulate matter emissions from loading and pushing operations because of the higher removal efficiencies. ESPs are effective for final tar removal from coke oven gas.

### Wastewater Treatment

Wastewater treatment systems include screens and settling tanks to remove total suspended solids, oil, and tar; steam stripping to remove ammonia, hydrogen sulfide, and hydrogen cyanide; biological treatment; and final polishing with filters.

The levels presented in Table 2 should be achieved.

### Solid Waste Treatment

All process hazardous wastes except for coke fines should be recycled to coke ovens. Wastewater treatment sludges should be dewatered. If toxic organics are detectable, dewatered sludges are to be charged to coke ovens or disposed in a secure landfill or an appropriate combustion unit.

## Emissions Guidelines

Emissions levels for the design and operation of each project must be established through the environmental assessment (EA) process on the basis of country legislation and the *Pollution Prevention and Abatement Handbook*, as applied to local conditions. The emissions levels selected must be

## Table 2. Target Wastewater Loads per Unit of Production, Coke Manufacturing

*(grams per ton of coke produced, unless otherwise specified)*

| Parameter | Maximum value |
|---|---|
| COD | 100 |
| Benzene | 0.015 |
| Benzo(a)pyrene | 0.009 |
| Naphthalene | 0.0008 |
| Nitrogen (total) | 12 |
| Cyanide (free) | 0.03 |
| Phenol | 0.15 |
| Wastewater | 0.3 m³/t of coke produced |

justified in the EA and acceptable to the World Bank Group.

The guidelines given below present emissions levels normally acceptable to the World Bank Group in making decisions regarding provision of World Bank Group assistance. Any deviations from these levels must be described in the World Bank Group project documentation. The emissions levels given here can be consistently achieved by well-designed, well-operated, and well-maintained pollution control systems.

The guidelines are expressed as concentrations to facilitate monitoring. Dilution of air emissions or effluents to achieve these guidelines is unacceptable.

All of the maximum levels should be achieved for at least 95% of the time that the plant or unit is operating, to be calculated as a proportion of annual operating hours.

*Air Emissions*

Benzene emissions should not be more than 5 milligrams per normal cubic meter ($mg/Nm^3$) in leaks from light oil processing, final cooler, tar decanter, tar storage, weak ammonia liquor storage, and the tar/water separator. VOC emissions should be less than 20 $mg/Nm^3$. Particulate matter emissions from the stacks should not exceed 50 $mg/Nm^3$. Sulfur recovery from coke oven gas should be at least 97% but preferably over 99%.

*Liquid Effluents*

The effluent levels presented in Table 3 should be achieved.

*Solid and Hazardous Wastes*

Solid hazardous wastes containing toxic organics should be recycled to a coke oven or treated

**Table 3. Effluents, Coke Manufacturing**

*(milligrams per liter, unless otherwise specified)*

| Parameter | Maximum value |
| --- | --- |
| BOD | 30 |
| COD | 150 |

in a combustion unit, with residues disposed of in a secure landfill.

*Ambient Noise*

Noise abatement measures should achieve either the levels given below or a maximum increase in background levels of 3 decibels (measured on the A scale) [dB(A)]. Measurements are to be taken at noise receptors located outside the project property boundary.

| Receptor | Maximum allowable log equivalent (hourly measurements), in dB(A) | |
| --- | --- | --- |
| | Day (07:00–22:00) | Night (22:00–07:00) |
| Residential, institutional, educational | 55 | 45 |
| Industrial, commercial | 70 | 70 |

## Monitoring and Reporting

Stack air emissions should be monitored continuously for particulate matter. Alternatively, opacity measurements of stack gases could suffice. Fugitive emissions should be monitored annually for VOCs. Wastewater discharges should be monitored daily for flow rate and for all parameters, except for dibenz(a,h)anthracene and benzo(a)pyrene. The latter should be monitored at least on a monthly basis or when there are process changes. Frequent sampling may be required during start-up and upset conditions.

Monitoring data should be analyzed and reviewed at regular intervals and compared with the operating standards so that any necessary corrective actions can be taken. Records of monitoring results should be kept in an acceptable format. The results should be reported to the responsible authorities and relevant parties, as required.

## Key Issues

The key production and control practices that will lead to compliance with emissions guidelines can be summarized as follows:

- Use cokeless iron- and steel-making processes, such as the direct reduction process for iron-making, to eliminate the need for coke manufacturing.
- Where feasible, use dry quenching instead of wet quenching.
- Use vapor-recovery systems in light oil processing, tar processing and storage, naphthalene processing, and phenol and ammonia recovery operations.
- Recover sulfur from coke oven gas.
- Segregate process and cooling water.
- Recycle process solid wastes to the coke oven.

## Sources

Bounicore, Anthony J., and Wayne T. Davis, eds. 1992. *Air Pollution Engineering Manual.* New York: Van Nostrand Reinhold.

European Community. 1993. "Technical Note on the Best Available Technologies to Reduce Emissions into Air from Coke Plants." Paper presented to BAT Exchange of Information Committee, Brussels.

————. 1993. "Study on the Technical and Economic Aspects of Measures to Reduce the Pollution from the Industrial Emissions of Cokeries." Paper presented to BAT Exchange of Information Committee, Brussels.

USEPA (United States Environmental Protection Agency). 1982. *Development Document for Effluent Limitations Guidelines and Standards for the Iron and Steel Manufacturing Point Source Subcategory.* EPA 440/1-82/024. Washington, D.C.

United States. 1992. *Federal Register,* vol. 57, no. 160, August 18. Washington, D.C.: Government Printing Office.

World Bank. 1995. "Industrial Pollution Prevention and Abatement: Coke Manufacturing." Draft Technical Background Document. Washington, D.C.

WHO (World Health Organization). 1989. *Management and Control of the Environment.* WHO/PEP/89.1. Geneva.

# Copper Smelting

## Industry Description and Practices

Copper can be produced either pyrometallurgically or hydrometallurgically. The hydrometallurgical route is used only for a very limited amount of the world's copper production and is normally only considered in connection with in-situ leaching of copper ores; from an environmental point of view, this is a questionable production route. Several different processes can be used for copper production. The traditional process is based on roasting, smelting in reverbatory furnaces (or electric furnaces for more complex ores), producing matte (copper-iron sulfide), and converting for production of blister copper, which is further refined to cathode copper. This route for production of cathode copper requires large amounts of energy per ton of copper: 30–40 million British thermal units (Btu) per ton cathode copper. It also produces furnace gases with low sulfur dioxide ($SO_2$) concentrations from which the production of sulfuric acid or other products is less efficient. The sulfur dioxide concentration in the exhaust gas from a reverbatory furnace is about 0.5–1.5%; that from an electric furnace is about 2–4%. So-called flash smelting techniques have therefore been developed that utilize the energy released during oxidation of the sulfur in the ore. The flash techniques reduce the energy demand to about 20 million Btu/ton of produced cathode copper. The $SO_2$ concentration in the off gases from flash furnaces is also higher, over 30%, and is less expensive to convert to sulfuric acid. (Note that the INCO process results in 80% sulfur dioxide in the off gas.) Flash processes have been in use since the 1950s.

In addition to the above processes, there are a number of newer processes such as Noranda, Mitsubishi, and Contop, which replace roasting, smelting, and converting, or processes such as ISA-SMELT and KIVCET, which replace roasting and smelting. For converting, the Pierce-Smith and Hoboken converters are the most common processes.

The matte from the furnace is charged to converters, where the molten material is oxidized in the presence of air to remove the iron and sulfur impurities (as converter slag) and to form blister copper.

Blister copper is further refined as either fire-refined copper or anode copper (99.5% pure copper), which is used in subsequent electrolytic refining. In fire refining, molten blister copper is placed in a fire-refining furnace, a flux may be added, and air is blown through the molten mixture to remove residual sulfur. Air blowing results in residual oxygen, which is removed by the addition of natural gas, propane, ammonia, or wood. The fire-refined copper is cast into anodes for further refining by electrolytic processes or is cast into shapes for sale.

In the most common hydrometallurgical process, the ore is leached with ammonia or sulfuric acid to extract the copper. These processes can operate at atmospheric pressure or as pressure leach circuits. Copper is recovered from solution by electrowinning, a process similar to electrolytic refining. The process is most commonly used for leaching low-grade deposits in situ or as heaps.

Recovery of copper metal and alloys from copper-bearing scrap metal and smelting residues requires preparation of the scrap (e.g., removal of insulation) prior to feeding into the primary process. Electric arc furnaces using scrap as feed are also common.

## Waste Characteristics

The principal air pollutants emitted from the processes are sulfur dioxide and particulate matter.

The amount of sulfur dioxide released depends on the characteristics of the ore—complex ores may contain lead, zinc, nickel, and other metals—and on whether facilities are in place for capturing and converting the sulfur dioxide. $SO_2$ emissions may range from less than 4 kilograms per metric ton (kg/t) of copper to 2,000 kg/t of copper. Particulate emissions can range from 0.1 kg/t of copper to as high as 20 kg/t of copper.

Fugitive emissions occur at furnace openings and from launders, casting molds, and ladles carrying molten materials. Additional fugitive particulate emissions occur from materials handling and transport of ores and concentrates.

Some vapors, such as arsine, are produced in hydrometallurgy and various refining processes. Dioxins can be formed from plastic and other organic material when scrap is melted. The principal constituents of the particulate matter are copper and iron oxides. Other copper and iron compounds, as well as sulfides, sulfates, oxides, chlorides, and fluorides of arsenic, antimony, cadmium, lead, mercury, and zinc, may also be present. Mercury can also be present in metallic form. At higher temperatures, mercury and arsenic could be present in vapor form. Leaching processes will generate acid vapors, while fire-refining processes result in copper and $SO_2$ emissions. Emissions of arsine, hydrogen vapors, and acid mists are associated with electrorefining.

Wastewater from primary copper production contains dissolved and suspended solids that may include concentrations of copper, lead, cadmium, zinc, arsenic, and mercury and residues from mold release agents (lime or aluminum oxides). Fluoride may also be present, and the effluent may have a low pH. Normally there is no liquid effluent from the smelter other than cooling water; wastewaters do originate in scrubbers (if used), wet electrostatic precipitators, cooling of copper cathodes, and so on. In the electrolytic refining process, by-products such as gold and silver are collected as slimes that are subsequently recovered. Sources of wastewater include spent electrolytic baths, slimes recovery, spent acid from hydrometallurgy processes, cooling water, air scrubbers, washdowns, stormwater, and sludges from wastewater treatment processes that require reuse/recovery or appropriate disposal.

The main portion of the solid waste is discarded slag from the smelter. Discard slag may contain 0.5–0.7% copper and is frequently used as construction material or for sandblasting. Leaching processes produce residues, while effluent treatment results in sludges, which can be sent for metals recovery. The smelting process typically produces less than 3 tons of solid waste per ton of copper produced.

## Pollution Prevention and Control

Process gas streams containing sulfur dioxide are processed to produce sulfuric acid, liquid sulfur dioxide, or sulfur. The smelting furnace will generate process gas streams with $SO_2$ concentrations ranging from 0.5% to 80%, depending on the process used. It is important, therefore, that a process be selected that uses oxygen-enriched air (or pure oxygen) to raise the $SO_2$ content of the process gas stream and reduce the total volume of the stream, thus permitting efficient fixation of sulfur dioxide. Processes should be operated to maximize the concentration of the sulfur dioxide. An added benefit is the reduction of nitrogen oxides ($NO_x$).

Closed-loop electrolysis plants will contribute to prevention of pollution.

Continuous casting machines should be used for cathode production to avoid the need for mold release agents.

Furnaces should be enclosed to reduce fugitive emissions, and dust from dust control equipment should be returned to the process.

Energy efficiency measures (such as waste heat recovery from process gases) should be applied to reduce fuel usage and associated emissions.

Recycling should be practiced for cooling water, condensates, rainwater, and excess process water used for washing, dust control, gas scrubbing, and other process applications where water quality is not a concern.

Good housekeeping practices are key to minimizing losses and preventing fugitive emissions. Such losses and emissions are minimized by enclosed buildings, covered or enclosed conveyors and transfer points, and dust collection equipment. Yards should be paved and runoff water routed to settling ponds. Regular sweeping of yards and indoor storage or coverage of concentrates and other raw materials also reduces materials losses and emissions.

## Treatment Technologies

Fabric filters are used to control particulate emissions. Dust that is captured but not recycled will need to be disposed of in a secure landfill or other acceptable manner.

Vapors of arsenic and mercury present at high gas temperatures are condensed by gas cooling and removed. Additional scrubbing may be required.

Effluent treatment by precipitation, filtration, and so on of process bleed streams, filter backwash waters, boiler blowdown, and other streams may be required to reduce suspended and dissolved solids and heavy metals. Residues that result from treatment are sent for metals recovery or to sedimentation basins. Stormwaters should be treated for suspended solids and heavy metals reduction.

Slag should be landfilled or granulated and sold.

Modern plants using good industrial practices should set as targets total dust releases of 0.5–1.0 kg/t of copper and $SO_2$ discharges of 25 kg/t of copper. A double-contact, double-absorption plant should emit no more than 0.2 kg of sulfur dioxide per ton of sulfuric acid produced (based on a conversion efficiency of 99.7%).

## Emissions Guidelines

Emissions levels for the design and operation of each project must be established through the environmental assessment (EA) process on the basis of country legislation and the *Pollution Prevention and Abatement Handbook,* as applied to local conditions. The emissions levels selected must be justified in the EA and acceptable to the World Bank Group.

The guidelines given below present emissions levels normally acceptable to the World Bank Group in making decisions regarding provision of World Bank Group assistance. Any deviations from these levels must be described in the World Bank Group project documentation. The emissions levels given here can be consistently achieved by well-designed, well-operated, and well-maintained pollution control systems.

The guidelines are expressed as concentrations to facilitate monitoring. Dilution of air emissions or effluents to achieve these guidelines is unacceptable.

All of the maximum levels should be achieved for at least 95% of the time that the plant or unit is operating, to be calculated as a proportion of annual operating hours.

### Air Emissions

The air emissions levels presented in Table 1 should be achieved.

The EA should address the buildup of heavy metals from particulate fallout in the vicinity of the plant over its projected life.

### Liquid Effluents

The effluent emissions levels presented in Table 2 should be achieved.

### Ambient Noise

Noise abatement measures should achieve either the levels given below or a maximum increase in background levels of 3 decibels (measured on the A scale) [dB(A)]. Measurements are to be taken

### Table 1. Emissions from Copper Smelting
*(milligrams per normal cubic meter)*

| Parameter | Maximum value |
| --- | --- |
| Sulfur dioxide | 1,000 |
| Arsenic | 0.5 |
| Cadmium | 0.05 |
| Copper | 1 |
| Lead | 0.2 |
| Mercury | 0.05 |
| Particulates, smelter | 20 |
| Particulates, other sources | 50 |

**Table 2. Effluents from Copper Smelting**
*(milligrams per liter, except for pH and temperature)*

| Parameter | Maximum value |
|---|---|
| pH | 6–9 |
| Total suspended solids | 50 |
| Arsenic | 0.1 |
| Cadmium | 0.1 |
| Copper | 0.5 |
| Iron | 3.5 |
| Lead | 0.1 |
| Mercury (total) | 0.01 |
| Zinc | 1.0 |
| Total metals | 10 |
| Temperature increase | $\leq 3°C^a$ |

*Note:* Effluent requirements are for direct discharge to surface waters.
a. The effluent should result in a temperature increase of no more than 3° C at the edge of the zone where initial mixing and dilution take place. Where the zone is not defined, use 100 meters from the point of discharge.

at noise receptors located outside the project property boundary.

| Receptor | Maximum allowable log equivalent (hourly measurements), in dB(A) | |
|---|---|---|
| | Day (07:00–22:00) | Night (22:00–07:00) |
| Residential, institutional, educational | 55 | 45 |
| Industrial, commercial | 70 | 70 |

## Monitoring and Reporting

Frequent sampling may be required during start-up and upset conditions. Once a record of consistent performance has been established, sampling for the parameters listed in this document should be as described below.

Air emissions should be monitored continuously for sulfur dioxide and particulate matter. Other air emissions parameters should be monitored annually.

Liquid effluents should be monitored daily for pH and total suspended solids and at least monthly for all other parameters.

Monitoring data should be analyzed and reviewed at regular intervals and compared with the operating standards so that any necessary corrective actions can be taken. Records of monitoring results should be kept in an acceptable format. The reports should be reported to the responsible authorities and relevant parties, as required.

## Key Issues

The key production and control practices that will lead to compliance with emissions requirements can be summarized as follows:

- Give preference to processes that are energy efficient and that produce high $SO_2$ concentrations (e.g., flash smelting).
- Use oxygen for enrichment of sulfur dioxide.
- Use the double-contact, double-absorption process for sulfuric acid production.
- Reduce effluent discharge by maximizing wastewater recycling.
- Maximize the recovery of dust and sludges.
- Minimize fugitive emissions by encapsulation of process equipment and use of covered or enclosed conveyors.
- Give preference to dry dust collectors over wet scrubbers.

## Sources

Bounicore, Anthony J., and Wayne T. Davis, eds. 1992. *Air Pollution Engineering Manual.* New York: Van Nostrand Reinhold.

Environment Canada. 1980. "A Study of Sulphur Containment Technology in the Non-Ferrous Metallurgical Industries." Report EPS 3-AP-79-8. Ottawa.

European Commission. 1991. "Technical Note on Best Available Technologies Not Entailing Excessive Costs for Heavy Metal Emissions from Non-Ferrous Industrial Plants." Brussels.

————. 1993. "Study on the Technical and Economical Aspects of Measures to Reduce the Pollution of Water and Other Environmental Areas from the Non-Ferrous Metal Industry." Brussels.

World Bank. 1996. "Pollution Prevention and Abatement: Copper Smelting." Draft Technical Background Document. Environment Department, Washington, D.C.

# Dairy Industry

## Industry Description and Practices

The dairy industry involves processing raw milk into products such as consumer milk, butter, cheese, yogurt, condensed milk, dried milk (milk powder), and ice cream, using processes such as chilling, pasteurization, and homogenization. Typical by-products include buttermilk, whey, and their derivatives.

## Waste Characteristics

Dairy effluents contain dissolved sugars and proteins, fats, and possibly residues of additives. The key parameters are biochemical oxygen demand (BOD), with an average ranging from 0.8 to 2.5 kilograms per metric ton (kg/t) of milk in the untreated effluent; chemical oxygen demand (COD), which is normally about 1.5 times the BOD level; total suspended solids, at 100–1,000 milligrams per liter (mg/l); total dissolved solids: phosphorus (10–100 mg/l), and nitrogen (about 6% of the BOD level). Cream, butter, cheese, and whey production are major sources of BOD in wastewater. The waste load equivalents of specific milk constituents are: 1 kg of milk fat = 3 kg COD; 1 kg of lactose = 1.13 kg COD; and 1 kg protein = 1.36 kg COD. The wastewater may contain pathogens from contaminated materials or production processes. A dairy often generates odors and, in some cases, dust, which need to be controlled. Most of the solid wastes can be processed into other products and by-products.

## Pollution Prevention and Control

Good pollution prevention practices in the dairy industry include:

- Reduction of product losses by better production control.
- Use of disposable packaging (or bulk dispensing of milk) instead of bottles where feasible.
- Collection of waste product for use in lower-grade products such as animal feed where this is feasible without exceeding cattle feed quality limits.
- Optimization of use of water and cleaning chemicals; recirculation of cooling waters.
- Segregation of effluents from sanitary installations, processing, and cooling (including condensation) systems; this facilitates recycling of wastewater.
- Use of condensates instead of fresh water for cleaning.
- Recovery of energy by using heat exchangers for cooling and condensing.
- Use of high-pressure nozzles to minimize water usage.
- Avoidance of the use of phosphorus-based cleaning agents.

Continuous sampling and measuring of key production parameters allow production losses to be identified and reduced, thus reducing the waste load. Table 1 presents product losses for a well-run dairy.

Odor problems can usually be prevented with good hygiene and storage practices. Chlorinated fluorocarbons should not be used in the refrigeration system.

## Target Pollution Loads

Since the pollutants generated by the industry are very largely losses in production, improvements in production efficiency (as described in the previous section) are recommended to reduce pollutant loads.

**Table 1. Product Losses in the Dairy Industry**
*(percent)*

| Operation | Product losses | | |
| --- | --- | --- | --- |
| | Milk | Fat | Whey |
| Butter/transport of skimmed milk | 0.17 | 0.14 | n.a. |
| Butter and skimmed milk powder | 0.60 | 0.20 | n.a. |
| Cheese | 0.20 | 0.10 | 1.6 |
| Cheese and whey evaporation | 0.20 | 0.10 | 2.2 |
| Cheese and whey powder | 0.20 | 0.10 | 2.3 |
| Consumer milk | 1.9 | 0.7 | n.a. |
| Full-cream milk powder | 0.64 | 0.22 | n.a. |

n.a. Not applicable.
*Note:* Data are expressed as the percentage of the volume of milk, fat, or whey processed.

Wastewater loads are typically 1–2 cubic meters per metric ton (m³/t) of milk processed. The plant operators should aim to achieve rates of 1 m³/t or less at the intake of the effluent treatment system. The BOD level should be less than 2.5 kg/t of milk, with a target of 1–1.5 kg/t. The BOD level from butter and cheese production should be less than 2 kg/t of product.

## Treatment Technologies

Pretreatment of effluents consists of screening, flow equalization, neutralization, and air flotation (to remove fats and solids); it is normally followed by biological treatment. If space is available, land treatment or pond systems are potential treatment methods. Other possible biological treatment systems include trickling filters, rotating biological contactors, and activated sludge treatment.

Pretreated dairy effluents can be discharged to a municipal sewerage system, if capacity exists, with the approval of the relevant authority.

Odor control by ventilation and scrubbing may be required where cheese is stored or melted. Dust control at milk powder plants is provided by fabric filters.

## Emissions Guidelines

Emissions levels for the design and operation of each project must be established through the environmental assessment (EA) process on the basis of country legislation and the *Pollution Prevention and Abatement Handbook,* as applied to local conditions. The emissions levels selected must be justified in the EA and acceptable to the World Bank Group.

The guidelines given below present emissions levels normally acceptable to the World Bank Group in making decisions regarding provision of World Bank Group assistance. Any deviations from these levels must be described in the World Bank Group project documentation. The emissions levels given here can be consistently achieved by well-designed, well-operated, and well-maintained pollution control systems.

The guidelines are expressed as concentrations to facilitate monitoring. Dilution of air emissions or effluents to achieve these guidelines is unacceptable.

All of the maximum levels should be achieved for at least 95% of the time that the plant or unit is operating, to be calculated as a proportion of annual operating hours.

### Air Emissions

Odor controls (such as absorbents/biofilters on exhaust systems) should be implemented where necessary to achieve acceptable odor quality for nearby residents. Fabric filters should be used to control dust from milk powder production to below 50 milligrams per normal cubic meter (mg/Nm³).

### Liquid Effluents

The effluent levels presented in Table 2 should be achieved.

### Ambient Noise

Noise abatement measures should achieve either the levels given below or a maximum increase in

**Table 2. Effluents from the Dairy Industry**
*(milligrams per liter, except for pH, temperature, and bacteria)*

| Parameter | Maximum value |
|---|---|
| pH | 6 –9 |
| BOD | 50 |
| COD | 250 |
| TSS | 50 |
| Oil and grease | 10 |
| Total nitrogen | 10 |
| Total phosphorus | 2 |
| Temperature increase | $\leq 3^\circ C^a$ |
| Coliform bacteria | 400 MPN/100 ml |

*Note:* Effluent requirements are for direct discharge to surface waters. MPN, most probable number.
a. The effluent should result in a temperature increase of no more than 3° C at the edge of the zone where initial mixing and dilution take place. Where the zone is not defined, use 100 meters from the point of discharge.

background levels of 3 decibels (measured on the A scale) [dB(A)]. Measurements are to be taken at noise receptors located outside the project property boundary.

| Receptor | Maximum allowable log equivalent (hourly measurements), in dB(A) | |
|---|---|---|
| | Day (07:00–22:00) | Night (22:00–07:00) |
| Residential, institutional, educational | 55 | 45 |
| Industrial, commercial | 70 | 70 |

## Monitoring and Reporting

Monitoring of the final effluent for the parameters listed above should be carried out at least once per month, or more frequently if the flows vary significantly.

Monitoring data should be analyzed and reviewed at regular intervals and compared with the operating standards so that any necessary corrective actions can be taken. Records of monitoring results should be kept in an acceptable format. The results should be reported to the responsible authorities and relevant parties, as required.

## Key Issues

The key production and control practices that will lead to compliance with emissions guidelines can be summarized as follows:

- Monitor key production parameters to reduce product losses.
- Use disposable packaging (or bulk dispensing of milk) instead of bottles, where feasible.
- Design and operate the production system to achieve recommended wastewater loads.
- Recirculate cooling waters.
- Collect wastes for use in low-grade products.

## Sources

Economopoulos, Alexander P. 1993. *Assessment of Sources of Air, Water, and Land Pollution: A Guide to Rapid Source Inventory Techniques and Their Use in Formulating Environmental Control Strategies.* Part 1: *Rapid Inventory Techniques in Environmental Pollution.* WHO/PEP/GETNET/93.1-A. Geneva: World Health Organization.

Robinson, R. K. 1986. "Advances in Milk Products." In *Modern Dairy Technology*, Vol. 2. Amsterdam: Elsevier Applied Science Publishers.

World Bank. 1996. "Pollution Prevention and Abatement: Dairy Industry." Draft Technical Background Document. Environment Department, Washington, D.C.

# Dye Manufacturing

## Industry Description and Practices

This document discusses the synthesis of dyes and pigments used in textiles and other industries. Dyes are soluble at some stage of the application process, whereas pigments, in general, retain essentially their particulate or crystalline form during application. A dye is used to impart color to materials of which it becomes an integral part. An aromatic ring structure coupled with a side chain is usually required for resonance and thus to impart color. (Resonance structures that cause displacement or appearance of absorption bands in the visible spectrum of light are responsible for color.) Correlation of chemical structure with color has been accomplished in the synthesis of dye using a chromogen-chromophore with auxochrome. Chromogen is the aromatic structure containing benzene, naphthalene, or anthracene rings. A chromophore group is a color giver and is represented by the following radicals, which form a basis for the chemical classification of dyes when coupled with the chromogen: azo ($-N=N-$); carbonyl ($=C=O$); carbon ($=C=C=$); carbon-nitrogen ($>C=NH$ or $-CH=N-$); nitroso ($-NO$ or $N-OH$); nitro ($-NO_2$ or $=NO-OH$); and sulfur ($>C=S$, and other carbon-sulfur groups). The chromogen-chromophore structure is often not sufficient to impart solubility and cause adherence of dye to fiber. The auxochrome or bonding affinity groups are amine, hydroxyl, carboxyl, and sulfonic radicals, or their derivatives. These auxochromes are important in the use classification of dyes. A listing of dyes by use classification comprises the following:

- *Acetate rayon dyes:* developed for cellulose acetate and some synthetic fibers

- *Acid dyes:* used for coloring animal fibers via acidified solution (containing sulfuric acid, acetic acid, sodium sulfate, and surfactants) in combination with amphoteric protein
- *Azoic dyes:* contain the azo group (and formic acid, caustic soda, metallic compounds, and sodium nitrate); especially for application to cotton
- *Basic dyes:* amino derivatives (and acetic acid and softening agents); used mainly for application on paper
- *Direct dyes:* azo dyes, and sodium salts, fixing agents, and metallic (chrome and copper) compounds; used generally on cotton-wool, or cotton-silk combinations
- *Mordant or chrome dyes:* metallic salt or lake formed directly on the fiber by the use of aluminum, chromium, or iron salts that cause precipitation in situ
- *Lake or pigment dyes:* form insoluble compounds with aluminum, barium, or chromium on molybdenum salts; the precipitates are ground to form pigments used in paint and inks
- *Sulfur or sulfide dyes:* contain sulfur or are precipitated from sodium sulfide bath; furnish dull shades with good fastness to light, washing, and acids but susceptible to chlorine and light
- *Vat dyes:* impregnated into fiber under reducing conditions and reoxidized to an insoluble color.

Chemical classification is based on chromogen. For example, nitro dyes have the chromophore $-NO_2$. The *Color Index* (C.I.), published by the Society of Dyers and Colourists (United Kingdom) in cooperation with the American Association of

Textile Chemists and Colorists (AATC), provides a detailed classification of commercial dyes and pigments by generic name and chemical constitution. This sourcebook also gives useful information on technical performance, physical properties, and application areas.

Dyes are synthesized in a reactor, filtered, dried, and blended with other additives to produce the final product. The synthesis step involves reactions such as sulfonation, halogenation, amination, diazotization, and coupling, followed by separation processes that may include distillation, precipitation, and crystallization. In general, organic compounds such as naphthalene are reacted with an acid or an alkali along with an intermediate (such as a nitrating or a sulfonating compound) and a solvent to form a dye mixture. The dye is then separated from the mixture and purified. On completion of the manufacture of actual color, finishing operations, including drying, grinding, and standardization, are performed; these are important for maintaining consistent product quality.

## Waste Characteristics

The principal air pollutants from dye manufacturing are volatile organic compounds (VOCs), nitrogen oxides ($NO_x$), hydrogen chloride (HCl), and sulfur oxides ($SO_x$).

Liquid effluents resulting from equipment cleaning after batch operation can contain toxic organic residues. Cooling waters are normally recirculated. Wastewater generation rates are of the order of 1–700 liters per kg (l/kg) of product except for vat dyes. The wastewater generation rate for vat dyes can be of the order of 8,000 l/kg of product. Biochemical oxygen demand (BOD) and chemical oxygen demand (COD) levels of reactive and azo dyes can be of the order of 25 kg/kg of product and 80 kg/ kg of product, respectively. Values for other dyes are, for example, $BOD_5$, 6 kg/kg; COD, 25 kg/kg; suspending solids, 6 kg/kg; and oil and grease, 30 kg/kg of product.

Major solid wastes of concern include filtration sludges, process and effluent treatment sludges, and container residues. Examples of wastes considered toxic include wastewater treatment sludges, spent acids, and process residues from the manufacture of chrome yellow and orange pigments, molybdate orange pigments, zinc yellow pigments, chrome and chrome oxide green pigments, iron blue pigments, and azo dyes.

## Pollution Prevention and Control

Every effort should be made to substitute degradable and less toxic ingredients for highly toxic and persistent ingredients. Recommended pollution prevention measures are to:

- Avoid the manufacture of toxic azo dyes and provide alternative dyestuffs to users such as textile manufacturers.
- Meter and control the quantities of toxic ingredients to minimize wastage.
- Reuse by-products from the process as raw materials or as raw material substitutes in other processes.
- Use automated filling to minimize spillage.
- Use equipment washdown waters as makeup solutions for subsequent batches.
- Return toxic materials packaging to supplier for reuse, where feasible.
- Find productive uses for off-specification products to avoid disposal problems.
- Use high-pressure hoses for equipment cleaning to reduce the amount of wastewater generated.
- Label and store toxic and hazardous materials in secure, bunded areas.

A dye and pigment manufacturing plant should prepare and implement an emergency plan that takes into account neighboring land uses and the potential consequences of an emergency. Measures to avoid the release of harmful substances should be incorporated in the design, operation, maintenance, and management of the plant.

## Target Pollution Loads

Implementation of cleaner production processes and pollution prevention measures can yield both economic and environmental benefits.

Specific reduction targets for the different processes have not been determined. In the absence of specific pollution reduction targets, new plants should always achieve better than the industry averages cited in "Waste Characteristics," above.

## Treatment Technologies

### Air Emissions

Stack gas scrubbing and/or carbon adsorption (for toxic organics) are applicable and effective technologies for minimizing the release of significant pollutants to air. Combustion is used to destroy toxic organics. Combustion devices should be operated at temperatures above 1,100° C (when required for the effective destruction of toxic organics), with a residence time of at least 0.5 second.

### Liquid Effluents

Effluent treatment normally includes neutralization, flocculation, coagulation, settling, carbon adsorption, detoxification of organics by oxidation (using ultraviolet systems or peroxide solutions), and biological treatment. Exhausted carbon from adsorption processes may be sent for regeneration or combustion. Reverse osmosis, ultrafiltration, and other filtration techniques are used to recover and concentrate process intermediates.

### Solid Hazardous Wastes

Contaminated solid wastes are generally incinerated, and the flue gases, when acidic, are scrubbed.

## Emissions Guidelines

Emissions levels for the design and operation of each project must be established through the environmental assessment (EA) process on the basis of country legislation and the *Pollution Prevention and Abatement Handbook,* as applied to local conditions. The emissions levels selected must be justified in the EA and acceptable to the World Bank Group.

The guidelines given below present emissions levels normally acceptable to the World Bank Group in making decisions regarding provision of World Bank Group assistance. Any deviations

from these levels must be described in the World Bank Group project documentation. The emissions levels given here can be consistently achieved by well-designed, well-operated, and well-maintained pollution control systems.

The guidelines are expressed as concentrations to facilitate monitoring. Dilution of air emissions or effluents to achieve these guidelines is unacceptable.

All of the maximum levels should be achieved for at least 95% of the time that the plant or unit is operating, to be calculated as a proportion of annual operating hours.

### Air Emissions

The emissions levels presented in Table 1 should be achieved.

### Liquid Effluents

The effluent levels presented in Table 2 should be achieved.

**Table 1. Emissions from Dye Manufacturing**
*(milligrams per normal cubic meter)*

| Parameter | Maximum value |
|---|---|
| Chlorine (or chloride) | 10 |
| VOCs | 20 |

**Table 2. Effluents from Dye Manufacturing**
*(milligrams per liter, except for pH)*

| Parameter | Maximum value |
|---|---|
| pH | 6–9 |
| BOD | 30 |
| COD | 150 |
| TSS | 50 |
| Oil and grease | 10 |
| Phenol | 0.5 |
| Chromium (hexavalent) | 0.1 |
| Copper | 0.5 |
| Zinc | 2 |
| AOX | 1 |
| Toxic organics such as benzidine (each) | 0.05 |

*Note:* Effluent requirements are for direct discharge to surface waters.

*Solid Wastes*

Contaminated solid wastes should be incinerated under controlled conditions to reduce toxic organics to nondetectable levels, in no case exceeding 0.05 mg/kg or the health-based level.

*Ambient Noise*

Noise abatement measures should achieve either the levels given below or a maximum increase in background levels of 3 decibels (measured on the A scale) [dB(A)]. Measurements are to be taken at noise receptors located outside the project property boundary.

| Receptor | Maximum allowable log equivalent (hourly measurements), in dB(A) | |
| --- | --- | --- |
| | Day (07:00–22:00) | Night (22:00–07:00) |
| Residential, institutional, educational | 55 | 45 |
| Industrial, commercial | 70 | 70 |

## Monitoring and Reporting

Frequent sampling may be required during start-up and upset conditions. Once a record of consistent performance has been established, sampling for the parameters listed in this document should be as described below.

Monitoring of air emissions should be done on a continuous basis. Liquid effluents should be monitored for toxic ingredients at least once every shift. The remaining parameters should be monitored at least daily.

Monitoring data should be analyzed and reviewed at regular intervals and compared with the operating standards so that any necessary corrective actions can be taken. Records of monitoring results should be kept in an acceptable format. The results should be reported to the responsible authorities and relevant parties, as required.

## Key Issues

The key production and control practices that will lead to compliance with emissions guidelines can be summarized as follows:

- Avoid the manufacture of toxic azo dyes and provide alternative dyestuffs to users such as textile manufacturers.
- Replace highly toxic and persistent ingredients with less toxic and degradable ones.
- Control loss and wastage of toxic ingredients.
- Return packaging for refilling.
- Use equipment washdown waters as makeup solutions for subsequent batches.
- Minimize wastage by inventory control and find uses for off-specification products.

## Sources

Kirk, Raymond E., and Donald F. Othmer. 1980. *Kirk-Othmer Encyclopedia of Chemical Technology.* 3d ed. New York: John Wiley and Sons.

Austen, George T., R. N. Shreve, and Joseph A. Brink. 1984. *Shreve's Chemical Process Industries.* New York: McGraw-Hill.

# Electronics Manufacturing

## Industry Description and Practices

The electronics industry includes the manufacture of *passive components* (resistors, capacitors, inductors); *semiconductor components* (discretes, integrated circuits); *printed circuit boards* (single and multilayer boards); and *printed wiring assemblies*. This chapter addresses the environmental issues associated with the last three manufacturing processes. The manufacture of passive components is not included because it is similar to that of semiconductors. (A difference is that passive component manufacturing uses less of the toxic chemicals employed in doping semiconductor components and more organic solvents, epoxies, plating metals, coatings, and lead.)

*Semiconductors.* Semiconductors are produced by treating semiconductor substances with dopants such as boron or phosphorus atoms to give them electrical properties. Important semiconductor substances are silicon and gallium arsenide. Manufacturing stages include crystal growth; acid etch and epitaxy formation; doping and oxidation; diffusion and ion implantation; metallization; chemical vapor deposition; die separation; die attachment; postsolder cleaning; wire bonding; encapsulation packaging; and final testing, marking, and packaging. Several of these process steps are repeated several times, so the actual length of the production chain may well exceed 100 processing steps. Between the repetitions, a cleaning step that contributes to the amount of effluent produced by the process is often necessary. Production involves carcinogenic and mutagenic substances and should therefore be carried out in closed systems.

*Printed circuit board (PCB) manufacturing.* There are three types of boards: single sided (circuits on one side only), double sided (circuits on both sides), and multilayer (three or more circuit layers). Board manufacturing is accomplished by producing patterns of conductive material on a nonconductive substrate by subtractive or additive processes. (The conductor is usually copper; the base can be pressed epoxy, Teflon, or glass.) In the subtractive process, which is the preferred route, the steps include cleaning and surface preparation of the base, electroless copperplating, pattern printing and masking, electroplating, and etching.

*Printed wiring assemblies.* Printed wiring assemblies consist of components attached to one or both sides of the printed circuit board. The attachment may be by through-hole technology, in which the "legs" of the components are inserted through holes in the board and are soldered in place from underneath, or by surface mount technology (SMT), in which components are attached to the surface by solder or conductive adhesive. (The solder is generally a tin-lead alloy.) In printed circuit boards of all types, drilled holes may have to be copper-plated to ensure interconnections between the different copper layers. SMT, which eliminates the drilled holes, allows much denser packing of components, especially when components are mounted on both sides. It also offers higher-speed performance and is gaining over through-hole technology.

## Waste Characteristics

### Air Emissions

Potential air emissions from *semiconductor* manufacturing include toxic, reactive, and hazardous gases; organic solvents; and particulates from the process. The changing of gas cylinders may also result in fugitive emissions of gases. Chemicals in use may include hydrogen, silane, arsine, phosphine, diborane, hydrogen chloride, hydrogen fluoride, dichlorosilane, phosphorous oxychloride, and boron tribromide.

Potential air emissions from the manufacture of *printed circuit boards* include sulfuric, hydrochloric, phosphoric, nitric, acetic, and other acids; chlorine; ammonia; and organic solvent vapors (isopropanol, acetone, trichloroethylene; n-butyl acetate; xylene; petroleum distillates; and ozone-depleting substances).

In the manufacture of *printed wiring assemblies*, air emissions may include organic solvent vapors and fumes from the soldering process, including aldehydes, flux vapors, organic acids, and so on.

Throughout the electronics manufacturing sector, chlorofluorocarbons (CFCs) have been a preferred organic solvent for a variety of applications. CFCs are ozone-depleting substances (ODSs). Their production in and import into developing countries will soon be banned. Hydrochlorofluorocarbons (HCFCs) have been developed as a substitute for CFCs, but they too are ODSs and will be phased out. Methyl chloroform, another organic solvent, has also been used by the electronics industry; it too is an ODS and is being eliminated globally on the same schedule as CFCs. Chlorobromomethane and n-propyl bromide are also unacceptable because of their high ozone-depleting potential.

*Effluents*

Effluents from the manufacture of *semiconductors* may have a low pH from hydrofluoric, hydrochloric, and sulfuric acids (the major contributors to low pH) and may contain organic solvents, phosphorous oxychloride (which decomposes in water to form phosphoric and hydrochloric acids), acetate, metals, and fluorides.

Effluents from the manufacture of *printed circuit boards* may contain organic solvents, vinyl polymers; stannic oxide; metals such as copper, nickel, iron, chromium, tin, lead, palladium, and gold; cyanides (because some metals may be complexed with chelating agents); sulfates; fluorides and fluoroborates; ammonia; and acids.

Effluents from *printed wiring assemblies* may contain acids, alkalis, fluxes, metals, organic solvents, and, where electroplating is involved, metals, fluorides, cyanides, and sulfates.

*Solid and Hazardous Wastes*

Solid and hazardous wastes from *semiconductor* manufacture may include heavy metals, solder dross (solder pot skimmings), arsenic, spent epoxy, and waste organic solvents (contributing the largest volume of waste). In *printed circuit board* operations, solid wastes may include scrap board materials, plating and hydroxide sludges, and inks. In the manufacture of *printed wiring assemblies*, solid wastes may include solder dross, scrap boards, components, organic solvents, and metals. Boards may also be treated with brominated flame retardants, which may pose some environmental risk when boards are disposed of in landfills. All conventional electronics present additional hazards in landfills because of the presence of lead in cathode-ray tube envelopes and in solder, as well as lead and other metal salts, particularly if they have not been cleaned in a postsoldering operation.

All three manufacturing processes may generate sludges containing heavy metals from wastewater treatment plants. Organic solvent residues also require management and disposal.

## Pollution Prevention and Control

*Semiconductor Industry*

Measures such as plasma etching of silicon nitride (a dry process) in metal oxide semiconductor (MOS) technology replace the hot corrosive phosphoric acid ($H_3PO_4$) wet process and offer reductions in generated waste and better safety for workers while reducing the number of processing steps. Because of the reaction of the plasma with the substrate, several substances are formed that are regarded as carcinogenic or mutagenic and that may pose a danger to maintenance personnel. Risks are minimized by sweeping equipment with nitrogen before opening it. A gas mask with breathing equipment should be worn by personnel during repair and maintenance.

*Printed Circuit Board Manufacturing*

A number of process alternatives exist for the manufacture of printed circuit boards. These include:

- In board manufacture: SMT rather than plated through-hole technology; injection molded substrate; additive plating
- In cleaning and surface preparation: use of nonchelating cleaners; extension of bath life; improvement of rinse efficiency; countercurrent cleaning; recycling and reuse of cleaners and rinses
- In pattern printing and masking: aqueous processable resist; screen printing to replace photolithography; dry photoresist; recycling and reuse of photoresist strippers; segregation of streams; recovery of metals
- For electroplating and electroless plating: replacement of these processes by mechanical board production; use of noncyanide baths; extension of bath life; recycling and reuse of cleaners and rinses; improvement of rinse efficiency; countercurrent rinsing; segregation of streams; recovery of metals
- In etching: use of differential plating; use of nonchelated etchants and nonchrome etchant; use of pattern instead of panel plating; use of additive instead of subtractive processes; recycling and reuse of etchants.

Metal recovery by regenerative electrowinning results in a near-zero effluent discharge for segregated metal-bearing streams. Heavy metals are recovered to metal sheets, which eliminates 95% of sludge disposal. Metal-bearing sludges that are not treated for recovery of metals should be disposed of in secure landfills.

*Printed Wiring Assemblies*

In the printed wiring assembly process, non-ozone-depleting alternatives are readily available for cleaning printed wiring assemblies. These alternatives include other organic solvents, hydrocarbon/surfactant blends, alcohols, and organic solvent blends, as well as aqueous and semi-aqueous processes. More important, the industry has shown that even sophisticated printed wiring assemblies intended for military uses (where specifications are very exacting) can be made without cleaning by using low-residue fluxes that leave very little in the way of contamination on the boards. The no-clean concept does away with the use of organic solvents and the need to dispose of organic solvent waste, eliminates a process step and the corresponding equipment, and has been shown to give adequate product quality according to the application.

*General*

Organic solvent losses can be reduced by conservation and recycling, using closed-loop delivery systems, hoods, fans, and stills. Installation of activated carbon systems can achieve up to 90% capture and recycle of organic solvents used in the system. All solvents and hazardous chemicals (including wastes) require appropriate safe storage to prevent spills and accidental discharges. All tanks, pipework, and other containers should be situated over spill containment trays with dimensions large enough to contain the total volume of liquid over them. Containment facilities must resist all chemical attack from the products. In lieu of containment facilities, the floor and walls, to a reasonable height, may be treated (e.g., by an epoxy product, where chemically appropriate) to prevent the possibility of leakage of accidental spills into the ground, and there should be doorsills. (Untreated cement or concrete or grouted tile floors are permeable.) It is unacceptable to have a drain in the floor of any shop where chemicals of any description are used or stored, except where such a drain leads to an adequate water-treatment plant capable of rendering used or stored chemicals in its catchment area.

Waste organic solvents should be sent to a solvent recycling operation for reconstitution and reuse. Where recycling facilities are not available, waste solvents may need to be incinerated or destroyed as appropriate for their chemical composition.

**Target Pollution Loads**

Implementation of cleaner production processes and pollution prevention measures can yield both economic and environmental benefits. The following production-related targets can be achieved by measures such as those described in the previous section.

Ozone-depleting substances are not to be used in production operations unless no proven alternative exists. Discharges of organic solvents should be minimized, and alternative technologies should be considered where available. Solder dross should not be sent to landfills. (Waste can be sent to suppliers or approved waste recyclers for recovery of the lead and tin content of the dross.) Scrap boards and assemblies having soldered components should have their components and solder connections removed before they are sent to landfills or recycled for other uses.

## Treatment Technologies

Wet scrubbers, point-of-use control systems, and volatile organic compound (VOC) control units are used to control toxic and hazardous emissions of the chemicals used in semiconductor manufacturing. It is often appropriate to scrub acid and alkaline waste gases in separate scrubbers because different scrubber liquids can then be used, resulting in higher removal efficiencies.

Air emission concentrations of chemicals such as arsine, diborane, phosphine, silane, and other chemicals used in the process should be reduced below worker health levels for plant operations.

Because of the many chemicals used in the electronics industry, wastewater segregation simplifies waste treatment and allows recovery and reuse of materials. Organic wastes are collected separately from wastewater systems. (Note that solvent used in the semiconductor industry cannot be readily recycled because much of it is generated from complex mixtures such as photoresist.) Acids and alkalis are sent to onsite wastewater treatment facilities for neutralization, after segregation of heavy-metal-bearing streams for separate treatment. Fluoride-bearing streams in a semiconductor plant are segregated and treated on site or sent off site for treatment or disposal. Treatment steps for effluents from the electronics industry may include precipitation, coagulation, sedimentation, sludge dewatering, ion exchange, filtering, membrane purification and separation, and neutralization, depending on the particular stream. Sanitary wastes are treated separately (primary and secondary treatment followed by disinfection) or discharged to a municipal treatment system.

## Emissions Guidelines

Emissions levels for the design and operation of each project must be established through the environmental assessment (EA) process on the basis of country legislation and the *Pollution Prevention and Abatement Handbook,* as applied to local conditions. The emissions levels selected must be justified in the EA and acceptable to the World Bank Group.

The guidelines given below present emissions levels normally acceptable to the World Bank Group in making decisions regarding provision of World Bank Group assistance. Any deviations from these levels must be described in the World Bank Group project documentation. The emissions levels given here can be consistently achieved by well-designed, well-operated, and well-maintained pollution control systems.

The guidelines are expressed as concentrations to facilitate monitoring. Dilution of air emissions or effluents to achieve these guidelines is unacceptable.

All of the maximum levels should be achieved for at least 95% of the time that the plant or unit is operating, to be calculated as a proportion of annual operating hours.

*Air Emissions*

The air emissions levels presented in Table 1 should be achieved.

*Liquid Effluents*

The effluent levels presented in Table 2 should be achieved.

*Ambient Noise*

Noise abatement measures should achieve either the levels given below or a maximum increase in background levels of 3 decibels (measured on the

### Table 1. Air Emissions from Electronics Manufacturing
*(milligrams per normal cubic meter)*

| Parameter | Maximum value |
|---|---|
| VOC | 20 |
| Phosphine | 1 |
| Arsine | 1 |
| Hydrogen fluoride | 5 |
| Hydrogen chloride | 10 |

## Table 2. Effluents from Electronics Manufacturing

*(milligrams per liter, except for pH )*

| Parameter | Maximum value |
|---|---|
| pH | 6–9 |
| BOD | 50 |
| TSS | |
| Maximum | 50 |
| Monthly average | 20 |
| Oil and grease | 10 |
| Phosphorus | 5.0 |
| Fluoride | 20 |
| Ammonia | 10 |
| Cyanide | |
| Total | 1.0 |
| Free | 0.1 |
| Total chlorocarbons and hydrochlorocarbons | 0.5 |
| Metals, total | 10 |
| Arsenic | 0.1 |
| Chromium, hexavalent | 0.1 |
| Cadmium | 0.1 |
| Copper | 0.5 |
| Lead | 0.1 |
| Mercury | 0.01 |
| Nickel | 0.5 |
| Tin | 2.0 |

*Note:* Effluent requirements are for direct discharge to surface waters.

A scale) [dB(A)]. Measurements are to be taken at noise receptors located outside the project property boundary.

| Receptor | Day (07:00–22:00) | Night (22:00–07:00) |
|---|---|---|
| Residential, institutional, educational | 55 | 45 |
| Industrial, commercial | 70 | 70 |

*Maximum allowable log equivalent (hourly measurements), in dB(A)*

## Monitoring and Reporting

Monitoring of sources of toxic emissions (such as the toxic gases used in the semiconductor industry, should be continuous and part of the process. Effluents should be monitored continuously for pH, and other parameters should be tested once a month.

Monitoring data should be analyzed and reviewed at regular intervals and compared with the operating standards so that any necessary corrective actions can be taken. Records of monitoring results should be kept in an acceptable format. The results should be reported to the responsible authorities and relevant parties, as required.

## Key Issues

The key production and control practices that will lead to compliance with emissions requirements can be summarized as follows:

- Cylinders of toxic gases should be well secured and fitted with leak detection devices as appropriate. Well-designed emergency preparedness programs are required. Note that fugitive emissions occurring when gas cylinders are changed do not normally require capture for treatment, but appropriate safety precautions are expected to be in place.
- No ozone-depleting chemicals should be used in the process unless no proven alternatives are available.
- Equipment, such as refrigeration equipment, containing ozone-depleting chemicals should not be purchased unless no other option is available
- Toxic and hazardous sludges and waste materials must be treated and disposed of or sent to approved waste disposal or recycling operations
- Where liquid chemicals are employed, the plant, including loading and unloading areas, should be designed to minimize evaporation (other than water) and to eliminate all risk of chemicals entering the ground or any watercourse or sewerage system in the event of an accidental leak or spill.

## Source

World Bank. 1997. "Industrial Pollution Prevention and Abatement: Electronics Manufacturing." Draft Technical Background Document. Environment Department, Washington, D.C.

# Electroplating

## Industry Description and Practices

Electroplating involves the deposition of a thin protective layer (usually metallic) onto a prepared metal surface, using electrochemical processes. The process involves pretreatment (cleaning, degreasing, and other preparation steps), plating, rinsing, passivating, and drying. The cleaning and pretreatment stages involve a variety of solvents (often chlorinated hydrocarbons, whose use is discouraged) and surface-stripping agents, including caustic soda and a range of strong acids, depending on the metal surface to be plated. The use of halogenated hydrocarbons for degreasing is not necessary, as water-based systems are available. In the plating process, the object to be plated is usually used as the cathode in an electrolytic bath. Plating solutions are acid or alkaline and may contain complexing agents such as cyanides.

## Waste Characteristics

Any or all of the substances used in electroplating (such as acidic solutions, toxic metals, solvents, and cyanides) can be found in the wastewater, either via rinsing of the product or from spillage and dumping of process baths. The solvents and vapors from hot plating baths result in elevated levels of volatile organic compounds (VOCs) and, in some cases, volatile metal compounds, which may contain chromates. Approximately 30% of the solvents and degreasing agents used can be released as VOCs when baths are not regenerated.

The mixing of cyanide and acidic wastewaters can generate lethal hydrogen cyanide gas, and this must be avoided. The overall wastewater stream is typically extremely variable (1 liter to 500 liters per square meter of surface plated) but is usually high in heavy metals, including cadmium, chrome, lead, copper, zinc, and nickel, and in cyanides, fluorides, and oil and grease, all of which are process dependent. Air emissions may contain toxic organics such as trichloroethylene and trichloroethane.

Cleaning or changing of process tanks and treatment of wastewaters can generate substantial quantities of wet sludges containing high levels of toxic organics or metals.

## Pollution Prevention and Control

Plating involves different combinations of a wide variety of processes, and there are many opportunities to improve on traditional practices in the industry. The improvements listed below should be implemented where possible.

### Changes in Process

- Replace cadmium with high-quality, corrosion-resistant zinc plating. Use cyanide-free systems for zinc plating where appropriate. Where cadmium plating is necessary, use bright chloride, high-alkaline baths, or other alternatives. Note, however, that use of some alternatives to cyanides may lead to the release of heavy metals and cause problems in wastewater treatment.
- Use trivalent chrome instead of hexavalent chrome; acceptance of the change in finish needs to be promoted.
- Give preference to water-based surface-cleaning agents, where feasible, instead of organic cleaning agents, some of which are considered toxic.
- Regenerate acids and other process ingredients whenever feasible.

*Reduction in Dragout and Wastage*

- Minimize dragout through effective draining of bath solutions from the plated part, by, for example, making drain holes in bucket-type pieces, if necessary.
- Allow dripping time of at least 10 to 20 seconds before rinsing.
- Use fog spraying of parts while dripping.
- Maintain the density, viscosity, and temperature of the baths to minimize dragout.
- Place recovery tanks before the rinse tanks (also yielding makeup for the process tanks). The recovery tank provides for static rinsing with high dragout recovery.

*Minimizing Water Consumption in Rinsing Systems*

It is possible to design rinsing systems to achieve 50–99% reduction in traditional water usage. Testing is required to determine the optimum method for any specific process, but proven approaches include:

- Agitation of rinse water or work pieces to increase rinsing efficiency
- Multiple countercurrent rinses
- Spray rinses (especially for barrel loads).

*Management of Process Solutions*

- Recycle process baths after concentration and filtration. Spent bath solutions should be sent for recovery and regeneration of plating chemicals, not discharged into wastewater treatment units.
- Recycle rinse waters (after filtration).
- Regularly analyze and regenerate process solutions to maximize useful life.
- Clean racks between baths to minimize contamination.
- Cover degreasing baths containing chlorinated solvents when not in operation to reduce losses. Spent solvents should be sent to solvent recyclers and the residue from solvent recovery properly managed (e.g., blended with fuel and burned in a combustion unit with proper controls for toxic metals).

**Target Pollution Loads**

A key parameter is the water use in each process. Systems should be designed to reduce water use. Where electroplating is routinely performed on objects with known surface area in a production unit, water consumption of no more than 1.3 liters per square meter plated ($l/m^2$) for rack plating and $10\,l/m^2$ for drum plating should be achieved. The recommended pollution prevention and control measures can achieve the target levels listed below.

- Cadmium plating should be avoided. Where there are no feasible alternatives, a maximum cadmium load in the waste of 0.3 grams for every kilogram of cadmium processed is recommended.
- At least 90% of the solvent emissions to air must be recovered by the use of an air pollution control system such as a carbon filter.
- Ozone-depleting solvents such as chlorofluorocarbons and trichloroethane are not to be used in the process.

**Treatment Technologies**

Segregation of waste streams is essential because of the dangerous reactions that can occur. Strong acid and caustic reactions can generate boiling and splashing of corrosive liquids; acids can react with cyanides and generate lethal hydrogen cyanide gas. In addition, segregated streams that are concentrated are easier to treat.

*Air Emissions*

Exhaust hoods and good ventilation systems protect the working environment, but the exhaust streams should be treated to reduce VOCs and heavy metals to acceptable levels before venting to the atmosphere. Acid mists and vapors should be scrubbed with water before venting. In some cases, VOC levels of the vapors are reduced by use of carbon filters, which allow the reuse of solvents, or by combustion (and energy recovery) after scrubbing, adsorption, or other treatment methods.

## Liquid Effluents

Cyanide destruction, flow equalization and neutralization, and metals removal are required, as a minimum, for electroplating plants. Individual design is necessary to address the characteristics of the specific plant, but there are a number of common treatment steps. For small facilities, the possibility of sharing a common wastewater treatment plant should be considered. Cyanide destruction must be carried out upstream of the other treatment processes. If hexavalent chrome ($Cr^{+6}$) occurs in the wastewater, the wastewater is usually pretreated to reduce the chromium to a trivalent form using a reducing agent, such as a sulfide.

The main treatment processes are equalization, pH adjustment for precipitation, flocculation, and sedimentation/filtration. The optimum pH for metal precipitation is usually in the range 8.5–11, but this depends on the mixture of metals present. The presence of significant levels of oil and grease may affect the effectiveness of the metal precipitation process; hence, the level of oil and grease affects the choice of treatment options and the treatment sequence. It is preferred that the degreasing baths be treated separately. Flocculating agents are sometimes used to facilitate the filtration of suspended solids. Pilot testing and treatability studies may be necessary, and final adjustment of pH and further polishing of the effluent may be required. Modern wastewater treatment systems use ion exchange, membrane filtration, and evaporation to reduce the release of toxics and the quantity of effluent that needs to be discharged. The design can provide for a closed system with a minor bleed stream.

## Solid and Hazardous Wastes

Treatment sludges contain high levels of metals, and these should normally be managed as hazardous waste or sent for metals recovery. Electrolytical methods may be used to recover metals. Sludges are usually thickened, dewatered, and stabilized using chemical agents (such as lime) before disposal, which must be in an approved and controlled landfill. The high costs of proper sludge disposal are likely to become an increasing incentive for waste minimization.

## Emissions Guidelines

Emissions levels for the design and operation of each project must be established through the environmental assessment (EA) process on the basis of country legislation and the *Pollution Prevention and Abatement Handbook,* as applied to local conditions. The emissions levels selected must be justified in the EA and acceptable to the World Bank Group.

The guidelines given below present emissions levels normally acceptable to the World Bank Group in making decisions regarding provision of World Bank Group assistance. Any deviations from these levels must be described in the World Bank Group project documentation. The emissions levels given here can be consistently achieved by well-designed, well-operated, and well-maintained pollution control systems.

The guidelines are expressed as concentrations to facilitate monitoring. Dilution of air emissions or effluents to achieve these guidelines is unacceptable.

All of the maximum levels should be achieved for at least 95% of the time that the plant or unit is operating, to be calculated as a proportion of annual operating hours.

### Air Emissions

A 90% recovery of the quantity of VOCs released from the process is required.

### Liquid Effluents

Electroplating plants should use closed systems where feasible or attain the effluent levels presented in Table 1.

### Sludges

Wherever possible, the generation of sludges should be minimized. Sludges must be dewatered and stabilized and should be disposed of in an approved, secure landfill. Leachates from stabilized

## Table 1. Effluents from the Electroplating Industry

*(milligrams per liter, except for pH)*

| Parameter | Maximum value |
|---|---|
| pH | 7–10 |
| TSS | 25 |
| Oil and grease | 10 |
| Arsenic | 0.1 |
| Cadmium | 0.1 |
| Chromium (hexavalent) | 0.1 |
| Chromium (total) | 0.5 |
| Copper | 0.5 |
| Lead | 0.2 |
| Mercury | 0.01 |
| Nickel | 0.5 |
| Silver | 0.5 |
| Zinc | 2 |
| Total metals | 10 |
| Cyanides (free) | 0.2 |
| Fluorides | 20 |
| Trichloroethane | 0.05 |
| Trichloroethylene | 0.05 |
| Phosphorus | 5 |

*Note:* Effluent requirements are for direct discharge to surface waters.

sludges should not contain toxics at levels higher than those indicated for liquid effluents. Where feasible, sludges may be reused, provided that toxics are not released to the environment.

### Ambient Noise

Noise abatement measures should achieve either the levels given below or a maximum increase in background levels of 3 decibels (measured on the A scale) [dB(A)]. Measurements are to be taken at noise receptors located outside the project property boundary.

| Receptor | Maximum allowable log equivalent (hourly measurements), in dB(A) | |
|---|---|---|
| | Day (07:00–22:00) | Night (22:00–07:00) |
| Residential, institutional, educational | 55 | 45 |
| Industrial, commercial | 70 | 70 |

## Monitoring and Reporting

Equipment to continuously monitor pH should be installed to provide an indication of overall treatment reliability. For larger plants (with discharges of more than 10,000 liters per day), the effluent should be sampled daily for all parameters except metals. Sampling of metals should be carried out at least monthly and when there are process changes. For smaller plants (having discharges of less than 10,000 liters per day), monthly monitoring of all parameters except pH may be acceptable. Frequent sampling may be required during start-up and upset conditions.

Monitoring data should be analyzed and reviewed at regular intervals and compared with the operating standards so that any necessary corrective actions can be taken. Records of monitoring results should be kept in an acceptable format. The records should be reported to the responsible authorities and relevant parties, as required.

## Key Issues

The key production and control practices that will lead to compliance with emissions guidelines can be summarized as follows:

- Use cyanide-free systems.
- Avoid cadmium plating.
- Use trivalent chrome instead of hexavalent chrome.
- Prefer water-based surface cleaning agents where feasible, instead of organic cleaning agents, some of which are considered toxic.
- Minimize dragout.
- Use countercurrent rinsing systems; recycle rinse waters to the process after treatment.
- Regenerate and recycle process baths and rinse waters after treatment.
- Recycle solvent collected from air pollution control systems.
- Send spent solvents for recovery.
- Do not use ozone-depleting substances.
- Manage sludges as hazardous waste. Reuse sludges to the extent feasible but without releasing toxics to the environment.

## Sources

Cushnie, G. C., Jr. 1985. *Electroplating Wastewater Pollution Control Technology.* Park Ridge, N.J.: Noyes Data Corporation.

Nordic Council of Ministers. 1993. *Possible Ways of Reducing Environmental Pollution from the Surface-Treatment Industry.* Oslo.

Patterson, James W. 1985. *Industrial Wastewater Treatment Technology.* 2d ed. Boston: Butterworth.

UNEP (United Nations Environment Programme). 1992. *Environmental Aspects of the Metal Finishing Industry: A Technical Guide.* Paris.

World Bank. 1996. "Pollution Prevention and Abatement: Electroplating Industry." Draft Technical Background Document. Environment Department, Washington, D.C.

# Foundries

## Industry Description and Practices

In foundries, molten metals are cast into objects of desired shapes. Castings of iron, steel, light metals (such as aluminum), and heavy metals (such as copper and zinc) are made in units that may be independent or part of a production line. Auto manufacturing facilities usually have foundries within their production facilities or as ancillaries. The main production steps include:

- Preparation of raw materials
- Metal melting
- Preparation of molds
- Casting
- Finishing (which includes fettling and tumbling).

Electric induction furnaces are used to melt iron and other metals. However, large car-component foundries and some small foundries melt iron in gas or coke-fired cupola furnaces and use induction furnaces for aluminum components of engine blocks. Melting capacities of cupola furnaces generally range from 3 to 25 metric tons per hour (t/hr). Induction furnaces are also used in zinc, copper, and brass foundries. Electric arc furnaces are usually used in stainless steel and sometimes in copper foundries. Flame ovens, which burn fossil fuels, are often used for melting nonferrous metals. The casting process usually employs nonreusable molds of green sand, which consists of sand, soot, and clay (or water glass). The sand in each half of the mold is packed around a model, which is then removed. The two halves of the mold are joined, and the complete mold is filled with molten metal, using ladles or other pouring devices. Large foundries often have pouring furnaces with automatically controlled pouring. The mold contains channels for introducing and distributing the metal—a "gating system." For hollow casting, the mold is fitted with a core. Cores must be extremely durable, and so strong bonding agents are used for the core, as well as for the molds themselves. These bonding agents are usually organic resins, but inorganic ones are also used. Plastic binders are being used for the manufacture of high-quality products. Sand cores and chemically bonded sand molds are often treated with water-based or spirit-based blacking to improve surface characteristics. Aluminum and magnesium, as well as copper and zinc alloys, are frequently die-cast or gravity-cast in reusable steel molds. Die casting involves the injection of metal under high pressure by a plunger into a steel die. Centrifugal casting methods are used for pipes.

Finishing processes such as fettling involves the removal from the casting of the gating system, fins (burrs), and sometimes feeders. This is accomplished by cutting, blasting, grinding, and chiseling. Small items are usually ground by tumbling, carried out in a rotating or vibrating drum, usually with the addition of water, which may have surfactants added to it.

## Waste Characteristics

Emissions of particulate matter (PM) from the melting and treatment of molten metal, as well as from mold manufacture, shakeout, cleaning and after-treatment, is generally of greatest concern. PM may contain metals that may be toxic. Oil mists are released from the lubrication of metals. Odor and alcohol vapor (from surface treatment of alcohol-based blacking) and emissions of other volatile organic compounds (VOCs) are also of concern. Care must be exercised when handling halogenated organics, including aluminum scrap contaminated with chlorinated organics, polyvinyl chloride (PVC) scrap and turnings with chlorinated cutting oil, as dioxins may be emitted during melting operations.

Oil and suspended solids are released into process effluents, and treatment is warranted before their discharge. Wet scrubbers release wastewaters that may contain metals. Wastewater from tumbling may contain metals and surfactants. Cooling waters, used in amounts of up to 20 cubic meters per metric ton, may contain oil and some chemicals for the control of algae and corrosion.

Sand molding creates large quantities of waste sand. Other wastes include slag (300–500 kilograms per metric ton, kg/t, of metal), collected particulate matter, sludges from separators used in wastewater treatment, and spent oils and chemicals. Discarded refractory lining is another waste produced.

The primary hazardous components of collected dust are zinc, lead, and cadmium, but its composition can vary greatly depending on scrap composition and furnace additives. (Nickel and chromium are present when stainless steel scrap is used.) Generally, foundries produce 10 kg of dust per ton of molten metal, with a range of 5–30 kg/t, depending on factors such as scrap quality. However, induction furnaces (with emissions of 3 kg/t of molten metal) and flame ovens tend to have lower air emissions than cupolas and electric arc furnaces (EAF). Major pollutants present in the air emissions include particulates of the order of 1,000 milligrams per normal cubic meter (mg/Nm$^3$).

Foundries can generate up to 20 cubic meters of wastewater per metric ton of molten metal when cooling water, scrubber water, and process water are not regulated. Untreated wastewaters may contain high levels of total suspended solids, copper (0.9 milligrams per liter, mg/l), lead (2.5 mg/l), total chromium (2.5 mg/l), hexavalent chromium, nickel (0.25 mg/l), and oil and grease. The characteristics of the wastewater will depend on the type of metal and the quality of scrap used as feed to the process.

Solid wastes (excluding dust) are generated at a rate of 300–500 kg/t of molten metal. Sludges and scale may contain heavy metals such as chromium, lead, and nickel.

## Pollution Prevention and Control

The following pollution prevention measures should be considered:

- Prefer induction furnaces to cupola furnaces.
- Replace the cold-box method for core manufacture, where feasible.
- Improve feed quality: use selected and clean scrap to reduce the release of pollutants to the environment. Preheat scrap, with afterburning of exhaust gases. Store scrap under cover to avoid contamination of stormwater.
- Provide hoods for cupolas or doghouse enclosures for EAFs and induction furnaces.
- Use dry dust collection methods such as fabric filters instead of scrubbers.
- Use continuous casting for semifinished and finished products wherever feasible.
- Store chemicals and other materials in such a way that spills, if any, can be collected.
- Control water consumption by recirculating cooling water after treatment.
- Use closed-loop systems in scrubbers where the latter are necessary.
- Reduce nitrogen oxide (NO$_x$) emissions by use of natural gas as fuel, use low-NO$_x$ burners.
- Reclaim sand after removing binders.

## Pollution Reduction Targets

The recommended pollution prevention measures can achieve the target levels given below.

### Air Emissions

Recover metals from collected dust. The target value for PM from furnaces and die casting machinery is not to exceed 0.5 kg/t of molten metal (after controls). The oil aerosol should not exceed 5 mg/Nm3.

### Wastewaters

Recycle wastewaters, if any. Avoid allowing contamination of stormwater with oil; oil in stormwater is not to exceed 5 mg/l.

### Solid Wastes

Reclaim sand used in molding.

## Treatment Technologies

### Air Emissions

Dust emission control technologies include cyclones, scrubbers (with recirculating water), baghouses, and electrostatic precipitators (ESPs). Scrubbers are also used to control mists, acidic gases, and amines. Gas flame is used for incineration of gas from core manufacture. Target values for emissions passing through a fabric filter are normally around 10 mg/Nm3 (dry). Emissions of PM from furnaces (including casting machines used for die casting) should not exceed 0.1–0.3 kg/t of molten metal, depending on the nature of the PM and the melting capacity of the plant. At small iron foundries, a somewhat higher emission factor may be acceptable, while in large heavy-metal foundries, efforts should be made to achieve a target value lower than 0.1 kg PM per metric ton. Odors may be eliminated by using bioscrubbers.

### Wastewater Treatment

Recirculate tumbling water by sedimentation or centrifuging followed by filtering (using sand filters or ultrafilters); separate oil from surface water. In the very rare cases in which scrubbers are used, recirculate water and adjust its pH to precipitate metals. Precipitate metals in wastewater by using lime or sodium hydroxide. Cooling waters should be recirculated, and polluted stormwater should be treated before discharge.

## Emissions Guidelines

Emissions levels for the design and operation of each project must be established through the environmental assessment (EA) process on the basis of country legislation and the *Pollution Prevention and Abatement Handbook,* as applied to local conditions. The emissions levels selected must be justified in the EA and acceptable to the World Bank Group. Any deviations from these levels must be described in the World Bank Group project documentation. The emissions levels given here can be consistently achieved by well-designed, well-operated, and well-maintained pollution control systems.

The guidelines are expressed as concentrations to facilitate monitoring. Dilution of air emissions or effluents to achieve these guidelines is unacceptable.

All of the maximum levels should be achieved for at least 95% of the time that the plant or unit is operating, to be calculated as a proportion of annual operating hours.

### Air Emissions

Air emissions of PM should be below 20 mg/Nm$^3$ where toxic metals are present and 50 mg/Nm$^3$ in other cases. This would correspond to total dust emissions of less than 0.5 kg/t of molten metal.

### Liquid Effluents

For foundries, the effluent levels presented in Table 1 should be achieved.

Sludges from wastewater treatment operations should be disposed of in a secure landfill after stabilization.

### Ambient Noise

Noise abatement measures should achieve either the levels given below or a maximum increase in background levels of 3 decibels (measured on the A scale) [dB(A)]. Measurements are to be taken

## Table 1. Effluents from Foundries

*(milligrams per liter, except for pH and temperature)*

| Parameter | Maximum value |
|---|---|
| pH | 6–9 |
| TSS | 50 |
| Oil and grease | 10 |
| Copper | 0.5 |
| Zinc | 2 |
| Temperature increase | ≤ 3° C[a] |

a. The effluent should result in a temperature increase of no more than 3° C at the edge of the zone where initial mixing and dilution take place. Where the zone is not defined, use 100 meters from the point of discharge.

at noise receptors located outside the project property boundary.

| Receptor | Maximum allowable log equivalent (hourly measurements), in dB(A) | |
| | Day (07:00–22:00) | Night (22:00–07:00) |
| --- | --- | --- |
| Residential, institutional, educational | 55 | 45 |
| Industrial, commercial | 70 | 70 |

## Monitoring and Reporting

Air emissions should be monitored continuously for PM using an opacity meter (for an opacity level of less than 10%).

Wastewater discharges should be monitored daily for the parameters listed in this guideline, except for metals, which may be monitored monthly or when there are process changes.

Monitoring data should be analyzed and reviewed at regular intervals and compared with the operating standards so that any necessary corrective actions can be taken. Records of monitoring results should be kept in an acceptable format. The results should be reported to the responsible authorities and relevant parties, as required.

## Key Issues

The key production and control practices that will lead to compliance with emissions requirements can be summarized as follows:

- Use continuous casting, where feasible.
- Give preference to the use of induction furnaces, where appropriate.
- Use doghouse enclosures for furnaces and dry dust collection systems such as bag filters.
- Recycle at least 90% of the wastewater.
- Reclaim molding sand after the removal of binders

## Sources

Freeman, H. M. 1995. *Industrial Pollution Prevention Handbook.* New York: McGraw-Hill.

Swedish Environmental Protection Agency. 1991. "Informs on Foundries-Industry Fact Sheet." SNV 91-620-9377 0/91-03/500ex. Solna.

# Fruit and Vegetable Processing

## Industry Description and Practices

Processing (canning, drying, freezing, and preparation of juices, jams, and jellies) increases the shelf life of fruits and vegetables. Processing steps include preparation of the raw material (cleaning, trimming, and peeling followed by cooking, canning, or freezing. Plant operation is often seasonal.

## Waste Characteristics

The fruit and vegetable industry typically generates large volumes of effluents and solid waste. The effluents contain high organic loads, cleansing and blanching agents, salt, and suspended solids such as fibers and soil particles. They may also contain pesticide residues washed from the raw materials. The main solid wastes are organic materials, including discarded fruits and vegetables. Odor problems can occur with poor management of solid wastes and effluents; when onions are processed; and when ready-to-serve meals are prepared.

## Pollution Prevention and Control

Reductions in wastewater volumes of up to 95% have been reported through implementation of good practices. Where possible, measures such as the following should be adopted:

- Procure clean raw fruit and vegetables, thus reducing the concentration of dirt and organics (including pesticides) in the effluent.
- Use dry methods such as vibration or air jets to clean raw fruit and vegetables. Dry peeling methods reduce the effluent volume (by up to 35%) and pollutant concentration (organic load reduced by up to 25%).

- Separate and recirculate process wastewaters.
- Use countercurrent systems where washing is necessary.
- Use steam instead of hot water to reduce the quantity of wastewater going for treatment (taking into consideration, however, the tradeoff with increased use of energy).
- Minimize the use of water for cleaning floors and machines.
- Remove solid wastes without the use of water.
- Reuse concentrated wastewaters and solid wastes for production of by-products.

As an example, recirculation of process water from onion preparation reduces the organic load by 75% and water consumption by 95%. Similarly, the liquid waste load (in terms of biochemical oxygen demand, BOD) from apple juice and carrot processing can be reduced by 80%.

Good water management should be adopted, where feasible, to achieve the levels of consumption presented in Table 1.

Solid wastes, particularly from processes such as peeling and coring, typically have a high nutritional value and may be used as animal feed.

### Table 1. Water Usage in the Fruit and Vegetable Processing Industry
*(cubic meters per metric ton of product)*

| Product category | Water use |
|---|---|
| Canned fruit | 2.5–4.0 |
| Canned vegetables | 3.5–6.0 |
| Frozen vegetables | 5.0–8.5 |
| Fruit juices | 6.5 |
| Jams | 6.0 |
| Baby food | 6.0–9.0 |

## Target Pollution Loads

Implementation of cleaner production processes and pollution prevention measures can yield both economic and environmental benefits. The target loads per unit of production shown in Table 2 can be achieved by implementing measures such as those described above. The numbers are the waste loads arising from the production processes before the addition of pollution control measures. These levels are derived from the average loads recorded in a major study of the industry and should be used as maximum levels of unit pollution in the design of new plants.

## Treatment Technologies

Preliminary treatment of wastewaters should include screening (or sieving to recover pulp) and grit removal, if necessary. This is followed by pH adjustment and biological treatment of the organic load.

The flows are frequently seasonal, and robust treatment systems are preferred for onsite treatment. Pond systems are used successfully to treat fruit and vegetable wastes, but odor nuisance, soil deterioration, and groundwater pollution are to be avoided. The quality of the effluent is normally suitable for discharge to municipal systems, although peak hydraulic loads may cause a problem. Odor problems can be avoided by using gas scrubbers or biofilters.

## Emissions Guidelines

Emissions levels for the design and operation of each project must be established through the environmental assessment (EA) process on the basis of country legislation and the *Pollution Prevention and Abatement Handbook,* as applied to local conditions. The emissions levels selected must be justified in the EA and acceptable to the World Bank Group.

The guidelines given below present emissions levels normally acceptable to the World Bank Group in making decisions regarding provision of World Bank Group assistance. Any deviations from these levels must be described in the World Bank Group project documentation. The emissions levels given here can be consistently achieved by well-designed, well-operated, and well-maintained pollution control systems.

The guidelines are expressed as concentrations to facilitate monitoring. Dilution of air emissions or effluents to achieve these guidelines is unacceptable.

All of the maximum levels should be achieved for at least 95% of the time that the plant or unit is operating, to be calculated as a proportion of annual operating hours.

### Liquid Effluents

The effluent levels presented in Table 3 should be achieved.

Pesticides may be present in significant levels; testing should therefore be performed, and, if pesticides are present at levels above 0.05 milligrams per liter (mg/l), corrective action should be taken. The best course may be to switch to a supplier that provides raw materials without pesticide residues.

### Solid Wastes

Whenever possible, organic wastes should be used in the production of animal feed or organic fertilizers. Other solid wastes should be disposed of in a secure landfill to avoid contamination of surface and groundwater.

### Ambient Noise

Noise abatement measures should achieve either the levels given below or a maximum increase in background levels of 3 decibels (measured on the A scale) [dB(A)]. Measurements are to be taken at noise receptors located outside the project property boundary.

| Receptor | Maximum allowable log equivalent (hourly measurements), in dB(A) | |
| --- | --- | --- |
| | Day (07:00–22:00) | Night (22:00–07:00) |
| Residential, institutional, educational | 55 | 45 |
| Industrial, commercial | 70 | 70 |

**Table 2. Target Loads per Unit of Production, Fruit and Vegetable Processing Industry**

### Fruit

| Product | Waste volume (m³/U) | $BOD_5$ (kg/U) | TSS (kg/U) | Solid waste (kg/t product) |
|---|---|---|---|---|
| Apricots | 29.0 | 15.0 | 4.3 | |
| Apples | | | | |
| All products | | | | 90 |
| All except juice | 3.7 | 5.0 | 0.5 | |
| Juice | 5.4 | 6.4 | 0.8 | |
| Cranberries | 2.9 | 2.0 | 0.3 | 10 |
| Citrus | 5.8 | 2.8 | 0.6 | |
| Sweet cherries | 10.0 | 3.2 | 1.3 | |
| Sour cherries | 7.8 | 9.6 | 0.6 | |
| Bing cherries | 12.0 | 17.0 | 1.0 | |
| Cranberries | 20.0 | 22.0 | 1.4 | |
| Dried fruit | 12.0 | 10.0 | 1.4 | |
| Grapefruit | 13.0 | 12.0 | 1.9 | |
| Canned | 72.0 | 11.0 | 1.2 | |
| Pressed | 1.6 | 1.9 | 0.4 | |
| Olives | 38.0 | 44.0 | 7.5 | 20 |
| Peaches | | | | 180 |
| Canned | 13.0 | 14.0 | 2.3 | |
| Frozen | 5.4 | 12.0 | 1.8 | |
| Pears | 12.0 | 21.0 | 3.2 | 200 |
| Pickles | | | | |
| Fresh packed | 8.5 | 9.5 | 1.9 | |
| Process packed | 9.6 | 18.0 | 3.3 | |
| Salting stations | 1.1 | 8.0 | 0.4 | |
| Pineapples | 13.0 | 10.0 | 2.7 | |
| Plums | 5.0 | 4.1 | 0.3 | |
| Raisins | 2.8 | 6.0 | 1.6 | |
| Strawberries | 13.0 | 5.3 | 1.4 | 60 |
| Tomatoes | | | | |
| Peeled | 8.9 | 4.1 | 6.1 | |
| Products | 4.7 | 1.3 | 2.7 | |

### Vegetables

| Product | Waste vol. (m³/U) | $BOD_5$ (kg/U) | TSS (kg/U) | Solid waste (kg/t prod) |
|---|---|---|---|---|
| All vegetables | | | | 130 |
| Asparagus | 69.0 | 2.1 | 3.4 | |
| Beets | 5.0 | 20.0 | 3.9 | |
| Broccoli | 11.0 | 9.8 | 5.6 | 200 |
| Brussels sprouts | 36.0 | 3.4 | 11.0 | |
| Carrots | 12.0 | 20.0 | 12.0 | 200 |
| Cauliflower | 89.0 | 5.2 | 2.7 | 40 |
| Corn | | | | |
| Canned | 4.5 | 14.0 | 6.7 | |
| Frozen | 13.0 | 20.0 | 5.6 | |
| Dehydrated onion and garlic | 20.0 | 6.5 | 5.9 | |
| Dehydrated vegetables | 22.0 | 7.9 | 5.6 | |
| Dry beans | 18.0 | 15.0 | 4.4 | |
| Lima beans | 27.0 | 14.0 | 10.0 | |
| Mushrooms | 22.0 | 8.7 | 4.8 | |
| Onions, canned | 23.0 | 23.0 | 9.3 | 40 |
| Peas | | | | |
| Canned | 20.0 | 22.0 | 5.4 | |
| Frozen | 15.0 | 18.0 | 4.9 | |
| Pimentos | 29.0 | 27.0 | 2.9 | |
| Potatoes | | | | 40 |
| All products | 10.0 | 18.0 | 16.0 | |
| Frozen products | 11.0 | 23.0 | 19.0 | |
| Dehydrated products | 8.8 | 11.0 | 8.6 | |
| Sauerkraut | | | | |
| Canned | 3.5 | 3.5 | 0.6 | |
| Cut | 0.4 | 1.2 | 0.2 | |
| Snap beans | | | | |
| Canned | 15.0 | 3.1 | 2.0 | |
| Frozen | 20.0 | 6.0 | 3.0 | |
| Spinach | | | | |
| Canned | 38.0 | 8.2 | 6.5 | |
| Frozen | 29.0 | 4.8 | 2.0 | |
| Squash | 5.6 | 17.0 | 2.3 | |
| Sweet potatoes | 4.1 | 30.0 | 12.0 | |

n.a. Not applicable.
*Source*: Adapted from Economopoulos 1993.

**Table 3. Effluents from the Fruit and Vegetable Processing Industry**

*(milligrams per liter, except for pH)*

| Parameter | Maximum value |
|---|---|
| pH | 6–9 |
| BOD | 50 |
| COD | 250 |
| TSS | 50 |
| Oil and grease | 10 |
| Total nitrogen | 10 |
| Total phosphorus | 5 |

*Note:* Effluent requirements are for direct discharge to surface waters.

## Monitoring and Reporting

Monitoring of the final effluent for the parameters listed in this document should be carried out at least once per month—more frequently, if the flows vary substantially. To estimate water usage in various production processes, the wastewaters from unit operations should be monitored during each product season or, at a minimum, annually.

Monitoring data should be analyzed and reviewed at regular intervals and compared with the operating standards so that any necessary corrective actions can be taken. Records of monitoring results should be kept in an acceptable format. The results should be reported to the responsible authorities and relevant parties, as required.

## Key Issues

The key production and control practices that will lead to compliance with emissions guidelines can be summarized as follows:

- Implement water conservation and recycling measures.
- Adopt dry cleaning and peeling methods.

## Sources

Economopoulos, Alexander P. 1993. *Assessment of Sources of Air, Water, and Land Pollution: A Guide to Rapid Source Inventory Techniques and their Use in Formulating Environmental Control Strategies.* Part 1: *Rapid Inventory Techniques in Environmental Pollution.* Geneva: World Health Organization.

World Bank. 1996. "Pollution Prevention and Abatement: Fruit and Vegetable Processing." Draft Technical Background Document. Environment Department, Washington, D.C.

# Glass Manufacturing

## Industry Description and Practices

This document describes the manufacture of flat glass and pressed and blown glass. Flat glass includes plate and architectural glass, automotive windscreens, and mirrors. Pressed and blown glass includes containers, machine-blown and hand-blown glassware, lamps, and television tubing. In both categories, a glass melt is prepared from silica sand, other raw materials such as lime, dolomite, and soda, and cullet (broken glass). The use of recycled glass is increasing. It reduces the consumption of both raw materials and energy but necessitates extensive sorting and cleaning prior to batch treatment to remove impurities.

For the manufacture of special and technical glass, lead oxide, potash, zinc oxide, and other metal oxides are added. Refining agents include arsenic trioxide, antimony oxide, nitrates, and sulfates. Metal oxides and sulfides are used as coloring or decoloring agents.

The most common furnace used for manufacturing glass melt is the continuous regenerative type, with either the side or the end ports connecting brick checkers to the inside of the melter. Checkers conserve fuel by acting as heat exchangers; the fuel combustion products heat incoming combustion air. The molten glass is refined (heat conditioning) and is then pressed, blown, drawn, rolled, or floated, depending on the final product. Damaged and broken product (cullet) is returned to the process.

The most important fuels for glass-melting furnaces are natural gas, light and heavy fuel oil, and liquefied petroleum gas. Electricity (frequently installed as supplementary heating) is also used. Energy requirements range from 3.7 to 6.0 kilojoules per metric ton (kJ/t) glass produced.

## Waste Characteristics

Two types of air emissions are generated: those from the combustion of fuel for operating the glass-melting furnaces, and fine particulates from the vaporization and recrystallization of materials in the melt. The main emissions are sulfur oxides ($SO_x$), nitrogen oxides ($NO_x$), and particulates, which can contain heavy metals such as arsenic and lead. Particulates from lead crystal manufacture can have a lead content of 20–60% and an arsenic content of 0.5–2%. Certain specialty glasses can produce releases of hydrogen chloride (HCl), hydrogen fluoride (HF), arsenic, boron, and lead from raw materials. Container, pressing, and blowing operations produce a periodic mist when the hot gob comes into contact with the release agent used on the molds.

Cold-top electric furnaces, in which the melt surface is covered by raw material feed, release very little particulate matter, as the blanket acts as a filter to prevent the release of particulate matter. Some releases of particulates will take place in tapping, but furnace releases should be of the order of 0.1 kilogram per ton (kg/t) when operated this way.

Lead glass manufacture may result in lead emissions of about 2–5 kg/t.

In all cases, the concentration of heavy metals and other pollutants in the raw flue gas mainly depends on the type of fuel used, the composition of the feed material, and the portion of recycled glass. High input of sulfates or potassium nitrate may increase emissions of sulfur dioxide and nitrogen oxides, respectively. Where nitrate is used, more than two thirds of the introduced nitrogen may be emitted as nitrogen oxides. The use of heavy metals as coloring or decoloring agents will increase emissions of these metals.

The grinding and polishing of flat glass to produce plate glass have become obsolete since the development of the float glass process. The chemical makeup of detergents that may be used in float glass manufacturing can vary significantly—some may contain phosphorus. In blowing and pressing, pollutants in effluents are generated by finishing processes such as cutting, grinding, polishing, and etching. The pollutants include suspended solids, fluorides, lead, and variations in pH.

Liquid effluents also result from forming, finishing, coating, and electroplating operations. Heavy metal concentrations in effluents occur where silvering and copperplating processes are in use.

**Pollution Prevention and Control**

Oxygen-enriched and oxyfuel furnaces are used in specialty glass operations to reduce emissions or to make possible higher production rates with the same size furnace. Although oxyfuel furnaces may produce higher $NO_x$ emissions on a concentration basis, they are expected to yield very low levels of nitrogen oxides on a mass basis (kg/t of product). Low-$NO_x$ furnaces, staged firing, and flue gas recirculation are available to reduce both concentration and the mass of nitrogen oxide emissions. These techniques are also available for air-fuel-fired furnaces. Nitrogen oxide levels can be controlled to 500–800 milligrams per cubic meter ($mg/m^3$).

The type of combustion fuel used affects the amount of sulfur oxides and nitrogen oxides emitted. Use of natural gas results in negligible sulfur dioxide emissions from the fuel compared with high-sulfur fuel oils. Fuel oil with a low sulfur content is preferable to fuel oil with a high sulfur content if natural gas is not available.

An efficient furnace design will reduce gaseous emissions and energy consumption. Examples of improvements include modifications to the burner design and firing patterns, higher preheater temperatures, preheating of raw material, and electric melting.

Changing the composition of the raw materials can, for example, reduce chlorides, fluorides, and sulfates used in certain specialty glasses. The use of outside-sourced cullet and recycled glass will reduce energy requirements (for an estimated 2% savings for each 10% of cullet used in the manufacture of melt) and thus air emissions (up to 10% for 50% cullet in the mix). Typical recycling rates are 10–20% in the flat glass industry and over 50% for the blown and pressed glass industries.

The amount of heavy metals used as refining and coloring or decoloring agents, as well as use of potassium nitrate, should be minimized to the extent possible.

In the furnace, particulates are formed through the volatilization of materials, leading to formation of condensates and of slag that clogs the furnace checkers. Disposal of the slag requires testing to determine the most suitable disposal method. It is important to inspect the checkers regularly to determine whether cleaning is required.

Particulate matter is also reduced, for example, by enclosing conveyors, pelletizing raw material, reducing melt temperatures, and blanketing the furnace melt with raw material.

Reductions in wastewater volumes are possible through closed cooling water loops and improved blowoff techniques.

**Target Pollution Loads**

Modern plants using good industrial practices are able to achieve the pollutant loads given here. Because of the lack of nitrogen in the oxidant, using oxyfuel-fired furnaces produces four to five times less flue gas volume than regenerative furnaces. As a result nitrogen oxides are reduced by 80%, and particulates are reduced by 20–80%.

For furnaces that operate with a cover of raw material, a target of 0.1 kg/t for particulates is realistic. Reductions in sulfur dioxide are achieved by choosing natural gas over fuel oil where possible.

**Treatment Technologies**

ESPs are the preferred choice for removing particulates, although fabric filters are also used. Dry scrubbing using calcium hydroxide is used to reduce sulfur dioxide, hydrogen fluoride, and hydrogen chloride. Secondary measures for $NO_x$ control include selective catalytic reduction

(SCR), selective noncatalytic reduction (SNCR), and certain proprietary processes such as the Pilkington 3R process.

## Emissions Guidelines

Emissions levels for the design and operation of each project must be established through the environmental assessment (EA) process on the basis of country legislation and the *Pollution Prevention and Abatement Handbook,* as applied to local conditions. The emissions levels selected must be justified in the EA and acceptable to the World Bank Group.

The guidelines given below present emissions levels normally acceptable to the World Bank Group in making decisions regarding provision of World Bank Group assistance. Any deviations from these levels must be described in the World Bank Group project documentation. The emissions levels given here can be consistently achieved by well-designed, well-operated, and well-maintained pollution control systems.

The guidelines are expressed as concentrations to facilitate monitoring. Dilution of air emissions or effluents to achieve these guidelines is unacceptable.

All of the maximum levels should be achieved for at least 95% of the time that the plant or unit is operating, to be calculated as a proportion of annual operating hours.

### Air Emissions

The air emissions presented in Table 1 should be achieved.

### Liquid Effluents

The effluent levels presented in Table 2 should be achieved.

### Ambient Noise

Noise abatement measures should achieve either the levels given below or a maximum increase in background levels of 3 decibels (measured on the A scale) [dB(A)]. Measurements are to be taken

## Table 1. Air Emissions from Glass Manufacturing

*(milligrams per normal cubic meter)*

| Parameter | Maximum value |
|---|---|
| Nitrogen oxides | 1,000 (up to 2,000 may be acceptable, depending on furnace technology and if justified in the EA) |
| Sulfur oxides | |
| Gas fired | 700 |
| Oil fired | 1,800 |
| Particulates | 50 (20 where toxic metals are present) |
| Lead and cadmium (total) | 5 |
| Arsenic | 1 |
| Total of other heavy metals | 5 |
| Fluoride | 5 |
| Hydrogen chloride | 50 |

## Table 2. Effluents from Glass Manufacturing

*(milligrams per liter, except for pH)*

| Parameter | Maximum value |
|---|---|
| pH | 6–9 |
| TSS | 50 |
| COD | 150 |
| Oil and grease | 10 |
| Lead | 0.1 |
| Arsenic | 0.1 |
| Antimony | 0.5 |
| Fluorides | 20 |
| Total metals | 10 |

*Note:* Effluent requirements are for direct discharge to surface waters.

at noise receptors located outside the project property boundary.

| | Maximum allowable log equivalent (hourly measurements), in dB(A) | |
|---|---|---|
| Receptor | Day (07:00–22:00) | Night (22:00–07:00) |
| Residential, institutional, educational | 55 | 45 |
| Industrial, commercial | 70 | 70 |

## Monitoring and Reporting

Frequent sampling may be required during start-up and upset conditions. Once a record of consistent performance has been established, sampling for the parameters listed in this document should be as described below.

Opacity should be monitored continuously. The maximum opacity level should be set to correspond to 50 mg/Nm$^3$. Other air emissions parameters should be measured annually. Liquid effluents should be continuously monitored for pH, and other parameters should be tested weekly.

Monitoring data should be analyzed and reviewed at regular intervals and compared with the operating standards so that any necessary corrective actions can be taken. Records of monitoring results should be kept in an acceptable format. The results should be reported to the responsible authorities and relevant parties, as required.

## Key Issues

The key production and control practices that will lead to compliance with emissions requirements can be summarized as follows:

- Consider using oxyfuel-fired furnaces for specialty glass manufacturing.
- Use low-NO$_x$ burners, staged firing, and flue gas recirculation.
- Consider natural gas rather than oil as the fuel of choice.
- Select raw materials to minimize emissions of fluorides and other pollutants such as chlorides and sulfates.
- Maximize water reuse.
- For reductions in particulate emissions, pelletize raw materials, enclose conveyors, reduce melt temperatures, and blanket the melt surface with raw material.

## Sources

Bounicore, Anthony J., and Wayne T. Davis, eds. 1992. *Air Pollution Engineering Manual.* New York: Van Nostrand Reinhold.

Economopoulos, Alexander P. 1993. *Assessment of Sources of Air, Water, and Land Pollution: A Guide to Rapid Source Inventory Techniques and Their Use in Formulating Environmental Control Strategies.* Part 1: *Rapid Inventory Techniques in Environmental Pollution.* Geneva, World Health Organization.

Sittig, Marshall. 1975. *Pollution Control in the Asbestos, Cement, Glass, and Allied Mineral Industries.* Park Ridge, N.J.: Noyes Data Corporation.

World Bank. 1996. "Pollution Prevention and Abatement: Glass Manufacturing Plants." Draft Technical Background Document. Environment Department, Washington, D.C.

# Industrial Estates

## Industrial Estate Development

Industrial estates are specific areas zoned for industrial activity in which infrastructure such as roads, power, and other utility services is provided to facilitate the growth of industries and to minimize impacts on the environment. The infrastructure may include effluent treatment; solid and toxic waste collection, treatment, and disposal; air pollution and effluent monitoring; technical services on pollution prevention; quality management (quality assurance and control); and laboratory services. There should be appropriate emergency preparedness and prevention plans and liaison with local fire and emergency services. This document covers the management of activities on an established estate.

Selection of sites for industrial estates should take into account social and environmental issues, as well as economic considerations. The key document would normally be an industrial estate development plan covering issues such as:

- Details of the location
- Mix of industries on the site (to ensure that the industries are compatible—for example, that neighbors of food processing plants do not pose a risk of contaminating food products)
- Layout and design
- Transport services
- Fuel storage
- Air quality management
- Water quality management, including the provision of common effluent treatment facilities, as required
- Solid waste management, including recycling
- Management of hazardous materials and hazardous wastes
- Noise control

- Occupational health and safety
- Hazard and emergency planning and response.

Industrial estates should maintain safe distances from residential areas (for example, 100 meters for small industries with minimal environmental hazard and at least 1 kilometer for very polluting industries). Definition of institutional responsibilities is an essential component of a development plan. The key environmental issues to be addressed in the development plan should be identified through an environmental assessment process.

### Pretreatment and Common Treatment

A significant environmental benefit of industrial estates is the opportunity to take advantage of economies of scale by providing common effluent and waste management facilities. Individual units. however, must still meet specific discharge or pretreatment guidelines.

The guidelines at a particular estate will depend on the industry mix and the type and scale of common facilities. The guidelines for each plant should be described in detail as part of the plant's contract with the estate.

## Target Pollution Loads

The following measures have been recommended for industries on industrial estates:

- Encourage the use of vapor recovery systems, where applicable, to control losses of volatile organic compounds (VOCs) from storage tanks and achieve 90–100% recovery.
- Encourage the use of low–nitrogen oxide ($NO_x$) burners in combustion systems. Plants should

be encouraged to use fuel with low sulfur content (or an emissions level of 2,000 milligrams per normal cubic meter, mg/Nm³) for sulfur oxides, $SO_x$). A sulfur recovery system may be feasible for large facilities when the hydrogen sulfide concentration in the tail gases exceeds 230 mg/Nm³.

- Institute spill prevention and control measures. Liquid fuels and chemicals should be stored in areas where there are provisions for containment of spills.
- Encourage the segregation of stormwater from process water. Cooling water should generally be recycled. Sewage effluent should be segregated from wastewaters containing heavy metals.

## Emissions Guidelines

Emissions levels for the design and operation of each project must be established through the environmental assessment (EA) process on the basis of country legislation and the *Pollution Prevention and Abatement Handbook,* as applied to local conditions. The emissions levels selected must be justified in the EA and acceptable to the World Bank Group.

The guidelines given below present emissions levels normally acceptable to the World Bank Group in making decisions regarding provision of World Bank Group assistance. Any deviations from these levels must be described in the World Bank Group project documentation. The emissions levels given here can be consistently achieved by well-designed, well-operated, and well-maintained pollution control systems.

The guidelines are expressed as concentrations to facilitate monitoring. Dilution of air emissions or effluents to achieve these guidelines is unacceptable.

All of the maximum levels should be achieved for at least 95% of the time that the plant or unit is operating, to be calculated as a proportion of annual operating hours.

### Air Emissions

For individual or common stacks, the maximum emissions levels presented in Table 1 should be achieved.

## Table 1. Air Emissions from Facilities in Industrial Estates

*(milligrams per normal cubic meter)*

| Parameter | Maximum value |
|---|---|
| PMª | 50 for large facilities<br>Up to 150 for small facilities with energy consumption of less than 10 gigajoules per hour (fuel used) |
| Nitrogen oxides | 750 (solid fuels)<br>460 (liquid fuels)<br>320 (gaseous fuels) |
| Sulfur oxides | 2,000 |
| Hydrogen sulfide | 15 |

a. For facilities emitting significant quantities of toxic metals, the emissions limit should be 20 mg/Nm³.

### Liquid Effluents

The maximum effluent levels presented in Table 2 should be achieved by discharges from common effluent treatment units:

Common effluent treatment units should be designed to handle the characteristics and load-

## Table 2. Effluents from Industrial Estates

*(milligrams per liter, except for pH and temperature)*

| Parameter | Maximum value |
|---|---|
| pH | 6–9 |
| BOD | 50 |
| COD | 250 |
| TSS | 50 (20 if toxic metals are present at significant levels) |
| Oil and grease | 10 |
| Cadmium | 0.1 |
| Chromium | |
|    Hexavalent | 0.1 |
|    Total | 0.5 |
| Copper | 0.5 |
| Lead | 0.1 |
| Nickel | 0.5 |
| Zinc | 2 |
| Phenol | 0.5 |
| AOX | 1 |
| Benzene | 0.05 |
| Benzo(a)pyrene | 0.05 |
| Sulfide | 1 |
| Temperature increase | ≤ 3°Cª |

a. The effluent should result in a temperature increase of no more than 3° C at the edge of the zone where initial mixing and dilution take place. Where the zone is not defined, use 100 meters from the point of discharge.

ing of wastewaters generated from the industrial estate. In some cases, different types of treatment units will be needed to handle different types of wastewaters. (For example, chemical precipitation units may be required to handle toxic metallic wastewaters, and biological treatment units for handling organic wastewaters.)

*Solid Wastes and Sludges*

Where possible, generation of sludges should be minimized. Sludges must be treated, and if toxic metals are present, the sludges must be stabilized.

*Ambient Noise*

Noise abatement measures should achieve either the levels given below or a maximum increase in background levels of 3 decibels (measured on the A scale) [dB(A)]. Measurements are to be taken at noise receptors located outside the project property boundary.

| Receptor | Maximum allowable log equivalent (hourly measurements), in dB(A) | |
|---|---|---|
| | Day (07:00–22:00) | Night (22:00–07:00) |
| Residential, institutional, educational | 55 | 45 |
| Industrial, commercial | 70 | 70 |

## Monitoring and Reporting

Frequent sampling should be recommended to plants during start-up and upset conditions. Once a record of consistent performance has been established, sampling for the parameters listed in this document can be as described below.

Daily monitoring of particulate emissions from stacks, using an opacity meter (with a target level of less than 10%), is recommended. Monthly monitoring of the sulfur content of the fuels used in combustion sources is also recommended.

Daily monitoring of liquid effluents is recommended for all the applicable parameters cited above, except for aromatics, metals, and sulfides, which should be monitored at least monthly.

Industrial estates should encourage units to analyze monitoring data, review it at regular intervals, and compare it with the operating standards so that any necessary corrective actions can be taken. Records of monitoring results should be kept in an acceptable format. The results should be reported to the responsible authorities and relevant parties, as required. Industrial estates should maintain a record of accidental releases of pollutants to the environment and should take appropriate corrective action to be better prepared for future occurrences. Where feasible, industrial estates should educate the industrial units on ways to mitigate environmental problems.

## Key Issues

Good environmental practices for industrial estates can be summarized as follows:

- Encourage the use of vapor recovery systems to reduce VOC emissions.
- Encourage the use of sulfur recovery systems where considered feasible.
- Encourage the use of low-$NO_x$ burners.
- Encourage the recovery and recycle of oily wastes.
- Encourage the regeneration and reuse of spent catalysts and solvents.
- Encourage the recycling of cooling water and the reuse of wastewaters.
- Institute segregation of stormwater from process wastewater.
- Encourage the use of nonchrome additives to cooling water.
- Institute spill prevention and control measures.
- Include properly designed storage facilities for hazardous chemicals and wastes, including provision for containment of contaminated water in case of fire.

## Source

World Bank. 1995. "Industrial Pollution Prevention and Abatement: Industrial Estates." Draft Technical Background Document. Environment Department, Washington, D.C.

# Iron and Steel Manufacturing

## Industry Description and Practices

Steel is manufactured by the chemical reduction of iron ore, using an integrated steel manufacturing process or a direct reduction process. In the conventional integrated steel manufacturing process, the iron from the blast furnace is converted to steel in a basic oxygen furnace (BOF). Steel can also be made in an electric arc furnace (EAF) from scrap steel and, in some cases, from direct reduced iron. BOF is typically used for high-tonnage production of carbon steels, while the EAF is used to produce carbon steels and low-tonnage specialty steels. An emerging technology, direct steel manufacturing, produces steel directly from iron ore. This document deals only with integrated iron and steel manufacturing; that on Mini Steel Mills addresses the electric arc steel process and steel finishing processes. Steel manufacturing and finishing processes discussed in that document are also employed in integrated steel plants. See also Coke Manufacturing.

In the BOF process, coke making and iron making precede steel making; these steps are not necessary with an EAF. Pig iron is manufactured from sintered, pelletized, or lump iron ores using coke and limestone in a blast furnace. It is then fed to a BOF in molten form along with scrap metal, fluxes, alloys, and high-purity oxygen to manufacture steel. In some integrated steel mills, sintering (heating without melting) is used to agglomerate fines and so recycle iron-rich material such as mill scale.

## Waste Characteristics

Sintering operations can emit significant dust levels of about 20 kilograms per metric ton (kg/t) of steel. Pelletizing operations can emit dust levels of about 15 kg/t of steel. Air emissions from pig iron manufacturing in a blast furnace include particulate matter (PM), ranging from less than 10 kg/t of steel manufactured to 40 kg/t; sulfur oxides ($SO_x$), mostly from sintering or pelletizing operations (1.5 kg/t of steel); nitrogen oxides ($NO_x$), mainly from sintering and heating (1.2 kg/t of steel); hydrocarbons; carbon monoxide; in some cases dioxins (mostly from sintering operations); and hydrogen fluoride.

Air emissions from steel manufacturing using the BOF may include PM (ranging from less than 15 kg/t to 30 kg/t of steel). For closed systems, emissions come from the desulfurization step between the blast furnace and the BOF; the particulate matter emissions are about 10 kg/t of steel.

In the conventional process without recirculation, wastewaters, including those from cooling operations, are generated at an average rate of 80 cubic meters per metric ton ($m^3/t$) of steel manufactured. Major pollutants present in untreated wastewaters generated from pig iron manufacture include total organic carbon (typically 100–200 milligrams per liter, mg/l); total suspended solids (7,000 mg/l, 137 kg/t); dissolved solids; cyanide (15 mg/l); fluoride (1,000 mg/l); chemical oxygen demand, or COD (500 mg/l); and zinc (35 mg/l).

Major pollutants in wastewaters generated from steel manufacturing using the BOF include total suspended solids (up to 4,000 mg/l, 1030 kg/t), lead (8 mg/l), chromium (5 mg/l), cadmium (0.4 mg/l), zinc (14 mg/l), fluoride (20 mg/l), and oil and grease. Mill scale may amount to 33 kg/t. The process generates effluents with high temperatures.

Process solid waste from the conventional process, including furnace slag and collected dust, is generated at an average rate ranging from 300 kg/t of steel manufactured to 500 kg/t, of which 30 kg may be considered hazardous depending on the concentration of heavy metals present. Approximately, 65% of BOF slag from steel manufacturing can be recycled in various industries such as building materials and, in some cases, mineral wool.

## Pollution Prevention and Control

Where technically and economically feasible, direct reduction of iron ore for the manufacture of iron and steel is preferred because it does not require coke manufacturing and has fewer environmental impacts. Wherever feasible, pelletizing should be given preferences over sintering for the agglomeration of iron ore. The following pollution prevention measures should be considered.

### Pig Iron Manufacturing

- Improve blast furnace efficiency by using coal and other fuels (such as oil or gas) for heating instead of coke, thereby minimizing air emissions.
- Recover the thermal energy in the gas from the blast furnace before using it as a fuel. Increase fuel efficiency and reduce emissions by improving blast furnace charge distribution.
- Improve productivity by screening the charge and using better taphole practices.
- Reduce dust emissions at furnaces by covering iron runners when tapping the blast furnace and by using nitrogen blankets during tapping.
- Use pneumatic transport, enclosed conveyor belts, or self-closing conveyor belts, as well as wind barriers and other dust suppression measures, to reduce the formation of fugitive dust.
- Use low-$NO_x$ burners to reduce $NO_x$ emissions from burning fuel in ancillary operations.
- Recycle iron-rich materials such as iron ore fines, pollution control dust, and scale in a sinter plant.
- Recover energy from sinter coolers and exhaust gases.
- Use dry $SO_x$ removal systems such as caron absorption for sinter plants or lime spraying in flue gases.

### Steel Manufacturing

- Use dry dust collection and removal systems to avoid the generation of wastewater. Recycle collected dust.
- Use BOF gas as fuel.
- Use enclosures for BOF.
- Use a continuous process for casting steel to reduce energy consumption.

### Other

Use blast furnace slag in construction materials. Slag containing free lime can be used in iron making.

## Target Pollution Loads

The recommended pollution prevention and control measures can achieve the following target levels.

### Liquid Effluents

Over 90% of the wastewater generated can be reused. Discharged wastewaters should in all cases be less than 5 m³/t of steel manufactured and preferably less than 1 m³/t.

### Solid Wastes

Blast furnace slag should normally be generated at a rate of less than 320 kg/t of iron, with a target of 180 kg/t. The generation rate, however, depends on the impurities in the feed materials. Slag generation rates from the BOF should be between 50 and 120 kg/t of steel manufactured, but this will depend on the impurity content of feed materials. Zinc recovery may be feasible for collected dust.

## Treatment Technologies

### Air Emissions

Air emission control technologies for the removal of particulate matter include scrubbers (or semidry systems), baghouses, and electrostatic precipitators (ESPs). The latter two technologies can achieve 99.9% removal efficiencies for particulate matter and the associated toxic metals: chromium (0.8 milligrams per normal cubic meter, mg/Nm³), cadmium (0.08 mg/Nm³), lead (0.02 mg/Nm³), and nickel (0.3 mg/Nm³).

Sulfur oxides are removed in desulfurization plants, with a 90% or better removal efficiency. However, the use of low-sulfur fuels and ores may be more cost-effective.

The acceptable levels of nitrogen oxides can be achieved by using low-$NO_x$ burners and other combustion modifications.

For iron and steel manufacturing, the emissions levels presented in Table 1 should be achieved.

### Wastewater Treatment

Wastewater treatment systems typically include sedimentation to remove suspended solids, physical or chemical treatment such as pH adjustment to precipitate heavy metals, and filtration.

The target levels presented in Table 2 can be achieved for steel-making processes.

### Solid Waste Treatment

Solid wastes containing heavy metals may have to be stabilized, using chemical agents, before disposal.

## Emissions Guidelines

Emissions levels for the design and operation of each project must be established through the en-

### Table 1. Load Targets per Unit of Production, Iron and Steel Manufacturing

| Parameter | Maximum value |
|---|---|
| $PM_{10}$ | 100 g/t of product (blast furnace, basic oxygen furnace); 300 g/t from sintering process |
| Sulfur oxides | For sintering: 1,200 g/t; 500 mg/m³ |
| Nitrogen oxides | For pelletizing plants: 500 g/t; 250–750 mg/Nm³; for sintering plants: 750 mg/Nm³ |
| Fluoride | 1.5 g/t; 5 mg/Nm³ |

### Table 2. Target Load per Unit of Production, Steel Manufacturing
*(emissions per metric ton of product)*

| Parameter | Blast furnace | Basic oxygen furnace |
|---|---|---|
| Wastewater | 0.1 m³ | 0.5 m³ |
| Zinc | 0.6 g | 3 g |
| Lead | 0.15 g | 0.75 g |
| Cadmium | 0.08 g | n.a. |

n.a. Not applicable.

vironmental assessment (EA) process on the basis of country legislation and the *Pollution Prevention and Abatement Handbook,* as applied to local conditions. The emissions levels selected must be justified in the EA and acceptable to the World Bank Group.

The guidelines given below present emissions levels normally acceptable to the World Bank Group in making decisions regarding provision of World Bank Group assistance. Any deviations from these levels must be described in the World Bank Group project documentation. The emissions levels given here can be consistently achieved by well-designed, well-operated, and well-maintained pollution control systems.

The guidelines are expressed as concentrations to facilitate monitoring. Dilution of air emissions or effluents to achieve these guidelines is unacceptable.

All of the maximum levels should be achieved for at least 95% of the time that the plant or unit is operating, to be calculated as a proportion of annual operating hours.

### Air Emissions

For integrated iron and steel manufacturing plants, the emissions levels presented in Table 3 should be achieved.

### Liquid Effluents

The effluent levels presented in Table 4 should be achieved.

## Table 3. Air Emissions from Iron and Steel Manufacturing

*(milligrams per normal cubic meter)*

| Parameter | Maximum value |
| --- | --- |
| PM | 50 |
| Sulfur oxides | 500 (sintering) |
| Nitrogen oxides | 750 |
| Fluorides | 5 |

### Sludges

Sludges should be disposed of in a secure land-fill after stabilization of heavy metals to ensure that heavy metal concentration in the leachates do not exceed the levels presented for liquid effluents.

### Ambient Noise

Noise abatement measures should achieve either the levels given below or a maximum increase in background levels of 3 decibels (measured on the A scale) [dB(A)]. Measurements are to be taken at noise receptors located outside the project property boundary.

| Receptor | Maximum allowable log equivalent (hourly measurements), in dB(A) | |
| --- | --- | --- |
| | Day (07:00–22:00) | Night (22:00–07:00) |
| Residential, institutional, educational | 55 | 45 |
| Industrial, commercial | 70 | 70 |

## Table 4. Effluents from Iron and Steel Manufacturing

*(milligrams per liter, except pH and temperature)*

| Parameter | Maximum value |
| --- | --- |
| pH | 6–9 |
| TSS | 50 |
| Oil and grease | 10 |
| COD | 250 |
| Phenol | 0.5 |
| Cadmium | 0.1 |
| Chromium (total) | 0.5 |
| Lead | 0.2 |
| Mercury | 0.01 |
| Zinc | 2 |
| Cyanide | |
| Free | 0.1 |
| Total | 1 |
| Temperature increase | ≤ 3°C[a] |

*Note:* Effluent requirements are for direct discharge to surface waters.
a. The effluent should result in a temperature increase of no more than 3° C at the edge of the zone where initial mixing and dilution take place. Where the zone is not defined, use 100 meters from the point of discharge.

## Monitoring and Reporting

Air emissions should be monitored continuously after the air pollution control device for particulate matter (or alternatively an opacity level of less than 10%) and annually for sulfur oxides, nitrogen oxides (with regular monitoring of sulfur in the ores), and fluoride. Wastewater discharges should be monitored daily for the listed parameters, except for metals, which should be monitored at least on a quarterly basis. Frequent sampling may be required during start-up and upset conditions.

Monitoring data should be analyzed and reviewed at regular intervals and compared with the operating standards so that any necessary corrective actions can be taken. Baseline data on fugitive PM emissions should be collected and used for comparison with future emissions estimates, which should be performed every three years based on samples collected. Records of monitoring results should be kept in an acceptable format. The results should be reported to the responsible authorities and relevant parties, as required.

## Key Issues

The key production and control practices that will lead to compliance with emissions guidelines are summarized here.

- Prefer the direct steel manufacturing process where technically and economically feasible.
- Use pelletized feed instead of sintered feed where appropriate.

- Replace a portion of the coke used in the blast furnace by injecting pulverized coal or by using natural gas or oil.
- Achieve high-energy efficiency by using blast furnace and basic oxygen furnace off-gas as fuels.
- Implement measures (such as encapsulation) to reduce the formation of dust, including iron oxide dust; where possible, recycle collected dust to a sintering plant.
- Recirculate wastewaters. Use dry air pollution control systems where feasible. Otherwise, treat wastewaters.
- Use slag in construction materials to the extent feasible.

## Sources

British Steel Consultants. 1993. "Research Study, International Steel Industry." Prepared for the International Finance Corporation, Washington, D.C.

The Netherlands. 1991. "Progress Report on the Study of the Primary Iron and Steel Industry." Third Meeting of the Working Group on Industrial Sectors, Stockholm, January 22–24.

Paris Commission. 1991. *Secondary Iron and Steel Production: An Overview of Technologies and Emission Standards Used in the* PARCOM *Countries.*

World Bank. 1996. "Pollution Prevention and Abatement: Iron and Steel Manufacturing". Draft Technical Background Document. Environment Department, Washington, D.C.

# Lead and Zinc Smelting

## Industry Description and Practices

Lead and zinc can be produced pyrometallurgically or hydrometallurgically, depending on the type of ore used as a charge. In the pyrometallurgical process, ore concentrate containing lead, zinc, or both is fed, in some cases after sintering, into a primary smelter. Lead concentrations can be 50–70%, and the sulfur content of sulfidic ores is in the range of 15–20%. Zinc concentration is in the range of 40–60%, with sulfur content in sulfidic ores in the range of 26–34%. Ores with a mixture of lead and zinc concentrate usually have lower respective metal concentrations. During sintering, a blast of hot air or oxygen is used to oxidize the sulfur present in the feed to sulfur dioxide ($SO_2$). Blast furnaces are used in conventional processes for reduction and refining of lead compounds to produce lead. Modern direct smelting processes include QSL, Kivcet, AUSMELT, and TBRC.

### Primary Lead Processing

The conventional pyrometallurgical primary lead production process consists of four steps: sintering, smelting, drossing, and refining. A feedstock made up mainly of lead concentrate is fed into a sintering machine. Other raw materials may be added, including iron, silica, limestone flux, coke, soda, ash, pyrite, zinc, caustic, and particulates gathered from pollution control devices. The sintering feed, along with coke, is fed into a blast furnace for reducing, where the carbon also acts as a fuel and smelts the lead-containing materials. The molten lead flows to the bottom of the furnace, where four layers form: "speiss" (the lightest material, basically arsenic and antimony), "matte" (copper sulfide and other metal sulfides), blast furnace slag (primarily silicates), and lead bullion (98% by weight). All layers are then drained off. The speiss and matte are sold to copper smelters for recovery of copper and precious metals. The blast furnace slag, which contains zinc, iron, silica, and lime, is stored in piles and is partially recycled. Sulfur oxide emissions are generated in blast furnaces from small quantities of residual lead sulfide and lead sulfates in the sinter feed.

Rough lead bullion from the blast furnace usually requires preliminary treatment in kettles before undergoing refining operations. During drossing, the bullion is agitated in a drossing kettle and cooled to just above its freezing point, 370°–425°C (700°–800°F). A dross composed of lead oxide, along with copper, antimony, and other elements, floats to the top and solidifies above the molten lead. The dross is removed and is fed into a dross furnace for recovery of the nonlead mineral values.

The lead bullion is refined using pyrometallurgical methods to remove any remaining nonlead materials (e.g., gold, silver, bismuth, zinc, and metal oxides such as oxides of antimony, arsenic, tin, and copper). The lead is refined in a cast-iron kettle in five stages. First, antimony, tin, and arsenic are removed. Next, gold and silver are removed by adding zinc. The lead is then refined by vacuum removal of zinc. Refining continues with the addition of calcium and magnesium, which combine with bismuth to form an insoluble compound that is skimmed from the kettle. In the final step, caustic soda, nitrates, or both may be added to remove any remaining traces of metal impurities. The refined lead will have a purity of 99.90–99.99%. It may be mixed with other metals to form alloys, or it may be directly cast into shapes.

332

*Secondary Lead Processing*

The secondary production of lead begins with the recovery of old scrap from worn-out, damaged, or obsolete products and with new scrap. The chief source of old scrap is lead-acid batteries; other sources include cable coverings, pipe, sheet, and other lead-bearing metals. Solder, a tin-based alloy, may be recovered from the processing of circuit boards for use as lead charge.

Prior to smelting, batteries are usually broken up and sorted into their constituent products. Fractions of cleaned plastic (such as polypropylene) case are recycled into battery cases or other products. The dilute sulfuric acid is either neutralized for disposal or recycled to the local acid market. One of the three main smelting processes is then used to reduce the lead fractions and produce lead bullion.

Most domestic battery scrap is processed in blast furnaces, rotary furnaces, or reverberatory furnaces. A reverberatory furnace is more suitable for processing fine particles and may be operated in conjunction with a blast furnace.

Blast furnaces produce hard lead from charges containing siliceous slag from previous runs (about 4.5% of the charge), scrap iron (about 4.5%), limestone (about 3%), and coke (about 5.5%). The remaining 82.5% of the charge is made up of oxides, pot furnace refining drosses, and reverberatory slag. The proportions of rerun slags, limestone, and coke vary but can run as high as 8% for slags, 10% for limestone, and 8% for coke. The processing capacity of the blast furnace ranges from 20 to 80 metric tons per day (tpd).

Newer secondary recovery plants use lead paste desulfurization to reduce sulfur dioxide emissions and generation of waste sludge during smelting. Battery paste containing lead sulfate and lead oxide is desulfurized with soda ash, yielding market-grade sodium sulfate as a by-product. The desulfurized paste is processed in a reverberatory furnace, and the lead carbonate product may then be treated in a short rotary furnace. The battery grids and posts are processed separately in a rotary smelter.

*Zinc Manufacturing*

In the most common hydrometallurgical process for zinc manufacturing, the ore is leached with sulfuric acid to extract the lead/zinc. These processes can operate at atmospheric pressure or as pressure leach circuits. Lead/zinc is recovered from solution by electrowinning, a process similar to electrolytic refining. The process most commonly used for low-grade deposits is heap leaching. Imperial smelting is also used for zinc ores.

**Waste Characteristics**

The principal air pollutants emitted from the processes are particulate matter and sulfur dioxide ($SO_2$). Fugitive emissions occur at furnace openings and from launders, casting molds, and ladles carrying molten materials, which release sulfur dioxide and volatile substances into the working environment. Additional fugitive particulate emissions occur from materials handling and transport of ores and concentrates. Some vapors are produced in hydrometallurgy and in various refining processes. The principal constituents of the particulate matter are lead/zinc and iron oxides, but oxides of metals such as arsenic, antimony, cadmium, copper, and mercury are also present, along with metallic sulfates. Dust from raw materials handling contains metals, mainly in sulfidic form, although chlorides, fluorides, and metals in other chemical forms may be present. Off-gases contain fine dust particles and volatile impurities such as arsenic, fluorine, and mercury. Air emissions for processes with few controls may be of the order of 30 kilograms lead or zinc per metric ton (kg/t) of lead or zinc produced. The presence of metals in vapor form is dependent on temperature. Leaching processes will generate acid vapors, while refining processes result in products of incomplete combustion (PICs). Emissions of arsine, chlorine, and hydrogen chloride vapors and acid mists are associated with electrorefining.

Wastewaters are generated by wet air scrubbers and cooling water. Scrubber effluents may contain lead/zinc, arsenic, and other metals. In the electrolytic refining process, by-products such as gold and silver are collected as slimes and are subsequently recovered. Sources of wastewater include spent electrolytic baths, slimes recovery, spent acid from hydrometallurgy processes, cooling water, air scrubbers, washdowns, and stormwater. Pollutants include dissolved and suspended solids, metals, and oil and grease.

The larger proportion of the solid waste is discarded slag from the smelter. Discard slag may contain 0.5–0.7% lead/zinc and is frequently used as fill or for sandblasting. Slags with higher lead/zinc) content—say, 15% zinc—can be sent for metals recovery. Leaching processes produce residues, while effluent treatment results in sludges that require appropriate disposal. The smelting process typically produces less than 3 tons of solid waste per ton of lead/zinc produced.

## Pollution Prevention and Control

The most effective pollution prevention option is to choose a process that entails lower energy usage and lower emissions. Modern flash-smelting processes save energy, compared with the conventional sintering and blast furnace process. Process gas streams containing over 5% sulfur dioxide are usually used to manufacture sulfuric acid. The smelting furnace will generate gas streams with $SO_2$ concentrations ranging from 0.5% to 10%, depending on the method used. It is important, therefore, to select a process that uses oxygen-enriched air or pure oxygen. The aim is to save energy and raise the $SO_2$ content of the process gas stream by reducing the total volume of the stream, thus permitting efficient fixation of sulfur dioxide. Processes should be operated to maximize the concentration of the sulfur dioxide An added benefit is the reduction (or elimination) of nitrogen oxides ($NO_x$).

- Use doghouse enclosures where appropriate; use hoods to collect fugitive emissions.
- Mix strong acidic gases with weak ones to facilitate production of sulfuric acid from sulfur oxides, thereby avoiding the release of weak acidic gases.
- Maximize the recovery of sulfur by operating the furnaces to increase the $SO_2$ content of the flue gas and by providing efficient sulfur conversion. Use a double-contact, double-absorption process.
- Desulfurize paste with caustic soda or soda ash to reduce $SO_2$ emissions.
- Use energy-efficient measures such as waste heat recovery from process gases to reduce fuel usage and associated emissions.

- Recover acid, plastics, and other materials when handling battery scrap in secondary lead production.
- Recycle condensates, rainwater, and excess process water for washing, for dust control, for gas scrubbing, and for other process applications where water quality is not of particular concern.
- Give preference to natural gas over heavy fuel oil for use as fuel and to coke with lower sulfur content.
- Use low-$NO_x$ burners.
- Use suspension or fluidized bed roasters, where appropriate, to achieve high $SO_2$ concentrations when roasting zinc sulfides.
- Recover and reuse iron-bearing residues from zinc production for use in the steel or construction industries.
- Give preference to fabric filters over wet scrubbers or wet electrostatic precipitators (ESPs) for dust control.

Good housekeeping practices are key to minimizing losses and preventing fugitive emissions. Losses and emissions are minimized by enclosed buildings, covered conveyors and transfer points, and dust collection equipment. Yards should be paved and runoff water routed to settling ponds.

## Pollution Reduction Targets

Implementation of cleaner production processes and pollution prevention measures can yield both economic and environmental benefits. The following production-related targets can be achieved by measures such as those described above. The figures relate to the production processes before the addition of pollution control measures.

The target pollutant load for lead and zinc smelting operations for particulate matter is 0.5 kg/t of concentrated ore processed. ESPs are used to recover dust. Pollutant load factors for lead in air emissions are 0.08 kg/t from roasting, 0.08 kg/t from smelting, and 0.13 kg/t from refining.

A double-contact, double-absorption plant should emit no more than 2 kg of sulfur dioxide per ton of sulfuric acid produced, based on a conversion efficiency of 99.7%. Sulfur dioxide should be recovered to produce sulfuric acid, thus yielding a marketable product and reducing $SO_2$ emissions. Fugitive emissions are controlled by using enclosed conveyors.

## Treatment Technologies

ESPs and baghouses are used for product recovery and for the control of particulate emissions. Dust that is captured but not recycled will need to be disposed of in a secure landfill or in another acceptable manner.

Arsenic trioxide or pentoxide is in vapor form because of the high gas temperatures and must be condensed by gas cooling so that it can be removed in fabric filters.

Collection and treatment of vent gases by alkali scrubbing may be required when sulfur dioxide is not being recovered in an acid plant.

Effluent treatment of process bleed streams, filter backwash waters, boiler blowdown, and other streams is required to reduce suspended and dissolved solids and heavy metals and to adjust pH. Residues that result from treatment are recycled to other industries such as the construction industry, sent to settling ponds (provided that groundwater and surface water contamination is not a concern), or disposed of in a secure landfill.

Slag should be either landfilled or granulated and sold for use in building materials.

## Emissions Guidelines

Emissions levels for the design and operation of each project must be established through the environmental assessment (EA) process on the basis of country legislation and the *Pollution Prevention and Abatement Handbook,* as applied to local conditions. The emissions levels selected must be justified in the EA and acceptable to the World Bank Group.

The guidelines given below present emissions levels normally acceptable to the World Bank Group in making decisions regarding provision of World Bank Group assistance. Any deviations from these levels must be described in the World Bank Group project documentation. The emissions levels given here can be consistently achieved by well-designed, well-operated, and well-maintained pollution control systems.

The guidelines are expressed as concentrations to facilitate monitoring. Dilution of air emissions or effluents to achieve these guidelines is unac-

ceptable. All of the maximum levels should be achieved for at least 95% of the time that the plant or unit is operating, to be calculated as a proportion of annual operating hours.

### Air Emissions

The air emissions levels presented in Table 1 should be achieved.

The environmental assessment should address the buildup of heavy metals from particulate fallout in the vicinity of the plant over its projected life.

### Liquid Effluents

The effluent emissions levels presented in Table 2 should be achieved.

### Table 1. Emissions from Lead/Zinc Smelting
*(milligrams per normal cubic meter)*

| Parameter | Maximum value |
|---|---|
| Sulfur dioxide | 400 |
| Arsenic | 0.1 |
| Cadmium | 0.05 |
| Copper | 0.5 |
| Lead | 0.5 |
| Mercury | 0.05 |
| Zinc | 1.0 |
| Particulates | 20 |

### Table 2. Effluents from Lead/Zinc Smelting
*(milligrams per liter, except for pH and temperature)*

| Parameter | Maximum value |
|---|---|
| pH | 6–9 |
| TSS | 20 |
| Arsenic | 0.1 |
| Cadmium | 0.1 |
| Copper | 0.5 |
| Iron | 3.5 |
| Lead | 0.1 |
| Mercury | 0.01 |
| Zinc | 2.0 |
| Total metals[a] | 5 |
| Temperature increase | ≤ 3°C[b] |

a. Includes arsenic, beryllium, cadmium chromium, gold, lead, mercury, nickel, selenium, silver, thallium, and vanadium.
b. The effluent should result in a temperature increase of no more than 3° C at the edge of the zone where initial mixing and dilution take place. Where the zone is not defined, use 100 meters from the point of discharge.

*Ambient Noise*

Noise abatement measures should achieve either the levels given below or a maximum increase in background levels of 3 decibels (measured on the A scale) [dB(A)]. Measurements are to be taken at noise receptors located outside the project property boundary.

| Receptor | Maximum allowable log equivalent (hourly measurements), in dB(A) | |
| --- | --- | --- |
| | Day (07:00–22:00) | Night (22:00–07:00) |
| Residential, institutional, educational | 55 | 45 |
| Industrial, commercial | 70 | 70 |

## Monitoring and Reporting

Frequent sampling may be required during start-up and upset conditions. Once a record of consistent performance has been established, sampling for the parameters listed in this document should be as described below.

Air emissions should be monitored continuously for sulfur dioxide and particulate matter. Other air emissions parameters should be monitored monthly. Fugitive emissions should be monitored annually.

Liquid effluents should be monitored daily for pH and total suspended solids and at least weekly for all other parameters.

All solid waste, tailings, and leachates should be monitored for toxic metals. Contamination of groundwater and surface waters should be avoided.

Monitoring data should be analyzed and reviewed at regular intervals and compared with the operating standards so that any necessary corrective actions can be taken. Records of monitoring results should be kept in an acceptable format. The results should be reported to the responsible authorities and relevant parties, as required.

## Key Issues

The key production and control practices that will lead to compliance with emissions requirements can be summarized as follows:

- Give preference to the flash-smelting process where appropriate.
- Choose oxygen enrichment processes that allow higher $SO_2$ concentrations in smelter gases to assist in sulfur recovery; use the double-contact, double-absorption process.
- Improve energy efficiency to reduce fuel usage and associated emissions; use low-$NO_x$ burners; give preference to natural gas as fuel.
- Reduce air emissions of toxic metals to acceptable levels.
- Maximize the recovery of dust and minimize fugitive emissions; use hoods and doghouse enclosures.
- Reduce effluent discharge by maximizing wastewater recycling.
- Avoid contamination of groundwater and surface waters by leaching of toxic metals from tailings, process residues, slag, and other wastes.

## Sources

Bounicore, Anthony J., and Wayne T. Davis, eds. 1992. *Air Pollution Engineering Manual.* New York: Van Nostrand Reinhold.

Environment Canada. 1980. "A Study of Sulphur Containment Technology in the Non-Ferrous Metallurgical Industries." Report EPS 3-AP-79-8. Ottawa.

# Meat Processing and Rendering

## Industry Description and Practices

The meat processing and rendering industry includes the slaughter of animals and fowl, processing of the carcasses into cured, canned, and other meat products, and the rendering of inedible and discarded remains into useful by-products such as lards and oils. A wide range of processes is used. Table 1 provides information on water usage in the industry.

## Waste Characteristics

The meat industry has the potential for generating large quantities of solid wastes and wastewater with a biochemical oxygen demand (BOD) of 600 milligrams per liter (mg/l). BOD can be as high as 8,000 mg/l, or 10–20 kilograms per metric ton (kg/t) of slaughtered animal; and suspended solids levels can be 800 mg/l and higher. In some cases, offensive odors may occur. The amounts of wastewater generated and the pollutant load depend on the kind of meat being processed. For example, the processing of gut has a significant impact on the quantity and quality (as measured by levels of BOD and of chemical oxygen demand, COD) of wastewater generated. The wastewater from a slaughterhouse can contain blood, manure, hair, fat, feathers, and bones. The wastewater may be at a high temperature and may contain organic material and nitrogen, as well as such pathogens as salmonella and shigella bacteria, parasite eggs, and amoebic cysts. Pesticide residues may be present from treatment of animals or their feed. Chloride levels from curing and pickling may be very high—up to 77,000 mg/l. Smoking operations can release toxic organics into air. Rendering is an evaporative process that produces a condensate stream with a foul odor.

All slaughtering wastes (generally, 35% of the animal weight) can be used as by-products or for rendering. The only significant solid waste going for disposal is the manure from animal transport and handling areas.

## Pollution Prevention and Control

Separation of product from wastes at each stage is essential for maximizing product recovery and reducing waste loads. The materials being handled are all putrescible; hence, cleanliness is essential. Water management should achieve the necessary cleanliness without waste. The amounts and strength of wastes can be reduced by good practices such as dry removal of solid wastes and installation of screens on wastewater collection channels.

In-plant measures that can be used to reduce the odor nuisance and the generation of solid and liquid wastes from the production processes include the following:

- Recover and process blood into useful by-products. Allow enough time for blood draining (at least seven minutes).
- Process paunches and intestines and utilize fat and slime.

## Table 1. Typical Water Usage in the Meat Industry

(cubic meters per metric ton of product)

| Process | Water use |
| --- | --- |
| Slaughterhouse | |
| Pigs | 1.5–10 |
| Cattle | 2.5–40 |
| Poultry | 6–30 |
| Meat processing | 2–60 |

- Minimize water consumed in production by, for example, using taps with automatic shutoff, using high water pressure, and improving the process layout.
- Eliminate wet transport (pumping) of wastes (for example, intestines and feathers) to minimize water consumption.
- Reduce the liquid waste load by preventing any solid wastes or concentrated liquids from entering the wastewater stream.
- Cover collection channels in the production area with grids to reduce the amount of solids entering the wastewater.
- Separate cooling water from process water and wastewaters, and recirculate cooling water.
- Implement dry precleaning of equipment and production areas prior to wet cleaning.
- Equip the outlets of wastewater channels with screens and fat traps to recover and reduce the concentration of coarse material and fat in the combined wastewater stream.
- Optimize the use of detergents and disinfectants in washing water.
- Remove manure (from the stockyard and from intestine processing) in solid form.
- Dispose of hair and bones to the rendering plants.
- Reduce air emissions from ham processing through some degree of air recirculation, after filtering.
- Isolate and ventilate all sources of odorous emissions. Oxidants such as nitrates can be added to wastes to reduce odor.

In *rendering plants*, odor is the most important air pollution issue. To reduce odor:

- Minimize the stock of raw material and store it in a cold, closed, well-ventilated place.
- Pasteurize the raw material before processing it in order to halt biological processes that generate odor.
- Install all equipment in closed spaces and operate under partial or total vacuum.
- Keep all working and storage areas clean.

## Target Pollution Loads

Implementation of cleaner production processes and pollution prevention measures can provide both economic and environmental benefits. The

**Table 2. Target Loads for Meat Processing and Rendering**

| Parameter | Maximum level |
|---|---|
| Water used | 3–6 m³/t of slaughtered animal |
| BOD | 10–20 kg/t |
| Total nitrogen | 100–200 mg/l |
| Total phosphorus | 10–20 mg/l |
| Suspended solids | 100–500 mg/l |

production-related targets presented in Table 2 can be achieved by measures such as those described above. The numbers relate to the production processes before the addition of pollution control measures.

## Treatment Technologies

Wastewaters from meat processing are suitable for biological treatment and (except for the very odorous rendering wastewater) could be discharged to a municipal sewer system after flow equalization, if the capacity exists. Sewer authorities usually require pretreatment of the wastewater before it is discharged into the sewer.

Screens and fat traps are the minimum means of pretreatment in any system. Flotation, in some cases aided by chemical addition, may also be carried out to remove suspended solids and emulsified fats, which can be returned to the rendering plant. The choice of an appropriate biological treatment system will be influenced by a number of factors, including wastewater load and the need to minimize odors. Rendering wastewater typically has a very high organic and nitrogen load. Extended aeration is an effective form of treatment, but care must be taken to minimize odors.

Disinfection of the final effluent may be required if high levels of bacteria are detected. Ponding is a simple solution but requires considerable space. Chemical methods, usually based on chlorine compounds, are an alternative.

Biofilters, carbon filters, and scrubbers are used to control odors and air emissions from several processes, including ham processing and rendering. Recycling exhaust gases from smoking may be feasible in cases where operations are not carried out manually and smoke inhalation by workers is not of concern.

## Emissions Guidelines

Emissions levels for the design and operation of each project must be established through the environmental assessment (EA) process on the basis of country legislation and the *Pollution Prevention and Abatement Handbook,* as applied to local conditions. The emissions levels selected must be justified in the EA and acceptable to the World Bank Group.

The guidelines given below present emissions levels normally acceptable to the World Bank Group in making decisions regarding provision of World Bank Group assistance. Any deviations from these levels must be described in the World Bank Group project documentation. The emissions levels given here can be consistently achieved by well-designed, well-operated, and well-maintained pollution control systems.

The guidelines are expressed as concentrations to facilitate monitoring. Dilution of air emissions or effluents to achieve these guidelines is unacceptable.

All of the maximum levels should be achieved at least 95% of the time that the plant or unit is operating, to be calculated as a proportion of annual operating hours.

### Air Emissions

Odor controls should be implemented, where necessary, to minimize odor impacts on nearby residents. Particulate matter emissions of smokehouses should be kept below 150 milligrams per normal cubic meter (mg/Nm³), with a carbon content of less than 50 mg/Nm³.

### Liquid Effluents

The liquid effluent levels presented in Table 3 should be achieved.

### Ambient Noise

Noise abatement measures should achieve either the levels given below or a maximum increase in background levels of 3 decibels (measured on the

**Table 3. Effluents from Meat Processing and Rendering Industry**
*(milligrams per liter, except for pH and bacteria)*

| Parameter | Maximum value |
|---|---|
| pH | 6–9 |
| BOD | 50 |
| COD | 250 |
| TSS | 50 |
| Oil and grease | 10 |
| Nitrogen (total) | 10 |
| Total phosphorus | 5 |
| Coliform bacteria | 400 MPN/100 ml |

*Note:* Effluent requirements are for direct discharge to surface waters. MPN, most probable number.

A scale) [dB(A)]. Measurements are to be taken at noise receptors located outside the project property boundary.

| Receptor | Maximum allowable log equivalent (hourly measurements), in dB(A) | |
|---|---|---|
| | Day (07:00–22:00) | Night (22:00–07:00) |
| Residential, institutional, educational | 55 | 45 |
| Industrial, commercial | 70 | 70 |

## Monitoring and Reporting

Monitoring of the final effluent for the parameters listed in this document should be carried out at least once a month—more frequently. if the flows vary significantly. Effluents should be analyzed for pesticides annually; if pesticides are present above 0.05 mg/l, appropriate corrective actions should be taken. Records of monitoring results should be kept in an acceptable format. The records should be reported to the responsible authorities and relevant parties, as required.

## Key Issues

The key production and control practices that will lead to compliance with emissions guidelines may be summarized as follows:

- Design and operate the production systems to achieve target water consumption levels.
- Separate cooling water from process water.
- Dry-clean production areas before washing, and provide grids and fat traps on collection channels.
- Eliminate wet transport of waste.
- Recover blood and other materials and process into useful by-products.
- Send organic material to the rendering plant.
- Design and operate the rendering plant to minimize odor generation.

## Sources

Economopoulos, Alexander P. 1993. *Assessment of Sources of Air, Water, and Land Pollution: A Guide to Rapid Source Inventory Techniques and their Use in Formulating Environmental Control Strategies*. Part 1: *Rapid Inventory Techniques in Environmental Pollution*. Geneva: World Health Organization.

World Bank. 1996. "Pollution Prevention and Abatement: Meat Processing and Rendering." Draft Technical Background Document. Environment Department, Washington, D.C.

# Mini Steel Mills

## Industry Description and Practices

Mini steel mills normally use the electric arc furnace (EAF) to produce steel from returned steel, scrap, and direct reduced iron. EAF is a batch process with a cycle time of about two to three hours. Since the process uses scrap metal instead of molten iron, coke-making and iron-making operations are eliminated. EAFs can economically serve small, local markets.

Further processing of steel can include continuous casting, hot rolling and forming, cold rolling, wire drawing, coating, and pickling. The *continuous casting* process bypasses several steps of the conventional ingot teeming process by casting steel directly into semifinished shapes. The casting, rolling, and steel finishing processes are also used in iron and steel manufacturing.

Hot steel is transformed in size and shape through a series of *hot rolling* and *forming* steps to manufacture semifinished and finished steel products. The hot rolling process consists of slab-heating (as well as billet and bloom), rolling, and forming operations. Several types of hot forming mills (primary, section, flat, pipe and tube, wire, rebar, and profile) manufacture a variety of steel products.

For the manufacture of a very thin strip or a strip with a high-quality finish, *cold rolling* must follow the hot rolling operations. Lubricants emulsified in water are usually used to achieve high surface quality and to prevent overheating of the product.

*Wire drawing* includes heat treatment of rods, cleaning, and sometimes coating. Water, oil, or lead baths are used for cooling and to impart desired features.

To prepare the steel for cold rolling or drawing, *acid pickling* is performed to chemically remove oxides and scale from the surface of the steel through use of inorganic acid water solutions. Mixed acids (nitric and hydrofluoric) are used for stainless steel pickling; sulfuric or hydrochloric acid is used for other steels. Other methods for removing scale include salt pickling, electrolytic pickling, and blasting; blasting is environmentally desirable, where feasible.

## Waste Characteristics

EAFs produce metal dusts, slag, and gaseous emissions. The primary hazardous components of EAF dust are zinc, lead, and cadmium; nickel and chromium are present when stainless steels are manufactured. The composition of EAF dust can vary greatly, depending on scrap composition and furnace additives. EAF dust usually has a zinc content of more than 15%, with a range of 5–35%. Other metals present in EAF dust include lead (2–7%), cadmium (generally 0.1–0.2% but can be up to 2.5% where stainless steel cases of nickel-cadmium batteries are melted), chromium (up to 15%), and nickel (up to 4%). Generally, an EAF produces 10 kilograms of dust per metric ton (kg/t) of steel, with a range of 5–30 kg/t, depending on factors such as furnace characteristics and scrap quality. Major pollutants present in the air emissions include particulates (1,000 milligrams per normal cubic meter, mg/Nm$^3$), nitrogen oxides from cutting, scarfing, and pickling operations, and acid fumes (3,000 mg/Nm$^3$) from pickling operations. Both nitrogen oxides and acid fumes vary with steel quality.

Mini mills generate up to 80 cubic meters of wastewater per metric ton (m$^3$/t) of steel product. Untreated wastewaters contain high levels of total suspended solids (up to 3,000 milligrams per liter, mg/l), copper (up to 170 mg/l), lead (10 mg/l), total chromium (3,500 mg/l), hexavalent chromium (200 mg/l), nickel (4,600 mg/l), and oil and grease (130 mg/l). Chrome and nickel concentrations result mainly from pickling operations. The characteristics of the wastewater depend on the type of steel, the forming and finishing operations, and the quality of scrap used as feed to the process.

Solid wastes, excluding EAF dust and wastewater treatment sludges, are generated at a rate of 20 kg/t of steel product. Sludges and scale from acid pickling, especially in stainless steel manufacturing, contain heavy metals such as chromium (up to 700 mg/kg), lead (up to 700 mg/kg), and nickel (400 mg/kg). These levels may be even higher for some stainless steels.

## Pollution Prevention and Control

The following pollution prevention measures should be considered:

- Locate EAFs in enclosed buildings.
- Improve feed quality by using selected scrap to reduce the release of pollutants to the environment.
- Use dry dust collection methods such as fabric filters.

Replace ingot teeming with continuous casting. Use continuous casting for semifinished and finished products wherever feasible. In some cases, continuous charging may be feasible and effective for controlling dust emissions.

- Use bottom tapping of EAFs to prevent dust emissions.
- Control water consumption by proper design of spray nozzles and cooling water systems.
- Segregate wastewaters containing lubricating oils from other wastewater streams and remove oil.
- Recycle mill scale to the sinter plant in an integrated steel plant.
- Use acid-free methods (mechanical methods such as blasting) for descaling, where feasible.
- In the pickling process, use countercurrent flow of rinse water; use indirect methods for heating and pickling baths.
- Use closed-loop systems for pickling; regenerate and recover acids from spent pickling liquor using resin bed, retorting, or other regeneration methods such as vacuum crystallization of sulfuric acid baths.

- Use electrochemical methods in combination with pickling to lower acid consumption.
- Reduce nitrogen oxide ($NO_x$) emissions by use of natural gas as fuel, use low-$NO_x$ burners, and use hydrogen peroxide and urea in stainless steel pickling baths.
- Recycle slags and other residuals from manufacturing operations for use in construction and other industries.
- Recover zinc from EAF dust containing more than 15% total zinc; recycle EAF dust to the extent feasible.

## Target Pollution Loads

High water use is associated with cooling. Recycle wastewaters to reduce the discharge rate to less than 5 m³/t of steel produced, including indirect cooling waters.

The recommended pollution prevention measures can achieve the target levels.

## Treatment Technologies

### Air Emissions

Dust emission control technologies include cyclones, baghouses, and electrostatic precipitators (ESPs). Scrubbers are used to control acid mists. Fugitive emissions from charging and tapping of EAFs should be controlled by locating the EAF in an enclosed building or using hoods and by evacuating the dust to dust arrestment equipment to achieve an emissions level of less than 0.25 kg/t.

### Wastewater Treatment

Spent pickle liquor containing hydrochloric acid is treated by spraying it into a roasting chamber and scrubbing the vapors. If hexavalent chrome is present in salt pickling or electrolytic pickling baths, it can be reduced with a sulfide reagent, iron salts, or other reducing agents. The remaining wastewaters are typically treated using oil-water separation flotation, precipitation, chemical flocculation, sedimentation/parallel plate separation/hydrocycloning, and filtration. Methods such as ultrafiltration may be used for oil emulsions. For continuous casting and cold rolling, oil should be less than 5 g/t and total suspended solids less than 10 g/t. For hot rolling, the corresponding values are 10 g/t and 50 g/t, respectively.

## Emissions Guidelines

Emissions levels for the design and operation of each project must be established through the environmental assessment (EA) process on the basis of country legislation and the *Pollution Prevention and Abatement Handbook,* as applied to local conditions. The emissions levels selected must be justified in the EA and acceptable to the World Bank Group.

The guidelines given below present emissions levels normally acceptable to the World Bank Group in making decisions regarding provision of World Bank Group assistance. Any deviations from these levels must be described in the World Bank Group project documentation. The emissions levels given here can be consistently achieved by well-designed, well-operated, and well-maintained pollution control systems.

The guidelines are expressed as concentrations to facilitate monitoring. Dilution of air emissions or effluents to achieve these guidelines is unacceptable.

All of the maximum levels should be achieved for at least 95% of the time that the plant or unit is operating, to be calculated as a proportion of annual operating hours.

### Air Emissions

Air emissions of particulate matter (PM) should be less than 20 mg/Nm³ where toxic metals are present and less than 50 mg/Nm³ in other cases. This would correspond to total dust emissions of less than 1 kg/t of steel. Sulfur oxides should be less than 2,000 mg/Nm³ and nitrogen oxides, less than 750 mg/Nm³.

### Liquid Effluents

For mini steel mills, the effluent levels presented in Table 1 should be achieved.

Sludges from wastewater treatment and steel finishing operations should be disposed of in a secure landfill after chrome reduction and stabilization. Levels of heavy metals in the leachates should be less than those presented for liquid

**Table 1. Effluents from Mini Steel Mills**
*(milligrams per liter, except for pH and temperature)*

| Parameter | Maximum value |
|---|---|
| pH | 6–9 |
| TSS | 50 |
| Oil and grease | 10 |
| Cadmium | 0.1 |
| Chromium | |
|     Hexavalent | 0.1 |
|     Total | 0.5 |
| Copper | 0.5 |
| Lead | 0.1 |
| Nickel | 0.5 |
| Temperature increase | ≤ 3°C[a] |

a. The effluent should result in a temperature increase of no more than 3° C at the edge of the zone where initial mixing and dilution take place. Where the zone is not defined, use 100 meters from the point of discharge.

effluents. Solid wastes such as slag, dust, and scale should be sent for metals recovery or recycled to the extent feasible.

### Ambient Noise

Noise abatement measures should achieve either the levels given below or a maximum increase in background levels of 3 decibels (measured on the A scale) [dB(A)]. Measurements are to be taken at noise receptors located outside the project property boundary.

| Receptor | Maximum allowable log equivalent (hourly measurements), in dB(A) | |
|---|---|---|
| | Day (07:00–22:00) | Night (22:00–07:00) |
| Residential, institutional, educational | 55 | 45 |
| Industrial, commercial | 70 | 70 |

## Monitoring and Reporting

Stack air emissions should be monitored continuously for PM, using an opacity meter (for an opacity level of less than 10%) or a dust detector.

Wastewater discharges should be monitored daily for the parameters listed in Table 1 except for metals, which should be monitored at least weekly or whenever there are process changes.

Monitoring data should be analyzed and reviewed at regular intervals and compared with the operating standards so that any necessary corrective actions can be taken. A baseline data set should be developed for fugitive emissions, and periodic review (once every three years) of such emissions should be performed. Records of monitoring results should be kept in an acceptable format. The results should be reported to the responsible authorities and relevant parties, as required.

## Key Issues

The key production and control practices that will lead to compliance with emissions guidelines can be summarized as follows:

- Replace ingot teeming with continuous casting.
- Locate EAFs in enclosed buildings or install dry dust collection systems such as bag filters.
- Use countercurrent flow of rinse water in acid pickling.
- Regenerate and reuse acid from spent pickle liquor or sell pickle liquor for use as a wastewater treatment reagent.
- Recycle at least 90% of the wastewater.
- Use hydrogen peroxide or urea to reduce nitrogen oxide emissions from nitric and hydrofluoric acid pickling baths.

## Sources

British Steel Consultants. 1993. "Research Study, International Steel Industry." Prepared for the International Finance Corporation, Washington, D.C.

Paris Commission. 1991. *Secondary Iron and Steel Production: An Overview of Technologies and Emission Standards Used in the PARCOM Countries.*

World Bank. 1996 "Pollution Prevention and Abatement: Mini Steel Mills." Draft Technical Background Document. Environment Department, Washington, D.C.

# Mixed Fertilizer Plants

## Industry Description and Practices

Mixed fertilizers contain two or more of the elements nitrogen, phosphorus, and potassium (NPK), which are essential for good plant growth and high crop yields. This document addresses the production of ammonium phosphates (monoammonium phosphate, or MAP, and diammonium phosphate, or DAP), nitrophosphates, potash, and compound fertilizers.

Ammonium phosphates are produced by mixing phosphoric acid and anhydrous ammonia in a reactor to produce a slurry. (This is the mixed-acid route for producing NPK fertilizers; potassium and other salts are added during the process.) The slurry is sprayed onto a bed of recycled solids in a rotating granulator, and ammonia is sparged into the bed from underneath. Granules pass to a rotary dryer followed by a rotary cooler. Solids are screened and sent to storage for bagging or for bulk shipment.

Nitrophosphate fertilizer is made by digesting phosphate rock with nitric acid. This is the nitrophosphate route leading to NPK fertilizers; as in the mixed-acid route, potassium and other salts are added during the process. The resulting solution is cooled to precipitate calcium nitrate, which is removed by filtration. The filtrate is neutralized with ammonia, and the solution is evaporated to reduce the water content. Prilling may follow. The calcium nitrate filter cake can be further treated to produce a calcium nitrate fertilizer, pure calcium nitrate, or ammonium nitrate and calcium carbonate. Nitrophosphate fertilizers are also produced by the mixed-acid process, through digestion of the phosphate rock by a mixture of nitric and phosphoric acids.

Potash (potassium carbonate) and sylvine (potassium chloride) are solution-mined from deposits and are refined through crystallization processes to produce fertilizer. Potash may also be dry-mined and purified by flotation.

Compound fertilizers can be made by blending basic fertilizers such as ammonium nitrate, MAP, DAP, and granular potash; this route may involve a granulation process.

## Waste Characteristics

### Air Emissions

The principal pollutants from the production of MAP and DAP are ammonia and fluorides, which are given off in the steam from the reaction. Fluorides and dust are released from materials-handling operations. Ammonia in uncontrolled air emissions has been reported to range from 0.1 to 7.8 kilograms of nitrogen per metric ton (kg/t) of product, with phosphorus ranging from 0.02 to 2.5 kg/t product (as phosphorous pentoxide, $P_2O_5$).

In nitrophosphate production, dust will also contain fluorides. Nitrogen oxides ($NO_x$) are given off at the digester. In the evaporation stage, fluorine compounds and ammonia are released. Unabated emissions for nitrogen oxides from selected processes are less than 1,000 milligrams per cubic meter ($mg/m^3$) from digestion of phosphate rock with nitric acid, 50–200 $mg/m^3$ from neutralization with ammonia, and 30–200 $mg/m^3$ from granulation and drying.

Dust is the primary air pollutant from potash manufacturing.

### Liquid Effluents

The volumes of liquid effluents from mixed fertilizer plants are reported to range from 1.4 to 50 cubic meters per metric ton ($m^3/t$) of product. Where water is used in scrubbers, the scrubbing liquors can usually be returned to the process. Effluents can contain nitrogen, phosphorus, and fluorine; the respective ranges of concentrations can be 0.7–15.7 kg/t of product (as N), 0.1–7.8 kg/t of product (as $P_2O_5$), and 0.1–3.2 kg/t of product.

*Solid Wastes*

Generally, there is little solid waste from a fertilizer plant, since dust and fertilizer spillage can be returned to the process.

## Pollution Prevention and Control

Materials handling and milling of phosphate rock should be carried out in closed buildings. Fugitive emissions can be controlled by, for example, hoods on conveying equipment, with capture of the dust in fabric filiters.

In the ammonium phosphate plant, the gas streams from the reactor, granulator, dryer, and cooler should be passed through cyclones and scrubbers, using phosphoric acid as the scrubbing liquid, to recover particulates, ammonia, and other materials for recycling.

In the nitrophosphate plant, nitrogen oxide ($NO_x$) emissions should be avoided by adding urea to the digestion stage. Fluoride emissions should be prevented by scrubbing the gases with water. Ammonia should be removed by scrubbing. Phosphoric acid may be used for scrubbing where the ammonia load is high. The process-water system should be balanced, if necessary, by the use of holding tanks to avoid the discharge of an effluent.

## Treatment Technologies

Additional pollution control devices—beyond the scrubbers, cyclones, and baghouses that are an integral part of the plant design and operations—are generally not required for mixed fertilizer plants. Good housekeeping practices are essential to minimize the amount of spilled material. Spills or leaks of solids and liquids should be returned to the process. Liquid effluents, if any, need to be controlled for total suspended solids, fluorides, phosphorus, and ammonia.

## Table 1. Emissions Loadings for Mixed Fertilizer Plants, Nitrophosphate Process
*(kilograms per ton of NPK fertilizer produced)*

| Parameter | Loading |
|---|---|
| Ammonia ($NH_3$ as N) | 0.3 |
| Nitrogen oxides (as $NO_2$) | 0.2 |
| Fluoride (as fluorine) | 0.02 |
| PM | 0.3 |

## Table 2. Emissions Loadings for Mixed Fertilizer Plants, Mixed-Acid Process
*(kilograms per ton of NPK fertilizer produced)*

| Parameter | Loading |
|---|---|
| Ammonia nitrogen ($NH_4$–N, including free ammonia) | 0.01 |
| Fluoride (as fluorine) | 0.01 |
| PM | 0.2 |

*Note:* Loadings can vary widely, depending on the grade of fertilizer produced.

Modern plants using good industrial practices are able to achieve the pollutant loads discussed below.

*Air Emissions*

Table 1 shows the emissions values that have been reported for the manufacture of NPK fertilizers by the nitrophosphate route and that should be attained in a well-operated plant. For NPK fertilizers produced by the mixed-acid route, the emissions loadings presented in Table 2 are attainable.

*Liquid Effluents*

An effluent discharge of less than 1.5 $m^3/t$ product as $P_2O_5$ is realistic, but use of holding ponds makes feasible a discharge approaching zero. Table 3 shows the pollutant loads in effluents reported for NPK fertilizers produced by the nitrophosphate route.

## Emissions Guidelines

Emissions levels for the design and operation of each project must be established through the

**Table 3. Pollutant Loads in Effluents, Mixed Fertilizer Plants, Nitrophosphate Process**

*(kilograms per ton of NPK fertilizer produced)*

| Parameter | Loading |
|---|---|
| $P_2O_5$ | 0.06 |
| $NH_4$–N | 0.012 |
| Nitrate nitrogen ($NO_3$–N) | 0.03 |
| Fluoride (as fluorine) | 0.05 |

environmental assessment (EA) process on the basis of country legislation and the *Pollution Prevention and Abatement Handbook,* as applied to local conditions. The emissions levels selected must be justified in the EA and acceptable to the World Bank Group.

The guidelines given below present emissions levels normally acceptable to the World Bank Group in making decisions regarding provision of World Bank Group assistance. Any deviations from these levels must be described in the World Bank Group project documentation. The emissions levels given here can be consistently achieved by well-designed, well-operated, and well-maintained pollution control systems.

The guidelines are expressed as concentrations to facilitate monitoring. Dilution of air emissions or effluents to achieve these guidelines is unacceptable.

All of the maximum levels should be achieved for at least 95% of the time that the plant or unit is operating, to be calculated as a proportion of annual operating hours.

*Air Emissions*

The emissions levels presented in Table 4 should be achieved.

**Table 4. Air Emissions from Mixed Fertilizer Plants**

*(milligrams per normal cubic meter)*

| Parameter | Maximum value |
|---|---|
| PM | 50 |
| Ammonia ($NH_3$ as N) | 50 |
| Fluorides (as fluorine) | 5 |
| Nitrogen oxides (as $NO_2$) | |
| Nitrophosphate unit | 500 |
| Mixed-acid unit | 70 |

**Table 5. Effluents from Mixed Fertilizer Plants**

*(milligrams per liter, except for pH)*

| Parameter | Maximum value |
|---|---|
| pH | 6–9 |
| TSS | 50 |
| Fluorides (as fluorine) | 20 |
| Total metals | 10 |
| Cadmium | 0.1 |
| Phosphorus | 5 |
| Ammonia ($NH_4$–N) | 10 |

*Note:* Effluent requirements are for direct discharge to surface waters.

*Liquid Effluents*

The effluent levels presented in Table 5 should be achieved.

Wastewater treatment discharges are sometimes used for agricultural purposes and may contain heavy metals. Of particular concern is the cadmium content.

*Ambient Noise*

Noise abatement measures should achieve either the levels given below or a maximum increase in background levels of 3 decibels (measured on the A scale) [dB(A)]. Measurements are to be taken at noise receptors located outside the project property boundary.

| Receptor | Maximum allowable log equivalent (hourly measurements), in dB(A) | |
|---|---|---|
| | Day (07:00–22:00) | Night (22:00–07:00) |
| Residential, institutional, educational | 55 | 45 |
| Industrial, commercial | 70 | 70 |

## Monitoring and Reporting

Frequent sampling may be required during start-up and upset conditions. Once a record of consistent performance has been established, sampling for the parameters listed in the tables should be as described below.

Air emissions at point of discharge are to be monitored continuously for fluorides and particulates and annually for ammonia and nitrogen oxides.

Liquid effluents should be continuously monitored for pH. Other parameters are to be monitored at least weekly.

Monitoring data should be analyzed and reviewed at regular intervals and compared with the operating standards so that any necessary corrective actions can be taken. Records of monitoring results should be kept in an acceptable format. The results should be reported to the responsible authorities and relevant parties, as required.

## Key Issues

The key production and control practices that will lead to compliance with emissions requirements can be summarized as follows:

- Maximize product recovery and minimize air emissions by appropriate maintenance and operation of scrubbers and baghouses.
- Eliminate effluent discharges by operating a balanced process water system.
- Prepare and implement an emergency preparedness and response plan. Such a plan is required because of the large quantities of ammonia and other hazardous materials stored and handled on site.

## Sources

Bounicore, Anthony J., and Wayne T. Davis, eds. 1992. *Air Pollution Engineering Manual*. New York: Van Nostrand Reinhold.

European Fertilizer Manufacturers' Association. 1995a. "Production of NPK Fertilizers by the Nitrophosphate Route." Booklet 7 of 8. Brussels.

————. 1995b. "Production of NPK Fertilizers by the Mixed Acid Route." Booklet 8 of 8. Brussels.

Sauchelli, Vincent. 1960. *Chemistry and Technology of Fertilizers*. New York: Reinhold Publishing.

Sittig, Marshall. 1979. *Fertilizer Industry; Processes, Pollution Control and Energy Conservation*. Park Ridge, N.J.: Noyes Data Corporation.

UNIDO (United Nations Industrial Development Organization). 1978. *Process Technologies for Nitrogen Fertilizers*. New York.

————. 1978. *Process Technologies for Phosphate Fertilizers*. New York.

World Bank. 1996. "Pollution Prevention and Abatement: Mixed Fertilizer Plants." Draft Technical Background Document. Environment Department, Washington, D.C.

# Nickel Smelting and Refining

## Industry Description and Practices

Primary nickel is produced from two very different ores, lateritic and sulfidic. Lateritic ores are normally found in tropical climates where weathering, with time, extracts and deposits the ore in layers at varying depths below the surface. Lateritic ores are excavated using large earth-moving equipment and are screened to remove boulders. Sulfidic ores, often found in conjunction with copper-bearing ores, are mined from underground. Following is a description of the processing steps used for the two types of ores.

### Lateritic Ore Processing

Lateritic ores have a high percentage of free and combined moisture, which must be removed. Drying removes free moisture; chemically bound water is removed by a reduction furnace, which also reduces the nickel oxide. Lateritic ores have no significant fuel value, and an electric furnace is needed to obtain the high temperatures required to accommodate the high magnesia content of the ore. Some laterite smelters add sulfur to the furnace to produce a matte for processing. Most laterite nickel processers run the furnaces so as to reduce the iron content sufficiently to produce ferronickel products. Hydrometallurgical processes based on ammonia or sulfuric acid leach are also used. Ammonia leach is usually applied to the ore after the reduction roast step.

### Sulfidic Ore Processing

Flash smelting is the most common process in modern technology, but electric smelting is used for more complex raw materials when increased flexibility is needed. Both processes use dried concentrates. Electric smelting requires a roasting step before smelting to reduce sulfur content and volatiles. Older nickel-smelting processes, such as blast or reverberatory furnaces, are no longer acceptable because of low energy efficiencies and environmental concerns.

In flash smelting, dry sulfide ore containing less than 1% moisture is fed to the furnace along with preheated air, oxygen-enriched air (30–40% oxygen), or pure oxygen. Iron and sulfur are oxidized. The heat that results from exothermic reactions is adequate to smelt concentrate, producing a liquid matte (up to 45% nickel) and a fluid slag. Furnace matte still contains iron and sulfur, and these are oxidized in the converting step to sulfur dioxide and iron oxide by injecting air or oxygen into the molten bath. Oxides form a slag, which is skimmed off. Slags are processed in an electric furnace prior to discard to recover nickel. Process gases are cooled, and particulates are then removed by gas-cleaning devices.

### Nickel Refining

Various processes are used to refine nickel matte. Fluid bed roasting and chlorine-hydrogen reduction produce high-grade nickel oxides (more than 95% nickel). Vapor processes such as the carbonyl process can be used to produce high-purity nickel pellets. In this process, copper and precious metals remain as a pyrophoric residue that requires separate treatment. Use of electrical cells equipped with inert cathodes is the most common technology for nickel refining. Electrowinning, in which nickel is removed from solution in cells equipped with inert anodes, is the more common refining process. Sulfuric acid solutions or, less commonly, chloride electrolytes are used.

## Waste Characteristics

### Air Emissions

Sulfur dioxide ($SO_2$) is a major air pollutant emitted in the roasting, smelting, and converting of sulfide ores. (Nickel sulfide concentrates contain 6–20% nickel and up to 30% sulfur.) $SO_2$ releases can be as high as 4 metric tons (t) of sulfur dioxide per metric ton of nickel produced, before controls. Reverberatory furnaces and electric furnaces produce $SO_2$ concentrations of 0.5–2.0%, while flash furnaces produce $SO_2$ concentrations of over 10%—a distinct advantage for the conversion of the sulfur dioxide to sulfuric acid. Particulate emission loads for various process steps include 2.0–5.0 kilograms per metric ton (kg/t) for the multiple hearth roaster; 0.5–2.0 kg/t for the fluid bed roaster; 0.2–1.0 kg/t for the electric furnace; 1.0–2.0 kg/t for the Pierce-Smith converter; and 0.4 kg/t for the dryer upstream of the flash furnace. Ammonia and hydrogen sulfide are pollutants associated with the ammonia leach process; hydrogen sulfide emissions are associated with acid leaching processes. Highly toxic nickel carbonyl is a contaminant of concern in the carbonyl refining process. Various process off-gases contain fine dust particles and volatilized impurities. Fugitive emissions occur at furnace openings, launders, casting molds, and ladles that carry molten product. The transport and handling of ores and concentrates produce windborne dust.

### Liquid Effluents

Pyrometallurgical processes for processing sulfidic ores are generally dry, and effluents are of minor importance, although wet electrostatic precipitators (ESPs) are often used for gas treatment, and the resulting wastewater could have high metal concentrations. Process bleed streams may contain antimony, arsenic, or mercury. Large quantities of water are used for slag granulation, but most of this water should be recycled.

### Solid Wastes and Sludges

The smelter contributes a slag that is a dense silicate. Sludges that require disposal will result when neutralized process effluents produce a precipitate.

## Pollution Prevention and Control

Pollution prevention is always preferred to the use of end-of-pipe pollution control facilities. Therefore, every attempt should be made to incorporate cleaner production processes and facilities to limit, at source, the quantity of pollutants generated.

The choice of flash smelting over older technologies is the most significant means of reducing pollution at source.

Sulfur dioxide emissions can be controlled by:

* Recovery as sulfuric acid
* Recovery as liquid sulfur dioxide (absorption of clean, dry off-gas in water or chemical absorbtion by ammonium bisulfite or dimethyl aniline)
* Recovery as elemental sulfur, using reductants such as hydrocarbons, carbon, or hydrogen sulfide

Toxic nickel carbonyl gas is normally not emitted from the refining process because it is broken down in decomposer towers. However, very strict precautions throughout the refining process are required to prevent the escape of the nickel carbonyl into the workplace. Continuous monitoring for the gas, with automatic isolation of any area of the plant where the gas is detected, is required. Impervious clothing is used to protect workers against contact of liquid nickel carbonyl with skin.

Preventive measures for reducing emissions of particulate matter include encapsulation of furnaces and conveyors to avoid fugitive emissions. Covered storage of raw materials should be considered.

Wet scrubbing should be avoided, and cooling waters should be recirculated. Stormwaters should be collected and used in the process. Process water used to transport granulated slag should be recycled. To the extent possible, all process effluents should be returned to the process.

## Treatment Technologies

The discharge of particulate matter emitted during drying, screening, roasting, smelting, and converting is controlled by using cyclones followed by wet scrubbers, ESPs, or bag filters. Fabric filters may require reduction of gas temperatures by, for example, dilution with low-temperature gases from hoods used for fugitive dust control. Preference should be given to the use of fabric filters over wet scrubbers.

Liquid effluents are used to slurry tailings to the tailings ponds, which act as a reservoir for the storage and recycle of plant process water. However, there may be a need to treat bleed streams of some process effluents to prevent a buildup of various impurities. Solid wastes from nickel sulfide ores often contain other metals such as copper and precious metals, and consideration should be given to further processing for their recovery. Slag can be used as construction material after nickel recovery, as appropriate (e.g., return of converter slag to the furnace). Sanitary sewage effluents require treatment in a separate facility or discharge to a municipal sewer.

Modern plants using good industrial practices are able to achieve the pollutant loads described below: The double-contact, double-absorption plant should emit no more than 0.2 kg of sulfur dioxide per metric ton of sulfuric acid produced (based on a conversion efficiency of 99.7%).

## Emission Guidelines

Emissions levels for the design and operation of each project must be established through the environmental assessment (EA) process on the basis of country legislation and the *Pollution Prevention and Abatement Handbook,* as applied to local conditions. The emissions levels selected must be justified in the EA and acceptable to the World Bank Group.

The following guidelines present emissions levels normally acceptable to the World Bank

Group in making decisions regarding provision of World Bank Group assistance. Any deviations from these levels must be described in the World Bank Group project documentation. The emissions levels given here can be consistently achieved by well-designed, well-operated, and well-maintained pollution control systems.

The guidelines are expressed as concentrations to facilitate monitoring. Dilution of air emissions or effluents to achieve these guidelines is unacceptable.

All of the maximum levels should be achieved for at least 95% of the time that the plant or unit is operating, to be calculated as a proportion of annual operating hours.

*Air Emissions*

The air emissions levels presented in Table 1 should be achieved.

*Liquid Effluents*

The effluent emissions levels presented in Table 2 should be achieved.

### Table 1. Air Emissions from Nickel Smelting
*(milligrams per normal cubic meter, unless otherwise specified)*

| Parameter | Maximum value |
|---|---|
| PM | 20 |
| Nickel | 1 |
| Sulfur dioxide | 2 kg/t sulfuric acid |

### Table 2. Effluents from Nickel Smelting
*(milligrams per liter, except for pH)*

| Parameter | Maximum value |
|---|---|
| pH | 6–9 |
| TSS | 50 |
| Nickel | 0.5 |
| Iron | 3.5 |
| Total metals | 10 |

*Note:* Effluent requirements are for direct discharge to surface waters.

*Ambient Noise*

Noise abatement measures should achieve either the levels given below or a maximum increase in background levels of 3 decibels (measured on the A scale) [dB(A)]. Measurements are to be taken at noise receptors located outside the project property boundary.

| Receptor | Maximum allowable log equivalent (hourly measurements), in dB(A) | |
| --- | --- | --- |
| | Day (07:00–22:00) | Night (22:00–07:00) |
| Residential, institutional, educational | 55 | 45 |
| Industrial, commercial | 70 | 70 |

## Key Issues

The key production and control practices that will lead to compliance with emission requirements can be summarized as follows:

- Use flash smelting for sulfidic ores; electric furnaces should only be used where regenerative energy is available.
- Choose oxygen enrichment processes that allow higher $SO_2$ concentrations in smelter gases to assist in sulfur recovery.
- Recover as much sulfur dioxide as possible by producing sulfuric acid, liquid sulfur dioxide, or other sulfur products.
- Reuse process waters, recirculate cooling waters, and use stormwater for the process.
- Enclose processes and conveyors to minimize fugitive emissions; cover raw material storage.

## Sources

Bounicore, Anthony J., and Wayne T. Davis, eds. 1992. *Air Pollution Engineering Manual.* New York: Van Nostrand Reinhold.

UNEP (United Nations Environment Programme). 1993. *Environmental Management of Nickel Production. A Technical Guide.* Technical Report 15. Paris.

World Bank. 1995. "Industrial Pollution Prevention and Abatement: Nickel Smelting and Refining." Draft Technical Background Document. Environment Department, Washington, D.C.

# Nitrogenous Fertilizer Plants

## Industry Description and Practices

This document addresses the production of ammonia, urea, ammonium sulfate, ammonium nitrate (AN), calcium ammonium nitrate (CAN), and ammonium sulfate nitrate (ASN). The manufacture of nitric acid used to produce nitrogenous fertilizers typically occurs on site and is therefore included here.

### Ammonia

Ammonia ($NH_3$) is produced from atmospheric nitrogen and hydrogen from a hydrocarbon source. Natural gas is the most commonly used hydrocarbon feedstock for new plants; other feedstocks that have been used include naphtha, oil, and gasified coal. Natural gas is favored over the other feedstocks from an environmental perspective.

Ammonia production from natural gas includes the following processes: desulfurization of the feedstock; primary and secondary reforming; carbon monoxide shift conversion and removal of carbon dioxide, which can be used for urea manufacture; methanation; and ammonia synthesis. Catalysts used in the process may include cobalt, molybdenum, nickel, iron oxide/chromium oxide, copper oxide/zinc oxide, and iron.

### Urea

Urea fertilizers are produced by a reaction of liquid ammonia with carbon dioxide. The process steps include solution synthesis, where ammonia and carbon dioxide react to form ammonium carbamate, which is dehydrated to form urea; solution concentration by vacuum, crystallization, or evaporation to produce a melt; forma-tion of solids by prilling (pelletizing liquid droplets) or granulating; cooling and screening of solids; coating of the solids; and bagging or bulk loading. The carbon dioxide for urea manufacture is produced as a by-product from the ammonia plant reformer.

### Ammonium Sulfate

Ammonium sulfate is produced as a caprolactam by-product from the petrochemical industry, as a coke by-product, and synthetically through reaction of ammonia with sulfuric acid. Only the third process is covered in this document. The reaction between ammonia and sulfuric acid produces an ammonium sulfate solution that is continuously circulated through an evaporator to thicken the solution and to produce ammonium sulfate crystals. The crystals are separated from the liquor in a centrifuge, and the liquor is returned to the evaporator. The crystals are fed either to a fluidized bed or to a rotary drum dryer and are screened before bagging or bulk loading.

### Ammonium Nitrate, Calcium Ammonium Nitrate, and Ammonium Sulfate Nitrate

Ammonium nitrate is made by neutralizing nitric acid with anhydrous ammonia. The resulting 80–90% solution of ammonium nitrate can be sold as is, or it may be further concentrated to a 95–99.5% solution (melt) and converted into prills or granules. The manufacturing steps include solution formation, solution concentration, solids formation, solids finishing, screening, coating, and bagging or bulk shipping. The processing steps depend on the desired finished product. Calcium ammonium nitrate is made by adding calcite or dolomite to the ammonium nitrate melt before prilling or granulating. Ammonium sulfate nitrate is made by granulating a solution of ammonium nitrate and ammonium sulfate.

## Nitric Acid

The production stages for nitric acid manufacture include vaporizing the ammonia; mixing the vapor with air and burning the mixture over a platinum/rhodium catalyst; cooling the resultant nitric oxide (NO) and oxidizing it to nitrogen dioxide ($NO_2$) with residual oxygen; and absorbing the nitrogen dioxide in water in an absorption column to produce nitric acid ($HNO_3$).

Because of the large quantities of ammonia and other hazardous materials handled on site, an emergency preparedness and response plan is required.

## Waste Characteristics

### Air Emissions

Emissions to the atmosphere from *ammonia plants* include sulfur dioxide ($SO_2$), nitrogen oxides ($NO_x$), carbon monoxide (CO), carbon dioxide ($CO_2$), hydrogen sulfide, volatile organic compounds (VOCs), particulates, methane, hydrogen cyanide, and ammonia. The two primary sources of pollutants, with typical reported values, in kilograms per ton (kg/t) for the important pollutants, are as follows:

- Flue gas from primary reformer
  $CO_2$: 500 kg/t $NH_3$
  $NO_x$: 0.6–1.3 kg/t $NH_3$ as $NO_2$
  $SO_2$: less than 0.1 kg/t
  CO: less than 0.03 kg/t
- Carbon dioxide removal
  $CO_2$: 1,200 kg/t

Nitrogen oxide emissions depend on the process features. Nitrogen oxides are reduced, for example, when there is low excess oxygen, with steam injection; when postcombustion measures are in place; and when low-$NO_x$ burners are in use. Other measures will also reduce the total amount of nitrogen oxides emitted. Concentrations of sulfur dioxide in the flue gas from the reformer can be expected to be significantly

higher if a fuel other than natural gas is used. Energy consumption ranges from 29 to 36 gigajoules per metric ton (GJ/t) of ammonia. Process condensate discharged is about 1.5 cubic meters per metric ton ($m^3$/t) of ammonia. Ammonia tank farms can release upward of 10 kg of ammonia per ton of ammonia produced. Emissions of ammonia from the process have been reported in the range of less than 0.04 to 2 kg/t of ammonia produced.

In a *urea plant*, ammonia and particulate matter are the emissions of concern. Ammonia emissions are reported as recovery absorption vent (0.1–0.5 kg/t), concentration absorption vent (0.1–0.2 kg/t), urea prilling (0.5–2.2 kg/t), and granulation (0.2–0.7 kg/t). The prill tower is a source of urea dust (0.5–2.2 kg/t), as is the granulator (0.1–0.5 kg/t).

Particulates are the principal air pollutant emitted from *ammonium sulfate plants*. Most of the particulates are found in the gaseous exhaust of the dryers. Uncontrolled discharges of particulates may be of the order of 23 kg/t from rotary dryers and 109 kg/t from fluidized bed dryers. Ammonia storage tanks can release ammonia, and there may be fugitive losses of ammonia from process equipment.

The production of *ammonium nitrate* yields emissions of particulate matter (ammonium nitrate and coating materials), ammonia, and nitric acid. The emission sources of primary importance are the prilling tower and the granulator. Total quantities of nitrogen discharged are in the range of 0.01–18.4 kg/t of product. Values reported for *calcium ammonium nitrate* are in the range of 0.1–3.3 kg nitrogen per ton of product.

*Nitric acid plants* emit nitric oxide, nitrogen dioxide (the visible emissions), and trace amounts of nitric acid mist. Most of the nitrogen oxides are found in the tail gases of the absorption tower. Depending on the process, emissions in the tail gases can range from 215 to 4,300 milligrams per cubic meter ($mg/m^3$) for nitrogen oxides. Flow may be of the order of 3,200 $m^3$ per ton of 100% nitric acid. Nitrogen oxide values will be in the low range when high-pressure absorption is used; medium-pressure absorption yields nitrogen oxide emissions at the high end of the range. These values are prior to the addition of any abatement hardware.

*Liquid Effluents*

Ammonia plant effluents may contain up to 1 kg of ammonia and up to 1 kg of methanol per cubic meter prior to stripping. Effluent from urea plants may discharge from less than 0.1 kg to 2.6 kg nitrogen per ton product. Effluents from ammonium nitrate plants have been reported to discharge 0.7–6.5 kg nitrogen per ton product. Comparable values for CAN plants are 0–10 kg nitrogen per ton of product. Nitric acid plants may have nitrogen in the effluent of the order of 0.1–1.7 kg nitrogen per ton of nitric acid.

*Solid Wastes*

Solid wastes are principally spent catalysts that originate in ammonia production and in the nitric acid plant. Other solid wastes are not normally of environmental concern.

## Pollution Prevention and Control

*Ammonia Plant*

The following pollution prevention measures are recommended:

- Where possible, use natural gas as the feedstock for the ammonia plant, to minimize air emissions.
- Use hot process gas from the secondary reformer to heat the primary reformer tubes (the exchanger-reformer concept), thus reducing the need for natural gas
- Direct hydrogen cyanide (HCN) gas in a fuel oil gasification plant to a combustion unit to prevent its release.
- Consider using purge gases from the synthesis process to fire the reformer; strip condensates to reduce ammonia and methanol.
- Use carbon dioxide removal processes that do not release toxics to the environment. When monoethanolamine (MEA) or other processes, such as hot potassium carbonate, are used in carbon dioxide removal, proper operation and maintenance procedures should be followed to minimize releases to the environment.

*Urea Plant*

Use total recycle processes in the synthesis process; reduce microprill formation and carryover of fines in prilling towers.

*Ammonium Nitrate Plant*

The following pollution prevention measures are recommended:

- *Prill tower:* reduce microprill formation and reduce carryover of fines through entrainment.
- *Granulators:* reduce dust emissions from the disintegration of granules.
- *Materials handling:* where feasible use covers and hoods on conveyors and transition points. Good cleanup practices must be in place to minimize contamination of stormwater runoff from the plant property.

It is important to note that hot ammonium nitrate, whether in solid or in concentrated form, carries the risk of decomposition and may even detonate under certain circumstances. Suitable precautions are therefore required in its manufacture.

*Ammonium Sulfate Plant*

Ammonium sulfate plants are normally fitted with fabric filters or scrubbers as part of the process.

## Target Pollution Loads

Implementation of cleaner production processes and pollution prevention measures can yield both economic and environmental benefits. The following production-related targets can be achieved by measures such as those described above. The numbers relate to the production processes before the addition of pollution control measures.

*Ammonia Plant*

New ammonia plants should set as a target the achievement of nitrogen oxide emissions of not more than 0.5 kg/t of product (expressed as $NO_2$

at 3% $O_2$). Ammonia releases in liquid effluents can be controlled to 0.1 kg/t of product. Condensates from ammonia production should be reused.

*Nitric Acid Plant*

Nitrogen oxide levels should be controlled to a maximum of 1.6 kg/t of 100% nitric acid.

## Treatment Technologies

In *urea plants,* wet scrubbers or fabric filters are used to control fugitive emissions from prilling towers; fabric filters are used to control dust emissions from bagging operations. These devices are an integral part of the operations, to retain product. New urea plants should achieve levels of particulate matter in air emissions of less than 0.5 kg/t of product for both urea and ammonia.

In *ammonium sulfate plants,* use of fabric filters, with injection of absorbent as necessary, is the preferred means of control. Discharges of not more than 0.1 kg/t of product should be attainable for particulate matter.

In *ammonium nitrate plants,* wet scrubbers can be considered for prill towers and the granulation plant. Particulate emissions of 0.5 kg/t of product for the prill tower and 0.25 kg/t of product for granulation should be the target. Similar loads for ammonia are appropriate.

In *nitric acid plants,* extended absorption and technologies such as nonselective catalytic reduction (NSCR) and selective catalytic reduction (SCR) are used to control nitrogen oxides in tail gases. To attain a level of 150 parts per million by volume (ppmv) of nitrogen oxides in the tail gases, the following approaches should be considered:

- High-pressure, single-pressure process with absorbing efficiency high enough to avoid additional abatement facilities
- Dual-absorption process with an absorption efficiency high enough to avoid additional treatment facilities
- Dual-pressure process with SCR
- Medium-pressure, single-pressure process with SCR.

Other effluents that originate in a nitrogenous fertilizer complex include boiler blowdown, water treatment plant backwash, and cooling tower blowdown from the ammonia and nitric acid plants. They may require pH adjustment and settling. These effluents should preferably be recycled or reused.

Spent catalysts are sent for regeneration or disposed of in a secure landfill.

Modern plants using good industrial practices are able to achieve the pollutant loads described below.

## Emissions Guidelines

Emissions levels for the design and operation of each project must be established through the environmental assessment (EA) process on the basis of country legislation and the *Pollution Prevention and Abatement Handbook,* as applied to local conditions. The emissions levels selected must be justified in the EA and acceptable to the World Bank Group.

The guidelines given below present emissions levels normally acceptable to the World Bank Group in making decisions regarding provision of World Bank Group assistance. Any deviations from these levels must be described in the World Bank Group project documentation. The emissions levels given here can be consistently achieved by well-designed, well-operated, and well-maintained pollution control systems.

The guidelines are expressed as concentrations to facilitate monitoring. Dilution of air emissions or effluents to achieve these guidelines is unacceptable.

All of the maximum levels should be achieved for at least 95% of the time that the plant or unit is operating, to be calculated as a proportion of annual operating hours.

*Air Emissions*

The emissions levels presented in Table 1 should be achieved.

*Liquid Effluents*

The effluent levels presented in Table 2 should be achieved.

## Table 1. Air Emissions from Nitrogenous Fertilizer Plants

*(milligrams per normal cubic meter)*

| Parameter | Maximum value |
|---|---|
| Nitrogen oxides (as $NO_2$) | 300 |
| Urea | 50 |
| Ammonia ($NH_3$) | 50 |
| PM | 50 |

## Table 2. Effluents from Nitrogenous Fertilizer Plants

*(milligrams per liter, except for pH and temperature)*

| Parameter | Maximum value |
|---|---|
| pH | 6–9 |
| TSS | 50 |
| Ammonia (as nitrogen) | 10 |
| Urea | 1 |
| Temperature increase | < 3°C[a] |

*Note:* Effluent requirements are for direct discharge to surface waters.

a. The effluent should result in a temperature increase of no more than 3°C at the edge of the zone where initial mixing and dilution take place. Where the zone is not defined, use 100 meters from the point of discharge.

### Ambient Noise

Noise abatement measures should achieve either the levels given below or a maximum increase in background levels of 3 decibels (measured on the A scale) [dB(A)]. Measurements are to be taken at noise receptors located outside the project property boundary.

| Receptor | Maximum allowable log equivalent (hourly measurements), in dB(A) | |
|---|---|---|
| | Day (07:00–22:00) | Night (22:00–07:00) |
| Residential, institutional, educational | 55 | 45 |
| Industrial, commercial | 70 | 70 |

## Monitoring and Reporting

Frequent sampling may be required during start-up and upset conditions. Once a record of consistent performance has been established, sampling for the parameters listed in this document should be as described below.

Air emissions should be monitored annually, except for nitrate acid plants, where nitrogen oxides should be monitored continuously. Effluents should be monitored continuously for pH and monthly for other parameters.

Monitoring data should be analyzed and reviewed at regular intervals and compared with the operating standards so that any necessary corrective actions can be taken. Records of monitoring results should be kept in an acceptable format. The results should be reported to the responsible authorities and relevant parties, as required.

## Key Issues

The key production and control practices that will lead to compliance with emissions requirements can be summarized as follows:

- Choose natural gas, where possible, as feedstock for the ammonia plant.
- Give preference to high-pressure processes or absorption process in combination with catalytic reduction units.
- Use low-dust-forming processes for solids formation.
- Reuse condensates and other wastewaters.
- Maximize product recovery and minimize air emissions by appropriate maintenance and operation of scrubbers and baghouses.

## Sources

Bounicore, Anthony J., and Wayne T. Davis, eds. 1992. *Air Pollution Engineering Manual.* New York: Van Nostrand Reinhold.

European Fertilizer Manufacturers' Association. 1995a. "Production of Ammonia." Booklet 1 of 8. Brussels.

————. 1995b. "Production of Nitric Acid." Booklet 2 of 8. Brussels.

————. 1995c. "Production of Urea and Urea Ammonium Nitrate." Booklet 5 of 8. Brussels.

————. 1995d. "Production of Ammonium Nitrate and Calcium Ammonium Nitrate." Booklet 6 of 8. Brussels.

European Union. 1990. "Best Available Technologies Not Entailing Excessive Costs for Ammonia Production." Technical Note. Brussels.

Sauchelli, Vincent. 1960. *Chemistry and Technology of Fertilizers*. New York: Reinhold Publishing.

Sittig, Marshall. 1979. *Fertilizer Industry: Processes, Pollution Control and Energy Conservation*. Park Ridge, N.J.: Noyes Data Corporation.

UNIDO (United Nations Industrial Development Organization). 1978. *Process Technologies for Nitrogen Fertilizers*. Vienna.

World Bank. 1995. "Industrial Pollution Prevention and Abatement: Nitrogenous Fertilizer Plants." Draft Technical Background Document. Environment Department, Washington, D.C.

# Oil and Gas Development (Onshore)

## Industry Description and Practices

This document deals with *onshore* oil and gas exploration, drilling, and production operations. Refining operations are covered in a separate document.

Testing, delineation, and production drilling are integral to hydrocarbon reservoir development, which involves the use of drilling rigs, associated equipment such as casing and tubing, large quantities of water, and drilling muds. In the process, oil and gas are moved to the surface through the well bore either through natural means (if the reservoir has enough pressure to push the oil and gas to the surface) or through induced pressure by means of a pump or other mechanism. At the surface, oil, gas, and water are separated. Crude oils with associated gas containing more than 30 milligrams per cubic meter ($mg/m^3$) of hydrogen sulfide are normally classified as "sour crude." The crude oil may require further processing, including the removal of associated gas. Oil produced at the wells is piped or shipped for use as feedstock in petroleum refineries.

Natural gas is predominantly methane with smaller amounts of ethane, propane, butanes, pentanes, and heavier hydrocarbons. Gas wells produce small quantities of condensate, which may require processing. Separation processes generally use pressure reduction, gravity separation, and emulsion "breaking" techniques. The gas that is produced may be used directly as fuel or as feedstock for the manufacture of petrochemicals. It may also contain small amounts of sulfur compounds such as mercaptans and hydrogen sulfide. Sour gas is sweetened by processes such as amine scrubbing.

## Waste Characteristics

The main wastes of environmental concerns associated with onshore oil and gas production are drilling-waste fluids or muds, drilling-waste solids, produced water, and volatile organic compounds. The drilling-waste muds may be freshwater gel, salt water (potassium chloride or sodium chloride), or oil invert–based systems. The oil invert mud systems may contain up to 50%, by volume, of diesel oil.

Drilling wastes may contain drilling muds (bentonite), borehole cuttings, additives (polymers, oxygen scavengers, biocides, and surfactants), lubricants, diesel oil, emulsifying agents, and various other wastes that are specifically related to the drilling activities. Drilling-waste solids, which are made up of the bottom layer of drilling-mud sump materials, may contain drill cuttings, flocculated bentonite, and weighting materials and other additives. Additional wastes from the drilling process include used oils, cementing chemicals, and toxic organic compounds.

Field processing of crude oil generates several waste streams, including contaminated wastewater, tank bottoms that may contain lead, emulsions, and heavy hydrocarbon residues, which may contain polynuclear aromatic hydrocarbons (PAHs). Cooling tower blowdown, boiler water, scrubber liquids, and steam production wastes are also generated, as well as contaminated soil, used oil, and spent solvents.

Wastewaters typically contain suspended solids. To control the growth of microorganisms in sour water, a biocide or hydrogen sulfide scavenger (for example, sodium hypochlorite) is generally used prior to reinjection or disposal of the

## Table 1. Wastewater from Crude Processing

*(milligrams per liter)*

| Parameter | Typical values (average) |
|---|---|
| Oil and grease | 7–1,300 (200) |
| Total organic carbon | 30–1,600 (400) |
| TSS | 20–400 (70) |
| Total dissolved solids (TDS) | 30,000–200,000 (100,000) |
| BOD | 120–340 |
| COD | 180–580 |
| Phenols | 50 |
| Cadmium | 0.7 |
| Chromium | 2.3 |
| Copper | 0.4 |
| Lead | 0.2 |
| Mercury | 0.1 |
| Nickel | 0.4 |

## Table 2. Air Emissions from Oil and Gas Production

| *Gas production (grams per cubic meter gas produced)* | |
|---|---|
| Sulfur oxides | < 0.1 |
| Nitrogen oxides | 10–12 |
| VOCs | 0.1–14 |
| Methane | 0.2–10 |
| *Oil production (grams per cubic meter oil produced)* | |
| Nitrogen oxides | 3.7 |
| VOCs | 3.3–26 |

water. Crude pipelines are routinely cleaned by pigging operations, which can lead to spills and to the generation of sludge containing heavy metals. Solid wastes that do not contain toxics are used as backfill material.

Table 1 presents a summary of the characteristics of the overall wastewater stream from crude processing.

Among the main sources of air emissions (see Table 2) are fired equipment, vents, flares (including those from compressor stations), and fugitive emissions. The emissions may contain volatile organic compounds (VOCs), sulfur oxides ($SO_x$), hydrogen sulfide, and nitrogen oxides ($NO_x$).

## Pollution Prevention and Control

Pollution prevention programs should focus on reducing the impacts of wastewater discharges, oil spills, and soil contamination and on minimizing air emissions. Minimizing the quantity of discharge should be stressed. Process changes might include the following:

- Maximize the use of freshwater gel–based mud systems.
- Eliminate the use of invert (diesel-based) muds. If the use of diesel-based muds is necessary, reuse the muds.
- Recycle drilling mud decant water.
- Use hydrogen sulfide scavengers to prevent degradation of sweet wells by sulfate-reducing bacteria.
- Select less toxic biocides, corrosion inhibitors, and other chemicals.
- Minimize gas flaring. (Note, however, that flaring is preferred to venting.)
- Store crude oil in tanks; tanks larger than 1,590 $m^3$ should have secondary (double) seals.
- Minimize and control leakage from tanks and pipelines.
- Practice corrosion prevention and monitor above- and below-ground tanks, vessels, pipes, etc.
- Remove hydrogen sulfide and mercaptans from sour gases (releasing greater than 1.8 kg of reduced sulfur compounds per hour) before flaring.
- Use knockout drums on flares to prevent condensate emissions.
- Regenerate spent amines and spent solvents, or send offsite for recovery.
- Use low-$NO_x$ burners in process heaters, especially in those with a design heat input of 4.2 X $10^{10}$ joules per hour.
- Provide spill prevention and control measures (bunds, berms, and hard surfacing for storage tanks; pressure relief valves; high-level alarms).
- Recover oil from process wastewaters.
- Segregate stormwater from process water.
- Implement leak detection and repair programs.
- Practice good housekeeping and ensure that appropriate operating and maintenance programs are in place.

A reclamation and closure plan for the site is required. This plan should be developed early in the project and should address the removal and disposal of production facilities in an environmentally sensitive manner, the restoration of the site, and provisions for any ongoing maintenance issues. Where possible, progressive restoration should be implemented.

## Target Pollution Loads

Implementation of cleaner production processes and pollution prevention measures can yield both economic and environmental benefits. In drilling operations, the use of fresh water should be minimized by maximizing the use of drilling mud pond decant water. Eliminate sour gas emissions by sweetening and reuse.

## Treatment Technologies

Typically, air emissions of toxic organics are minimized by routing such vapors to recovery systems, flares, or boilers. Tail gases are scrubbed to remove sulfur compounds.

The decant from the drilling mud disposal sump is treated by coagulation and settling before discharge. Alternatively, the sump fluids may be injected downhole into an approved disposal formation.

The drained and settled drilling-mud solids are disposed of on land by capping; by mixing, burying, and covering; by trenching; or by encapsulating. Other options include land spreading, land filling, incineration (for destruction of toxic organics), or in situ solidification/fixation.

Effluents from the crude process may be treated using coagulation, de-emulsification, settling, and filtration. Stormwater is settled and if necessary, treated (by coagulation, flocculation, and sedimentation) before discharge.

## Emissions Guidelines

Emissions levels for the design and operation of each project must be established through the environmental assessment (EA) process on the basis of country legislation and the *Pollution Prevention and Abatement Handbook*, as applied to local conditions. The emissions levels selected must be justified in the EA and acceptable to the World Bank Group.

The guidelines given below present emissions levels normally acceptable to the World Bank Group in making decisions regarding provision of World Bank Group assistance. Any deviations from these levels must be described in the World Bank Group project documentation. The emissions levels given here can be consistently achieved by well-designed, well-operated, and well-maintained pollution control systems.

The guidelines are expressed as concentrations to facilitate monitoring. Dilution of air emissions or effluents to achieve these guidelines is unacceptable.

All of the maximum levels should be achieved for at least 95% of the time that the plant or unit is operating, to be calculated as a proportion of annual operating hours.

### Air Emissions

The emissions levels presented in Table 3 should be achieved.

### Liquid Effluents

The effluent levels presented in Table 4 should be achieved.

### Ambient Noise

Noise abatement measures should achieve either the levels given below or a maximum increase in background levels of 3 decibels (measured on the A scale) [dB(A)]. Measurements are to be taken at noise receptors located outside the project property boundary.

### Table 3. Emissions from Onshore Oil and Gas Production

*(milligrams per normal cubic meter, unless otherwise specified)*

| Parameter | Maximum value |
|---|---|
| VOCs, including benzene | 20 |
| Hydrogen sulfide | 30 |
| Sulfur oxides (for oil production) | 1,000 |
| Nitrogen oxides | |
|    Gas fired | 320 (or 86 ng/J) |
|    Oil fired | 460 (or 130 ng/J) |
| Odor | Not offensive at the receptor end[a] |

*Note:* ng/J, nanograms per joule.
a. Hydrogen sulfide at the property boundary should be less than 5 mg/m³.

### Table 4. Liquid Effluents from Onshore Oil and Gas Production
*(milligrams per liter, except for pH and temperature)*

| Parameter | Maximum value |
|---|---|
| pH | 6-9 |
| BOD | 50 |
| TSS | 50 |
| Oil and grease[a] | 20 |
| Phenol | 1 |
| Sulfide | 1 |
| Total toxic metals[b] | 5 |
| Temperature increase | < 3°C[c] |

*Note:* Effluent requirements are for direct discharge to surface waters.
a. Up to 40 mg/l is acceptable for facilities producing less than 10,000 tons per day.
b. Toxic metals Include antimony, arsenic, beryllium, cadmium, chromium, copper, lead, mercury, nickel, selenium, silver, thallium, vanadium, and zinc.
c. The effluent should result in a temperature increase of no more than 3° C at the edge of the zone where initial mixing and dilution take place. Where the zone is not defined, use 100 meters from the point of discharge.

| Receptor | Maximum allowable log equivalent (hourly measurements), in dB(A) | |
|---|---|---|
| | Day (07:00–22:00) | Night (22:00–07:00) |
| Residential, institutional, educational | 55 | 45 |
| Industrial, commercial | 70 | 70 |

### Monitoring and Reporting

Frequent sampling may be required during start-up and upset conditions. Once a record of consistent performance has been established, sampling for the parameters listed in this document should be as described below.

Air emissions of the parameters should be assessed annually. Liquid effluents from production operations should be analyzed for the parameters on a daily basis, except for metals, which can be monitored monthly or when there are significant process changes.

Monitoring data should be analyzed and reviewed at regular intervals and compared with the operating standards so that any necessary corrective actions can be taken. Records of monitoring results should be kept in an acceptable format. The results should be reported to the responsible authorities and relevant parties, as required.

### Key Issues

The key production and control practices that will lead to compliance with emissions requirements can be summarized as follows:

- Maximize the use of freshwater gel–based mud systems.
- Dispose of drilling muds in a manner that minimizes the impact on the environment. Reuse invert (diesel-based) muds.
- Reuse drilling-mud pond decant water.
- Encourage the reuse of produced water for steam generation when steam is used to stimulate reservoir production.
- Minimize gas flaring.
- Scrub sour gases.

### Sources

Alberta Land Conservation and Reclamation Council. 1990. *Literature Review on the Disposal of Drilling Waste Solids.* Alberta Land Conservation and Reclamation Research Technical Advisory Committee Report 90-9. Edmonton.

API (American Petroleum Institute). 1989. *Onshore Solid Waste Management in Exploration and Production Operations.* API Environmental Guidance Document. Washington, D.C.

United Kingdom, Her Majesty's Inspectorate of Pollution. 1992. "Chief Inspector's Guidance to Inspectors, Environment Protection Act 1990. Process Guidance Note IPR 1/16: Petroleum Processes Onshore Oil Production." Her Majesty's Stationery Office, London.

# Pesticides Formulation

## Industry Description and Practices

This document addresses the formulation of pesticides from active ingredients. Manufacture of pesticides is the subject of a separate document.

The major chemical groups that are formulated include:

- Insecticides (organophosphates, carbamates, organochlorines, pyrethroids, biorationals, and botanicals)
- Fungicides (dithiocarbamates, triazoles, MBCs, morpholines, pyrimidines, phthalamides, and inorganics)
- Herbicides (triazines, carbamates, phenyl ureas, phenoxy acids, bipyridyls, glyphosates, sulfonyl ureas, amide xylenols, and imidazole inones)
- Rodenticides (coumarins).

The main purpose of pesticide formulation is to manufacture a product that has optimum biological efficiency, is convenient to use, and minimizes environmental impacts. The active ingredients are mixed with solvents, adjuvants (boosters), and fillers as necessary to achieve the desired formulation. The types of formulations include wettable powders, soluble concentrates, emulsion concentrates, oil-in-water emulsions, suspension concentrates, suspoemulsions, water-dispersible granules, dry granules, and controlled release, in which the active ingredient is released into the environment from a polymeric carrier, binder, absorbent, or encapsulant at a slow and effective rate. The formulation steps may generate air emissions, liquid effluents, and solid wastes.

## Waste Characteristics

The principal air pollutants are particulate matter (PM) and volatile organic compounds (VOCs). These are released from mixing and coating operations.

Most liquid effluents result from spills, the cleaning of equipment, and process wastewaters. The effluents may contain toxic organics, including pesticide residues.

Major solid wastes of concern include contaminated discarded packaging and process residues. There will also be effluent treatment sludges. The solid wastes generated depend on the process. They can be amount to about 3.3 grams per kilogram (g/kg) of product and may contain 40% active ingredient.

## Pollution Prevention and Control

The recommended pollution prevention measures are as follows:

- Use equipment washdown waters as makeup solutions for subsequent batches.
- Use dedicated dust collectors to recycle recovered materials.
- Use suction hoods to collect vapors and other fugitive emissions.
- Return toxic materials packaging to the supplier for reuse.
- Find productive uses for off-specification products to avoid disposal problems.
- Minimize raw material and product inventory to avoid degradation and wastage.
- Label and store toxic and hazardous materials in secure, bunded areas.

A pesticide formulation plant should prepare and implement an emergency preparedness and response plan that takes into account neighboring land uses and the potential consequences of an emergency or accidental release of harmful substances. Measures to avoid the release of harmful substances should be incorporated in the design, operation, maintenance, and management of the plant. Additional guidance on the selection and use of pesticides is provided in Guidelines and Best Practice, GB 4.03, "Agricultural Pest Management" (World Bank 1993).

## Treatment Technologies

Baghouses for removal of particulate matter and carbon adsorption for removal of VOCs are applicable and effective technologies.

Reverse osmosis or ultrafiltration is used to recover process materials from wastewater. Effluent treatment may include carbon adsorption, detoxification of pesticides by oxidation (using ultraviolet systems or peroxide solutions), and biological treatment. Exhausted carbon from absorption processes may be sent for regeneration or combustion.

Due to the relatively small volumes of solid wastes, it is difficult to find acceptable and affordable methods of disposal. Ideally, solid wastes should be incinerated in a facility where combustion conditions such as 1,100°C and at least 0.5 second flame residence time are maintained, to ensure effective destruction of toxics.

## Emissions Guidelines

Emissions levels for the design and operation of each project must be established through the environmental assessment (EA) process on the basis of country legislation and the *Pollution Prevention and Abatement Handbook*, as applied to local conditions. The emissions levels selected must be justified in the EA and acceptable to the World Bank Group.

The guidelines given below present emissions levels normally acceptable to the World Bank Group in making decisions regarding provision of World Bank Group assistance. Any deviations from these levels must be described in the World Bank Group project documenta-

tion. The emissions levels given here can be consistently achieved by well-designed, well-operated, and well-maintained pollution control systems.

The guidelines are expressed as concentrations to facilitate monitoring. Dilution of air emissions or effluents to achieve these guidelines is unacceptable.

All of the maximum levels should be achieved for at least 95% of the time that the plant or unit is operating, to be calculated as a proportion of annual operating hours.

### Air Emissions

The emissions levels presented in Table 1 should be achieved.

### Liquid Effluents

The effluent levels presented in Table 2 should be achieved.

### Solid Wastes

Toxic solid wastes should be treated to destroy toxic organics and bring them to levels below 0.05 milligrams per kilogram (mg/kg).

### Ambient Noise

Noise abatement measures should achieve either the levels given below or a maximum increase in background levels of 3 decibels (measured on the A scale) [dB(A)]. Measurements are to be taken at noise receptors located outside the project property boundary.

### Table 1. Emissions from Pesticides Formulation
*(milligrams per normal cubic meter)*

| Parameter | Maximum value |
|---|---|
| PM | 20; 5 where very toxic compounds are present[a] |
| VOCs | 20 |
| Chlorine (or chloride) | 5 |

a. See the World Health Organization's list of extremely hazardous substances (WHO 1996).

## Table 2. Effluents from Pesticides Formulation

*(milligrams per liter, except for pH)*

| Parameter | Maximum value |
|---|---|
| pH | 6–9 |
| AOX | 1 |
| COD | 150 |
| TSS[a] | 20 |
| Oil and grease | 10 |
| Organochlorines | 0.05 |
| Nitroorganics | 0.05 |
| Pyrethroids | 0.05 |
| Phenoxy compounds | 0.05 |
| Active ingredients (each) | 0.05 |
| Arsenic and hexavalent chrome (each) | 0.1 |
| Copper | 0.5 |
| Mercury | 0.01 |

*Note:* Effluent requirements are for direct discharge to surface waters.
a. Monthly average, but in no case more than 50 mg/l.

| Receptor | Maximum allowable log equivalent (hourly measurements), in dB(A) | |
|---|---|---|
| | Day (07:00–22:00) | Night (22:00–07:00) |
| Residential, institutional, educational | 55 | 45 |
| Industrial, commercial | 70 | 70 |

## Monitoring and Reporting

Frequent sampling may be required during start-up and upset conditions. Once a record of consistent performance has been established, sampling for the parameters listed in this document should be as described below:

- Continuously monitor air emissions exiting the air pollution control system where toxic organics are being emitted at rates greater than 0.5 kilograms per hour (kg/h).
- Analyze liquid effluents generated from the process before discharge (or at least once per shift). Where the effluents are suspected to be toxic, a bioassay test should be performed to assess their acceptability in the environment. The toxicity factor for fish should not be

greater than 2; toxicity to *Daphnia* = 8; toxicity to algae = 16; and toxicity to bacteria = 8.)

Monitoring data should be analyzed and reviewed at regular intervals and compared with the operating standards so that any necessary corrective actions can be taken. Records of monitoring results should be kept in an acceptable format. The results should be reported to the responsible authorities and relevant parties, as required.

## Key Issues

The key production and control practices that will lead to compliance with emissions guidelines can be summarized as follows:

- Good management practices, especially cleanliness and materials control, are essential and must be put in place.
- Return packaging for refilling.
- Incinerate all toxic organic wastes (except those containing toxic volatile metals).

## References and Sources

ACS (American Chemical Society). 1983. *Advances in Pesticide Formulation Technology.* ACS Symposium Series 254. Washington, D.C.

Seaman, D. 1990. "Trends in the Formulation of Pesticides: An Overview." *Pesticide Science* 29: 437–49.

Sittig, Marshall. 1980. *Pesticides Manufacturing and Toxic Materials Control Encyclopedia.* Park Ridge, N.J.: Noyes Data Corporation.

UNIDO (United Nations Industrial Development Organization). 1992. *International Safety Guidelines for Pesticide Formulation in Developing Countries.* Vienna.

USEPA (United States Environmental Protection Agency). 1990. *Guides to Pollution Prevention: The Pesticide Formulating Industry.* EPA/625/7-90/004. Washington, D.C.

———. 1992. "Development Document for Best Available Technology and New Source Performance for the Pesticide Chemical Industry." Proposed. EPA/821-R-92.005. Washington, D.C.

WHO (World Health Organization). 1996. *International Programme on Chemical Safety (IPCS): The WHO Recommended Classification of Pesticides by Hazard and Guidelines to Classification 1996–1997.* Geneva.

World Bank. 1993. "Agricultural Pest Management." Guidelines and Best Practice, GB 4.03. *World Bank Operational Manual.* April. Washington, D.C.

———. 1996. "Pollution Prevention and Abatement: Pesticides Formulation." Draft Technical Background Document. Environment Department, Washington, D.C.

# Pesticides Manufacturing

## Industry Description and Practices

This document deals with the synthesis of the active ingredients used in pesticide formulations. The formulation of pesticides from the active ingredients is covered in a separate document.

The major chemical groups manufactured include:

- Carbamates and dithiocarbamates (carbofuran, carbaryl, ziram, and benthiocarb)
- Chlorophenoxy compounds (2,4-D, 2,4,5-T, and silvex)
- Organochlorines (dicofol and endosulfan)
- Organophosphorus compounds (malathion, dimethoate, phorate, and parathion methyl)
- Nitro compounds (trifluralin)
- Miscellaneous compounds such as biopesticides (for example, *Bacillus thuringiensis* and pherhormones), heterocycles (for example, atrazine), pyrethroids (for example, cypermethrin), and urea derivatives (for example, diuron).

*Special attention must be given to restricted substances.* Production proposals for the following pesticides should be carefully evaluated: hexachlorobenzene, toxaphene, chlordane, aldrin, DDT, mirex, dieldrin, endrin, and heptachlor. (See the UN-ECE list of restricted substances and the international agreements on pesticides considered acceptable for manufacturing and use, for example, WHO 1996.)

The principal manufacturing steps are (a) preparation of process intermediates; (b) introduction of functional groups; (c) coupling and esterification; (d) separation processes, such as washing and stripping; and (e) purification of the final product. Each of these steps may generate air emissions, liquid effluents, and solid wastes.

## Waste Characteristics

The principal air pollutants are volatile organic compounds (VOCs) and particulate matter (PM).

Liquid effluents resulting from equipment cleaning after batch operation contain toxic organics and pesticide residues. Cooling waters are normally recirculated. Wastewater concentrations are: chemical oxygen demand (COD), 13,000 milligrams per liter (mg/l), with a range of 0.4–73, 000 mg/l; oil and grease, 800 mg/l, (with a range of 1–13,000 mg/l; total suspended solids, 2,800 mg/l, with a range of 4–43,000 mg/l. Major solid wastes of concern include process and effluent treatment sludges, spent catalysts, and container residues. Approximately 200 kilograms (kg) of waste is generated per metric ton of active ingredient manufactured.

## Pollution Prevention and Control

Every effort should be made to replace highly toxic and persistent ingredients with degradable and less toxic ones. Recommended pollution prevention measures are as follows:

- Meter and control the quantities of active ingredients to minimize wastage.
- Reuse by-products from the process as raw materials or as raw material substitutes in other processes.
- Use automated filling to minimize spillage.
- Use "closed" feed systems for batch reactors.
- Use nitrogen blanketing where appropriate on pumps, storage tanks, and other equipment to minimize the release of toxic organics.
- Give preference to nonhalogenated and nonaromatic solvents where feasible.
- Use high-pressure hoses for equipment cleaning to reduce wastewater.

- Use equipment washdown waters and other process waters (such as leakages from pump seals) as makeup solutions for subsequent batches.
- Use dedicated dust collectors to recycle recovered materials.
- Vent equipment through a recovery system.
- Maintain losses from vacuum pumps (such as water ring and dry) at low levels.
- Return toxic materials packaging to the supplier for reuse or incinerate/destroy in an environmentally acceptable manner.
- Minimize storage time of off-specification products through regular reprocessing.
- Find productive uses for off-specification products to avoid disposal problems.
- Minimize raw material and product inventory to avoid degradation and wastage that could lead to the formation of inactive but toxic isomers or by-products.
- Label and store toxic and hazardous materials in secure, bunded areas.

A pesticide manufacturing plant should prepare a hazard assessment and operability study and also prepare and implement an emergency preparedness and response plan that takes into account neighboring land uses and the potential consequences of an emergency. Measures to avoid the release of harmful substances should be incorporated in the design, operation, maintenance, and management of the plant.

Guidance on the selection and use of pesticides is provided in Guidelines and Best Practice, GB 4.03, "Agricultural Pest Management" (World Bank 1993).

## Target Pollution Loads

Implementation of cleaner production processes and pollution prevention measures can yield both economic and environmental benefits.

Specific reduction targets for the different processes have not been determined. In the absence of specific pollution reduction targets, new plants should always achieve better than the industry averages quoted in the section on waste characteristics and should approach the load-based effluent levels. Certain publications such as the EU reports give the pollution loads achieved for each type of pesticide and may be used as a reference.

Table 3, below, presents the maximum load-based levels for active ingredients in the effluent after the addition of pollution control measures.

## Treatment Technologies

### Air Emissions

Stack gas scrubbing and/or carbon adsorption (for toxic organics) and baghouses (for particulate matter removal) are applicable and effective technologies for minimizing the release of significant pollutants to air. Combustion is used to destroy toxic organics. Combustion devices should be operated at temperatures above 1,100° C with a flame residence time of at least 0.5 second to achieve acceptable destruction efficiency of toxics. However, temperatures of around 900° C are acceptable provided that at least 99.99% destruction/removal efficiency of toxics is achieved.

### Liquid Effluents and Solid Wastes

Reverse osmosis or ultrafiltration is used to recover and concentrate active ingredients. Effluent treatment normally includes flocculation, coagulation, settling, carbon adsorption, detoxification of pesticides by oxidation (using ultraviolet systems or peroxide solutions), and biological treatment. Exhausted carbon from absorption processes may be sent for regeneration or combustion. When the wastewater volumes are small and an onsite incinerator is appropriate, combustion of toxic wastewaters may be feasible.

Contaminated solid wastes are generally incinerated, and the flue gases are scrubbed.

## Emissions Guidelines

Emissions levels for the design and operation of each project must be established through the environmental assessment (EA) process on the basis of country legislation and the *Pollution Prevention and Abatement Handbook,* as applied to local conditions. The emissions levels selected must be justified in the EA and acceptable to the World Bank Group.

The guidelines given below present emissions levels normally acceptable to the World Bank

Group in making decisions regarding provision of World Bank Group assistance. Any deviations from these levels must be described in the World Bank Group project documentation. The emissions levels given here can be consistently achieved by well-designed, well-operated, and well-maintained pollution control systems.

The guidelines are expressed as concentrations to facilitate monitoring. Dilution of air emissions or effluents to achieve these guidelines is unacceptable.

All of the maximum levels should be achieved for at least 95% of the time that the plant or unit is operating, to be calculated as a proportion of annual operating hours.

*Air Emissions*

The emissions levels presented in Table 1 should be achieved.

*Liquid Effluents*

Table 2 presents the load-based levels for active ingredients in the effluent after pollution control measures have been applied. However, effluent discharges should be minimized to the extent feasible. These data have been provided to assist in computing pollution reduction targets before the addition of pollution control measures.

The effluent levels presented in Table 3 should be achieved.

Bioassay testing should be performed to ensure that the toxicity of the effluent is acceptable (toxicity to fish = 2; toxicity to *Daphnia* = 8; toxicity to algae = 16; and toxicity to bacteria = 8).

## Table 1. Emissions from Pesticides Manufacturing

*(milligrams per normal cubic meter)*

| Parameter | Maximum value |
|---|---|
| PM | 20; 5 where very toxic compounds are present[a] |
| VOCs | 20 |
| Chlorine (or chloride) | 5 |

a. See the World Health Organization's list of extremely hazardous substances (WHO 1996).

## Table 2. Load-Based Levels for Active Ingredients (AIs) in Effluents after Treatment in Pesticides Manufacture

*(milligrams per kilogram active ingredient produced, or ppm of AI produced)*

| Active ingredient | Daily maximum[a] | Monthly average[b] |
|---|---|---|
| Atrazine | 2.6 | 1.0 |
| Carbaryl[c] | | 0.73 |
| Carbofuran | 0.12 | 0.028 |
| 2,4-D[1c] | 0.12 | 0.034 |
| Diuron | 32 | 14 |
| Malathion | 0.24 | 0.095 |
| Parathion methyl | 0.77 | 0.34 |
| Trifluralin[c] | 0.32 | 0.11 |
| Ziram[d] | 5.7 | 1.9 |

a. Daily maximum not to be exceeded.
b. Monthly average not to be exceeded.
c. As total toluidine AIs, as trifluralin; after in-plant treatment before mixing with other wastewaters.
d. As total dithiocarbamates, as ziram.

## Table 3. Effluents from Pesticides Manufacturing

*(milligrams per liter, except for pH)*

| Parameter | Maximum value |
|---|---|
| pH | 6–9 |
| BOD[a] | 30 |
| COD | 150 |
| AOX | 1 |
| TSS | 10 |
| Oil and grease | 10 |
| Phenol | 0.5 |
| Arsenic | 0.1 |
| Chromium (hexavalent) | 0.1 |
| Copper | 0.5 |
| Mercury | 0.01 |
| Active ingredient (each) | 0.05 |

*Note:* Effluent requirements are for direct discharge to surface waters.
a. A BOD test is to be performed only in cases where the effluent does not contain any substance toxic to the microorganisms used in the test.

*Solid Wastes*

Contaminated solid wastes should be treated to achieve toxic organic levels of no more than 0.05 milligrams per kilogram.

*Ambient Noise*

Noise abatement measures should achieve either the levels given below or a maximum increase in background levels of 3 decibels (measured on the A scale) [dB(A)]. Measurements are to be taken at noise receptors located outside the project property boundary.

| | Maximum allowable log equivalent (hourly measurements), in dB(A) | |
|---|---|---|
| Receptor | Day (07:00–22:00) | Night (22:00–07:00) |
| Residential, institutional, educational | 55 | 45 |
| Industrial, commercial | 70 | 70 |

## Monitoring and Reporting

Frequent sampling may be required during start-up and upset conditions. Once a record of consistent performance has been established, sampling for the parameters listed in this document should be as described below.

Monitoring of air emissions should be done on a continuous basis when the mass flow of toxic substances exceeds 0.5 kg per hour. Otherwise, it can be done annually. Liquid effluents should be monitored for active ingredients at least once every shift. The remaining parameters should be monitored at least daily.

Monitoring data should be analyzed and reviewed at regular intervals and compared with the operating standards so that any necessary corrective actions can be taken. Records of monitoring results should be kept in an acceptable format. The results should be reported to the responsible authorities and relevant parties, as required.

## Key Issues

The key production and control practices that will lead to compliance with emissions guidelines can be summarized as follows:

- Replace highly toxic and persistent ingredients with less toxic, degradable ones.
- Control loss and wastage of active ingredients.
- Return packaging for refilling.
- Use equipment washdown waters as makeup solutions for subsequent batches.
- Minimize wastage by inventory control and find uses for off-specification products.

## References and Sources

European Union. 1996. "Best Available Technology Notes on Various Pesticides Manufacturing Processes." Brussels.

Sittig, Marshall. *Pesticide Manufacturing and Toxic Materials Control Encyclopedia.* Park Ridge, N.J.: Noyes Data Corporation.

UNIDO (United Nations Industrial Development Organization). 1992. *International Safety Guidelines for Pesticides Formulation in Developing Countries.* Vienna.

United Kingdom, Her Majesty's Inspectorate of Pollution. 1993. "Chief Inspector's Guidance to Inspectors, Environmental Protection Act 1990. Process Guidance Note IPR 4/B: Pesticide Processes." Her Majesty's Stationery Office, London.

USEPA (U.S. Environmental Protection Agency). 1988. *Pesticide Waste Control Technology.* Park Ridge, N.J.: Noyes Data Corporation.

WHO (World Health Organization). 1996. *International Programme on Chemical Safety (IPCS): The WHO Recommended Classification of Pesticides by Hazard and Guidelines to Classification 1996–1997.* Geneva.

World Bank. 1993. "Agricultural Pest Management." Guidelines and Best Practice, GB 4.03. *World Bank Operational Manual.* April. Washington, D.C.

————. 1996. "Pollution Prevention and Abatement: Pesticides Manufacturing." Draft Technical Background Document. Environment Department, Washington, D.C.

# Petrochemicals Manufacturing

## Industry Description and Practices

Natural gas and crude distillates such as naphtha from petroleum refining are used as feedstocks to manufacture a wide variety of petrochemicals that are in turn used in the manufacture of consumer goods. The description of petrochemical processes and products presented here is for illustrative purposes only. The basic petrochemicals manufactured by cracking, reforming, and other processes include olefins (such as ethylene, propylene, butylenes, and butadiene) and aromatics (such as benzene, toluene, and xylenes). The capacity of naphtha crackers is generally of the order of 250,000–750,000 metric tons per year (tpy) of ethylene production. Some petrochemical plants also have alcohol and oxo-compound manufacturing units on site. The base petrochemicals or products derived from them, along with other raw materials, are converted to a wide range of products. Among them are:

- Resins and plastics such as low-density polyethylene (LDPE), high-density polyethylene (HDPE), linear low-density polyethylene (LLDPE), polypropylene, polystyrene, and polyvinyl chloride (PVC)
- Synthetic fibers such as polyester and acrylic
- Engineering polymers such as acrylonitrile butadiene styrene (ABS)
- Rubbers, including styrene butadiene rubber (SBR) and polybutadiene rubber (PBR)
- Solvents
- Industrial chemicals, including those used for the manufacture of detergents such as linear alkyl benzene (LAB) and of coatings, dyestuffs, agrochemicals, pharmaceuticals, and explosives.

A number of alternative methods for manufacturing the desired products are available. Details on typical processes and products are provided in the Annex.

## Waste Characteristics

Fugitive air emissions from pumps, valves, flanges, storage tanks, loading and unloading operations, and wastewater treatment are of greatest concern. Some of the compounds released to air are carcinogenic or toxic. Ethylene and propylene emissions are of concern because their release can lead to the formation of extremely toxic oxides. Compounds considered carcinogenic that may be present in air emissions include benzene, butadiene, 1,2-dichloroethane, and vinyl chloride. A typical naphtha cracker at a petrochemical complex may release annually about 2,500 metric tons of alkenes, such as propylenes and ethylene, in producing 500,000 metric tons of ethylene. Boilers, process heaters, flares, and other process equipment (which in some cases may include catalyst regenerators) are responsible for the emission of particulates, carbon monoxide, nitrogen oxides (200 tpy), based on 500,000 tpy of ethylene capacity, and sulfur oxides (600 tpy).

The release of volatile organic compounds (VOCs) into the air depends on the products handled at the plant. VOCs released may include acetaldehyde, acetone, benzene, toluene, trichloroethylene, trichlorotoluene, and xylene. VOC emissions are mostly fugitive and depend on the production processes, materials-handling and effluent-treatment procedures, equipment maintenance, and climatic conditions. VOC emissions from a naphtha cracker range from 0.6 to 10 kilograms per metric ton (kg/t) of ethylene produced. Of these emissions, 75% consists of alkanes, 20% of unsaturated hydrocarbons, about half of which is ethylene, and 5% of aromatics. For a vinyl chloride plant, VOC emissions are 0.02–2.5 kg/t of product; 45% is ethylene dichloride, 20% vinyl chloride, and 15% chlorinated organics; for an SBR plant, VOC emissions are 3–10 kg/t of product; for an ethyl benzene plant, 0.1-2 kg/t of product; for an ABS plant, 1.4–27 kg/t of product; for a styrene plant, 0.25–18 kg/t of product; and for a polystyrene plant, 0.2–5 kg/t of product. Petrochemical units generate wastewaters from process operations such as vapor condensation, from cooling tower blowdown, and from stormwater runoff. Process wastewaters are generated at a rate of about 15 cubic meters per hour (m³/hr), based on 500,000 tpy ethylene production, and may contain biochemical oxygen demand (BOD) levels of 100 mg/l, as well as chemical oxygen demand (COD) of 1,500–6,000 mg/l, suspended solids of 100–400 mg/l, and oil and grease of 30–600 mg/l. Phenol levels of up to 200 mg/l and benzene levels of up to 100 mg/l may also be present.

Petrochemical plants generate solid wastes and sludges, some of which may be considered hazardous because of the presence of toxic organics and heavy metals. Spent caustic and other hazardous wastes may be generated in significant quantities; examples are distillation residues associated with units handling acetaldehyde, acetonitrile, benzyl chloride, carbon tetrachloride, cumene, phthallic anhydride, nitrobenzene, methyl ethyl pyridine, toluene diisocyanate, trichloroethane, trichloroethylene, perchloroethylene, aniline, chlorobenzenes, dimethyl hydrazine, ethylene dibromide, toluenediamine, epichlorohydrin, ethyl chloride, ethylene dichloride, and vinyl chloride.

*Accidental discharges* as a result of abnormal operation, especially from polyethylene and ethylene-oxide-glycol plants in a petrochemical complex, can be a major environmental hazard, releasing large quantities of pollutants and products into the environment. Plant safety and fire prevention and control procedures should be in place.

## Pollution Prevention and Control

Petrochemical plants are typically large and complex, and the combination and sequence of processes are usually specific to the characteristics of the products manufactured. Specific pollution prevention or source reduction measures are best determined by technical staff. However, there are a number of broad areas where improvements are often possible, and site-specific emission reduction measures in these areas should be designed into the plant and targeted by plant management. Areas where efforts should be concentrated are discussed below.

### Reduction of Air Emissions

- Minimize leakages of volatile organics, including benzene, vinyl chloride, and ethylene oxide, from valves, pump glands (through use of mechanical seals), flanges, and other process equipment by following good design practices and equipment maintenance procedures.
- Use mechanical seals where appropriate.
- Minimize losses from storage tanks, product transfer areas, and other process areas by adopting methods such as vapor recovery systems and double seals (for floating roof tanks).
- Recover catalysts and reduce particulate emissions.
- Reduce nitrogen oxide ($NO_x$) emissions by using low-$NO_x$ burners. Optimize fuel usage.

In some cases, organics that cannot be recovered are effectively destroyed by routing them to flares and other combustion devices.

### Elimination or Reduction of Pollutants

- Use nonchrome-based additives in cooling water.
- Use long-life catalysts and regeneration to extend the cycle.

### Recycling and Reuse

- Recycle cooling water and treated wastewater to the extent feasible.
- Recover and reuse spent solvents and other chemicals to the extent feasible.

### Improved Operating Procedures

- Segregate process wastewaters from stormwater systems.

- Optimize the frequency of tank and equipment cleaning.
- Prevent solids and oily wastes from entering the drainage system.
- Establish and maintain an emergency preparedness and response plan.

## Target Pollution Loads

Implementation of cleaner production processes and pollution prevention measures can yield both economic and environmental benefits. The following production-related targets can be achieved by measures such as those described in the previous section. The figures relate to the production processes before the addition of pollution control measures.

A good practice target for petrochemical complex is to reduce total organic emissions (including VOCs) from the process units to 0.6% of the throughput. Target maximum levels for air releases, per ton of product, are, for ethylene, 0.06 kg; for ethylene oxide, 0.02 kg; for vinyl chloride, 0.2 kg; and for 1,2-dichloroethane, 0.4 kg. Methods of estimating these figures include ambient and emissions monitoring, emission factors, and inventories of emissions sources. Design assumptions should be recorded to allow for subsequent computation and reduction of losses.

Vapor recovery systems to control losses of VOCs from storage tanks and loading areas should achieve close to 100% recovery.

A wastewater generation rate of 15 cubic meters per 100 tons of ethylene produced is achievable with good design and operation; and new petrochemical complexes should strive to achieve this.

## Treatment Technologies

### Air Emissions

Control of air emissions normally includes the capturing and recycling or combustion of emissions from vents, product transfer points, storage tanks, and other handling equipment.

Catalytic cracking units should be provided with particulate removal devices. Particulate removal technologies include fabric filters, ceramic filters, wet scrubbers, and electrostatic precipitators. Gaseous releases are minimized by con-

densation, absorption, adsorption (using activated carbon, silica gel, activated alumina, and zeolites), and, in some cases, biofiltration and bioscrubbing (using peat or heather, bark, composts, and bioflora to treat biodegradable organics), and thermal decomposition.

### Liquid Effluents

Petrochemical wastewaters often require a combination of treatment methods to remove oil and other contaminants before discharge. Separation of different streams (such as stormwater) is essential to minimize treatment requirements. Oil is recovered using separation techniques. For heavy metals, a combination of oxidation/reduction, precipitation, and filtration is used. For organics, a combination of air or steam stripping, granular activated carbon, wet oxidation, ion exchange, reverse osmosis, and electrodialysis is used. A typical system may include neutralization, coagulation/flocculation, flotation/sedimentation/filtration, biodegradation (trickling filter, anaerobic, aerated lagoon, rotating biological contactor, and activated sludge), and clarification. A final polishing step using filtration, ozonation, activated carbon, or chemical treatment may also be required. Examples of pollutant loads that can be achieved are: COD, less than 1 kg per 100 tons of ethylene produced; suspended solids, less than 0.4 kg/100 t; and dichloroethane, than 0.001 kg/100 t.

### Solid and Hazardous Wastes

Combustion (preceded in some cases by solvent extraction) of toxic organics is considered an effective treatment technology for petrochemical organic wastes. Steam stripping and oxidation are also used for treating organic waste streams. Spent catalysts are generally sent back to the suppliers. In some cases, the solid wastes may require stabilization to reduce the leachability of toxic metals before disposal of in an approved, secure landfill.

## Emissions Guidelines

Emissions levels for the design and operation of each project must be established through the environmental assessment (EA) process on the basis of country legislation and the *Pollution Prevention and Abatement Handbook,* as applied to local conditions. The emissions levels selected must be justified in the EA and acceptable to the World Bank Group.

The guidelines given below present emissions levels normally acceptable to the World Bank Group in making decisions regarding provision of World Bank Group assistance. Any deviations from these levels must be described in the World Bank Group project documentation. The emissions levels given here can be consistently achieved by well-designed, well-operated, and well-maintained pollution control systems.

The guidelines are expressed as concentrations to facilitate monitoring. Dilution of air emissions or effluents to achieve these guidelines is unacceptable. All of the maximum levels should be achieved for at least 95% of the time that the plant or unit is operating, to be calculated as a proportion of annual operating hours.

*Air Emissions*

The emissions levels presented in Table 1 should be achieved.

*Liquid Effluents*

The effluent levels presented in Table 2 should be achieved.

### Table 1, Emissions from Petrochemicals Manufacturing and Target Ambient Levels

*(miligrams per normal cubic meter)*

| Parameter | Maximum value |
|---|---|
| PM | 20 |
| Nitrogen oxides | 300 |
| Hydrogen chloride | 10 |
| Sulfur oxides | 500 |
| Benzene | 5 mg/m³ for emissions; 0.1 ppb at the plant fence |
| 1,2-dichloroethane | 5 mg/m³ for emissions; 1.0 ppb at the plant fence |
| Vinyl chloride | 5 mg/m³ for emissions; 0.4 ppb at the plant fence |
| Ammonia | 15 mg/m³ |

*Note:* Maximum ambient levels for ethylene oxide are 0.3 parts per billion (ppb) at the plant fence. Maximum total emissions of the VOCs acetaldehyde, acrylic acid, benzyl chloride, carbon tetrachloride, chlorofluorocarbons, ethyl acrylate, halons, maleic anhydride, 1, 1, 1 trichlorethane, trichloroethylene, and trichlorotoluene are 20 mg/Nm³. Maximum total heavy metals emissions are 1.5 mg/Nm³.

### Table 2. Effluents from Petrochemicals Manufacturing

*(milligrams per liter, except for pH and temperature)*

| Parameter | Maximum value |
|---|---|
| pH | 6–9 |
| BOD | 30 |
| COD | 150 |
| TSS | 30 |
| Oil and grease | 10 |
| Cadmium | 0.1 |
| Chromium (hexavalent) | 0.1 |
| Copper | 0.5 |
| Phenol | 0.5 |
| Benzene | 0.05 |
| Vinyl chloride | 0.05 |
| Sulfide | 1 |
| Nitrogen (total) | 10 |
| Temperature increase | $\leq 3°C^a$ |

*Note:* Effluent requirements are for direct discharge to surface waters.
a. The effluent should result in a temperature increase of no more than 3° C at the edge of the zone where initial mixing and dilution take place. Where the zone is not defined, use 100 meters from the point of discharge.

*Solid Wastes and Sludges*

Wherever possible, generation of sludges should be minimized. Sludges must be treated to reduce toxic organics to nondetectable levels. Wastes containing toxic metals should be stabilized before disposal.

*Ambient Noise*

Noise abatement measures should achieve either the levels given below or a maximum increase in background levels of 3 decibels (measured on the A scale) [dB(A)]. Measurements are to be taken at noise receptors located outside the project property boundary.

| Receptor | Maximum allowable log equivalent (hourly measurements), in dB(A) | |
|---|---|---|
| | Day (07:00–22:00) | Night (22:00–07:00) |
| Residential, institutional, educational | 55 | 45 |
| Industrial, commercial | 70 | 70 |

## Monitoring and Reporting

Frequent sampling may be required during start-up and upset conditions. Once a record of consistent performance has been established, sampling for the parameters listed in this document should be as described below.

Air emissions from stacks should be visually monitored for opacity at least once every eight hours. Annual emissions monitoring of combustion sources should be carried out for sulfur oxides, nitrogen oxides, and the organics listed above, with fuel sulfur content and excess oxygen maintained at acceptable levels during normal operations. Leakages should be visually checked every eight hours and at least once a week using leak detection equipment.

Liquid effluents should be monitored at least once every eight hours for all the parameters cited above except metals, which should be monitored at least monthly.

Each shipment of solid waste going for disposal should be monitored for toxics.

Monitoring data should be analyzed and reviewed at regular intervals and compared with the operating standards so that any necessary corrective actions can be taken. Records of monitoring results should be kept in an acceptable format. The results should be reported to the responsible authorities and relevant parties, as required.

## Key Issues

The key production and control practices that will lead to compliance with emissions guidelines can be summarized as follows:

- Implement an equipment maintenance program that minimizes releases of volatile organics, including ethylene oxide, benzene, vinyl chloride, and 1,2-dichloroethane.
- Install vapor recovery systems to reduce VOC emissions.
- Use low-$NO_x$ burners.
- Optimize fuel usage.
- Regenerate and reuse spent catalysts, solvents, and other solutions to the extent feasible.
- Recycle cooling water and reuse wastewaters.
- Segregate stormwater from process wastewater.
- Use nonchrome-based additives in cooling water.
- Design and practice emergency preparedness and prevention measures.

## Annex. Typical Processes and Products in Petrochemical Manufacturing

$C_1$ compounds (with one carbon atom in their molecule) manufactured at petrochemical plants include methanol, formaldehyde, and halogenated hydrocarbons. Formaldehyde is used in the manufacture of plastic resins, including phenolic, urea, and melamine resins. Halogenated hydrocarbons are used in the manufacture of silicone, solvents, refrigerants, and degreasing agents.

Olefins (organics having at least one double bond for carbon atoms) are typically manufactured from the steam cracking of hydrocarbons such as naphtha. Major olefins manufactured include ethylene ($C_2$, since it has two carbon atoms), propylene ($C_3$), butadiene ($C_4$), and acetylene. The olefins manufactured are used in the manufacture of polyethylene, including low-density polyethylene (LDPE) and high-density polyethylene (HDPE), and for polystyrene, polyvinyl chloride, ethylene glycol (used along with dimethyl terphthalate, DMT, as feedstock to the polyester manufacturing process), ethanol amines (used as solvents), polyvinyl acetate (used in plastics), polyisoprene (used for synthetic rubber manufacture), polypropylene, acetone (used as a solvent and in cosmetics), isopropanol (used as a solvent and in pharmaceuticals manufacturing), acrylonitrile (used in the manufacture of acrylic fibers and nitrile rubber), propylene glycol (used in pharmaceuticals manufacturing), and polyurethane.

Butadiene is used in the manufacture of polybutadiene rubber (PBR) and styrene butadiene rubber (SBR). Other $C_4$ compounds manufactured include butanol, which is used in the manufacture of solvents such as methyl ethyl ketone.

The major aromatics (organics having at least one ring structure with six carbon atoms) manufactured include benzene, toluene, xylene, and naphthalene. Other aromatics manufactured include phenol, chlorobenzene, styrene, phthalic and maleic anhydride, nitrobenzene, and aniline. Benzene is generally recovered from cracker streams at petrochemical plants and is used for the manufacture of phenol, styrene, aniline, nitrobenzene, sulfonated detergents, pesticides such as hexachlorobenzene, cyclohexane (an important intermediate in synthetic fiber manufacture), and caprolactam, used in the manufacture of nylon. Benzene is also used as a solvent.

The main uses of toluene are as a solvent in paints, rubber, and plastic cements and as a feedstock in the manufacture of organic chemicals, explosives, detergents, and polyurethane foams. Xylenes (which exist as three isomers) are used in the manufacture of DMT, alkyd resins, and plasticizers. Naphthalene is mainly used in the manufacture of dyes, pharmaceuticals, insect repellents, and phthalic anhydride (used in the manufacture of alkyd resins, plasticizers, and polyester).

The largest user of phenol in the form of thermosetting resins is the plastics industry. Phenol is also used as a solvent and in the manufacture of intermediates for pesticides, pharmaceuticals, and dyestuffs. Styrene is used in the manufacture of synthetic rubber and polystyrene resins. Phthalic anhydride is used in the manufacture of DMT, alkyd resins, and plasticizers such as phthalates. Maleic anhydride is used in the manufacture of polyesters and, to some extent, for alkyd resins. Minor uses include the manufacture of malathion and soil conditioners. Nitrobenzene is used in the manufacture of aniline, benzidine, and dyestuffs and as a solvent in polishes. Aniline is used in the manufacture of dyes, including azo dyes, and rubber chemicals such as vulcanization accelerators and antioxidants.

## Sources

Bounicore, Anthony J., and Wayne T. Davis, eds. 1992. *Air Pollution Engineering Manual*. New York: Van Nostrand Reinhold.

Cortes, Mariluz, and Peter Bocock. 1984. *North-South Technology Transfer: A Case Study of Petrochemicals in Latin America*. Baltimore, Md.: The John Hopkins University Press

Langley, Roger. 1991. *Petrochemicals: An Industry and Its Future*. Special Report 2067. London: Economist Intelligence Unit.

National Swedish Environmental Protection Board. 1987. "Focus on Environmental Impacts of Petrochemical Plants in Stenungsund. SNV." Report 3209. Solna.

UNIDO (United Nations Industrial Development Organization). 1994. "Report on Consultation on Downstream Petrochemical Industries in Developing Countries in Tehran, Islamic Republic of Iran during November 7 through 11, 1993." Vienna.

United Kingdom, Her Majesty's Inspectorate of Pollution. 1993. "Chief Inspector's Guidance to Inspectors, Environmental Protection Act 1990. Process Guidance Note IPR 4/1: Petrochemical Processes." London: Her Majesty's Stationery Office.

Vergara, Walter, and Dominique Babelon. 1990. *The Petrochemical Industry in Developing Asia: A Review of the Current Situation and Prospects for Development in the 1990s*. World Bank Technical Paper 113. Washington, D.C.: World Bank.

Vergara, Walter, and Donald Brown. 1988. *The New Face of the World Petrochemical Sector: Implications for Developing Countries*. World Bank Technical Paper 84. Washington, D.C.: World Bank.

# Petroleum Refining

## Industry Description and Practices

The petroleum industry is organized into four broad sectors: exploration and production of crude oil and natural gas; transport; refining; and marketing and distribution. This document addresses only petroleum refining.

Crude oil is fractionated into liquefied petroleum gas, naphtha (used to produce gasoline by blending with octane boosters), kerosene/aviation turbine fuel, diesel oil, and residual fuel oil. Catalytic cracking and reforming, thermal cracking, and other secondary processes are used to achieve the desired product specifications. Certain refineries also produce feedstocks for the manufacture of lubricating oils and bitumens. Some refineries also manufacture coke.

## Waste Characteristics

Boilers, process heaters, and other process equipment are responsible for the emission of particulates, carbon monoxide, nitrogen oxides ($NO_x$), sulfur oxides ($SO_x$), and carbon dioxide. Catalyst changeovers and cokers release particulates. Volatile organic compounds (VOCs) such as benzene, toluene, and xylene are released from storage, product loading and handling facilities, and oil-water separation systems and as fugitive emissions from flanges, valves, seals, and drains. For each ton of crude processed, emissions from refineries may be approximately as follows:

- Particulate matter: 0.8 kilograms (kg), ranging from less than 0.1 to 3 kg.
- Sulfur oxides: 1.3 kg, ranging 0.2–06 kg; 0.1 kg with the Claus sulfur recovery process.
- Nitrogen oxides: 0.3 kg, ranging 0.06–0.5 kg.

- Benzene, toluene, and xylene (BTX): 2.5 grams (g), ranging 0.75 to 6 g; 1 g with the Claus sulfur recovery process. Of this, about 0.14 g benzene, 0.55 g toluene, and 1.8 g xylene may be released per ton of crude processed.
- VOC emissions depend on the production techniques, emissions control techniques, equipment maintenance, and climate conditions and may be 1 kg per ton of crude processed (ranging from 0.5 to 6 kg/t of crude).

Petroleum refineries use relatively large volumes of water, especially for cooling systems. Surface water runoff and sanitary wastewaters are also generated. The quantity of wastewaters generated and their characteristics depend on the process configuration. As a general guide, approximately 3.5–5 cubic meters ($m^3$) of wastewater per ton of crude are generated when cooling water is recycled. Refineries generate polluted wastewaters, containing biochemical oxygen demand (BOD) and chemical oxygen demand (COD) levels of approximately 150–250 milligrams per liter (mg/l) and 300–600 mg/l, respectively; phenol levels of 20–200 mg/l; oil levels of 100–300 mg/l in desalter water and up to 5,000 mg/l in tank bottoms; benzene levels of 1–100 mg/l; benzo(a)pyrene levels of less than 1 to 100 mg/l; heavy metals levels of 0.1–100 mg/l for chrome and 0.2–10 mg/l for lead; and other pollutants. Refineries also generate solid wastes and sludges (ranging from 3 to 5 kg per ton of crude processed), 80% of which may be considered hazardous because of the presence of toxic organics and heavy metals.

*Accidental discharges of large quantities of pollutants can occur as a result of abnormal operation in a refinery and potentially pose a major local environmental hazard.*

## Pollution Prevention and Control

Petroleum refineries are complex plants, and the combination and sequence of processes is usually very specific to the characteristics of the raw materials (crude oil) and the products. Specific pollution prevention or source reduction measures can often be determined only by the technical staff. However, there are a number of broad areas where improvements are often possible, and site-specific waste reduction measures in these areas should be designed into the plant and targeted by management of operating plants. Areas where efforts should be concentrated are discussed here.

### Reduction of Air Emissions

- Minimize losses from storage tanks and product transfer areas by methods such as vapor recovery systems and double seals.
- Minimize $SO_x$ emissions either through desulfurization of fuels, to the extent feasible, or by directing the use of high-sulfur fuels to units equipped with $SO_x$ emissions controls.
- Recover sulfur from tail gases in high-efficiency sulfur recovery units.
- Recover non-silica-based (i.e., metallic) catalysts and reduce particulate emissions.
- Use low-$NO_x$ burners to reduce nitrogen oxide emissions.
- Avoid and limit fugitive emissions by proper process design and maintenance.
- Keep fuel usage to a minimum.

### Elimination or Reduction of Pollutants

- Consider reformate and other octane boosters instead of tetraethyl lead and other organic lead compounds for octane boosting.
- Use non-chrome-based inhibitors in cooling water, where inhibitors are needed.
- Use long-life catalysts and regenerate to extend the catalysts' life cycle.

### Recycling and Reuse

- Recycle cooling water and, where cost-effective, treated wastewater.
- Maximize recovery of oil from oily wastewaters and sludges. Minimize losses of oil to the effluent system.
- Recover and reuse phenols, caustics, and solvents from their spent solutions.
- Return oily sludges to coking units or crude distillation units.

### Operating Procedures

- Segregate oily wastewaters from stormwater systems.
- Reduce oil losses during tank drainage carried out to remove water before product dispatch.
- Optimize frequency of tank and equipment cleaning to avoid accumulating residue at the bottom of the tanks.
- Prevent solids and oily wastes from entering the drainage system.
- Institute dry sweeping instead of washdown to reduce wastewater volumes.
- Establish and maintain an emergency preparedness and response plan and carry out frequent training.
- Practice corrosion monitoring, prevention, and control in underground piping and tank bottoms.
- Establish leak detection and repair programs.

## Target Pollution Loads

Implementation of pollution prevention measures can yield both economic and environmental benefits. However, a balance on energy usage and environmental impacts may have to be struck. The production-related targets described below can be achieved by measures such as those detailed in the previous section. The values relate to the production processes before the addition of pollution control measures.

New refineries should be designed to maximize energy conservation and reduce hydrocarbon losses. A good practice target for simple refineries (i.e., refineries with distillation, catalytic reforming, hydrotreating, and offsite facilities) is that the total quantity of oil consumed as fuel and lost in production operations should not exceed 3.5% of the throughput. For refineries with secondary conversion units (i.e., hydrocrackers or lubricating oil units), the target should be 5–6% (and, in some cases, up to 10%) of the throughput. Fugitive VOC emissions from the process units can be reduced to 0.05% of the throughput, with total VOC emissions of less than 1 kg per ton of crude (or 0.1% of throughput). Methods of estimating these figures include emissions monitoring, mass balance, and inventories of emissions sources. Design assumptions should be recorded to allow for subsequent computation and reduction of losses.

Vapor recovery systems to control losses of VOCs from storage tanks and loading areas should achieve 90–100% recovery.

Plant operators should aim at using fuel with less than 0.5% sulfur (or an emissions level corresponding to 0.5% sulfur in fuel). High-sulfur fuels should be directed to units equipped with $SO_x$ controls. Fuel blending is another option. A sulfur recovery system that achieves at least 97% (but preferably over 99%) sulfur recovery should be used when the hydrogen sulfide concentration in tail gases exceeds 230 mg/$Nm^3$. The total release of sulfur dioxide should be below 0.5 kg per ton for a hydroskimming refinery and below 1 kg per ton for a conversion refinery.

A wastewater generation rate of 0.4 $m^3$/t of crude processed is achievable with good design and operation, and new refineries should achieve this target as a minimum.

The generation rate of solid wastes and sludges should be less than 0.5% of the crude processed, with a target of 0.3%.

## Treatment Technologies

### Air Emissions

Control of air emissions normally includes the capture and recycling or combustion of emissions from vents, product transfer points, storage tanks, and other handling equipment. Boilers, heaters, other combustion devices, cokers, and catalytic units may require particulate matter controls. Use of a carbon monoxide boiler is normally a standard practice in the fluidized catalytic cracking units. Catalytic cracking units should be provided with particular removal devices. Steam injection in flaring stacks can reduce particulate matter emissions.

### Liquid Effluents

Refinery wastewaters often require a combination of treatment methods to remove oil and contaminants before discharge. Separation of different streams, such as stormwater, cooling water, process water, sanitary, sewage, etc., is essential for minimizing treatment requirements. A typical system may include sour water stripper, gravity separation of oil and water, dissolved air flotation, biological treatment, and clarification. A final polishing step using filtration, activated carbon, or chemical treatment may also be required. Achievable pollutant loads per ton of crude processed include BOD, 6 g; COD, 50 g; suspended solids, 10 g; and oil and grease, 2 g.

### Solid and Hazardous Wastes

Sludge treatment is usually performed using land application (bioremediation) or solvent extraction followed by combustion of the residue or by use for asphalt, where feasible. In some cases, the residue may require stabilization prior to disposal to reduce the leachability of toxic metals.

Oil is recovered from slops using separation techniques such as gravity separators and centrifuges.

## Emissions Guidelines

Emissions levels for the design and operation of each project must be established through the environmental assessment (EA) process on the basis of country legislation and the *Pollution Prevention and Abatement Handbook,* as applied to local conditions. The emissions levels selected must be justified in the EA and acceptable to the World Bank Group.

The guidelines given below present emissions levels normally acceptable to the World Bank Group in making decisions regarding provision of World Bank Group assistance. Any deviations from these levels must be described in the World Bank Group project documentation. The emissions levels given here can be consistently achieved by well-designed, well-operated, and well-maintained pollution control systems.

The guidelines are expressed as concentrations to facilitate monitoring. Dilution of air emissions or effluents to achieve these guidelines is unacceptable.

All of the maximum levels should be achieved for at least 95% of the time that the plant or unit is operating, to be calculated as a proportion of annual operating hours.

*Air Emissions*

The emissions levels presented in Table 1 should be achieved.

*Liquid Effluents*

The emissions levels presented in Table 2 should be achieved.

Effluent requirements are for direct discharge to surface waters. Discharge to an offsite wastewater treatment plant should meet applicable pretreatment requirements.

*Solid Wastes and Sludges*

Wherever possible, generation of sludges should be minimized to 0.3 kg per ton of crude processed, with a maximum of 0.5 kg per ton of crude processed. Sludges must be treated and stabilized to reduce concentrations of toxics (such as benzene and lead) in leachate to acceptable levels, for example, below 0.05 milligram per kg.

*Ambient Noise*

Noise abatement measures should achieve either the levels given below or a maximum increase in background levels of 3 decibels (measured on the

### Table 1. Emissions from the Petroleum Industry
*(milligrams per normal cubic meter)*

| Parameter | Maximum value |
|---|---|
| PM | 50 |
| Nitrogen oxides[a] | 460 |
| Sulfur oxides | 150 for sulfur recovery units; 500 for other units |
| Nickel and vanadium (combined) | 2 |
| Hydrogen sulfide | 152 |

a. Excludes NO$_x$ emissions from catalytic units.

### Table 2. Effluents from the Petroleum Industry
*(milligrams per liter)*

| Parameter | Maximum value |
|---|---|
| pH | 6–9 |
| BOD | 30 |
| COD | 150 |
| TSS | 30 |
| Oil and grease | 10 |
| Chromium | |
|   Hexavalent | 0.1 |
|   Total | 0.5 |
| Lead | 0.1 |
| Phenol | 0.5 |
| Benzene | 0.05 |
| Benzo(a)pyrene | 0.05 |
| Sulfide | 1 |
| Nitrogen (total)[a] | 10 |
| Temperature increase | ≤ 3°C[b] |

a. The maximum effluent concentration of nitrogen (total) may be up to 40 mg/l in processes that include hydrogenation.
b. The effluent should result in a temperature increase of no more than 3° C at the edge of the zone where initial mixing and dilution take place. Where the zone is not defined, use 100 meters from the point of discharge, provided there are no sensitive ecosystems within this range.

A scale) [dB(A)]. Measurements are to be taken at noise receptors located outside the project property boundary.

| Receptor | Day (07:00–22:00) | Night (22:00–07:00) |
|---|---|---|
| Residential, institutional, educational | 55 | 45 |
| Industrial, commercial | 70 | 70 |

Maximum allowable log equivalent (hourly measurements), in dB(A)

## Monitoring and Reporting

Frequent sampling may be required during startup and upset conditions. Once a record of consistent performance has been established, sampling for the parameters listed in this document should be as described below.

Air emissions from stacks should be monitored once every shift, if not continuously, for opacity (maximum level, 10%). Air emissions of hydrogen sulfide from a sulfur recovery unit should be monitored on a continuous basis. Annual emissions monitoring of combustion sources should be carried out for sulfur oxides (sulfur content of the fuel monitored on a supply-tank basis) and for nitrogen oxides.

Liquid effluents should be monitored daily for all the parameters listed above, except that metals should be monitored at least monthly.

Monitoring data should be analyzed and reviewed at regular intervals and compared with the operating standards so that any necessary corrective actions can be taken. Records of monitoring results should be kept in an acceptable format. The results should be reported to the responsible authorities and relevant parties, as required.

## Key Issues

The key production and control practices that will lead to compliance with emissions guidelines can be summarized as follows:

- Use vapor recovery systems to reduce VOC emissions.
- Install sulfur recovery systems, where feasible.
- Use low-$NO_x$ burners.
- Maintain fuel and losses to 3.5% for simple refineries and below 6% (with 10% as the maximum) for refineries with secondary processing.
- Recover and recycle oily wastes.

- Regenerate and reuse spent catalysts and solvents.
- Recycle cooling water and minimize wastewaters.
- Segregate storm water from process wastewater.
- Use nonchrome-based inhibitors (use only to the extent needed in cooling water).
- Minimize the generation of sludges.
- Install spill prevention and control measures.

## Sources

Bounicore, Anthony J., and Wayne T. Davis, eds. 1992. *Air Pollution Engineering Manual*. New York: Van Nostrand Reinhold.

Commission of the European Communities. DG XI A3. 1991. "Technical Note on the Best Available Technologies to Reduce Emissions of Pollutants into the Air from the Refining Industry." Brussels.

_____. DG XI A3. 1993. "Technoeconomic Study on the Reduction Measures, based on Best Available Technology, of Water Discharges and Waste Generation from Refineries." Brussels.

USEPA (U.S. Environmental Protection Agency). 1982. "Development Document for Effluent Limitations Guidelines and Standards for the Petroleum Refining Point Source Category." Washington, D.C.

World Bank. 1996. "Pollution Prevention and Abatement: Petroleum Refining." Draft Technical Background Document. Environment Department, Washington, D.C.

# Pharmaceuticals Manufacturing

## Industry Description and Practices

The pharmaceutical industry includes the manufacture, extraction, processing, purification, and packaging of chemical materials to be used as medications for humans or animals. Pharmaceutical manufacturing is divided into two major stages: the production of the active ingredient or drug (primary processing, or manufacture) and secondary processing, the conversion of the active drugs into products suitable for administration. This document deals with the synthesis of the active ingredients and their usage in drug formulations to deliver the prescribed dosage. Formulation is also referred to as galenical production.

The main pharmaceutical groups manufactured include:

- Proprietary ethical products or prescription-only medicines (POM), which are usually patented products
- General ethical products, which are basically standard prescription-only medicines made to a recognized formula that may be specified in standard industry reference books
- Over-the counter (OTC), or nonprescription, products.

The products are available as tablets, capsules, liquids (in the form of solutions, suspensions, emulsions, gels, or injectables), creams (usually oil-in-water emulsions), ointments (usually water-in-oil emulsions), and aerosols, which contain inhalable products or products suitable for external use. Propellants used in aerosols include chlorofluorocarbons (CFCs), which are being phased out. Recently, butane has been used as a propellant in externally applied products.

The major manufactured groups include:

- Antibiotics such as penicillin, streptomycin, tetracyclines, chloramphenicol, and antifungals
- Other synthetic drugs, including sulfa drugs, antituberculosis drugs, antileprotic drugs, analgesics, anesthetics, and antimalarials
- Vitamins
- Synthetic hormones
- Glandular products
- Drugs of vegetable origin such as quinine, strychnine and brucine, emetine, and digitalis glycosides
- Vaccines and sera
- Other pharmaceutical chemicals such as calcium gluconate, ferrous salts, nikethamide, glycerophosphates, chloral hydrate, saccharin, antihistamines (including meclozine, and buclozine), tranquilizers (including meprobamate and chloropromoazine), antifilarials, diethyl carbamazine citrate, and oral antidiabetics, including tolbutamide and chloropropamide
- Surgical sutures and dressings.

The principal manufacturing steps are (a) preparation of process intermediates; (b) introduction of functional groups; (c) coupling and esterification; (d) separation processes such as washing and stripping; and (e) purification of the final product. Additional product preparation steps include granulation; drying; tablet pressing, printing, and coating; filling; and packaging. Each of these steps may generate air emissions, liquid effluents, and solid wastes.

The manufacture of penicillin, for example, involves the batch fermentation—using 100–200 cubic meter ($m^3$) batches—of maize steep liquor or a similar base, with organic precursors added to control the yield. Specific mold culture such as *Penicillium chrysogenum* for Type II is inoculated into the fermentation medium. Penicillin is separated from the fermentation broth by solvent extraction. The product is further purified using acidic extraction. This is followed by treatment with a pyrogen-free distilled water solution containing the alkaline salt of the desired element. The purified aqueous concentrate is separated from the solvent in a supercentrifuge and pressurized through a biological filter to remove the final traces of bacteria and pyrogens. The solution can be concentrated by freeze drying or vacuum spray drying. Oil-soluble procaine penicillin is made by reacting a penicillin concentrate (20–30%) with a 50% aqueous solution of procaine hydrochloride. Procaine penicillin crystallizes from this mixture.

The manufacture of pharmaceuticals is controlled by Good Management Practices (GMP) in some countries. (See, for example, United Kingdom 1993.) Some countries require an environmental assessment (EA) report addressing the fate and toxicity of drugs and their metabolized by-products. The EA data relate to the parent drug, not to all metabolites, and include (a) physical and chemical properties; (b) biodegradability; (c) photolysis propensity; (d) aqueous toxicity to fish; (e) prediction of existing or planned treatment plant to treat wastes and wastewaters; and (f) treatment sequences that are capable of treating wastes and wastewaters.

## Waste Characteristics

The principal air pollutants are volatile organic compounds (VOCs) and particulate matter (PM).

Liquid effluents resulting from equipment cleaning after batch operation contain toxic organic residues. Their composition varies, depending on the product manufactured, the materials used in the process, and other process details. Cooling waters are normally recirculated. Some wastewaters may contain mercury, in a range of 0.1–4 milligrams per liter (mg/l), cadmium (10–600 mg/l), isomers of hexachlorocyclohexane, 1,2-dichloroethane, and solvents. Typical amounts released with the wastewater are 25 kilograms of biochemical oxygen demand (BOD) per metric ton of product (kg/t), or 2,000 mg/l; 50 kg/t chemical oxygen demand (COD), or 4,000

mg/l; 3 kg/t of suspended solids; and up to 0.8 kg/t of phenol.

The principal solid wastes of concern include process and effluent treatment sludges, spent catalysts, and container residues. Approximately 200 kg wastes per ton of product of waste are generated. Some solid wastes contain significant concentrations of spent solvents and other toxic organics.

## Pollution Prevention and Control

Every effort should be made to replace highly toxic and persistent ingredients with degradable and less toxic ones. Recommended pollution prevention measures are as follows:

- Meter and control the quantities of active ingredients to minimize wastage.
- Reuse by-products from the process as raw materials or as raw material substitutes in other processes.
- Recover solvents used in the process by distillation or other methods.
- Give preference to the use of nonhalogenated solvents.
- Use automated filling to minimize spillage.
- Use "closed" feed systems into batch reactors.
- Use equipment washdown waters and other process waters (such as leakages from pump seals) as makeup solutions for subsequent batches.
- Recirculate cooling water.
- Use dedicated dust collectors to recycle recovered materials.
- Vent equipment through a vapor recovery system.
- Use loss-free vacuum pumps.
- Return toxic materials packaging to the supplier for reuse, or incinerate/destroy it in an environmentally acceptable manner.
- Minimize storage time of off-specification products through regular reprocessing.
- Find productive uses for off-specification products to avoid disposal problems.
- Minimize raw material and product inventory to avoid degradation and wastage.
- Use high-pressure hoses for equipment cleaning to reduce wastewater.
- Provide stormwater drainage and avoid contamination of stormwater from process areas.

- Label and store toxic and hazardous materials in secure, bunded areas. Spillage should be collected and reused.

Where appropriate, a pharmaceutical manufacturing plant should prepare a hazard assessment and operability study and also prepare and implement an emergency plan that takes into account neighboring land uses and the potential consequences of an emergency. Measures to avoid the release of harmful substances should be incorporated in the design, operation, maintenance, and management of the plant.

**Pollution Reduction Targets**

Implementation of cleaner production processes and pollution prevention measures can yield both economic and environmental benefits.

Specific reduction targets for the different processes have not been determined. In the absence of specific pollution reduction targets, new plants should always achieve better than the industry averages quoted in the section on Waste Characteristics. Table 2, below, presents the maximum effluent levels after the addition of pollution control measures.

Vapor recovery systems should be installed to control air emissions. Wastewaters and treated effluents should be recycled to the extent feasible.

**Treatment Technologies**

*Air Emissions*

Stack gas scrubbing, carbon adsorption (for toxic organics), and baghouses (for particulate matter removal) are applicable and effective technologies for minimizing the release of significant pollutants to air. In some cases, biological filters are also used to reduce emissions of organics. Combustion is used for the destruction of toxic organics.

*Liquid Effluents*

Reverse osmosis or ultrafiltration is used to recover and concentrate active ingredients. Effluent treatment normally includes neutralization, flocculation, flotation, coagulation, filtration, settling, ion exchange, carbon adsorption, detoxification of active ingredients by oxidation (using ozone wet air oxidation ultraviolet systems or peroxide solutions), and biological treatment (using trickling filters, anaerobic, activated sludge, and rotating biological contactors). Exhausted carbon from adsorption processes may be sent for regeneration or combustion. In some cases, air or steam stripping is performed to remove organics. Toxic metals are precipitated and filtered out.

*Solid Wastes*

Contaminated solid wastes are generally incinerated, and the flue gases are scrubbed. Combustion devices should be operated at temperatures above 1,000° C, with a residence time of at least 1 second, to achieve acceptable destruction efficiency (over 99.99%) of toxics. However, temperatures of around 900° C are acceptable provided that at least 99.99% destruction/removal efficiency of toxics is achieved.

**Emissions Guidelines**

Emissions levels for the design and operation of each project must be established through the environmental assessment (EA) process on the basis of country legislation and the *Pollution Prevention and Abatement Handbook,* as applied to local conditions. The emissions levels selected must be justified in the EA and acceptable to the World Bank Group.

The following guidelines present emissions levels normally acceptable to the World Bank Group in making decisions regarding provision of World Bank Group assistance. Any deviations from these levels must be described in the World Bank Group project documentation. The emissions levels given here can be consistently achieved by well-designed, well-operated, and well-maintained pollution control systems.

The guidelines are expressed as concentrations to facilitate monitoring. Dilution of air emissions or effluents to achieve these guidelines is unacceptable.

All of the maximum levels should be achieved for at least 95% of the time that the plant or unit is operating, to be calculated as a proportion of annual operating hours.

## Air Emissions

The emissions levels presented in Table 1 should be achieved.

*Class A compounds* are those that may cause significant harm to human health and the environment. They include Montreal Protocol substances, as well as others identified from a review of the Group B compounds in the proposed EU directive "The Limitation of Organic Solvents from Certain Processes and Industrial Installations" and other international standards. Examples of Class A compounds include acetaldehyde, acrylic acid, benzyl chloride, carbon tetrachloride, chlorofluorocarbons (being phased out), ethyl acrylate, halons (being phased out), maleic anhydride, 1,1,1 trichlorethane, tichloromethane, trichloroethylene, and trichlorotoluene.

*Class B compounds* are organic compounds of with less environmental impact than Class A compounds. Examples include toluene, acetone, and propylene. Odors should be acceptable at the plant boundary.

## Liquid Effluents

The effluent levels presented in Table 2 should be achieved.

### Table 1. Emissions from Pharmaceutical Manufacturing
*(milligrams per normal cubic meter)*

| Parameter | Maximum value |
|---|---|
| Active ingredient (each)[a] | 0.15 |
| PM | 20 |
| Total Class A[b] | 20 |
| Total Class B[c] | 80 |
| Benzene, vinyl chloride, dichloroethane (each) | 5 |

a. Releases below these mass emissions limits may not be trivial and so may still require controls and setting of appropriate release limits.
b. Applicable when total Class A compounds (see text) exceed 100g/hr.
b. Applicable when total Class B compounds (see text), expressed as toluene, exceed the lower of 5 t/year or 2 kg/hr.

### Table 2. Effluents from Pharmaceutical Manufacturing
*(milligrams per liter, except for pH)*

| Parameter | Maximum value |
|---|---|
| pH | 6–9 |
| BOD[a] | 30 |
| COD | 150 |
| AOX | 1 |
| TSS | 10 |
| Oil and grease | 10 |
| Phenol | 0.5 |
| Arsenic | 0.1 |
| Cadmium | 0.1 |
| Chromium (hexavalent) | 0.1 |
| Mercury | 0.01 |
| Active ingredient (each) | 0.05 |

a. A BOD test is to be performed only in cases where the effluent does not contain any substance toxic to the microorganisms used in the test.

Bioassay testing should be performed to ensure that toxicity of the effluent is acceptable (toxicity to fish = 2; toxicity to *Daphnia* = 8; toxicity to algae = 16; and toxicity to bacteria = 8).

## Solid Wastes

Contaminated solid wastes should be incinerated under controlled conditions at a minimum temperature of 1,000°C and a residence time of 1 second for liquid feed, so as to achieve over 99.99% reduction in toxic organics. Halogenated organics should not normally be incinerated. Where incineration of such organics is required, the release of dioxins and furans is restricted to levels below 1 nanogram per normal cubic meter (ng/Nm³), as measured using a toxicity equivalent factor for 2, 3, 7, 8-TCDD.

## Ambient Noise

Noise abatement measures should achieve either the levels given below or a maximum increase in background levels of 3 decibels (measured on the A scale) [dB(A)]. Measurements are to be taken at noise receptors located outside the project property boundary.

| Receptor | Maximum allowable log equivalent (hourly measurements), in dB(A) | |
|---|---|---|
| | Day (07:00–22:00) | Night (22:00–07:00) |
| Residential, institutional, educational | 55 | 45 |
| Industrial, commercial | 70 | 70 |

## Monitoring and Reporting

Frequent sampling may be required during start-up and upset conditions. Once a record of consistent performance has been established, sampling for the parameters listed in this document should be as described below.

Monitoring of air emissions should be on a continuous basis. Liquid effluents should be monitored for active ingredients at least once every shift. The remaining parameters should be monitored at least daily.

Monitoring data should be analyzed and reviewed at regular intervals and compared with the operating standards so that any necessary corrective actions can be taken. Records of monitoring results should be kept in an acceptable format. The results should be reported to the responsible authorities and relevant parties, as required.

## Key Issues

The key production and control practices that will lead to compliance with emissions requirements can be summarized as follows:

- Replace highly toxic and persistent ingredients with less toxic, degradable ones.
- Control loss and wastage of active ingredients.
- Return packaging for refilling.
- Use vapor recovery systems to prevent the release of toxic organics into air.
- Recover solvents and avoid the use of halogenated solvents.
- Use equipment washdown waters as makeup solutions for subsequent batches.
- Minimize wastage by inventory control, and find uses for off-specification products.

## Reference

United Kingdom, Her Majesty's Inspectorate of Pollution. 1993. "Chief Inspector's Guidance to Inspectors, Environment Protection Act 1990, Process Guidance Note IPR 4/9: Pharmaceutical Processes." Her Majesty's Stationery Office, London.

# Phosphate Fertilizer Plants

## Industry Description and Practices

Phosphate fertilizers are produced by adding acid to ground or pulverized phosphate rock. If sulfuric acid is used, single or normal, phosphate (SSP) is produced, with a phosphorus content of 16–21% as phosphorous pentoxide ($P_2O_5$). If phosphoric acid is used to acidulate the phosphate rock, triple phosphate (TSP) is the result. TSP has a phosphorus content of 43–48% as $P_2O_5$.

SSP production involves mixing the sulfuric acid and the rock in a reactor. The reaction mixture is discharged onto a slow-moving conveyor in a den. The mixture is cured for 4 to 6 weeks before bagging and shipping.

Two processes are used to produce TSP fertilizers: run-of-pile and granular. The run-of-pile process is similar to the SSP process. Granular TSP uses lower-strength phosphoric acid (40%, compared with 50% for run-of-pile). The reaction mixture, a slurry, is sprayed onto recycled fertilizer fines in a granulator. Granules grow and are then discharged to a dryer, screened, and sent to storage.

Phosphate fertilizer complexes often have sulfuric and phosphoric acid production facilities. Sulfuric acid is produced by burning molten sulfur in air to produce sulfur dioxide, which is then catalytically converted to sulfur trioxide for absorption in oleum. Sulfur dioxide can also be produced by roasting pyrite ore. Phosphoric acid is manufactured by adding sulfuric acid to phosphate rock. The reaction mixture is filtered to remove phosphogypsum, which is discharged to settling ponds or waste heaps.

## Waste Characteristics

Fluorides and dust are emitted to the air from the fertilizer plant. All aspects of phosphate rock processing and finished product handling generate dust, from grinders and pulverizers, pneumatic conveyors, and screens. The mixer/reactors and dens produce fumes that contain silicon tetrafluoride and hydrogen fluoride. Liquid effluents are not normally expected from the fertilizer plant, since it is feasible to operate the plant with a balanced process water system. The fertilizer plant should generate minimal solid wastes.

A sulfuric acid plant has two principal air emissions: sulfur dioxide and acid mist. If pyrites ore is roasted, there will also be particulates in air emissions that may contain heavy metals such as cadmium, mercury, and lead. Sulfuric acid plants do not normally discharge liquid effluents except where appropriate water management measures are absent. Solid wastes from a sulfuric acid plant will normally be limited to spent vanadium catalyst. Where pyrite ore is roasted, there will be pyrite residue, which will require disposal. The residue may contain a wide range of heavy metals such as zinc, copper, lead, cadmium, mercury, and arsenic.

The phosphoric acid plant generates dust and fumes, both of which contain hydrofluoric acid, silicon tetrafluoride, or both.

Phosphogypsum generated in the process (at an approximate rate of about 5 tons per ton of phosphoric acid produced) is most often disposed of as a slurry to a storage/settling pond or waste heap. (Disposal to a marine environment is practiced at some existing phosphoric acid plants.)

Process water used to transport the waste is returned to the plant after the solids have settled out. It is preferable to use a closed-loop operating system, where possible, to avoid a liquid effluent. In many climatic conditions, however, this is not possible, and an effluent is generated that contains phosphorus (as $PO_4$), fluorides, and suspended solids. The phosphogypsum contains trace metals, fluorides, and radionuclides (especially radon gas) that have been carried through from the phosphate rock.

## Pollution Prevention and Control

In a fertilizer plant, the main source of potential pollution is solids from spills, operating upsets, and dust emissions. It is essential that tight operating procedures be in place and that close attention be paid to constant cleanup of spills and to other housecleaning measures. Product will be retained, the need for disposal of waste product will be controlled, and potential contamination of stormwater runoff from the property will be minimized.

The discharge of sulfur dioxide from sulfuric acid plants should be minimized by using the double-contact, double-absorption process, with high efficiency mist eliminators. Spills and accidental discharges should be prevented by using well-bunded storage tanks, by installing spill catchment and containment facilities, and by practicing good housekeeping and maintenance. Residues from the roasting of pyrites may be used by the cement and steel manufacturing industries.

In the phosphoric acid plant, emissions of fluorine compounds from the digester/reactor should be minimized by using well-designed, well-operated, and well-maintained scrubbers. Design for spill containment is essential for avoiding inadvertent liquid discharges. An operating water balance should be maintained to avoid an effluent discharge.

The management of phosphogypsum tailings is a major problem because of the large volumes and large area required and because of the potential for release of dust and radon gases and of fluorides and cadmium in seepage. The following measures will help to minimize the impacts:

- Maintain a water cover to reduce radon gas release and dust emissions.
- Where water cover cannot be maintained, keep the tailings wet or revegetate to reduce dust. (Note, however, that the revegetation process may increase the rate of radon emissions.)
- Line the tailings storage area to prevent contamination of groundwater by fluoride.

- Where contamination of groundwater is a concern, a management and monitoring plan should be implemented.

Phosphogypsum may find a use in the production of gypsum board for the construction industry.

## Target Pollution Loads

Implementation of cleaner production processes and pollution prevention measures can yield both economic and environmental benefits. The following production-related targets can be achieved by measures such as those described above. The numbers relate to the production processes before the addition of pollution control measures.

In sulfuric acid plants that use the double-contact, double-absorption process, emissions levels of 2–4 kilograms of sulfur dioxide per metric ton (kg/t) of sulfuric acid can be achieved, and sulfur trioxide levels of the order of 0.15–0.2 kg/t of sulfuric acid are attainable.

## Treatment Technologies

Scrubbers are used to remove fluorides and acid from air emissions. The effluent from the scrubbers is normally recycled to the process. If it is not possible to maintain an operating water balance in the phosphoric acid plant, treatment to precipitate fluorine, phosphorus, and heavy metals may be necessary. Lime can be used for treatment. Spent vanadium catalyst is returned to the supplier for recovery, or, if that cannot be done, is locked in a solidification matrix and disposed of in a secure landfill.

Opportunities to use gypsum wastes as a soil conditioner (for alkali soil and soils that are deficient in sulfur) should be explored to minimize the volume of the gypsum stack.

## Emissions Guidelines

Emissions levels for the design and operation of each project must be established through the environmental assessment (EA) process on the basis of country legislation and the *Pollution Prevention and Abatement Handbook,* as applied to local conditions. The emissions levels selected must be justified in the EA and acceptable to the World Bank Group.

The following guidelines present emissions levels normally acceptable to the World Bank Group in making decisions regarding provision of World Bank Group assistance. Any deviations from these levels must be described in the World Bank Group project documentation. The emissions levels given here can be consistently achieved by well-designed, well-operated, and well-maintained pollution control systems.

The guidelines are expressed as concentrations to facilitate monitoring. Dilution of air emissions or effluents to achieve these guidelines is unacceptable.

All of the maximum levels should be achieved for at least 95% of the time that the plant or unit is operating, to be calculated as a proportion of annual operating hours.

### Air Emissions

The emissions levels presented in Table 1 should be achieved.

### Liquid Effluents

The effluent levels presented in Table 2 should be achieved.

### Ambient Noise

Noise abatement measures should achieve either the levels given below or a maximum increase in

### Table 1. Air Emissions from Phosphate Fertilizer Production

*(milligrams per normal cubic meter)*

| Pollutant | Maximum value |
|---|---|
| *Fertilizer plant* | |
| Fluorides | 5 |
| PM | 50 |
| *Sulfuric acid plant* | |
| Sulfur dioxide | 2 kg/t acid |
| Sulfur trioxide (SO$_3$) | 0.15 kg/t acid |
| *Phosphoric acid plant* | |
| Fluorides | 5 |
| PM | 50 |

### Table 2. Effluents from Phosphate Fertilizer Production

*(milligrams per liter, except for pH)*

| Pollutant | Maximum value |
|---|---|
| pH | 6–9 |
| TSS | 50 |
| Phosphorus | 5 |
| Fluoride | 20 |
| Cadmium | 0.1 |

*Note:* Effluent requirements are for direct discharge to surface waters.

background levels of 3 decibels (measured on the A scale) [dB(A)]. Measurements are to be taken at noise receptors located outside the project property boundary.

| Receptor | Maximum allowable log equivalent (hourly measurements), in dB(A) | |
|---|---|---|
| | Day (07:00–22:00) | Night (22:00–07:00) |
| Residential, institutional, educational | 55 | 45 |
| Industrial, commercial | 70 | 70 |

## Monitoring and Reporting

Fluoride and particulate emissions to the atmosphere from the fertilizer plant should be monitored continuously. In the sulfuric acid plant, sulfur dioxide and acid mist in the stack gas should be monitored continuously.

Liquid effluents should be monitored continuously for pH. All other parameters may be monitored monthly.

Monitoring data should be analyzed and reviewed at regular intervals and compared with the operating standards so that any necessary corrective actions can be taken. Records of monitoring results should be kept in an acceptable format. The results should be reported to the responsible authorities and relevant parties, as required.

For land storage of phosphogypsum, the following monitoring parameters and frequency are recommended for the stack drainage and runoff:

continuously for pH; daily for fluorides; and monthly for phosphorus, sulfates, and gross alpha-particle activity.

## Key Issues

The key production and control practices that will lead to compliance with emissions requirements can be summarized as follows:

- Achieve the highest possible sulfur conversion rate; use the double-contact, double-absorption process for sulfuric acid production.
- Consider the use of phosphogypsum to produce gypsum board for the construction industry.
- Design and operate phosphogypsum disposal facilities to minimize impacts.
- Maximize product recovery and minimize air emissions by appropriate maintenance and operation of scrubbers and baghouses.
- Eliminate effluent discharges by operating a balanced process water system.
- Prepare and implement an emergency preparedness and response plan (required because of the large quantities of sulfuric and phosphoric acids and other hazardous materials stored and handled on the site).

- Consider providing pyrite-roasting residues to the cement- or steel-making industry.

## Sources

Bounicore, Anthony J., and Wayne T. Davis, eds. 1992. *Air Pollution Engineering Manual.* New York: Van Nostrand Reinhold.

European Fertilizer Manufacturers' Association. 1995a. "Production of Sulphuric Acid." Booklet 3 of 8. Brussels.

————. 1995b. "Production of Phosphoric Acid." Booklet 4 of 8. Brussels.

Sauchelli, Vincent. 1960. *Chemistry and Technology of Fertilizers.* New York: Reinhold Publishing.

Sittig, Marshall. 1979. *Fertilizer Industry: Processes, Pollution Control and Energy Conservation.* Park Ridge, N.J.: Noyes Data Corporation.

UNIDO (United Nations Industrial Development Organization). 1978. *Process Technologies for Phosphate Fertilizers.* New York.

World Bank. 1996. "Pollution Prevention and Abatement: Phosphate Fertilizer Plants." Draft Technical Background Document. Environment Department, Washington, D.C.

# Printing

The printing industry is very diverse, as can be seen in the multitude of different products that bear some form of printing—books, daily newspapers, periodicals, packaging, cartons, carrier bags, drink containers, signs, forms, brochures, advertisements, wallpaper, textiles, sheeting, metal foil, and so on.

Text, diagrams, pictures, and so on are designed and composed on, for example, a newspaper page. If pictures and/or text are to be printed in several colors, these must be separated. The pictures are also often screened, producing an image that consists of a large number of very small dots instead of a solid field. Photographic techniques are used for setting and working on pictures.

The page is then transferred to a printing form, a printing block (high-intensity, flexography), plate (offset), roller (rotogravure), or stencil (screen printing). This is done by means of exposure to a light-sensitive coating. In the case of offset and screen printing, the printing form is developed by washing away part of the coating; the form may then, in theory, be used immediately. The offset plate is coated with rubber to protect it from oxidation. The screen sheet's sides are masked with protective paint.

Other printing methods require further stages. The small grooves in the gravure roller are etched or, increasingly, engraved, and the surface is chromed for better durability. The rubber printing block for flexographic printing is cast or engraved by laser.

Printing is done on single sheets or paper web, using one or more printing units, depending on the number of colors required. The dyeing agent is, in most cases, a solvent that evaporates from the paper. (In some cases, it is necessary to hasten evaporation by feeding in warm air.) Clear varnish is sometimes added to the printed surface.

The printed matter is processed off-press, where it is cut, jointed, folded, sewn, bound, packaged, and so on.

Printing may also be a step in another manufacturing process—for example, laminating at package printing works, in which layers of paper, plastic and metal foil are joined.

Plastic surfaces are treated to facilitate printing using electrical discharges from an electrode system, the "corona treatment."

## Waste Characteristics

Emissions into the air mainly consist of organic solvents and other organic compounds. Some substances may cause unpleasant odors or affect health and the environment.

Discharges to water bodies mainly consist of silver, copper, chromium, organic solvents, and other toxic organic compounds.

Noise comes principally from fans, printing presses, and transport.

Wastes consist of environmentally hazardous wastes such as photographic and residual chemicals, metal hydroxide sludge, dyestuff and solvent residues, wiping material containing dyes and solvents, and oil spills. There are also bulky wastes such as paper.

## Pollution Prevention and Control

The recommended pollution prevention measures are as follows:

- Estimate and control, typically on an annual basis, the quantities of volatile organic solvents used, including the amount used in dyes, inks, glues, and damping water. Estimate and control the proportion that is made up of chlorinated organic solvents.

- Replace solvent-based dyes and glues with solvent-free or water-based dyes and glues, where feasible. Water-based dyes are preferred for flexographic printing on paper and plastic and for screen printing and rotogravure.
- Give preference to the use of radiation-setting dyes.
- Engrave, rather than etch, gravure cylinders to reduce the quantity of heavy metals used.
- Enclose presses and ovens to avoid diffuse evaporation of organic substances entering the general ventilation system, where feasible. Use suction hoods to collect vapors and other fugitive emissions.
- Evacuate air from printing presses and drying ovens into a ventilation system.
- Where possible, replace chemicals used for form preparation and cleaning with more environmentally friendly alternatives. Maintain a record of chemicals and environmentally hazardous waste. Do not use halogenated solvents and degreasing agents in new plants. Replace them with nonhalogenated substances in existing facilities.
- Estimate the quantity of developing bath and fixing bath used per year and maintain these at acceptable levels.
- Minimize the rinse water flow in the developing machines by, for example, use of "stand-by."
- Collect fixing bath, developer, used film, photographic paper, and blackened ends of photosetting paper and manage them properly.
- Use countercurrent flow fixing processes.
- Aim for a closed washing system.
- Store chemicals and environmentally hazardous waste such as dyes, inks, and solvents so that the risk of spillage into the wastewater system is minimized. Examples of measures that should be considered are retaining dikes or areas with no outlet, as a means of absorbing spillage. Minimize noise disturbance from fans and presses.
- Use equipment washdown waters as makeup solutions for subsequent batches. Use countercurrent rinsing.
- Recover energy from combustion systems, when they are used.

- Return toxic materials packaging to the supplier for reuse.
- Recover plates by remelting.
- Label and store toxic and hazardous materials in secure, bunded areas.

## Treatment Technologies

### Air Emissions

- Control emissions of gases from web offset with heat-setting thermic or catalytic incineration. Recover toluene from rotogravure by absorption, using active carbon. Carry out adsorption of solvents, using zeolites, and recover organic solvents.
- Treat organic solvents by using trickling filters. Use biological scrubbers to treat discharges of water-soluble solvents.
- Treat metal-containing effluents from the manufacture of gravure cylinders and printing blocks by applying the established methods of chemical precipitation, sedimentation, and filtration. Collect fixing baths for recovery or destruction. Evaporate solvents from regeneration of active carbon filters. Perform closed-screen chase washing; recirculate solvents and separate sludge. Fit developing machines with counterflow fixing or connect them to an organic ion exchanger. Collect film-developing agents for destruction. Carry out high-pressure water jet cleaning. Use ultrafiltration to treat washing water.

### Solid Wastes

Because of the relatively small volumes of solid wastes, it is difficult to find acceptable and affordable methods of disposal. Ideally, solid wastes should be sent for incineration in a facility where combustion conditions (1,100° C and at least 0.5 second residence time) that ensure effective destruction of toxics are maintained.

## Emissions Guidelines

Emissions levels for the design and operation of each project must be established through the environmental assessment (EA) process on the basis of country legislation and the *Pollution Prevention and Abatement Handbook,* as applied to local conditions. The emissions levels selected must be justified in the EA and acceptable to the World Bank Group.

The following guidelines present emissions levels normally acceptable to the World Bank Group in making decisions regarding provision of World Bank Group assistance. Any deviations from these levels must be described in the World Bank Group project documentation. The emissions levels given here can be consistently achieved by well-designed, well-operated, and well-maintained pollution control systems.

The guidelines are expressed as concentrations to facilitate monitoring. Dilution of air emissions or effluents to achieve these guidelines is unacceptable.

All of the maximum levels should be achieved for at least 95% of the time that the plant or unit is operating, to be calculated as a proportion of annual operating hours.

### Air Emissions

The maximum value for emissions of volatile organic compounds (VOCs) should be below 20 milligrams per normal cubic meter (mg/Nm³), calculated as total carbon. Chlorine (chloride/chlorinated hydrocarbons) emissions should be below 10 mg/Nm³.

### Liquid Effluents

The effluent levels presented in Table 1 should be achieved.

### Solid Wastes

Toxic solid wastes should be treated to destroy toxic organics to levels below 0.05 milligrams per kilograms (mg/kg). Wastes containing toxic metals should be stabilized to achieve levels in the leachate below those indicated in Table 1.

### Ambient Noise

Noise abatement measures should achieve either the levels given below or a maximum increase in background levels of 3 decibels (measured on the A scale) [dB(A)]. Measurements are to be taken

**Table 1. Effluents from Printing Plants**
*(milligrams per liter, except for pH)*

| Parameter | Maximum value |
|---|---|
| pH | 6.5–10 |
| BOD | 30 |
| COD | 150 |
| TSS | 50 |
| Oil and grease | 10 |
| Cadmium | 0.1 |
| Chromium | |
|   Hexavalent | 0.1 |
|   Total | 0.5 |
| Copper | 0.5 |
| Silver | 0.5 |
| Zinc | 2 |

*Note:* Effluent requirements are for direct discharge to surface waters.

at noise receptors located outside the project property boundary.

| | Maximum allowable log equivalent (hourly measurements), in dB(A) | |
|---|---|---|
| Receptor | Day (07:00–22:00) | Night (22:00–07:00) |
| Residential, institutional, educational | 55 | 45 |
| Industrial, commercial | 70 | 70 |

## Monitoring and Reporting

Frequent sampling may be required during start-up and upset conditions. Once a record of consistent performance has been established, sampling for the parameters listed in this document should be as described below:

- Continuously monitor air emissions exiting the air pollution control system where toxic organics are being emitted at rates greater than 0.1 kilogram/hour.
- Analyze liquid effluents generated from the process at least monthly, and analyze solid waste before sending it for disposal.

Monitoring data should be analyzed and reviewed at regular intervals and compared with the operating standards so that any necessary corrective actions can be taken. Records of monitoring results should be kept in an acceptable format. The results should be reported to the responsible authorities and relevant parties, as required.

## Key Issues

The key production and control practices that will lead to compliance with emissions guidelines can be summarized as follows:

- Put in place and use good management practices, especially cleanliness and materials control.
- Collect spent fixing solution. Reuse it, or manage it as hazardous waste.
- Recirculate liquid effluents.
- Do not use halogenated solvents.
- Use organic, solvent-free dyes and glues, where feasible.

- Minimize air emissions and generation of toxic wastes, especially organics.
- Incinerate all toxic organic wastes except those containing toxic volatile metals.
- Collect solvent vapors, including toluene. Recover solvents or incinerate them in a combustion unit.
- Manage as hazardous waste spent photographic chemicals, plate developer, dye residues, and other wastes containing toxic organics or metals.

## Sources

Swedish Environmental Protection Agency. 1991. "The Graphic Industry, Industry Fact Sheet." SNV 91-620-9305-3/91-03/500ex. Solna.

USEPA (United States Environmental Protection Agency). 1995. "Printing and Publishing: Sector Notebook, EPA Envirosense Bulletin Board." EPA/310-R-95-014. Office of Compliance, Washington, D.C.

# Pulp and Paper Mills

## Industry Description and Practices

Pulp and paper are manufactured from raw materials containing cellulose fibers, generally wood, recycled paper, and agricultural residues. In developing countries, about 60% of cellulose fibers originate from nonwood raw materials such as bagasse (sugar cane fibers), cereal straw, bamboo, reeds, esparto grass, jute, flax, and sisal. This document addresses environmental issues in pulp and paper manufacturing with unit production capacities greater than 100 metric tons per day (tpd).

The main steps in pulp and paper manufacturing are raw material preparation, such as wood debarking and chip making; pulp manufacturing; pulp bleaching; paper manufacturing; and fiber recycling. Pulp mills and paper mills may exist separately or as integrated operations. Manufactured pulp is used as a source of cellulose for fiber manufacture and for conversion into paper or cardboard.

Pulp manufacturing starts with raw material preparation, which includes debarking (when wood is used as raw material), chipping, and other processes such as depithing (for example, when bagasse is used as the raw material). Cellulosic pulp is manufactured from the raw materials, using chemical and mechanical means.

The manufacture of pulp for paper and cardboard employs mechanical (including thermomechanical), chemimechanical, and chemical methods. Mechanical pulping separates fibers by such methods as disk abrasion and billeting. Chemimechanical processes involve mechanical abrasion and the use of chemicals. Thermomechanical pulps, which are used for making products such as newsprint, are manufactured from raw materials by the application of heat, in addition to mechanical operations. Chemimechanical pulping and chemithermomechanical pulping (CTMP) are similar but use less mechanical energy, softening the pulp with sodium sulfite, carbonate, or hydroxide.

Chemical pulps are made by cooking (digesting) the raw materials, using the kraft (sulfate) and sulfite processes. Kraft processes produce a variety of pulps used mainly for packaging and high-strength papers and board. Wood chips are cooked with caustic soda to produce brownstock, which is then washed with water to remove cooking (black) liquor for the recovery of chemicals and energy. Pulp is also manufactured from recycled paper.

Mechanical pulp can be used without bleaching to make printing papers for applications in which low brightness is acceptable—primarily, newsprint. However, for most printing, for copying, and for some packaging grades, the pulp has to be bleached. For mechanical pulps, most of the original lignin in the raw pulp is retained but is bleached with peroxides and hydrosulfites. In the case of chemical pulps (kraft and sulfite), the objective of bleaching is to remove the small fraction of the lignin remaining after cooking. Oxygen, hydrogen peroxide, ozone, peracetic acid, sodium hypochlorite, chlorine dioxide, chlorine, and other chemicals are used to transform lignin into an alkali-soluble form. An alkali, such as sodium hydroxide, is necessary in the bleaching process to extract the alkali-soluble form of lignin. Pulp is washed with water in the bleaching process.

In modern mills, oxygen is normally used in the first stage of bleaching. The trend is to avoid the use of any kind of chlorine chemicals and employ "total chlorine-free" (TCF) bleaching. TCF processes allow the bleaching effluents to be fed to the recovery boiler for steam generation; the steam is then used to generate electricity, thereby reducing the amount of pollutants discharged. Elemental chlorine-free (ECF) processes, which use chlorine dioxide, are required for bleaching certain grades of pulp.

*The use of elemental chlorine for bleaching is not recommended.* Only ECF processes are acceptable, and, from an environmental perspective, TCF processes are preferred.

The soluble organic substances removed from the pulp in bleaching stages that use chlorine or chlorine compounds, as well as the substances removed in the subsequent alkaline stages, are chlorinated. Some of these chlorinated organic substances are toxic; they include dioxins, chlorinated phenols, and many other chemicals. It is generally not practical to recover chlorinated organics in effluents, since the chloride content causes excessive corrosion.

The finished pulp may be dried for shipment (market pulp) or may be used to manufacture paper on site (in an "integrated" mill).

Paper and cardboard are made from pulp by deposition of fibers and fillers from a fluid suspension onto a moving forming device that also removes water from the pulp. The water remaining in the wet web is removed by pressing and then by drying, on a series of hollow-heated cylinders (for example, calender rolls). Chemical additives are added to impart specific properties to paper, and pigments may be added for color.

## Waste Characteristics

The significant environmental impacts of the manufacture of pulp and paper result from the pulping and bleaching processes. In some processes, sulfur compounds and nitrogen oxides are emitted to the air, and chlorinated and organic compounds, nutrients, and metals are discharged to the wastewaters.

### Air Emissions

In the kraft pulping process, highly malodorous emissions of reduced sulfur compounds, measured as total reduced sulfur (TRS) and including hydrogen sulfide, methyl mercaptan, dimethyl sulfide, and dimethyl disulfide, are emitted, typically at a rate of 0.3–3 kilograms per metric ton (kg/t) of air-dried pulp (ADP). (Air-dried pulp is defined as 90% bone-dry fiber and 10% water.) Other typical generation rates are: particulate matter, 75–150 kg/t; sulfur oxides, 0.5–30 kg/t; nitrogen oxides, 1–3 kg/t; and volatile organic compounds (VOCs), 15 kg/t from black liquor oxidation. In the sulfite pulping process, sulfur oxides are emitted at rates ranging from 15 kg/t to over 30 kg/t. Other pulping processes, such as the mechanical and thermomechanical methods, generate significantly lower quantities of air emissions.

Steam- and electricity-generating units using coal or fuel oil emit fly ash, sulfur oxides, and nitrogen oxides. Coal burning can emit fly ash at the rate of 100 kg/t of ADP.

### Liquid Effluents

Wastewaters are discharged at a rate of 20–250 cubic meters per metric ton ($m^3$/t) of ADP. They are high in biochemical oxygen demand (BOD), at 10–40 kg/t of ADP; total suspended solids, 10–50 kg/t of ADP; chemical oxygen demand (COD), 20–200 kg/t of ADP; and chlorinated organic compounds, which may include dioxins, furans, and other adsorbable organic halides, AOX, at 0–4 kg/t of ADP.

Wastewater from chemical pulping contains 12–20 kg of BOD/t of ADP, with values of up to 350 kg/t. The corresponding values for mechanical pulping wastewater are 15–25 kg BOD/t of ADP. For chemimechanical pulping, BOD discharges are 3 to 10 times higher than those for mechanical pulping. Pollution loads for some processes, such as those using nonwood raw materials, could be significantly different.

Phosphorus and nitrogen are also released into wastewaters. The main source of nutrients, nitrogen, and phosphorus compounds is raw material such as wood. The use of peroxide, ozone, and other chemicals in bleaching makes it necessary to use a complexing agent for heavy metals such as manganese.

### Solid Wastes

The principal solid wastes of concern include wastewater treatment sludges (50–150 kg/t of ADP). Solid materials that can be reused include waste paper, which can be recycled, and bark, which can be used as fuel. Lime sludge and ash may need to be disposed of in an appropriate landfill.

## Pollution Prevention and Control

The most significant environmental issues are the discharge of chlorine-based organic compounds (from bleaching) and of other toxic organics. The unchlorinated material is essentially black liquor that has escaped the mill recovery process. Some mills are approaching 100% recovery. Industry developments demonstrate that total chlorine-free bleaching is feasible for many pulp and paper products but cannot produce certain grades of paper. The adoption of these modern process developments, wherever feasible, is encouraged.

Pollution prevention programs should focus on reducing wastewater discharges and on minimizing air emissions. Process recommendations may include the following:

- Use energy-efficient pulping processes wherever feasible. Acceptability of less bright products should be promoted. For less bright products such as newsprint, thermomechanical processes and recycled fiber may be considered.
- Minimize the generation of effluents through process modifications and recycle wastewaters, aiming for total recycling.
- Reduce effluent volume and treatment requirements by using dry instead of wet debarking; recovering pulping chemicals by concentrating black liquor and burning the concentrate in a recovery furnace; recovering cooking chemicals by recausticizing the smelt from the recovery furnace; and using high-efficiency washing and bleaching equipment.
- Minimize unplanned or nonroutine discharges of wastewater and black liquor, caused by equipment failures, human error, and faulty maintenance procedures, by training operators, establishing good operating practices, and providing sumps and other facilities to recover liquor losses from the process.
- Reduce bleaching requirements by process design and operation. Use the following measures to reduce emissions of chlorinated compounds to the environment: before bleaching, reduce the lignin content in the pulp (Kappa number of 10) for hardwood by extended cooking and by oxygen delignification under elevated pressure; optimize pulp washing prior to bleaching; use TCF or at a minimum, ECF bleaching systems; use oxygen, ozone, peroxides (hydrogen peroxide), peracetic acid, or enzymes (cellulose-free xylanase) as substitutes for chlorine-based bleaching chemicals; recover and incinerate maximum material removed from pulp bleaching; where chlorine bleaching is used, reduce the chlorine charge on the lignin by controlling pH and by splitting the addition of chlorine.
- Minimize sulfur emissions to the atmosphere by using a low-odor design black liquor recovery furnace.
- Use energy-efficient processes for black liquor chemical recovery, preferably aiming for a high solid content (say, 70%).

### Target Pollution Loads

Implementation of cleaner production processes and pollution prevention measures can yield both economic and environmental benefits. The following production-related targets can be achieved by measures such as those described above. The values relate to the production processes before the addition of pollution control measures.

For air emissions, the target is 1.5 kg $NO_x$ per ton for both kraft and sulfite processes; for mechanical and chemimechanical processes used in newsprint manufacture, 260 nanograms per joule (ng/J) of $NO_x$ for coal; 130 ng/J for oil; and 86 ng/J for gas used as fuel.

Wastewater generation rates should not exceed 50 m³/t of ADP, and levels of 20 m³/t of ADP (or product) should be targeted. For paper mills, effluent discharges should be less than 5 m³/t of ADP. Wherever feasible, use a total wastewater recycling system, along with a TCF pulp-bleaching system, and incinerate bleaching effluents in the recovery boiler. As a minimum, use chlorine dioxide as a substitute for elemental chlorine in pulp bleaching.

### Treatment Technologies

Sulfur oxide emissions are scrubbed with slightly alkaline solutions. The reduced sulfur-compounds gases are collected using headers, hoods, and venting equipment. Condensates from the digester relief condenser and evaporation of black liquor are stripped of reduced sulfur compounds. The stripper overhead and noncondensable are incinerated in a lime kiln or a dedicated combustion unit. Approximately, 0.5 kg sulfur per ton of pulp for the kraft process and 1.5 kg sulfur per ton for the sulfite process are considered acceptable emissions levels. Electrostatic precipitators are used to control the release of particulate matter into the atmosphere.

Wastewater treatment typically includes (a) neutralization, screening, sedimentation, and floatation/hydrocycloning to remove suspended solids and (b) biological/secondary treatment to reduce the organic content in wastewater and destroy toxic organics. Chemical precipitation is also used to remove certain cations. Fibers collected in primary treatment should be recovered and recycled. A mechanical clarifier or a settling pond is used in primary treatment. Flocculation to assist in the removal of suspended solids is also sometimes necessary. Biological treatment systems, such as activated sludge, aerated lagoons, and anaerobic fermentation, can reduce BOD by over 99% and achieve a COD reduction of 50% to 90%. Tertiary treatment may be performed to reduce toxicity, suspended solids, and color.

Solid waste treatment steps include dewatering of sludge and combustion in an incinerator, bark boiler, or fossil-fuel-fired boiler. Sludges from a clarifier are dewatered and may be incinerated; otherwise, they are landfilled.

The following levels can be achieved by adopting good industrial practices: COD, 35 kg/t (aim for 15 kg/t); AOX, 2 kg/t of ADP (aim for 0.2 kg/t); total phosphorus, 0.02 kg/t; total nitrogen, 0.15 kg/t; and solid waste generation, 150 kg/t of ADP.

## Emissions Guidelines

Emissions levels for the design and operation of each project must be established through the environmental assessment (EA) process on the basis of country legislation and the *Pollution Prevention and Abatement Handbook*, as applied to local conditions. The emissions levels selected must be justified in the EA and acceptable to the World Bank Group.

The following guidelines present emissions levels normally acceptable to the World Bank Group in making decisions regarding provision of World Bank Group assistance. Any deviations from these levels must be described in the World Bank Group project documentation. The emissions levels given here can be consistently achieved by well-designed, well-operated, and well-maintained pollution control systems.

The guidelines are expressed as concentrations to facilitate monitoring. Dilution of air emissions or effluents to achieve these guidelines is unacceptable.

All of the maximum levels should be achieved for at least 95% of the time that the plant or unit is operating, to be calculated as a proportion of annual operating hours.

### Air Emissions

Air emissions from pulp and paper manufacturing should achieve the levels presented in Table 1.

### Liquid Effluents

Liquid effluents from pulp and paper manufacturing should achieve the levels presented in Table 2.

### Solid Wastes

Solid wastes should be sent to combustion devices or disposed of in a manner that avoids odor generation and the release of toxic organics to the environment.

### Table 1. Air Emissions from Pulp and Paper Manufacturing

*(milligrams per normal cubic meter)*

| Parameter | Maximum value |
| --- | --- |
| PM[a] | 100 for recovery furnace |
| Hydrogen sulfide | 15 (for lime kilns) |
| Total sulfur emitted | |
|    Sulfite mills | 1.5 kg/t ADP |
|    Kraft and other | 1.0 kg/t ADP |
| Nitrogen oxides | 2 kg/t ADP |

a. Where achieving 100 mg/Nm$^3$ is not cost-effective, an emissions level up to 150 mg/Nm$^3$ is acceptable. Air emissions requirements are for dry gas, at 0°C and 1 atmosphere.

## Table 2. Liquid Effluents from New Pulp and Paper Manufacturing

| Parameter | Maximum value |
|---|---|
| pH | 6–9 |
| COD | 300 mg/l and 15 kg/t for kraft and CTMP pulp mills; 700 mg/l and 40 kg/t for sulfite pulp mills; 10 mg/l and 5 kg/t for mechanical and recycled fiber pulp; 250 mg/l for paper mills |
| AOX | 40 mg/l and 2 kg/t (aim for 8 mg/l and 0.4 kg/t for retrofits and for 4 mg/l and 0.2 kg/t for new mills) and 4 mg/l for paper mills |
| Total phosphorus | 0.05 kg/t |
| Total nitrogen | 0.4 kg/t |
| Temperature | < 3°C[a] |

*Note:* Molecular chlorine should not be used in the process. Effluent requirements are for direct discharge to surface waters.

a. The effluent should not result in a temperature increase of more than 3° C at the edge of the zone where initial mixing and dilution take place. Where the zone is not defined, use 100 meters from the point of discharge.

### *Ambient Noise*

Noise abatement measures should achieve either the levels given below or a maximum increase in background levels of 3 decibels (measured on the A scale) [dB(A)]. Measurements are to be taken at noise receptors located outside the project property boundary.

| Receptor | Maximum allowable log equivalent (hourly measurements), in dB(A) | |
|---|---|---|
| | Day (07:00–22:00) | Night (22:00–07:00) |
| Residential, institutional, educational | 55 | 45 |
| Industrial, commercial | 70 | 70 |

## Monitoring and Reporting

Frequent sampling may be required during startup and upset conditions. Once a record of consistent performance has been established, sampling for the parameters listed in this document should be as described below.

Monitoring of air emissions for opacity (maximum level of 10%) should be continuous; daily monitoring should be conducted for hydrogen sulfide and annual monitoring for other pollutants. Liquid effluents should be monitored for the listed parameters at least daily, or more often when there are significant process changes.

Monitoring data should be analyzed and reviewed at regular intervals and compared with the operating standards so that any necessary corrective actions can be taken. Records of monitoring results should be kept in an acceptable format. The results should be reported to the responsible authorities and relevant parties, as required.

## Key Issues

The key production and control practices that will lead to compliance with emissions guidelines can be summarized as follows:

- Prefer dry debarking processes.
- Prevent and control spills of black liquor.
- Prefer total chlorine-free processes, but at a minimum, use elemental chlorine-free bleaching systems.
- Reduce the use of hazardous bleaching chemicals by extended cooking and oxygen delignification.
- Aim for zero-effluent discharge where feasible. Reduce wastewater discharges to the extent feasible. Incinerate liquid effluents from the pulping and bleaching processes.
- Reduce the odor from reduced sulfur emissions by collection and incineration and by using modern, low-odor recovery boilers fired at over 75% concentration of black liquor.
- Dewater and properly manage sludges.
- Where wood is used as a raw material to the process, encourage plantation of trees to ensure sustainability of forests.

## Sources

Kirkpatrick, N. 1991. *Environmental Issues in the Pulp and Paper Industries.* Surrey, U.K.: Pira International.

Nordic Council of Ministers. 1993. "Study of Nordic Pulp and Paper Industry and the Environment." *Nordiske Seminar-g Arbejds-rapporter* 1993:638. Copenhagen.

UNEP (United Nations Environment Programme). 1987. "Pollution Abatement and Control Technology (PACT), Publication for the Pulp and Paper Industry." UNEP Industry and Environment Information Transfer Series. Paris.

UNIDO (United Nations Industrial Development Organization). 1992. "Draft Pulp and Paper Industrial Pollution Guidelines." Vienna.

————. 1991. "Case Study No. 1, Pulp and Paper." Conference on Ecologically Sustainable Industrial Development, Copenhagen, October 1991. Vienna.

USEPA (United States Environmental Protection Agency). 1993. *Pulp, Paper, and Paperboard Industry Background Information for Proposed Air Emission Standards, Manufacturing Processes at Kraft, Sulfite, Soda, and Semi-Chemical Mills.* EPA-453 R-93-050a. Office of Air Quality Planning and Standards. Research Triangle Park, N.C.

————. 1993. *Development Document for Proposed Effluent Limitations Guidelines and Standards for the Pulp, Paper and Paperboard Point Source Category.* EPA-821-R-93-019. Office of Water, Mail Code 4303, Washington, D.C.

World Bank. 1996. "Pollution Prevention and Abatement: Pulp and Paper Mills." Draft Technical Background Document. Environment Department, Washington, D.C.

# Sugar Manufacturing

## Industry Description and Practices

The sugar industry processes sugar cane and sugar beet to manufacture edible sugar. More than 60% of the world's sugar production is from sugar cane; the balance is from sugar beet. Sugar manufacturing is a highly seasonal industry, with season lengths of about 6 to 18 weeks for beets and 20 to 32 weeks for cane.

Approximately 10% of the sugar cane can be processed to commercial sugar, using approximately 20 cubic meters of water per metric ton ($m^3$/t) of cane processed. Sugar cane contains 70% water; 14% fiber; 13.3% saccharose (about 10 to 15% sucrose), and 2.7% soluble impurities. Sugar canes are generally washed, after which juice is extracted from them. The juice is clarified to remove mud, evaporated to prepare syrup, crystallized to separate out the liquor, and centrifuged to separate molasses from the crystals. Sugar crystals are then dried and may be further refined before bagging for shipment. In some places (for example, in South Africa), juice is extracted by a diffusion process that can give higher rates of extraction with lower energy consumption and reduced operating and maintenance costs.

For processing sugar beet (water, 75%; sugar, 17%), only the washing, preparation, and extraction processes are different. After washing, the beet is sliced, and the slices are drawn into a slowly rotating diffuser where a countercurrent flow of water is used to remove sugar from the beet slices. Approximately 15 cubic meters ($m^3$) of water and 28 kilowatt-hours (kWh) of energy are consumed per metric ton of beet processed.

Sugar refining involves removal of impurities and decolorization. The steps generally followed include affination (mingling and centrifugation),
melting, clarification, decolorization, evaporation, crystallization, and finishing. Decolorization methods use granular activated carbon, powdered activated carbon, ion exchange resins, and other materials.

## Waste Characteristics

The main air emissions from sugar processing and refining result primarily from the combustion of bagasse (the fiber residue of sugar cane), fuel oil, or coal. Other air emission sources include juice fermentation units, evaporators, and sulfitation units. Approximately 5.5 kilograms of fly ash per metric ton (kg/t) of cane processed (or 4,500 mg/$m^3$ of fly ash) are present in the flue gases from the combustion of bagasse.

Sugar manufacturing effluents typically have biochemical oxygen demand (BOD) of 1,700–6,600 milligrams per liter (mg/l) in untreated effluent from cane processing and 4,000–7,000 mg/l from beet processing; chemical oxygen demand (COD) of 2,300–8,000 mg/l from cane processing and up to 10,000 mg/l from beet processing; total suspended solids of up to 5,000 mg/l; and high ammonium content. The wastewater may contain pathogens from contaminated materials or production processes. A sugar mill often generates odor and dust, which need to be controlled. Most of the solid wastes can be processed into other products and by-products. In some cases, pesticides may be present in the sugar cane rinse liquids.

## Pollution Prevention and Control

Good pollution prevention practices in sugar manufacturing focus on the following main areas:

- Reduce product losses to less than 10% by better production control. Perform sugar auditing.
- Discourage spraying of molasses on the ground for disposal.
- Minimize storage time for juice and other intermediate products to reduce product losses and discharge of product into the wastewater stream.
- Give preference to less polluting clarification processes such as those using bentonite instead of sulfite for the manufacture of white sugar.
- Collect waste product for use in other industries—for example, bagasse for use in paper mills and as fuel. Cogeneration systems for large sugar mills generate electricity for sale. Beet chips can be used as animal feed.
- Optimize the use of water and cleaning chemicals. Procure cane washed in the field. Prefer the use of dry cleaning methods.
- Recirculate cooling waters.

Continuous sampling and measurement of key production parameters allow production losses to be identified and reduced, thus reducing the waste load. Fermentation processes and juice handling are the main sources of leakage. Odor problems can usually be prevented with good hygiene and storage practices.

**Target Pollution Loads**

Since the pollutants generated by the industry are largely losses in production, improvements in production efficiency are recommended to reduce pollutant loads. Approximately 90% of the saccharose should be accounted for, and 85% of the sucrose can be recovered. Recirculation of water should be maximized.

Wastewater loads can be reduced to at least 1.3 m³/t of cane processed, and plant operators should aim at rates of 0.9 m³/t or less through recirculation of wastewater. Wastewater loads from beet processing should be less than 4m³/t of sugar produced or 0.75 m³/t of beet processed, with a target of 0.3 to 0.6 m³/t of beet processed.

**Treatment Technologies**

Pretreatment of effluents consists of screening and aeration, normally followed by biological treatment. If space is available, land treatment or pond systems are potential treatment methods. Other possible biological treatment systems include activated sludge and anaerobic systems. which can achieve a reduction in the BOD level of over 95%.

Odor control by ventilation and sanitation may be required for fermentation and juice-processing areas. Biofilters may be used for controlling odor. Cyclones, scrubbers, and electrostatic precipitators are used for dust control.

**Emissions Guidelines**

Emissions levels for the design and operation of each project must be established through the environmental assessment (EA) process on the basis of country legislation and the *Pollution Prevention and Abatement Handbook,* as applied to local conditions. The emissions levels selected must be justified in the EA and acceptable to the World Bank Group.

The guidelines given below present emissions levels normally acceptable to the World Bank Group in making decisions regarding provision of World Bank Group assistance. Any deviations from these levels must be described in the World Bank Group project documentation. The emissions levels given here can be consistently achieved by well-designed, well-operated, and well-maintained pollution control systems.

The guidelines are expressed as concentrations to facilitate monitoring. Dilution of air emissions or effluents to achieve these guidelines is unacceptable.

All of the maximum levels should be achieved for at least 95% of the time that the plant or unit is operating, to be calculated as a proportion of annual operating hours.

*Air Emissions*

Particulate matter and sulfur oxide emissions should be less than 100 milligrams per normal cubic meter (mg/Nm3). in some cases, emissions of particulate matter may be up to 150 mg/Nm³ for small mills with less than 8.7 megawatts (MW) heat input to the boiler, and emissions of sulfur oxides may be up to 2,000 mg/Nm³. Nitrogen oxide emissions should be less than 260 nanograms per joule (ng/J), or 750 mg/Nm³, for solid

## Table 1. Effluents from Sugar Manufacturing

*(milligrams per liter, except for pH and temperature)*

| Parameter | Maximum value |
|-----------|---------------|
| pH | 6–9 |
| BOD | 50 |
| COD | 250 |
| TSS | 50 |
| Oil and grease | 10 |
| Total nitrogen ($NH_4$–N) | 10 |
| Total phosphorus | 2 |
| Temperature increase | $\leq 3° C^a$ |

*Note:* Effluent requirements are for direct discharge to surface waters.

a. The effluent should result in a temperature increase of no more than 3° C at the edge of the zone where initial mixing and dilution take place. Where the zone is not defined, use 100 meters from the point of discharge.

fuels and 130 ng/J (460 mg/Nm³) for liquid fuels. Odor controls should be implemented where necessary to achieve acceptable odor quality for nearby residents.

### Liquid Effluents

The effluent levels presented in Table 1 should be achieved.

Biocides should not be present above detection levels or should be less than 0.05 mg/l.

### Ambient Noise

Noise abatement measures should achieve either the levels given below or a maximum increase in background levels of 3 decibels (measured on the A scale) [dB(A)]. Measurements are to be taken at noise receptors located outside the project property boundary.

| Receptor | Maximum allowable log equivalent (hourly measurements), in dB(A) | |
|----------|---------|---------|
| | Day (07:00–22:00) | Night (22:00–07:00) |
| Residential, institutional, educational | 55 | 45 |
| Industrial, commercial | 70 | 70 |

## Monitoring and Reporting

Monitoring of air emissions should be on an annual basis, with continuous monitoring of the fuel used. Only fuels with acceptable levels of ash and sulfur should be used. Monitoring of the final effluent for the parameters listed in this document should be carried out at least daily, or more frequently if the flows vary significantly. Effluents should be sampled annually to ensure that biocides are not present at significant levels.

Monitoring data should be analyzed and reviewed at regular intervals and compared with the operating standards so that any necessary corrective actions can be taken. Records of monitoring results should be kept in an acceptable format. The results should be reported to the responsible authorities and relevant parties, as required.

### Key Issues

The key production and control practices that will lead to compliance with emissions guidelines can be summarized as follows:

- Monitor key production parameters to reduce product losses to less than 10%.
- Design and operate the production system to achieve recommended wastewater loads.
- Recirculate cooling waters.
- Collect wastes for use in low-grade products.

### Sources

Economomopoulos, Alexander P. 1993. *Assessment of Sources of Air, Water, and Land Pollution: A Guide to Rapid Source Inventory Techniques and their Use in Formulating Environmental Control Strategies. Part 1: Rapid Inventory Techniques in Environmental Pollution.* Geneva: World Health Organization.

World Bank. 1995. "Industrial Pollution Prevention and Abatement: Sugar Manufacturing." Draft Technical Background Document. Environment Department, Washington, D.C.

# Tanning and Leather Finishing

## Industry Description and Practices

Hides and skins are sometimes preserved by drying, salting, or chilling, so that raw hides and skins will reach leather tanneries in an acceptable condition. The use of environmentally persistent toxics for preservation of raw hides and skins is to be avoided.

In the tanning process, animal hides and skins are treated to remove hair and nonstructured proteins and fats, leaving an essentially pure collagen matrix. The hides are then preserved by impregnation with tanning agents. Leather production usually involves three distinct phases: preparation (in the beamhouse); tanning (in the tanyard); and finishing, including dyeing and surface treatment. A wide range of processes and chemicals, including chrome salts, is used in the tanning and finishing processes.

The tanning and finishing process generally consists of:

- Soaking and washing to remove salt, restore the moisture content of the hides, and remove any foreign material such as dirt and manure
- Liming to open up the collagen structure by removing interstitial material
- Fleshing to remove excess tissue from the interior of the hide
- Dehairing or dewooling to remove hair or wool by mechanical or chemical means
- Bating and pickling to delime the skins and condition the hides to receive the tanning agents
- Tanning to stabilize the hide material and impart basic properties to the hides
- Retanning, dyeing, and fat-liquoring to impart special properties to the leather, increase penetration of tanning solution, replenish oils in the hides, and impart color to the leather
- Finishing to attain final product specifications.

## Waste Characteristics

The potential environmental impacts of tanning are significant. Composite untreated wastewater, amounting to 20–80 cubic meters per metric ton ($m^3$/t) of hide or skin, is turbid, colored, and foul smelling. It consists of acidic and alkaline liquors, with chromium levels of 100–400 milligrams per liter (mg/l); sulfide levels of 200–800 mg/l; nitrogen levels of 200–1,000 mg/l; biochemical oxygen demand (BOD) levels of 900–6,000 mg/l, usually ranging from 160 to 24,000 mg/l; chemical oxygen demand (COD) ranging from 800 to 43,000 mg/l in separate streams, with combined wastewater levels of 2,400 to 14,000 mg/l; chloride ranging from 200 to 70,000 mg/l in individual streams and 5,600 to 27,000 mg/l in the combined stream; and high levels of fat. Suspended solids are usually half of chloride levels. Wastewater may also contain residues of pesticides used to preserve hides during transport, as well as significant levels of pathogens. Significant volumes of solid wastes are produced, including trimmings, degraded hide, and hair from the beamhouse processes. The solid wastes can represent up to 70% of the wet weight of the original hides. In addition, large quantities of sludges are generated. Decaying organic material produces strong odors. Hydrogen sulfide is released during dehairing, and ammonia is released in deliming. Air quality may be further degraded by release of solvent vapors from spray application, degreasing, and finishing (for example, dye application).

## Pollution Prevention and Control

The design of new plants should address the following process modifications:

- Process fresh hides or skins to reduce the quantity of salt in wastewater, where feasible.
- Reduce the quantities of salt used for preservation. When salted skins are used as raw material, pretreat the skins with salt elimination methods.
- Use salt or chilling methods to preserve hides, instead of persistent insecticides and fungicides.
- When antiseptics or biocides are necessary, avoid toxic and less degradable ones, especially those containing arsenic, mercury, lindane, or pentachlorophenol or other chlorinated substances.
- Flesh green hides instead of limed hides.
- Use sulfide and lime as a 20–50% solution to reduce sulfide levels in wastewater.
- Split limed hides to reduce the amount of chrome needed for tanning.
- Consider the use of carbon dioxide in deliming to reduce ammonia in wastewater.
- Use only trivalent chrome when required for tanning.
- Inject tanning solution in the skin using high-pressure nozzles; recover chrome from chrome-containing wastewaters, which should be kept segregated from other wastewaters. Recycle chrome after precipitation and acidification. Improve fixation of chrome by addition of dicarboxylic acids.
- Recycle spent chrome liquor to the tanning process or to the pickling vat.
- Examine alternatives to chrome in tanning, such as titanium, aluminum, iron, zirconium, and vegetable tanning agents.
- Use nonorganic solvents for dyeing and finishing.
- Recover hair by using hair-saving methods to reduce pollution loads. For example, avoid dissolving hair in chemicals by making a proper choice of chemicals and using screens to remove hair from wastewater.

- Use photocell-assisted paint-spraying techniques to avoid overspraying.
- Precondition hides before vegetable tanning.

Through good management, water use can be reduced by 30–50%, to 25 liters per kilograms (l/kg) of raw material. Recommendations for reducing water consumption include the following:

- Monitor and control process waters; reductions of up to 50% can be achieved.
- Use batch washing instead of continuous washing, for reductions of up to 50%.
- Use low-float methods (for example, use 40–80% floats). Recycle liming, pickling, and tanning floats. Recycle sulfide in spent liming liquor after screening to reduce sulfide losses (by, say, 20–50%) and lime loss (by about 40–60%).
- Use drums instead of pits for immersion of hides.
- Reuse wastewaters for washing—for example, by recycling lime wash water to the soaking stage. Reuse treated wastewaters in the process to the extent feasible (for example, in soaking and pickling).

Waste reduction measures should include the following:

- Recover hide trimmings for use in the manufacture of glue, gelatin, and similar products.
- Recover grease for rendering. Use aqueous degreasing methods.
- Recycle wastes to the extent feasible in the manufacture of fertilizer, animal feed, and tallow, provided the quality of these products is not compromised.
- Use tanned shavings in leather board manufacture.
- Control odor problems by good housekeeping methods such as minimal storage of flesh trimmings and organic material.
- Recover energy from the drying process to heat process water.

## Target Pollution Loads

Implementation of cleaner production processes and pollution prevention measures can yield both economic and environmental benefits. The production-related waste load figures presented in

## Table 1. Target Loads per Unit of Production

*(kilogram per ton of raw material)*

| Parameter | Maximum value |
|---|---|
| BOD | 40 |
| COD | 140 |
| Nitrogen | 7 |
| Chromium | 6 |
|  | (aim for 1.5) |
| Sulfide | 1 |
| Solid waste | 500 |
| Effluent flow rate | 30,000 |
|  | (aim for 15,000) |

*Sources:* Indian Standards Institution 1977; UNEP 1991.

Table 1 can be achieved by implementing measures such as those described above. The figures are for the waste loads arising from production processes before the addition of pollution control measures. These levels are derived from typical loads recorded in industry studies and should be used as maximum levels of unit pollution in the design of new plants.

Use of techniques such as water-based paint and roller coating can help achieve emissions of volatile organic compounds (VOCs) from finishing of less than 4 kg/t (aim for 2 kg/t).

### Treatment Technologies

Treatment of tannery wastewaters is always required. Some streams, such as soaking liquor (which has high salinity), sulfide-rich lime liquor, and chrome wastewaters should be segregated. Preliminary screening of wastewaters is required because of the large quantities of solids present. Recovery of hair from the dehairing and liming process reduces the BOD of the process effluent. Physical-chemical treatment precipitates metals and removes a large portion of solids, BOD, and COD. Biological treatment is usually required to reduce the remaining organic loads to acceptable levels (0.3 kg BOD, 2 kg COD, and 0.004 kg chromium per metric ton of raw hide).

Good ventilation and minimization of solvent release can avoid the need to collect and treat vapors in carbon adsorption beds. VOC emissions from finishing are approximately 30 kg/t if pollution prevention measures are not adopted.

Maximum upstream pollutant reduction is essential for tanneries, but treatment is also required.

### Emissions Guidelines

Emissions levels for the design and operation of each project must be established through the environmental assessment (EA) process on the basis of country legislation and the *Pollution Prevention and Abatement Handbook,* as applied to local conditions. The emissions levels selected must be justified in the EA and acceptable to the World Bank Group.

The guidelines given below present emissions levels normally acceptable to the World Bank Group in making decisions regarding provision of World Bank Group assistance. Any deviations from these levels must be described in the World Bank Group project documentation. The emissions levels given here can be consistently achieved by well-designed, well-operated, and well-maintained pollution control systems.

The guidelines are expressed as concentrations to facilitate monitoring. Dilution of air emissions or effluents to achieve these guidelines is unacceptable.

All of the maximum levels should be achieved for at least 95% of the time that the plant or unit is operating, to be calculated as a proportion of annual operating hours.

#### Air Emissions

Odor controls should be implemented to reduce impacts on nearby residents.

#### Liquid Effluents

The effluent levels presented in Table 2 should be achieved.

#### Solid Wastes

Solid wastes and sludges must be disposed of in a secure landfill.

#### Ambient Noise

Noise abatement measures should achieve either the levels given below or a maximum increase in

## Table 2. Effluents from Tanning and Leather-Finishing Processes

*(milligrams per liter, except for pH and bacteria)*

| Parameter | Maximum value |
|---|---|
| pH | 6–9 |
| BOD | 50 |
| COD | 250 |
| TSS | 50 |
| Oil and grease | 10 |
| Sulfide | 1.0 |
| Chromium | |
|   Hexavalent | 0.1 |
|   Total | 0.5 |
| Nitrogen ($NH_4$–N) | 10 |
| Phosphorus (total) | 2 |
| Coliform bacteria | 400 MPN/100 ml |

*Note:* Effluent requirements are for direct discharge to surface waters. MPN, most probable number.

background levels of 3 decibels (measured on the A scale) [dB(A)]. Measurements are to be taken at noise receptors located outside the project property boundary.

| Receptor | Maximum allowable log equivalent (hourly measurements), in dB(A) | |
|---|---|---|
| | Day (07:00–22:00) | Night (22:00–07:00) |
| Residential, institutional, educational | 55 | 45 |
| Industrial, commercial | 70 | 70 |

## Monitoring and Reporting

Frequent sampling may be required during start-up and upset conditions. Once a record of consistent performance has been established, sampling for the parameters listed in this document should be conducted monthly.

Annual monitoring for pesticides should be carried out, and, if pesticides are present at levels of 0.05 mg/l and above, corrective actions should be taken.

Monitoring data should be analyzed and reviewed at regular intervals and compared with the operating standards so that any necessary corrective actions can be taken. Records of monitoring results should be kept in an acceptable format. The results should be reported to the responsible authorities and relevant parties, as required.

## Key Issues

The key production and control practices that will lead to compliance with emissions guidelines can be summarized as follows:

- Minimize chrome use; avoid the use of hexavalent chrome and use trivalent chrome instead; recover and recycle chrome.
- Avoid the use of hides treated with persistent insecticides and fungicides.
- Use nonorganic solvents for dyeing and finishing.
- Minimize storage of flesh trimmings and organic material.
- To reduce water use, monitor and control process waters; use batch instead of continuous washing; use drums for immersion of hides; reuse wash water and recycle floats; and segregate wastewater streams to simplify treatment.
- Minimize solid waste by recovery and reuse of hide trimmings.

## References and Sources

Danish Technological Institute. 1992. *Possibilities for a Reduction of the Pollution Load from Tanneries.* Final Report, Nordic Council of Ministers. Copenhagen.

Indian Standards Institution. 1977. *Guide for Treatment and Disposal of Effluents of Tanning Industry.* New Delhi.

UNEP (United Nations Environment Programme). 1991. *Tanneries and the Environment: A Technical Guide to Reducing the Environmental Impact of Tannery Operations.* Paris.

World Bank. 1996. "Pollution Prevention and Abatement: Tanning and Leather Finishing." Draft Technical Background Document. Environment Department, Washington, D.C.

# Textiles

## Industry Description and Practices

The textile industry uses vegetable fibers such as cotton; animal fibers such as wool and silk; and a wide range of synthetic materials such as nylon, polyester, and acrylics. The production of natural fibers is approximately equal in amount to the production of synthetic fibers. Polyester accounts for about 50% of synthetics. (Chemical production of the polymers used to make synthetic fiber is not covered in this document.)

The stages of textile production are fiber production, fiber processing and spinning, yarn preparation, fabric production, bleaching, dyeing and printing, and finishing. Each stage generates wastes that require proper management.

This document focuses on the wet processes (including wool washing, bleaching, dyeing, printing, and finishing) used in textile processing.

## Waste Characteristics

Textile production involves a number of wet processes that may use solvents. Emissions of volatile organic compounds (VOCs) mainly arise from textile finishing, drying processes, and solvent use. VOC concentrations vary from 10 milligrams of carbon per cubic meter ($mg/m^3$) for the thermosol process to 350 mg carbon/$m^3$ for the drying and condensation process. Process wastewater is a major source of pollutants (see Table 1). It is typically alkaline and has high BOD—from 700 to 2,000 milligrams per liter (mg/l)—and high chemical oxygen demand (COD), at approximately 2 to 5 times the BOD level. Wastewater also contains solids, oil, and possibly toxic organics, including phenols from dyeing and finishing and halogenated organics from processes such as bleaching. Dye wastewaters are frequently highly colored and may contain heavy metals such as copper and chromium. Wool processing may release bacteria and other pathogens. Pesticides are sometimes used for the preservation of natural fibers, and these are transferred to wastewaters during washing and scouring operations. Pesticides are used for mothproofing, brominated flame retardants are used for synthetic fabrics, and isocyanates are used for lamination *The use of pesticides and other chemicals that are banned in OECD countries is discouraged and in general, is not acceptable.* Wastewaters should be checked for pesticides such as DDT and PCP and for metals such as mercury, arsenic, and copper.

Air emissions include dust, oil mists, acid vapors, odors, and boiler exhausts. Cleaning and production changes result in sludges from tanks and spent process chemicals, which may contain toxic organics and metals.

## Pollution Prevention and Control

Pollution prevention programs should focus on reduction of water use and on more efficient use of process chemicals. Process changes might include the following:

- Match process variables to type and weight of fabric (reduces wastes by 10–20%).
- Manage batches to minimize waste at the end of cycles.
- Avoid nondegradable or less degradable surfactants (for washing and scouring) and spinning oils.
- Avoid the use, or at least the discharge, of alkylphenol ethoxylates. Ozone-depleting substances should not be used, and the use of organic solvents should be minimized.

**Table 1. Wastewater Characteristics in the Textiles Industry**

| Process and unit (U) | Waste volume (m³/U) | BOD (kg/U) | TSS (kg/U) | Other pollutants (kg/U) | |
|---|---|---|---|---|---|
| *Wool processing (metric ton of wool)*[a] | | | | | |
| Average unscoured stock[b] | 544 | 314 | 196 | Oil | 191 |
| Average scoured stock | 537 | 87 | 43 | Cr | 1.33 |
| Process-specific | | | | Phenol | 0.17 |
|   Scouring | 17 | 227 | 153 | Cr | 1.33 |
|   Dyeing | 25 | 27 | | Phenol | 0.17 |
|   Washing | 362 | 63 | | | |
|   Carbonizing | 138 | 2 | 44 | Oil | 191 |
|   Bleaching | 12.5 | 1.4 | | Cr | 1.33 |
| | | | | Phenol | 0.17 |
| *Cotton processing (metric ton of cotton)* | | | | | |
| Average compounded[c] | 265 | 115 | 70 | | |
| Process-specific | | | | | |
|   Yarn sizing | 4.2 | 2.8 | | | |
|   Desizing | 22 | 58 | 30 | | |
|   Kiering | 100 | 53 | 22 | | |
|   Bleaching | 100 | 8 | 5 | | |
|   Mercerizing | 35 | 8 | 2.5 | | |
|   Dyeing | 50 | 60 | 25 | | |
|   Printing | 14 | 54 | 12 | | |
| *Other fibers (metric ton of product)* | | | | | |
| Rayon processing | 42 | 30 | 55 | | |
| Acetate processing | 75 | 45 | 40 | | |
| Nylon processing | 125 | 45 | 30 | | |
| Acrylic processing | 210 | 125 | 87 | | |
| Polyester processing | 100 | 185 | 95 | | |

a. The pH varies widely, from 1.9 to 10.4.
b. The average compounded load factors listed are based on the assumption that only 20% of the product is mercerized (only nonwoolen components are mercerized) and 10% is bleached.
c. The average compounded load factors listed are based on the assumption that only 35% of the product is mercerized, 50% of the product is dyed, and 14% of the product is printed.
*Source:* Economopoulos 1993.

- Use transfer printing for synthetics (reduces water consumption from 250 l/kg to 2 l/kg of material and also reduces dye consumption). Use water-based printing pastes, when feasible.
- Use pad batch dyeing (saves up to 80% of energy requirements and 90% of water consumption and reduces dye and salt usage). For knitted goods, exhaust dyeing is preferred.
- Use jet dyers, with a liquid-to-fabric ratio of 4:1 to 8:1, instead of winch dyers, with a ratio of 15:1, where feasible.
- Avoid benzidine-based azo dyes and dyes containing cadmium and other heavy metals. Do not use chlorine-based dyes.
- Use less toxic dye carriers and finishing agents. Avoid carriers containing chlorine, such as chlorinated aromatics.
- Replace dichromate oxidation of vat dyes and sulfur dyes with peroxide oxidation.
- Reuse dye solution from dye baths.
- Use peroxide-based bleaches instead of sulfur- and chlorine-based bleaches, where feasible.
- Control makeup chemicals.
- Reuse and recover process chemicals such as caustic (reduces chemical costs by 30%) and size (up to 50% recovery is feasible).
- Replace nondegradable spin finish and size with degradable alternatives.
- Use biodegradable textile preservation chemicals. Do not use polybrominated diphe-

nylethers, dieldrin, arsenic, mercury, or pentachlorophenol in mothproofing, carpet backing, and other finishing processes. Where feasible, use permethrin for mothproofing instead.
- Control the quantity and temperature of water used.
- Use countercurrent rinsing.
- Improve cleaning and housekeeping measures (which may reduce water usage to less than 150 m³/t of textiles produced).
- Recover heat from wash water (reduces steam consumption).

**Target Pollution Loads**

Implementation of cleaner production processes and pollution prevention measures can yield both economic and environmental benefits. The following production-related waste load figures can be achieved by implementing measures such as those described above. The figures are the waste loads arising from the production processes before the addition of pollution control measures.

*Air Emissions*

VOC emissions should be less than 1 kilogram carbon per ton of fabric.

*Wastewater*

Wastewater load levels should preferably be less than 100 cubic meters per ton of fabric, but up to 150 m³ is considered acceptable.

**Treatment Technologies**

VOC abatement measures include using scrubbers, employing activated carbon adsorbers, and routing the vapors through a combustion system. A common approach to wastewater treatment consists of screening, flow equalization, and settling to remove suspended solids, followed by biological treatment. Physical-chemical treatment is also practiced: careful control of pH, followed by the addition of a coagulant such as alum before settling, can achieve good first-stage treatment. Further treatment to reduce BOD, if required, can be carried out using oxidation ponds (if space permits) or another aerobic process; up to 95% removal of BOD can be achieved.

Average effluent levels of 30–50 mg/l BOD will be obtained. Anaerobic treatment systems are not widely used for textile wastes. Carbon adsorption is sometimes used to enhance removal. In some cases, precipitation and filtration may also be required. Up to 90% recovery of size is feasible by partial recycling of prewash and additional ultrafiltration of diluted wash water. Disinfection of wastewaters from wool processing may be required to reduce coliform levels.

Residues and sludges often contain toxic organic chemicals and metals. These should be properly managed, with final disposal in an approved, secure landfill. Sludges containing halogenated organics and other toxic organics should be effectively treated by, for example, incineration before disposal of the residue in a secure landfill.

**Emissions Guidelines**

Emissions levels for the design and operation of each project must be established through the environmental assessment (EA) process on the basis of country legislation and the *Pollution Prevention and Abatement Handbook*, as applied to local conditions. The emissions levels selected must be justified in the EA and acceptable to the World Bank Group.

The following guidelines present emissions levels normally acceptable to the World Bank Group in making decisions regarding provision of World Bank Group assistance. Any deviations from these levels must be described in the World Bank Group project documentation. The emissions levels given here can be consistently achieved by well-designed, well-operated, and well-maintained pollution control systems.

The guidelines are expressed as concentrations to facilitate monitoring. Dilution of air emissions or effluents to achieve these guidelines is unacceptable.

All of the maximum levels should be achieved for at least 95% of the time that the plant or unit is operating, to be calculated as a proportion of annual operating hours.

*Air Emissions*

VOC emissions should be reduced to less than 1 kg carbon per metric ton of fabric, or 20 milligrams per normal cubic meter (mg/Nm³), by implementing measures such as routing the extracted air from the solvent usage areas through a combustion system (such as a boiler).

*Liquid Effluents*

The effluent levels presented in Table 2 should be achieved.

*Sludges*

Sludges containing chromium or other toxics should be treated and disposed of in a secure landfill. Incineration of toxic organics should effectively destroy or remove over 99.99% of toxic organics.

*Ambient Noise*

Noise abatement measures should achieve either the levels given below or a maximum increase in background levels of 3 decibels (measured on the A scale) [dB(A)]. Measurements are to be taken

**Table 2. Effluents from the Textiles Industry**
*(milligrams per liter, except for pH, temperature, and bacteria)*

| Parameter | Maximum value |
|---|---|
| pH | 6–9 |
| BOD | 50 |
| COD | 250 |
| AOX | 8 |
| TSS | 50 |
| Oil and grease | 10 |
| Pesticides (each) | 0.05 |
| Chromium (total) | 0.5 |
| Cobalt | 0.5 |
| Copper | 0.5 |
| Nickel | 0.5 |
| Zinc | 2 |
| Phenol | 0.5 |
| Sulfide | 1 |
| Temperature increase | < 3°C[a] |
| Coliform bacteria | 400 MPN/100 ml |

*Note:* Effluent requirements are for direct discharge to surface waters. Mercury should not be used in the process. The liquid effluent should not be colored. MPN, most probable number.
a. The effluent should result in a temperature increase of no more than 3° C at the edge of the zone where initial mixing and dilution take place. Where the zone is not defined, use 100 meters from the point of discharge.

at noise receptors located outside the project property boundary.

| | Maximum allowable log equivalent (hourly measurements), in dB(A) | |
|---|---|---|
| Receptor | Day (07:00–22:00) | Night (22:00–07:00) |
| Residential, institutional, educational | 55 | 45 |
| Industrial, commercial | 70 | 70 |

**Monitoring and Reporting**

Frequent sampling may be required during startup. Once a record of consistent performance has been established, sampling for the parameters listed above should be done at least weekly. Only those metals that are detected or are suspected to be present should be monitored. If the presence of other heavy metals such as arsenic, cadmium, lead, mercury, and nickel is suspected, those substances should be included in the monitoring program and treated to achieve the levels mentioned in the "General Industry Guidelines" in this volume.

Monitoring data should be analyzed and reviewed at regular intervals and compared with the operating standards so that any necessary corrective actions can be taken. Records of monitoring results should be kept in an acceptable format. The results should be reported to the responsible authorities and relevant parties, as required.

**Key Issues**

The key production and control practices that will lead to compliance with emissions guidelines can be summarized as follows:
• Avoid the use of less degradable surfactants (in washing and scouring operations) and spinning oils.
• Consider the use of transfer printing for synthetics. Use water-based printing pastes, where feasible.
• Consider the use of pad batch dyeing.
• Use jet dyers instead of winch dyers, where feasible.

- Avoid the use of benzidine-based azo dyes and dyes containing cadmium and other heavy metals. Chlorine-based dyes should not be used.
- Do not use mercury, arsenic, and banned pesticides in the process.
- Control the makeup of chemicals and match process variables to the type and weight of the fabric.
- Recover and reuse process chemicals and dye solution.
- Substitute less-toxic dye carriers wherever possible. Avoid carriers containing chlorine.
- Use peroxide-based bleaches instead of sulfur- and chlorine-based bleaches, where feasible.
- Adopt countercurrent rinsing and improved cleaning and housekeeping.

## References and Sources

Economopoulos, Alexander P. 1993. *Assessment of Sources of Air, Water, and Land Pollution: A Guide to Rapid Source Inventory Techniques and their Use in Formulating Environmental Control Strategies.* Part 1: *Rapid Inventory Techniques in Environmental Pollution.* Geneva: World Health Organization.

Gherzi Textile Organization. 1990. "The Spinning, Weaving, Knitting, and Processing Sectors to 2000 AD: A Period of Further Dynamic Global Changes." Report prepared under Contract 3090 for the International Finance Corporation, Washington, D.C.

IFC (International Finance Corporation). 1994. "Textile Waste Treatment Seminar, June 21," Presentation by Piedmond Olsen Hensley. Washington, D.C.

Modak. 1991. *Environmental Aspects of the Textile Industry: A Technical Guide.* Paris: United Nations Environment Programme, Industry and Environment Office. Paris.

Paris Convention for the Prevention of Marine Pollution. 1994. "Draft Report on Best Available Techniques and Best Environmental Practice for Wet Processes in the Textile Processing Industry." Presented by Belgium at the Sixth Meeting of the Working Group on Industrial Sectors, Oslo, January 17–21. INDSEC 6/12/2-E. Agenda Item 12.

UNEP (United Nations Environment Programme). 1994. *The Textile Industry and the Environment.* Technical Report 16. Paris.

World Bank, 1996. "Pollution Prevention and Abatement: Textiles Industry." Draft Technical Background Document. Environment Department, Washington, D.C.

# Thermal Power: Guidelines for New Plants

## Industry Description and Practices

This document sets forth procedures for establishing maximum emissions levels for all fossil-fuel-based thermal power plants with a capacity of 50 or more megawatts of electricity (MWe) that use coal, fuel oil, or natural gas.[1]

*Conventional steam-producing thermal power plants* generate electricity through a series of energy conversion stages: fuel is burned in boilers to convert water to high-pressure steam, which is then used to drive a turbine to generate electricity.

*Combined-cycle units* burn fuel in a combustion chamber, and the exhaust gases are used to drive a turbine. Waste heat boilers recover energy from the turbine exhaust gases for the production of steam, which is then used to drive another turbine. Generally, the total efficiency of a combined-cycle system in terms of the amount of electricity generated per unit of fuel is greater than for conventional thermal power systems, but the combined-cycle system may require fuels such as natural gas.

*Advanced coal utilization technologies* (e.g., fluidized-bed combustion and integrated gasification combined cycle) are becoming available, and other systems such as cogeneration offer improvements in thermal efficiency, environmental performance, or both, relative to conventional power plants. The economic and environmental costs and benefits of such advanced technologies need to be examined case by case, taking into account alternative fuel choices, demonstrated commercial viability, and plant location. The criteria spelled out in this document apply regardless of the particular technology chosen.

*Engine-driven power plants* are usually considered for power generation capacities of up to 150 MWe. They have the added advantages of shorter building period, higher overall efficiency (low fuel consumption per unit of output), optimal matching of different load demands, and moderate investment costs, compared with conventional thermal power plants. Further information on engine-driven plants is given in Annex A.

## Waste Characteristics

The wastes generated by thermal power plants are typical of those from combustion processes. The exhaust gases from burning coal and oil contain primarily particulates (including heavy metals, if they are present in significant concentrations in the fuel), sulfur and nitrogen oxides ($SO_x$ and $NO_x$), and volatile organic compounds (VOCs). For example, a 500 MWe plant using coal with 2.5% sulfur (S), 16% ash, and 30,000 kilojoules per kilogram (kJ/kg) heat content will emit each day 200 metric tons of sulfur dioxide ($SO_2$), 70 tons of nitrogen dioxide ($NO_2$), and 500 tons of fly ash if no controls are present. In addition, the plant will generate about 500 tons of solid waste and about 17 gigawatt-hours (GWh) of thermal discharge.

This document focuses primarily on emissions of particulates less than 10 microns (mm) in size ($PM_{10}$, including sulfates), of sulfur dioxide, and of nitrogen oxides. Nitrogen oxides are of concern because of their direct effects and because they are precursors for the formation of ground-level ozone. Information concerning the health and other damage caused by these and other pollutants, as well as on alternative methods of emissions control, is provided in the relevant pollutant and pollutant control documents.

The concentrations of these pollutants in the exhaust gases are a function of firing configuration, operating practices, and fuel composition. Gas-fired plants generally produce negligible quantities of particulates and sulfur oxides, and levels of nitrogen oxides are about 60% of those from plants using coal. Gas-fired plants also release lower quantities of carbon dioxide, a greenhouse gas.

Ash residues and the dust removed from exhaust gases may contain significant levels of heavy metals and some organic compounds, in addition to inert materials. Fly ash removed from exhaust gases makes up 60–85% of the coal ash residue in pulverized-coal boilers. Bottom ash includes slag and particles that are coarser and heavier than fly ash. The volume of solid wastes may be substantially higher if environmental measures such as flue gas desulfurization (FGD) are adopted and the residues are not reused in other industries.

Steam turbines and other equipment may require large quantities of water for cooling, including steam condensation. Water is also required for auxiliary station equipment, ash handling, and FGD systems. The characteristics of the wastewaters generated depend on the ways in which the water has been used. Contamination arises from demineralizers, lubricating and auxiliary fuel oils, and chlorine, biocides, and other chemicals used to manage the quality of water in cooling systems. Once-through cooling systems increase the temperature of the receiving water.

## Policy Framework

The development of a set of environmental requirements for a new thermal power plant involves decisions of two distinct kinds. First, there are the specific requirements of the power plant itself. These are the responsibility of the project developer in collaboration with relevant local or other environmental authorities. This document focuses on the issues that should be addressed in arriving at project-specific emissions standards and other requirements.

Second, there are requirements that relate to the operation of the power system as a whole. These strategic issues must be the concern of national or regional authorities with the responsibility for setting the overall policy framework for the development of the power sector. Examples of such requirements include measures to promote energy conservation via better demand-side management, to encourage the use of renewable sources of energy rather than fossil fuels, and to meet overall targets for the reduction of emissions of sulfur dioxide, nitrogen oxides, or greenhouse gases.

In the context of its regular country dialogue on energy and environmental issues, the World Bank is willing to assist its clients to develop the policy framework for implementing such environmental requirements for the power sector as a whole. One step in this process might be the preparation of a sectoral environmental assessment. This document assumes that the project is consistent with broad sectoral policies and requirements that have been promulgated by the relevant authorities in order to meet international obligations and other environmental goals affecting the power sector.

In some cases, strategies for meeting system-wide goals may be developed through a power-sector planning exercise that takes account of environmental and social factors. This would, for instance, be appropriate for a small country with a single integrated utility. In other cases, governments may decide to rely on a set of incentives and environmental standards designed to influence the decisions made by many independent operators.

## Determining Site-Specific Requirements

This document spells out the process—starting from a set of maximum emissions levels acceptable to the World Bank Group—that should be followed in determining the site-specific emissions guidelines. The guidelines could encompass both controls on the plant and other measures, perhaps outside the plant, that may be necessary to mitigate the impact of the plant on the airshed or watershed in which it is located. The process outlines how the World Bank Group's policy on Environmental Assessment (OP 4.01) for thermal power plants can be implemented. The guidelines are designed to protect human health; reduce mass loading to the environment to acceptable levels; achieve emissions levels based on commercially proven and widely used technologies; follow current regulatory and technology trends; be cost-effective; and promote the use of cleaner fuels and good-management practices that increase energy efficiency and productivity.

It is important to stress that the results of the environmental assessment (EA) are critical to defining many of the design parameters and other assumptions, such as location, fuel choice, and the like, required to develop the detailed specification of a project. The assessment results must be integrated with economic analyses of the key design options. Thus, it is essential that the work of preparing an environmental assessment be initiated during the early stages of project conception and design so that the initial results of the study can be used in subsequent stages of project development. It is not acceptable to prepare an environmental assessment that considers a small number of options in order to justify a predetermined set of design choices.

*Evaluation of Project Alternatives*

The EA should include an analysis of reasonable alternatives that meet the ultimate objective of the project. The assessment may lead to alternatives that are sounder, from an environmental, sociocultural, and economic point of view, than the originally proposed project. Alternatives need to be considered for various aspects of the system, including:

- Fuels used
- Power generation technologies
- Heat rejection systems
- Water supply or intakes
- Solid waste disposal systems
- Plant and sanitary waste discharge
- Engineering and pollution control equipment (see Annex B for some examples)
- Management systems.

The alternatives should be evaluated as a part of the conceptual design process. Those alternatives that provide cost-effective environmental management are preferred.

*Clean Development Mechanism (CDM)*

The Kyoto Protocol provisions allow for the use of the clean development mechanism (CDM), under which, beginning in 2000, greenhouse gas emissions from projects in non–Annex I countries that are certified by designated operating entities can be acquired by Annex I countries and credited against their emissions binding commit-

ments. The availability of CDM financing may alter, in some cases, the choice of the least-cost project alternative. Once the CDM is enacted, it will be advisable to incorporate the following steps into the process of evaluating project alternatives:

- Identification and assessment of alternatives that are eligible for CDM-type financing (e.g., alternatives that are not economical without carbon offsets and whose incremental costs above the least-cost baseline alternative, taking account of local environmental externalities, are smaller than the costs of resulting carbon offsets).
- Negotiation with Annex I parties of possible offset arrangements, if CDM-eligible alternatives exist. The World Bank Group will be prepared to assist in the process of identifying the CDM-eligible alternatives and negotiating offset arrangements for projects that are partly financed or guaranteed by the World Bank Group.

*Environmental Assessment*

An EA should be carried out early in the project cycle in order to establish emissions requirements and other measures on a site-specific basis for a new thermal power plant or unit of 50 MWe or larger. The initial tasks in carrying out the EA should include:

- Collection of baseline data on ambient concentrations of $PM_{10}$ and sulfur oxides (for oil and coal-fired plants), nitrogen oxides, (and ground-level ozone, if levels of ambient exposure to ozone are thought to be a problem) within a defined airshed encompassing the proposed project.[2]
- Collection of similar baseline data for critical water quality indicators that might be affected by the plant.
- Use of appropriate air quality and dispersion models to estimate the impact of the project on the ambient concentrations of these pollutants, on the assumption that the maximum emissions levels described below apply. (See the chapters on airshed models in Part II of this *Handbook*.)

When there is a reasonable likelihood that in the medium or long term the power plant will be expanded or other pollution sources will increase significantly, the analysis should take account of the impact of the proposed plant design both immediately and after any probable expansion in capacity or in other sources of pollution. The EA should also include impacts from construction work and other activities that normally occur, such as migration of workers when large facilities are built. Plant design should allow for future installation of additional pollution control equipment, should this prove desirable or necessary.

The EA should also address other project-specific environmental concerns, such as emissions of cadmium, mercury, and other heavy metals resulting from burning certain types of coal or heavy fuel oil. If emissions of this kind are a concern, the government (or the project sponsor) and the World Bank Group will agree on specific measures for mitigating the impact of such emissions and on the associated emissions guidelines.

The quality of the EA (including systematic cost estimates) is likely to have a major influence on the ease and speed of project preparation. A good EA prepared early in the project cycle should make a significant contribution to keeping the overall costs of the project down.

## Emissions Guidelines

Emissions levels for the design and operation of each project must be established through the EA process on the basis of country legislation and the *Pollution Prevention and Abatement Handbook,* as applied to local conditions. The emissions levels selected must be justified in the EA and acceptable to the World Bank Group.

The following maximum emissions levels are normally acceptable to the World Bank Group in making decisions regarding the provision of World Bank Group assistance for new fossil-fuel-fired thermal power plants or units of 50 MWe or larger (using conventional fuels). The emissions levels have been set so they can be achieved by adopting a variety of cost-effective options or technologies, including the use of clean fuels or washed coal. For example, dust controls capable of over 99% removal efficiency, such as electrostatic precipitators (ESPs) or baghouses, should always be installed for coal-fired power plants.

Similarly, the use of low-$NO_x$ burners with other combustion modifications such as low excess air (LEA) firing should be standard practice. The range of options for the control of sulfur oxides is greater because of large differences in the sulfur content of different fuels and in control costs. In general, for low-sulfur (less than 1% S), high-calorific-value fuels, specific controls may not be required, while coal cleaning, when feasible, or sorbent injection (in that order) may be adequate for medium-sulfur fuels (1–3% S). FGD may be considered for high-sulfur fuels (more than 3% S). Fluidized-bed combustion, when technically and economically feasible, has relatively low $SO_x$ emissions. The choice of technology depends on a benefit-cost analysis of the environmental performance of different fuels and the cost of controls.

Any deviations from the following emissions levels must be described in the World Bank Group project documentation.

*Air Emissions*

The maximum emissions levels given here can be consistently achieved by well-designed, well-operated, and well-maintained pollution control systems. In contrast, poor operating or maintenance procedures affect actual pollutant removal efficiency and may reduce it to well below the design specification. The maximum emissions levels are expressed as concentrations to facilitate monitoring. Dilution of air emissions to achieve these guidelines is unacceptable. Compliance with ambient air quality guidelines should be assessed on the basis of good engineering practice (GEP) recommendations. See Annex C for ambient air quality guidelines to be applied if local standards have not been set.[3] Plants should not use stack heights less than the GEP recommended values unless the air quality impact analysis has taken into account building downwash effects. All of the maximum emissions levels should be achieved for at least 95% of the time that the plant or unit is operating, to be calculated as a proportion of annual operating hours.[4] The remaining 5% of annual operating hours is assumed to be for start-up, shutdown, emergency fuel use, and unexpected incidents. For peaking units where the start-up mode is expected to be longer than 5% of the annual operating hours, exceedance should be justified by the EA with regard to air quality impacts.

*Power plants in degraded airsheds.* The following definitions apply in airsheds where there already exists a significant level of pollution.

An airshed will be classified as having *moderate air quality* with respect to particulates, sulfur dioxide, or nitrogen dioxide if either 1 or 2 applies:

1. (a) The annual mean value of $PM_{10}$ exceeds 50 micrograms per cubic meter ($mg/m^3$) for the airshed (80 $mg/m^3$ for total suspended particulates, TSP); (b) the annual mean value of sulfur dioxide exceeds 50 $mg/m^3$; or (c) the annual mean value of nitrogen dioxide exceeds 100 $mg/m^3$ for the airshed.

2. The 98th percentile of 24-hour mean values of $PM_{10}$, sulfur dioxide, or nitrogen dioxide for the airshed over a period of a year exceeds 150 $mg/m^3$ (230 $mg/m^3$ for TSP).

An airshed will be classified as having *poor air quality* with respect to particulates, sulfur dioxide, or nitrogen dioxide if either 1 or 2 applies:

1. (a) The annual mean of $PM_{10}$ exceeds 100 $mg/m^3$ for the airshed (160 $mg/m^3$ for TSP); (b) the annual mean of sulfur dioxide exceeds 100 $mg/m^3$ for the airshed; or (c) the annual mean of nitrogen dioxide exceeds 200 $mg/m^3$ for the airshed.

2. The 95th percentile of 24-hour mean values of $PM_{10}$, sulfur dioxide, or nitrogen dioxide for the airshed over a period of a year exceeds 150 $mg/m^3$ (230 $mg/m^3$ for TSP).

*Plants smaller than 500 MWe in airsheds with moderate air quality* are subject to the maximum emissions levels indicated below, provided that the EA shows that the plan will not lead *either* to the airshed dropping into the "poor air quality" category *or* to an increase of more than 5 $mg/m^3$ in the annual mean level of particulates ($PM_{10}$ or TSP), sulfur dioxide, or nitrogen dioxide for the entire airshed. If either of these conditions is not satisfied, lower site-specific emissions levels should be established that would ensure that the conditions can be satisfied. The limit of a 5 $mg/m^3$ increase in the annual mean will apply to the cumulative total impact of all power plants built in the airshed within any 10-year period beginning on or after the date at which the guidelines come into effect.

*Plants larger than or equal to 500 MWe in airsheds with moderate air quality and all plants in airsheds with poor air quality* are subject to site-specific requirements that include offset provisions to ensure that (a) there is no net increase in the total emissions of particulates or sulfur dioxide within the airshed and (b) the resultant ambient levels of nitrogen dioxide do not exceed the levels specified for moderately degraded airsheds.[5] The measures agreed under the offset provisions must be implemented before the power plant comes fully on stream. Suitable offset measures could include reductions in emissions of particulates, sulfur dioxide, or nitrogen dioxide as a result of (a) the installation of new or more effective controls at other units within the same power plant or at other power plants in the same airshed, (b) the installation of new or more effective controls at other large sources, such as district heating plants or industrial plants, in the same airshed, or (c) investments in gas distribution or district heating systems designed to substitute for the use of coal for residential heating and other small boilers.[6] The monitoring and enforcement of the offset provisions would be the responsibility of the local or national agency responsible for granting and supervising environmental permits. Such offset provisions would normally be described in detail in a specific covenant in the project loan agreement.

Project sponsors who do not wish to engage in the negotiations necessary to put together an offset agreement would have the option of relying on an appropriate combination of clean fuels, controls, or both.

*Particulate matter.* For all plants or units, PM emissions (all sizes) should not exceed 50 $mg/Nm^3$.[7] The EA should pay specific attention to particulates smaller than 10 mm in aerodynamic diameter ($PM_{10}$) in the airshed, since these are inhaled into the lungs and are associated with the most serious effects on human health. Where possible, ambient levels of fine particulates (less than 2.5 mm in diameter) should be measured. Recent epidemiologic evidence suggests that much of the health damage caused by exposure to particulates is associated with these fine particles, which penetrate most deeply into the lungs. Emissions of $PM_{10}$ and fine particulates include ash, soot, and carbon compounds (often the results of incomplete combustion), acid condensates, sulfates, and nitrates, as well as lead, cadmium, and other metals. Fine particulates, including sulfates, nitrates, and carbon compounds, are also formed by chemical processes in the atmosphere, but they tend to disperse over the whole airshed.

*Sulfur dioxide.* Total sulfur dioxide emissions from the power plant or unit should be less than 0.20 metric tons per day (tpd) per MWe of capacity for the first 500 MWe, plus 0.10 tpd for each additional MWe of capacity over 500 MWe.[8] In addition, the concentration of sulfur dioxide in flue gases should not exceed 2,000 mg/Nm$^3$ (see note 4 for assumptions), with a maximum emissions level of 500 tpd. Construction of two or more separate plants in the same airshed to circumvent this cap is not acceptable.

*Nitrogen oxides.* The specific emissions limits for nitrogen oxides are 750 mg/Nm$^3$, or 260 nanograms per joule (ng/J), or 365 parts per million parts (ppm) for a coal-fired power plant, and up to 1,500 mg/Nm$^3$ for plants using coal with volatile matter less than 10%; 460 mg/Nm$^3$ (or 130 ng/J, or 225 ppm) for an oil-fired power plant; and 320 mg/Nm$^3$ (or 86 ng/J, or 155 ppm) for a gas-fired power plant.

For combustion turbine units, the maximum NO$_x$ emissions levels are 125 mg/Nm$^3$ (dry at 15% oxygen) for gas; 165 mg/Nm$^3$ (dry at 15% oxygen) for diesel (No. 2 oil); and 300 mg/Nm$^3$ (dry at 15% oxygen) for fuel oil (No. 6 and others).[9] Where there are technical difficulties, such as scarcity of water available for water injection, an emissions variance allowing a maximum emissions level of up to 400 mg/Nm$^3$ dry (at 15% oxygen) is considered acceptable, provided there are no significant environmental concerns associated with ambient levels of ozone or nitrogen dioxide.

For engine-driven power plants, the EA should pay particular attention to levels of nitrogen oxides before and after the completion of the project. Provided that the resultant maximum ambient levels of nitrogen dioxide are less than 150 mg/m$^3$ (24-hour average), the specific emissions guidelines are as follows: (a) for funding applications received after July 1, 2000, the NO$_x$ emissions levels should be less than 2,000 mg/Nm$^3$ (or 13 grams per kilowatt-hour, g/kWh dry at

15% oxygen); and (b) for funding applications received before July 1, 2000, the NO$_x$ emissions levels should be less than 2,300 mg/Nm$^3$ (or 17 g/kWh dry at 15% oxygen). In all other cases, the maximum emissions level of nitrogen oxides is 400 mg/Nm$^3$ (dry at 15% oxygen).

*Offsets and the role of the World Bank Group.* Large power complexes should normally not be developed in airsheds with moderate or poor air quality, or, if they must be developed, then only with appropriate offset measures. The costs of identifying and negotiating offsets for large power complexes are not large in relation to the total cost of preparing such projects. In the context of its regular country dialogue on energy and environmental issues, the World Bank is prepared to assist the process of formulating and implementing offset agreements for projects that are partly financed or guaranteed by the World Bank Group. If the offsets for a particular power project that will be financed by a World Bank Group loan involve specific investments to reduce emissions of particulates, sulfur oxides, or nitrogen oxides, these may be included within the scope of the project and may thus be eligible for financing under the loan.[10]

*Long-range transport of acid pollutants.* Where ground-level ozone or acidification is or may in future be a significant problem, governments are encouraged to undertake regional or national studies of the impact of sulfur dioxide, nitrogen oxides, and other pollutants that damage sensitive ecosystems, with, in appropriate cases, support from the World Bank (see Policy Framework, above). The aim of such studies is to identify least-cost options for reducing total emissions of these pollutants from a region or a country so as to achieve load targets, as appropriate.[11]

A possible (but not the only) approach to identifying sensitive ecosystems is to estimate critical loads for acid depositions and critical levels for ozone in different geographic areas. The analysis must, however, take into account the large degree of uncertainty involved in making such estimates.

In appropriate cases, governments should develop cost-effective strategies, as well as legal instruments, to protect sensitive ecosystems or to reduce transboundary flows of pollutants.

Where such regional studies have been carried out, the environmental assessment should take account of their results in assessing the overall impact of a proposed power plant.

The site-specific emissions requirements should be consistent with any strategy and applicable legal framework that have been adopted by the host country government to protect sensitive ecosystems or to reduce transboundary flows of pollutants.

*Liquid Effluents*

The effluent levels presented in Table 1 (for the applicable parameters) should be achieved daily without dilution.

Coal pile runoff and leachate may contain significant concentrations of toxics such as heavy metals. Where leaching of toxics to groundwater or their transport in surface runoff is a concern, suitable preventive and control measures such as protective liners and collection and treatment of runoff should be put in place.

*Solid Wastes*

Solid wastes, including ash and FGD sludges, that do not leach toxic substances or other con-

taminants of concern to the environment may be disposed in landfills or other disposal sites provided that they do not impact nearby water bodies. Where toxics or other contaminants are expected to leach out, they should be treated by, for example, stabilization before disposal.

*Ambient Noise*

Noise abatement measures should achieve either the levels given below or a maximum increase in background levels of 3 decibels (measured on the A scale) [dB(A)]. Measurements are to be taken at noise receptors located outside the project property boundary.

| Receptor | Maximum allowable log equivalent (hourly measurements), in dB(A) Day (07:00–22:00) | Night (22:00–07:00) |
|---|---|---|
| Residential, institutional, educational | 55 | 45 |
| Industrial, commercial | 70 | 70 |

## Monitoring and Reporting

For measurement methods, see the chapter on Monitoring in this *Handbook*.

Maintaining the combustion temperature and the excess oxygen level within the optimal band in which particulate matter and $NO_x$ emissions are minimized simultaneously ensures the greatest energy efficiency and the most economic plant operation. Monitoring should therefore aim at achieving this optimal performance as consistently as possible. Systems for continuous monitoring of particulate matter, sulfur oxides, and nitrogen oxides in the stack exhaust can be installed and are desirable whenever their maintenance and calibration can be ensured. Alternatively, surrogate performance monitoring should be performed on the basis of initial calibration. The following surrogate parameters are relevant for assessing environmental performance. (They require no changes in plant design but do call for appropriate training of operating personnel.)

**Table 1. Effluents from Thermal Power Plants**
*(milligrams per liter, except for pH and temperature)*

| Parameter | Maximum value |
|---|---|
| pH | 6–9 |
| TSS | 50 |
| Oil and grease | 10 |
| Total residual chlorine[a] | 0.2 |
| Chromium (total) | 0.5 |
| Copper | 0.5 |
| Iron | 1.0 |
| Zinc | 1.0 |
| Temperature increase | ≤ 3°C[b] |

a. "Chlorine shocking" may be preferable in certain circumstances. This involves using high chlorine levels for a few seconds rather than a continuous low-level release. The maximum value is 2 mg/l for up to 2 hours, not to be repeated more frequently than once in 24 hours, with a 24-hour average of 0.2 mg/l. (The same limits would apply to bromine and fluorine.)
b. The effluent should result in a temperature increase of no more than 3° C at the edge of the zone where initial mixing and dilution take place. Where the zone is not defined, use 100 meters from the point of discharge when there are no sensitive aquatic ecosystems within this distance.

- *Particulate matter.* Ash and heavy metal content of fuel; maximum flue gas flow rate; minimum power supply to the ESP or minimum pressure drop across the baghouse; minimum combustion temperature; and minimum excess oxygen level.
- *Sulfur dioxide.* Sulfur content of fuel.
- *Nitrogen oxides.* Maximum combustion temperature and maximum excess oxygen level.

Direct measurement of the concentrations of emissions in samples of flue gases should be performed regularly (for example, on an annual basis) to validate surrogate monitoring results or for the calibration of the continuous monitor (if used). The samples should be monitored for PM and nitrogen oxides and may be monitored for sulfur oxides and heavy metals, although monitoring the sulfur and heavy metal content of fuel is considered adequate. At least three data sets for direct emissions measurements should be used, based on an hourly rolling average.

Automatic air quality monitoring systems measuring ambient levels of $PM_{10}$, sulfur oxides, and nitrogen oxides outside the plant boundary should be installed where maximum ambient concentration is expected or where there are sensitive receptors such as protected areas and population centers. ($PM_{10}$ and $SO_x$ measurements are, however, not required for gas-fired plants.) The number of air quality monitors should be greater if the area in which the power plant is located is prone to temperature inversions or other meteorological conditions that lead to high levels of air pollutants affecting nearby populations or sensitive ecosystems. The purpose of such ambient air quality monitoring is to help assess the possible need for changes in operating practices (including burning cleaner fuels to avoid high short-term exposures), especially during periods of adverse meteorological conditions. The pollutant guidelines specify short-term ambient air quality guideline values which, if exceeded, call for emergency measures such as burning cleaner fuels.

Any measures should be taken in close collaboration with local authorities. The specific design of the ambient monitoring system should be based on the findings of the EA. The frequency of ambient measurements depends on prevailing conditions; ambient measurements, when taken, should normally be averaged daily.

The pH and temperature of the wastewater discharges should be monitored continuously. Levels of suspended solids, oil and grease, and residual chlorine should be measured daily, and heavy metals and other pollutants in wastewater discharges should be measured monthly if treatment is provided.

Monitoring data should be analyzed and reviewed at regular intervals and compared with the operating standards so that any necessary corrective actions can be taken. Records of monitoring results should be kept in an acceptable format. The results should be reported in summary form, with notification of exceptions, if any, to the responsible government authorities and relevant parties, as required. In the absence of specific national or local government guidelines, actual monitoring or surrogate performance data should be reported at least annually. The government may require additional explanation and may take corrective action if plants are found to exceed maximum emissions levels for more than 5% of the operating time, or on the occasion of a plant audit. The objective is to ensure continuing compliance with the emissions limits agreed at the outset, based on sound operation and maintenance. Exceedances of the maximum emissions levels would normally be reviewed in light of the enterprise's good-faith efforts in this regard.

As part of the Framework Convention on Climate Change, countries will be asked to record their emissions of greenhouse gases (GHG). As an input to this, and to facilitate possible future activities implemented jointly with Annex I countries, the emissions of individual projects should be estimated on the basis of the chemical composition of the fuel or measured directly. Table 2 in the chapter on Greenhouse Gas Abatement and Climate Change in Part II of this *Handbook* provides relevant emissions factors.

In order to develop institutional capacity, training should be provided with adequate budgets to ensure satisfactory environmental performance. The training may include education on environmental assessment, environmental mitigation plans, and environmental monitoring. In some cases, it may be appropriate to include the staff from the environmental implementation agencies, such as the state pollution control board, in the training program

## Key Issues

The key production and emissions control practices that will lead to compliance with the above guidelines are summarized below. It is assumed that the proposed project represents a least-cost solution, taking into account environmental and social factors.

- Choose the cleanest fuel economically available (natural gas is preferable to oil, which is preferable to coal).
- Give preference to high-heat-content, low-ash, low-sulfur coal (or high-heat-content, high-sulfur coal, in that order) and consider beneficiation for high-ash, high-sulfur coal.
- Select the best power generation technology for the fuel chosen to balance the environmental and economic benefits. The choice of technology and pollution control systems will be based on the site-specific environmental assessment.

  Keep in mind that particulates smaller than 10 microns in size are most important from a health perspective. Acceptable levels of particulate matter removal are achievable at relatively low cost.

  Consider cost-effective technologies such as pre-ESP sorbent injection, along with coal washing, before in-stack removal of sulfur dioxide.

  Use low-$NO_x$ burners and other combustion modifications to reduce emissions of nitrogen oxides.

- Before adopting expensive control technologies, consider using offsetting reductions in emissions of critical pollutants at other sources within the airshed to achieve acceptable ambient levels.
- Use $SO_x$ removal systems that generate less wastewater, if feasible; however, the environmental and cost characteristics of both inputs and wastes should be assessed case by case.
- Manage ash disposal and reclamation so as to minimize environmental impacts—especially the migration of toxic metals, if present, to nearby surface and groundwater bodies, in addition to the transport of suspended solids in surface runoff. Consider reusing ash for building materials.
- Consider recirculating cooling systems where thermal discharge to water bodies may be of concern.
- Note that a comprehensive monitoring and reporting system is required.

## Annex A. Engine-Driven Power Plants

Engine-driven power plants use fuels such as diesel oil, fuel oil, gas, orimulsion, and crude oil. The two types of engines normally used are the medium-speed four-stroke trunk piston engine and the low-speed two-stroke crosshead engine. Both types of engine operate on the air-standard diesel thermodynamic cycle. Air is drawn or forced into a cylinder and is compressed by a piston. Fuel is injected into the cylinder and is ignited by the heat of the compression of the air. The burning mixture of fuel and air expands, pushing the piston. Finally the products of combustion are removed from the cylinder, completing the cycle. The energy released from the combustion of fuel is used to drive an engine, which rotates the shaft of an alternator to generate electricity. The combustion process typically includes preheating the fuel to the required viscosity, typically 16–20 centiStokes (cSt), for good fuel atomization at the nozzle. The fuel pressure is boosted to about 1,300 bar to achieve a droplet distribution small enough for fast combustion and low smoke values. The nozzle design is critical to the ignition and combustion process. Fuel spray penetrating to the liner can damage the liner and cause smoke formation. Spray in the vicinity of the valves may increase the valve temperature and contribute to hot corrosion and burned valves. If the fuel timing is too early, the cylinder pressure will increase, resulting in higher nitrogen oxide formation. If injection is timed too late, fuel consumption and turbocharger speed will increase. $NO_x$ emissions can be reduced by later injection timing, but then particulate matter and the amount of unburned species will increase.

*Ignition quality.* For distillate fuels, methods for establishing ignition quality include cetane number and cetane index for diesel. The CCAI number, based on fuel density and viscosity, gives a rough indication of the ignition behavior of heavy fuel oil.

*Fuel quality.* Fuel ash constituents may lead to abrasive wear, deposit formation, and high-temperature corrosion, in addition to emissions of particulate matter. The properties of fuel that may affect engine operation include viscosity, specific gravity, stability (poor stability results in the precipitation of sludge, which may block the filters), cetane number, asphaltene content, carbon residue, sulfur content, vanadium and sodium content (an indicator of corrosion, especially on exhaust valves), presence of solids such as rust, sand, and aluminum silicate, which may result in blockage of fuel pumps and liner wear, and water content.

*Waste characteristics.* The wastes generated are typical of those from combustion processes. The exhaust gases contain particulates (including heavy metals if present in the fuel), sulfur and nitrogen oxides, and, in some cases, VOCs. Nitrogen oxides are the main concern after particulate matter in the air emissions. $NO_x$ emissions levels are (almost exponentially) dependent on the temperature of combustion, in addition to other factors. Most of the $NO_x$ emissions are formed from the air used for combustion and typically range from 1,100 to 2,000 ppm at 15% oxygen. Carbon dioxide emissions are approximately 600 g/kWh of electricity, and total hydrocarbons (calculated as methane equivalent) are 0.5 g/kWh of electricity.

The exhaust gases from an engine are affected by (a) the load profile of the prime mover; (b) ambient conditions such as air humidity and temperature; (c) fuel oil quality, such as sulfur content, nitrogen content, viscosity, ignition ability, density, and ash content; and (d) site conditions and the auxiliary equipment associated with the prime mover, such as cooling properties and exhaust gas back pressure. The engine parameters that affect nitrogen oxide emissions are (a) fuel injection in terms of timing, duration, and atomization; (b) combustion air conditions, which are affected by valve timing, the charge air system, and charge air cooling before cylinders; and (c) the combustion process, which is affected by air and fuel mixing, combustion chamber design, and the compression ratio. The particulate matter emissions are dependent on

the general conditions of the engine, especially the fuel injection system and its maintenance, in addition to the ash content of the fuel, which is in the range 0.05–0.2%. $SO_x$ emissions are directly dependent on the sulfur content of the fuel. Fuel oil may contain around 0.3% sulfur and, in some cases, up to 5%.

## Annex B. Illustrative Pollution Prevention and Control Technologies

A wide variety of control technology options is available. As usual, these options should be considered after an adequate assessment of broader policy options, including pricing and institutional measures. Additional information is provided in the relevant documents on pollution control technologies.

### Cleaner Fuels

The simplest and, in many circumstances, most cost-effective form of pollution prevention is to use cleaner fuels. For new power plants, combined-cycle plants burning natural gas currently have a decisive advantage in terms of their capital costs, thermal efficiency, and environmental performance. Natural gas is also the preferred fuel for minimizing GHG emissions because it produces lower carbon dioxide emissions per unit of energy and enhances energy efficiency.

If availability or price rule out natural gas as an option, the use of low-sulfur fuel oil or high-heat-content, low-sulfur, low-ash coal should be considered. Typically, such fuels command a premium price over their dirtier equivalents, but the reductions in operating or environmental costs that they permit are likely to outweigh this premium. In preparing projects, an evaluation of alternative fuel options should be conducted at the outset to establish the most cost-effective combination of fuel, technology, and environmental controls for meeting performance and environmental objectives.

If coal is used, optimal environmental performance and economic efficiency will be achieved through an integrated approach across the whole coal-energy chain, including the policy and investment aspects of mining, preparation, transport, power generation and heat conversion, and clean coal technologies. Coal washing, in particular, has a beneficial impact in terms of reducing the ash content and ash variability of coal used in thermal power plants, which leads to consistent boiler performance, reduced emissions, and less maintenance.

### Abatement of Particulate Matter

The options for removing particulates from exhaust gases are cyclones, baghouses (fabric filters), and ESPs. Cyclones may be adequate as precleaning devices; they have an overall removal efficiency of less than 90% for all particulate matter and considerably lower for $PM_{10}$. Baghouses can achieve removal efficiencies of 99.9% or better for particulate matter of all sizes, and they have the potential to enhance the removal of sulfur oxides when sorbent injection, dry-scrubbing, or spray dryer absorption systems are used. ESPs are available in a broad range of sizes for power plants and can achieve removal efficiencies of 99.9% or better for particulate matter of all sizes.

The choice between a baghouse and an ESP will depend on fuel and ash characteristics, as well as on operating and environmental factors. ESPs can be less sensitive to plant upsets than fabric filters because their operating effectiveness is not as sensitive to maximum temperatures and they have a low pressure drop. However, ESP performance can be affected by fuel characteristics. Modern baghouses can be designed to achieve very high removal efficiencies for $PM_{10}$ at a capital cost that is comparable to that for ESPs, but it is necessary to ensure appropriate training of operating and maintenance staff.

### Abatement of Sulfur Oxides

The range of options and removal efficiencies for $SO_x$ controls is wide. Pre-ESP sorbent injection can remove 30–70% of sulfur oxides, at a cost of US$50–$100 per kW. Post-ESP sorbent injection can achieve 70–90% $SO_x$ removal, at a cost of US$80–$170 per kW. Wet and semidry FGD units consisting of dedicated $SO_x$ absorbers can remove 70–95%, at a cost of US$80–$170 per kW (1997 prices). The operating costs of most FGDs are substantial because of the power consumed (of the order of 1–2% of the electricity generated), the chemicals used, and disposal of residues. Es-

timates by the International Energy Agency (IEA) suggest that the extra levelized annual cost for adding to a coal-fired power plant an FGD designed to remove 90% of sulfur oxides amounts to 10–14% depending on capacity utilization.

An integrated pollution management approach should be adopted that does not involve switching from one form of pollution to another. For example, FGD scrubber wastes, when improperly managed, can lead to contamination of the water supply, and such $SO_x$ removal systems could result in greater emissions of particulate matter from materials handling and windblown dust. This suggests the need for careful benefit-cost analysis of the types and extent of $SO_x$ abatement.

### Abatement of Nitrogen Oxides

The main options for controlling $NO_x$ emissions are combustion modifications: low-$NO_x$ burners with or without overfire air or reburning, water/steam injection, and selective catalytic or noncatalytic reduction (SCR/SNCR). Combustion modifications can remove 30–70% of nitrogen oxides, at a capital cost of less than US$20 per kW and a small increase in operating costs. SNCR systems can remove 30–70% of nitrogen oxides, at a capital cost of US$20–$40 per kW and a moderate increase in operating cost. However, plugging of the preheater because of the formation of ammonium bisulfate may pose some problems. SCR units can remove 70–90% of nitrogen oxides but involve a much larger capital cost of US$40–$80 per kW and a significant increase in operating costs, especially for coal-fired plants. Moreover, SCR may require low-sulfur fuels (less than 1.5% sulfur content) because the catalyst elements are sensitive to the sulfur dioxide content in the flue gas.

### Fly Ash Handling

Fly ash handling systems may be generally categorized as dry or wet, even though the dry handling system involves wetting the ash to 10–20% moisture to improve handling characteristics and to mitigate the dust generated during disposal. In wet systems, the ash is mixed with water to produce a liquid slurry containing 5–10% solids by weight. This is discharged to settling ponds, often with bottom ash and FGD sludges, as well. The ponds may be used as the final disposal site, or the settled solids may be dredged and removed for final disposal in a landfill. Wherever feasible, decanted water from ash disposal ponds should be recycled to formulate ash slurry. Where heavy metals are present in ash residues or FGD sludges, care must be taken to monitor and treat leachates and overflows from settling ponds, in addition to disposing of them in lined places to avoid contamination of water bodies. In some cases, ash residues are being used for building materials and in road construction. Gradual reclamation of ash ponds should be practiced.

*Water Use*

It is possible to reduce the fresh water intake for cooling systems by installing evaporative recirculating cooling systems. Such systems require a greater capital investment, but they may use only 5% of the water volume required for once-through cooling systems. Where once-through cooling systems are used, the volume of water required and the impact of its discharge can be reduced by careful siting of intakes and outfalls, by minimizing the use of biocides and anticorrosion chemicals (effective nonchromium-based alternatives are available to inhibit scale and products of corrosion in cooling water systems), and by controlling discharge temperatures and thermal plumes. Wastewaters from other processes, including boiler blowdown, demineralizer backwash, and resin regenerator wastewater, can also be recycled, but again, this requires careful management and treatment for reuse. Water use can also be reduced in certain circumstances through the use of air-cooled condensers.

## Annex C. Ambient Air Quality

The guidelines presented in Table C.1 are to be used only for carrying out an environment assessment in the absence of local ambient standards. They were constructed as consensus values taking particular account of WHO, USEPA, and EU standards and guidelines. *They do not in any way substitute for a country's own ambient air quality standards.*

### Table C.1. Ambient Air Quality in Thermal Power Plants

*(micrograms per cubic meter)*

| Pollutant | 24-hour average | Annual average |
|---|---|---|
| $pM_{10}$ | 150 | 50 |
| TSP[a] | 230 | 80 |
| Nitrogen dioxide | 150 | 100 |
| Sulfur dioxide | 150 | 80 |

a. Measurement of $PM_{10}$ is preferable to measurement of TSP.

### Notes

1. For plants smaller than 50 MWe, including those burning nonfossil fuels, PM emissions levels may be as much as 100 mg/Nm³. If justified by the EA, PM emissions levels up to 150 mg/Nm³ may be acceptable in special circumstances. The maximum emissions levels for nitrogen oxides remain the same, while for sulfur dioxide, the maximum emissions level is 2,000 mg/Nm³.

2. *Airshed* refers to the local area around the plant whose ambient air quality is directly affected by emissions from the plant. The size of the relevant local airshed will depend on plant characteristics, such as stack height, as well as on local meteorological conditions and topography. In some cases, airsheds are defined in legislation or by the relevant environmental authorities. If not, the EA should clearly define the airshed on the basis of consultations with those responsible for local environmental management.

In collecting baseline data, qualitative assessments may suffice for plants proposed in greenfield sites. For nondegraded airsheds, quantitative assessment using models and representative monitoring data may suffice.

3. See, e.g., United States, 40 CFR, Part 51, 100 (ii). Normally, GEP stack height = $H + 1.5L$, where $H$ is the height of nearby structures and $L$ is the lesser dimension of either height or projected width of nearby structures.

4. The assumptions are as follows: for coal, flue gas dry 6% excess oxygen—assumes 350 Nm³/GJ. For oil, flue gas dry 3% excess oxygen—assumes 280 Nm³/GJ. For gas, flue gas dry 3% excess oxygen—assumes 270 Nm³/GJ (see annex D). The oxygen level in engine exhausts and combustion turbines is assumed to be 15%, dry. See the document on Monitoring for measurement methods.

5. Gas-fired plants (in which the backup fuel contains less than 0.3% sulfur) and other plants that achieve emissions levels of less than 400 mg/Nm³ for sulfur oxides and nitrogen oxides are exempt from the offset requirements, since their emissions are relatively lower.

## Annex D. Conversion Chart

**Table D.1. SO$_2$ and NO$_x$ Emissions Conversion Chart for Steam-Based Thermal Power Plants**

| To convert | To (multiply by): | | | | | | | | |
|---|---|---|---|---|---|---|---|---|---|
| | | *ppm* | *ppm* | *g/GJ* | | | *lb/10⁶ Btu* | | |
| *From* | *Mg/Nm³* | *NO$_x$* | *SO$_2$* | *Coal* [a] | *Oil* [b] | *Gas* [c] | *Coal* [a] | *Oil* [b] | *Gas* [c] |
| Mg/Nm³ | 1 | 0.487 | 0.350 | 0.350 | 0.280 | 0.270 | 8.14 x 10-4 | 6.51 x 10-4 | 6.28 x 10-4 |
| ppm NO$_x$ | 2.05 | 1 | | 0.718 | 0.575 | 0.554 | 1.67 x 10-3 | 1.34 x 10-3 | 1.29 x 10-3 |
| ppm SO$_2$ | 2.86 | | 1 | 1.00 | 0.801 | 0.771 | 2.33 x 10-3 | 1.86 x 10-3 | 1.79 x 10-3 |
| G/GJ | | | | | | | | | |
| Coal[a] | 2.86 | 1.39 | 1.00 | 1 | | | 2.33 x 10-3 | | |
| Oil[b] | 3.57 | 1.74 | 1.25 | | 1 | | | 2.33 x 10-3 | |
| Gas[c] | 3.70 | 1.80 | 1.30 | | | 1 | | | 2.33 x 10-3 |
| lb/10⁶ Btu | | | | | | | | | |
| Coal[a] | 1,230 | 598 | 430 | 430 | | | 1 | | |
| Oil[b] | 1,540 | 748 | 538 | | 430 | | | 1 | |
| Gas[c] | 1,590 | 775 | 557 | | | 430 | | | 1 |

*Note:* g/GJ, grams per gigajoule; lb/10⁶ Btu, pounds per 100,000 British thermal units; Mg/Nm³, megagrams per normal cubic meter; ppm, parts per million.
a. Flue gas dry 6% excess O$_2$; assumes 350 Nm³/GJ.
b. Flue gas dry 3% excess O$_2$; assumes 280 Nm³/GJ.
c. Flue gas dry 3% excess O$_2$; assumes 270 Nm³/GJ.
*Source:* International Combustion Ltd.; data for coal, oil, and gas based on IEA 1986.

6. Wherever possible, the offset provisions should be implemented within the framework of an overall air quality management strategy designed to ensure that air quality in the airshed is brought into compliance with ambient standards.

7. A normal cubic meter (Nm³) is measured at 1 atmosphere and 0° C. The additional cost of controls designed to meet the 50 mg/Nm³ requirement, rather than one of 150 mg/Nm³ (e.g., less than 0.5% of total investment costs for a 600 MW plant) is expected to be less than the benefits of reducing ambient exposure to particulates. The high overall removal rate is necessary to capture PM$_{10}$ and fine particulates that seriously affect human health. Typically about 40% of PM by mass is smaller than 10 μm, but the collection efficiency of ESPs drops considerably for smaller particles. A properly designed and well-operated plant can normally achieve the lower emissions levels as easily as it can achieve higher emissions levels.

An exception to the maximum PM emissions level may be granted to engine-driven power plants for which funding applications are received before January 1, 2001. PM emissions levels of up to 75 mg/Nm³ would be allowed, provided that the EA presents documentation to show that (a) lower-ash grades of fuel oil are not commercially available; (b) emissions control technologies are not commercially available; and (c) the resultant ambient levels for PM$_{10}$ (annual average of less than 50 μg/m³ and 24-hour mean of less than

150 μg/m³) will be maintained for the entire duration of the project.

8. The maximum SO$_x$ emissions levels were back-calculated using the USEPA Environmental Protection Agency Industrial Source Complex (ISC) Model, with the objective of complying with the 1987 WHO Air Quality Guidelines for acceptable one-hour (peak) ambient concentration levels (350 μg/m³). The modeling results show that, in general, an emissions level of 2,000 mg/m³ (equivalent to 0.2 tpd per MWe) results in a one-hour level of 300 μg/m³, which, when added to a typical existing background level of 50 μg/m³ for greenfield sites, produces a one-hour level of 350 μg/m³ (see the discussion of degraded airsheds in the text). Compliance with the WHO one-hour level is normally the most significant, as short-term health impacts are considered to be the most important; compliance with this level also, in general, implies compliance with the WHO 24-hour and annual average guidelines. For large plants, the emissions guidelines for sulfur dioxide were further reduced to 0.1 tpd per MWe for capacities above 500 MWe to maintain acceptable mass loadings to the environment and thus address ecological concerns (acid rain). This results in a sulfur dioxide emissions level of 0.15 tpd/MWe (or 1.275 lb/mm Btu) for a 1,000 MWe plant.

9. Where the nitrogen content of the liquid fuel is greater than 0.015% and the selected equipment manufacturer cannot guarantee the emissions levels pro-

vided in the text, an $NO_x$ emissions allowance (i.e., added to the maximum emissions level) can be computed based on the following data as exceptions:

| Nitrogen content (percentage by weight) | Correction factor ($NO_x$ percentage by volume) |
|---|---|
| 0.015–0.1 | 0.04 N |
| 0.1–0.25 | 0.004 + 0.0067 (N − 0.1) |
| > 0.25 | 0.005 |

*Note:* Correction factor, 0.004% = 40 ppm = 80 mg / $Nm^3$.

There may be cases in which cost-effective $NO_x$ controls may not be technically feasible. Exceptions to the $NO_x$ emissions requirements (including those given in this note) are acceptable provided it can be shown that (a) for the entire duration of the project, the alternative emissions level will not result in ambient conditions that have a significant impact on human health and the environment, and (b) cost-effective techniques such as low-$NO_x$ burners, LEA, water or steam injection, and reburning are not feasible.

10. It should be noted that the offset requirement, which focuses on the level of total emissions, should result in an improvement in ambient air quality within the airshed, compared with the baseline scenario (as documented with ambient air monitoring data), if the offset measures are implemented for non-power-plant sources. Such sources typically emit from stacks of a lower average height than those for the new power plant.

11. Part II of this *Handbook* provides guidance on possible approaches for dealing with acid emissions. There is substantial scope for exploiting the synergies between the local and long-range benefits of emissions reductions.

## References and Sources

Homer, John. 1993. *Natural Gas in Developing Countries: Evaluating the Benefits to the Environment.* World Bank Discussion Paper 190. Washington, D.C.

IEA (International Energy Agency.) 1992. *Coal Information.* Paris.

Jechoutek, Karl G., S. Chattopadhya, R. Khan, F. Hill, and C. Wardell. 1992. "Steam Coal for Power and Industry." Industry and Energy Department Working Paper, Energy Series 58. World Bank, Washington, D.C.

MAN B & W. 1993. "The MAN B & W Diesel Group: Their Products, Market Successes, and Market Position in the Stationary Engines Business." Presentation to the World Bank, October 14.

OECD (Organisation for Economic Co-operation and Development). 1981. *Costs and Benefits of Sulphur Oxides Control.* Paris.

Rentz, O., H. Sasse, U. Karl, H. J. Schleef, and R. Dorn. 1997. "Emission Control at Stationary Sources in the Federal Republic of Germany." Vols. I and 2. Scientific Program of the German Ministry of Environment. Report 10402360. Bonn.

Stultz, S. C., and John B. Kitto, eds. 1992. *Steam: Its Generation and Use.* 40th ed. Barberton, Ohio: The Babcock & Wilcox Co.

Tavoulareas, E. Stratos, and Jean-Pierre Charpentier. 1995. *Clean Coal Technologies for Developing Countries.* World Bank Technical Paper 286, Energy Series. Washington, D.C.

United States. CFR (*Code of Federal Regulations*). Washington, D.C.: Government Printing Office.

Wartsila Diesel. 1996. "Successful Power Generation Operating on Residual Fuels." Presentation to the World Bank, May 16.

WHO (World Health Organization). 1987. *Air Quality Guidelines for Europe.* Copenhagen: WHO Regional Office for Europe.

World Bank. 1991. "Guideline for Diesel Generating Plant Specification and Bid Evaluation." Industry and Energy Department Working Paper, Energy Series Paper 43. Washington, D.C.

# Thermal Power: Rehabilitation of Existing Plants

## Key Issues

The range of circumstances in which the rehabilitation of an existing thermal power plant may be considered is extremely large. It is neither possible nor desirable to attempt to prescribe specific environmental guidelines for all of the different cases that may arise in the World Bank's operational work. Hence, this document focuses on the process that should be followed in order to arrive at an agreed set of site-specific standards that should be met by the plant after its rehabilitation.

At the heart of this process is the preparation of a combined environmental audit of the existing plant and assessment of alternative rehabilitation options relevant to the future impact of the plant on nearby populations and ecosystems. The coverage of the environmental assessment component of the study will depend on the rehabilitation activities involved and may be similar to that required for a new thermal power plant when major portions of the plant are being replaced or retrofitted. The amount of data required, the range of options considered, and the coverage of the environmental analysis will typically be less than appropriate for a new plant. At the same time, the initial environmental audit should not be restricted to those parts of the existing plant that may be affected by the rehabilitation. It should review all the major aspects of the plant's equipment and operating procedures in order to identify environmental problems and recommend cost-effective measures that would improve the plant's environmental performance.

The time and resources devoted to preparing the environmental audit and assessment should be appropriate to the nature and scale of the proposed rehabilitation. It would, for example, not be appropriate to carry out an extensive environmental assessment in cases involving minor modifications or the installation or upgrading of environmental controls such as a wastewater treatment plant or dust filters or precipitators. For larger projects, such as the installation of flue gas desulfurization (FGD) equipment, the environmental assessment might focus particularly on the range of options for reducing sulfur emissions and for disposing of the gypsum or solid waste generated by the equipment.

It is, however, recommended that an environmental audit be undertaken in almost all cases. Experience suggests that such investigations will often pay for themselves by identifying zero- or low-cost options for energy conservation and waste minimization. In addition, such an audit may indicate ways in which the project could be redesigned in order to address the most serious environmental problems associated with the plant.

Major rehabilitations that imply a substantial extension (10 years or more) of the expected operating life of the plant should be subject to an environmental assessment similar in depth and coverage to one that would be prepared for a new plant. In such cases, the plant will normally be expected to meet the basic guidelines that apply to new thermal power plants for emissions of particulates, nitrogen oxides ($NO_x$), wastewater discharges, and solid wastes. Where the rehabilitated plant would be unable to meet the basic guidelines for sulfur dioxide ($SO_2$) without additional and potentially expensive controls, the environmental assessment should review the full range of options for reducing $SO_2$ emissions, both from the plant itself and from other sources within the same airshed or elsewhere in the country. On the basis of this analysis, the government, the enterprise, and the World Bank Group will agree on specific measures, either at the plant or elsewhere, to mitigate the impact of these emissions and will also agree on the associated emissions requirements.

Any rehabilitation that involves a shift in fuel type—i.e., from coal or oil to gas, as distinguished from a change from one grade or quality of coal or oil to another—will be subject to the same basic emissions guidelines as would apply to a new plant burning the same fuel.

## Environmental Audit

An audit of the environmental performance of the existing plant should do at least the following:

- Review the actual operating and environmental performance of the plant in relation to its original design parameters.
- Examine the reasons for poor performance to identify measures that should be taken to address specific problems or to provide a basis for more appropriate assumptions about operating conditions in the future—for example, with respect to average fuel characteristics.
- Assess the scope for making improvements in maintenance and housekeeping inside and around the plant (e.g., check for excess oxygen levels, actual emissions levels, fuel spills, coal pile runoff, fugitive dust from coal piles, recordkeeping, monitoring, and other indicators of operation and maintenance of thermal power plants).
- Evaluate the readiness and capacity of the plant's emergency management systems to cope with incidents varying from small spills to major accidents (check storage of flammables, safe boiler and air pollution control system operation, and so on).
- Examine the plant's record with respect to worker safety and occupational health.

The report on the environmental audit should provide recommendations on the measures required to rectify any serious problems that were identified in the course of the study. These recommendations should be accompanied by approximate estimates of the capital and operating costs that would be involved and by an indication of the actions that should be taken either to implement the recommendations or to evaluate alternative options.

The management of the plant or the borrower should submit the report on the environmental audit to the World Bank Group, along with a statement of the steps taken to address the problems that were identified and to ensure that such problems do not recur in the future. Implementation of the actions outlined in the statement will be treated as one of the elements of the site-specific requirements for the project.

## Environmental Assessment

An environmental assessment of the proposed rehabilitation should be carried out early in the process of preparing the project in order to allow an opportunity to evaluate alternative rehabilitation options before key design decisions are finalized. The assessment should examine the impacts of the existing plant's operations on nearby populations and ecosystems, the changes in these impacts that would result under alternative specifications for the rehabilitation, and the estimated capital and operating costs associated with each option.

Depending on the scale and nature of the rehabilitation, the environmental assessment may be relatively narrow in scope, focusing on only a small number of specific concerns that would be affected by the project, or it may be as extensive as would be appropriate for the construction of a new unit at the same site. Normally, it should cover the following points:

- Ambient environmental quality in the airshed or water basin affected by the plant, together with approximate estimates of the contribution of the plant to total emissions loads of the main pollutants of concern
- The impact of the plant, under existing operating conditions and under alternative scenarios for rehabilitation, on ambient air and water quality affecting neighboring populations and sensitive ecosystems
- The likely costs of achieving alternative emissions standards or other environmental targets for the plant as a whole or for specific aspects of its operations
- Recommendations concerning a range of cost-effective measures for improving the environmental performance of the plant within the

framework of the rehabilitation project and any associated emissions standards or other requirements implied by the adoption of specific measures.

These issues should be covered at a level of detail appropriate to the nature and scale of the proposed project.

If the plant is located in an airshed or water basin that is polluted as a result of emissions from a range of sources, including the plant itself, comparisons should be made of the relative costs of improving ambient air or water quality by reducing emissions from the plant or by reducing emissions from other sources. As a result of such an analysis, the government, the enterprise, and the World Bank Group would agree to set site-specific emissions standards for the plant after it has been rehabilitated that take account of actions to reduce other emissions elsewhere in the airshed or water basin.

## Emissions Guidelines

The following measures must be incorporated when rehabilitating thermal power plants:
- Normally, the energy conversion efficiency of the plant should be increased by at least 25% of its current level.
- Baseline emissions levels for particulate matter, nitrogen oxides, and sulfur oxides should be computed.

- An analysis of the feasibility (including benefits) of switching to a cleaner fuel should be conducted. Gas is preferred where its supply can be assured at or below world average prices. Coal with high heat content and low sulfur content is preferred over coal with high heat content and high sulfur content, which in turn is preferred over coal with low heat content and high sulfur content.
- Washed coal should be used, if feasible.
- Low-$NO_x$ burners should be used, where feasible.
- Either the emissions levels recommended for new plants, or at least a 25% reduction in baseline level, should be achieved for the pollutant being addressed by the rehabilitation project.
- The maximum emissions level for PM is 100 milligrams per normal cubic meter ($mg/Nm^3$), but the target should be 50 $mg/Nm^3$. In rare cases, an emissions level of up to 150 $mg/Nm^3$ may be acceptable.
- $SO_2$ emissions levels should meet regional load targets. Cleaner fuels should be used, to avoid short-term exposure to sulfur dioxide.

## Monitoring and Reporting

Monitoring and reporting requirements for a thermal power plant that has been rehabilitated should be the same as those for a new thermal power plant of similar size and fuel type.

# Vegetable Oil Processing

## Industry Description and Practices

The vegetable oil processing industry involves the extraction and processing of oils and fats from vegetable sources. Vegetable oils and fats are principally used for human consumption but are also used in animal feed, for medicinal purposes, and for certain technical applications. The oils and fats are extracted from a variety of fruits, seeds, and nuts. The preparation of raw materials includes husking, cleaning, crushing, and conditioning. The extraction processes are generally mechanical (boiling for fruits, pressing for seeds and nuts) or involve the use of solvent such as hexane. After boiling, the liquid oil is skimmed; after pressing, the oil is filtered; and after solvent extraction, the crude oil is separated and the solvent is evaporated and recovered. Residues are conditioned (for example, dried) and are reprocessed to yield by-products such as animal feed. Crude oil refining includes degumming, neutralization, bleaching, deodorization, and further refining.

## Waste Characteristics

Dust is generated in materials handling and in the processing of raw materials, including in the cleaning, screening, and crushing operations. For palm fruit, about 2–3 cubic meters of wastewater is generated per metric ton of crude oil ($m^3/t$). The wastewater is high in organic content, resulting in a biochemical oxygen demand (BOD) of 20,000–35,000 milligrams per liter (mg/l) and a chemical oxygen demand (COD) of 30,000–60,000 mg/l. In addition, the wastewaters are high in dissolved solids (10,000 mg/l), oil and fat residues (5,000–10,000 mg/l), organic nitrogen (500–800 mg/l), and ash residues (4,000–

to 5,000 mg/l). Seed dressing and edible fat and oil processing generate approximately 10–25 $m^3$ of wastewater per metric ton (t) of product. Most of the solid wastes (0.7–0.8 t/t of raw material), which are mainly of vegetable origin, can be processed into by-products or used as fuel. Molds may be found on peanut kernels, and aflatoxins may be present.

## Pollution Prevention and Control

Good pollution prevention practices in the industry focus on the following main areas:

- Prevent the formation of molds on edible materials by controlling and monitoring air humidity.
- Use citric acid instead of phosphoric acid, where feasible, in degumming operations.
- Where appropriate, give preference to physical refining rather than chemical refining of crude oil, as active clay has a lower environmental impact than the chemicals generally used.
- Reduce product losses through better production control.
- Maintain volatile organic compounds (VOCs) well below explosive limits. Hexane should be below 150 $mg/m^3$ of air (its explosive limit is 42,000 $mg/m^3$).
- Provide dust extractors to maintain a clean workplace, recover product, and control air emissions.
- Recover solvent vapors to minimize losses.
- Optimize the use of water and cleaning chemicals.
- Recirculate cooling waters.
- Collect waste product for use in by-products such as animal feed, where feasible without exceeding cattle-feed quality limits.

Continuous sampling and measuring of key production parameters allow production losses to be identified and reduced, thus reducing the waste load.

Odor problems can usually be prevented through good hygiene and storage practices. Chlorinated fluorocarbons should not be used in the refrigeration system.

## Pollution Reduction Targets

Since the pollutants generated by the industry are very largely losses in production, improvements in production efficiency, as described above, are recommended to reduce pollutant loads.

Wastewater loads are typically 3–5 m³/t of feedstock; plant operators should aim to achieve lower rates at the intake of the effluent treatment system. Hexane, if used, should be below 50 mg/l in wastewater. The BOD level should be less than 2.5 kg/t of product, with a target of 1–1.5 kg/t.

## Treatment Technologies

Pretreatment of effluents comprises screening and air flotation to remove fats and solids; it is normally followed by biological treatment. If space is available, land treatment or pond systems are potential treatment methods. Other possible biological treatment systems include trickling filters, rotating biological contactors, and activated sludge treatment.

Pretreated effluents can be discharged to a municipal sewerage system, if capacity exists, with the approval of the relevant authority. Proper circulation of air, using an extractive and cleaning system, is normally required to maintain dust at acceptable levels. Dust control is provided by fabric filters. Odor control is by ventilation, but scrubbing may also be required.

## Emissions Guidelines

Emissions levels for the design and operation of each project must be established through the environmental assessment (EA) process on the basis of country legislation and the *Pollution Prevention and Abatement Handbook,* as applied to local con-

ditions. The emissions levels selected must be justified in the EA and acceptable to the World Bank Group.

The guidelines given below present emissions levels normally acceptable to the World Bank Group in making decisions regarding provision of World Bank Group assistance. Any deviations from these levels must be described in the World Bank Group project documentation. The emissions levels given here can be consistently achieved by well-designed, well-operated, and well-maintained pollution control systems.

The guidelines are expressed as concentrations to facilitate monitoring. Dilution of air emissions or effluents to achieve these guidelines is unacceptable.

All of the maximum levels should be achieved for at least 95% of the time that the plant or unit is operating, to be calculated as a proportion of annual operating hours.

### Air Emissions

Odor controls should be implemented where necessary to achieve acceptable odor quality for nearby residents. Fabric filters should be used to control dust from production units to below 50 milligrams per normal cubic meter (mg/Nm³).

### Liquid Effluents

The effluent levels presented in Table 1 should be achieved.

**Table 1. Effluents from Vegetable Oil Processing**
*(milligrams per liter, except for pH and temperature)*

| Parameter | Maximum value |
|---|---|
| pH | 6–9 |
| BOD | 50 |
| COD | 250 |
| TSS | 50 |
| Oil and grease | 10 |
| Total nitrogen | 10 |
| Temperature increase | ≤ 3°C[a] |

a. The effluent should result in a temperature increase of no more than 3° C at the edge of the zone where initial mixing and dilution take place. Where the zone is not defined, use 100 meters from the point of discharge.

*Ambient Noise*

Noise abatement measures should achieve either the levels given below or a maximum increase in background levels of 3 decibels (measured on the A scale) [dB(A)]. Measurements are to be taken at noise receptors located outside the project property boundary.

| Receptor | Maximum allowable log equivalent (hourly measurements), in dB(A) | |
| --- | --- | --- |
| | *Day (07:00–22:00)* | *Night (22:00–07:00)* |
| Residential, institutional, educational | 55 | 45 |
| Industrial, commercial | 70 | 70 |

## Monitoring and Reporting

Monitoring of the final effluent for the parameters listed in this document should be carried out at least weekly, or more frequently, if the flows vary significantly.

Monitoring data should be analyzed and reviewed at regular intervals and compared with the operating standards so that any necessary corrective actions can be taken. Records of monitoring results should be kept in an acceptable format. The results should be reported to the responsible authorities and relevant parties, as required.

## Key Issues

The key production and control practices that will lead to compliance with emissions requirements can be summarized as follows:

- Monitor key production parameters to reduce product losses.
- Prefer citric acid to phosphoric acid in degumming operations.
- Give preference to physical refining over chemical refining of crude oil, where appropriate.
- Hold levels of hexane, if used, below 150 mg/m$^3$.
- Design and operate the production system to achieve recommended wastewater loads.
- Recirculate cooling waters.
- Collect wastes for use in by-products or as fuel.

## Source

German Federal Ministry for Economic Cooperation and Development (BMZ). 1995. *Environmental Handbook, Documentation on Monitoring and Evaluating Environmental Impacts.* Vol. 2. Bonn.

# Wood Preserving

## Industry Description and Practices

Wood preserving involves imparting protective properties to wood to guard against weathering and attack by pests. Three main types of preservatives are used: water based (for example, sodium phenylphenoxide, benzalconium chloride, guazatin, and copper chrome arsenate); organic solvent based (for example, pentachlorophenol and such substitutes as propiconazol, tebuconazol, lindane, permethrin, triazoles, tributyltin compounds, and copper and zinc naphthenates); borates; and tar oils (such as creosote). *Note that some of the preservatives mentioned here (for example, lindane, tributyltin, and pentachlorophenol) are banned in some countries and are not to be used.*

The preservatives are applied to the surface of wood by pressure impregnation, with a pressure range of 800 kilopascals (kPa) to 1,400 kPa; by deluging (mechanical application by flooding or spraying), by dipping or immersion; and by thermal processing (immersion in a hot bath of preservative). Application of vacuum helps to improve the effectiveness of the process and to recover some of the chemicals used. Pesticides are applied using appropriate protective clothing, including gloves, aprons, overalls, and inhalation protection.

## Waste Characteristics

Any or all of the substances used in wood preserving, such as preservatives and solvents, can be found in the drips and the surface runoff streams. Air emissions of solvents and other volatile organics result from the surface treatment steps, drying of the treated wood, and storage and transfer of chemicals. Soil contamination may result from the drippage and surface runoff, and this may happen near the process areas and the treated wood storage areas. Some of the major pollutants present in drips, surface runoff, and contaminated soil include polynuclear aromatic hydrocarbons, pentachlorophenol, pesticides, dioxins, chrome, copper, and arsenic.

## Pollution Prevention and Control

Wood preserving involves different combinations of a wide variety of processes, and there are many opportunities to improve on the traditional practices in the industry. The following improvements should be implemented where feasible.

- Do not use pentachlorophenol, lindane, tributyltin, or copper chrome arsenate (or its derivatives).
- Give preference to pressurized treatment processes to minimize both wastage of raw materials and the release of toxics that may be present.
- Minimize drippage by effective removal of extra preservative from the wood surface by mechanical shaking until no drippage is noticeable. Provide sufficient holding time after preservative application to minimize free liquid.
- Recycle collected drips after treatment, if necessary.
- Heat treated wood when water-based preservatives are used.
- Use concrete pads for the wood treatment area and intermediate storage areas to ensure proper collection of drippage. Treated wood should be sent for storage only after drippage has completely stopped.
- Minimize surface runon by diversion of stormwater away from the process areas.
- Cover process areas and collect surface runoff for recycling and treatment. Where water-based preservatives are used, prevent freshly

treated wood from coming into contact with rainwater.
- Sites should be selected that are not prone to flooding or adjacent to water intake points or valuable groundwater resources.
- Preservatives and other hazardous substances should be stored safely, preferably under a roof with a spill collection system.
- Proper labels should be applied, and used packaging should be returned to the supplier for reuse or sent for other acceptable uses or destruction.

## Target Pollution Loads

Minimize contamination of surface runoff and soil. Have a closed system for managing liquids to avoid the discharge of liquid effluents.

## Treatment Technologies

### Air Emissions

Exhaust streams should be treated, using carbon filters that allow the reuse of solvents, to reduce volatile organic compounds (VOCs) to acceptable levels before venting to the atmosphere. Where VOC recovery is not feasible, destruction is carried out in combustion devices or bio-oxidation systems.

### Liquid Effluents

The main treatment process is recycling of collected drips and surface runoff after evaporation. Other processes include detoxification (using ultraviolet oxidation) and precipitation or stabilization of heavy metals.

### Solid and Hazardous Wastes

Contaminated soil may contain heavy metals and toxic organics and should normally be managed as hazardous waste. Treatment methods include incineration of toxic organics and stabilization of heavy metals.

## Emissions Guidelines

Emissions levels for the design and operation of each project must be established through the envi-

ronmental assessment (EA) process on the basis of country legislation and the *Pollution Prevention and Abatement Handbook*, as applied to local conditions. The emissions levels selected must be justified in the EA and acceptable to the World Bank Group.

The guidelines given below present emissions levels normally acceptable to the World Bank Group in making decisions regarding provision of World Bank Group assistance. Any deviations from these levels must be described in the World Bank Group project documentation. The emissions levels given here can be consistently achieved by well-designed, well-operated, and well-maintained pollution control systems.

The guidelines are expressed as concentrations to facilitate monitoring. Dilution of air emissions or effluents to achieve these guidelines is unacceptable.

All of the maximum levels should be achieved for at least 95% of the time that the plant or unit is operating, to be calculated as a proportion of annual operating hours.

### Air Emissions

The maximum air emission level from wood impregnation areas for VOC is 20 milligrams per normal cubic meter ($mg/Nm^3$).

### Liquid Effluents

Wood-preserving plants should use closed systems, where feasible, or should attain the effluent levels presented in Table 1.

### Sludges

Wherever possible, generation of sludges and contaminated soil should be minimized. Contaminated soil and sludges must be treated, stabilized, and disposed of in an approved, secure landfill. The levels of toxics in the leachate should be the same as for liquid effluents.

### Ambient Noise

Noise abatement measures should achieve either the levels given below or a maximum increase in background levels of 3 decibels (measured on the A scale) [dB(A)]. Measurements are to be taken

**Table 1. Effluents (Including Surface Runoff) from the Wood-Preserving Industry**

*(milligrams per liter, except for pH)*

| Parameter | Maximum value |
|---|---|
| pH | 6–9 |
| TSS | 50 |
| COD | 150 |
| Oil and grease | 10 |
| Phenol | 0.5 |
| Arsenic | 0.1 |
| Chromium | |
|   Hexavalent | 0.1 |
|   Total | 0.5 |
| Copper | 0.5 |
| Fluorides | 20 |
| Polynuclear aromatic hydrocarbons | |
|   (PAHs), such as benzo(a)pyrene (each) | 0.05 |
| Dioxins/furans (total) | 0.0005 |
| Pesticides (each) | 0.05 |

*Note:* Effluent requirements are for direct discharge to surface waters.

at noise receptors located outside the project property boundary.

| | Maximum allowable log equivalent (hourly measurements), in dB(A) | |
|---|---|---|
| *Receptor* | *Day* (07:00–22:00) | *Night* (22:00–07:00) |
| Residential, institutional, educational | 55 | 45 |
| Industrial, commercial | 70 | 70 |

## Monitoring and Reporting

Daily monitoring of the parameters listed in this document, except for metals, should be carried out to provide an indication of overall treatment reliability. Metals should be sampled at least monthly. More frequent sampling may be required for certain batches and during wet weather conditions.

Monitoring data should be analyzed and reviewed at regular intervals and compared with the operating standards so that any necessary corrective actions can be taken. Records of monitoring results should be kept in an acceptable format. The results should be reported to the responsible authorities and relevant parties, as required.

## Key Issues

The key production and control practices that will lead to compliance with emissions guidelines can be summarized as follows:

- Do not use pentachlorophenol, lindane, tributyltin, copper chrome arsenate, or other preservatives that are considered toxic and for which less toxic alternatives are available for wood treatment systems.
- Use pressurized treatment processes.
- Heat treated wood when water-based preservatives are used.
- Minimize drippage carryover by ensuring that drippage has completely stopped before removing the treated wood from the process area. Collect and recycle drip solutions, and put in place total recycle systems for liquids and effluents.
- Use concrete pads for the wood treatment and intermediate storage areas.
- Divert stormwater away from process areas. Collect and treat surface runoff.
- Recycle solvent vapors, where feasible; otherwise, they should be destroyed in a combustion device or in a bio-oxidation system.
- Manage contaminated soil and sludges as hazardous wastes.

## Sources

United States. 1990. "Wood Preserving; Identification and Listing of Hazardous Waste: Final Rule." *Federal Register, vol.* 55, no. 235, December 6.

World Bank. 1995. "Industrial Pollution Prevention and Abatement: Wood Preserving Industry." Draft Technical Background Document. Environment Department, Washington, D.C.

# General Environmental Guidelines

The World Bank Group may finance commercial and industrial projects for which no specific environmental guidelines have been written. In such cases, the general environmental guidelines outlined in this chapter can be used, but, depending on the project, the requirements contained here may need to be supplemented by additional requirements.

Projects must comply with World Bank Group policies and guidelines, which emphasize pollution prevention, including the use of cleaner production technologies. The intent of the guidelines is to minimize resource consumption, including energy use, and to eliminate or reduce pollutants at the source. For ease of monitoring, maximum permitted emissions limits are often expressed in concentration terms—for example, milligrams per liter (mg/l) for liquid effluents and, for air emissions, milligrams per normal cubic meter (mg/Nm³), where "normal" is measured at one atmosphere and 0° Celsius. The focus, however, should continue to be on reducing the mass of pollutants emitted to the environment. *Dilution of effluents and air emissions to achieve maximum permitted values is unacceptable.* Occasionally, emissions limits are specified in mass of pollutants per unit of production or some other process parameter. In such cases, the limits include leaks and fugitive emissions.

Pollution control systems may be required in order to meet specified emissions limits. These systems must be well maintained and operated and must not be fitted with overflow or bypass devices unless such devices are required for emergencies or for safety purposes.

The following sections contain requirements for air emissions, liquid effluents, hazardous chemicals and wastes, and solid wastes. Sections on ambient noise and monitoring requirements are included. The final section summarizes the key steps that will contribute to minimizing the impact of the project on the environment.

## Emissions Guidelines

Emissions levels for the design and operation of each project must be established through the environmental assessment (EA) process on the basis of country legislation and the *Pollution Prevention and Abatement Handbook,* as applied to local conditions. The emissions levels selected must be justified in the EA and acceptable to the World Bank Group.

The guidelines given below present emissions levels normally acceptable to the World Bank Group in making decisions regarding provision of World Bank Group assistance. Any deviations from these levels must be described in the World Bank Group project documentation.

All of the maximum levels should be achieved for at least 95% of the time that the plant or unit is operating, calculated as a proportion of annual operating hours.

### Air Emissions

Most of the air emissions from commercial and general industrial facilities originate with the fuel used for heating purposes or for generating steam for process purposes. Particular emissions that may originate in the process are addressed case by case. Concentrations of contaminants emitted from the stacks of significant sources with an equivalent heat input of more than 10 million British thermal units per hour (Btu/hr), including boilers, furnaces, incinerators, and electrical generating equipment, should not exceed the limits presented in Table 1.

## Table 1. Air Emissions Limits for General Application

*(milligrams per normal cubic meter)*

| Pollutant or parameter | Limit |
|---|---|
| PM | 50 for units with $\geq$ 50 MWe input |
| | 100 for units with < 50 MWe input |
| Nitrogen oxides, as $NO_2$ | |
| Coal fired | 750 (260 ng/J) |
| Oil fired | 460 (130 ng/J) |
| Gas fired | 320 (86 ng/J) |
| Sulfur dioxide | Not to exceed 2,000 |

*Note:* MWe, megawatts electricity; ng/J, nanograms/joule.

The project sponsor is required to demonstrate compliance with the emissions limits specified in Table 1. The following methods may be used to demonstrate compliance:

- For sources less than 100 million Btu/hr, compliance with the guidelines for particulate matter may be demonstrated by maintaining the stack emissions opacity below 20%. Opacity can be determined visually by a qualified observer, with a continuous opacity meter, or with a mobile light detection and ranging (LIDAR) system.
- The sulfur content of fuels may be used to demonstrate compliance with the sulfur dioxide ($SO_2$) emissions guidelines. The guidelines are met by the use of liquid fuels with a sulfur content of 0.5% or less or of solid fuels with a sulfur content of 0.8% or less and a heat content of 7,000 kilocalories per kilogram (kcal/kg). The use of solid fuels burned in underfired-feed stoker units meets the $SO_2$ emissions guideline if the sulfur content of the solid fuel is 1.0% or less. The sponsor must maintain records of fuel analyses to demonstrate that the sulfur content of the fuel is at or below the specified levels.
- Manufacturers' performance guarantees can be used to demonstrate that the emissions guidelines for nitrogen oxides ($NO_x$) are met. The performance guarantees must be verified by conducting an initial performance test after the equipment has been commissioned. The sponsor must maintain records to demonstrate that the equipment is operated within manufacturers' specifications.

- Alternatively, stack emissions can be monitored for specified contaminants. The monitoring must be sufficiently frequent to demonstrate continued compliance with the guidelines.

Table 2 may be used to determine equivalent source sizes.

The World Bank's "Pollution Prevention and Abatement Guidelines for Thermal Power Plants" apply to sources larger than 50 MWe or with an equivalent heat input greater than 170 million Btu/hr. Sources with an equivalent heat input of 10 million Btu/hr are generally not subject to the above limits. However, the World Bank Group may in particular cases specify emissions limits for such sources to protect the local environment.

To ensure that ambient air conditions are not compromised, concentrations of contaminants, measured immediately outside the project property boundary, should not exceed the limits shown in Table 3.

Pollutants such as dioxins and furans, toxic organics, and toxic metals should not exceed risk-specific doses or reference air concentrations at the receptor end. The dioxin emissions level for 2,3,7,8-TCDD equivalent should be less than 1 nanogram per normal cubic meter.

## Table 2. Equivalent Source Sizes

| In millions of Btu/hr | In tons of steam/hr | In MWe |
|---|---|---|
| 10 | 4.2 | 2.9 |
| 50 | 21.0 | 14.5 |
| 100 | 42.0 | 29.0 |
| 200 | 84.0 | 58.0 |

## Table 3. Ambient Air Conditions at Property Boundary, for General Application

*(micrograms per cubic meter)*

| Pollutant | Concentration |
|---|---|
| *Particulate matter* | |
| Annual arithmetic mean | 50 |
| Maximum 24-hour average | 70 |
| *Nitrogen oxides* | |
| Maximum 24-hour average | 150 |
| *Sulfur dioxide* | |
| Annual arithmetic mean | 50 |
| Maximum 24-hour average | 125 |

*Liquid Effluents*

Process wastewater, domestic sewage, and contaminated stormwater and runoff must meet the maximum limits shown in Table 4 before being

### Table 4. Limits for Process Wastewater, Domestic Sewage, and Contaminated Stormwater Discharged to Surface Waters, for General Application

*(milligrams per liter, except for pH, bacteria, and temperature)*

| Pollutant or parameter | Limit |
|---|---|
| pH | 6–9 |
| BOD | 50 |
| COD | 250 |
| Oil and grease | 10 |
| TSS | 50 |
| *Metals* | |
| Heavy metals, total | 10 |
| Arsenic | 0.1 |
| Cadmium | 0.1 |
| Chromium | |
|   Hexavalent | 0.1 |
|   Total | 0.5 |
| Copper | 0.5 |
| Iron | 3.5 |
| Lead | 0.1 |
| Mercury | 0.01 |
| Nickel | 0.5 |
| Selenium | 0.1 |
| Silver | 0.5 |
| Zinc | 2.0 |
| *Cyanide* | |
|   Free | 0.1 |
|   Total | 1.0 |
| Ammonia | 10 |
| Fluoride | 20 |
| Chlorine, total residual | 0.2 |
| Phenols | 0.5 |
| Phosphorus | 2.0 |
| Sulfide | 1.0 |
| Coliform bacteria | < 400 MPN/100 ml |
| Temperature increase | Maximum 3°C above ambient temperature of receiving waters[a] |

Note: MPN, most probable number.
a. The effluent should result in a temperature increase of no more than 3° C at the edge of the zone where initial mixing and dilution take place. Where the zone is not defined, use 100 meters from the point of discharge.

discharged to surface waters. Where there is a leachate from a solid waste disposal site, the toxic metals contained in the leachate should not exceed the levels shown in the table for pollutants in liquid effluents. Pollutants of concern for a project that are not included in Table 4 will be specified by the World Bank Group. Levels of pesticides, dioxins, furans, and other toxics, such as polynuclear aromatic hydrocarbons (PAHs), in effluent discharges should not exceed either 100 times the WHO guidelines for drinking water or 0.05 mg/l.

Liquid effluent may be discharged to a public or private central wastewater treatment system. Where this is the case, information from the local authority or private central wastewater treatment company is to be provided to confirm that the treatment system has the capacity and is managed to adequately treat the project's liquid effluents. The World Bank Group may require pretreatment prior to such discharge.

*Hazardous Materials and Wastes*

Sponsors shall, whenever possible, use nonhazardous instead of hazardous materials. All hazardous wastes, process residues, solvents, oils, and sludges must be properly disposed of. Leachates that contain hazardous pollutants must not exceed the liquid effluent levels given in Table 4.

The following management measures for handling hazardous wastes and materials should be implemented:

- All hazardous (ignitable, reactive, flammable, radioactive, corrosive, and toxic) materials must be stored in clearly labeled containers or vessels.
- Storage and handling of hazardous materials must be in accordance with local regulations or international standards and appropriate to their hazard characteristics. Storage and liquid impoundment areas for fuels, raw and in-process materials, solvents, wastes, and finished products should be designed with secondary containment (e.g., dikes and berms) to prevent spills and the contamination of soil, groundwater, and surface waters.
- Fire prevention systems and secondary containment should be provided for storage fa-

cilities, where necessary or required by regulations, to prevent fires or the release of hazardous materials to the environment.

New installations or manufactured products should not contain unbonded asbestos fibers. The need to remove asbestos and asbestos-containing materials (ACMs) from existing applications shall be evaluated case by case. Disposal of removed asbestos and ACMs should be carried out in accordance with host country requirements or following internationally recognized best practices.

Formulations containing chromates should not be used in water treatment processes.

Transformers or equipment containing polychlorinated biphenyls (PCBs) or PCB-contaminated oil should not be installed. Existing equipment containing PCBs or PCB-contaminated oil should be phased out and disposed of in a manner consistent with the requirements of the host country or internationally recognized best practices.

Several chemicals classified as ozone-depleting substances (ODSs) are scheduled for phase-out under the Montreal Protocol on Substances That Deplete the Ozone Layer. They include chloro-fluorocarbons (CFCs); halons; 1,1,1-trichloroethane (methyl chloroform); carbon tetrachloride; hydrochlorofluorocarbons (HCFCs); hydrobromofluorocarbons (HBFCs); and methyl bromide. These chemicals are currently used in a variety of applications, including domestic, commercial, and process refrigeration (CFCs and HCFCs); domestic, commercial, and motor vehicle air conditioning (CFCs and HCFCs); manufacturing of foam products (CFCs); solvent cleaning applications (CFCs, HCFCs, methyl chloroform, and carbon tetrachloride); aerosol propellants (CFCs); fire protection systems (halons and HBFCs); and crop fumigants (methyl bromide). No systems or processes are to be installed using CFCs, halons, 1,1,1-trichloroethane, carbon tetrachloride, methyl bromide, or HBFCs unless it can be shown that no alternative exists. (There are few applications worldwide that require any of these chemicals.) HCFCs should be considered only as interim or bridging alternatives, since they too are to be phased out.

*Solid Wastes*

Project sponsors are to implement the following practices for managing solid wastes generated in the course of operating the facility:

- Recycle or reclaim materials where possible.
- If recycling or reclamation is not practical, wastes must be disposed of in an environmentally acceptable manner and in compliance with local laws and regulations.

## Other Environmental Requirements: Ambient Noise

Noise abatement measures should achieve either the levels given below or a maximum increase in background levels of 3 decibels (measured on the A scale) [dB(A)]. Measurements are to be taken at noise receptors located outside the project property boundary.

| Receptor | Maximum allowable log equivalent (hourly measurements), in dB(A) | |
|---|---|---|
| | Day (07:00–22:00) | Night (22:00–07:00) |
| Residential, institutional, educational | 55 | 45 |
| Industrial, commercial | 70 | 70 |

## Monitoring

Liquid effluents should be sampled and measured weekly, or as agreed between the borrower and the World Bank Group, for common parameters such as BOD, suspended solids, pH, oils and grease, and flow. The World Bank Group will specify sampling frequencies for project-specific pollutants that are present in the effluent. Leachates from solid waste disposal sites should be sampled and tested monthly, using strategically located sampling points. The parameters to be tested will depend on the nature of the potential leachate and will be specified by the World Bank Group.

The World Bank Group will specify the frequency and method for monitoring pollutants in the stack discharge.

## Recordkeeping and Reporting

The project sponsor is required to maintain records of air emissions, effluents, and hazardous wastes sent off site, as well as significant environmental events such as spills, fires, and other emergencies that may have an impact on the environment. The information should be reviewed and evaluated to improve the effectiveness of the environmental protection plan.

## Key Issues for Environmental Control

The key production and control practices that will assist in meeting emissions requirements can be summarized as follows:

- Where feasible, choose energy-efficient and environmentally sound processes.
- Ensure that control, treatment, and monitoring facilities are properly maintained and that they are operated according to their instruction manuals.

# Glossary of Environmental Terms

**Abatement.** Reducing the degree or intensity of, or eliminating, pollution.

**Absorption.** The passage of one substance into or through another; e.g., an operation in which one or more soluble components of a gas mixture are dissolved in a liquid.

**Accident site.** The location of an unexpected occurrence, failure, or loss, either at a plant or along a transportation route, resulting in a release of hazardous materials.

**Acid deposition.** A complex chemical and atmospheric phenomenon that occurs when emissions of sulfur and nitrogen compounds and other substances are transformed by chemical processes in the atmosphere, often far from the original sources, and then deposited on earth in either a wet or a dry form. The wet forms, popularly called "acid rain," can fall as rain, snow, or fog. The dry forms are acidic gases or particulates.

**Acid rain.** *See* Acid deposition

**Activated carbon.** A highly adsorbent form of carbon used to remove odors and toxic substances from liquid or gaseous emissions. In waste treatment, it is used to remove dissolved organic matter from wastewater. It is also used in motor vehicle evaporative control systems.

**Activated sludge.** Residue that results when primary effluent is mixed with bacteria-laden sludge and then agitated and aerated to promote biological treatment. This speeds breakdown of organic matter in raw sewage undergoing secondary wastewater treatment.

**Active ingredient.** In any pesticide product, the component that kills, or otherwise controls, target pests. Pesticides are regulated primarily on the basis of active ingredients.

**Acute exposure.** A single exposure to a toxic substance that results in severe biological harm or death. Acute exposures are usually characterized as lasting no longer than a day.

**Acute toxicity.** The ability of a substance to cause poisonous effects resulting in severe biological harm or death soon after a single exposure or dose; also, any severe poisonous effect resulting from a single short-term exposure to a toxic substance. *See also* Chronic toxicity; Toxicity

**Adaptation.** Changes in an organism's structure or habit that help it adjust to its surroundings.

**Add-on control device.** An air pollution control device such as a carbon adsorber or incinerator that reduces the pollution in an exhaust gas. The control device usually does not affect the process being controlled and thus is "add-on" technology as opposed to a scheme to control pollution by making some alteration to the basic process.

**Adsorption.** 1. Adhesion of molecules of gas, liquid, or dissolved solids to a surface. 2. An advanced method of treating wastes in which

*Note:* This glossary is based on United States Environmental Protection Agency, Office of Communications and Public Affairs, "Glossary of Environmental Terms and Acronym List," 19K-1002 (Washington, D.C., December 1989).

activated carbon removes organic matter from wastewater.

**Advanced wastewater treatment.** Any treatment of sewage that goes beyond the secondary or biological water treatment stage and includes the removal of nutrients such as phosphorus and nitrogen and a high percentage of suspended solids. *See also* Primary wastewater treatment; Secondary wastewater treatment

**Aeration.** A process that promotes biological degradation of organic water. The process may be passive (as when waste is exposed to air), or active (as when a mixing or bubbling device introduces the air).

**Aerobic.** Life or processes that require, or are not destroyed by, the presence of oxygen. *See also* Anaerobic

**Aerobic treatment.** Process by which microbes decompose complex organic compounds in the presence of oxygen and use the liberated energy for reproduction and growth. Types of aerobic processes include extended aeration, trickling filtration, and rotating biological contactors.

**Aerosol.** A suspension of liquid or solid particles in a gas.

**Agricultural pollution.** The liquid and solid wastes from farming, including runoff and leaching of pesticides and fertilizers; erosion and dust from plowing; animal manure and carcasses; and crop residues and debris.

**Airborne particulates.** Total suspended particulate matter found in the atmosphere as solid particles or liquid droplets. The chemical composition of particulates varies widely, depending on location and time of year. Airborne particulates include windblown dust, emissions from industrial processes, smoke from the burning of wood and coal, and the exhaust of motor vehicles.

**Air mass.** A widespread body of air that gains certain meteorological or polluted characteristics—

for example, a heat inversion or smokiness—while standing in one location. The characteristics can change as the air mass moves away. *See also* Inversion

**Air monitoring.** See Monitoring.

**Air pollutant.** Any substance in air that could, in high enough concentration, harm human beings, other animals, vegetation, or material. Pollutants may include almost any natural or artificial composition of matter capable of being airborne. They may be in the form of solid particles, liquid droplets, gases, or combinations of these states. Generally, they fall into two main groups: (a) those emitted directly from identifiable sources and (b) those produced in the air by interaction between two or more primary pollutants or by reaction with normal atmospheric constituents, with or without photoactivation. Exclusive of pollen, fog, and dust, which are of natural origin, about 100 contaminants have been identified. They fall into the following categories: solids, sulfur compounds, volatile organic chemicals, nitrogen compounds, oxygen compounds, halogen compounds, radioactive compounds, and odors.

**Air pollution.** The presence of contaminant or pollutant substances in the air that do not disperse properly and interfere with human health or welfare or produce other harmful environmental effects.

**Air pollution episode.** A period of abnormally high concentration of air pollutants, often due to low winds and temperature inversion, that can cause illness and death. *See also* Inversion

**Algae.** Simple rootless plants that grow in sunlit waters in relative proportion to the amounts of nutrients available. They can affect water quality adversely by lowering the dissolved oxygen in the water. Algae are food for fish and small aquatic animals.

**Algal blooms.** Sudden spurts of algal growth that can affect water quality adversely and that indicate potentially hazardous changes in local water chemistry.

**Ambient air.** Any unconfined portion of the atmosphere: open air, surrounding air.

**Anaerobic.** A life or process that occurs in, or is not destroyed by, the absence of oxygen.

**Aquifer.** An underground geological formation, or group of formations, containing usable amounts of groundwater that can supply wells and springs.

**Assimilation.** The ability of a body of water to purify itself of pollutants.

**Atmosphere** (as a measurement). A standard unit of pressure representing the pressure exerted by a 29.92-inch column of mercury at sea level at 45° latitude and equal to 1,000 grams per square centimeter.

**Attenuation.** The process by which a compound is reduced in concentration over time, through adsorption, degradation, dilution, or transformation.

**Background level.** In air pollution control, the concentration of air pollutants in a definite area during a fixed period of time prior to the starting up or on the stoppage of a source of emission under control. In toxic substances monitoring, the average presence in the environment, originally referring to naturally occurring phenomena.

**Bacteria** (singular: bacterium). Microscopic living organisms that can aid in pollution control by consuming or breaking down organic matter in sewage or by similarly acting on oil spills or other water pollutants. Bacteria in soil, water, or air can cause human, animal, and plant health problems.

**Baghouse filter.** Large fabric bag, usually made of glass fibers, used to eliminate intermediate and large (greater than 20 microns in diameter) particles. This device operates in a way similar to the bag of an electric vacuum cleaner, passing the air and smaller particulate matter while entrapping the larger particulates.

**Bar screen.** In wastewater treatment, a device used to remove large solids.

**Benthic organism (benthos).** A form of aquatic plant or animal life found on or near the bottom of a stream, lake, or ocean.

**Bioaccumulative.** Substances that are very slowly metabolized or excreted by living organisms and thus increase in concentration within the organisms as the organisms breathe contaminated air, drink contaminated water, or eat contaminated food. *See also* Biological magnification

**Bioassay.** Using living organisms to measure the effect of a substance, factor, or condition by comparing before-and-after data; often used to mean cancer bioassays.

**Biochemical oxygen demand (BOD).** A measure of the amount of oxygen consumed in the biological processes that break down organic matter in water. The greater the BOD, the greater the degree of pollution. In this *Handbook*, BOD is understood to be $BOD_5$, the amount of dissolved oxygen so consumed in five days.

**Biodegradable.** The ability to break down or decompose rapidly under natural conditions and processes.

**Biological control.** In pest control, the use of animals and organisms that eat or otherwise kill or outcompete pests.

**Biological magnification.** Refers to the process whereby certain substances such as pesticides or heavy metals move up the food chain, work their way into a river or lake, and are eaten by aquatic organisms such as fish, which in turn are eaten by large birds, animals, or humans. The substances become concentrated in tissues or internal organs as they move up the chain.

**Biological oxidation.** The way bacteria and microorganisms feed on and decompose complex organic materials; used in self-purification of water bodies and in activated sludge wastewater treatment.

**Biological treatment.** A treatment technology that uses bacteria to consume waste and thus break down organic materials.

**Biomass.** All the living material in a given area; often refers to vegetation. Also called *biota.*

**Biomonitoring.** 1. The use of living organisms to test the suitability of effluents for discharge into receiving waters and to test the quality of such waters downstream from the discharge. 2. Analysis of blood, urine, tissues, etc., to measure chemical exposure in humans.

**Biotechnology.** Techniques that use living organisms or parts of organisms to produce a variety of products—from medicines to industrial enzymes–to improve plants or animals or to develop microorganisms for specific uses such as removing toxics from bodies of water or for pesticides.

**BOD₅.** The amount of dissolved oxygen consumed in five days by biological processes breaking down organic matter.

**Brackish water.** A mixture of fresh and salt water.

**Bubble.** A system under which existing emissions sources can propose alternate means for complying with a set of emissions limitations; under the bubble concept, sources can hold emissions to a lower level, where this is cost-effective, in return for a comparable realization of controls at a second emission point where costs are higher.

**By-product.** Material, other than the principal product, that is generated as a consequence of an industrial process.

**Cadmium (Cd).** A heavy metal element that accumulates in the environment.

**Carbon adsorber.** An add-on control device that uses activated carbon to absorb volatile organic compounds (VOCs) from a gas stream. The VOCs are later recovered from the carbon.

**Carbon dioxide ($CO_2$).** A colorless, odorless, non-poisonous gas that results from fossil fuel combustion and is normally a part of the ambient air.

**Carbon monoxide (CO).** A colorless, odorless, poisonous gas produced by incomplete fossil fuel combustion.

**Carcinogen.** Any substance that can cause or contribute to the production of cancer.

**Catalytic converter.** An air pollution abatement device that removes pollutants from motor vehicle exhaust, either by oxidizing them into carbon dioxide and water or by reducing them to nitrogen and oxygen.

**Catalytic incinerator.** A control device that oxidizes volatile organic compounds (VOCs) by using a catalyst to promote the combustion process. Catalytic incinerators require lower temperatures than conventional thermal incinerators, yielding fuel and cost savings.

**Cells.** 1. In solid waste disposal, holes in which waste is dumped, compacted, and covered with layers of dirt on a daily basis. 2. The smallest structural part of living matter capable of functioning as an independent unit.

**Chemical oxygen demand (COD).** A measure of the oxygen required to oxidize all compounds in water, both organic and inorganic.

**Chemical treatment.** Any one of a variety of technologies that use chemicals or a variety of chemical processes to treat waste.

**Chlorinated hydrocarbons.** A category which includes a class of persistent, broad-spectrum insecticides that linger in the environment and accumulate in the food chain. Among them are DDT, aldrin, dieldrin, heptaclor, chlordane, lindane, endrin, mirex, hexachloride, and toxaphene. Trichloroethylene (TCE), used as an industrial solvent, is also a chlorinated hydrocarbon.

**Chlorinated solvent.** An organic solvent containing chlorine atoms, e.g., methylene chloride and 1,1,1-trichloromethane, which is used in aerosol spray containers and in roadway paint.

**Chlorination.** The application of chlorine to drinking water, sewage, or industrial waste to disinfect or to oxidize undesirable compounds.

**Chlorofluorocarbons (CFCs).** A family of inert, nontoxic, and easily liquefied chemicals used in refrigeration, air conditioning, packaging, and insulation or as solvents and aerosol propellants. Because CFCs are not destroyed in the lower atmosphere, they drift into the upper atmosphere, where their chlorine components destroy ozone.

**Chromium.** *See* Heavy metals

**Chronic toxicity.** The capacity of a substance to cause long-term poisonous human health effects. *See also* Acute toxicity

**Cleanup.** Actions taken to deal with a release or threat of release of a hazardous substance that could affect humans, the environment, or both. The term is sometimes used interchangeably with the terms *remedial action, removal action, response action,* or *corrective action.*

**Coagulation.** A clumping of particles in wastewater to settle out impurities; often induced by chemicals such as lime, alum, and iron salts.

**Coliform index.** A rating of the purity of water based on a count of fecal bacteria.

**Coliform organism.** Microorganisms found in the intestinal tracts of humans and animals. Their presence in water indicates fecal pollution and potentially dangerous bacterial contamination by disease-causing microorganisms.

**Combined sewers.** A sewer system that carries both sewage and stormwater runoff. Normally, its entire flow goes to a waste treatment plant, but during a heavy storm the stormwater volume may be so great as to cause overflows. When this happens, untreated mixtures of stormwater and sewage may flow into receiving waters. Stormwater runoff may also carry toxic chemicals from industrial areas or streets into the sewer system.

**Comminution.** Mechanical shredding or pulverizing of waste; used in both solid waste management and wastewater treatment.

**Compaction.** Reduction of the bulk of solid waste by rolling and tamping.

**Composting.** The natural biological decomposition of organic material in the presence of air to form a humus-like material. Controlled methods of composting include mechanical mixing and aerating, ventilating the materials by dropping them through a vertical series of aerated chambers, or placing the compost in piles in the open air and mixing or turning it periodically.

**Contaminant.** Any physical, chemical, biological, or radiological substance or matter that has an adverse affect on air, water, or soil.

**Conventional systems.** Sewerage systems that have been traditionally used to collect municipal wastewater in gravity sewers and convey it to a central primary or secondary treatment plant prior to discharge to surface waters.

**Cooling tower.** A structure that helps remove heat from water used as a coolant, e.g., in electric power generating plants.

**Corrosion.** The dissolving and wearing away of metal caused by a chemical reaction that occurs between water and the pipes that the water contacts, or when chemicals touching a metal surface, or when two metals are in contact.

**Cover material.** Soil used to cover compacted solid waste in a sanitary landfill.

**Cubic feet per minute (cfm).** A measure of the volume of a substance flowing through air within a fixed period of time. With regard to indoor air, refers to the amount of air, in cubic feet, that is exchanged with indoor air in a minute's time, or an air exchange rate.

**Curie.** A quantitative measure of radioactivity equal to $3.7 \times 10^{10}$ disintegrations per second.

**Cyclone collector.** A device that uses centrifugal force to pull large particles from polluted air.

**Decomposition.** The breakdown of matter by bacteria and fungi; changes the chemical makeup and physical appearance of materials.

**Degradation.** The process by which a chemical is reduced to a less complex form.

**Denitrification.** The anaerobic biological reduction of nitrate nitrogen to nitrogen gas.

**Desulfurization.** Removal of sulfur from fossil fuels to reduce pollution.

**Detergent.** Synthetic washing agent that helps to remove dirt and oil. Some detergents contain compounds that kill useful bacteria and encourage algal growth when they are discharged in wastewater that reaches receiving waters.

**Digester.** In wastewater treatment, a closed tank; in solid waste conversion, a unit in which bacterial action is induced and accelerated to break down organic matter and establish the proper carbon-to-nitrogen ratio.

**Dilution ratio.** The relationship between the volume of water in a stream and the volume of incoming water; it affects the ability of the stream to assimilate waste.

**Dioxin.** Any of a family of compounds known chemically as dibenzo-p-dioxins. Concern about them arises from their potential toxicity and contamination in commercial products. Tests on laboratory animals indicate that it is one of the more toxic man-made chemicals known.

**Disinfectant.** A chemical or physical process that kills pathogenic organisms in water. Chlorine is often used to disinfect sewage treatment effluent, water supplies, wells, and swimming pools.

**Dispersant.** A chemical agent used to break up concentrations of organic material such as spilled oil.

**Disposal.** Final placement or destruction of toxic, radioactive, or other wastes; surplus or banned pesticides or other chemicals; polluted soils; and drums containing hazardous materials from removal actions or accidental releases. Disposal may be accomplished through use of approved secure landfills, surface impoundments, land farming, deep well injection, ocean dumping, or incineration.

**Dissolved oxygen (DO).** The oxygen freely available in water; vital to fish and other aquatic life and for the prevention of odors. Traditionally, the level of dissolved oxygen has been accepted as the single most important indicator of the ability of a water body to support desirable aquatic life. Secondary wastewater treatment and advanced wastewater treatment are generally designed to protect DO in waste-receiving waters.

**Dissolved solids.** Disintegrated organic and inorganic material contained in water. Excessive amounts make water unfit for drinking or for use in industrial processes.

**Distillation.** The act of purifying liquids through boiling so that the steam condenses to a pure liquid and the pollutants remain in a concentrated residue.

**Dump.** A site used to dispose of solid wastes without environmental controls.

**Ecology.** The relationship of living things to one another and their environment, or the study of such relationships.

**Ecosystem.** The interacting system of a biological community and its nonliving environmental surroundings.

**Effluent.** Wastewater—treated or untreated—that flows out of a treatment plant, sewer, or industrial outfall; generally refers to wastes discharged into surface waters.

**Effluent limitation.** Restrictions established by a national environmental agency or by a subnational jurisdiction on quantities, rates, and concentrations in wastewater discharges.

**Electrostatic precipitator (ESP).** An air pollution control device that removes particles from a gas stream (smoke) after combustion occurs. The ESP imparts an electrical charge to the particles, causing them to adhere to metal plates inside the precipitator. Rapping on the plates causes the particles to fall into a hopper for disposal.

**Emission.** Pollution discharged into the atmosphere from smokestacks, other vents, and surface areas of commercial or industrial facilities, from residential chimneys; and from motor vehicle, locomotive, or aircraft exhausts.

**Emission factor.** The relationship between the amount of pollution produced and the amount of raw material processed. For example, an emission factor for a blast furnace making iron would be the number of pounds of particulates per ton of raw material.

**Emission standard.** The maximum amount of air-polluting discharge legally allowed from a single source, mobile or stationary.

**Enrichment.** The addition of nutrients (e.g., nitrogen, phosphorus, or carbon compounds) from sewage effluent or agricultural runoff to surface water. This process greatly increases the growth potential of algae and aquatic plants.

**Environment.** The sum of all external conditions affecting the life, development, and survival of an organism.

**Environmental assessment (EA).** A process whose breadth, depth, and type of analysis depend on the proposed project. EA evaluates a project's potential environmental risks and impacts in its area of influence and identifies ways of improving project design and implementation by preventing, minimizing, mitigating, or compensating for adverse environmental impacts and by enhancing positive impacts.

**Environmental audit.** 1. An independent assessment of the current status of a party's compliance with applicable environmental requirements. 2. An independent evaluation of a party's environmental compliance policies, practices, and controls.

**Eutrophication.** The slow aging process during which a lake, estuary, or bay evolves into a bog or marsh and eventually disappears. During the later stages of eutrophication the water body is choked by abundant plant life as the result of increased amounts of nutritive compounds such as nitrogen and phosphorus. Human activities can accelerate the process.

**Evapotranspiration.** The loss of water from the soil both by evaporation and by transpiration from the plants growing in the soil.

**Exposure.** A potential health threat to the living organisms in the environment due to the amount of radiation or pollutant present in the environment.

**Fabric filter.** A cloth device that catches dust particles from industrial emissions.

**Fecal coliform bacteria.** Bacteria found in the intestinal tracts of mammals. Their presence in water or sludge is an indicator of pollution and possible contamination by pathogens.

**Fertilizer.** Materials such as nitrogen and phosphorus that provide nutrients for plants. Commercially sold fertilizers may contain other chemicals or may be in the form of processed sewage sludge.

**Filtration.** A treatment process, under the control of qualified operators, for removing solid (particulate) matter from water by passing the water through porous media such as sand or a manmade filter. The process is often used to remove particles that contain pathogenic organisms.

**Flocculation.** The process by which clumps of solids in water or sewage are made to increase in size by biological or chemical action so that they can be separated from the water.

**Flowmeter.** A gauge that shows the speed of wastewater moving through a treatment plant; also used to measure the speed of liquids moving through various industrial processes.

**Flue gas.** Vented air coming out of a chimney after combustion in the burner; can include nitrogen oxides, carbon oxides, water vapor, sulfur oxides, particles, and many chemical pollutants.

**Flue gas desulfurization.** A technology that uses a sorbent, usually lime or limestone, to remove sulfur dioxide from the gases produced by burning fossil fuels. Flue gas desulfurization is currently the state-of-the-art technology in use by major sulfur dioxide emitters such as power plants.

**Fluorides.** Gaseous, solid, or dissolved compounds containing fluorine that result from industrial processes; excessive amounts in food can lead to fluorosis.

**Fluorocarbon (FCs).** Any of a number of organic compounds analogous to hydrocarbons in which one or more hydrogen atoms are replaced by fluorine. Once used in the United States as a propellant in aerosols, they are now primarily used in coolants and some industrial processes. FCs containing chlorine are called chlorofluorocarbons (CFCs). They are believed to be modifying the ozone layer in the stratosphere, thereby allowing more harmful solar radiation to reach the Earth's surface.

**Fly ash.** Noncombustible residual particles from the combustion process carried by flue gas.

**Food chain.** A sequence of organisms each of which uses the next lower member of the sequence as a food source.

**Fugitive emissions.** Emissions not caught by a capture system.

**Geiger counter.** An electrical device that detects the presence of certain types of radioactivity.

**Generator.** A facility or mobile source that emits pollutants into the air or releases hazardous wastes into water or soil.

**Granular activated carbon (GAC) treatment.** A filtering system often used in small water systems and individual homes to remove organics. GAC can be highly effective in removing elevated levels of radon from water.

**Greenhouse effect.** The warming of the Earth's atmosphere caused by a buildup of carbon dioxide or other trace gases; many scientists believe that this buildup allows light from the sun's rays to heat the Earth but prevents a counterbalancing loss of heat.

**Groundwater.** The supply of fresh water found beneath the Earth's surface (usually in aquifers), which is often used for supplying wells and springs. Because groundwater is a major source of drinking water, there is growing concern about areas where leaching agricultural or industrial pollutants or substances from leaking underground storage tanks are contaminating it.

**Habitat.** The place where a population (e.g., human, animal, plant, or microorganism) lives, and its surroundings, both living and nonliving.

**Half-life.** 1. The time required for a pollutant to lose half its effect on the environment. For example, the half-life of DDT in the environment is 15 years and that of radium is 1,580 years. 2. The time required for half of the atoms of a radioactive element to undergo decay. 3. The time required for the elimination of half of a total dose from the body.

**Hazardous wastes.** By-products of society that can pose a substantial or potential hazard to human health or the environment when improperly managed. Substances classified as hazardous wastes possess at least one of four characteristics—ignitability, corrosivity, reactivity, or toxicity—or appear on special lists.

**Heavy metals.** Metallic elements with atomic number greater than 20, such as mercury and lead. They can damage living things at low concentrations and tend to accumulate in the food chain.

**Herbicide.** A chemical pesticide designed to control or destroy plants, weeds, or grasses.

**Holding pond.** A pond or reservoir, usually made of earth, built to store polluted runoff.

**Hydrocarbons (HC).** Chemical compounds that consist entirely of carbon and hydrogen.

**Hydrogen sulfide (HS).** Gas emitted during organic decomposition and as a by-product of oil refining and burning. It smells like rotten eggs and, in heavy concentration, can cause illness.

**Hydrology.** The science dealing with the properties, distribution, and circulation of water.

**Impoundment.** A body of water or sludge confined by a dam, dike, floodgate, or other barrier.

**Incineration.** 1. Burning of certain types of solid, liquid, or gaseous materials. 2. A treatment technology involving destruction of waste by controlled burning at high temperatures, e.g., burning sludge to remove the water and reduce the remaining residues to a safe, nonburnable ash that can be disposed of safely on land, in some waters, or in underground locations.

**Incinerator.** A furnace for burning wastes under controlled conditions.

**Indicator.** In biology, an organism, species, or community whose characteristics show the presence of specific environmental conditions.

**Indirect discharge.** Introduction of pollutants from a nondomestic source into a publicly owned waste treatment system. Indirect dischargers can be commercial or industrial facilities whose wastes go into the local sewers.

**Infiltration.** 1. The penetration of water through the ground surface into subsurface soil or the penetration of water from the soil into sewer or other pipes through defective joints, connections, or manhole walls. 2. A land application technique whereby large volumes of wastewater are applied to land and allowed to penetrate the surface and percolate through the underlying soil. *See also* Percolation

**Inorganic chemicals.** Chemical substances of mineral origin, not of basically carbon structure.

**Insecticide.** A pesticide compound specifically used to kill or control the growth of insects.

**Instream use.** Water use taking place within a stream channel, e.g., hydroelectric power generation, navigation, water quality improvement, fish propagation, or recreation.

**Inversion.** An atmospheric condition that occurs when a layer of warm air prevents the rise of cooling air trapped beneath it. This in turn prevents the rise of pollutants that might otherwise be dispersed and can cause an air pollution episode.

**Ion exchange treatment.** A water-softening method often found on a large scale at water purification plants; the treatment removes some organics and radium by adding calcium oxide or calcium hydroxide to increase the pH to a level at which the metals will precipitate out.

**Irrigation.** Technique for applying water or wastewater to land areas to supply the water and nutrient needs of plants.

**Lagoon.** 1. A shallow pond in which sunlight, bacterial action, and oxygen work to purify wastewater; also used for storage of wastewaters or spent nuclear fuel rods. 2. A shallow body of water, often separated from the sea by coral reefs or sandbars.

**Land application.** Discharge of wastewater onto the ground for treatment or reuse. *See also* Irrigation

**Landfills.** 1. *Sanitary landfills* are land disposal sites for nonhazardous solid wastes at which wastes are spread in layers, compacted to the smallest practical volume, and covered at the end of each operating day. 2. *Secure chemical landfills* are disposal sites for hazardous wastes that are selected and designed to minimize the chance of release of hazardous substances into the environment.

**Leachate.** A liquid that results when water collects contaminants as it trickles through wastes, agricultural pesticides, or fertilizers.

**Leaching.** The process by which soluble constituents are dissolved and carried down through the soil by a percolating fluid. Leaching may occur in farming areas, feedlots, and landfills and may result in hazardous substances entering surface water, groundwater, or soil. *See also* Leachate

**Limnology.** The study of the physical, chemical, meteorological, and biological aspects of fresh water.

**Liner.** 1. A relatively impermeable barrier designed to prevent leachate from leaking from a landfill. Liner materials include plastic and dense clay. 2. An insert or sleeve for sewer pipes to prevent leakage or infiltration.

**Mechanical aeration.** Use of mechanical energy to inject air into water, causing a waste stream to absorb oxygen.

**Methane.** A colorless, nonpoisonous, flammable gas created by anaerobic decomposition of organic compounds.

**Microbes.** Microscopic organisms such as algae, viruses, bacteria, fungi, and protozoa, some of which cause disease.

**Mitigation.** Measures taken to reduce adverse impacts on the environment.

**Mixed liquor.** A mixture of activated sludge and water containing organic matter undergoing activated sludge treatment in an aeration tank.

**Mobile source.** A moving producer of air pollution, mainly forms of transport such as cars, trucks, motorcycles, and airplanes.

**Modeling.** An investigative technique using a mathematical or physical representation of a system or theory that accounts for all or some of its known properties. Models are often used to test the effect of changes in system components on the overall performance of the system.

**Monitoring.** Periodic or continuous surveillance or testing to determine the level of compliance with statutory requirements or pollutant levels in various media or in humans, animals, and other living things.

**Monitoring wells.** Wells drilled at a site to collect groundwater samples for the purpose of physical, chemical, or biological analysis to determine the amounts, types, and distribution of contaminants in the groundwater beneath the site.

**Mutagen.** Any substance that can cause a change in genetic material.

**Neutralization.** Decreasing the acidity or alkalinity of a substance by adding to it alkaline or acidic materials, respectively.

**Nitrate.** A compound containing nitrogen that can exist in the atmosphere or as a dissolved gas in water and can have harmful effects on humans and animals. Nitrates in water can cause severe illness in infants and cows.

**Nitric oxide (NO).** A gas formed by combustion under high temperature and high pressure in an internal combustion engine. It changes to nitrogen dioxide in the ambient air and contributes to photochemical smog.

**Nitrification.** The process whereby ammonia in wastewater is oxidized to nitrite and then to nitrate by bacterial or chemical reactions.

**Nitrogen dioxide ($NO_2$).** The result of nitric oxide combining with oxygen in the atmosphere; a major component of photochemical smog.

**Nitrogenous wastes.** Animal or vegetable residues that contain significant amounts of nitrogen.

**Nitrogen oxides ($NO_x$).** Products of combustion from transport and stationary sources and major contributors to acid deposition and the formation of ground-level ozone in the troposphere.

**Nonpoint sources.** Pollution sources that are diffuse and do not have a single point of origin or are not introduced into a receiving stream from a specific outlet. The pollutants are generally carried off the land by storm-water runoff. The commonly used categories for nonpoint sources are agriculture, forestry, urban, mining, construction, dams and channels, land disposal, and saltwater intrusion.

**Nutrient.** Any substance assimilated by living things that promotes growth. The term is generally applied to nitrogen and phosphorus in wastewater but is also applied to other essential and trace elements.

**Organic.** 1. Referring to or derived from living organisms. 2. In chemistry, any compound containing carbon.

**Organic chemicals/compounds.** Animal- or plant-produced substances containing mainly carbon, hydrogen, and oxygen.

**Organophosphates.** Pesticide chemicals that contain phosphorus; used to control insects. They are short-lived, but some can be toxic when first applied.

**Outfall.** The place where an effluent is discharged into receiving waters.

**Overburden.** The rock and soil cleared away before mining.

**Overland flow.** A land application technique that cleanses waste by allowing it to flow over a sloped surface. As the water flows over the surface, the contaminants are removed. The water is collected at the bottom of the slope for reuse.

**Oxidation.** 1. The addition of oxygen, which breaks down organic waste or chemicals such as cyanides, phenols, and organic sulfur compounds in sewage by bacterial and chemical means. 2. Oxygen combining with other elements. 3. The process in chemistry whereby electrons are removed from a molecule.

**Oxidation pond.** A man-made lake or body of water in which liquid waste is consumed by bacteria. It is used most frequently with other water-treatment processes. An oxidation pond is basically the same as a sewage lagoon.

**Ozone ($O_3$).** Found in two layers of the atmosphere, the troposphere and the stratosphere. In the troposphere (the layer extending 7 to 10 miles up from the Earth's surface), ozone is a chemical oxidant and major component of photochemical smog. In the stratosphere (the atmospheric layer beginning 7 to 10 miles above the Earth's surface), ozone is a form of oxygen found naturally that provides a protective layer shielding the Earth from the harmful health effects of ultraviolet radiation on humans and the environment.

**Ozone depletion.** Destruction of the stratospheric ozone layer that shields the Earth from ultraviolet radiation harmful to biological life. This destruction of ozone is caused by the breakdown of certain chlorine- or bromine-containing compounds (chlorofluorocarbons or halons) that break down when they reach the stratosphere and catalytically destroy ozone molecules.

**Particulates.** Fine liquid or solid particles, such as dust, smoke, mist, fumes, or smog, found in air or emissions.

**Pathogenic.** Capable of causing disease.

**Pathogens.** Microorganisms that can cause disease in other organisms or in humans, other animals, and plants. They may be bacteria, viruses, or parasites and are found in sewage, in runoff from animal farms or rural areas populated with domestic or wild animals, and in water used for swimming. Fish and shellfish contaminated by pathogens, or the contaminated water itself, can cause serious illness.

**Percolation.** The movement of water downward and radially through the subsurface soil layers, usually continuing downward to the groundwater.

**Permeability.** The rate at which liquids pass through soil or other materials in a specified direction.

**Permit.** An authorization, license, or equivalent control document issued by an approved agency to implement the requirements of an environmental regulation; e.g., a permit to operate a wastewater treatment plant or to operate a facility that may generate harmful emissions.

**Persistence.** Refers to the length of time a compound, once introduced into the environment, stays there. A compound may persist for less than a second or indefinitely.

**Pesticide.** Substance or mixture of substances intended for preventing, destroying, repelling, or mitigating any pest. Also, any substance or mixture of substances intended for use as a plant regulator, defoliant, or desiccant. Pesticides can accumulate in the food chain or contaminate the environment if misused.

**pH.** A measure of the acidity or alkalinity of a liquid or solid material.

**Phenols.** Organic compounds that are byproducts of petroleum refining, tanning, and textile, dye, and resin manufacturing. Low concentrations cause taste and odor problems in water; higher concentrations can kill aquatic life and humans.

**Phosphates.** Certain chemical compounds containing phosphorus.

**Phosphorus.** An essential chemical food element that can contribute to the eutrophication of lakes and other water bodies. Increased phosphorus levels result from discharge of phosphorus-containing materials into surface waters.

**Photochemical oxidants.** Air pollutants formed by the action of sunlight on oxides of nitrogen and hydrocarbons.

**Photosynthesis.** The manufacture of carbohydrates and oxygen by plants from carbon dioxide and water in the presence of chlorophyll, using sunlight as an energy source.

**Physical and chemical treatment.** Processes generally used in large-scale wastewater treatment facilities. Physical processes may involve air stripping or filtration. Chemical treatment includes coagulation, chlorination, or ozone addition. The term can also refer to treatment of toxic materials in surface waters and groundwater, oil spills, and some methods of dealing with hazardous materials on or in the ground.

**Phytoplankton.** That portion of the plankton community comprised of tiny plants, e.g., algae, diatoms.

**Phytotoxic.** Something that harms plants.

**Plume.** 1. Visible or measurable discharge of a contaminant from a given point of origin; can be visible or thermal in water or visible in the air as, for example, a plume of smoke. 2. The area of measurable and potentially harmful radiation leaking from a damaged reactor. 3. The distance from a toxic release considered dangerous for those exposed to the leaking fumes.

**Point source.** A stationary location or fixed facility from which pollutants are discharged or emitted; any single identifiable source of pollution, e.g., a pipe, ditch, ship, ore pit, or factory smokestack.

**Pollutant.** Generally, the presence of matter or energy whose nature, location, or quantity produces undesired environmental effects. Under the U.S. Clean Water Act, for example, the term is defined as the man-made or man-induced alteration of the physical, biological, and radiological integrity of water.

**Polychlorinated biphenyls (PCBs).** a group of toxic, persistent chemicals used in transformers and capacitators for insulating purposes and in gas pipeline systems as a lubricant.

**Polyelectrolytes.** Synthetic chemicals that help solids to clump during sewage treatment.

**Polymers.** The basic molecular ingredients in plastic.

**Polyvinyl chloride (PVC).** A tough, environmentally indestructible plastic that releases hydrochloric acid when burned.

**Potable water.** Water that is safe for drinking and cooking.

**ppm/ppb.** Parts per million/parts per billion, a way of expressing tiny concentrations of pollutants in air, water, soil, human tissue, and food and or other products.

**Precipitation.** Removal of solids from liquid waste so that the hazardous solid portion can be disposed of safely; removal of particles from airborne emissions.

**Precipitators.** Air pollution control devices that collect particles from an emission.

**Precursor.** In photochemical terminology, a compound such as a volatile organic compound (VOC) that "precedes" an oxidant. Precursors react in sunlight to form ozone or other photochemical oxidants.

**Pretreatment.** Processes used to reduce, eliminate, or alter the nature of wastewater pollutants from nondomestic sources before they are discharged into publicly owned treatment works.

**Prevention.** Measures taken to minimize the release of wastes to the environment.

**Primary wastewater treatment.** First steps in wastewater treatment; screens and sedimentation tanks are used to remove most materials that float or will settle. Primary treatment results in the removal of about 30% of carbonaceous biochemical oxygen demand (BOD) from domestic sewage. *See also* Secondary wastewater treatment; tertiary wastewater treatment

**Putrescible.** Able to rot quickly enough to cause odors and attract flies.

**Pyrolysis.** Decomposition of a chemical by extreme heat.

**Radiobiology.** The study of the effects of radiation on living things.

**Radiation.** Any form of energy propagated as rays, waves, or streams of energetic particles. The term is frequently used in relation to the emission of rays from the nucleus of an atom.

**Raw sewage.** Untreated wastewater.

**Receiving waters.** A river, lake, ocean, stream, or other watercourse into which wastewater or treated effluent is discharged.

**Recycle/reuse.** The process of minimizing the generation of waste by recovering usable products that might otherwise become wastes. Examples are the recycling of aluminum cans, waste paper, and bottles.

**Red tide.** A proliferation of a marine plankton that is toxic and often fatal to fish. This natural phenomenon may be stimulated by the addition of nutrients. A tide can be called red, green, or brown, depending on the coloration of the plankton.

**Refuse.** *See* Solid waste

**Residual.** Amount of a pollutant remaining in the environment after a natural or technological process has taken place, e.g., the sludge remaining after initial wastewater treatment, or particulates remaining in air after the air passes through a scrubbing or other pollutant removal process.

**Resistance.** For plants and animals, the ability to withstand poor environmental conditions or attacks by chemicals or disease. The ability may be inborn or developed.

**Resource recovery.** The process of obtaining matter or energy from materials formerly discarded.

**Reverse osmosis.** A water treatment process used in small water systems by adding pressure to force water through a semipermeable membrane, Reverse osmosis removes most drinking water contaminants. It is also used in wastewater treatment. Large-scale reverse osmosis plants are now being developed.

**Risk assessment.** The qualitative and quantitative evaluation performed in an effort to define the risk posed to human health or the environment by the presence or potential presence and use of specific pollutants.

**Rubbish.** Solid waste, excluding wood waste and ashes, from homes, institutions, and workplaces.

**Runoff.** That part of precipitation, snowmelt, or irrigation water that runs off the land into streams or other surface water; can carry pollutants from the air and land into the receiving waters.

**Salinity.** The degree of salt in water.

**Salts.** Minerals that water picks up as it passes through the air and over and under the ground and as it is used by households and industry.

**Sand filters.** Devices that remove some suspended solids from sewage. Air and bacteria decompose additional wastes filtering through the sand so that cleaner water drains from the bed.

**Sanitary landfill.** *See* Landfills

**Sanitary sewers.** Underground pipes that carry off only domestic or industrial waste, not stormwater.

**Sanitation.** Control of physical factors in the environment that could harm human development, health, or survival.

**Screening.** Use of screens to remove coarse floating and suspended solids from sewage.

**Scrubber.** An air pollution device that uses a spray of water or reactant or a dry process to trap pollutants in emissions.

**Secondary wastewater treatment.** The second step in most publicly owned water treatment systems, in which bacteria consume the organic parts of the waste. It is accomplished by bringing together waste, bacteria, and oxygen in trickling filters or in the activated sludge process. This treatment removes floating and settleable solids and about 90% of the oxygen-demanding substances and suspended solids. Disinfection is the final stage of secondary treatment. *See also* Primary wastewater treatment; Tertiary wastewater treatment

**Sedimentation.** Letting solids settle out of wastewater by gravity during wastewater treatment.

**Sedimentation tanks.** Holding areas for wastewater in which floating wastes are skimmed off and settled solids are removed for disposal.

**Sediments.** Soil, sand, and minerals washed from land into water, usually after rain. Sediments pile up in reservoirs, rivers, and harbors, destroying fish-nesting areas and holes of water animals and clouding the water so that needed sunlight may not reach aquatic plants. Careless farming, mining, and building activities will expose sediment materials, allowing them to be washed off the land after rainfalls.

**Septic tank.** An underground storage tank for wastes from homes having no sewer line to a treatment plant. The wastes go directly from the home to the tank, where the organic waste is decomposed by bacteria and the sludge settles to the bottom. The effluent flows out of the tank into the ground through drains; the sludge is pumped out periodically.

**Settleable solids.** Material heavy enough to sink to the bottom of a wastewater treatment tank.

**Settling tank.** A holding area for wastewater in which heavier particles sink to the bottom for removal and disposal.

**Sewage.** The waste and wastewater produced by residential and commercial establishments and discharged into sewers.

**Sewage sludge.** Sludge produced at a municipal treatment works.

**Sewer.** A channel or conduit that carries wastewater and stormwater runoff from the source to a treatment plant or receiving stream. Sanitary sewers carry household, industrial, and commercial wastes. Storm sewers carry runoff from rain or snow. Combined sewers are used for both purposes.

**Silt.** Fine particles of sand or rock that can be picked up by the air or water and deposited as sediment.

**Siting.** The process of choosing a location for a facility.

**Skimming.** Using a machine to remove oil or scum from the surface of the water.

**Slow sand filtration.** Treatment process involving passage of raw water through a bed of sand at low velocity that results in the substantial removal of chemical and biological contaminants.

**Sludge.** A semisolid residue from any of a number of air or water treatment processes. Sludge can be a hazardous waste.

**Slurry.** A watery mixture of insoluble matter that results from some pollution control techniques.

**Smelter.** A facility that melts or fuses ore, often with an accompanying chemical change, to separate the metal. Emissions from smelters are known to cause pollution.

**Smog.** Fog made heavier and darker by smoke. Air pollution associated with oxidants. *See also* Photochemical oxidants

**Smoke.** Particles suspended in air after incomplete combustion of materials.

**Solid wastes.** Nonliquid, nonsoluble materials, ranging from municipal garbage to industrial wastes, that contain complex, and sometimes hazardous, substances. Solid wastes include sewage sludge, agricultural refuse, demolition wastes, and mining residues. Technically, solid wastes also refer to liquids and gases in containers.

**Solid waste disposal.** The final placement of refuse that is not salvaged or recycled.

**Solid waste management.** Supervised handling of waste materials from their source through recovery processes to disposal.

**Solidification and stabilization.** Removal of wastewater from a waste or changing it chemically to make the waste less permeable and less susceptible to transport by water.

**Solvent.** Substance (usually liquid) capable of dissolving or dispersing one or more other substances.

**Stabilization.** Conversion of the active organic matter in sludge into inert, harmless material.

**Stable air.** A mass of air that is not moving normally, so that it holds rather than disperses pollutants.

**Stack.** A chimney or smokestack; a vertical pipe that discharges used air.

**Stack effect.** Used air, as in a chimney, that moves upward because it is warmer than the surrounding atmosphere.

**Sterilization.** 1. In pest control, the use of radiation and chemicals to damage body cells needed for reproduction. 2. The destruction of all living organisms in water or on the surface of various materials. In contrast, disinfection is the destruction of most living organisms in water or on surfaces.

**Strip mining.** A process that uses machines to scrape soil or rock away from mineral deposits just under the earth's surface.

**Sulfur dioxide ($SO_2$).** A heavy, pungent, colorless, gaseous air pollutant formed primarily by processes involving fossil fuel combustion.

**Sump.** A pit or tank that catches liquid runoff for drainage or disposal.

**Surface water.** All water naturally open to the atmosphere (rivers, lakes, reservoirs, streams, impoundments, seas, estuaries, etc.); also refers to springs, wells, or other collectors that are directly influenced by surface water.

**Surfactant.** A surface-active agent used in detergents to cause lathering.

**Suspended solids.** Small particles of solid pollutants that float on the surface of or are suspended in sewage or other liquids. They resist removal by conventional means. *See also* Total suspended solids

**Tailings.** Residue of raw materials or waste separated out during the processing of crops or mineral ores.

**Teratogen.** Substance that causes malformation or serious deviation from normal development of embryos and fetuses.

**Tertiary wastewater treatment.** Advanced cleaning of wastewater that goes beyond the secondary or biological stage to remove nutrients such as phosphorus and nitrogen and most biochemical oxygen demand (BOD) and suspended solids. *See also* Primary wastewater treatment; Secondary wastewater treatment

**Thermal pollution.** Discharge of heated water from industrial processes that can affect the life processes of aquatic organisms.

**Total suspended solids (TSS).** A measure of the suspended solids in wastewater, effluent, or water bodies. *See also* Suspended solids

**Toxic pollutants.** Materials contaminating the environment that cause death, disease, or birth defects in organisms that ingest or absorb them. The quantities and length of exposure necessary to cause these effects can vary widely.

**Toxic substance.** A chemical or mixture that may present an unreasonable risk of injury to health or the environment.

**Toxicity.** The degree of danger posed by a substance to animal or plant life. *See also* Acute toxicity; Chronic toxicity

**Trichloroethylene (TCE).** A stable, low-boiling-point colorless liquid, toxic by inhalation. TCE is used as a solvent, as a metal degreasing agent, and in other industrial applications.

**Trickling filter.** A coarse biological treatment system in which wastewater trickles over a bed of stones or other material covered with bacterial growth. The bacteria break down the organic waste in the sewage and produce clean water.

**Turbidity.** 1. Haziness in air caused by the presence of particles and pollutants. 2. A similar cloudy condition in water due to suspended silt or organic matter.

**Underground storage tank.** A tank located wholly or partially under ground that is designed to hold gasoline or other petroleum products or chemical solutions.

**Urban runoff.** Stormwater from city streets and adjacent domestic or commercial properties that may carry pollutants of various kinds into sewer systems or receiving waters.

**Vapor.** The gaseous phase of substances that are liquid or solid at atmospheric temperature and pressure, e.g., steam.

**Vapor capture system.** Any combination of hoods and ventilation system that captures or contains organic vapors so that they may be directed to an abatement or recovery device.

**Vector.** 1. An organism, often an insect or rodent, that carries disease. 2. An object (e.g., plasmids, viruses, or other bacteria) used to transport genes into a host cell. A gene is placed in the vector; the vector then "infects" the bacterium.

**Vinyl chloride.** A chemical compound, used in producing some plastics, that is believed to be carcinogenic.

**Volatile.** Description of any substance that evaporates readily.

**Volatile organic compound (VOC).** Any organic compound that participates in atmospheric photochemical reactions; generally have a boiling point of less than 145° Celsius. See Anthony J. Buonicore and Wayne T. Davis, eds., *Air Pollution Engineering Manual* (New York: Van Nostrand Reinhold,1992), Table 7, p. 45.

**Wastes.** 1. Unwanted materials left over from a manufacturing process. 2. Refuse from places of human or animal habitation.

**Wastewater treatment plant.** A facility containing a series of tanks, screens, filters, and other processes by which pollutants are removed from water.

**Wastewater treatment stream.** The continuous movement of wastes from generator to treater and disposer.

**Wastewater.** Spent or used water from individual homes, communities, farms, or industries that contains dissolved or suspended matter.

**Wastewater operations and maintenance.** Actions taken after construction to ensure that facilities constructed to treat wastewater will be properly operated, maintained, and managed to achieve efficiency levels and prescribed effluent levels in an optimum manner.

**Water pollution.** The presence in water of enough harmful or objectionable material to damage water quality.

**Water quality criteria.** Specific levels of water quality that, if reached, are expected to render a body of water suitable for its designated use. The criteria are based on specific levels of pollutants that would make the water harmful if used for drinking, swimming, farming, fish production, or industrial processes.

**Watershed.** The land area that drains into a stream.

**Wetlands.** An area that is regularly saturated by surface water or groundwater and is subsequently characterized by a prevalence of vegetation adapted for life in saturated soil conditions. Examples include swamps, bogs, fens, marshes, and estuaries.

# Distributors of World Bank Group Publications

ices and credit terms vary from
untry to country. Consult your
cal distributor before placing an
der.

**RGENTINA**
orld Publications SA
., Cordoba 1877
20 Ciudad de Buenos Aires
l: (54 11) 4815-8156
x: (54 11) 4815-8156
mail: wpbooks@infovia.com.ar

**JSTRALIA, FIJI, PAPUA NEW**
**UINEA, SOLOMON ISLANDS,**
**NUATU, AND SAMOA**
A. Information Services
8 Whitehorse Road
itcham 3132, Victoria
l: (61) 3 9210 7777
x: (61) 3 9210 7788
mail: service@dadirect.com.au
RL: http://www.dadirect.com.au

**JSTRIA**
erold and Co.
eihburggasse 26
1011 Wien
: (43 1) 512-47-31-0
x: (43 1) 512-47-31-29
RL: http://www.gerold.co/at.online

**NGLADESH**
cro Industries Development
sistance Society (MIDAS)
ouse 5, Road 16
anmondi R/Area
aka 1209
: (880 2) 326427
x: (880 2) 811188

**LGIUM**
an De Lannoy
du Roi 202
60 Brussels
: (32 2) 538-5169
x: (32 2) 538-0841

**AZIL**
blicacoes Tecnicas Internacionais
.tda.
a Peixoto Gomide, 209
409 Sao Paulo, SP.
: (55 11) 259-6644
x: (55 11) 258-6990
nail: postmaster@pti.uol.br
L: http://www.uol.br

**NADA**
nouf Publishing Co. Ltd.
59 Canotek Road
awa, Ontario K1J 9J3
: (613) 745-2665
x: (613) 745-7660
nail:
rder.dept@renoufbooks.com
L: http://www.renoufbooks.com

**INA**
na Financial & Economic
ublishing House
Da Fo Si Dong Jie
jing
(86 10) 6401-7365
x: (86 10) 6401-7365
na Book Import Centre
. Box 2825
jing
nese Corporation for Promotion
Humanities
You Fang Hu Tong,
an Nei Da Jie
jing
(86 10) 660 72 494
x: (86 10) 660 72 494

**OMBIA**
enlace Ltda.
rera 6 No. 51-21
rtado Aereo 34270
tafé de Bogotá, D.C.
(57 1) 285-2798
(57 1) 285-2798

**TE D'IVOIRE**
ter d'Edition et de Diffusion
ricaines (CEDA)
B.P. 541
jan 04
(225) 24 6510; 24 6511
(225) 25 0567

**PRUS**
ter for Applied Research
rus College
iogenes Street, Engomi
Box 2006
osia
(357 2) 59-0730
(357 2) 66-2051

**CZECH REPUBLIC**
USIS, NIS Prodejna
Havelkova 22
130 00 Prague 3
Tel: (420 2) 2423 1486
Fax: (420 2) 2423 1114
URL: http://www.nis.cz/

**DENMARK**
SamfundsLitteratur
Rosenoerns Allé 11
DK-1970 Frederiksberg C
Tel: (45 35) 351942
Fax: (45 35) 357822
URL: http://www.sl.cbs.dk

**ECUADOR**
Libri Mundi
Libreria Internacional
P.O. Box 17-01-3029
Juan Leon Mera 851
Quito
Tel: (593 2) 521-606; (593 2) 544-
185
Fax: (593 2) 504-209
E-mail: librimu1@librimundi.com.ec
E-mail: librimu2@librimundi.com.ec

**CODEU**
Ruiz de Castilla 763, Edif. Expocolor
Primer piso, Of. #2
Quito
Tel/Fax: (593 2) 507-383; 253-091
E-mail: codeu@impsat.net.ec

**EGYPT, ARAB REPUBLIC OF**
Al Ahram Distribution Agency
Al Galaa Street
Cairo
Tel: (20 2) 578-6083
Fax: (20 2) 578-6833

The Middle East Observer
41, Sherif Street
Cairo
Tel: (20 2) 393-9732
Fax: (20 2) 393-9732

**FINLAND**
Akateeminen Kirjakauppa
P.O. Box 128
FIN-00101 Helsinki
Tel: (358 0) 121 4418
Fax: (358 0) 121-4435
E-mail: akatilaus@stockmann.fi
URL: http://www.akateeminen.com

**FRANCE**
Editions Eska; DBJ
48, rue Gay Lussac
75005 Paris
Tel: (33-1) 55-42-73-08
Fax: (33-1) 43-29-91-67

**GERMANY**
UNO-Verlag
Poppelsdorfer Allee 55
53115 Bonn
Tel: (49 228) 949020
Fax: (49 228) 217492
URL: http://www.uno-verlag.de
E-mail: unoverlag@aol.com

**GHANA**
Epp Books Services
P.O. Box 44
TUC
Accra
Tel: 223 21 778843
Fax: 223 21 779099

**GREECE**
Papasotiriou S.A.
35, Stournara Str.
106 82 Athens
Tel: (30 1) 364-1826
Fax: (30 1) 364-8254

**HAITI**
Culture Diffusion
5, Rue Capois
C.P. 257
Port-au-Prince
Tel: (509) 23 9260
Fax: (509) 23 4858

**HONG KONG, CHINA; MACAO**
Asia 2000 Ltd.
Sales & Circulation Department
302 Seabird House
22-28 Wyndham Street, Central
Hong Kong, China
Tel: (852) 2530-1409
Fax: (852) 2526-1107
E-mail: sales@asia2000.com.hk
URL: http://www.asia2000.com.hk

**HUNGARY**
Euro Info Service
Margitszgeti Europa Haz
H-1138 Budapest
Tel: (36 1) 350 80 24, 350 80 25
Fax: (36 1) 350 90 32
E-mail: euroinfo@mail.matav.hu

**INDIA**
Allied Publishers Ltd.
751 Mount Road
Madras - 600 002
Tel: (91 44) 852-3938
Fax: (91 44) 852-0649

**INDONESIA**
Pt. Indira Limited
Jalan Borobudur 20
P.O. Box 181
Jakarta 10320
Tel: (62 21) 390-4290
Fax: (62 21) 390-4289

**IRAN**
Ketab Sara Co. Publishers
Khaled Eslamboli Ave., 6th Street
Delafrooz Alley No. 8
P.O. Box 15745-733
Tehran 15117
Tel: (98 21) 8717819; 8716104
Fax: (98 21) 8712479
E-mail: ketab-sara@neda.net.ir

Kowkab Publishers
P.O. Box 19575-511
Tehran
Tel: (98 21) 258-3723
Fax: (98 21) 258-3723

**IRELAND**
Government Supplies Agency
Oifig an tSoláthair
4-5 Harcourt Road
Dublin 2
Tel: (353 1) 661-3111
Fax: (353 1) 475-2670

**ISRAEL**
Yozmot Literature Ltd
P.O. Box 56055
3 Yohanan Hasandlar Street
Tel Aviv 61560
Tel: (972 3) 5285-397
Fax: (972 3) 5285-397

R.O.Y. International
PO Box 13056
Tel Aviv 61130
Tel: (972 3) 649 9469
Fax: (972 3) 648 6039
E-mail: royil@netvision.net.il
URL: http://www.royint.co.il

Palestinian Authority/Middle East
Index Information Services
P.O.B. 19502 Jerusalem
Tel: (972 2) 6271219
Fax: (972 2) 6271634

**ITALY, LIBERIA**
Licosa Commissionaria Sansoni SPA
Via Duca Di Calabria, 1/1
Casella Postale 552
50125 Firenze
Tel: (39 55) 645-415
Fax: (39 55) 641-257
E-mail: licosa@ftbcc.it
URL: http://www.ftbcc.it/licosa

**JAMAICA**
Ian Randle Publishers Ltd.
206 Old Hope Road, Kingston 6
Tel: 876-927-2085
Fax: 876-977-0243
E-mail: irpl@colis.com

**JAPAN**
Eastern Book Service
3-13 Hongo 3-chome, Bunkyo-ku
Tokyo 113
Tel: (81 3) 3818-0861
Fax: (81 3) 3818-0864
E-mail: orders@svt-ebs.co.jp
URL:
http://www.bekkoame.or.jp/~svt-
ebs

**KENYA**
Africa Book Service (E.A.) Ltd.
Quaran House, Mfangano Street
P.O. Box 45245
Nairobi
Tel: (254 2) 223 641
Fax: (254 2) 330 272

Legacy Books
Loita House
Mezzanine 1
P.O. Box 68077
Nairobi
Tel: (254) 2-330853, 221426
Fax: (254) 2-330854, 561654
E-mail: Legacy@form-net.com

**KOREA, REPUBLIC OF**
Dayang Books Trading Co.
International Division
783-20, Pangba Bon-Dong,
Socho-ku
Seoul
Tel: (82 2) 536-9555
Fax: (82 2) 536-0025
E-mail: seamap@chollian.net

Eulyoo Publishing Co., Ltd.
46-1, Susong-Dong
Jongro-Gu
Seoul
Tel: (82 2) 734-3515
Fax: (82 2) 732-9154

**LEBANON**
Librairie du Liban
P.O. Box 11-9232
Beirut
Tel: (961 9) 217 944
Fax: (961 9) 217 434
E-mail: hsayegh@librairie-du-
liban.com.lb
URL: http://www.librairie-du-
liban.com.lb

**MALAYSIA**
University of Malaya Cooperative
Bookshop, Limited
P.O. Box 1127
Jalan Pantai Baru
59700 Kuala Lumpur
Tel: (60 3) 756-5000
Fax: (60 3) 755-4424
E-mail: umkoop@tm.net.my

**MEXICO**
INFOTEC
Av. San Fernando No. 37
Col. Toriello Guerra
14050 Mexico, D.F.
Tel: (52 5) 624-2800
Fax: (52 5) 624-2822
E-mail: infotec@rtn.net.mx
URL: http://rtn.net.mx

Mundi-Prensa Mexico S.A. de C.V.
c/Rio Panuco, 141-Colonia
Cuauhtemoc
06500 Mexico, D.F.
Tel: (52 5) 533-5658
Fax: (52 5) 514-6799

**NEPAL**
Everest Media International Services
(P.) Ltd.
GPO Box 5443
Kathmandu
Tel: (977 1) 416 026
Fax: (977 1) 224 431

**NETHERLANDS**
De Lindeboom/Internationale
Publicaties b.v.-
P.O. Box 202, 7480 AE Haaksbergen
Tel: (31 53) 574-0004
Fax: (31 53) 572-9296
E-mail: lindeboo@worldonline.nl
URL: http://www.worldonline.nl/~lin-
deboo

**NEW ZEALAND**
EBSCO NZ Ltd.
Private Mail Bag 99914
New Market
Auckland
Tel: (64 9) 524-8119
Fax: (64 9) 524-8067

Oasis Official
P.O. Box 3627
Wellington
Tel: (64 4) 499 1551
Fax: (64 4) 499 1972
E-mail: oasis@actrix.gen.nz
URL: http://www.oasisbooks.co.nz/

**NIGERIA**
University Press Limited
Three Crowns Building Jericho
Private Mail Bag 5095
Ibadan
Tel: (234 22) 41-1356
Fax: (234 22) 41-2056

**PAKISTAN**
Mirza Book Agency
65, Shahrah-e-Quaid-e-Azam
Lahore 54000
Tel: (92 42) 735 3601
Fax: (92 42) 576 3714

Oxford University Press
5 Bangalore Town
Sharae Faisal
PO Box 13033
Karachi-75350
Tel: (92 21) 446307
Fax: (92 21) 4547640
E-mail: ouppak@TheOffice.net

Pak Book Corporation
Aziz Chambers 21, Queen's Road
Lahore
Tel: (92 42) 636 3222; 636 0885
Fax: (92 42) 636 2328
E-mail: pbc@brain.net.pk

**PERU**
Editorial Desarrollo SA
Apartado 3824, Ica 242 OF. 106
Lima 1
Tel: (51 14) 285380
Fax: (51 14) 286628

**PHILIPPINES**
International Booksource Center Inc.
1127-A Antipolo St. Barangay,
Venezuela
Makati City
Tel: (63 2) 896 6501; 6505; 6507
Fax: (63 2) 896 1741

**POLAND**
International Publishing Service
Ul. Piekna 31/37
00-677 Warzawa
Tel: (48 2) 628-6089
Fax: (48 2) 621-7255
E-mail: books%ips@ikp.atm.com.pl
URL:
http://www.ipscg.waw.pl/ips/export

**PORTUGAL**
Livraria Portugal
Apartado 2681, Rua Do Carm
o 70-74
1200 Lisbon
Tel: (1) 347-4982
Fax: (1) 347-0264

**ROMANIA**
Compani De Librarii Bucuresti S.A.
Str. Lipscani no. 26, sector 3
Bucharest
Tel: (40 1) 313 9645
Fax: (40 1) 312 4000

**RUSSIAN FEDERATION**
Isdatelstvo <Ves Mir>
9a, Kolpachniy Pereulok
Moscow 101831
Tel: (7 095) 917 87 49
Fax: (7 095) 917 92 59
ozimarin@glasnet.ru

**SINGAPORE; TAIWAN, CHINA**
**MYANMAR; BRUNEI**
Hemisphere Publication Services
41 Kallang Pudding Road #04-03
Golden Wheel Building
Singapore 349316
Tel: (65) 741-5166
Fax: (65) 742-9356
E-mail: ashgate@asianconnect.com

**SLOVENIA**
Gospodarski vestnik Publishing
Group
Dunajska cesta 5
1000 Ljubljana
Tel: (386 61) 133 83 47; 132 12 30
Fax: (386 61) 133 80 30
E-mail: repansekj@gvestnik.si

**SOUTH AFRICA, BOTSWANA**
For single titles:
Oxford University Press Southern
Africa
Vasco Boulevard, Goodwood
P.O. Box 12119, N1 City 7463
Cape Town
Tel: (27 21) 595 4400
Fax: (27 21) 595 4430
E-mail: oxford@oup.co.za

For subscription orders:
International Subscription Service
P.O. Box 41095
Craighall
Johannesburg 2024
Tel: (27 11) 880-1448
Fax: (27 11) 880-6248
E-mail: iss@is.co.za

**SPAIN**
Mundi-Prensa Libros, S.A.
Castello 37
28001 Madrid
Tel: (34 91) 4 363700
Fax: (34 91) 5 753998
E-mail: libreria@mundiprensa.es
URL: http://www.mundiprensa.com/

Mundi-Prensa Barcelona
Consell de Cent, 391
08009 Barcelona
Tel: (34 3) 488-3492
Fax: (34 3) 487-7659
E-mail: barcelona@mundiprensa.es

**SRI LANKA, THE MALDIVES**
Lake House Bookshop
100, Sir Chittampalam Gardiner
Mawatha
Colombo 2
Tel: (94 1) 32105
Fax: (94 1) 432104
E-mail: LHL@sri.lanka.net

**SWEDEN**
Wennergren-Williams AB
P. O. Box 1305
S-171 25 Solna
Tel: (46 8) 705-97-50
Fax: (46 8) 27-00-71
E-mail: mail@wwi.se

**SWITZERLAND**
Librairie Payot Service Institutionnel
C(tm)tes-de-Montbenon 30
1002 Lausanne
Tel: (41 21) 341-3229
Fax: (41 21) 341-3235

ADECO Van Diermen
EditionsTechniques
Ch. de Lacuez 41
CH1807 Blonay
Tel: (41 21) 943 2673
Fax: (41 21) 943 3605

**THAILAND**
Central Books Distribution
306 Silom Road
Bangkok 10500
Tel: (66 2) 2336930-9
Fax: (66 2) 237-8321

**TRINIDAD & TOBAGO**
**AND THE CARRIBBEAN**
Systematics Studies Ltd.
St. Augustine Shopping Center
Eastern Main Road, St. Augustine
Trinidad & Tobago, West Indies
Tel: (868) 645-8466
Fax: (868) 645-8467
E-mail: tobe@trinidad.net

**UGANDA**
Gustro Ltd.
PO Box 9997, Madhvani Building
Plot 16/4 Jinja Rd.
Kampala
Tel: (256 41) 251 467
Fax: (256 41) 251 468
E-mail: gus@swiftuganda.com

**UNITED KINGDOM**
Microinfo Ltd.
P.O. Box 3, Omega Park, Alton,
Hampshire GU34 2PG
England
Tel: (44 1420) 86848
Fax: (44 1420) 89889
E-mail: wbank@microinfo.co.uk
URL: http://www.microinfo.co.uk

The Stationery Office
51 Nine Elms Lane
London SW8 5DR
Tel: (44 171) 873-8400
Fax: (44 171) 873-8242
URL: http://www.the-stationery-
office.co.uk/

**VENEZUELA**
Tecni-Ciencia Libros, S.A.
Centro Cuidad Comercial Tamanco
Nivel C2, Caracas
Tel: (58 2) 959 5547; 5035; 0016
Fax: (58 2) 959 5636

**ZAMBIA**
University Bookshop, University of
Zambia
Great East Road Campus
P.O. Box 32379
Lusaka
Tel: (260 1) 252 576
Fax: (260 1) 253 952

**ZIMBABWE**
Academic and Baobab Books (Pvt.)
Ltd.
4 Conald Road, Graniteside
P.O. Box 567
Harare
Tel: 263 4 755035
Fax: 263 4 781913